MILES BEYOND

The Electric Explorations of

Miles Davis, 1967–1991

PAUL TINGEN

BILLBOARD BOOKS

an imprint of Watson-Guptill Publications

New York

First published in 2001 by Billboard Books
an imprint of Watson-Guptill Publications
a division of BPI Communications, Inc.
770 Broadway, New York, NY 10003
www.watsonguptill.com

Library of Congress Cataloging-in-Publication Data

Tingen, Paul.
Miles beyond : the electric explorations of Miles Davis,
1967–1991 / by Paul Tingen.
    p.   cm.
Includes bibliographical references and indexes.
Discography: p.
ISBN: 0-8230-8346-2
1. Davis, Miles. 2. Jazz musicians—United States—Biography. I.
Title.
ML419.D39 T56 2001
788.9'2165'092—dc21
[B]
                        2001016194

The principal typefaces used in the composition of this book
were 10-point Adobe Garamond and 7-point Avenir Light.

Manufactured in the United States of America

First printing, 2001

1 2 3 4 5 6 7 8 9 / 08 07 06 05 04 03 02 01

Senior Acquisitions Editor: Bob Nirkind
Editor: Alison Hagge
Production Manager: Hector Campbell
Cover and interior design: Jay Anning

CONTENTS

ACKNOWLEDGEMENTS

To begin with, I'd like to thank the three people who have been consistently present throughout the researching and writing of this book, and without whom it would either not have happened, or would have taken an entirely different form.

First, Elisabeth Tønsberg gave daily support, transcribed the vast majority of the interviews, provided constant feedback and inspiration, and introduced me to the ideas of Ken Wilber. Second, Enrico Merlin invited me to stay at his house and rummage through his enormous collection of private Miles Davis recordings, as well as his library of Miles articles and videos. The fruits of Enrico's decades-long research into Miles's music greatly helped me with my understanding of the electric music. Third, my editor at Billboard, Bob Nirkind, gracefully guided me through the whole two-year process of researching and writing this book. I'm indebted to his tenacity, which ensured that I delivered the best book that I could write.

This book would not have been possible without the contributions of all those interviewed. I'd like to acknowledge and thank: Bob Belden, Bob Berg, Paul Buckmaster, Leon "Ndugu" Chancler, Mino Cinelu, Chick Corea, Pete Cosey, Erin Davis, Jack and Lydia DeJohnette, George Duke, Marguerite Eskridge, Bill Evans, Sonny Fortune, Robert Fripp, Jo Gelbard, Steve Grossman, Herbie Hancock, Michael Henderson, Dave Holland, Adam Holzman, Karl Hyde, Robert Irving III, Mark Isham, Darryl Jones, Henry Kaiser, Bill Laswell, Dave Liebman, Reggie Lucas, Teo Macero, Marilyn Mazur, Palle Mikkelborg, Jason Miles, Marcus Miller, James Mtume, Bennie Rietveld, Mark Rothbaum, Badal Roy, Wayne Shorter, Jim Rose, John Scofield, Wadada Leo Smith, Mike Stern, Peter Shukat, Dorothy Weber, Ricky Wellman, Lenny White, Vince Wilburn Jr., Mark Wilder, and Jah Wobble.

Some of the above were also helpful in other ways. Vince Wilburn Jr. put me in touch with several interviewees. Jack and Lydia DeJohnette, Marguerite Eskridge, Jo Gelbard, Mark Rothbaum, Paul Buckmaster, James Mtume, Pete Cosey, Peter Shukat, Bill Laswell, Adam Holzman, and Robert Irving III read through sections of the unfinished manuscript and provided comments, corrections, and/or additional information.

In addition, Bob Doerschuk made the initial link between Bob Nirkind and myself; Billboard Books's Alison Hagge edited and improved my final manuscript, and was a joy to work with; British Miles Davis enthusiast Martin Booth read the entire manuscript and gave many invaluable comments; his daughter Jeannie provided a priceless quote; Steve Wilson provided a tape; Jan Lohmann and Peter Losin both answered queries via e-mail; Losin's *Miles Ahead* Web site was a source of valuable data; Gordon Meltzer connected me with a few interviewees; Collanene Cosey put me in touch with her son Pete; Brian Jacobs e-mailed some helpful material; Hi-Grade in London provided the excellent ASUS laptop on which this book was written, and were second to none for technical support; Ole Ry Nielsen gave valuable feedback on Chapter 6; Mark Riva commented on Chapter 1; Bill Murphy and Bill Laswell provided useful information; Lucia Viola read part of the manuscript and shared some of her knowledge of Ornette Coleman; Tom Cording at Sony/Legacy in New York and Sharon Kelly at Sony Music in London were both extremely helpful, providing information and many CDs; Seth Rothstein of Sony/Legacy sent musical material; Florence Halfon at Warner Bros. in London provided all of Miles's available Warner Bros. CDs; Palle Mikkelborg lent a video recording of the making of *Aura*; Jacqueline Palmer and Janice Eddy transcribed several interview tapes; John Szwed corrected some mistakes; Hector Zazou, Holger Czukay, Paul Schütze, Peter Hammill, Marc Ribot, Rupert Hine, Blair Jackson, and Jon Hassell discussed aspects of Miles with me that influenced the book's final outcome; my brother Bart offered practical assistance; my brother Rob provided some videos; my parents also lent practical support; Rich Kenny handed me the piece by Michael Ventura on voodoo and rock 'n' roll that played an invaluable part in Chapter 11; and Jörg Trommer and Renate Berretz provided constant listening support and encouragement.

In terms of the eleven places in which this book was researched and written, I'd like to highlight a few of the names of those who graciously welcomed me into their residences and/or communities: all at the Glen Ivy community in Corona, California; Caítriona Reed and Michele Benzamin-Masuda at Manzanita Village, Warner Springs, California; Benedicte, Michala, and Cecilie Tønsberg in Mors, Denmark; Susanne André and Ole Ry Nielsen in Brovst, Denmark; Wendy and Fynn Stirm in York, England; Roberta Wall in New York; Sid Kemp and Kris Lindbeck in Morristown, New Jersey; Jeremy Jacobsen in Forres, Scotland; and all at the Findhorn Foundation Community, near Findhorn, Scotland.

And finally, thank you, Miles, for being a constant source of inspiration, wonder, and puzzlement.

To all of you, and to anyone I may have forgotten, as well as to any other seen and unseen forces that have supported the creation of this book, my heartfelt gratitude.

—PAUL TINGEN

I would like to thank all the people who helped me to realize the sessionography: Bob Belden, John Cottrell, Laurent Cugny, Franco D'Andrea, Adam Holzman, Henry Kaiser, Dave Liebman, Jan Lohmann, Peter Losin, Teo Macero, Albert McMahill, Gordon Meltzer, Veniero Rizzardi, John Scofield, and Mark White.

And a very special thanks to Paul Tingen, who shared many hours with me in correcting, improving, and discussing the sessionography.

—ENRICO MERLIN

INTRODUCTION

Where were you the first time you heard the music of Miles Davis? And where were you when you heard that he had died? Since you are reading these words, chances are that you will know the answers to both questions.

The memories of the big moments in our lives, whether personal or historical, remain with us forever, and are often embedded in seemingly irrelevant details: how things smelled at the time, what music we were listening to, what the weather was like. This is often called the "JFK effect," illustrated by the proverbial question: "where were you when you heard that John F. Kennedy was shot?" Such memories mark the momentous moments when history touched us personally, leaving an indelible mark.

Miles Davis never achieved the household fame of the likes of JFK. Yet an amazing number of people remember where they were and what they were doing when they first heard his music, and when they heard he had died, illustrating Miles Davis's huge impact.

"I first heard his music pulsating out of a juke box, one warm summer day in 1954, in a fish joint back in St. Louis, Missouri," author and poet Quincy Troupe recalled.[1] It's a remarkably detailed memory of something that happened forty-five years ago, and illustrative of how deeply it affected Troupe. The writer Joel Lewis remembered in detail the moment when he heard Miles's music for the first time, on FM radio in early 1970. The track was "Spanish Key" from *Bitches Brew,* and it made enough of an impression for him to remember the deejay who played it (Rosko) and the following "segue into a soft drink advert. I made a note to find this album the next day."[2]

Miles's death also stirred unusually strong emotions in people. The effect, of course, was strongest in people who had known him personally. Mark Rothbaum, Miles's business associate and manager from 1973 to 1983, recounted, "It was a Saturday afternoon in late September. I was driving back from shopping, and you know how, when the sun is very bright and flickers through the leaves, you can get almost hypnotized. I was driving on this country road and I was mesmerized by the light. At 5 P.M. a news program came on the radio that usually started with a theme tune. But this time the first note was Miles. I immediately started crying . . . the minute I heard that first note I knew he had died. I cried hysterically. I had to stop the car, pull over. I never believed he would die, even though I'd seen him near death several times. I thought he'd always pull through. Miles brought out every tear I ever should have cried. I never did cry, because of being a man, and so on. But that time I was sobbing. I couldn't control it."

People who had never met him were also strongly affected. Blair Jackson, author of the biography *Garcia: An American Life* and executive editor of *Mix* magazine, remembered, "I was visiting New York, walking up First Avenue late at night, looking for a restaurant when my eye fell on a newspaper headline in a newsstand that said: 'Miles David is dead.' I was deeply shocked." And in a poetic and poignant variation on this theme, the Buddhist meditation teacher Caítriona Reed recalled that she had a dream about Miles around the time he died "in which he made a new album, and it was entirely silent. . . ."

My own answers to the above two questions will bring my reasons for writing this book into focus. I remember first hearing Miles's music as a teenager in the late 1970s at my parent's home. It was a sunny afternoon in the middle of summer and a Dutch radio station was playing some seriously weird stop-start rock music fronted by a screaming electric guitar. Since I was into experimental and avant-garde rock music at the time, bands like King Crimson and Henry Cow, and loved screaming electric guitars, I listened attentively, and made a mental note of the artist mentioned after the piece finished, wondering 'Miles Davis, isn't he a jazz artist?' I went to the local music library a week or so later and among the great number of Miles Davis jazz recordings I found one double album with a cover that looked more likely to contain the kind of music I'd heard on the radio. It was a red and gold psychedelic affair with a night vision of a large city seen through what looked like an aquarium. I took it home, placed it on my record player, and my jaw dropped. This was the weirdest, totally over-the-top funk I'd ever heard. I was initially put off by the nerve-racking density and seeming monotony of the music. This was nothing like the engaging, open, stop-start stuff I'd heard on the radio. But since *Agharta,* the record I'd brought home, was all I had, and since the cover looked so cool, I persevered. The insurgent cover instruction to play the album at the loudest possible volume was further encouragement, much to my parents' dismay.

Soon I discovered that astonishing moment, fourteen minutes and forty-three seconds into Side 1, where the band cuts out and Pete Cosey's guitar solo goes into total overdrive. Being a guitarist myself, I thought I was an insider on the outer fringes of crazy electric-guitar playing, but this was beyond my comprehension. From that moment on Side 1 until the middle of Side 4, the music was continuously interesting, provocative, unbelievable, and highly exciting. I was sold. For the next months *Agharta* rarely left my record player.

It bewildered me that I didn't have a clue as to how the music and the solos were structured or conceived. There was clearly a large element of improvisation going on, but the music was too structured and too melodic and there was too much flawless interplay between the musicians for it to be totally improvised. I was baffled by this dense and bizarre music, because I had no frame of reference. Nothing I knew sounded even remotely like it, not even the other electric Miles Davis albums I sought out and enjoyed, *Get up with It* and *Bitches Brew.* (Fifteen years later I finally found the piece I had first heard on the Dutch radio station. It turned out to be "Gemini/Double Image" from *Live-Evil.* It was testimony to the strong impression that piece made on me that I could still recognize it after all that time.)

The moment I learned Miles had died was late October 1991, around 7:30 in the evening. For most of September and October I'd been visiting a place where there was no easy access to newspapers or television. Now I had moved out of London to an idyllic home in the countryside near Canterbury. When laying out old newspapers on the floor as a base for a new carpet, my eye fell on writer/trumpeter Ian Carr's excellent full-page obituary in *The Independent* of September 30. I was stunned and silenced, and reread the piece several times over, somehow hoping that, miraculously, it was a joke. It had seemed as is Miles would be around forever. And now it turned out that he wouldn't. I felt a sense of deep loss, and no more work was done on the carpet that evening. Instead I put on his records and tried to come to grips with him having gone.

❖

Miles Davis touches something very profound in many of us, leaving an enduring mark on our psyches. He represents something larger than life, something of archetypal significance, something of which we aren't always wholly conscious. Miles deeply affected people the world over. He changed our perceptions, he repeatedly set new directions in music, he brought new sounds into being, he changed the way musicians think about themselves and about music, he changed the position of black people in our society and the way many black people think about themselves. One of my aims in this book is to uncover and describe the marks that Miles made on us.

I will attempt to do this with one important self-imposed restriction, which follows almost inevitably from my first encounter with Miles's music. Being someone who grew up listening to and playing mainly rock music, I was most affected by the rock-influenced music. I will therefore focus exclusively on Miles's electric period, often using the term "electric" as shorthand, since the common denominator of all Miles's explorations in this direction is the application of at least one electric instrument. (More commonly used terms are "jazz-rock" or "fusion," but they don't describe Miles's electric music well. The former is too narrow, since Miles also incorporated influences from African, Latin, Indian, and classical music, while the latter conjures up associations with sterile pyrotechnics and the dreaded smooth jazz and jazz-lite genres of the 1980s and 1990s.)

Miles explicitly began exploring rock influences with the second great quintet, which featured Wayne Shorter, Herbie Hancock, Ron Carter, and Tony Williams—specifically on December 4, 1967, when electric guitarist Joe Beck came in for a session. Because the musical history of the quintet forms an unbroken line, I will extend the story slightly backwards in time, and begin going into detail when the first members of the second quintet entered Miles's band, in 1963. After dealing with the quintet, I will describe how Miles went deeper and deeper into electric territory during the late 1960s and the first half of the 1970s. Following a touch-in with his "silent" period (from 1975 to 1980), during which Miles descended into drugs, despair, and darkness, I'll detail his musical adventures of the 1980s and very early 1990s, until his death on September 28, 1991.

This self-imposed restriction to the electric music of Miles Davis is the first raison d'être of this book. There are already plenty of Miles Davis biographies around. Regardless of their quality, they all have one thing in common: they were written by people whose musical and cultural outlooks center on jazz. And, since there is no way of putting this subtly, I'll put it straight: With regards to the electric music, these writers, generally speaking, simply don't "get it." At best their portrayals and narratives lack depth and substance, at worst they are rife with snobbery and narrow-mindedness, expressing the prejudice that rock music is inferior to jazz.

Mercifully, the school of thought that recognizes just two categories of music—good music and bad music—is increasingly gaining ground. Yet amazingly, expressions of musical snobbery that have the audacity to devalue whole musical genres are still around.[3] Bassist Marcus Miller made an interesting comment about this. As someone who plays several different styles of music, he has often been subjected to incompetent criticism. His response is to compare music genres to different languages, all with their own vocabulary, grammar, and inner logic. To him, criticizing someone for playing rock, soul, or jazz is like criticizing him or her for speaking French, Spanish, or Japanese.

Taking Miller's analogy a step further, we determine that, just as one has to understand French to be able to assess the merits or faults of a piece of French writing, so one has to know the inner logic and vocabulary of a certain music genre to be a competent critic. Of course, given how eagerly people now switch from the "language" of rock to, say, the "languages" of world music or jazz or classical, the divisions in music aren't quite as extreme.[4]

This doesn't necessarily mean that switching is easy. Miles Davis, for example, admitted in his autobiography that learning the "language" of rock was a stretch for him: "When I started playing against that new rhythm . . . first I had to get used to it. At first there was no feeling because I was used to the old way of playing things like with Bird and Trane. Playing the new shit was a gradual process. You don't stop playing the way you used to play. You don't hear the sound at first. It takes time."[5] Miles eventually "got it" and went on to do great things with this "new shit."

All this is not intended to widen musical divisions or to create oppositions where there aren't any. I know there are people for whom the boundaries between jazz and rock don't exist, who prefer to focus on the common ground between the two musical "languages." My own instinct is in this direction. My point here is simply that we need to know our own limits. If we don't understand a musical idiom, if we don't speak its "language," it is better to maintain a respectful silence on the subject.

Although I appreciate some forms of jazz, the jazz "language" as a whole is largely foreign to me. Mindful of my own limitations, I will therefore only provide a brief overview of Miles's rich jazz period, purely to place his development into electric music in context. Accepting that jazz is not my native "language," I would not dare to attempt a critique. This decision is simply based on my respect for a great art form.

This book aims to be the first to thoroughly cover the music of the whole electric period (1967 to 1991) from the sympathetic perspective of someone who "speaks" rock. I'd like to stress that this does not make my observations and opinions absolute, nor does it express an intention to launch a polemic against Miles Davis's jazz critics. Accepting the premise that we are speaking rather different "languages," I see little point in lengthy comparisons or discussions. But I will occasionally touch base with their evaluations and criticisms of Miles's electric music, to demonstrate the difference in emphasis, interpretation, and language, and to address some widely held misinterpretations. To survey the territory and illustrate why this book is necessary, I'd like to offer a few examples.

The bias of *Miles: The Autobiography* towards the jazz period is illustrated by the 239 pages spent on the twenty-three-year period from September 1944 (when Miles arrived in New York) to December 4, 1967, (the first introduction of rock, funk, and folk music elements). Less than half this amount, 103 pages, is dedicated to the twenty-two years from the latter date till 1989, when the book was published. Another example is that Miles's pivotal '70–'75 bassist, Michael Henderson, receives only three name checks, whereas bassist Ron Carter, who was with Miles from 1963 to 1968, is mentioned twenty-one times. Rather than exemplifying a predisposition on Miles's part, this more likely reflects the preferences of ghostwriter Quincy Troupe, who appears better versed in and more familiar with jazz music. He was also part of the team that put together the eight-part radio program *The Miles Davis Radio Project,* broadcast in 1990, which contained many musical examples and interviews with Miles's former sidemen, but didn't even mention the music of 1972 to 1975.

Ian Carr's *Miles Davis: The Definitive Biography* and Jack Chambers's *Milestones: The Music and Times of Miles Davis* were both republished in 1998. Both books contain additional material about Miles's last decade, but remain deeply flawed in their treatment of the electric Miles, for different reasons. Ian Carr is indiscriminately positive about most of the '80s electric period, turning his book into a fanzine in places, but virtually ignores the '73–'75 period. The pivotal guitarist Pete Cosey only gets two name checks in his six-hundred-page book. *Milestones* is more balanced than *Miles Davis* in its treatment of Miles's electric music until 1984, when the two-part biography was completed, although Chambers clearly does not know what to say about *On the Corner,* one of Miles's most influential recordings. Rather than give his own opinion, he simply quotes saxophonist Stan Getz: "That music is worthless."[6]

In addition, Chambers's new introduction is a vendetta laced with inaccuracies and condescending nonsense. Some examples are: "His music repertoire was dominated by three-chord riffs tunes,"[7] and "In a hokey routine at the end of his concerts Davis used to raise a large Styrofoam board with the sideman's name on it, milking applause from the funk-sated audience. When he came to [Vince] Wilburn [Jr.], he took to holding the board in one hand while holding his nose with the other." The truth is, Miles's music from the 1980s contained elaborate melodic and chordal structures, while during the time Wilburn played with the band (from 1985 to 1987), Miles had not yet developed the holding-up-name-signs routine. One wonders whether the writer was venting hurt and bitterness over his claim that large sections of his two-part book were copied and rewritten in Miles's autobiography.

None of the biographies of Miles Davis currently on the market delves deeper or with significantly more understanding into Miles's electric period. Eric Nisenson's *'Round about Midnight* is the best and the fairest, but the electric period is not the primary focus of the book. There are also two collections of essays and articles written on Miles Davis: *The Miles Davis Companion* and *A Miles Davis Reader.* They contain some interesting new information on the electric period, but again, it is thin on the ground. This led the editor of *A Miles Davis Reader,* Bill Kirchner, to remark in his introduction: ". . . serious writing about his music of the '60s, '70s and '80s is not exactly voluminous. Much work remains to be done in analyzing all periods of Davis's career, most of all concerning the later developments."[8] This book aims to do exactly that.

Miles Beyond's second raison d'être concerns the fact that no systematic inventory of the views and experiences of those who played with and knew Miles has ever been made in book form. I set out to talk to as many of the many musicians and associates in Miles's life as I could find, and was fortunate enough to interview almost fifty people, including six from the '73–'75 band, the least covered and least understood of all of Miles's bands. Much of what was discussed happened twenty-five to thirty years ago, and memories fade and people die. So it seemed a matter of urgency to interview them now, before it's too late. This was borne out by the fact that the amount of detail interviewees could remember was directly proportional to the time that had passed since the described events had happened. Recollections covering the '60s, '70s, and even the '80s are often vague, and sometimes conflicting.

In drawing all these interviews together I was able to give a more comprehensive picture of Miles's working methods, as well as of the man behind the public mask, than has been shown so far. Even as this book focuses mainly on the music, the man and his music are to a large degree inseparable, and consequently I will also cover aspects of the man. Many people are preoccupied with the invulnerable macho mask that Miles Davis put on for the world, and perceive him as a total enigma. My opinion is that it is crucial to be able to have at least a peek behind the mask and gain some sense of him as a person, with all his strengths and vulnerabilities. Although some may feel this detracts from the legend, I feel this makes him more human, and makes his achievements more alive and meaningful for us.

Miles Davis's greatness lies in the fact that he achieved some extraordinary things and was a deeply flawed human being at the same time. Fleshing out his human side increases the depth and meaning of his legacy. Therefore, I will be forthright about covering various aspects of his personality, including the darker side. After all, brutal honesty was part of Miles's method. It's an essential element of his autobiography, which, plagiarized in parts or not, rings with an authentic voice. There's no reason why we should be any less honest.

By being coy or overly respectful or by denying his humanity, we only contribute to Miles Davis's current transformation into a cultural icon, which threatens to flatten him into one of the many respectable and neutered American pinups that are safely contained in the status quo and have lost their capacity to challenge and transform. Miles Davis was an agent of change, in the words of Blair Jackson "a musical provocateur," always gnawing away at the certainties that make us too comfortable and impede our creativity. Every agent of change inevitably carries a degree of threat and risk to the status quo, and we honor Miles Davis's legacy best by keeping this aspect of the man and his work alive.

I'd like to end with some more personal notes. First, at various places in this book parallels are drawn between Miles's presence and working methods and those of Zen teachers. In this context, it is important that I declare a possible bias. Although I do not regard myself as a Buddhist, I have practiced in a Zen Buddhist tradition since 1990 with the Vietnamese poet, teacher, writer, and peace activist Thich Nhat Hanh (who was nominated for the 1967 Nobel Peace Prize by Dr. Martin Luther King Jr.). In 1997 I was ordained as a lay member in Nhat Hanh's core, Order of Interbeing. I have also written a body of acoustic guitar pieces that have emerged from this practice and because of this I was labeled a "Zen guitarist" by the London listings magazine *Time Out.*

We tend to see what we look for, and my background may give rise to suspicions that I have been putting the cart before the horse (i.e., have tried to fit aspects of Miles into my own preconceived ideas). It is therefore important to stress that when I embarked on this project the thought of relating Miles to Zen had not occurred to me. I was alerted to this angle when several interviewees unexpectedly made the parallel with Zen. I also found that several writers mention the Zen aspect. For example, writer Gene Santoro stated: "Miles Davis as leader is the epitome of Zen."[9] Naturally, my interest was piqued, and I explored the parallel further. I reasoned that if there was something to this, at least I was well placed to describe it.

Second, some aesthetic and political points. I have critically assessed all the music described in this book. This raises a number of issues. Some interviewees questioned whether evaluating this music is necessary at all. As a musician, I share their reservations. Because of the bad name music critics have among musicians, and out of a resulting sense of solidarity, most musicians are reluctant to go public with negative opinions on the work of their colleagues. Being a musician as well as a writer, I have in my journalistic work preferred to stay silent about music I do not like, choosing to cover only those musicians I respected.

For a reporter this position may be sufficient. However, it is not sufficient when writing a book. Apart from the fact that a purely descriptive book risks being utterly boring, a book writer's task is not only to inform but also to enlighten, stimulate, and engage the reader, bringing new perspectives and insights. The reader may not always agree, but these new perspectives should deepen the reader's understanding of the subject at hand. This simply cannot be achieved by trying to appear objective and impartial and by avoiding expressing opinions.

In any case, both "impartiality" and "objectivity" are nonstarters in this instance. The very act of writing a book requires strong engagement with the subject matter. This kind of engagement is also most likely the reason why you are reading this book at this moment. Strong feelings and opinions are inevitable. In practice, trying to be "objective" results in disguising these feelings and opinions, which will inevitably seep through in other ways: the tone of the narrative, the amount of space allotted to certain pieces of music, the questions asked of the interviewees, the selections of their answers that are included, etc. Rather than write by suggestion and implication, I feel it is more honorable for a writer to be explicit and forthright about his opinions and limitations, and leave it to readers to make up their own minds.

This leads to a point about the nature of music critique. I firmly side with the aesthetic position that beauty, or quality, is in the eye—or in this context, the ear—of the beholder. Arguments that state that certain proportions, colors, harmonies, and rhythms inherently have universal and quantifiable effects on human beings are fascinating, and may well hold deep truths. I do not dismiss them. My reasons for taking "beauty is in the ear of the beholder" as my critical adage are political. They spring from the work of the American psychologist Marshall Rosenberg, who has pioneered a revolutionary new approach to language called nonviolent communication.

Rosenberg argues that the language and the thinking in which we have all been educated are based on the premise that people and situations outside of us are responsible for how we feel. The result is a plethora of right–wrong judgements: When we feel upset because someone shouts at us, or creates a piece of music we don't like, we denounce him or her or it as being "wrong" and deserving of punishment. We tend to enforce our values through blame, shame, and coercion. Rosenberg argues convincingly that this is a form of violence that lies at the root of all the human violence that plagues our planet.[10]

The alternative presented in nonviolent communication involves a paradigm shift in perspective. It suggests that we relate our feelings to our needs, values, and wants, rather than to outside events. For example, when people shout at us, we may feel scared and angry, because we're not getting the respect and safety we want. We don't like what the they are doing one bit, but at no point do we assume that they are wrong for doing what they do, or to blame for our feelings. Instead of trying to coerce them into acting the way we want them to, we express our like or dislike through stating our feelings and needs. Nonviolent communication, also called "a language of the heart," springs from this deceptively simple premise.

It falls outside the scope of this book to elaborate further on this issue. The relevance here is that I do not wish to further thinking that implies that there can be something inherently right or wrong with the actions I'm seeing or the piece of music I'm hearing. Hence my position that our reactions, emotional or mental, to a piece of music are never caused by this piece of music, but always by the needs and values we hold dear. In the course of history, riots have broken out, and composers and performers have been physically and verbally attacked, over pieces of music. The absolutist judgements of critics are exactly what have made them so unpopular with musicians. The attacks on Miles and his electric music are merely among the most recent expressions of a way of thinking that assumes that an artist and his art can be inherently "wrong," and if so, need to be punished.

I have found that articulating my emotional responses and the values that cause them has not only prevented me from going down similar routes but has also greatly elucidated my thinking in assessing Miles's music, as well as some of the less likeable aspects of his personality. Nevertheless, I have not always expressed myself in this book in the ways recommended by nonviolent communication. The reason is simple. Nonviolent communication is still a little-known approach to language and thinking, and I do not wish to confuse the reader with sometimes cumbersome phraseology, stating that "I like this piece of music, because it meets my need for beauty," or something to that effect. Instead, I have sometimes chosen to follow customary protocol and describe music as "beautiful" or "boring." This invariably means that I have felt pleasure or boredom in listening to it, because it conformed to or conflicted with a number of things I value in music: certain aesthetics, instrumental colors, harmonic, melodic, or rhythmic variety, structural logic, consistency, atmosphere, and so on. But I'd like to impress on the reader that I never intend to say that there's something inherently or objectively right or wrong with a piece of music, a statement, someone's actions, or a person. My responses are always rooted in my own needs and values.

I hope that these personal, aesthetic, and political points add to the reader's understanding, and that this book will meet each reader's needs for entertainment, information, and inspiration.

Chapter One

LISTEN

"I was put here to play music, and interpret music. . . . I might do a lot of things, but the main thing that I love, that comes before everything, even breathing, is music."

—MILES DAVIS[1]

"Listen." *Miles: The Autobiography* opens with this word, immediately hitting a bull's-eye. It goes straight to the heart of Miles Davis.

Listen before breathing. Miles had a different way of listening. To music. To sound. To people. To the rhythm of the times. To time and space. To understand Miles we have to listen to the way he expressed himself, in music, words, lifestyle, and life choices. Listening is central. It's what he taught the musicians who played with him. It's what he taught his audiences as well.

Bassist Gary Peacock described Miles as "by far the greatest listener that I have ever experienced in a musical group."[2] His colleague Dave Holland observed that Miles had "the best understanding of time, space, and movement of anybody I have ever worked with." Keyboardist Adam Holzman stated, "It may be a funny thing to say for a musician, but Miles taught me how to listen." Percussionist Badal Roy said that the main thing he learned from Miles was "to play from the heart and to listen."

Miles used to tell his musicians, "When you play music, don't play the idea that's there, play the next idea. Wait. Wait another beat, or maybe two, and maybe you'll have something that's more fresh. Don't just play from the top of your head, but listen and try to play a little deeper."[3] Miles also advised his musicians, "Don't play what's there. Play what's not there."[4] He might have said: "Don't listen to what's there, listen to what's not there."

Other than during the second half of the '80s, Miles rarely rehearsed his bands. Instead, he instructed his musicians to practice on the bandstand. He got angry with them if they practiced at home or in their hotel rooms, saying "How are you going to rehearse the future?"[5] He wanted them to be fully present with, to listen to, the music in the present moment. "Of all of those in the band, Miles is the most easily influenced by outside events. He reflects everything he feels in his playing immediately," remarked an unnamed band member.[6]

Miles wanted his sidemen to enter into a relationship with music using what Zen calls "beginner's mind"—never being on autopilot, never just following habit energy, but always alert, ready for the unexpected, right here, right now. "Miles did not want me to come to the rehearsals," guitarist Pete Cosey recalled. "He wanted to keep things fresh. Part of that is knowing what to play and what not to play. The way you do that is to be able to listen to what is going on around you. When you come into any situation, it's the best thing to do: to listen. That is how you learn."

Listening requires awareness, paying attention. Miles taught both by example. A word used by many musicians who worked with him is "focus." Dave Holland said, "There was a tremendous sense of focus coming from him that influenced everybody. We were all drawn in by it, it was almost like a vortex. Once you were in its sphere of influence, there was a certain magic that seemed to be happening." Drummer Jack DeJohnette remarked, "Playing with Miles was about being focused, and about being open to where the music takes you. His sound focused your attention on him and the music. Sometimes this meant leading and sometimes this meant following. He just had that magic, he had that power, that special gift."

Miles's unique listening awareness rubbed off on the musicians around him. In his presence they often found themselves raising their awareness and playing to new and unexpected heights. In doing so they exemplified Miles's adage: "Play what you know and play above what you know."[7] Guitarist Sonny Sharrock only played with Miles for one day in 1970, but this was enough to change his approach to the guitar, making him realize that playing music is about "really listening, the way Miles listened; to hear the piece to the end right from the first note, and to see what the space is going to be in the piece."[8] Guitarist John McLaughlin commented, "Miles has the capacity to draw out of people things that even surprise the musicians themselves. He's been a guru of sorts to a lot of people. He was certainly a musical mentor to me."[9]

Miles stated that when listening to his music, "I always listen to what I can leave out."[10] He listened to what's not there—to the space behind the notes, to the silence from which music emerges and in which it is framed—trying to find the best balance between that space and the notes that furnish it. One of Miles's big discoveries was that this often requires fewer notes, rather than more. As a result, his economy of playing and usage of space became legendary. Miles always played between the lines, implying notes, suggesting a mood with minimal material, stretching the "less is more" maxim to new levels.

Early in 1985, when working on the album *Aura,* Miles told a Danish interviewer: "I don't believe in wasting any phrases, no matter how small, how soft. With phrases comes rhythm. I don't waste rhythm either. The rhythm can throw off the melody and it gets lost. So you have to know what the phrases mean, what the notes mean. A lot of musicians don't! They play a note, and they don't know what it means, they just know 'that's a raised ninth, that's a . . . ' whatever. You should tell them what it means, then musicians won't go to sleep. That's very important."[11]

Guitarist John Scofield said, "He expressed himself in a virtuoso way, but not with a lot of notes. He had this ability to strip things down and to make it profound. When most people play just one note, it's not so hot. But he found the right one to play. It was impossible for anybody else to do what he did because he was so unique. He was a teacher for us all." Keith Jarrett, Gary Peacock, and Jack DeJohnette wrote, "Miles was *the* authentic minimalist (where, although there are so few notes, there was so much *in* those notes). No matter how much noise there was around him, Miles always came from silence, the notes existing in a purity all their own."[12] Producer and arranger Quincy Jones concurred, "Miles always played the most unexpected note, and the one that is the perfect note."[13]

By contrast, many musicians tend to overplay, and Miles joked that because "they play too many fucking notes" they need to go to "Notes Anonymous."[14] He spent much of his life teaching musicians the virtues of space, of silence, of phrasing, of waiting, of economy of notes and ideas, and most of all, of focus and listening. He remembered about percussionist Airto Moreira, "When he first came with me he played too loud and didn't listen to what was happening with the music. I would tell him to stop banging and playing so loud, and just to listen more."[15] According to Moreira, Miles just instructed him with the aphorism, "Don't bang, just play,"[16] leaving him to figure out what this meant. Moreira concluded, "He wanted me to hear the music, and *then* play some sounds."[17]

Illustrating how his listening awareness was always present—not just in music, but in everyday life—Miles once remarked, "Rhythm is all around us, even if you stumble."[18] An anecdote from his time in Malibu in the late '80s illustrates the same point. One day Miles was stopped by a police officer for speeding. "I wasn't speeding, and in any case, my speedometer isn't working," Miles protested. "So how can you know how fast you're going?" the officer asked. "I can hear it," Miles replied.

So listen. Listen to what's not there. Listen between the lines, of words, of music, of Miles.

❖

"Listen. The greatest feeling I ever had in my life—with my clothes on—was when I first heard Diz and Bird together in St. Louis, Missouri, back in 1944. . . . Music all up in my body, and that's what I wanted to hear. . . . I'm always looking for it, listening and feeling for it, though, trying to feel it in and through the music I play every day."[19]

Throughout his life, Miles's main focus was unearthing the meaning of music, delving for the feeling of that moment in 1944, which is the ultimate a musician can experience. Guitarist Robert Fripp described it as the point at which "we are fully alive in the present moment and totally alert to the musical impulse." Miles was single-minded and egoless in the pursuit of this aim, saying, "You gotta get rid of your ego,"[20] and "Men have the biggest egos! . . . All of them will listen, but if they do it, they'll do it once. Then the ego comes back. A man's ego is something else."[21]

Jo Gelbard, the artist who worked with Miles when he got into painting during the '80s and who was also his partner from 1986 to his death, commented, "He had no ego in music. That's why he had his back to the audience, because he could hear the band better and direct them. As opposed to, 'This is Miles Davis, and who cares who's behind me.' It was never just about him and his horn. He was always part of the group that was with him."

Lydia DeJohnette, wife of Jack, knew Miles well. "In music there was no arrogance to his ego," she remarked. "Being on stage was never about him, but always about musical inspiration, no matter where it came from. It made him happy to feel that inspiration. Sometimes he'd look at Jack and say, 'You know?' and Jack would go, 'Yeah, I know.' There was a knowing that they shared about the musical field, and it is where Miles felt connected with other people."

Jack DeJohnette added: "People were often worried about their personal contributions and their egos, but Miles was thinking of it as a team. He also knew that, whatever was going on, the sound of his horn could galvanize everything. Miles heard the finished thing." Keyboardist Herbie Hancock made a similar point: "Miles is an incredible team worker. He listens to what everybody does, and he uses that and what he plays makes what everybody does sound better."[22]

Miles's ability to focus and raise the level of awareness of the members of his bands was perplexing. Countless musicians who worked with Miles recounted stories of how he had a life-changing impact on them, and many talk about him in near-transcendental terms. Jarrett, Peacock, and DeJohnette called Miles "a medium, a transformer, a touchstone, a magnetic field."[23] The people who were interviewed for this book used words like "mystical," "guru," "sorcerer," "shaman," "teacher," "magician," "Merlin," or "Zen teacher."

"Miles gave me myself," bassist Michael Henderson said. "He gave me something that belonged to me. When I came to play with him, I became 'me.' Like everybody else who was with him. We all found ourselves. We found exactly who we were and what we should be doing as far as being in the music industry, and in life."

"I found my musical identity through playing with Miles," echoed Henderson's colleague Marcus Miller. "The first time I played with him, in 1980, I was scared like hell. We were recording a track called 'Aïda.' He played me F-sharp and G and said, 'That's it.' So I asked, 'That's it?' 'Yeah.' So I played only F-sharp and G. Miles stopped the band and asked, 'What are you doing, man? Are you just going to play these two notes? Is that all you're going to do?' So I started to do all sorts of variations. He stopped the band again, and said, 'Man, why are you playing so much? Just play F-sharp and G, and then shut up.' So I thought, 'Oh, he's just playing with me. This is a test.' I realized I just had to play and not worry about him. That's what I did and this time he let the whole take go by. Miles had great people skills in the sense of bringing out the best in you as a musician. He was great precisely because he wasn't communicating that much verbally. He made you find it on your own. Just like those martial arts teachers who point you in a direction and tell you a puzzling story that you have to analyze yourself. Or like those student-master relationships where the student can't understand why the master has him painting fences, and later on realizes, 'Oh yes, it's because . . .' It was the same thing with Miles."

Miller's analogy with fence painting comes from the movie *The Karate Kid*, in which a Zen-like Asian martial arts teacher has his pupil painting fences as part of his apprenticeship. John McLaughlin also drew the Zen parallel, saying "Miles in the studio directed very closely, but with very obscure statements. He was like a Zen master. He would give you very strange directions that were very difficult to understand, very obscure. But I think that was his intention, as it is with a Zen master. They will say something to you, and your mind will not be able to deal with it on a rational level. And so he made you act in a subconscious way, which was the best way. He had this great gift of pulling the best things out of people, without them even realizing."[24]

Palle Mikkelborg, the Danish trumpeter and composer who worked with Miles on *Aura,* wrote in his liner notes, "Musically, Miles is to me what a Zen teacher is spiritually."[25] Mikkelborg explained, "I have talked to a lot of people who have been to Japan and who have studied Zen. They say that sometimes in Zen you'll be told things which you don't understand, but you just have a feeling that what they say . . . is right. The same with Miles, he often said things that were very cryptic, but had a deeper meaning. During our first rehearsal for the performance of *Aura* in December 1984 he said to me about the drummer, 'Let him play as if he plays to a tap dancer.' We were working on 'Violet,' the last piece for the album, a very, very slow piece. I told the drummer what Miles had said and he asked me, 'What does he mean?' And I said, 'I don't know.' We thought about it, and we guessed that Miles wanted him to keep some energy back, and play with a mental awareness of a hidden, faster energy. It changed something in our attitude, and made the very slow rhythm lift off. I don't see it as anything else than a way of getting the best out of the present musical situation. I think it was an intuitive feeling he had for getting where he wanted to go. He once said to me, 'When you conduct an orchestra, you have to smell good.' At the time, I thought, 'What the hell does he mean?' Later on I understood that it means to be 'on' all the time. 'Smell good' means 'be aware,' awareness. He was 'on' all the time."

By being "'on' all the time," Miles exemplified the unsurpassed dedication and concentration with which he approached music. His attitude expressed a deep reverence and respect, demanding his total, egoless, here-and-now presence, almost as if music was sacred to him. Pianist Chick Corea touched on this when he said, "Miles set an example by the way he loved to make music. He was about making music. That kind of attitude created an atmosphere in which we all joined, because we all wanted to make music in such a very concentrated way." Guitarist Robben Ford recalled, "His presence created such an edge. I'd never been with anyone who could be so demanding just by his mere presence."[26]

Twenty-five years after working with Miles, saxophonist Sonny Fortune's voice dropped to a whisper when he said, "The whole time I worked with him I was in awe over the magic he had. I walked away from the experience of playing with him feeling that it was something that I would never forget. I can't explain it at all. Because of this magic, he didn't have to say much, and he didn't say much. He was one of the persons that I've met who expressed the least amount of trivia. He didn't talk about much, he didn't gossip, he didn't seem to be affected by a whole lot of things. He was a cat who only said one or two phrases, but it would summarize what you were trying to get to. And he had a knowing about music that you could sense and feel, even if it wasn't necessarily visible or describable."

These quotes all describe the same essence, the same attitude, from different perspectives. The analogy with Zen, alluded to by Miller, McLaughlin, and Mikkelborg, is a good way of portraying this. It makes it possible to draw together the perspectives of many observers and to create a comprehensive framework for understanding the many characteristics that made Miles such a great musical teacher and innovator. Minimalism, here-and-now presence, being awake, awareness, going beyond habit energies, egoless service to a greater purpose, teaching by example—these are all at the heart of Zen. Miles's love of boxing has parallels with the martial arts aspects of Zen. And like Miles, Zen teachers are traditionally men of few words, while Miles's penchant for cryptic one-liners has parallels with Zen koans.

The listening sense, especially inner listening, is also often associated with Zen, and with spiritual awareness in general. "Be still, and know that I am God" is a central phrase in Christianity. The original title of *The Tibetan Book of the Dead* contains the word hearing, and its most-used invocation is "Listen, ye man of noble birth."[27] In his book

The World Is Sound, the German author and jazz critic Joachim-Ernst Berendt elaborated on many aspects of the listening sense in a widely known chapter called "The Temple in the Ear" (after a phrase by the German poet Rainer Maria Rilke). Berendt argued that our television-obsessed culture has become overly focused on the visual sense, reducing the ears to an "auxiliary organ."[28] He quoted scientific evidence suggesting that the listening sense is more pronounced in women and reasoned that listening reflects feminine qualities of receptivity and awareness, whereas the penetrating and projecting visual-spatial sense is a masculine trait. According to Berendt, revaluing our listening sense is crucial if we want to rebalance and heal our off-kilter culture; he saw Zen practice as one way of achieving this, since it is about "wakefulness" and "listening to silence."[29] With his focus on the listening sense, Miles contributed to this rebalancing process.

❖

The aim of introducing spiritual perspectives and making the analogy with Zen is not to put Miles on a spiritual pedestal. To his great credit, Miles undermined any attempts by others to turn him into a guru. "I stood next to him in Japan when somebody began kissing his feet, literally," Lydia DeJohnette remembered. "Miles was like, 'Stop it!' Miles was aware of levels that other people aren't. He understood the vibration of music, what Jack called the 'essence' of music. So he could have been a guru if he wanted to. The '60s and the '70s were the era of gurus. But he didn't want to be a guru. I think some of his obnoxious side came from that."

The era of gurus may be over, but the spiritual and transcendental aspects of Miles's being are hinted at too frequently to be ignored. Things transcendental get dozens of mentions in Miles's autobiography, for example when he says that he believes in "mystery and the supernatural," "superstition," and "numerology," and that he can "predict the future." Miles also stated, "I do believe in being spiritual and do believe in spirits . . . music is about the spirit and the spiritual, and about feeling,"[30] and repeatedly referred to his clairvoyant side.

Eric Nisenson related how Miles often knew who called before he picked up the phone and could sense someone walking towards his house when they were still a block away. "Real *Twilight Zone* stuff,"[31] Nisenson commented. Quincy Troupe claimed in *Miles and Me* that Miles had a "spiritual, mystical" effect on him, and related how Miles talked to Gil Evans, John Coltrane, Charlie Parker, and others after they died. "He saw and understood things differently," Troupe wrote, "and he seemed to feel and know things spiritually, almost to the point of having extrasensory perception."[32]

Miles always seemed to know much more than he articulated, and his often-short expressions were so enticing because they always hinted at a much larger, hidden awareness, an intuitive "knowing," as Sonny Fortune and Lydia DeJohnette called it. Miles's nephew, drummer Vince Wilburn Jr., said, "It was innate, a 'knowing' gifted people have. With Miles it was almost a clairvoyant thing." And Miles's companion from 1969 to 1971, Marguerite Eskridge, remembered how he always gave the impression of knowing much more than he expressed. She added, "I honestly couldn't say whether this was because he was searching for the right words, or didn't want to talk about it, or maybe thought something like, 'doesn't everybody also know these things and understand them?'"

Spirituality does not necessarily overlap with organized religion, for which Miles had little time. "He was not one for God," Jo Gelbard commented, "but he was convinced that all the concerts and all the sounds he'd ever made were still there, floating around somewhere. That, for instance, his concert on November 12, 1956, was intact somewhere in space, and that they would one day invent a machine to play it again. He loved that idea!" Miles's idea of music floating around in eternity conjures up associations with the notion of "music of the spheres" and has a striking parallel with the idea of the "Akashic Records"—an alleged huge cosmic database of everything that ever happened, and a popular concept in New Age circles.

Robert Fripp, who, like Miles, has a predilection for cryptic but captivating statements, wrote about the difference between the "understanding musician" and the "knowing musician." "Knowing is an ordering of experience on the outside of our perceptions; understanding is an ordering of our experience on the inside of our perceptions."[33]

In this sense, Miles was a "knowing musician." When listening to the essence of music, Miles had the capacity to hear things that eluded others. He heard "meaning" in notes other musicians missed. He was the aural equivalent of a visionary. This made Miles a great teacher and a great musician. It gave him the ability to spot potentially great musicians, and also to play the kid in the story of the emperor's clothes, ruthlessly pointing out when music or musicians were out of touch with "the musical impulse." Yet, crucially, his strength was not in musical conception. He didn't conceive of the many musical innovations that he spearheaded. Instead, he recognized the unique creative possibilities in what was being done by his contemporaries, appropriated and developed these in highly imaginative ways, and communicated his findings to a worldwide audience.

Miles's role was reminiscent of that of the English writer John Aubrey who, one day in 1648, walked up a hill next to the English village of Avebury, looked down, and saw something that no one had ever seen before. As long as people could remember, Avebury had included a mysterious circular earthwork and a collection of huge stones. On that day Aubrey suddenly saw the meaning of the stones and earthwork: they made up a prehistoric site—a larger sister to Stonehenge. When his contemporaries went up to have a look, they invariably recognized it, too, and could hardly believe that they had never noticed it before.

A shift in perspective like this is often known as an "aha" or "eureka" experience; we suddenly "get" something. Moreover, insofar as the new outlook also changed the view the villagers had of themselves and of their world, it can be called a "paradigm shift." The scientist Thomas Kuhn introduced the idea of paradigm shifts, defining paradigms as sets of fundamental assumptions and concepts on which particular views of the world are based. Most of the time, human knowledge is deepened by working from a particular set of generally agreed premises. But periodically new paradigms emerge. For example, at one point describing the movements of the sun and the planets based on the premise that the earth is the center of the universe became too complex, and a new scientific paradigm was accepted that sees the earth as circling around the sun. What made this into a paradigm shift, rather than just a shift in perspective on a particular issue, was the enormous ramifications for the way mankind looked at itself and its place in the universe. Another, very literal, example, is the discovery of the law of perspective in the early Renaissance. Suddenly, all earlier drawings and paintings with their wrong perspectives appeared hopelessly naive. Human evolution progresses through these kinds of paradigm shifts. The term can apply as much to new ways of looking at the world, art, or music, as to, on a smaller scale, new ways of looking at our village, or our personal life. To discover, say, that we have a different father than we thought we had, can be a paradigm shift for an individual.

Paradigm shifts are usually preceded by a prolonged period of personal, political, or cultural turmoil, signaling that the old paradigm doesn't fit anymore. We tend to forget about these wider cultural contexts in which paradigm shifts occur, only remembering the individual pioneers. Their names are familiar. Albert Einstein brought about a paradigm shift in our thinking about the universe at a time when the natural sciences were feverishly trying to find new solutions to emerging problems. As part of the rising political awareness in the 1960s, Martin Luther King Jr. helped shift the American psyche on race issues. Charles Darwin changed our thinking about our origins in a society that was trying to make sense of the data provided by numerous fossil finds. The Beatles, embedded in the historic events of the '60s, brought about a paradigm shift in the music and culture of their era.

Miles Davis, surrounded by the cascading musical and political developments of 1945 to 1975, was one of the select group of twentieth-century musicians who initiated several paradigm shifts. He had a remarkable capacity for capturing and transforming the zeitgeist, for pointing his finger at the stone circle at a time when people were ready to recognize it. It was this that made him into one of the great artists of the twentieth century, rather than an obscure visionary remembered only by music historians.

Miles's cool jazz, hardbop, and modal jazz experiments each changed the musical perspective of the jazz community, causing respected jazz writer Leonard Feather to proclaim, "He has manifestly changed the entire course of an art form three or four times in twenty-five years—an accomplishment no other jazz musician can claim."[34] Miles's explorations into jazz-rock and ambient jazz were paradigm shifts that affected not only the jazz community but also those beyond. In the context of a visually orientated culture, his listening awareness can also be described in paradigm terms.

In addition, as the first black jazz musician who consistently crossed over into other music genres, other cultures, and other countries, Miles transcended the paradigm of musical, cultural, and racial segregation. He was one of the first truly universal musicians, going beyond categories, boundaries, and borders of any kind. The effects of his musical and personal odyssey rippled into the whole of twentieth-century music and culture, and are still with us today.

And finally, Miles instigated a paradigm shift on his musical instrument. Before Miles, the jazz trumpet was mostly played with a bright, brassy sound, rich in vibrato. But through Miles's stylistic developments we today hear the jazz trumpet being played very differently, sounding more vulnerable, soulful, like a cri de coeur. Trumpeter Olu Dara observed, "He's singing rather than playing the trumpet. He was using it like the human voice. He transformed the mechanical aspect of the instrument. He made it sound like a breath."[35] Saxophonist Wayne Shorter remembered simply, "They called him the guy with the strange sound on the trumpet."[36]

The absence of vibrato was the most characteristic aspect of Miles's style, resulting in an unadorned, introverted sound, often with a crack at the beginning of his notes, giving the impression of vulnerability. Miles also tended to play in the gentler, rounder-sounding middle and low registers, because he couldn't "hear" the trumpet's high notes. And in 1954 Miles popularized the sound of the trumpet played with a Harmon mute without the stem. Combined with the lack of vibrato, and played close to a microphone, this allows for an intimate, tender, but very expressive sound.

There is a widespread misunderstanding that Miles conceived of these approaches because of limitations in his trumpet technique, but he already displayed awesome chops on some recordings in the '40s.[37] It is more likely that his innovations emerged from his astute listening awareness, which made him recognize the significance of sound. "Sound is the most important thing a musician can have, because you can't do anything without a sound," Miles remarked. "If a musician is interested in his sound, then you can look for some good playing."[38]

Miles kept developing as a trumpeter until he reached his technical peak in the late '60s, playing an extroverted and virtuoso form of power trumpet that included its high register. He also established a very personal, wah-wah–inspired electric trumpet style in the '70s. Both his power and his electric trumpet styles retained recognizable elements of his characteristic cracked, voicelike, vibratoless sound, but neither was as influential. In the '80s Miles returned to his original trumpet style, often sounding more cracked and vulnerable than before because his technique only occasionally rose to its previous heights.

It was Miles's "strange" cri de coeur on the trumpet that had the most universal resonance and added another color to the palette of human experience. Even if he hadn't spearheaded several musical revolutions, his place in posterity would be secured purely for introducing this horn sound. It was the focal point, the pivot that drew everything he did together, the common thread at the heart of all the disparate musical styles and experiments that he traversed during his epic, forty-six-year-long recording career. Echoing the story of the Pied Piper of Hameln, the charismatic sound of Miles's horn made millions follow him into the undiscovered territory he probed.

"When Miles played his horn, everything fell into place . . . [and] he spoke to the whole world," Jack DeJohnette remarked. His wife Lydia added, "Miles spoke more with his horn than with his mouth. His inner life came out in his music. When you listen to his horn you can hear sadness, you can hear pain, you can hear everything else. This is where he revealed himself."

Miles's touching, deeply human trumpet sound is so moving and compelling because of its apparent contradiction with the tough, inscrutable, macho persona that he displayed to the world. The poignant irony that the hard man with the legendary rough, raspy, almost demonic voice—the aftermath of a throat operation in the '50s—played his instrument with voicelike lyricism has inflated this contradiction to almost mythical proportions.

Miles's many contradictions, his fierce independence and his leadership abilities, his sensitive, vulnerable sound, his awareness, his listening capacities, and his violence and drug addiction, epitomized some of the extremes of our human nature.

Marguerite Eskridge recounted how Miles expressed aspects of these extremes privately. "Miles was the epitome of the Gemini, Jekyll and Hyde personality. The positive one was golden; [he] would give anybody anything that they needed, open his door and take in guys who were out of work, or homeless. The opposite one was just as extreme; [he] had a very violent temper and could be very violent."

A sense of unfathomable darkness and imminent danger often surrounded Miles. It is hinted at by the more ominous epithets that he received, such as "dark magus," "prince of darkness," and "a puzzle wrapped in an enigma."[39] But the melancholy and vulnerability always shone through. In Miles's horn sound we can always sense the delicate sensitivity that was also there. We sense his spiritual qualities, the fire of his creativity, and the light of his authenticity and "knowing," as much as the surrounding looming shadows. We sense his deep humanity, which makes us feel for him and sympathize with him, and we sense the "unexplainable," larger-than-life qualities that urged him to go into places where most of us wouldn't dream of going. He was both one of us and a stranger in a strange land. He was someone on the brink of several paradigms conveying mysterious tales to which we cannot but listen.

Chapter Two

CHANGES

"I have to change. It's like a curse."

—MILES DAVIS[1]

Life is only available to us in the present moment. Being fully in touch with life means being fully present with each of an endless succession of ever-changing present moments. This is the essence of mindfulness practice in Zen. If we can remain in the present moment, and be aware of the impermanent nature of this present moment, we will be better prepared for the inevitable changes that continuously face us. Miles's extraordinary presence, focus, and penchant for change demonstrated his capacity to walk this tightrope.

For Miles, short-term and long-term changes were a way of life. Short-term change occurred in the way his musical performances would alter night by night, week by week, month by month. Although Miles is reported to have said, with a aphorism often quoted among musicians, "I'm happy if I can play one new idea on a night,"[2] many of his bands were renowned for developing new ideas moment by moment. Miles's second great quintet—featuring saxophonist Wayne Shorter, keyboardist Herbie Hancock, bassist Ron Carter, and drummer Tony Williams—was especially famous for this. Miles commented in his autobiography that he learned something new every night and that the songs they played at the beginning of the year were often unrecognizable by the end of the year.

"Miles would create something and record it in the studio," Marguerite Eskridge reminisced. "Then he'd take it home and listen to it, sometimes for days. And then it would be over. It was time for something new, and he didn't really care to go back and listen to those things again. It was always, 'what's the next thing?' It was the creating that was important, not the 'now I have it, let's enjoy it.'" Lydia DeJohnette commented, "Miles was a true artist. His art was always a work in progress. It was always in the moment, and moving forward. He would rarely go back and listen to his old stuff." And Dave Liebman opined, "He couldn't keep repeating. See, that would be the cardinal sin for Miles. He could not be a classicist. A classicist is one who makes his art classic and continues to refine it and stays with it. . . . Miles would never do that."[3]

Without impermanence there is no life, no growth, just static sterility. For an artist, stagnation is synonymous with creative death. Acutely aware of this, Miles initiated change not only moment by moment but also over much larger time frames, spearheading cool jazz from 1949 to 1950, hardbop in the mid-1950s, modal jazz and orchestral jazz in the late 1950s, something that's been called avant-bop in the mid-1960s, and jazz-rock in the late 1960s, 1970s, and 1980s. Like Picasso, to whom he is often compared, Miles went through several radically different creative phases. Normally, innovative artists are celebrated if they manage to change the course of music only once, but astonishingly, Miles was at the forefront of several new musical directions, a feat unparalleled in the history of music.

Miles summarized the urgency of his need for change in the aphorism "If I ever look back, I'll die." Of course, this was a tongue-in-cheek quip made to emphasize a point, and was not to be taken literally. It nevertheless gained tragic significance in the summer of 1991 when Miles Davis did look back, for the first time in his life, at two concerts in Montreux and Paris. Less than twelve weeks later, on September 28, he died. Rather than dramatize the situation, and assume that he died because he looked back, it appears that he looked back because he was aware that he was dying.

"Miles knew he didn't have long to live," Jo Gelbard said. "Death permeated every minute of his day and his decision making. There was a finality to the whole period that gave it a type of closure."

It may seem a distraction to dwell on the two occasions that were uncharacteristic of Miles's career. But they were indeed a closure, a winding down, a summing up of his kaleidoscopic career, and they offer a good starting point for a career overview. They also demonstrate how crucial his "never-look-back" ethos was for his creative survival, and how alive and relevant the electric direction he was negotiating still is.

During the first event, on July 8, 1991, at the Montreux Jazz Festival, Miles played some of the legendary music he had recorded earlier in his career with his musical soul mate, the arranger and composer Gil Evans. These works had been released on classic albums like *The Birth of the Cool, Miles Ahead, Porgy and Bess,* and *Sketches of Spain. The Birth of the Cool,* recorded in 1949 and 1950, contained the first serious answer to the bebop revolution that had swept through the jazz world in the years after the Second World War. About a decade later, Miles and Evans recorded the other three albums. It is hard to overstate the importance of the music Miles performed on that night in Montreux with an impromptu orchestra conducted by Quincy Jones. And since this was the first time in more than three decades that he had played it, one can understand that many in the jazz world viewed it with the rose-tinted glasses of nostalgia.

Warner Bros. Records released both a video and a CD of Miles's Montreux performance, and they show that the rose-tinted glasses were really of the high-tech type described in *The Hitchhiker's Guide to the Galaxy*—the ones that turn black at the first sign of danger. To the dispassionate viewer, the small and stooping figure of Miles Davis looked fragile and ill at ease. Even someone who doesn't speak the jazz "language" can hear that the oversized orchestra does less than full justice to Gil Evans's delicate arrangements, and that Miles's playing was shaky. Given that the man who never looked back hadn't played this music for more than thirty years, and given that he only turned up for the rehearsal the night before, at 11 P.M., it's amazing that he played as well as he did.

Herbie Hancock may have spoken for many when he agreed that it "wasn't his finest playing" but that he "just cried" when he saw the video of the event, and that "Miles's worst playing sounds better than everybody else's best playing. It still has a sound and an honesty that attracts." At the same time, many other musicians who had played with

Miles had feelings ranging from grave doubts to utter frustration. Saxophonist Steve Grossman said, "The Montreux thing was very sad. He looked real ill there." Another musician, who declined to go on the record, refused Miles's invitation to come to Montreux because he felt the concert "should never have been done."

Jo Gelbard accompanied Miles to both concerts. "Miles didn't like doing Montreux, he was very unhappy there," she reminisced. "Why did he do it? I talked him into it. Miles was tired, and he was dying, but Montreux gave good money and it was supposed to be his retirement money. You know, we were also in denial, thinking that maybe he won't die after all, and maybe we'll get another five years and buy a ranch and live together. Montreux was a very heavy time. He was in a terrible mood. The trip to Montreux was a slide into hell for him. He was up for that summer tour in general [with his regular band], but given how sick and weak he was it took all he had. And redoing anything from the past was not his favorite thing. I don't remember whose idea the Paris concert two days later was, but Miles was very up for that. We worked very hard and far in advance at painting the backdrop for it, so he didn't associate the concert with Montreux. He was particularly concerned with getting the set design exact, more than usual."

The Paris concert took place in an outdoor venue called La Villette, where an impressive conglomeration of world-class players had descended to join Miles's working band and pay tribute to the master. They were all musicians who had once played with him, and their names read like a who's who of late-twentieth-century jazz, including John McLaughlin, Steve Grossman, Herbie Hancock, Joe Zawinul, Wayne Shorter, Chick Corea, Dave Holland, Al Foster, and John Scofield. Almost all of these artists had come to fruition during the time they played with Miles, integrated the lessons, and applied them in successful careers of their own. The musicians who rose to greatness during their time with Miles easily numbers a few dozen, leading to ironic talk about the "University of Miles Davis." Here were some of its graduates, providing living testimony of Miles's enormous influence on his fellow musicians and, since most are known for playing rock-influenced jazz music, exemplifying the richness and creative success of the jazz-rock direction.

An abbreviated version of the show was televised in many countries around the world,[4] but neither the music nor the video of the La Villette concert have been officially released. This is a frustrating hiatus, because the concert was superlative. An upright Miles looked a million miles from death. He was clearly at ease and in his element, playing relatively little. But when he did play, he played well. Moreover, although it did not contain any of his classic work with Gil Evans, the La Villette concert covered much larger sections of Miles Davis's career. It featured his 1947 bebop composition "Donna Lee," a piece called "Out of the Blue" that he first recorded in 1951, and three pieces that changed the course of music. They were "All Blues" from *Kind of Blue* (Miles's 1959 venture into modal jazz, which is still widely regarded as the best jazz album of all time) and "In a Silent Way" and "It's about That Time" from the 1969 album *In a Silent Way* (Miles's first genuine jazz-rock album, which also became one of the blueprints for ambient music).

The video shies away from the distracting visual pyrotechnics that have become common in music videos and instead focuses on the interaction between the musicians. The awe and respect with which they regarded Miles is evident. They watched his every move and facial expression, waiting for cues to start performing, or for an indication of whether he approved of what they played. Miles was continuously in the center of attention. His commanding here-and-now presence forced the musicians, once again, to "play above what they normally play." Most of the musicians present rose to the occasion, and even Miles's regular band, featuring ace saxophonist Kenny Garrett and a very supple Richard Patterson on bass, played with increased intensity. Moreover, the jazz-rock sections shone most brightly, notably Prince's "Penetration," Hancock's "Watermelon Man," McLaughlin's angular soloing in "Katia," and saxophonist's Kenny Garrett's stirring solo in "Human Nature." By contrast, "All Blues" sounded rushed and sloppy, and "Out of the Blue" sounded irrelevant. Overall, the concert showcased all the things that had made Miles Davis one of the most influential musicians of the twentieth century: the trumpet sound, the musical innovations, and the amazing presence that brought out great performances in the musicians present. La Villette was a worthy crowning of a glorious career.

"The Paris gig was a celebration of all the people who had been with him, and we were all there to celebrate him and his music," Holland recalled. "There was a wonderful atmosphere! Everybody was there on time, even Herbie, who is known to always be a little late. It was great. The Montreux thing had a very different premise, being a production recreating the Gil Evans collaboration. Except that Gil wasn't there. Except it wasn't the same band. Except it was another time and another place."

Chick Corea's memories of Paris were equally positive. "The concert was wonderful!" Corea exclaimed. "Miles had the vibe of recounting his life. He was a very unsentimental guy, but during that concert, he embraced all his old friends. It looked like he really enjoyed himself while making a review of his past. He didn't do much playing. He let the band play. But he was directing strongly."

Twelve weeks later, Miles was dead. Almost all the musicians who had ever worked with him expressed deep shock and total surprise; like many, they had assumed that Miles would always be there. He'd survived through so many decades, had come back from the dead so often, and had been part of so many musical mutations, he had seemed to transcend the laws that apply to the rest of us.

Whatever larger-than-life qualities had been ascribed to him, Miles turned out to be as human, mortal, and vulnerable as all of us. He suffered enormous pain, both physical and emotional, during his lifetime. But despite this he achieved great things as a musician. The tales of his inheritance and his jazz inventions, and of his "darkness" and his light, have been told many times. The main facts are well known, so I will not dwell on the details, but I will paint his story in broad brush strokes for readers less familiar with his childhood and jazz background.

Miles Dewey Davis III was born on May 26, 1926, in Alton, Illinois. When he was one year old, his parents moved twenty-five miles down the Mississippi River to East St. Louis. Miles came from a line of proud and independent black men: his paternal grandfather, Miles Dewey Davis I, was a prosperous bookkeeper who became a landowner; his father, Miles Dewey Davis II, a successful dentist and landowner. As a result the young Miles Davis grew up with a high sense of self-esteem in a well-to-do black middle-class family. This made the indignities of racism even harder for him to bear, something that had a huge influence on his outlook in life. Miles did not get on well with his mother, Cleota Henry. In his autobiography Miles stated that he got his looks and artistic talent from her, but other than that she seemed to have been an aloof figure for him, one who frequently tried to thwart his musical ambitions, and often, in his words, "slapped the shit out of me."[5] His parents' marriage was deeply dysfunctional, and they separated when he was eighteen. Miles had an older sister, Dorothy, and a younger brother, Vernon.

Miles was an extremely intelligent and talented child, with a photographic memory; he started playing trumpet when he was nine or ten. He was influenced by the strong trumpet-playing tradition in St. Louis and East St. Louis, featuring a more controlled, softer style than came upstream from New Orleans. Miles's trumpet teacher, Elwood Buchanan, helped Miles develop his own sound by advising him not to use vibrato. The period until *The Birth of the Cool* in 1949 can be seen as a formative period during which Miles soaked up as many influences as he could and formed his own sound and approach to music. There are many endearing examples in his autobiography of his total commitment to music, such as his attempts to name the pitch of squeaking doors, or, when listening to gigs, his attempts to write down chords on matchboxes or guess the note played the moment a flipped coin hit a table.

Miles's first professional engagement was in East St. Louis, with the local R&B band Eddie Randle's Blue Devils, during 1943 and 1944. When the famous Billy Eckstine Band came to St. Louis in 1944, Miles's two-week sitting-in stint became one of the big events in his life, not least because it was the first time he saw Charlie Parker and Dizzie Gillespie play. This was when he had, in his words, "the greatest feeling I ever had—with my clothes on." Parker and Gillespie told him to look them up if he came to New York City. Although his mother was opposed to his going to New York City, Miles convinced his father by stating that he wanted to attend the Juilliard School of Music. But when Miles arrived in the city in September of 1944, Juilliard took second place to the jazz clubs in Harlem and on the legendary jazz street of the time, Fifty-second Street, often simply called "The Street." It was here that bebop was being developed, and it was here that Miles played next to Charlie Parker for the first time. Parker and Gillespie became Miles's main teachers, continuing a long-standing tradition among jazz musicians of freely sharing knowledge. Parker taught by example; Gillespie was more involved, engaging in lengthy discussions and practical demonstrations, such as showing him harmony on the piano.

Miles dropped out of Juilliard after a year, an event that would upset most parents. However, it prompted his father to simply declare his belief in his son and to encourage him to find his own voice. With this kind of support behind him, it did not take long for Miles's education to bear fruit. His first recording with Parker in November of 1945 immediately gave rise to several bebop classics, such as "Now's the Time" and "Billie's Bounce." Miles played with Parker until the end of the '40s. It says much about the courage, vision, and self-belief of the young Miles that he held his own next to the virtuoso Parker and, in the face of much disapproval from Parker fans and critics, continued to develop his own trumpet voice.

Despite leaving Juilliard, Miles continued to receive financial support from his father during his first years in New York. It was a luxury that set him apart from most of the black musicians he met in New York, who usually came from impoverished black ghettos. In St. Louis, Miles had already grown up perched on the fence between the white middle-class American dream and his black ethnic background, assimilating the values and cultural outlooks of both. In addition, Miles mentioned in passing, "My family got a lot of Indian blood."[6] This became apparent in his later life, when his Native American genes seemed to increasingly manifest themselves in his facial features. Quincy Troupe noted, when sitting with Miles on a Malibu beach in 1986, "I remember thinking when I looked at him from the side that I could see a lot of Native American Indian in his profile."[7] It suggests a triple heritage of African, European, and Native American influences, making Miles a quintessentially modern American.

Miles's rich heritage put him in a very unusual position, further epitomized by his dual education—his formal music tuition at Juilliard and his informal assimilation from his jazz colleagues. According to Gary Tomlinson, professor of music at the University of Pennsylvania, this led Miles into an acute fascination with *differences.* "Perhaps more than any other contemporary musician, Davis made this stylistic, cultural, and ethnic mix the stuff of his music."[8] One of Miles's great strengths became his capacity for transforming differences into unifying bridges, a characteristic that was epitomized by his music, his work with musicians of a wide variety of musical, ethnic, racial, and cultural origins, and his appeal to audiences of equally varied backgrounds.

Miles first entered the studio as a leader in August of 1947, at the age of twenty-one, when he recorded his compositions "Milestones" and "Half Nelson." During the late 1940s he gained international recognition as Parker's sideman and as one of the main exponents of the bebop style, but by the turn of the decade he began to formulate his own musical direction. Miles's post-1948 recording career has often been described as an attempt to distance himself from his bebop days, to find alternatives to bebop's fast and frenzied style, even though he would regularly draw upon it until the late '60s. From late 1948 onwards he certainly appeared to be stripping his music down at many steps of the way, exemplifying his ethos "I always listen for what I can leave out."

The Birth of the Cool sessions were his first move in this direction, and the first time he assumed his John Aubrey role, recognizing a stone circle where few others had. Miles acted as the bandleader and figurehead who brought to fruition existing ideas of arrangers Gil Evans, Gerry Mulligan, John Lewis, and John Caresi. The twelve songs they recorded in 1949 and 1950 contained music that was a combination of the slower "cool" style that had already been developed in jazz and of European orchestral-style arrangements. The music had a far-reaching effect on the jazz world that resonates to this day.

The young Miles Davis seemed on course towards great things, but he first took a painful and lengthy detour following his first foreign concert performances in Paris in May of 1949. The respect and adulation he received there caught him by surprise. He met the likes of Jean Paul Sartre, Simone de Beauvoir, and Pablo Picasso, and fell deeply in love with the singer Julliette Greco.[9] When he returned to New York he sank into a deep depression, and within weeks heroin had taken over his life. It was the beginning of a four-year nightmare, during which he changed from "a nice, quiet, honest, caring person into someone who was the complete opposite."[10] His playing suffered and he produced only a few things of lasting value during this period. The main light on the horizon was a recording session for Prestige Records in October of 1951. Miles was one of the first jazz musicians to record for the new 33 1/3 rpm long-play record medium and transcend the constraints of the three-minute maximum time limit that dogged 78 rpm records. He rose to the occasion with the acclaimed track "Dig."

These four years were a tragic and painful experience for Miles. He became a pimp, stole from his friends, ended up in jail, was found in the gutter, and separated from his childhood sweetheart Irene Cawthon,[11] with whom he had three children, Cheryl (b. 1944), Gregory (b. 1946), and Miles IV (b. 1950). By the end of 1953, after four years of suffering and humiliations, he decided he had had enough, went back to his father's farm in Millstadt, Illinois, and kicked heroin cold turkey. Much has been made of this amazing demonstration of will and self-discipline. However, it was not as decisive as it seemed. He described in his autobiography how he couldn't stop completely, and went back to pimping and using heroin in Detroit, where he had exiled himself early in 1954 to get away from the drug scene. On his return to New York he still used cocaine, a drug that would remain a part of his life until the '80s. Miles hit the nail on the head when he described himself as having an "addictive personality," and skepticism has to be applied to any claim after his cold-turkey episode that he was drug free. Moreover, the drug addiction episode left lasting scars on his psyche, and he went from being an open and trusting person to distrusting everybody. His often cold and aloof behavior, combined with his tendencies to turn his back to the audience, or walk off stage during his sidemen's solos, and his refusal to be an entertainer on stage and announce song titles, led to a lot of controversy, and the birth of the Miles Davis persona.

The real value of Miles going cold turkey was that, drugs or no drugs, he was in control of his life again. The results were dramatic. The period from 1954 to 1960 is one of the richest, most innovative, and influential periods any artist has enjoyed in the twentieth century. It began with Miles's recording of the thirteen-minute-long track "Walkin'" in April of 1954, which set the tone for the whole hardbop movement of the '50s. During this time Miles gained his reputation for discovering new talent, the pianist Horace Silver being one of his first major discoveries. Towards the end of 1954 Miles recorded some legendary tracks with pianist Thelonious Monk, one of them being "Bag's Groove," in which he applied his leaving-things-out motto by excluding the piano in certain places. He also was influenced by the piano playing of Ahmad Jamal, admiring him for his light touch and use of space.

Things moved increasingly fast for Miles during 1955. There was a performance at the Newport Jazz Festival that earned him headlines and put him back in the public eye. Following this, he formed his first great quintet, featuring saxophonist John Coltrane, pianist Red Garland, bassist Paul Chambers, and drummer Philly Joe Jones. All were relative unknowns, and Coltrane received a lot of flak from the critics for his "hard" tone. But Miles spotted Coltrane's huge talent at a time when no one else did, and he nurtured and protected Coltrane, just as Parker had once done with him. The development of the quintet into the most revered and influential small band in jazz history elevated Miles's name as a talent spotter to legendary proportions. The quintet recorded five albums during 1956 that have become jazz classics: *Cookin'*, *Relaxin'*, *Workin'*, *Steamin'* (all on Prestige), and *'Round about Midnight*. The last-named album was his first for Columbia Records, the record company with which he forged an extremely fruitful thirty-year relationship. These five albums contain music that was a continuation and expansion of the hardbop, or "neo-bop," that was in vogue at the time. While the style was not especially groundbreaking, the quintet played it with more authority, variety, and invention than anyone else.

In December of 1957, Miles added alto saxophonist Julian "Cannonball" Adderley, an R&B–based player, to the band. The dichotomy between Adderley and the experimental Coltrane has been analyzed by writer and poet Amiri Baraka as laying the first foundations for the two major currents that have dominated jazz since the '60s: fusion (which sprang from a mixture of jazz, gospel, funk, R&B, and pop) and free-jazz (which emerged in 1959 from the chromatic and avant-garde "out" playing of the likes of Ornette Coleman and Don Cherry).[12] However, these polarities were no more than tendencies in the Miles Davis Sextet, and for now they joined forces in the creation of the ultimate hardbop album, *Milestones,* recorded in April of 1958. The following year, during two sessions in March and August, and with Bill Evans on piano and Jimmy Cobb on drums, the sextet recorded the seminal jazz record *Kind of Blue.* The big breakthrough of this album was Miles's application of the modal ideas pioneered by composer/writer George Russell. Modal music is based on scales (or modes), rather than chord structures, and until *Kind of Blue* nobody had been able to make it work. But Miles once more discovered meaning where few others had.

The modal form allowed Miles to completely free himself from the yoke of bebop's harmonic constraints. Once again, he had managed to bring new music into being by leaving out certain elements and working creatively with the remaining essence. Until he hit upon circular bass lines and layered rhythms a decade later, it seemed as if it was not possible to simplify jazz music any further. The legacy of Miles's time with Charlie Parker in the 1940s, particularly the saxophonist's approach to organizing music, provided another important influence on *Kind of Blue.* "Bird was never organized about telling people what he wanted them to do," Miles said. "He just got who he thought could play the shit he wanted and left it at that. Nothing was written down, maybe a sketch of a melody. . . . He was real spontaneous, went on instinct."[13]

In early 1957, Miles applied Parker's method during a session with ad hoc musicians in Paris to record the score for Louis Malle's movie *Ascenseur pour l'Échafaud.* He created the music by getting the musicians to improvise on the most minimal of musical material. In the case of *Kind of Blue,* Miles again wrote down a few musical sketches, placed them in front of musicians who had never seen them before, and recorded their first takes. This forced the musicians to be totally alert to what was happening in the present moment. Sensing the Zen connection, pianist Bill Evans drew an analogy with the Japanese Zen art form of the uninterrupted line in his sleeve notes. The fact that such minimal material could result in successful music provided an important lesson that Miles would apply during the rest of his career, especially during the period from 1968 to 1975 and from 1980 to 1983.

At the same time that he pushed the boundaries of hardbop with the quintet and sextet, Miles had a parallel career, creating the three classic records with Gil Evans that were the main focus of the Montreux concert in July of 1991. In May of 1957 he recorded *Miles Ahead* with an eighteen-piece orchestra. The music was in many ways an extension of the *The Birth of the Cool* sessions, only it was played with more expression, and was musically more developed, with greater dissonances in the harmony and richer textures.

Evans arranged the music, and Miles was the only soloist, breaking new ground by playing the softer-sounding flügelhorn on all tracks. He did the same on their next collaboration, *Porgy and Bess,* which was based on George Gershwin's musical and recorded in July and August of 1958. Finally, in November of 1959 and March of 1960, Miles and Evans recorded a third collaboration, called *Sketches of Spain.* Inspired by "Concierto de Aranjuez," by the Spanish classical composer Joaquín Rodrigo, it became one of Miles's best-selling albums. Other innovations on these three albums include the introduction of what is today called world music (in the Latin-American and flamenco sounds) and prominent bass lines that have as much a melodic as a harmonic function. These innovations would become important features of Miles's electric music.

However, just like ten year earlier, Miles's band, music, and personal life were slowly disintegrating by late 1959, and it would take him until 1964 to get his act back together. There were several reasons for his decline. Adderley had left the quintet soon after the recording of *Kind of Blue,* and Coltrane left in March of 1960. Both departures were huge creative blows, because there were no saxophonists available who could replace them to Miles's satisfaction. In August of 1959 the infamous Birdland incident took place, during which a policeman asked Miles to move on when he was taking a breather in front of the club. When Miles refused, he ended up in jail with blood running down his head. The incident left him with considerable bitterness. On top of this emotional scar, he was also starting to have many physical problems. In 1961 he discovered that he was suffering from sickle-cell anemia, causing him great pain in his joints, especially his left hip. The pain led him to increase his drug use, particularly alcohol, cocaine, and painkillers. Then his father died in May of 1962, his mother in February of 1964, and his marriage to Frances Taylor collapsed during the same period. Miles described himself as "something like the Phantom of the Opera . . . all paranoid and shit . . . I was a mess and getting worse."[14]

In the midst of all this it was not surprising that his music was suffering. After Coltrane left, Miles went through a string of saxophonists, and in March of 1961 he recorded an unsatisfactory album called *Someday My Prince Will Come.* He and Gil Evans abandoned *Quiet Nights,* an attempt to capitalize on the Latin music that was in vogue at the time, because their hearts weren't in it. After their great achievements a few years earlier, this must have been disheartening. Apart from a one-day session in 1968, they never recorded large-scale orchestral projects again. To Miles's dismay and against his explicit wishes, Columbia released *Quiet Nights,* which led to him falling out with producer Teo Macero for two years.

Meanwhile, other events in the jazz world seemed to be overtaking Miles. The free-jazz movement was out on the cutting edge, bitterly dividing the jazz world into conservatives and progressives. For the first time in his creative life, Miles found himself siding with the conservatives. He critiqued free-jazz on regular occasions, like to journalist Les Tomkins: "You have to have some kind of form. You have to start *somewhere.*"[15] Miles appeared out of step with the times, and come 1964, few would have put any money on Miles's ability to rise from the ashes again to take the lead. Yet, he was on the verge of rebuilding another band that would not only reestablish his position at the forefront of jazz but would also be his first to employ rock influences, thereby paving the way for his explorations into jazz-rock.

Chapter Three

FREEDOM JAZZ DANCE

*"There's nothing magical about the electric period.
There's nothing mysterious about how we put things
together. There was just more courage involved. The
courage to say: 'To hell with the critics.'"*
—WAYNE SHORTER

1964. Change was in the air in the Western world. After the economically stable, but socially stifling, decades following World War II, the status quo was showing cracks. The signs were inescapable enough for Bob Dylan to write a prophetic album called *The Times They Are A-Changin'*. Increased political awareness gave rise to a genuine protest movement, and questions were being asked about the quagmire of the Vietnam War and about the roles of authorities. Rebellion became the modus operandi of the baby boomer generation, which changed its style of clothing, grew its hair, and experimented with drugs and Eastern religions. People with short hair and suits were labeled "straight," "square," or "stiff," and since most jazz musicians wore suits and had short hair, they were dismissed accordingly.

Only a few years earlier, jazz had been the vanguard of the hip, the young, and the arty, but now it was perceived as a relic of an anachronistic and antiquated era. Rock 'n' roll music had become the voice of the new generation. During the early 1960s it dominated the charts in a popularized form, known as "pop," that had few artistic merits or pretensions. But by 1964, a more serious and sophisticated form of rock 'n' roll, called "rock," started to develop. Spearheaded by British bands like The Beatles, The Rolling Stones, and The Who, it drew heavily on American music styles such as blues, soul, R&B, and the '50s rock 'n' roll of Elvis Presley, Buddy Holly, Little Richard, and Chuck Berry. In return, the "British Invasion" revitalized an American rock music scene featuring bands like The Byrds, Jefferson Airplane, The Doors, and The Allman Brothers Band. All founded in 1965, these bands were also influenced by American folk and country music. Meanwhile, Jimi Hendrix was cutting his teeth playing with The Isley Brothers, Little Richard, Ike and Tina Turner, and Sam Cooke, getting himself into shape to stun the world a few years later.

One of the maxims of this worldwide youth movement was poignantly captured by The Who in their 1965 protopunk anthem "My Generation." The line "I hope I die before I get old" gave rock music one of its first entries in the *Oxford Dictionary of*

Quotations. Miles Davis turned thirty-eight in 1964, and from the perspective of the rebellious young he was already old, one of yesterday's men. He was also an icon of the '40s and '50s, the era that was now being rejected. Moreover, since Miles was not leading the way anymore within his own jazz community, people were increasingly expecting him to rest on his laurels and play out his time emulating his earlier achievements.

But as he had done so often, Miles defied expectations. He was about to embark on the most adventurous decade of his musical career, leading him almost inexorably from music still wholly within the jazz tradition towards the African-influenced funk he pursued in the mid-1970s. During the eleven years from 1964 to 1975, Miles traveled such a long distance and explored so many different corners that his beginning and end points seem like different worlds. But those who look closely can spot an underlying continuity that stretches all the way from his beginnings in St. Louis to his experiments of *On the Corner* and *Agharta.*

In 1964 there were few indications of great things to come. Miles hadn't yet expressed much interest in the dramatic social events that would soon overtake Western culture, nor in the rock music that was its main artistic expression. When queried, he usually made a few derogatory comments about the inferior skills of rock musicians, and carried on with business as usual, which was breathing life into the jazz idiom. Sharp suits and haircuts remained the name of the game. The outrageous clothes and sunglasses of the '70s still belonged to a different, faraway universe.

Initiating change was second nature to Miles, but uncharacteristically, he did not instigate the adventure he embarked on in the '60s. Whether Miles was burnt out or distracted by his personal problems is unclear, but this time his tried-and-true leaving-things-out approach was done for him, when drummer Jimmy Cobb and pianist Wynton Kelly left his band in 1962. They were the last remaining members of the legendary sextet of the late '50s—which had featured John Coltrane and Cannonball Adderley—and their departure forced Miles's hand.

True to form, he rose to the occasion, and by May of 1963 he had formed a new quintet that satisfied his high standards. The rhythm section consisted of twenty-six-year-old bassist Ron Carter, twenty-three-year-old pianist Herbie Hancock, and seventeen-year-old drummer Tony Williams, establishing a pattern of working with much younger musicians that Miles would continue for the rest of his life. Younger musicians offered him a better connection to the music of the present, and were open-minded. "Coleman Hawkins once told me not to play with anybody old because they'll be hard to bend the way you want them to play,"[1] Miles commented in 1982.

Ron Carter was a rock steady player with a beautiful round tone. He had emerged as the only good news from an unsatisfactory recording session for the album *Seven Steps to Heaven* in April of 1963, which also featured saxophonist George Coleman. Realizing that the music wasn't happening, Miles moved fast. A month later he recruited Williams and Hancock. (The latter had been introduced to Miles a year earlier by trumpeter Donald Byrd, in whose band Hancock was playing at the time.) Hancock gave Miles the light touch of Ahmad Jamal and Wynton Kelly, as well as a classical harmonic and melodic resourcefulness. Tony Williams was a drum prodigy discovered by Miles's friend and '50s playing partner, saxophonist Jackie McLean. Miles said that he knew "right away that this was going to be one of the baddest motherfuckers who had ever played a set of drums."[2] As so often, his observations were prescient. Williams's driving feel and amazing polyrhythmic improvisations would gain him recognition as one of the world's most innovative and influential drummers.

When they came together, Williams, Carter, and Hancock clicked immediately. Their first recording session with Miles, in May of 1963, again with George Coleman on tenor sax, was also included on *Seven Steps to Heaven* and was well received. Miles appeared happy with this quintet. Their live performances reinvigorated him, while the rhythm section was already beginning to deconstruct the hardbop formula. Yet not all the elements necessary to take the quintet to the next level were in place. Coleman's smooth perfectionism jarred with the band's risk-taking tendencies; he seemed to lack their natural curiosity for musical experimentation. When the rhythm section spent hours after concerts analyzing what had happened, Coleman would retreat to his hotel room, and practice ideas for the next night. This led to conflicts with Miles.

"We were playing three shows a night in Philadelphia in a hotel bar and stayed in the same hotel," Herbie Hancock remembered. "Coleman had worked out these tricky little figures in his hotel room, and during the night he'd find a place to put these things. Miles got angry and said: 'I pay you to practice *on* the bandstand.' In other words, he was not concerned about getting a slick and perfect sound. He wanted you to try out things in front of the audience, and was vehemently opposed to us prerehearsing things, and trying to fit them in while playing live. It was about trying to capture the moment, how you're feeling in that moment."

Recognizing his differences with the band, George Coleman left in the spring of 1964. Tenor saxophonist Sam Rivers replaced him for a summer tour of Japan, but left afterwards for reasons that remain unclear. As luck would have it, when Miles came back to the States, Wayne Shorter had just left Art Blakey and the Jazz Messengers, and was available and willing to fill the saxophone spot. Shorter was a masterful saxophonist who combined a broad, silken tone with exceptionally fluid phrasing. His considerable compositional talents and penchant for reckless experimentation were instrumental in lifting the quintet's music to unsurpassed levels.

Today the quintet consisting of Miles, Wayne Shorter, Herbie Hancock, Ron Carter, and Tony Williams is regarded as one of the finest ensembles in the history of jazz, and is known as the "second great quintet," the successor to Miles's late '50s "first great quintet," which featured John Coltrane, Red Garland, Paul Chambers, and Philly Joe Jones. But unlike the first great quintet, the second great quintet was relatively underappreciated during its existence. It was out of step with the tempestuous '60s musical frontlines of free-jazz and rock.

At a time when people were getting ready to storm the barricades, free themselves from the stifling straitjackets of the "stiffs," and party, Miles chose to delve into some of the most cerebral and abstract jazz ever produced. With the benefit of hindsight, he put it, succinctly as always, like this: "We were playing a searching kind of music, but the times had changed. Everybody was dancing."[3] This is not to say that the quintet didn't storm any barricades of its own. It's just that few people at the time recognized this, let alone its significance.

❖

Musician and educator Bill Kirchner remarked that it took until the '80s and '90s for the full importance of the second quintet to be appreciated within the jazz community, and that "its lessons are still being absorbed."[4] During these belated reevaluations the period from 1964 to 1968 has been likened to Miles's creative plateau of 1955 to 1960 in terms of creativity and innovation. It was also noted that until 1964 Miles's studio albums contained a combination of original compositions and covers. The quintet, by contrast, composed almost all of the music it recorded, with contributions shared among all five members. Although common in rock, this was new in jazz. The nature of the quintet's compositions was also groundbreaking. Rather than set up melodic, harmonic, and rhythmic structures in the traditional twelve- or thirty-two-bar format with A, B, bridge, and/or turnaround sections, the quintet improvised with few defined elements—a melody, a mood, and a scale. Bridges, turnarounds, and even B sections tended to be left out altogether. The harmonic content was usually minimal, veering towards the modal instead of consisting of chord progressions.

This approach fulfilled the prophetic words Miles had uttered in the late '50s. "When you go this way, you can go on forever," Miles had said of his modal experiments of the time. "You don't have to worry about changes and you can do more with the line. It becomes a challenge to see how melodically inventive you are. When you're based on chords, you know at the end of thirty-two bars that the chords have run out and there's nothing to do but repeat what you have just done—with variations. I think a movement in jazz is beginning away from conventional strings of chords, and [there is] a return to an emphasis on melodic rather than harmonic variation. There will be fewer chords but infinite possibilities as to what to do with them."[5]

Interestingly, Miles also once stressed the influence of Western classical music in this context, which is a rather unexpected twist, since the latter is usually associated with harmonic complexity. He made this reference in 1987, when he explained how he instructed Herbie Hancock to leave harmonic elements out of his playing. Miles recalled that Hancock would often play too much and play chords that were "too thick," and that he sometimes made joking gestures of cutting Hancock's hands off to emphasize the point. Miles said, "I used to tell Herbie: 'You don't need all those notes in a chord. If you got the bass playing bass, and your voicings are right, the bass is on the bottom. If you can play three notes in a chord with that, you can get that sound.' I found that out years ago when I took [Paul] Hindemith's *Kleine Klaviermusik* (Op.45/4) apart to see how much harmony you got."[6]

The quintet only gradually and belatedly integrated the new studio material into its live repertoire, instead mostly covering Miles's '50s and early '60s repertoire, as can be heard on the eight-CD set *The Complete Live at the Plugged Nickel*, recorded on December 22 and 23, 1965. The innovations on the live stage were more focused on pushing the boundaries in the way this fairly traditional repertoire could be played in a small band, radically altering things night by night. This led to a discrepancy between the quintet's studio recordings and its live music. The rhythm section experimented with tempo changes, meter changes, and modulations, taking such liberties with the material that the band sometimes veered into free-jazz territory. The quintet's collective improvisation in effect harked back to the collective group improvisations of 1920s jazz. But by placing the rhythm section instruments on equal footing with the solo instruments, they developed it to a new level. The degree of independence and interaction among all the instruments was stupendous, and seemed to be based on a near-telepathic rapport among the musicians.

"We were already doing unusual stuff behind George Coleman, even before Wayne Shorter joined the band," Herbie Hancock remarked. "One day Miles said: 'Why don't you play like that behind me?' Tony and I looked at each other and said: 'Okay.' So we started doing these counter rhythms and overlapping things, all kinds of crazy stuff. The first night we did this Miles was actually having a difficult time finding his way around all this. But the next day he had no trouble at all with it. And the third day Miles had already moved it in a forward direction. I found myself in a new place, and had to change my role. We called this approach 'controlled freedom,' and it was one of the reasons why the first album was called *E.S.P.*, because our approach depended totally on how we reacted and listened to each other. Moreover, Miles was able to extract elements from the core of what his sidemen were playing, and somehow include that in his own solos. We were constantly trying to cook up new things, and he would pick a phrase or a response to a phrase that was being played behind him, and transform that in such a way that it would make the band sound really like a team."

Like his focus on making the band sound good, Miles's willingness to learn as much from his rhythm section as they learned from him, despite being a musical generation older than they were, was a demonstration of his egoless attitude towards music. When Tony Williams criticized him that his trumpet playing had slackened and told him to start practicing again, instead of feeling threatened or offended, Miles reveled in the challenge. His controversial stage manners expressed the same attitude. There was no arrogance in his turning his back on the audience, or his walking off stage during his sidemen's solos. He acted like this respectively to be able to hear his band better and to direct it, and because he was aware of his great charisma and did not want to attract the audience's attention during his sidemen's solos.

"He wanted to have interesting stuff coming from everybody," Herbie Hancock added. "He never thought he was out there by himself and that the other men were just in the background. And he did not care whether you sounded good or not. He just cared that you were working on something, striving for something, reaching for something. This was his primary focus of attention, and the primary thing that he tried to encourage all musicians who worked with him to do. It's a form of risk taking that he demonstrated in his own playing. He wanted us all to have the daring and conviction to go for it, even if we didn't make it."

There is an anecdote that beautifully captures how Miles dealt with one of his sidemen not making it. It must have been a defining moment for Hancock, because he has described in many interviews how he once played a completely "wrong" chord in the middle of one of Miles's solos. Cringing with embarrassment, Hancock heard Miles instantly change his notes, to make Hancock's chord sound "right." "My mouth dropped," Hancock commented, "I was so stunned, I couldn't play for a few minutes. I just let the music go by. But Miles didn't even look at me. He just carried on. He didn't hear what I'd done as 'wrong.' He just heard it as part of the reality of the present moment, a reality he could shape any way he wanted to. It illustrated the kind of openness that he had towards anything that happened."

Held in this kind of awareness, Miles's sidemen developed qualities that they didn't know they had, and Miles unified their remarkable outpourings of creativity into something that was much more than the sum of the already considerable parts. Both live and in the studio Miles and his sidemen had differentiated and yet integrated their instruments to the highest possible degree, and had pared the song form down to its most basic elements. The second great quintet had arrived at the culmination of small-band jazz, distilling the core of hardbop to its very essence. Having taken jazz to its limits, Miles found that there was nowhere to go but "playing that tired old shit over and over again,"[7] moving into free-jazz, or looking to other genres for inspiration. The second great quintet would come close to playing free-jazz, but Miles was deeply suspicious of this direction. Rather than repeat himself, or space out further into free-jazz's abstraction, he decided to come down to earth and make music for the heart and the feet again. Rock, funk, soul, and folk music were about to enter Miles's studio music, and neither his nor anybody else's music would ever be the same again.

Columbia's lavish six-CD boxed set—*Miles Davis Quintet, 1965–1968,* released in 1998 and containing the quintet's entire studio recordings in chronological order—clarifies the development of the group's studio music enormously, making it easy to see that it consists of two distinct periods. The first period begins with the quintet's studio baptism on January 20, 1965, and includes music previously released on the albums *E.S.P, Miles Smiles, Sorcerer,* and *Nefertiti.* The music falls almost exclusively within jazz territory and consists of twenty-nine different titles (counting alternate and final takes of the same tracks as one). Miles composed only four of them, including two co-composed with Carter. The rest are by Shorter (fourteen), Hancock (four), Carter (three), and Williams (two). In addition, there are two covers, one of them a celebrated version of Eddie Harris's "Freedom Jazz Dance." During this first period Miles was happy to surf the wave of his sidemen's energy and talents, an approach summarized when he described Williams as the "creative spark," Shorter as the "idea person," Hancock and Carter as the "anchors," and himself as "just the leader who put it all together."[8]

But by 1967 there were signs that Miles was starting to find the quintet format restrictive and was looking for new creative angles. In January he hired tenor saxophonist Joe Henderson, who recalled, "The time I was there, the only constant was Miles, Wayne Shorter, and myself. I never knew who would be playing piano, bass, or drums from night to night."[9] According to Henderson, live guest musicians included pianist Chick Corea, drummer Jack DeJohnette, and bassists Miroslav Vitous and Eddie Gomez. "I think Miles was just evolving in some kind of way," Henderson commented.[10] The experiments were aborted, and Henderson left by the end of March. Another indication of Miles's desire for change during this time was that he began performing his live sets as one continuous piece of music, sequencing from one song into another without breaks. This freed him from requests to introduce the songs on the bandstand and thus from part of the controversy that had been surrounding his noncommunicative stage manners. But the main reason for doing away with breaks between tracks was musical. In his autobiography Miles explained that performing an uninterrupted set allowed more space for improvisations and turned his performances into "musical suites."

In December of 1967 Miles steered the quintet's studio music in a wholly new direction, initiating its second period, which lasted until the group's dissolution in July of 1968. Much of the music from this second period was released on the albums *Miles in the Sky* and *Filles de Kilimanjaro*. Of the fifteen titles recorded during these seven months, Miles is credited as composer of nine, including one track co-written with Gil Evans.[11] One of Miles's new compositions was "Circle in the Round," which was recorded on December 4, 1967, and which resulted in arguably the most unusual track the quintet ever recorded, introducing the electric guitar in a prominent role in his music. Three weeks later, on December 28, the group recorded "Water on the Pond," again featuring electric guitar and, significantly, electric keyboard, which had never been heard before in Miles's music. These two tracks mark the first instances of the influence of the '60s counterculture explicitly entering Miles's music, a development that would soon gain momentum and turn his music upside down.

There has been much speculation over the causes of this dramatic and unexpected shift. From the increase in the number of compositions Miles contributed, it appears that he decided to enter into a different relationship with his group. Instead of steering the maelstrom of ideas that poured out of them, he tightened the reins and took back direct control, most likely because of his desire to explore the music of the '60s counterculture. Miles's interest in the electric guitar comes out of his fascination with the guitar-driven music of James Brown, to which he started listening at this time, and from his love of the blues, especially the guitar playing of Muddy Waters and B. B. King. He said that he first took notice of the electric keyboard through Joe Zawinul's use of it on Cannonball Adderley's Top 20 hit "Mercy, Mercy, Mercy," released in March of 1967.[12] Adderley played a style known in the early '60s as "soul jazz," mixing blues, soul, and bop. The influence of his band on Miles gives substance to Amiri Baraka's claim that when the saxophonist played with Miles in the late '50s, he represented the earliest tendencies in Miles's bands towards mixing jazz with rock, soul, and folk music.[13]

There have been suggestions that Miles's sidemen in the second great quintet—in particular the young Tony Williams, who was sympathetic to the music of the counterculture—urged him towards the new direction. But looking back to himself in 1967, Herbie Hancock said that he was a "jazz snob" who frowned on rock and electric instruments. "One day I came into the studio and there was no acoustic piano to be seen," Hancock recalled, "but in the corner was a Fender Rhodes, an instrument I'd never played before. So I asked Miles what he wanted me to play, and he said: 'Play that!' I was thinking, 'That toy? Oh, okay then . . .' I turned it on and played a chord, and it sounded beautiful, with a really warm, bell-like sound. I learned that night not to form an opinion about things you have no experience of. I also found out that Miles was already listening to Jimi Hendrix and other rock artists, as well as flamenco and classical music, and when I saw that my hero, my musical mentor, was open to these things, I changed my whole attitude."

It is possible that the death of John Coltrane in July of 1967 also contributed to Miles's shift in direction. Coltrane had been one of the leaders of the free-jazz movement, and by all accounts some of the spirit of jazz died with his passing. Miles still felt close to Coltrane and he was deeply shocked by his former band member's death. The sense of an era having ended, combined with the personal loss, makes it possible that

Coltrane's death was another prompt for Miles to rethink his position. And on a larger scale, by 1967 the musical, cultural, and social events that had still been bubbling just beneath the surface in 1964 had exploded into the limelight, heralding the beginning of a new era. The Vietnam and Civil Rights protest movements were in full swing, The Beatles had released their groundbreaking *Sgt. Pepper's* album, and Jimi Hendrix had ignited America with his performance at the Monterey International Pop Festival.

Miles also claims that his young wife, Betty Mabry, influenced him in his new musical tastes. Mabry was a twenty-three-year-old singer and songwriter when they met in late '67 or early '68. They married in September of 1968. The marriage lasted for only a year, but Miles asserted, "Betty was a big influence on my personal life as well as my musical life. She introduced me to the music of Jimi Hendrix—and to Jimi Hendrix himself—and other black music and musicians. She knew Sly Stone and all those guys. . . . She also helped me change the way I was dressing."[14]

Over the years various jazz commentators have used the influence of Mabry and of the '60s counterculture to suggest that nonmusical reasons were behind Miles's venture into the music genre they seem to hate most: rock. To them rock is by definition an inferior music genre, and they appear to find it inconceivable that Miles genuinely liked rock and included its influences purely for musical reasons. This attitude may sound archaic, but amazingly, is still being endorsed in the twenty-first century by Ken Burns and Geoffrey C. Ward in their otherwise excellent book *Jazz: A History of America's Music,* which accompanied the much-publicized PBS television series of the same name. Jazz-rock is given only five pages in the book's near-five-hundred pages, and Ward—who wrote the book—dismisses the genre by quoting the prejudices of the likes of trumpeter Lester Bowie and critic Martin Williams. The former claims that "Rock 'n' roll is entry-level music. . . . You're supposed to develop beyond that. To us hardcore musicians, we always considered [fusion] a little lightweight."[15] While the latter asserts that "the beat in jazz moves forward . . . jazz *goes* somewhere. . . . Rock *stays* somewhere."[16] Williams uses this as an argument to pronounce jazz superior to rock.

These snobbish and ignorant points of view echo those of Leonard Feather thirty years ago. On June 13, 1968, Feather, one of the most intelligent and erudite jazz critics of the time, found records and tapes by James Brown, Aretha Franklin, Dionne Warwick, The Byrds, and Fifth Dimension scattered throughout Miles's hotel room. Two weeks later, on June 27, he visited Miles again, saw a similar collection of recordings, and pondered the enigma: "There are several explanations, but the simplest and most logical, it seems to me, is that when you have reached an aesthetic mountaintop, there is no place to look but down."[17] The 1990 interpretation by Stanley Crouch, one of Miles's most vociferous critics, was equally prejudiced ("[Miles] was intimidated into mining the fool's gold of rock 'n' roll"[18]), as is the rubbish he was allowed to proclaim in Ward and Burns's book ("Jazz is a music of adult emotion while rock focused on adolescent passion").[19]

Rife as they were in the 1960s, these attitudes, sadly, still exist and are considered worthy of publication and discussion decades later. It means that Wayne Shorter's assertion that it takes "more courage" to incorporate musical elements controversial in one's own milieu and, to say "to hell with the critics" is still relevant. The controversy over Miles's move into electric music will be dealt with in more detail in Chapter 6. For now Shorter's additional comment is apt: "You have to do that [display 'more courage'], and don't let anything stop you. Certainly don't let the critics stop you. When Charlie Parker came out he was playing different kinds of notes, and really fast stuff. And they were saying: 'Oh, it's not legitimate,' 'He's squeaking,' 'He doesn't have a legitimate tone.' The puppet masters have all these gatekeepers trying to stop anything new, because if the standard of enlightenment is raised or widened, their mediocre products are in jeopardy."

❖

Some of the "gatekeepers" and "puppet masters" must have already raised an eyebrow when the quintet first dipped its toe in some jazz-alien flavors on its second recording date, on January 21, 1965, with the track "Eighty-One." The arranged section of the track, credited to Carter and Miles, has a straight feel instead of jazz's triplet swing time, and the bass line and brass stabs have echoes of R&B. In addition, the delightful "Footprints," recorded on October 25, 1966, combines an evocative, African-sounding melody with a melodic bass vamp rather than changes. And dated May 17, 1967, the studio recording of "Masqualero" features a straight rhythm, and an ostinato-like melodic bass line that sounds and functions like a rock bass riff. The scale, melody, and atmosphere set out by composer Wayne Shorter have a strong Spanish/Arabic quality, which is reinforced by the straight rhythm and striking bass line.

At the time of their release, the crossover elements of "Eighty-One," "Footprints," and "Masqualero" were barely noted. But with hindsight they add weight to the view that Miles's venture into rock was much more gradual and happened over a much longer period of time than has long been assumed. The reason Miles's experimentation with rock elements seemed rather sudden at the time was that his next steps into this territory went unreleased for more than a decade. One wonders whether these steps were so radical that they shocked the "gatekeepers" and "puppet masters" at Columbia Records into holding the recorded tracks back. The sessions in question occurred between December of 1967 and February of 1968, with the main turning point being the aforementioned tracks that initiated the second period of the quintet, "Circle in the Round" and "Water on the Pond," both recorded in December of 1967. The former was not released until 1979, on the compilation of outtakes from 1955 to 1970 of the same name, while the latter was issued in 1981 on a collection of unreleased recordings from 1960 to 1970 called *Directions*.

"Circle in the Round" marks a pivotal moment in Miles's musical development because it introduced many of the ingredients that would inform Miles's music until 1975, in particular the musical influences of the '60s counterculture, his search for a dense and complex bottom end, and the application of postproduction technology. Examining these elements, one detects that—in addition to the electric guitar, played by the then up-and-coming jazz guitarist Joe Beck—Miles also introduced other textures new to his music on "Circle in the Round," such as celeste and chimes. Like that of "Masqualero," the melody has a Spanish/Arabic quality. The general feel is fairly loose, and the folklike melody, the new acoustic textures, and Joe Beck's clean sound and polite approach all indicate that the main musical influence of the music of the '60s counterculture on "Circle in the Round" came from folk, not rock.

Although Beck's part is restricted—he plays an insistent tremolo throughout—his inclusion is crucial: It was the first expression of Miles's search for a heavy bottom end.

This in turn was the logical outcome of Miles's thirty-year history of stripping his music of its harmonic elements. As we have seen, with the second great quintet the result of this leaving-things-out process was that the complexity and interest had to come from the improvised interactions among all five players, who had now all reached equal footing. Making the rhythm section the most important element of the music and adding other instruments to it, like electric guitar and electric keyboard, were the next logical steps. "I wanted to hear the bass line a little stronger. If you can hear a bass line, then any note in a sound that you play can be heard,"[20] Miles explained in his usual cryptic way. "We change the bass line quite a bit on all the songs we play," he continued. "It varies. So I figured if I wrote a bass line, we could vary it so that it would have a sound a little larger than a five-piece group. By using the electric piano and having Herbie play the bass line and the chords with the guitar and Ron also playing with him in the same register, I thought that it would sound good. It came out all right. It was a nice sound."[21]

With the rhythm section center stage, the soloists had to weave their improvisations in and out of an increasingly dense and polyrhythmic bottom end. Rather than being leaders who set the atmosphere and structure of the music, they became strands in a web of rhythm. This role division is the essence of much African music. It can operate in this way because its rhythms have a central element that is missing in most Western music: repetition of depth and complexity.

Here we arrive at another logic underlying the introduction of electric instruments in Miles's music in December of 1967 and rock rhythms in the following years. Miles often maintained that his new direction was the result of his desire to strengthen the African elements in his music. "I started putting the backbeat in the drums out in front and on top of everything, like in African music," Miles explained. "In Western music, white people at this time were trying to suppress rhythm because of where it comes from—Africa—and its racial overtones. But rhythm is like breathing. So that's what I began to learn in this group and it just pointed the way forward."[22]

And what a way forward it was. Less than two years later, on *Bitches Brew,* the bottom end would reach critical mass with three electric keyboardists, two drummers, two bassists, two percussionists, one bass clarinetist, and an electric guitarist. Incorporating African elements remained an important focus for Miles until 1975. He was inspired by the emerging pride of black Americans in their African origins and by developments in 1960s black popular music. The latter was experimenting in the same direction: for example, with the doubling up of the bass line in Motown, and the bottom-heavy funk rhythms of James Brown. By contrast, at the time, most rock rhythm sections were still locked in a fairly primitive, subordinate role. The story of rock through the '70s and '80s is to an important extent the story of the emancipation of the rhythm section.

The other essential new ingredient in the making of "Circle in the Round" was the use of the studio as a creative tool, rather than just a technical facility to register sound. The latter had been the traditional approach to recording music. But in the '50s and '60s new technologies made it possible to use the studio creatively and to dramatically change the nature of the recorded music. One such tool is tape editing, which had been applied since magnetic tape was introduced in America in 1946 (as one of the spoils of war; the Germans had developed the technology in the '30s). But it was initially purely used as a means of creating an idealized performance through splicing together the best sections of different recording takes. This approach was still based on the paradigm of creating an approximation of reality.

Around 1967 a shift occurred in Western popular music culture towards looking at recordings as aural fantasies that were only restrained by the imagination of the recording's creator and the limitations of technology. This happened mainly because of the Beach Boys's *Pet Sounds* and The Beatles's *Sgt. Pepper's Lonely Hearts Club Band.* The Beach Boys and The Beatles experimented with all sorts of postproduction techniques (overdubbing, varying tape speed, playing the tape backwards, cutting up the tape, adding effects, and so on) that created results that at the time would have been impossible for a live band to reproduce. Both albums hit the rock music world like a bomb because of the daring way in which they made the shift from reproduction to fantasy. *Pet Sounds* is "generally credited as establishing the idea of the rock album as legitimate art,"[23] whereas the commercially more successful *Sgt. Pepper's* conveyed the concept to a worldwide audience. As a direct result, the sound of rock recordings changed dramatically. Suddenly the studio became an instrument in its own right, and it didn't take long for musicians to start to occupy the chairs of the engineer and producer, a practice that would have been regarded as heresy by the white-coated studio personnel of the previous era.

Significantly, this is another point where the worlds of rock and jazz parted company. Jack Chambers is a typical exponent of the fairly negative jazz view on these postproduction editing tools, calling into question the validity of the whole process in general, and the edits done to Miles's music after 1967 in particular. He rightly noted that since jazz is such a performance-orientated music, studio trickery is not its most obvious bedfellow. But he missed the point when he discarded the approach by concluding ". . . those devices contributed very little to the quality of *Sgt. Pepper.*"[24] The studio trickery may not have improved the songs themselves, but it certainly created a unique and influential sonic fantasy. The result was that *Sgt. Pepper's,* in conjunction with *Pet Sounds,* and in the context of several decades of tumultuous studio experimentation, contributed to a paradigm shift in the way Western popular music culture perceives studio recordings. Studio technology had been applied in a creative way in small pockets for years, by Les Paul in the '50s and Frank Zappa in the mid-1960s, as well as by various people in the classical avant-garde, such as Edgard Varèse, Karlheinz Stockhausen, and Pierre Henry. But the Beach Boys and The Beatles had the opportunity and capacity to make all of us see its value and potential. They gave this technology a purpose and a meaning that was suddenly recognized and understood by millions.

It is likely that Miles Davis and producer Teo Macero were two of these millions. Macero had begun working with Miles again in October of 1966, after a hiatus of four years following their falling out over *Quiet Nights.* Macero is also an accomplished composer and musician, and someone who loves to experiment with studio technology. With the abundance of studio experimentation surrounding them, it is not surprising that Miles and Macero set out for a brave new experiment in December of 1967: creating a structure for a jazz track through postproduction. Macero had worked with tape editing in Miles's music since the recording of *Sketches of Spain* in 1959 and 1960,[25] but always to construct the ideal performance of an existing piece, never to create a fantasy structure. However, from December 1967 onwards, postproduction methods would become an important compositional tool in Miles and Macero's work together.

As a first experiment with these methods, "Circle in the Round" was not entirely successful. The basic ideas and execution of the track are compelling enough, but the evocative, melancholic atmosphere becomes dreary due to the endless repeats and the gargantuan length of the track—26:10 in the 1979 edit by engineer Stan Tonkel, released on the eponymous compilation album, and 33:30 in Macero's original 1968 version, included in the quintet's boxed set.[26] Miles himself expressed dissatisfaction with "Circle in the Round" on various occasions. He blamed Joe Beck in his autobiography, saying that the guitarist "couldn't give me what I wanted."[27] And he is reported to have said a month after the session, "I was so mad, they gave me a royalty check and I didn't even look at it."[28] Miles's frustration with Beck was probably caused by the fact that the guitarist didn't introduce anything original that lifted the music, something Miles's quintet members did all the time. Miles thrived on musicians giving him back the unexpected, and it is true that Beck's unguitaristic and tightly prescribed contribution never steps out of its basic parameters. This has a deadening effect on the music. In an interview in 1996, Beck confirmed that it was a problematic session for him: "I just flailed around like a drowning man."[29]

It seems unfair to pin the failure of the session on Beck, however. The guitarist was most likely not the only one who was confounded. Miles had introduced several new, not yet fully formed ideas, and the other musicians, as well as Macero, may well have struggled to come to terms with the novel approach. Miles also did not give Macero an easy task to begin with by recording "Circle in the Round" in thirty-five segments. The tape recorder, like the camera, can imply meaning where no meaning exists, and sifting through hours of musical material and finding the best moments, let alone putting them in a new order, is inevitably challenging. A large amount of recorded material puts more responsibility on the shoulders of the editor and, for one reason or another, neither Macero nor Tonkel did a particularly good job. A sign of the experimental nature of the edits are the crude and jarring edits in Macero's version (at 12:12 and 21:22, for example). Tonkel abridged the track by seven minutes, but his version is still way too long. Although some may like the duration for its hypnotic quality, the material does not justify a length of more than maybe seven or eight minutes.

Despite its flaws, the track "Circle in the Round" still contained enough promise for Miles to carry on with his new course. He employed Beck again on "Water on the Pond," recorded on December 28, 1967, and for two sessions in January and February of 1968. During these latter two months Miles also used guitarists Bucky Pizzarelli and George Benson, on respectively one and two recording dates.[30] After this he abandoned his initial experiments with the electric guitar. Listening to the evidence on *Miles Davis Quintet, 1965–1968* it is not hard to see why. These experiments are rarely genuinely successful in the sense that something new and substantial is added to the music.

"Water on the Pond" is one of the better tracks. An enjoyable but rather light Latinesque romp, Hancock's first use of an electric keyboard is the important new element.

Beck's guitar largely doubles Carter's bass and only adds a little sharpness and depth to the bass line. Two weeks later, on January 12, the quintet recorded the track "Fun," with Bucky Pizzarelli on guitar. Another relatively insubstantial but pleasant enough track, "Fun" is influenced by calypso rather than rock, and the electric guitar again largely doubles the bass line. However, the electric guitar adds enough depth and elegance to the bass line to justify its addition.

Four days later the quintet recorded another detour into postbebop territory, namely Hancock's "The Collector," for some reason called "Teo's Bag" and credited to Miles. On that same day, guitarist George Benson added his recognizable tone to Shorter's "Paraphernalia," a hardbop track with Hancock on acoustic piano. Benson comps and solos in a very traditional jazz fashion at a point when Miles was attempting to break the jazz mold, making it ironic that this track contains the most effective application of the electric guitar in Miles's earliest experiments with the instrument.

On January 25 the quintet plus Beck recorded two Herbie Hancock Latin-jazz originals that were never completed—"I Have a Dream" and "Speak like a Child." Benson's last session with the quintet was on February 15, when Miles's jazz composition "Side Car" was recorded, as was Shorter's "Sanctuary." The latter track is notable in this context because it was recorded again one-and-a-half years later on the sessions for *Bitches Brew*. The powerful, stark melody gets a subtle, delicate rendition, despite Benson's hesitant comping. Bob Belden's conclusion in the annotations for the quintet's boxed set is apt: "It seems that Miles was looking for something in a guitarist that just wasn't happening at that time in jazz."[31]

Just as Miles did not expect perfection from his sidemen, he was undeterred by the mixed results of his own experiments. Regarding these sessions as learning experiences, he continued his search for a deeper and denser bottom end with increased intensity. The following day, February 16, marked his last orchestral studio session with Gil Evans. They recorded "Falling Water," and thickened the low end with bass, drums, tuba, bassoon, marimba, and timpani, Hancock on Wurlitzer piano, and Joe Beck and Herb Bushler on guitar. There's an interesting suspended feeling to this track, but it does not make a lasting impression.

Three months later, on May 15, the quintet was back in the studio to record Miles's "Country Son," a strange concoction of hardbop and rocklike grooves, featuring Hancock in some places playing funk riffs on acoustic piano. The following day they worked on Tony Williams's "Black Comedy," a track firmly in the avant-bop style that the quintet had developed to its extremity. One wonders whether the band members had any inkling that this recording would mark the end of an era, for the very next day, May 17, 1968, there was another defining session.

Miles introduced a composition called "Stuff," which contained rhythms and riffs lifted directly from rock and soul music. Herbie Hancock played electric piano, and rather than disturb the creative chemistry of the quintet by adding an extra player, Miles chose to fortify the bottom end by asking Ron Carter to play electric bass. Taken together, these elements set up a tight, R&B–like groove that forms the main foundation of the piece. For the first time in Miles's music, groove had become more important than melody or mode. At the same time, the sound, aesthetic, structure, and playing approaches of "Stuff" are still rooted in the jazz tradition, exemplified in Miles's and

Shorter's solos, the near-seventeen-minute length of this instrumental track, and the alternating theme/solo structure. Hancock and Carter groove along using many elements of rock and soul, though Williams doesn't appear to be able to decide whether he's going to lock in a groove or take the jazz approach of continuous improvised rolls and accents.

"Stuff" was released in 1968 as the opening track of the *Miles in the Sky* album, and in combination with the psychedelic 1960s cover and the reference of the title to The Beatles's "Lucy in the Sky with Diamonds," it should have been immediately apparent to jazz listeners that huge changes were in the air. Strangely, this was not the case. Most commentators noted that something was different, but generally speaking couldn't pinpoint what it was. The clues were even stronger with the next album, *Filles de Kilimanjaro,* released in 1969, on which electric bass, electric piano, and folk, soul, and R&B influences dominate. Miles emphasized his new course by having the text "Directions in Music by Miles Davis" prominently displayed on the cover. "It means I tell everybody what to do," he explained to journalist Don DeMicheal in 1969, ". . . it's my date, y'understand? . . . I got tired of seeing 'Produced by this person or that person.' When I'm on a date, I'm usually supervising everything."[32]

Filles de Kilimanjaro has been described as Miles's first fusion album, though it also did not stir any controversy at the time of its release. Even Stanley Crouch likes it and wrote that the album was "the trumpeter's last important jazz record." The reason is that, like *Miles in the Sky, Filles de Kilimanjaro* still falls within a jazz aesthetic. For example, the frantic execution of "Petits Machins"—recorded on June 19, 1968, and based on a composition by Gil Evans—has its roots in the quintet's hardbop origins, even as it features a lyrical, folksy melody. "Tout de Suite," recorded the next day, also has a graceful, folklike melody, but it is underpinned with a straight rock rhythm. Hancock plays many blues-influenced figures on the electric piano and Carter holds down a deep and strong bottom end. This version also contains a faster, busier middle section that again has echoes of hardbop in its aesthetic and atmosphere. On the alternate take of "Tout de Suite," released on *Miles Davis Quintet, 1965–1968,* the quintet stays with the folklike feel of the melody and arrangement throughout.

The track "Filles de Kilimanjaro" has a similar, almost pastoral feel, and a strong African influence in the rhythms and the gorgeous theme. The quintet takes an unusually long time repeating and developing the melody, and the soloists keep referring to it. Moreover, the solos and the simple chord changes are to some degree idiomatic of folk and rock music, and at the same time transcend them. Unlike "Stuff," on which the quintet sounds as if it's mainly having fun experimenting with funk and soul influences without adding anything new, "Filles de Kilimanjaro" and, to a lesser degree, "Tout de Suite," indicate for the first time a real integration of these influences. The quintet started to find its own voice in relation to them by creating a unique musical landscape. Furthermore, the static atmosphere that they explored in these two tracks became a blueprint for the ambient direction to which Miles would return on many occasions, most famously on *In a Silent Way.*

The quintet dissolved not long after its final recording session on June 21, 1968. The reason usually given is that the same thing happened as with all of Miles's great bands:

Once his sidemen developed to a certain level, they wanted to branch out and play their own music. The reputation musicians gained from working with Miles Davis was so powerful that it was usually enough to ensure a successful career. Carter was the first to leave, by the end of July 1968, because he was highly in demand as a session bassist and was reluctant to tour. This is why the quintet had intermittently been using half a dozen stand-in bassists in live performance during the period from 1966 to 1968. This solution had become untenable.

Herbie Hancock was aware in early August of 1968 that his time had come, but instead of jumping he was pushed. "We had a gig I was supposed to be back for, but I got food poisoning on my honeymoon in Brazil, and couldn't make it," Hancock said. "Miles knew that Tony, Wayne, and myself had talked about leaving. Chick Corea replaced me when I was in Brazil, and when Miles realized that he was an effective replacement, rather than risk having to rebuild a band from scratch, he preferred to let me go. He'd just enlisted Dave Holland as a bass player, and when I got home Miles's manager explained to me that if I made my break with the quintet then, Miles would have at least two people to build a band around. I said 'fine,' although I actually wasn't planning to make the break yet. It was a hard band to leave!"

Understandably, Miles was eager to avoid a repeat of the difficulties he had encountered in assembling a fitting quintet in the early '60s. He had seen many times how musicians outgrew his groups, leaving him scrambling for replacements. But in the case of the second great quintet there was another factor: the band had become too limited for Miles's purposes. For more than three years, Miles's primary objective had been developing the quintet's potential; in December of 1967 this objective became secondary to that of integrating the music of the '60s counterculture. The quintet now had to serve an exterior purpose that was more important than the particular gifts of any of its individual members, and it is not surprising that it lasted for only six months after this change in course.

Herbie Hancock related how much the musical goalposts had moved during his time with Miles. "In the beginning we knew whether something we played was good or not. Even though we were trying out new things, our approach was still pretty much tied in with a more traditional way of playing. But the more the stuff developed, the harder it became to tell if what we were doing was working or not. For one thing, Miles more and more recorded things in bits and pieces, just little ideas here and there that were later on strung together. It was fascinating to work like that, but during the recording sessions we couldn't tell if the stuff was good or bad, or what it was at all. We'd play and then we'd wonder, 'What was that? What did we do?'"

This is where the paradigm shift to a new musical direction occurred, and Miles was one of the few who recognized the meaning of the emerging stone circles. It would take most others a little while longer to recognize them, too. Wayne Shorter reflected on the same process when he stated that by "raising the standards of enlightenment" music can "enable someone to awake. We figured, maybe there's someone out there listening who is also waking up." By 1968 it appeared that many of those who listened to Miles Davis were still asleep. They would soon be woken up—first by a whisper, then by a storm.

Chapter Four

NEW DIRECTIONS

"Miles was brilliant as a bandleader. He allowed the musicians to play just as they are and deal with the music from their own choices and their own judgements. Therefore the music that came out was very strong."
—CHICK COREA

In 1968 rude awakenings were the order of the day. A steady flow of earthshaking events raised "the standards of enlightenment," bringing changes that still reverberate decades later. The protest movement had acquired real political power, affecting the United States's Vietnam policy and nearly toppling the French government. Western culture was being turned inside out by an iconoclastic maelstrom that left no stone unturned, considered no sacred cow too holy and respected no ivory tower as off-limits. The hunger for change was as radical as it was deep, and it permeated every aspect of society. Since music was the counterculture's main vehicle of expression, this hunger affected the music world especially deeply.

The music of Miles Davis was no exception. The four years with his second great quintet had signaled a return to form as well as a tentative exploration of elements of folk, soul, and rock. He had been making his moves carefully and gradually, while remaining within a jazz aesthetic. But a few months after the quintet's dissolution in the summer of 1968, Miles's explorations into undiscovered musical country gained more momentum. In keeping with the spirit of the times, he gradually entered a period of intense experimentation. The sheer volume of studio recordings that resulted is an indication of the intensity of his explorations. During the two years between the dissolution of the second great quintet in mid-1968 and June 5, 1970, when a studio recording hiatus of nearly two years commenced, a staggering total of nearly nine hours of music was recorded and released, spread over eight albums. Apparently this is only the tip of the iceberg. Columbia still possesses many more hours of recordings in its vaults, and intends to release selections in historical boxed sets similar to *Miles Davis Quintet, 1965–1968* and *The Complete* Bitches Brew *Sessions*.[1]

This creative explosion was most likely driven by Miles's excitement about his latest musical direction and his discovery of the creative potential of the recording studio. Miles's comment, "For me, the changes that were happening in my music were very exciting and the music that was happening everywhere was incredible,"[2] seems to corroborate this.

In addition, several people have remarked on the parallels between the circumstances of Miles's personal life, in particular his relationship with women, and the state of his music. "Miles changed every five years, whenever he got a new girl friend," Teo Macero once commented.[3] And guitarist Carlos Santana recalled how the women surrounding Miles from 1969 to 1970 "changed the way he dressed, the places he went, and the music he listened to."[4] Miles has tried to discredit Macero's statements, but in his autobiography he repeatedly credited the tremendous influence of the women in his life, for example Frances Taylor's influence on *Kind of Blue,* and how Betty Mabry introduced him to Jimi Hendrix and the music of the counterculture. Moreover, in reviewing the history of his life it seems undeniable that he often faltered when he wasn't in a stable relationship (1950 to 1953, 1961 to 1964, and 1975 to 1979) or when his relationship was dysfunctional (as with Frances in the early 1960s). By contrast, he blossomed creatively when he was physically healthy and inspired by relationships.

The creative heights of 1965 to 1970 were a case in point. After the lows of the early '60s, the time with the second great quintet had paralleled an upward curve on a personal level, in part instigated by his relationship with Cicely Tyson from 1966 to 1967. During 1968 and 1969 he had an intense relationship with Betty Mabry, and after that with Marguerite Eskridge and Jackie Battle. Regarding the latter two Miles stated: "Both of them were real spiritual women, into health foods and things like that. They were both real quiet, but very strong women who had great confidence in themselves."[5]

"Miles and I didn't drink any alcohol and didn't do drugs of any kind," Marguerite Eskridge said. "I was at that time a very strict vegetarian and Miles liked fish, so we didn't always eat the same things, but he was very concerned about being healthy." Bassist Dave Holland recalled that when he was in the band, from mid-1968 to mid-1970, "Miles had a trainer that traveled with him, he went to the gym every day, he was boxing, and he was eating health food. He always gave the impression of being extremely healthy, aware, and sharp." Pianist Chick Corea was part of Miles's band during the same period as Holland, and recalled, "Miles was living the life of a health freak. He had stopped smoking cigarettes. He was in top form and playing very powerfully on the horn." Drummer Lenny White added, "The period I was with Miles, 1969 to 1970, he was constantly talking about 'blockages' and 'cleansing.' If you can get the 'blockages' out of your system, you become a conduit for the creative force. Miles was trying to achieve this around this time, because he was really clean."

Miles's health regime appears to have had the desired "cleansing" effect, because from 1968 to 1970 his creative focus was strong, and the results were dramatic. By the end of this period his studio music was transformed from a mixture of hardbop and free-jazz, spiced up by folk, soul, and rock influences, to a groundbreaking, strongly rock-influenced style driven by electric guitar and electric bass. These two years would prove to be extremely influential, in effect bringing a whole new genre of music—jazz-rock—into full bloom.

❖

Given that Miles's achievements from this period still loom large several decades later, it is easy to lose sight of the fact that his new musical direction did not develop in a vacuum. Miles did not invent jazz-rock. Fusions of jazz and rock had been attempted since the early '60s. Just as The Beatles had recognized and realized the potential of existing post-production techniques on *Sgt. Pepper's*, Miles recognized the potential of the early jazz-rock experiments in a way few others had, and he developed it to a degree that can be called a musical paradigm shift. As is common with paradigm shifts, this one also happened in a wider cultural context. To clarify this process, it may be helpful to briefly picture the embryonic jazz-rock culture surrounding Miles around 1968, from which he drew both inspiration and musicians.[6]

In Great Britain, pianist/guitarist Alexis Korner was mixing jazz and blues as early as 1962, and seeing future luminaries like John McLaughlin, Mick Jagger, and drummer Ginger Baker pass through his band. Baker went on to form Cream in 1966 with bassist Jack Bruce and blues/rock guitarist Eric Clapton. Baker and Bruce defined themselves as jazz musicians, and with sets featuring extensive collective improvisations, the band was one of the pioneers of jazz-rock. Other British bands exploring combinations of jazz and rock in the '60s were Colosseum, Soft Machine, Nucleus (with writer/trumpeter Ian Carr), Jethro Tull, and King Crimson.

From 1965 to 1966 there were regular gatherings of a group of jazz musicians in New York who aimed to expand their musical horizons and who experimented with elements of rock music. The musicians included guitarists Larry Coryell and Joe Beck, saxophonists Jim Pepper and Charles Lloyd, and trumpeters Randy Brecker and (free-jazz originator) Don Cherry. In 1969 Coryell made a highly regarded recording called *Spaces* with John McLaughlin, bassist Miroslav Vitous, and drummer Billy Cobham. Cobham in turn played with guitarist John Abercrombie in the group Dreams before joining McLaughlin in Mahavishnu Orchestra in 1971. Guitarists Cornell Dupree (who worked briefly with Miles in March of 1972) and Eric Gale, and drummer Steve Gadd combined forces in a jazz-rock band called Stuff. And guitarist Mike Bloomfield played the blues, the common ground between jazz and rock, with his band Electric Flag, which featured bassist Harvey Brooks, who would appear on *Bitches Brew*.

Several of the above-mentioned musicians were involved with Miles at some point, adding their creativity and experiences to his boiling experimental cauldron. The influence of Cannonball Adderley and his electric pianist Joe Zawinul has already been documented. Tony Williams's band Lifetime, featuring John McLaughlin and organist Larry Young, recorded a groundbreaking jazz-rock album called *Emergency!* in May of 1969 that also would not have escaped Miles's attention. In addition, Miles has commented repeatedly on the achievements of tenor sax player Charles Lloyd. Between 1966 and 1968 Lloyd had enormous success with a mixture of jazz and rock that *Billboard* called "psychedelic jazz."[7] Drummer Jack DeJohnette and pianist Keith Jarrett formed one half of Lloyd's band, and Miles eventually enlisted the formidable talents of both.

During the late '60s many American rock bands were influenced by free-jazz, adding touches of psychedelic-sounding improvisations to their live performances. Examples include The Grateful Dead, The Byrds, and Jefferson Airplane. Around the same time, West Coast jazz musicians like electric pianist Mike Nock of Fourth Way and saxophonist John Handy were incorporating elements of rock into their music. They were often found playing at rock concerts, gaining admirers on both sides of the rock/jazz divide. Meanwhile, chart-topping, horn-based rock bands like Blood, Sweat & Tears and Chicago were spicing up their music with jazz elements, while Santana was blending rock with Latin and jazz. Finally, there was rock guitarist Jimi Hendrix, who had a significant impact on many jazz musicians. Miles and Hendrix shared a huge mutual admiration, and apparently jammed together regularly at the former's house. Sadly, nothing ever came of the collaborations the two planned.

❖

The music scene in the late '60s consisted of a whirlwind of primarily young musicians experimenting with new ideas, influences, and combinations. When Miles's second great quintet dissolved, he turned to this adventurous, up-and-coming generation of young musicians for inspiration and recruitment, demonstrating his remarkable abilities as a talent scout. One of the most famous examples is his enlistment of Dave Holland.

In June of 1968 the British bassist was playing with vocalist Elaine Delmar at the Ronnie Scott Club in London. They were supporting pianist Bill Evans, who had Jack DeJohnette on drums in his band. The story goes that Miles was in London for a brief holiday and came to the club to see Evans and DeJohnette, although there are also suggestions that the two tipped him off about Holland and that Miles came specifically to see the bassist. However it happened, Miles was greatly impressed with Holland's performance and invited him to join his band. Flabbergasted, the twenty-one-year-old bass player agreed to come to New York. Ron Carter left the quintet by the end of July, and Holland flew over around the same time.[8]

"I was living in London at the time, finishing up a three-year course at the Guildhall School of Music and doing jazz gigs around London," Dave Holland recalled. "I knew Miles was in the audience, but I thought he was there purely to see Bill Evans and Jack DeJohnette. I didn't even think he was listening to me. We were just the support act. I understood later that he was looking for a new, regular, permanent bassist, because Ron [Carter] didn't want to travel, so the band was always using different bass players on gigs. But I don't know why he recruited *me*. I suspect he knew where I was coming from, what my musical intention was. The whole thing was my first lesson in how Miles was: he was always aware of what was going on. He was always listening, and once told me that from the way someone took their horn out of a case, he could tell what kind of musician they were. He was a great observer of people. After I arrived in New York, Herbie showed me some of the songs, but I was basically thrown into the deep end for the first gig. That was customary at the time. You were expected to have done your homework and know the music already. It was one of those tests that we musicians had for each other: 'Were you able to handle it?'"

A few weeks later, on September 24, Dave Holland recorded two additional tracks for *Filles de Kilimanjaro* with Miles, Shorter, Williams, and Chick Corea, who had joined in August, when Hancock was down with food poisoning in Brazil. Corea already had some credits to his name, including tenures with Stan Getz and Sarah Vaughan.

Although Carter and Hancock had migrated to the electric versions of their instruments for the second great quintet's last five recording sessions, Holland played acoustic bass and Corea played acoustic as well as electric piano on the two new tracks. This temporary throwback to acoustic instruments may appear puzzling, given Miles's assertion in his autobiography that Carter had left because he didn't want to play electric bass.

One wonders whether this was a case of confusion on Miles's part or whether this claim was taken by Troupe from an ancient and incorrect interview, because Dave Holland was hired by Miles as an acoustic bass player.

"Miles had seen me play acoustic bass in a very conventional jazz context," Dave Holland said. "As far as Miles knew, I only played acoustic bass. There was no electric bass at all in the music, and he never asked me to play electric bass. I was playing only acoustic for the first year. I still played acoustic bass on *Bitches Brew* [in August of 1969], and I volunteered to play the electric bass after that because I felt the music needed it." Despite having heard Holland in a "conventional jazz context," something of Holland's roots, which were as much in rock and R&B as in jazz, may have filtered through to Miles.

The changes of personnel and instrumentation halfway through the recording of *Filles de Kilimanjaro* didn't affect the sound and musical concept of the album significantly, and the new tracks, "Frelon Brun" and "Mademoiselle Mabry," both credited to Miles, are still firmly rooted in a jazz aesthetic. The accents and theme that open "Frelon Brun" have a Motown-esque soul flavor, not dissimilar to that of "Stuff." But Williams treats the track as pure jazz, accenting and improvising freely rather than holding down a groove, and the theme-solos-theme structure of the piece, along with the busy, improvisational middle section, echo the influence of bebop.

"Mademoiselle Mabry" was named after Miles's brand-new wife—he and Mabry married that same month (September). "The rhythm figures were written out, and we repeated them throughout the track," Holland recalled. "The embellishments were of course up to us, but there was a fairly formalized score with specific rhythmic phrases." Although this degree of circumscription was unusual, given Miles's tendency to let musicians deal creatively with only very basic sketches of material, the focus on the rhythm section is congruent with his search for the thickening of the bottom end.

Ironically, the bottom end of this piece is light and transparent. Williams spends most of his time adding color with tom-toms and drums, largely avoiding the cymbals and hi-hat, and Holland and Corea leave huge spaces in their playing. The piece is a teasing stop-start affair that continuously threatens to lock into a groove, only to dissolve the moment it does so. There are also moments when Miles's horn line and some of the chord structure resemble the classic Leiber and Stoller song "On Broadway" (for example, at 04:35 and 04:45). As a result, the piece comes across as a pastiche, someone borrowing elements from various places but not quite knowing how to fit them together. The players sound inhibited, and although the almost pastoral atmosphere is pleasant enough, the piece lacks the beautiful, folklike melody and coherent rhythm section playing that carry the title track.

Clearly Miles was still cautiously trying out new, but largely unformed, ideas in "Frelon Brun" and "Mademoiselle Mabry." Perhaps he proceeded so carefully because he wanted these two tracks to be consistent with the other three tracks on *Filles de Kilimanjaro*. Perhaps he was still working in his new quintet. Whatever the reasons, at the quintet's next session six weeks later, on November 11, Miles began to let go of the brakes. The quintet, with the addition of Herbie Hancock, recorded "Two Faced" and "Dual Mr. Anthony Tillmon Williams Process," which were released in 1976 on the album *Water Babies*.[9] This session marked a departure in style and approach, beginning with the fact that it was Miles's first-ever session with two keyboard players.[10]

"Two Faced" bears striking similarities to "Mademoiselle Mabry" in concept and atmosphere; Shorter's opening theme is played with the same stop-start approach, for instance. Fortunately, Dave Holland appears to have grown in confidence, or is allowed more free rein, and manages to lock into a convincing groove with Williams and the two electric keyboards. This lifts the piece out of the potential doldrums. The call-response canon between Miles and Shorter is also effective. Overall, "Two Faced" has much more coherence and substance than "Mademoiselle Mabry," although at eighteen minutes some more trimming wouldn't have harmed the piece. "Two Faced" is nevertheless a landmark, because it is Miles's last-known studio recording predominantly located within a jazz aesthetic.

With "Dual Mr. Anthony Tillmon Williams Process" Miles took his first decisive leap across whatever aesthetic divide separates the rock and jazz "languages." As well as carrying an unusual title, "Dual Mr. Anthony Tillmon" is also an oddity in Miles's catalog from other perspectives. The piece has a poppy '60s groove, almost like a twist, and is one of the few pieces Miles recorded that is completely locked in its era, making it sound rather dated. Hancock and Corea cheerfully overlay many blues, funk, and rock clichés over the pop rhythms and chord changes, and only Miles's inimitable spacing and choice of notes, and Shorter's fluid and mercurial phrasing, lift it out of the ordinary.

Nonetheless, Miles had made a decisive leap into the unknown. And in keeping with Hancock's description in Chapter 3 of how quickly the bandleader took new sounds and influences to a new level, it only took one day for Miles to find his feet, on November 12, during a session with Joe Zawinul instead of Chick Corea on electric piano. The resulting track, "Splash" (released in 1979 on *Circle in the Round*), is almost a cross between "Two Faced" and "Dual Mr. Anthony Tillmon Williams Process," employing both the stop-start device of the former and echoes of the twist rhythm of the latter. Here these elements are much better integrated, making the track sound more mature and cohesive. One starts to hear a musical vision, rather than some musicians having fun with musical elements with which they are not fully conversant. It is interesting to note that this is the same ensemble, minus guitarist John McLaughlin, that was to record *In a Silent Way* nearly three months later. Miles may well have judged that there was a compelling chemistry to this group of musicians.

Although Joe Zawinul never joined Miles's working band, he played a pivotal role in the development of Miles's music from 1968 to 1970. After the dissolution of the second great quintet, Wayne Shorter contributed few compositions, and it appears that Zawinul stepped to some degree into Shorter's shoes, supplying Miles with base material from which to shape his musical vision. There are other parallels. Zawinul and Shorter are essentially of the same generation as Miles, with Zawinul being born in 1932 and Shorter in 1933. Moreover, both already had impressive track records by the time they came to play with Miles. Zawinul, originally from Austria, had moved to the United States in 1959, and enjoyed success as a pianist and composer playing with Maynard Ferguson, Dinah Washington, and Cannonball Adderley (he actually penned "Mercy, Mercy, Mercy").

It appears that although Miles liked to enlist young and unformed musicians in his bands to help him shape his vision, he relied on older and more experienced musicians to hand him musical templates. Miles's long partnership with Gil Evans, who was fourteen years older and who wrote and arranged much music for him, is another case in point. Likewise, producer/musician Teo Macero, who helped him make sense of the material that emerged, was born in 1925.

❖

The first composition Zawinul provided Miles with, "Ascent," recorded on November 27, led to a dramatic new development. Like "Tout de Suite" and "Filles de Kiliman-jaro," "Ascent" is an exploration of the pastoral theme that seemed to occupy Miles's mind during this time. However, it takes the whole concept much further, since its focus is solely on achieving a suspended, timeless feel—it is Miles's first piece that can truly be called ambient. In recognition of its different nature, he called it a "tone poem" in his autobiography. Miles's ambient experiments were probably partly inspired by the "mood music" that had become popular during the musical experimentation of the '60s under the influence of the counterculture's interest in Indian culture and music and consciousness-altering drugs like marijuana and LSD.

Traditionally, music contains sequences of themes, solos, rhythms, and/or chord changes that are intended to be sufficiently interesting and engaging to hold the listener's attention. In the mid-1970s, producer and composer Brian Eno, one of rock's great mav-ericks and experimenters, articulated how what he called "ambient" can do away with these considerations. "Ambient" is primarily concerned with setting up an ambience, an aural backdrop in which the listener can submerge him or herself, whether listening to the music consciously or unconsciously. Eno suggested that music is like a scent, a color, or an environment, resulting in a different state of mind. "Ambient Music is intended to induce calm and a space to think . . . ," Eno wrote. "It must be as ignorable as it is inter-esting."[11] Significantly, Eno stated that Miles and Macero's last experiment with mood music, the 1974 epic "He Loved Him Madly," influenced him strongly. "Teo Macero's revolutionary production on that piece seemed to me to have the 'spacious' quality that I was after . . . it became a touchstone to which I returned frequently."[12]

Eno named his concept after the Latin word "ambire," meaning "to surround." The success of an ambient piece of music depends less on the interest generated by specific musical events and more on whether its atmosphere is powerful enough to put and keep the listener in this different state of mind. Another, related, aspect of ambient is the treat-ment of musical components as abstract blocks of sound that can be moved around quite independently of each other and are not looked at in the linear, developmental terms of "normal" music. This attitude was pioneered in avant-garde classical music during the first half of the twentieth century, most notably in musique concrète, and fit like a glove with the tape-editing technologies that emerged after the Second World War.

The abstract aspect of ambient music is analogous to abstract painting, and it is not surprising that both concepts emerged around the same time, the turn of the nine-teenth/twentieth century. One early pioneer was the French composer Eric Satie, who spoke of his music as "musique d'ameublement," or "music as furniture." John Cage, the American avant-garde composer, developed this idea to its logical extreme with "4:33" from 1952, during which the musician plays three movements of silence and the "per-formance" consists of random environmental noises.

The near-fifteen-minute-long "tone poem" "Ascent" stands right at the beginning of Miles's exploration of what later became known as the "ambient" approach. Dave Holland plays a very slow quarter note line and Jack DeJohnette restricts himself to accents and coloring. The three keyboards make no attempt at developing the music, playing thematic solos, or using the tension-release structure that typifies more traditional musical approaches. Like Miles and Shorter, they are more interested in creating and holding an atmosphere than in attracting interest. Given that this is a fairly new direction in Miles's music, the experiment is remarkably successful. The only problem is that after some time the mood begins to grate, perhaps due to the uniform sound of the electric keyboards. Despite its ambient nature, the piece doesn't offer enough depth in terms of texture and color to justify the allotted time span and would have benefited from being shortened through editing, or from the inclusion of another texture or musical idea.

The other piece recorded on November 27 is the total opposite of "Ascent." Miles again used a Joe Zawinul composition, "Directions," and the resulting hard-hitting, rock-influenced piece is a showcase for Jack DeJohnette, who has a remarkable capacity for combining powerful, driving grooves with the improvisational aspect of jazz drumming. Miles had been aware of his capacities since 1967, when DeJohnette played a few times with the second quintet. The drummer had now left Charles Lloyd's group, so it is likely that Miles hired him for the November 27 session with a view to replacing Tony Williams, who was developing more and more activities outside of Miles's band and getting ready to leave. Williams left by the end of 1968, and DeJohnette joined Miles's live band at an unknown date during the first three months of 1969.

With "Directions" Miles's explorations into jazz-rock suddenly took a great leap forward. Apart from DeJohnette's robust drumming, the decisive factor is the strong and repetitive ostinato bass line played by Dave Holland on acoustic bass and doubled by an electric keyboardist, probably Zawinul. It is maybe the first idiomatic application in Miles's music of the power of repetition and of circumscribing the role of elements of the rhythm section, which are essential features of rock as well as of African music. Miles must have sensed that he was onto something, because rather than just doing a few takes, as was his usual working method, he appears to have spent some time experimenting with the piece. As a result, two versions were released on *Directions* in 1981. "Directions II" is enhanced with an interesting new beginning, but Miles's and Shorter's solos are much less incisive. They seem to have less to say, and it's not surprising that "Directions I" clocks in at 06:46, whereas the alternative take only makes it to 04:49. The importance of "Directions" in Miles's oeuvre is illustrated by the fact that it became his set opener for three years.[13] (One also wonders whether there is a link between the title "Directions" and the subheading "Directions in Music by Miles Davis" that appeared on his records around this time.)

❖

By November of 1968 Miles had come to grips with the new musical direction he had initiated in December of 1967. The stumbling and awkwardness with the new medium were over. However, what the new direction was about remained elusive to some of the musicians.

"I was recently re-listening to the music of late 1968 and the remix of *Bitches Brew*, because at the time when I was making these records I didn't really listen to them," Chick Corea said in 1999. "My mind was simply not there. But when I listen now I can hear Miles's musical approach much more clearly than I did at the time, and it's so powerful, so continually adventurous. There was an artistic integrity that is very inspiring, because it is very necessary for an artist to go ahead and venture into new territories. You can't wait for someone to agree with what you're doing. That's why it's so ironic that he was being charged with 'selling out' when he went into this direction. But that was simply what happened around that time. Every time a jazz musician played an electric instrument, and it didn't matter what he played on it, he was being accused of 'not being honest' or something like that."

Like Hancock, Corea readily acknowledged the debt he owes Miles in opening his eyes to the potential of electric instruments. "The session on which we recorded 'Two Faced' and 'Dual Mr. [Anthony] Tillmon' was the first time Miles had two electric keyboards playing at the same time," Corea recalled. "I remember walking into the studio a few weeks earlier, and Miles showing me this electric piano to play. I thought 'What a toy!' But I grew to love the instrument. There was also one particular moment, I think it was when we played the Jazz Workshop in Boston [December 5 to 8], when I walked to the stage for the first set of the night, and the piano was set up, ready for me to play. But there was also a Fender Rhodes on the stage. My instinct was to go to the acoustic piano first, but Miles said, 'No, no. Play that,' and pointed to the Fender Rhodes. From that moment on he never wanted to hear the acoustic piano again."

As we have seen, Miles was alerted to the electric piano by Zawinul's playing on "Mercy, Mercy, Mercy," and he liked the instrument's capacity for deepening the bottom end. As he did in "Directions," he often asked the electric piano(s) to double the bass line. Miles's strong interest in the electric piano may appear odd, given that he wore his interest in the blues and the electric guitar on his sleeve around this time. The explanation was most likely purely practical. Miles had several top-class keyboardists available who could give him what he wanted, whereas the electric guitar experiments of late '67 and early '68 had shown him that he had yet to find an electric guitarist who could meet his needs. By adding extra keyboard players Miles found an alternative way of deepening the bottom end.

The additional keyboard players also exemplified the approach Miles had initiated with "Circle in the Round" nearly a year earlier of adding guest musicians to a recording session to fulfill a particular musical vision. He had already done this during some sessions before the second great quintet came together, but the scope of this method now expanded dramatically. After the initial experiments with one electric guitarist (December of 1967 to February of 1968) in November 1968 Herbie Hancock, Joe Zawinul, and Jack DeJohnette were invited to record alongside Miles's regular live group. In February of 1969, on *In a Silent Way*, three extra musicians complemented Miles's live quintet, and on the *Bitches Brew* sessions half a year later, there were eight additional musicians. Thereafter there would sometimes be as many as ten guest musicians in the studio and no members of Miles's current live band at all. The pool of musicians from which Miles drew became so large that it became known as "Miles's Stock Company Players."

The nonlive band musicians were invited not only for the color or slant they might add to the music but also because their inclusion introduced an element of the unexpected, just like the method of presenting musicians with rudimentary musical sketches that they've never seen before. The result was often a combination of unease and total concentration that has been called "the sound of men walking on eggshells."

"One of the things that created the sound of the studio recordings was that we were all trying to figure out what was going on," Dave Holland explained. "It wasn't something that was cut-and-dried, as in: 'Here's your part, you play from here to here.' Instead we were given a brief idea, and then we'd try to do something with it. In the sessions with Joe Zawinul . . . if you'd asked me at the time what was going on, I would not have been able to tell you. . . . All musicians were trying to find out what to do, and this created a certain space. It wasn't that it was tentative, but when you really know a piece of music, there's a tendency to overplay it sometimes. If you don't know the music, you're more careful and searching in your playing."

❖

This was eloquently demonstrated on Miles's first electric tour de force, *In a Silent Way*, which combined all the approaches he had developed from 1967 to 1968: ambient, rock, working with guest musicians, and postproduction techniques. The session from which the album was culled took place on Tuesday, February 18, 1969, and featured four members of Miles's live quintet: Miles himself, Corea, Shorter, and Holland. The additional musicians were Hancock, Zawinul, Tony Williams (rather than DeJohnette, because Miles wanted Williams's sound), and John McLaughlin. The then twenty-seven-year-old guitarist had come to New York only two weeks earlier, on February 3, on the invitation of Williams. McLaughlin had already gained some fame in Europe as a player who was well-versed in free-jazz, swing, R&B, and country blues, and he even enjoyed a stint as a pop session player, appearing on records by Tom Jones, Petula Clark, and David Bowie. By the time McLaughlin crossed the Atlantic he had developed a unique approach to playing jazz-rock guitar, which was characterized by a combination of a hard-edged, metallic, often distorted sound, normally associated with rock guitar, and a jazz guitarist's harmonic knowledge and single-note dexterity. The story goes that on the evening of his arrival in New York McLaughlin played at a jam witnessed by eminent jazz guitarist Larry Coryell, who immediately declared, "This is the best guitar player I have ever heard in my life."[14]

The historic events of February 18, 1969, began with the now-legendary tale of Miles calling Joe Zawinul in the morning, seemingly on the spur of the moment, and inviting him for the session. Miles called back a few minutes later with the instruction, "Bring some music." One of the charts Zawinul brought along was "In a Silent Way," which Miles proceeded to alter radically, as so often before, by leaving things out. "We changed what Joe had written," Miles recalled, "cut down all the chords and took his melody and used that. I wanted to make it sound more like rock. In rehearsal we had played it like Joe had written it, but it wasn't working for me because all the chords were cluttering it up. . . . When we recorded I just threw out the chord sheets and told everyone to play just the melody, just to play off that. They were surprised to be working that way."[15]

"It was quite an education to see Miles take a piece of material and adapt it to what he wanted it to be," Dave Holland concurred. "I don't remember Miles ever playing someone else's tune the way they had written it. He always changed it. He'd take a section, do something with it, and make it his. If there were many chords, he'd just have the bass play one note underneath all the moving chords, so that you get a pedal point. He did this with Zawinul's 'In a Silent Way' and also Shorter's 'Sanctuary.' One of the main things I learned from these sessions was how important process is to the end result. The way you put something together is as important as what you put together, and [it] influences what you end up with."

"His genius as a bandleader was in his group way of thinking, and in choosing the musicians and leading them forward by what he played, and by the way he used the ideas he or someone else brought to the band," Chick Corea commented.[16] "It was always interesting to see what he did with someone's composition. Miles would take the basic piece and often only play certain notes from it, and leave the rhythm section to play other notes. He didn't write that much as a composer, but he was an incredible, brilliant arranger. Miles suggested how to play the melodies, when to play them, how long to play them for. He'd open them up and then close them down and leave notes out. An example was the afternoon rehearsals we did at the Blue Coronet Club in Brooklyn [in April of 1969]. He asked me to bring some tunes, and I played a theme called 'This' for him, which had a quick rising line full of fast notes, and then a couple of slower notes at the end. After I played it a couple of times, he just picked out the couple of notes at the end to play on the trumpet, and let the rhythm section play the fast beginning. This immediately gave the piece a sound and identity."[17]

There were more surprises in store for the musicians during the *In a Silent Way* session. One was the cryptic instruction Miles gave to a nervous John McLaughlin: "Play as if you don't know how to play the guitar." Miles commented, "I didn't use John as a rock player, but for special effects."[18] The other surprise was Miles's direction to McLaughlin to play Zawinul's "In a Silent Way" theme on electric guitar over a pedal E. McLaughlin played through the score searchingly and hesitantly, thinking it was a tryout. To his astonishment, and probably to the amazement of the other musicians as well, it ended up being the master take. McLaughlin's searching playing had exactly the unhurried, fragile, and timeless feel Miles was looking for. "You never knew what was going to happen, so there was always an edge of nervousness. That's the way he pulled things out of you," recalled John McLaughlin.[19]

What Miles drew out of John McLaughlin during this session was remarkable. The guitarist's playing on *In a Silent Way*—and also on the follow-up album *Bitches Brew*—is among the freshest and most evocative of his career. Whether it was due to Miles's presence, his unusual instructions, or the chemistry between the musicians we will never know, but McLaughlin played with unsurpassed clarity, space, and elegance, almost as if he was rediscovering how to play the guitar. One innovation was the way he managed to comp and solo at the same time. After more than a year of searching, Miles had finally found the electric guitarist who could give him what he wanted, and he duly invited McLaughlin to join his working band. The guitarist declined, however, because he wanted the freedom to explore his own musical direction. Nevertheless, over the next two years he was to feature on several Miles studio sessions and live performances.

McLaughlin himself does not appear to have recognized the brilliance of his own playing, or that of the other musicians, on the *In a Silent Way* session. His bewilderment was illustrated by an anecdote told by Herbie Hancock. "After we finished we walked out of the studio," Hancock remembered. "And while we were standing in the hallway John came over and whispered to me, 'Can I ask you a question?' I answered, 'Sure.' He said, 'Herbie, I can't tell . . . was that any good what we did? I mean, what did we do? I can't tell what's going on!' So I told him, 'John, welcome to a Miles Davis session. Your guess is as good as mine. I have no idea, but somehow when the records come out, they end up sounding good.' Miles had a way of seeing straight through what happened and knowing that over time people would figure out what was really happening."

It was another sign of Miles's ability to recognize a new musical paradigm where others could not. The musicians had done exactly what the trumpeter always said he wanted them to do—"To be ready to play what you know and play above what you know"[20]— but the result was so far beyond what they knew that they were unable to make sense of the results. Miles was aware of the trailblazing nature of the record, declaring to a journalist just before its release that "this one will scare the shit out of them."[21]

In a Silent Way had a significant impact on its release and has since become known as the first milestone of the jazz-rock genre in terms of its musical influence and commercial appeal, and as an important forerunner of ambient music. Miles himself summarized, as always concisely, that *In a Silent Way* was a "tone poem very similar to 'Ascent,'" recorded three months earlier, dryly noting that "'Ascent' wasn't as compelling." He hit the nail right on the head. *In a Silent Way* is a logical development of the tracks "Ascent" and "Directions," incorporating the ambient, atmospheric quality of "Ascent," made more "compelling" by the structure and power of a rhythm section that's playing repetitive, ostinato patterns, as on "Directions."

Tony Williams was probably at his most disciplined ever, playing almost only high-hat shuffles on "Shhh/Peaceful," and a light but driving rimshot pattern on "It's about That Time." Williams's restrained playing has been a bone of contention among jazz critics. The astute writer Peter Keepnews wrote, "As much as I like *In a Silent Way,* I've never understood why the volcanic Tony Williams was reined in so tightly."[22] "There was no Tony Williams volcano on that session," Bob Belden explained. "Because Tony had been miffed at Miles for inviting Jack DeJohnette to the 'Directions' session [November 27], and when he saw John McLaughlin on the February 18 session, he was further pissed off. So he probably held back to keep Miles from recording Lifetime's star in the Lifetime way."

Serendipitously, Williams's ire-inspired restraint is one of the major reasons why the music works. Any deviation would have weakened the exquisite atmosphere of Miles's "tone poem," which is delicately balanced between the need for musical interest—supplied by trumpet, saxophone, and guitar—and for color and structure—supplied by the bass, drums, pianos, organ, and again the guitar. It's to support this precarious balance that Dave Holland's part on "Shhh/Peaceful" consists of only a two-note theme, with some agile variations in between; whereas on "It's about That Time" he alternates between a three-note riff and a proper bass melody (called "Section #3" in Merlin's sessionography). For the same reason Miles had McLaughlin adding color and movement by playing "special effects" instead of filling the spaces in the ways jazz or rock guitarists normally would.

As an ambient piece, or a "tone poem," *In a Silent Way* moves in a unique musical universe, where unconventional aesthetic and time laws apply. Not everybody appreciated or understood this approach. Stanley Crouch was probably not alone in viewing it as "droning wallpaper music," therewith touching on both ambient's ambition (i.e., to be a kind of wallpaper) and its potential weakness (i.e., the danger of a slide into Muzak). The distinction between ambient and Muzak is ultimately a matter of taste, but a ground rule may be that Muzak tends to be sentimental and aesthetically derivative, a form of aural kitsch.

Author Robert M. Pirsig memorably describes sentimentality as "a narrowing of experience to the emotionally familiar."[23] The music on *In a Silent Way* is original, unfamiliar, and decidedly nonsentimental, and therefore anything but Muzak. Its triumph lies in the fact that it not only lays open two new musical universes—jazz-rock and ambient—it also manages to poise itself perfectly on the meeting place between the two, working well as either. Apart from the clarity of the ideas and the masterful playing of the musicians, there are other secrets to its success. One is its innovative form: it was a new approach at the time to release an album with two continuous sides of music, with the two tracks on Side 2 fused together. It reflected the continuous "musical suite" form in which Miles had started to play his live performances from early 1967 onwards, and on record the structure is an essential aspect of why the hypnotic mood is sustained over the whole of the album. Another reason is the short length of 38:02, which is just long enough to carry the musical interest the material has to offer.

Most listeners and critics have long noticed the repeat of the 04:15-minute-long "In a Silent Way" section at the beginning and end of "It's about That Time," which seems to reduce the amount of new music to less than thirty-four minutes. But few appear to be aware of the almost shocking truth that underlies the album. In a 1976 interview, Teo Macero explained that the total amount of music recorded during the session was "well over two hours,"[24] although Bob Belden asserted that it was only one hour, which Macero and engineer John Guerriere trimmed to forty-nine minutes. When Macero asked Miles for feedback the trumpeter listened rather radically for what he could "leave out," because after he was done there were just twenty-seven minutes of music left. Macero and Guerriere then edited these twenty-seven minutes to a total length of thirty-eight minutes by repeating certain sections. The first 05:55 of "Shhh/Peaceful," for example, is repeated from 11:55 onwards, which means that the total amount of original material in this track is just 11:55, plus a nine-second fade-out.

"I used the same material over and over again,"[25] remembered Macero. This was an early example of the cut-and-paste and loop approach that's endemic in modern dance music. Some might call it a scam to sell an album with only twenty-seven minutes of original music, but Macero commented, with reason: "It was not done to deceive anyone. It was an attempt to develop the very best pieces that were recorded. Considering the favorable responses we got on the record, certainly no one felt cheated. It was a gas doing that album—a totally new approach."

The combination of Miles's leaving-things-out approach and Macero's compositional editing skills focused the direction of the music.[26] This was most likely the reason why large sections of the public recognized what *In a Silent Way* was about, while some of the musicians had trouble making sense of what they'd played immediately after the session: during the recording the final concept had not yet been established. Miles's and Macero's "totally new approach" consisted of taking an atmospheric snapshot of a session, almost like a still life. The harmonic and rhythmic development is virtually zero, and Macero filled this out in a way that beautifully sustains the captured atmosphere. Because the edits were done very skillfully, few people noticed that the album is based on such a minimal amount of material. Rather than a scam, *In a Silent Way* is a visionary masterpiece.

The story of *In a Silent Way* also illustrates something else. There have been some ruffles among a few of the musicians who played on Miles's sessions, most notably Joe Zawinul. They felt that Miles didn't give enough credit to the musicians who co-created with him in the studio. But although Zawinul delivered the main tune of the album, the way it came out was entirely the result of Miles's vision; the musicians and Macero were purely acting in its service.

In interviews, John McLaughlin has often stressed this point: "What happened with all the musicians who played with Miles in the studio was strictly Miles's doing. Let's make that perfectly clear. Miles's records were always carefully directed by him, orchestrated in a way that was not quite obvious. Because he had that thing, that ability to be able to make musicians play in a way that they would not normally think of. He had a way of pulling things out of them that they were unaware of. He certainly did it to me. So it was absolutely Miles's vision—the way the concepts would go. I think we have to put the credit on Miles. We all had ideas. Everybody would come up with things—a riff or a motif. But they were all really in the function of Miles and his music. We were only concerned with what we could do to contribute to what he was playing."[27]

"Whenever Joe or somebody would bring in something they wrote, I'd have to cut it all up because these guys get so hung up on what they write," Miles once noted. "They think it's complete the way they write it. Like the way he wanted that 'In a Silent Way' was completely different. I don't know what he was looking for when he wrote that tune, but it wasn't going to be on my record."[28] On another occasion he explained, "You write to establish a mood. That's all you need. Then we can go on for hours. If you complete something, you play it, and it's finished. Once you resolve it, there's nothing more to do. But when it's open, you can suspend it. . . ."[29]

Miles had developed the method of presenting musicians with unfamiliar and rudimentary musical sketches for more than a decade, leading to the creation of one of the all-time great jazz albums, *Kind of Blue*. Partly because the same method was used, *In a Silent Way* has a comparable pastoral, fragile, timeless feel, and its whispering wake-up call has often been compared to the modal delicacy of *Kind of Blue*. But due to personal problems and the disintegration of his band in late 1959, Miles had at the time not been able to develop his method any further, turning *Kind of Blue* into a creative end point. Ten years later things were different. The bandleader now managed to expand dramatically on the ideas that came into focus with *In a Silent Way*. Rather than a stand-alone peak, the album therefore turned out to be a stepping stone into undiscovered territory. Six months later, in August of 1969, Miles whipped up the scale and scope of his whisper to a storm.

Chapter Five

SORCERER'S BREW

*"Bitches Brew was like a big pot and Miles was the
sorcerer who was hanging over it. . . ."*
—LENNY WHITE

"He was like Merlin the magician."
—BILLY COBHAM

August of 1969 marked Miles Davis's boldest venture yet into undiscovered country. This time there was no more holding back, no more tentative experimentation, no more "walking on eggshells." The album that emerged, *Bitches Brew*, was groundbreaking, beginning with its stark title and Abdul Mati Klarwein's memorable cover painting. Made at Miles's personal invitation, Klarwein's expressionistic work captured the zeitgeist of free love and flower power, depicting a naked black couple looking expectantly at an ocean, a huge vibrant, red flower beside them. The background of the title is unknown, but a clue is provided by the absence of an apostrophe at the end of the word "bitches," making "brew" a verb, not a noun. Carlos Santana speculated that the album was a "tribute" to "the cosmic ladies" who surrounded Miles at the time and introduced him to some of the music, clothes, and attitudes of the '60s counterculture.[1] Gary Tomlinson, on the other hand, assumed that "bitches" referred to the musicians themselves.[2] Just like "motherfucker," the term "bitch" can be used as an accolade in African-American vernacular. Whatever the title meant, it sounded provocative. Teo Macero remarked, "The word 'bitches,' you know, probably that was the first time a title like that was ever used. . . . The title fit the music, the cover fit the music."[3]

The music on *Bitches Brew* is indeed provocative, and extraordinary. For Miles it meant a point of no return for the musical direction he had initiated with the recording of "Circle in the Round" in December of 1967. Until August of 1969 he had remained close enough to the jazz aesthetic and to jazz audiences to allow for a comfortable return into the jazz fold. But *Bitches Brew*'s ferocity and power carried a momentum that was much harder to turn around. The hypnotic grooves, which were rooted in rock and African music, heralded a dramatic new musical universe that not only gained Miles a new audience but also divided listeners into two groups—each side looking at this new music from totally different, and seemingly irreconcilable, perspectives. In the words of Quincy Troupe, these two groups were like "oil and water."[4]

Bitches Brew signaled a watershed in jazz, and had a significant impact on rock. In combination with Miles's fame and prestige, the album gave the budding jazz-rock genre visibility and credibility, which was instrumental in promoting it to the dominant direction in jazz. This is why, three decades after its making, *Down Beat* still called *Bitches Brew* "the most revolutionary jazz album in history."[5] The recording's enormous influence on the jazz music scene was bolstered by the fact that almost all the musicians involved progressed to high-profile careers in their own right. In the early 1970s, Joe Zawinul and Wayne Shorter (with percussionist Airto Moreira) were involved in Weather Report, Herbie Hancock and Bennie Maupin set up Mwandishi, John McLaughlin (with Billy Cobham) created Mahavishnu Orchestra, and Chick Corea founded Return to Forever with Lenny White. These bands became legendary names in the jazz-rock genre, and all of the aforementioned musicians, as well as Dave Holland and Jack DeJohnette, are still major players today.

Bitches Brew's influence has also been acknowledged by, or can be heard in the music of, artists as diverse as Carlos Santana, Henry Kaiser, Fred Frith, Bill Laswell, Vernon Reid, Talking Heads, Sonic Youth, David Sylvian, Sting, Mark Isham, Radiohead, and The Grateful Dead. Phil Lesh, the bassist for The Grateful Dead, said, "It was unlike any other jazz that had occurred before and it was revolutionary . . . it brought together many different ways of looking at music. One of the major achievements in the music of our century, if I may say so."[6] Thom Yorke, Radiohead's singer/guitarist, explained, "It was at the core of what we were trying to do with *OK Computer*."[7] And Jon Hassell, ambient trumpeter and one-time modern classical composer, spoke for many musicians when he declared, "Thank Goddess you were there, Miles. This music—as all great art must—extended the vocabulary of my imagination. I could dream and fantasize in a way that I couldn't before."[8]

Contrary to the impression given by these statements, *Bitches Brew* was not a sudden dramatic move in a completely new direction for Miles. In line with his long-standing, step-by-step working methods, the recording was maybe a large, but nevertheless logical, step forward on a course he had set almost two years earlier. In terms of personnel, musical conception, and sonic textures, the album was a direct descendant of its predecessor, *In a Silent Way*. Teo Macero remarked that with the latter album, the music "was just starting to jell. . . . It [*In a Silent Way*] was the one before [*Bitches Brew*]. Then all of a sudden all the elements came together."[9]

Bitches Brew and *In a Silent Way* are both dominated by circular grooves, John McLaughlin's angular guitar playing, and the sound of the Fender Rhodes electric piano. However, Miles related in his autobiography how he wanted to expand the canvas on *Bitches Brew* in terms of the length of the pieces and the number of musicians. While *In a Silent Way* featured eight musicians and was recorded in one single session, *Bitches Brew* included thirteen musicians and was the result of three days of recording. On the third day the rhythm section consisted of: three keyboardists, electric guitar, two basses, four drummers/percussionists, and a bass clarinet. Miles had pulled out the stops in his search for a heavier bottom end.

Uncharacteristically, Miles's live quintet also influenced *Bitches Brew*. Miles's live and studio directions continued to diverge around this time, with the studio experiments pioneering new material—incorporating elements of rock, soul, and folk that only gradually filtered through to the live stage. But in July of 1969 Miles's live quintet began performing "Spanish Key," "Miles Runs the Voodoo Down," and "Sanctuary," all of which would appear on *Bitches Brew*. ("Sanctuary" had, of course, already been recorded by the second great quintet on February 15, 1968.)

Having broken in this new material, Miles felt confident enough to book three successive days of studio time. He began by calling in the same crew that had recorded *In a Silent Way:* Wayne Shorter, Chick Corea, Joe Zawinul, John McLaughlin, and Dave Holland; only Tony Williams and Herbie Hancock were missing. Miles gave preference to live-band drummer Jack DeJohnette because of his "deep groove,"[10] invited Lifetime organist Larry Young instead of Hancock, and also added session bassist and Columbia producer Harvey Brooks. Together with Zawinul and McLaughlin, Young and Brooks had played on a session Miles organized for his wife, Betty Mabry, a few weeks earlier to record her first and ultimately unsuccessful solo album, *They Say I'm Different.* Miles also summoned nineteen-year-old drummer Lenny White who, like Tony Williams, is reported to have been brought to his attention by saxophonist Jackie McLean. Drummer/percussionist Don Alias had been introduced to Miles by Tony Williams, and he brought along percussionist Jim Riley, also known as "Jumma Santos." Tenor saxophonist and bass clarinettist Bennie Maupin was recommended by Jack DeJohnette. A finishing touch, and a stroke of genius, was Miles's instruction to Maupin to play only the bass clarinet, adding a very distinctive and enigmatic sound to the brew.

According to Miles, the approach he had developed of presenting musicians with musical sketches they had never seen before was also integral to the making of *Bitches Brew*. "I brought in these musical sketches that nobody had seen, just like I did on *Kind of Blue* and *In a Silent Way*."[11] However, this conflicts with the fact that three of the pieces had already been broken in during live concerts, as well as with his assertion that there had been rehearsals for the making of *Bitches Brew*, a fact that is confirmed by Joe Zawinul. "There was a lot of preparations for the sessions," the keyboardist recalled. "I went to Miles's house several times. I had ten tunes for him. He chose a few and then made sketches of them."[12]

"The night before the first studio session we rehearsed the first half of the track 'Bitches Brew,'" drummer Lenny White recalled. "I think we just rehearsed that one track. Jack DeJohnette, Dave Holland, Chick Corea, and Wayne Shorter were all there. I had a snare drum, and Jack had a snare drum and a cymbal. I was a nineteen-year-old kid, and I was afraid of Miles. My head was in the clouds! I was in awe. But he was really cool with me; he encouraged me and I ended up spending time with him at his home in later months. He was a real positive influence."

Since Miles was looking for more complex, larger-scale pieces, he probably felt that he needed some rehearsals to establish at least some structure and organization to keep more than a dozen musicians focused during three days of sessions. With none of the musicians aware of the whole picture, they would still react to the sessions with beginners' minds.

At 10 A.M. on Tuesday, August 19, 1969, twelve musicians, Teo Macero, and engineer Stan Tonkel gathered at Columbia Studio B for the first day of the recordings of *Bitches Brew*. Miles described the sessions as follows: "I would direct, like a conductor, once we started to play, and I would either write down some music for somebody or would tell

him to play different things I was hearing, as the music was growing, coming together. While the music was developing I would hear something that I thought could be extended or cut back. So that recording was a development of the creative process, a living composition. It was like a fugue, or motif, that we all bounced off of. After it had developed to a certain point, I would tell a certain musician to come in and play something else. . . . I wish we had thought of video taping that whole session. . . . That was a great recording session, man."[13]

"As the music was being played, as it was developing, Miles would get new ideas," Jack DeJohnette commented. "This was the beautiful thing about it. He'd do a take, and stop, and then get an idea from what had just gone before, and elaborate on it, or say to the keyboards 'play this sound. . . .' One thing fed the other. It was a process, a kind of spiral, a circular situation. The recording of *Bitches Brew* was a stream of creative musical energy. One thing was flowing into the next, and we were stopping and starting all the time, maybe to write a sketch out, and then go back to recording. The creative process was being documented on tape, with Miles directing the ensemble like a conductor an orchestra."

"During the session we'd start a groove, and we'd play," Lenny White remembered. "And then Miles would point to John McLaughlin and John would play for a while, and then Miles would stop the band. Then we'd start up again and he'd point to the keyboards, and someone would do another solo. All tracks were done in segments like that, with only the piano players possibly having a few written sketches in front of them. Miles said that he wanted Jack DeJohnette to be the leader of the rhythm section, because he was wearing the sunglasses! I'm from Jamaica, Queens, and I had played with other drummers before. I was trying to be very aware of wanting the music to sound very organic and congruent, real tight and seamless, so that people couldn't really hear that there were two drummers."

"*Bitches Brew* was like a big pot and Miles was the sorcerer," White continued. "He was hanging over it, saying, 'I'm going to add a dash of Jack DeJohnette, and a little bit of John McLaughlin, and then I'm going to add a pinch of Lenny White. And here's a teaspoonful of Bennie Maupin playing the bass clarinet.' He made that work. He got the people together who he thought would make an interesting combination. Harvey Brooks said he didn't know why he got the call, but he made an interesting pairing with Dave Holland on acoustic bass. It was a big, controlled experiment, and Miles had a vision that came true."

"The idea of using two basses and two drummers was very interesting," Dave Holland agreed. "The role division between Harvey and me depended on the piece, but as I remember it, Harvey was taking responsibility for laying down the main line on the electric bass, and I had a freer part embellishing things on the acoustic bass. Miles always gave the minimum amount of instructions. Usually he'd let you try and find something that you thought worked, and if it did, then that would be the end of it. His approach was that if he needed to tell someone what to do, he had the wrong musician. If we used any notation it was often a collage-type thing with a bass line and some chord movement, and maybe a melody related to that. But it was never something long or extended. It was always a fairly compact section, and then we'd move to another section. The recording of *Bitches Brew* was therefore often very fragmented. We'd have these sketches of ideas, and we'd play each for ten minutes or so, and then we'd sort of stop, come to an ending of sorts. And then we might do one more take like that, and then move on to the next thing. Often I didn't know whether we were rehearsing or recording, but Miles had a policy of recording everything."

"I think it was a lot of fun for him, with his favorite musicians on their respective instruments," DeJohnette added. "It was different and it was fun. There wasn't a lot said. Most of it was just directed with a word here and a word there. We were creating things and making them up on the spot, and the significant thing was that the tape recorder was always rolling and capturing it. Sometimes Miles said: 'This is not working. That's not it. Let's try something else.' But it was never because somebody had made a mistake or something. Miles was hearing the collective. He was trying to capture moods and feelings and textures. He always went for the essence of things, and that was much more important to him than going back and redoing a note that wasn't perfect. Perfection for him was really capturing the essence of something, and being in the moment with it. And then he and Teo later edited all these moments and put them all together. Some of the edits surprised me, but overall they were seamless, and captured the feeling and the intensity of the music."

Having been rehearsed the night before at Miles's house, "Bitches Brew" was the first track recorded on that initial day in Columbia Studio B. A beautiful example of Miles's directing and of the recording-in-sections approach can be heard at 07:28, when the ensemble appears to drift to a halt. Miles gives some indecipherable instructions, and the musicians carry on, clearly still not quite knowing where to go, because the music soon dissolves into entropy again. At this point, at 07:50, Miles simply says "John." McLaughlin begins to solo and the band picks up the groove again. Enough material was recorded in this way to create a separate track from an outtake (on which Miles did not play), titled "John McLaughlin."

After recording "Bitches Brew," the ensemble—without Maupin, Zawinul, McLaughlin, Brooks, and White[14]—performed "Sanctuary," a Wayne Shorter composition already recorded in a more gentle, sparser version by the second great quintet in February of 1968, with George Benson on guitar. Following this, the full complement of twelve musicians tried their hands on two Zawinul compositions, "Pharaoh's Dance" and "Orange Lady," but these takes were rejected.

"Miles Runs the Voodoo Down" (the title was a reference to Hendrix's "Voodoo Chile") was recorded the next day. In this case the previous performances of the live quintet of the track led to problems with the studio rhythm section. The addition of seven other musicians significantly altered the feel and dynamics of the piece, and Jack DeJohnette's medium-tempo, fairly loose live groove didn't appear to work.

"Lenny and Jack were playing and somehow things didn't jell," Don Alias explained. ". . . I think Miles really wanted that Buddy Miles sound; he was just gettin' into the funk thing. . . . He counted off the second time, and it wasn't happening. I couldn't take it any longer. I had been practicing this drum rhythm while I was in New Orleans for Mardi Gras . . . I'm sitting there thinking 'I've got the perfect rhythm for this tune.' . . . I can't take it any longer and Miles is about to count off for the third time and I interrupted and said, 'Miles, I've got this rhythm and I think it would go with the tune.' So he said: 'Go over and play it.' I sat down and played it, and he said: 'Show Jack . . . show Jack.' And it's one of those kind of rhythms where you don't need any chops . . . Jack couldn't get it, so Miles said to me: 'Just stay there' (on Lenny White's drumset). That's how I ended up being one of the drumset players on 'Miles Runs the Voodoo Down.'"[15]

On the third and final recording day, White was back in his drum seat and Alias was on congas. The thirteenth musician, Larry Young, was added to the ensemble on electric piano, creating once again a battery of three keyboard players, as on *In a Silent Way.* Two long tracks, "Spanish Key" and Zawinul's "Pharaoh's Dance," were put to tape. Altogether, a wealth of material had been recorded over the three days.

"The sessions would go till about three or four in the afternoon, and once the three days were over we went to Miles's house, and listened to all the unedited tapes," White remembered. "Half a year later a record came out that was totally different, because they'd taken the front end of one tune and put that in the middle and so on. Basically Teo Macero had made a whole other thing out of it. I suspect that Miles said to Teo: 'Go ahead and do what you think best,' and that Miles then approved or disapproved what had been done."

With his last comment, Lenny White touched on one of the many controversies that have become part of the legacy and the legend of *Bitches Brew,* namely the heavy postproduction applied to the album. The tape editing on the two opening pieces of the album, "Pharaoh's Dance" and the title track, is remarkably complex, and has a far-reaching effect on the music. In addition, Macero expanded his tool kit with studio effects like echo, reverb, and slap (tape) delay, the last courtesy of a machine called the Teo 1, made by technicians at Columbia. This effect can most clearly be heard on the trumpet in the beginning section of "Bitches Brew" and at 08:41 in "Pharaoh's Dance."

Enrico Merlin's research and the 1998 release of the four-CD boxed set *The Complete* Bitches Brew *Sessions* have cast important new light on the album's postproduction process. They show how Macero not only used tape editing to glue together large musical sections, as on "Circle in the Round" or *In a Silent Way,* he extended his scope to editing tiny musical segments to create brand-new musical themes. Courtesy of both approaches, "Pharaoh's Dance" contains an astonishing eighteen edits.[16] Its famous stop-start opening theme was entirely constructed during postproduction, using repeat loops of fifteen- and thirty-one-second fragments of tape, while thematic micro-edits occur between 08:53 and 09:00 where a one-second-long fragment appearing at 08:39 is repeated five times.

"I had carte blanche to work with the material," Macero explained. "I could move anything around and what I would do is record everything, right from beginning to end, mix it all down and then take all those tapes back to the editing room and listen to them and say: 'This is a good little piece here, this matches with that, put this here,' etc., and then add in all the effects—the electronics, the delays and overlays ... [I would] be working it out in the studio and take it back and re-edit it—front to back, back to front and the middle somewhere else and make it into a piece. I was a madman in the engineering room. Right after I'd put it together I'd send it to Miles and ask, 'How do you like it?' And he used to say, 'That's fine,' or 'That's OK,' or 'I thought you'd do that.' ... He never saw the work that had to be done on those tapes. I'd have to work on those tapes for four or five weeks to make them sound right."[17]

It appears that Macero found part of his inspiration for his postproduction treatments on *Bitches Brew* in classical music. The English composer Paul Buckmaster pointed out that on "Pharaoh's Dance" and "Bitches Brew" the producer created structures that have echoes of the sonata form that was at the heart of late-eighteenth- and nineteenth-century instrumental music. The basic elements of the sonata form, employed by composers like Mozart and Beethoven, are an opening exposition with two themes, a middle section called a development (in which the exposition material is worked through in many variations), a recapitulation (which contains a repetition of the two themes of the exposition), and a final coda.

In "Pharaoh's Dance" the section 00:00 to 02:32 can be called the exposition, since it contains two basic themes, with Theme #1 first played between 00:00 and 00:15 and Theme #2 at 00:46. Starting at 02:32 is a solo section, or development, containing references to the material of the exposition at 02:54 and 07:55. A dramatic section is edited in between 08:29 and 08:42, with tape delay added to Miles's horn, then repeated at 08:44 to 08:53, and followed by a one-second tape loop that repeats five times between 08:53 and 09:00. When Miles at long last plays Zawinul's stirring main theme (referred to earlier in the track, but never actually played), at 16:38, it can be considered the coda."(See Merlin's sessionography on pages 312 and 313 for detailed editing chart.)

The influence of the sonata form on the structure of "Bitches Brew" is not as clear-cut, but it is still apparent. Enrico Merlin's analysis notes fifteen edits in the piece, including (as in "Pharaoh's Dance") several short tape loops that create a new theme (in this case at 03:01, 03:07, 03:12, 03:17, and 03:27). Another section that leaps out at the listener is the tape loop from 10:36 to 10:52, where Macero creates excitement by looping a short trumpet phrase, making it sound like a precomposed theme. The section from 00:00 to 03:32 can be called the exposition, with the first theme appearing at 00:00 (the bass vamp) and at 00:41 (the corresponding melodic theme). The second theme is pasted in at 02:50. The development occurs between 03:32 and 14:36, with solos by Miles, McLaughlin, Shorter, and Corea. At 14:36 there's a recapitulation of the first theme, followed by another development, beginning at 17:20. The final recapitulation, a literal repeat of the first 02:50, can be interpreted as a coda.

Macero's strong editorial involvement in "Pharaoh's Dance" and "Bitches Brew," as well as his selection of "John McLaughlin" for inclusion on the album, may well have to do with the fact that these were the tracks that had not been broken in by the live band. Miles most likely did not have a clear vision for the final structure. By contrast, "Spanish Key," "Miles Runs the Voodoo Down," and "Sanctuary" had all been played live, giving Miles time to develop a functional structure. Only "Sanctuary" contains an edit, at 05:13, at which point Macero pasted in another take. It also seems likely that Macero was influenced in his edits by the form Miles had given to these three tracks, especially "Spanish Key," which has a circular structure, with Miles stating the main theme at 00:36, 09:17, and 16:48, and with the solo section containing several references to the main theme.

"There's very little dialogue . . . between Miles and myself," Macero elaborated on his working relationship with Miles. ". . . If we say 20 words in the course of a three-hour session, that's a lot. But there's no mystery . . . I spend as much time listening to it as he spent creating it. He may have gone over a composition in his mind, mentally, for weeks, and that's exactly what I do when I listen to the tape. . . . One thing about Miles and his music, in working with Miles you can experiment as much as you wish. You can take his music, you can cut it up, you can put the filters in, you can do anything you want to it as long as he knows who it is. I mean, he's not going to let just anyone do it. . . . I don't take liberties on my own, unless I check with him. . . . The final decision is up to the artist, because he has to live with the record."[18]

❖

The genius of Macero's editing on *Bitches Brew,* and his role in Miles's electric music in general, can be compared to that of George Martin's work with The Beatles. Like Martin, Macero often added a classical music sensibility to his protégé's music, and worked with him over a long period of time (from 1958 to 1983). Macero also worked with the likes of Dave Brubeck, Charlie Byrd, Duke Ellington, Ella Fitzgerald, Leonard Bernstein, Thelonious Monk, Charles Mingus, Lounge Lizards, Vernon Reid, and Robert Palmer, and has made an indelible mark on twentieth-century music. Yet his influence, especially in the case of Miles Davis, has not been widely recognized.[19]

Publicly, Miles rarely acknowledged Macero's role. He mentioned the producer just a few times in his autobiography, and only in passing. It's not hard to suspect that this may have had to do with their love-hate relationship, exemplified by Miles's refusal to talk to Macero for more than two years after the producer was involved in the release of *Quiet Nights* in 1964. Huge rows, as well as Macero's assertion that their relationship was like "matrimony,"[20] confirm the picture of a creatively fruitful, but personally tension-filled, connection.

In Macero's view, "Miles always wanted to take the credit for everything—on a lot of albums he didn't want the names of the musicians on the cover."[21] Once, when Macero asked for a bonus, he claims that Miles responded, "I don't think you deserve it. Anybody could have done it."[22] The most likely reason for Miles's reluctance to openly credit Macero was that he saw at several stages during his life how white men would take, or be given, the credit for black men's creative achievements. In his autobiography Miles stated, "Some people have written that doing *Bitches Brew* was Clive Davis's [head of Columbia at the time] or Teo Macero's idea. That's a lie, because they didn't have nothing to do with none of it. Again, it was white people trying to give some credit to other white people where it wasn't deserved, because the record became a breakthrough concept, very innovative. They were going to re-write history after the fact like they always do."[23] And in a 1973 interview Miles complained, "As long as I've been playing, they never say I done anything. They always say that some white guy did it."[24] (As mentioned earlier, this was the reason he had the text "Directions in Music by Miles Davis" placed on the covers of *Filles de Kilimanjaro* and *In a Silent Way. Bitches Brew* was his last recording to carry the legend.)

But just as the enormous influence of George Martin doesn't detract from the genius of The Beatles, emphasizing the importance of Macero in no way diminishes Miles's achievements. In reality, the freedom Miles gave to Macero is an illustration of the trumpeter's greatness. Many modern artists tend to want to control every aspect of record making, producing and sometimes engineering their own albums. This does not necessarily lead to better results. Macero once noted, "Miles would leave it up to me to make all the fucking decisions. People today, they want to be producer, writer, they want to do everything. I'm saying, Jesus Christ, then do it yourself. Save yourself some money."[25]

Great art has more chance of emerging when artists are acutely aware of their strengths and limitations. As an improvisational, here-and-now musician *pur sang* Miles did not have the inclination, the patience, or the skills to get deeply involved in the time-consuming, laborious postproduction process. Moreover, one of Miles's main strengths was the freedom he allowed the musicians with whom he worked. Delegating responsibility for the postproduction process to Macero reflects the same attitude. Given how sacrosanct music was to Miles, he must have trusted Macero deeply.

"Both of us have learned something from the things we've done together," Macero remarked. "I learned from the standpoint of editing, shifting the compositions around. . . . It's a creative process being a producer with Miles. In fact, it's more of a creative process than it is with any other artist. You have to know something about the music. You really need to be a composer, because for a lot of it he relies on you and your judgement. . . . I'm going through them as a composer, Miles as a composer-musician-performer. . . . You must be very creative along with the artist, because if you're not as creative as he is—forget it."[26]

It seems that Miles and Macero wanted to focus attention on the collaborative nature of their work by placing the two most-edited and experimental tracks, "Pharaoh's Dance" and "Bitches Brew," at the beginning of the album. They are like a declaration of intent. Macero's edits are not immediately apparent; they create a subliminal sense of both unrest and structure, something that's initially hard to grasp but immediately lifts the music out of the level of a jam. The edits are also successful in that they do not detract from the interaction between Miles and the ensemble. Although McLaughlin, the keyboardists, Maupin, Shorter, and Holland all take solos, they are mixed in a way that makes them float momentarily on top of the brew. Unlike Miles, they do not rise above it. This has led some jazz critics to complain that *Bitches Brew* doesn't really contain any solos, thereby not only missing the solos that were actually there, but—more importantly—missing the point that the musical essence of the album is not sequences of solos but the interplay between Miles and his ensemble.

Miles's trumpet is mixed much further to the front, like a singer. This makes it possible to hear the strength and range of his playing, the way he phrased his notes and guided the other musicians. After five years of being pushed to his limit in the second great quintet, and being in good health, he was at the peak of his trumpet-playing powers. Miles's sound is round, full, and powerful, and the way he drives the ensemble with often declamatory phrases that have predominantly a rhythmic rather than a melodic function, is remarkable. A good example is his solo in "Pharaoh's Dance" starting at 03:34, where he sounds as if he's wrestling, or perhaps boxing, with the band, pushing it, pulling it, steering it, and creating constant tension and release. Rather than a soloist playing over changes, Miles creates contrast, interest, and excitement in relation to a large mass of players who on their own could easily have sunk into amorphous anonymity.

Billy Cobham, an up-and-coming drummer at the time, played on the additional material on *The Complete Bitches Brew Sessions*.[27] Cobham still had the sound of awe in his voice when he remembered: "Miles was just coming out of the greatest band that he'd ever had, the second great quintet, and his trumpet playing was at a peak. He always played the ultimate musical phrase, even if it wasn't technically correct. It was unbelievable! When you listen to Freddie Hubbard you hear trumpet proficiency par excellence, and then you hear Miles and he had a way of taking what Freddie did and compacting it in five notes. Those five notes said it all. The air around them became musical, and the silence became more profound and important. You just don't learn that. Miles somehow could just do that. He was like Merlin the magician. It was based on Miles's innate ability to use space. Not playing became more important than playing. But it had to be the right spaces at the right time! It was uncanny how he'd play one note, and that note would carry through five or eight bars of changes. That note would be *the* note."

A major piece of work by any definition, "Pharaoh's Dance" was never performed live, and one wonders whether Miles had any doubts about the track's success. The album's title track, on the other hand, was a staple of the live band for more than two years, until October of 1971. It was invariably played at about half the length of the album time (26:58), thereby raising the issue of the extreme length of the two opening tracks of the album. ("Pharaoh's Dance" clocks in at 20:03.) There are two ways of looking at this. If one relates to the music as an "abstract," ambient atmosphere, a jungle environment that one can enter and roam, the length of these tracks becomes a significant aspect of their attraction. But from a more traditional, "figurative" perspective, in which the focus is on solos, themes, grooves, variety, development, "Pharaoh's Dance" and "Bitches Brew" are too long, and would both work better if cut substantially. The drastic cut in the length of "Bitches Brew" during live performances was partly due to the smaller size of the live band, but also suggests that Miles shared this opinion.

As with "Circle in the Round," Macero's editing was only partly successful. This is demonstrated by "John McLaughlin," the outtake from the track "Bitches Brew." At only 04:22 long it sustains interest from beginning to end, making it a good example of how this music works in a much tighter format. Moreover, the major tracks that weren't edited, "Spanish Key" and "Miles Runs the Voodoo Down," are much more focused, and contain Miles's best solos. "Spanish Key," a revisiting of the Spanish influences Miles had explored on *Sketches of Spain* and "Flamenco Sketches" on *Kind of Blue,* is a flowing, fluent boogie based around several different scales and tonal centers. Enrico Merlin has pointed out that the track employs what he calls "coded phrases," meaning musical cues with which the band is steered towards the next musical section. "[The] modulations are always initiated by the soloist who performs a phrase in the new key, thus signaling his own wish to change the tonal center," Merlin wrote. "This device was used for the first time in 'Flamenco Sketches.' I believe that Davis was trying, and he succeeded brilliantly, to adapt the idea of 'Flamenco Sketches' to the musical experimentation of that time [the late '60s]."[28] Sweltering and riveting throughout, "Spanish Key" would have been even stronger had it ended around thirteen minutes, when the music appears to come to a natural halt, rather than its full running time of 17:32. "Miles Runs the Voodoo Down" is probably the most successful track on *Bitches Brew,* courtesy of a beautiful, deep bass line, Alias's slow-burning, driving New Orleans drum groove, a tight structure, and excellent solos by Miles, McLaughlin, Shorter, and Zawinul. It remained a favorite of live performance until August of 1970. Finally, the version of "Sanctuary" on *Bitches Brew* is expressive and muscular but lacks the subtlety of the first recording with the second great quintet in February of 1968.

Regardless of how the quality of the music on *Bitches Brew* is judged, it is important to recognize the astonishing concoction of influences that had gone into Miles's cauldron. Miles had combined improvisational working methods that he developed in the late '50s with musical influences such as rock, folk, soul, and African music. Moreover, the ensemble's collective improvisation, which was based on the working methods developed by the second great quintet, and the call-and-response structure between Miles and the ensemble, both find their roots in early jazz. In his autobiography Miles likened *Bitches Brew*'s collective improvisations to the jam sessions he attended at Minton's in Harlem in the late '40s. Like many writers, Miles also made comparisons between the recording's kaleidoscopic sound world and the noises of New York City. Then, in the words of Lenny White, he mixed in a "dash" of this musician and that composer, not only skillfully blending their qualities, but also enlarging the sonic palette of jazz and rock with bass clarinet and extensive percussion. Both were novel sounds in jazz and rock music around 1969.

To this explosive mixture Teo Macero added mid-twentieth-century studio trickery, a nineteenth-century classical music awareness of musical structure, and a way of looking at music as abstract blocks of sound, which he freely cut and moved around. In other words, the two most heavily edited tracks on *Bitches Brew* were hybrids of "figurative" and "abstract" art. They combined, respectively, the traditional musical line of something akin to a sonata form with the cut-and-paste ideas that had come out of musique concrète, serial music, and studio technology, which later influenced ambient and dance music. Add to this the strongly chromatic improvising of the keyboard players, which has echoes of classical atonal music, and it is clear that an impressive amount of influences went into the making of *Bitches Brew*. This is no doubt one of the major reasons for the recording's immense success and influence. Virtually anyone willing to listen to it with an open mind is able to recognize something familiar in the music, despite the fact that it contains few easily identifiable melodies, hooks, or vamps.

Bitches Brew encompasses just about every musical polarity of the late '60s, whether jazz and rock, classical and African, improvised and notated music, live playing and postproduction editing. Its greatness lies in how it managed to bridge these polarities, transcending and including all the disparate ingredients into a completely new whole, and ended up with much more than the sum of its components. *Bitches Brew* explores a new, intangible musical universe, and any attempt to fully explain or define its "concept" and its music will inevitably diminish it to some degree. If one must find a label for the music, Lenny White probably had a good stab at it when he called it "African-American classical music—a combination of the harmonic language developed in the West over several hundreds of years, played from an African-American perspective, with an African-American approach to rhythm."

How *Bitches Brew* opened up a new, unknown musical paradigm is humorously illustrated by an anecdote told by Joe Zawinul that mirrors John McLaughlin's incomprehension during the *In a Silent Way* sessions. The keyboardist had been so baffled by the *Bitches Brew* sessions that he didn't even recognize the resulting music when he heard it later in another context. "I didn't really like the sessions at the time," Zawinul reminisced. "I didn't think they were exciting enough. But a short while later I was at the CBS offices, and a secretary was playing this incredible music. It was really smoking. So

I asked her, 'Who the hell is this?' And she replied, 'It's that *Bitches Brew* thing.' I thought, 'Damn, that's great.'"[29]

Of course, the recording also had its era on its side. The late '60s and early '70s were full of music that people didn't necessarily understand but that made them feel alive, that spoke to them. It was a time when audiences were prepared to go out of their way to enjoy the unusual and the controversial. The energy and mystery of the music, the title, the eye-catching and ultrahip cover, and the stream-of-consciousness liner notes by Ralph J. Gleason all perfectly expressed the zeitgeist. All elements came together in one seamless package, and the effect was powerful: The recording sold 400,000 copies in its first year and earned Miles a Grammy for "Best Jazz Performance, Soloist with Large Group." As a result, Gleason's showy words sounded prescient rather than hyped-up: "this music will change the world like *cool* and *walkin'* did and now that communication is faster and more complete it may change it more deeply and quickly."[30]

In addition to the music recorded during August of 1969, *The Complete* Bitches Brew *Sessions* also contains material from sessions in November of 1969, and from January and February of 1970. The total amount of music is dramatically extended from the 94 minutes of the original album to almost 266 minutes. Some of the additional material had already been issued on the albums *Big Fun, Circle in the Round,* and *Live-Evil,* but there are also nine previously unreleased tracks, totaling about 86 minutes of music.

Macero was invited by Sony/Columbia to participate in the creation of the boxed set, but he declined after a first meeting. The long collaboration between Miles and Macero created a deep bond between the two men, and it's understandable that since Miles's passing, Macero sees himself as a custodian of his legacy. In assuming this role he has loudly declared to anyone who wanted to listen that he disagrees with the way Sony/Columbia is reissuing the Miles Davis back catalog in general and *The Complete* Bitches Brew *Sessions* in particular. He boldly stated that "Miles Davis would never have agreed to the unreleased material being released, nor to the way the original material has been remixed and remastered," and that's to quote one of his milder statements. Macero has also supported the argument that the boxed set is a misnomer.

The original *Bitches Brew* sessions took place over the course of three days in August of 1969, and were complete in themselves. It appears a commercially inspired stretch to include material recorded several months later, with different personnel and a radically different musical feel, and declare it part of the *Bitches Brew* sessions. Reissue producer Bob Belden and executive producer Michael Cuscuna have reason to argue in the boxed set that Miles entered a new musical phase in March of 1970, when he started to work with a small, guitar-based group. However, the boxed set, awarded another Grammy in 1999 for "Best Boxed Recording Package," could have been called something like *The* Bitches Brew *Era,* since the additional material can easily be seen as a phase in itself, typified by the addition of Indian instruments like sitar, tamboura, and tabla. Most of this material has a pastoral atmosphere completely at odds with the storm of the original *Bitches Brew* sessions.

With regard to the issues that Macero raised concerning remixing and remastering, much of the Miles Davis music issued on CD by Sony during the late '90s has undergone this process, including all four boxed sets released to date. The triple-Grammy winning *Miles Davis & Gil Evans: The Complete Columbia Studio Recordings* and *Miles Davis & John Coltrane: The Complete Columbia Recordings, 1955–1961*, were remixed from three tracks, and the *Miles Davis Quintet, 1965–1968* was mixed from four tracks, by Sony staff engineer Mark Wilder. The small amount of tracks meant that Wilder's freedom to change the nature of the music was limited. However, *Bitches Brew* was recorded on eight-track and involved multitudes of complex edits and intricate sound effects. This made it more difficult to reconstruct the original version in a remix and it gave the remixer much more freedom to impose his own vision. In addition, some of the original effect equipment, like the Teo 1, was not available anymore, making an exact replication even harder. Finally, Wilder and Belden decided to make some fundamental changes to the sound and nature of the mix, leaving themselves open to accusations similar to those aimed at one time at the restorers of the Sistine Chapel.

"Let me make clear that when Sony told me that they wanted me to re-create the whole album, I knew immediately that we couldn't do any tinkering or release alternative takes or extend pieces," Belden explained in response. "I did not want to play Teo Macero. Instead, we wanted the boxed set to flow seamlessly. That is why we had to remix all the material. The two-track masters for the original *Bitches Brew* album were in bad shape, and there was a lot of disparity between them and the other material, whereas the previously unreleased stuff had not been mixed at all. Moreover, for the original LP they boosted the bottom and cut out the high end, taking out a lot of clarity. We put that clarity back in. We also decided to try to re-create what the musicians would have heard in the studio. There were always two distinct Fender Rhodes players, so we wanted to make sure that Chick Corea was always on the right and the guest on the left. That gives a sense of continuity. And we wanted to bring out the sound of Miles's trumpet and make it sound more in the pocket, the way you would have heard it during studio playbacks. We wanted to bring out the natural interplay between the musicians. At the same time we followed Teo's edits as faithfully as we could."

"Of course it's much more of a challenge to remix eight-tracks," Wilder agreed. "But I was able to get a very accurate approximation of the original mixes. We tried to pay homage to Teo's original edits and mixes as much as we could, but we also tried to bring out the musicality of the sessions. Those guys played some killing stuff that got a little lost in the technology of the mix and the postproduction. So yes, we tried to create a feeling of people playing music together. The musicality of what occurred during these sessions was paramount for us, and we wanted to remove some of the original mix technology to bring this out. They had made some very wild fader movements during the mix that we couldn't replicate anyway. But at the same time there are those signature things that were done during the mix, the slap [tape] echoes on Miles's trumpet, that we tried to replicate as best as we could. We would run my mixes and edits against the original LP version, and sometimes we'd compare with my version in one speaker and the original in the other to make sure that there were no edits that we had missed or mistimed. We worked amazingly hard on this."

Phrases like "removing some of the original mix technology" or "re-create what the musicians would have heard in the studio" will alarm purists. But as always, the proof of the pudding is in the eating, and from this perspective the work of Belden and Wilder is more than vindicated. All original edits are retained (although the new version of "Pharaoh's Dance" curiously loses four seconds that were in the original version, 08:29 to 08:33) and the instrumental balance of the mixes on *The Complete* Bitches Brew *Sessions* does not sound significantly different from that of the original album. The sound is greatly improved, however, displaying more aliveness, depth, and detail, partly because the Dolby that suppressed the high end (as well as the hiss) in the original is removed. There's a pleasant roundness to the new sound that was missing in the sometimes thin and abrasive-sounding original.

Belden and Wilder also succeeded in their aim of bringing out the interplay among the musicians. The improved high end especially has added a transparency that makes it easier to distinguish among the various percussion instruments and to imagine oneself in the studio with the musicians. It seems as if a cloud has lifted from the recordings, and some extra hiss is a small price to pay. Macero strongly criticized the new mixes, complaining that Miles sounded only "one inch tall," but the overall consensus, including from the musicians who played on the sessions, is that the new mixes sound excellent. The parallel with the restoration of the Sistine Chapel that appears apt is that of the brighter colors that emerged, which initially shocked traditionalists.

The additional material included in *The Complete* Bitches Brew *Sessions* begins with four tracks recorded on November 19. Wayne Shorter was replaced by the eighteen-year-old saxophonist Steve Grossman, Dave Holland with Ron Carter, and Jack DeJohnette with Billy Cobham. Guest musicians Bennie Maupin, Harvey Brooks, and John McLaughlin returned, and Herbie Hancock sat in as second keyboard player. Miles also added the exotic sounds of Brazilian percussionist Airto Moreira, plus Khalil Balakrishna on sitar and Bihari Sharma on tabla. Corea was the only musician from the live band at these sessions, and there is some historical confusion with regards to the reasons.

In his autobiography, Miles stated that Wayne Shorter left the band "in late fall 1969" and that he then "broke up the band to find replacements."[31] This is incorrect, because Shorter played with the live band until early March of 1970. Miles's assertion that Shorter had "told me ahead of time when he was leaving" and that he wanted to try out new musicians (thereby adding to his growing list of Stock Company Players) was probably closer to the mark.

The size of the band may suggest a direct line to the *Bitches Brew* sessions three months earlier, but the introduction of the Brazilian and Indian elements took things in a totally different direction. Indian music influences had become popular in the late '60s, mainly through The Beatles's and the counterculture's interest in Eastern mysticism, and sitars were occasionally employed in Western popular music, especially psychedelic rock. Miles was one of the few jazz musicians who did more than just flirt with this influence, and Indian instruments intermittently played an important part in his music from 1969 to 1973.

During this stage in his career Miles appeared almost obsessed with incorporating as many disparate musical influences as possible, seemingly using anything or anyone on which he could lay his hands. The question has often been asked whether Miles had a vision for the end result or was just randomly throwing things into his cauldron and was as surprised by the results as anyone else.

"I think that Miles definitely had a vision," Dave Holland commented, "but when you put together improvised music, you're dealing with musicians and their approach and style of playing. One of the things I learned from Miles is that you don't come in with a fixed vision. The vision is there, but it is not finished. The composition a classical composer writes is finished, and all musicians do is interpret it. Improvised music is different. Part of your palette is the musicians you're working with, and so with this group it will come out one way, and with that group it will come out another way. So if you ask me, 'Did Miles have a vision?' I'll say 'Yes.' But ask, 'Did he know what the end result would sound like?' and I'd have to say 'No.' He couldn't. When he was putting something together, he was listening and selecting what he liked. To me this is the great art of putting together improvised music. Miles worked in the tradition where you create a form that's clear, but that also has enough room for the musicians to be creative with. Miles was giving us a context for the music, and then we found what we could do within that context."

Still, throwing different musicians together to see what will happen is a risky approach, and this was demonstrated in a series of failures. The track "Great Expectations," recorded on November 19, is an example. It was first released on *Big Fun* in 1974, and has a structure similar to that of "Nefertiti" from June of 1967, with a repeating main melody underpinned by an ever-varying drum section. The bass relentlessly plays a rock riff not dissimilar to that of "Peter Gunn," and the Brazilian and Indian elements add some color and variation. But it's not enough to save the rather dreary and repetitive effort, which is weak on the figurative side (an unengaging melody and little melodic development) and offers little on the abstract side (the atmosphere is feeble and unfocused).

Zawinul's "Orange Lady," recorded on the same day and also first released on *Big Fun,* is better, partly because the melodic line is more interesting and partly because it is reasonably successful as a "tone poem," an exercise in creating a mood. The other two tracks recorded during this session were previously unreleased, and, as Macero argued, with good reason. "Yaphet" sounds as if it starts where "Orange Lady" left off, meanders for nearly ten minutes, and adds nothing significant whatsoever. "Corrado" is no more than a directionless thirteen-minute jam. Apart from Miles's incisive playing, it has no engaging features.

Things didn't get much better at the next session nine days later on November 28, with a similar ensemble. Organist Larry Young joined Hancock and Corea and, possibly to inject some energy from tried-and-true elements, Miles reinstated his live band rhythm section: Holland played bass and DeJohnette was on drums next to Cobham. The previously unreleased "Trevere" is a kernel of an idea that never takes off; halfway through the band comes to a halt—from the sound of it, because they had no clue where to take things next.

The same problems also apply to "The Big Green Serpent," which is basically a group of musicians trying out an idea and getting nowhere. Belden sounds almost apologetic about the inclusion of "The Little Blue Frog" and its alternate take ("A jam in G. That's all it really is. Just a jam"[32]), but at least the musicians sound as if they're having fun, and McLaughlin and the rhythm section lay down a satisfactory groove. A 02:42 section of "The Little Blue Frog" was released as a single in the United States in April of 1970, before the release of *Bitches Brew,* and in France in 1973. It must have left listeners completely at a loss. As Belden said, "What were they (and who were they?) thinking?"[33] Indeed.

The question arises as to why these two sessions were such failures. One explanation may be the shooting incident that occurred in October of 1969. The Birdland affair in August of 1959, when Miles was beaten and arrested by two New York police officers, had shown how devastating the impact of extramusical dramas on Miles's musical progress could be. That incident abruptly cut short the rising creative curve that culminated in *Kind of Blue* and marked the beginnings of a three-and-a-half-year creative wasteland. Although less directly related to racial issues, and therefore emotionally less close to the bone, the episode in October of 1969 was shocking enough, and it would not be surprising if it caused a creative dip in the months following.

In Miles's memory, he and Marguerite Eskridge were unexpectedly shot at when they were talking and kissing in front of her apartment.[34] Eskridge remembered the incident differently. "Miles was playing at the Blue Coronet Club in Brooklyn," she recounted. "He had supposedly been getting calls that he should not be playing there unless he booked through a particular agency. I had a premonition that night at the club that something was going to happen. At one stage I literally felt blood trickling down the side of my face, even though I was never shot. After the gig Miles drove me home in his Ferrari, and he kept looking in the rearview mirror. At one point he said, 'There's a gypsy cab following us.' He tried to lose it a few times, and then we pulled in next to the building where I lived in Brooklyn. A few moments later he saw the car coming in from the rear, and said, 'Duck down.' We both ducked. At that point a lot of shots were fired from the car, and then it drove away. We were still sitting in the car because I had been taking my time pulling out my keys and everything. If I had gotten right out and walked to the outside door I would have been standing unprotected, and I would clearly have been shot. Miles had been grazed slightly at his side. A bullet had gone through his leather jacket. The car had trapped a lot of the bullets. We went to the hospital and at about 5 A.M. the police came out and read me my rights! I mean, we were the victims! They wouldn't say what we were being charged for, but they took us to the police station, and then finally I found out that they believed that there was marijuana in the car. Later on, all charges were dropped because they found that it was nothing but herbal teas. . . ."

Miles said that he had been shot at because some black promoters were angry with him for using white promoters to do his bookings, but saxophonist Dave Liebman claimed it was the result of a drug deal gone wrong. "He was definitely involved in something, you know—questionable characters that's for sure."[35] The unfounded suspicions of the police also give this story a race-related slant and may well have heightened the impact the incident had on Miles. Whatever its background, the link between the shooting and the failure of the November sessions is speculative in the end. If we are to look for musical reasons, a possible explanation is that the many new, young musicians felt inhibited by Miles's presence and disorientated by his unorthodox working methods.

"When they [the musicians] are in that studio it's like God coming—oh, oh, here he comes," Macero recalled. "They stop talking, they don't fool around, they tend to business and they listen, and when he stops, they stop. . . . He is the teacher, he is the one who's sort of pulling the strings. He's the professor. He's the God that they look up to and they never disagreed, to my knowledge, in the studio. If they did, they got a goddamn drumstick over their head, and I've seen that happen, too."[36]

"As far as I was concerned, all the people around me were light years ahead of what I was capable of doing," Cobham explained, "so all I could do was shut up and absorb and hope that something would stick. For me it was like school time, ten times graduate school. Far beyond any institution. Everything was experimentation. There was not one moment when whatever was on a piece of paper was not changed. That's why there were no stems on the notes. Nothing was tied. There might be three notes and then a space and then four tones, and then a space, and then two notes. You'd have to generally know how it was phrased, but it didn't necessarily mean that it was going to stay like that. His instructions were very minimal, almost Zen. He would give me very little to work with. The very rare times he talked to me, it was something like: 'I need something from you. Give me something between the Latin and the jazz vein.' I was blown away by the fact that he even acknowledged that he liked what I did. I was just like, eyes open, ears open, absorbing as much as I could."

Cobham clearly was in awe, and this feeling was shared by several of the other new musicians, which possibly inhibited their playing. Miles's darker side was surely a contributing factor. According to many eyewitnesses he could be ruthless in the way he handled people, taking advantage of them if they allowed it, testing them to see how far he could go. He respected those who stood up to him, but musicians who couldn't, didn't last long. For this reason some musicians were not only in awe, but actively scared of him.

"His perceptions of people were so intuitive," explained Lydia DeJohnette. "In one second he would know who you were and what you wanted. And if he felt where you were coming from wasn't centered—if you couldn't look him in the eye, if he didn't think he could treat you as an equal—he would just put you away. He could destroy people emotionally."

"There was always a lot of magic in working with him," Jack DeJohnette added, "always a lot of challenges. You always had to be prepared for the unexpected. You had to be on your toes and alert. He kept you thinking all the time, and that was fun. You never knew what was going to happen, and that made it exciting, but also very challenging. Personally I was never afraid of Miles, but I've seen people who were. He had a bitter side and a very loving side. He was a visionary and very intuitive, and he could read people like he could read music. He immediately knew your vulnerabilities and could press your buttons."

Steve Grossman elaborated on the same theme when he remarked that, even though it was an incredible break for him to be playing with Miles at such a young age, it was also nerve-racking. "Miles was just such a great person and very encouraging. He really tried to make me feel at ease. But he was one of my favorite musicians since I was eight years old, so it was difficult. Also, I was used to playing straight-ahead jazz and to suddenly go into this environment where everyone had a lot more experience, I would say I was inhibited."

"I was terrified for the first month," Airto Moreira recalled.[37] And Billy Cobham commented, "I was never scared of Miles, but I was intimidated by his presence. Miles would sometimes try and see how far he could go with you. If he thought he could break your nose and you wouldn't respond, he would do it. Just to see what would happen. I was never that unfortunate to experience that kind of stuff, but I've seen him intimidate people to some degree. Of course, it had a rippling effect throughout the music. The music always is a sincere sonic mirror of what happened in the social environment in which it is played. And so some people would play . . . scared of Miles."

The air of danger and of the unexpected that always hung around Miles was one way in which he kept his musicians on their toes, fully alive to the present moment and to music. But it could be counterproductive. Perhaps this was the case in November of 1969, when several of the new musicians played "inhibited" and/or "scared of Miles." A pointer in this direction is the fact that the following sessions, on January 27 and 28 and February 6, 1970, are far superior. The new musicians may well have become accustomed to Miles's presence, gaining in confidence and daring to open up more. In addition, Miles seemed to have come to the conclusion that the experiments with a large group of musicians had run their course because his studio ensembles were getting smaller, and the music better.

On January 27, 1970, Grossman was absent and Shorter returned on soprano sax, Zawinul replaced Hancock and Young, and McLaughlin, Brooks, and Sharma were dropped. This reduced the ensemble from fourteen to ten players. "Lonely Fire," first released on *Big Fun,* starts in an ambient mood similar to that of "Orange Lady." Zawinul's theme sets up a powerful atmosphere and is repeated over and over again with the rhythm section playing variations underneath, as in "Nefertiti" and "Great Expectations." "Lonely Fire" threatens to meander too long for its own good as a "tone poem," but entices again when Holland embarks on a driving rhythm around the eleven-minute mark, with Chick Corea throwing in Eastern-sounding scales. It works, but it's not a great track, and overly long at more than twenty-one minutes.

"Guinnevere" was first released in 1979 as part of the *Circle in the Round* set. A composition by David Crosby of Crosby, Stills, Nash & Young, it is another showcase for Miles's interest in American folk music. Little happens in the twenty-one-minute-long track, and for much of the time the melody is played over a very slow four-note bass line. But the atmosphere is nevertheless gripping, probably due to the focus and simplicity of the playing. By contrast with the November sessions, the musicians now sound as if they're playing with a unified purpose. It may be a "period piece,"[38] but its pastoral atmosphere still carries some power decades later.

The session of January 28, with the same group as the day before but with McLaughlin instead of Balakrishna, was another improvement. Perhaps Miles also felt that his compositional ideas had not been giving him the results he wanted, because for this session and the session of February 6 he did not use his own material but tried his hand at one composition by Shorter and four by Zawinul.

Shorter's "Feio" is performed in a way similar to "Guinnevere," with Holland playing a slow, three-note bass line, the horns somberly blowing the top line, and the spaces being filled up by drums, Moreira's percussion, and some screaming electric guitar splashes by McLaughlin. It works still better than "Guinnevere," perhaps because the track is only half as long, and McLaughlin, Moreira, and DeJohnette create considerable interest as well as a potent atmosphere. Zawinul's "Double Image" completed the day's work in a version that's more straightforward and less raw than the one recorded on February 6 in 1971 on *Live-Evil.*

On February 6 Bennie Maupin was replaced by a sitar player, not credited on *The Complete* Bitches Brew *Sessions* but named as Balakrishna on the liner notes for *Live-Evil.* Suddenly and inexplicably everything fell into place. The track "Recollections," based on a Zawinul folk composition not dissimilar to "In a Silent Way," is simply gorgeous. It is beautifully executed, with a compelling, frozen-in-time atmosphere similar to Miles's version of said song, all the musicians are perfectly aligned with each other. McLaughlin also plays some graceful and elegant folk-influenced fills that are very different from the stabbing staccato riffs that sharpened "In a Silent Way." "Recollections" is among the most pastoral pieces Miles ever recorded and is entirely successful as an ambient piece of music. The same applies to the short "Take It or Leave It," which is actually the middle section of Zawinul's "In a Silent Way."

Finally, the version of "Double Image" recorded on this day, and released in 1971 on *Live-Evil*, is a triumph. The rhythm is opened up from the fairly standard way it had been played when the same track was recorded a week earlier and is transformed into a funky stop-start affair, with a screaming electric guitar filling the gaps. It's a format that Miles would explore several times during the early '70s. Although there is still a lot of improvisation going on, the role of the rhythm section is tightly circumscribed. The track is more firmly in rock territory than anything Miles had done up to this point, echoing rock avant-garde rather than free-jazz. This is the first sign of Miles formulating a new, rockier, guitar-centered studio direction, which he would bring to fruition in the months following on *A Tribute to Jack Johnson.*

Chapter Six

KIND OF BLUES

*"When I first started playing with Eddie Randle's
Blue Devils in St. Louis—[we] played the blues . . .
all the time."*

—MILES DAVIS[1]

Bitches Brew was released as a double LP in April of 1970. Its impact was immediate, and lasting. Not only did it earn Miles a Grammy and his first gold record, it was also the foremost jazz album to incorporate the music styles associated with the 1960s counterculture and to cross over to the counterculture marketplace. The rock world received the recording with particular enthusiasm. But the reaction from the jazz community was more guarded. Some jazz critics and musicians were positive, expressing admiration for what they recognized as a courageous and innovative answer to the stalemate between the conservatism of hardbop and the extremes of free-jazz; others denounced what they saw as "a bunch of noise,"[2] a "sellout,"[3] or "dollar-sign music."[4]

Had *Bitches Brew* failed commercially these critics might not have given it much attention, but its high public profile made it impossible to ignore and at the same time provided the ammunition to demonize the man and his intentions, rather than deal with the music itself. However, even a surface examination of the most basic facts surrounding *Bitches Brew* indicates that if the recording was a "sell-out," it surely was one of the most perverse and clumsy in the history of music. Before its release, there was no reason to believe that *Bitches Brew* would be commercially successful. On the contrary. In those days releasing a double album was regarded as decidedly noncommercial, because it was thought that the higher cost deterred potential music buyers. The album's extremely long tracks were deeply resistant to radio play, and the music itself was hardly catchy or easy on the ear. Nobody had ever heard jazz or rock like this.

In the light of this, it makes more sense to see Miles as displaying tremendous courage in exploring uncharted territory and in opting for an uncertain future in the music world of the '60s counterculture, which before *Bitches Brew* still regarded him as one of yesterday's men. By going electric he also risked becoming a contentious figure in the jazz community, where he could safely have lived out his days feted and respected. In short, the risks Miles took with *Bitches Brew* were immense, which is why Wayne Shorter's comment, "There's nothing magical about the electric period. . . . There was just more courage involved," is so appropriate. Dizzy Gillespie once made a similar point: "Miles should be commended for going off in a completely new direction. He's just as brave as shit."[5]

All this raises one simple question: why? Why did Miles move towards the music and marketplace of the '60s counterculture? Why did he risk derision, vilification, and commercial disaster? And why did Miles reject an alternative option, going into free-jazz? Why would a musician whose natural habitat was the cutting edge, who had been at the forefront of nearly every new development in jazz for nearly a quarter century, reject the latest development in jazz? This chapter attempts to answer these questions.

The controversy surrounding *Bitches Brew* has been a major reason why the above questions have often been overlooked and why in-depth and insightful analysis of Miles's electric direction has been scarce. Many of the reflections from Miles's supporters have been defenses made in relation to the "sell-out" allegations and they have not examined Miles's electric music on its own terms. (It is illustrative that an expert in Renaissance music, Professor Gary Tomlinson, has offered one of the few genuinely authoritative assessments of Miles's electric direction with his essay "Miles Davis: Musical Dialogician."[6] His outsider position allowed him a fresh perspective.) At the same time, Miles's detractors sound too prejudiced—too much as if they're coming from old-fashioned antirock and anti-electric instrument attitudes—to be taken seriously. It is tempting to simply ignore them, but their allegations have clouded the discussion so deeply that in order to obtain a clear space wherein the above questions can be answered, it is necessary to first deal with these allegations.

The charges against Miles are set in the context of much circumstantial evidence. In 1966 Miles turned forty, became a grandfather, had lost his long-standing position at the forefront of the jazz community, and was confronted with diminishing audience interest. By the mid- to late 1960s Miles was in a precarious situation, with sales of his recordings dropping to below 50,000, compared to highs of 150,000 in the late 1950s. Concert attendance was also dwindling dramatically, as Dave Holland observed when he joined Miles's band in the summer of 1968. "I was actually shocked at how few people were coming to his concerts," Holland said. "On an opening night in San Francisco there were maybe thirty to forty people. My expectation of Miles was that him being a great artist, everyplace he played would be absolutely packed. That was not the case."

None of these facts is in dispute, and their implication—that Miles faced major midlife, identity, and financial crises—may well be true. While in this uncertain situation, Miles sought the company of girlfriends and musicians between ten and twenty years his junior, changed his clothes, and played music influenced by the youth culture of the day. Not long afterwards his record sales increased again. Nobody will argue with these facts either. The disagreement begins with the interpretation that Miles was motivated mainly by desires for money, success, fame, eternal life, or worse, that he simply obeyed orders from above. The latter allegation sounds ridiculous, but jazz critic John Litweiler wrote that "Davis's bosses ordered him to make a hit record, or else; *Bitches Brew* was his response."[7] If this interpretation is taken seriously, one begins to understand why Stanley Crouch reached for hyperbole, calling Miles's move into jazz-rock "the fall,"[8] and adding that Miles "deserves the description that Nietzsche gave of Wagner: The greatest example of self-violation in the history of art."[9] Crouch's assertion prompted Gary Carner, editor of *The Miles Davis Companion,* to remark, with a hint of sarcasm, that Crouch portrays Miles's "sell-out" as "a fall from grace reminiscent of Adam's in the Bible."[10]

Litweiler referred to a story often quoted to support the sell-out charges. It concerned a well-publicized row between Miles and Clive Davis (no relation), who became vice president and general manager of Columbia Records in 1966. Columbia had been a rather conservative record company with a largely middle-of-the-road artist roster, and with the emergence of the music of the '60s counterculture sales were dropping dramatically. In response, Clive Davis set himself to signing adventurous new acts that reflected the spirit and music of the times, particularly artists who bridged the gap between jazz and rock. Some of his signings, such as Blood, Sweat & Tears, Chicago, Santana, and blues-rock guitarist Johnny Winter, were hugely successful, and Miles may well have looked with envy at the three-million-selling singles Blood, Sweat & Tears enjoyed in 1969.

Concerned by the combination of Miles's declining record sales and the large advances paid to him, Clive Davis called the trumpeter sometime in 1969 with the suggestion that, in order to reach a larger audience, he should play large rock venues and support rock bands. Miles was furious, accused Columbia and Davis of racial bias, and announced that he wanted to break off his relationship with the record company. Heated discussions between Columbia and Miles's manager, Jack Whittemore, followed, and reports about the conflict appeared in the press, suggesting that Miles intended to move to Motown Records. But in the end Miles made his peace with Clive Davis and Columbia, and when Davis connected Miles with the legendary rock concert organizer Bill Graham in early 1970, Miles agreed to do the very thing that had infuriated him so much: he appeared at the rock venues Fillmore East in New York in March (one of the two concerts issued in the summer of 2001 as *Live at the Fillmore East*), supporting the Steve Miller Blues Band and Neil Young & Crazy Horse, and at the Fillmore West in San Francisco in April, supporting Laura Nyro (which resulted in the live album *Black Beauty*). Following this, Miles played numerous rock venues throughout 1970, supporting many different rock acts. Miles remarked that playing these rock venues was an "eye-opening" experience because suddenly he was confronted with 5,000 people, a far cry from the small jazz clubs with a few dozen people that he had played only months previously.

Reports of Miles's successes at these venues vary. Biographer Jack Chambers claimed that Miles had some "lessons in humility"[11] when he opened for the likes for Crosby, Stills, Nash & Young, The Band, and Santana, and that the youthful audience found his music too difficult. The trumpeter himself admitted that his music "went right past a lot of that audience"[12] when he was on the same bill as The Band at the Hollywood Bowl in 1971. At the same time, Miles also boisterously recounted that his band had "torn the place down" on many other occasions. In Dave Holland's memory, the latter version of events is closer to the truth: "The rock audience reactions were very good. We did one show with The Grateful Dead, and I heard quite recently from one of the ex-members that they were very nervous that they had to play up next to Miles. It was a time when people were not that worried about musical categories. And this was some pretty strong in-your-face music. People loved it."

Nevertheless, the music Miles played around the turn of the decade, whether in the recording studio or live, was not easily accessible for rock audiences, and this is one of the main arguments made by people who have sprung to Miles's defense. His defenders also point to his fierce independence, artistic pride, commitment to music, continuous desire for change, and exhortations such as "If you sacrifice your art because of some woman, or some man, or for some color, or for some wealth, you can't be trusted."[13] As always, actions speak louder than words, and there is an anecdote that illustrates how Miles's focus remained on music, and not on image or commercial success. The popular and respected singer Laura Nyro asked Miles in 1969 to perform on an album that she was recording. He visited the recording studio, listened to the tracks, concluded that "all the holes where he could play had already been filled in,"[14] and declined to perform. This was not the action of a man who had sold his soul to commercialism. Performing on Nyro's album would have given Miles a lot of credibility with the young generation. But as always, musical considerations came first.

There are many other events that indicate that Miles's move into jazz-rock was not a response to record company pressures, financial crises, or other extramusical considerations. Several of these events have been outlined in previous chapters—such as the fact that he had already made his first steps in the direction of the music of the counterculture with the recording of "Circle in the Round" in December of 1967 (most likely before he got involved with Betty Mabry, who is said to have influenced him). This recording preceded the row with Clive Davis by more than a year. There were also no commercial reasons for the plethora of recordings in the middle of 1968 and in June of 1970. And the attractive cover of *Bitches Brew*, which seems to have prejudiced so many jazz commentators, was not a new development. The cover of Miles's album *Miles in the Sky*, released in 1968, was archetypal 1960s Pop art.

There is only one instance where the claim that Miles's new musical direction was deliberately conceived to reach a new audience holds some ground, and this is regarding his desire to achieve more popularity with black audiences. Until this point a large portion of his audience had been white. Influenced by the increasing political consciousness of blacks in the '60s, Miles grew unhappy with this. His attempts to reach a black audience in 1972 with his most controversial album, *On the Corner,* have been well documented. However, in 1969 he had already approached a black-owned marketing and public relations company called New Wave Communications with a view to promoting him to a black audience. Clive Davis recalled that Miles telephoned *him* as early as 1968 with the request to stop promoting him as a jazz musician, in order to widen and increase his audience.[15] But a desire to increase his black audience is hardly the same thing as a sell-out.

The above discussion reflects the arguments most commonly put forward to criticize, or defend, Miles's electric direction. None of these facts and interpretations convincingly support the idea of a commercially inspired change of direction in 1969. Of course we will never know with certainty what moved Miles during this crucial period, and perhaps financial considerations, a midlife crisis, and a reluctance to grow old were part of the equation. Miles was a human being as well as an artist, and he experienced feelings and temptations that affect us all. But when commentators propose that these were the driving forces that led Miles to behavior incongruous with numerous previous career choices, perhaps they are blinded by their own agendas.

On a deeper level, the misunderstanding of Miles's electric direction expresses a difference in musical "languages," or insofar as people look at music differently from their jazz or rock perspectives, a difference in musical paradigms. Most of Miles's jazz critics were and are unable to understand the jazz-rock vernacular because they're stuck in a jazz paradigm, from which rock looks unpleasant and incomprehensible. Rather than admit to their limitations, his detractors simply devalue and dismiss what they don't understand. This leaves them with little option but to reach for extramusical arguments, such as the sell-out charges. The tragedy is that, had Miles's opponents been able to follow him into his new direction, they would have recognized that it renewed and arguably salvaged jazz.

❖

In response to the question of *why* Miles went into electric music, I'd like to offer two interpretations of Miles's approach to music that have only occasionally been touched upon. The first interpretation is founded on the scientific axiom that accepts the simplest explanation of the known facts as the most plausible hypothesis. The hypothesis proposed here is that Miles is best understood as primarily a blues player who moved into jazz and then into jazz-rock, rather than a jazz player who was influenced by the blues. This makes sense of many aspects of his career and trumpet style that have so far seemed inexplicable. The second interpretation follows from the observation that Miles built every new musical step on his previous steps, and it asserts that the secret of his enormous success and influence is that he was a traditionalist and a revolutionary at the same time.

Jazz writers have often noted the strong blues elements in Miles's playing and music. For example, jazz critic Gary Giddins remarked, "The 1949 blues was heralded as birth of the cool, and the 1954 blues as a return to the hot"[16] and "[Miles] revitalized the blues with 'All Blues' and 'Freddie Freeloader.'"[17] Jack Chambers stated that when Miles surged to the forefront of the hardbop movement with the track "Walkin'" in 1954, he "quite literally filters the blues through bebop into a new style."[18] And Leonard Feather wrote that when Miles grew up in St. Louis, "the blues became second nature."[19]

Jazz writers tend to perceive these blues influences as external, as an early influence that Miles transcended in his music and sometimes returned to for inspiration. However, the blues influence was much more integral, permeating Miles's whole musical outlook. Miles hinted many times at the crucial importance of the blues for him and indicated that his musical formation was steeped in it. The place where he grew up, St. Louis, is the blues heartland. "The blues was always around when I was in St. Louis," Miles commented. "I heard blues played by the bands that came up from New Orleans on the riverboats, and by musicians from Oklahoma and Missouri and Kansas."[20]

The first group in which Miles played, Eddie Randle's Blue Devils, was an R&B band, and it had a huge formative impact on the young Miles. He also stated that his electric direction was really a return to the blues roots of his youth. "I was trying to play the music I grew up on now, that roadhouse, honky-tonk, funky thing that people used to dance to on Friday and Saturday nights."[21] Musing on the highly evolved music of the second great quintet he remarked, "I used to listen to Muddy Waters in Chicago. . . . I knew I had to get some of what he was doing up in my music. You know, the sound of the $1.50 drums and the harmonicas and the two-chord blues. I had to get back to that now because what we had been doing was just getting really abstracted. That was cool while I did it, but I just wanted to get back to that sound from where I had come."[22]

In an interview in 1969, when commenting on his time with Eddie Randle's Blue Devils, Miles virtually equated rock and blues: "You don't have to be a special kind of player to play rock. That's what we were playing when I first started playing with Eddie Randle's Blue Devils in St. Louis—[we] played the blues . . . *all* the time."[23] This remark isn't exactly complimentary to rock and requires a brief clarification. Miles was often heard talking in derogatory terms about rock. For example, in 1969 he told the *Washington Post*, "Those cats haven't done much yet. It's very easy to take a riff and vamp for three minutes, but when they get out there to solo, they ain't got nothing to say."[24]

In the '60s most rock musicians lagged far behind jazz musicians in terms of technical ability and knowledge of music theory. Their relative ignorance and limited skills frustrated Miles, who had gone through years of almost obsessive musical training, both classical at Juilliard and the hands-on knowledge shared by jazz musicians like Dizzie Gillespie and Charlie Parker. There were few rock musicians around at that time who were dedicated and focused enough to engage in naming the pitch of creaking doors or writing chords on matchboxes. (The rock virtuoso was a phenomenon that only became commonplace during the '70s, when the general technical standard of playing in rock greatly increased.) Consummate musicianship was something Miles greatly admired, and this was an area in which he resonated with the jazz community, laced as it was—and is—with virtuoso musicians. The relative lack of technical ability among rock musicians in the '60s was one of the major reasons why many in the jazz community rejected rock.

However, unlike many of his jazz colleagues, Miles did not throw out the rock baby with the nonvirtuoso bathwater. Instead, he recognized the creative potential of rock music as soon as it started coming of age in the mid-1960s. Miles was able to hear the meaning behind the notes played by rock musicians. Having spent much of his time reining in the virtuosity of jazz musicians and teaching them the importance of listening, of space, of sound, of economy of notes, he was able to listen to rock without prejudice, and he recognized its common ground with the blues. For example, he named the blues as the central factor in the mutual recognition and admiration he shared with rock innovator Jimi Hendrix.

The Miles Davis Radio Project highlighted the huge influence of the blues in Miles's music in a way few other commentators had, illustrating it with audio examples and with comments by Carlos Santana, trumpeter Olu Dara, and others. During the program an unidentified interviewee stated, "He sang the blues on the trumpet, rather than just play it as most other players," and another voice added, "He was a real blues player. . . ."[25] Olu Dara claimed, "He was singing the blues."[26]

"To learn to sustain and make a guitar sound like a voice is what we're all trying to do," Santana said. "The voice is the ultimate instrument, is the closest to the heart. I saw Miles as a singer. His music sounds like John Lee Hooker, when he moans. John Lee Hooker moaning says a hell of a lot more than a lot of people's poems. Just one moan. His voice and his tone are really crucial. . . . I don't know if people in this country have the experience of sucking out a sugar cane and getting the juice out. Miles does that in solos, and so do all the blues guitarists. Getting the juice out of the note, they're getting inside of the note. You know it and I know it and everybody knows it. The way Miles plays the blues is still with Lightnin' Hopkins, he has that tone. But he also combines that gut-bucket-cotton thing with the elegance of Duke Ellington. His phrasing brings it all together."[27]

On the radio program Santana demonstrated the sucking-a-sugar-cane sound on a guitar, which has an effect not unlike that of the wah-wah pedal. It's a matter of bending notes and varying their timbre by changing the way the note is picked. The program continued with a section of Miles's haunting performance in "Nuit sur les Champs-Élysées," the opening track of *Ascenseur pour l'Échafaud*, and Miles can be heard bending and changing the timbre of his notes in a very similar way. He's sucking the sugar cane out of his trumpet, getting right inside of the notes, stretching them, leaving spaces, playing slow, haunting lines, and concentrating on his sound.

Finding and expressing his sound was a lifelong endeavor for Miles. His acute awareness of sound was not only directly related to his extraordinary listening sense but also reflected his blues grounding. He repeatedly described his focus on sound in exactly the same words as Santana, as a matter of "getting inside of the note." On one occasion he remarked, "Sound is important to me. I have a mid-Western sound. I used to play the cornet, so I prefer a round sound with no attitude in the sound. If I can't get that sound, I can't play anything. The sound I have is like a round voice."[28] And he said, "I've practiced my tone for almost . . . fifty years, and if I can't hear my tone, I can't play. . . . If I lose my tone, I can't fuck, I can't make love, can't do nuthin'. I'll just walk into the ocean and die."[29]

Miles played many different notes inside of one note by varying the pitch and timbre, just as blues guitarists do. Miles's main tool in achieving this was his sound. It is one of the reasons that he's such an exquisite ballad player; it is also at the root of his minimalist, less-is-more approach to playing. Changing the sound of individual notes only works if these notes are held for a certain length of time, i.e., through playing slowly. By playing fewer notes in exactly the right places, he suggested additional notes, and his well-chosen spaces sound like musical notes in their own right. He not only had a capacity to play the "most unexpected but the right note" (as Quincy Jones has stated), he also played that note in the right way, in the right place, with the right phrasing, and with the right bend and timbre.

Miles performed with several blues greats—such as in November of 1973 when he appeared with B. B. King on Spanish television, performing King's "You Know I Love You." In 1989 Miles played with John Lee Hooker on the blues-based soundtrack for the movie *The Hot Spot,* sounding totally in his element and eloquently demonstrating his getting-the-juice-out-of-notes approach and his penchant for grouping his notes in rhythmically well-defined phrases, leaving plenty of space between the phrases. Exact rhythmic phrasing is one of the key aspects of blues improvisation and it is not necessarily an attribute of other forms of improvisation. (In rock and jazz music improvisers often fill up all the spaces, playing continuous streams of notes.) A blues guitarist can play all the right notes, but if they aren't phrased correctly, they won't pack a punch. Given his blues roots, Miles had an unusually strongly developed rhythmic awareness, and precise phrasing was among his fortes.

"He plays rhythm," saxophonist Dave Liebman remarked. "He plays off the beat. He plays on the upbeats. He'll play a rhythmic phrase in order to get the attention going. He's not just thinking harmonically and melodically. He's thinking rhythm. It's like a drummer. He would constantly talk about rhythm. . . . Coltrane was straight ahead, it wasn't about rhythm, it was about lines and motion. With Miles this thing was about up and down, get in between the beats, in between—like boxing. . . . When you think about Miles's playing. . . . It's a ballet. It's a dance. It's a ball bouncing. It's not like some stream of air or stream of water."[30]

Miles confirmed that he learned the art of phrasing during his R&B days in St. Louis: "Eddie Randle used to tell me to play a phrase and then breathe, or play the way you breathed."[31] Miles also repeatedly made references to the parallels between his trumpet style and guitar playing. For example, "I had always played the trumpet like a guitar and the wah-wah just made the sound closer."[32] Clearly, his use of the wah-wah pedal during the '70s was an attempt to amplify the effect of "sucking the sugar cane." It may be pushing the case for the blues guitar influence too far, but it is nevertheless possible that even his pioneering use of the metal Harmon mute was in part inspired by blues slide guitar playing, often performed with a metal bottleneck and sharing the same metallic and mellifluous quality.

I owe another important parallel to the British Miles Davis enthusiast Martin Booth, who pointed to the striking similarities between Miles's '70s wah-wah playing and that of blues harp players, particularly Little Walter's electric harmonica on classic '50s numbers like "Juke" and "Off the Wall." Little Walter played in Muddy Waters's late '40s/early '50s revolutionary electric blues band, which paved the way for the modern R&B sound and hence for rock music. The similarities between Miles's phrasing and bending the notes and that of the blues harmonica are indeed striking, and are particularly exemplified by his 1972's blues recording "Red China Blues," on which Miles appeared side by side with harmonica player Wally Chambers.

Many early blues musicians were singers who accompanied themselves on the guitar and harmonica, on which they developed a style rooted in imitations of the human voice. Being strongly influence by this approach, Miles made the trumpet sound as expressive as a voice. This has often been described as one of his biggest contributions to the instrument's stylistic development. However, there's a key aspect to this approach that has often gone unnoticed. The main stylist in jazz trumpet playing before Miles, Louis Armstrong, also attempted to humanize the sound of the trumpet, in his case by imitating the vibrato of the trained human voice. Until Miles came along, this approach was commonplace in jazz and in classical instrumental styles.

By contrast, the humanity of Miles's style has always been predominantly ascribed to the fact that he took *out* the vibrato. This seeming contradiction is about much more than just a stylistic development in trumpet playing. It represents two different attitudes towards artistic expression—the nineteenth-century romantic approach and the modern style that emerged in the course of the twentieth century. Before Miles there was a strong tendency to dramatize expressions, to overplay and overact. Overacting in silent movies is a prime example; the nineteenth-century novel—with its tendency for flowery language, extremely detailed descriptions, and stories loaded with subplots—is another. Similarly, the operatic singing style of the eighteenth and nineteenth centuries developed a strong, artificial vibrato that was designed to enlarge the volume of the voice and is in effect a form of oversinging.

These ornate stylistic approaches were part of the romantic art style, and, with the exception of the classical singer, if a modern musician, actor, or writer were to use them, his or her efforts would quickly be regarded as over the top, possibly even kitsch. By contrast, the modern approach is based on understatement and economy of means, on a more direct, no-frills, natural style, in which vibrato, or overacting, or flowery language, is discouraged.

With his sense for understatement, economy of means, and nonvibrato, Miles was one of the twentieth-century pioneers of the modern playing style. This is an important reason why so much of his music and playing hasn't dated. There's a parallel here with Pablo Picasso, who was one of the early architects of the modern style in the visual arts and who fought a lifelong war against what he regarded as the "prettiness" of romantic art. This resembled Miles's fight against what he called "sissified" musical stylistic tendencies. Miles's music could be emotional, tender, gentle, and melodic, but it was rarely pretty, kitsch, or sentimental, and there was no room for excessive ornamentation and vibrato.

Understatement and economy of means can strip away nuances, richness, and depth, and Miles's genius was the way he developed other devices to enrich the creative and emotional range of the modern style. Instead of imitating the vibrato of the trained human voice, he imitated, through the influence of the blues, the natural inflections of the human voice. It is ironic that by rejecting one of the prime means through which musicians in the '30s, '40s, and '50s tried to humanize their instrumental sound, Miles ultimately sounded more human to us than his predecessors.

Two more seemingly unrelated facts fall into place when we view Miles primarily as a blues musician. First, it makes it easier to comprehend how he was able to incorporate so many seemingly disparate musical influences. Almost all nonclassical American music forms—jazz, R&B, gospel, soul, funk, and rock—have their roots in the blues. Both jazz and rock were direct descendants of the blues, which explains why they were the two main constants of his music. Many other music styles—folk, classical, African, Latin, Spanish, and Indian—were also part of his music, but they were at least one step further removed from the blues; they were therefore more ephemeral influences, and often harder to integrate.

Second, emphasizing the blues influence makes sense of Miles's leaving-things-out approach to musical modernization. The traditional view, proposed by many jazz commentators and alluded to in Chapter 2, sees Miles's career as a reaction to the complexity of late '40s bebop, culminating in him grooving on one note in the '70s. However, this view offers no explanations as to why he reacted to bebop in such a way. Placing the blues center stage offers an elegant and simple explanation. Rather than bebop being a starting point to which he subsequently reacted, the blues were his underlying roots and his bebop period was an excursion into nonnative musical territory. Once Miles's formative period was over and he began to develop his own musical direction (from 1950 and the "cool" style onwards), he was always, consciously or unconsciously, looking for the simplicity and directness of the "sound of the $1.50 drums and the harmonicas and the two-chord blues."

This search culminated in Miles's electric music, which was saturated with the blues. Professor Gary Tomlinson noted that "All his fusion work sings the blues, its melodies pivoting again and again on flat-VII or playing subtly on flat-III/III exchanges. Indeed, Miles speaks the blues rather more plainly here than in many of his earlier styles; [writer Greg] Tate is right to say that Davis turned from 'post-bop modernism' to funky fusion, 'because he was bored fiddling with quantum mechanics and just wanted to play the blues again.'"[33]

In the sense that he was retracing his steps, Miles was a traditionalist. He appeared to be aware of this side of himself, because in 1969 he mused, "I'm straight. Actually, I think, old-fashioned, you know. I'm just straight."[34] But to reduce Miles to a conservative would be a great mistake. This brings us to the second vital interpretation of Miles's attitude to music. The foundations for his greatness lay in the fact that he was a traditionalist *as well as* a revolutionary. He included the blues influence in everything he did, yet he transcended the blues at the same time. This principle was exquisitely summarized in his aphorism: "Play what you know, and play above what you know." Most focus on the "play above what you know" part, because it has an intriguing, unexplainable quality. All musicians can play what they know, but few can play above what they know. However, emphasizing the latter aspect over "play what you know" misses the point. Miles could have just said "play above what you know." But he didn't. The simple reason is that to "play what you know" is as essential.

Miles had picked the principle of his aphorism up from Charlie Parker in the late '40s, remembering "Anything might happen musically when you were playing with Bird. So I learned to play what I knew and extend it upwards—a little *above* what I knew. You had to be ready for anything."[35] Miles repeated the principle in various guises, such as to Leonard Feather in 1972: "A cliché should be your musical foundation, but it shouldn't be what you do."[36]

It is hard to overstate the importance of Miles's aphorism. It summed up the whole creative tension from which Miles's music sprang. Some of the ideas proposed by the philosopher Ken Wilber may be helpful in explaining this. In his many books, Wilber undertakes to give an all-encompassing picture of the evolutionary processes of the cosmos. In essence, he attempts nothing short of giving "A Brief History of Everything," which is indeed the tongue-in-cheek title he gave to a popularized account of many of his ideas, and which is required reading for anyone interested in, well, everything. Wilber not only describes the physical evolution of humanity, he also elaborates at length on the evolution of our inner worlds (i.e., the evolution of our cultures and our consciousness). His ideas are therefore readily applicable to the realm of artistic expression and to Miles's musical development, and I ask the reader to bear with me as I attempt a brief history of everything in six paragraphs.

Wilber proposes that the whole universe can be interpreted in terms of building blocks called "holons"—meaning something that is whole in itself and yet part of a larger whole at the same time. For example, an electron is a holon, and is part of an atom (which is a holon), which can be part of a molecule (which is again a holon). This is called the vertical organization of holons: they can dissolve downwards into their building blocks—for instance, when molecules become atoms—or they can "transcend" to a higher level of organization, as when notes are strung together to form a melody.

Deepening the concept of form and content, Wilber also describes the "exterior" and "interior" facets of a holon. "Exterior" refers to its physical characteristics, its form, its outside, its surface, which can be instantly and relatively objectively viewed just by looking at it. "Interior" refers to the holon's inside, its content, its meaning, the consciousness with which it is imbued; perceiving the "interior" involves (inner) listening, intuition, and (when dealing with sentient beings) dialog. For instance, the "exterior," physical side of a human brain is composed of holons—such as brain cells, neuron cells, synapses, alpha and beta waves—that can be viewed through dissection or with brain scans. The brain's "interior" is made up of thoughts, feelings, perceptions, etc., and to get to know these we need to talk to and listen to the owner of the brain. Similarly, describing a chord progression as II-V-I refers to this holon's "exterior," a "surface" aspect that can be instantly and objectively established, whereas "hearing" the meaning of the notes, its "interior" aspect, involves a deeper intuitive awareness.

Other crucial concepts are "span" and "depth." The former refers to the "horizontal" aspect of holons, i.e., the number of same-level holons; the latter refers to the number of "vertical" layers a holon contains. Evolution is a drive towards more organization, more depth, and less span. There are trillions and trillions of bacteria (great span, little depth), but six billion humans (less span, more depth). The more depth a holon has, the more of the universe it contains, and the greater its significance is. Depth is synonymous with "interior," and with meaning, and hence with consciousness. Millions of random notes have great span, but little depth. However, when these notes are organized in musical phrases and chords, they form fewer holons (less span), but have more meaning (more depth). Humans, it can be argued, have more consciousness than bacteria.

Humanity has evolved over thousands of years through different types of economical, social, and political (exterior) structures, each usually with more organization and depth than the previous one. Each of these structures has a particular worldview or paradigm (interior). Contemplative philosophers (Buddha, Lao Tzu, Socrates, Plato, Confucius) emerged with the rise of agricultural societies, which suddenly allowed (some) people time to think about their existence. The rational paradigm, also called the Enlightenment (based on the ideas of Descartes, Locke, and Kant), went hand in hand with the technological and scientific advances of our industrial society. The rational worldview is deeply focused on the scientifically observable "exterior" and on the visual sense, and it tends to undervalue the "interior" and the listening sense.

The "interior" of the information technology society that has been taking shape since the late-twentieth century is the postmodern, "existential" paradigm, which acknowledges and values the interior as much as the exterior and aims to balance and integrate the two.[37] One obvious manifestation of this emerging worldview is holistic medicine. As late as the early 1980s, anyone suggesting that there was a relationship between physical disease (exterior) and people's thoughts and feelings (interior) was laughed away by medical scientists. But today the relationship between mind and body is accepted as so obvious that we can hardly credit that people once believed otherwise.

Wilber describes how evolution moves forwards through a process of "transcending and including," gaining more depth (consciousness) as it includes more of the universe. Newly emerging holons contain lower-level holons but are also more than the sum of these holons. This principle of "transcend and include" is crucially important. Without it, evolutionary steps forward are rarely stable or viable. Of course, inclusion without transcendence means evolutionary standstill. But transcendence without inclusion involves repression of lower-level holons, which results in unbalanced growth and often in dissolution into lower-level holons. Unintegrated traumatic childhood experiences leading to personality disorders are a good example. Another is the tendency of sections of the New Age culture—which is one expression of the nascent "existential" paradigm—to devalue rational argument and scientific methodology, thereby risking a throwback to the prerational worldview of the Middle Ages.

Wilber's concepts can add many fresh perspectives to a discussion of Miles's music and methods. For instance, Miles's "knowing," his capacity to hear meaning behind the notes, can be understood as an exceptional ability to listen beyond the "exterior" quality of music and perceive its "interior," its meaning. Miles told percussionist Mtume in the '70s, "Anybody can play. The note is only 20 percent. The attitude of the motherfucker who plays it is 80 percent." This is simply another way of saying that the interior of a note, its meaning, its "attitude," counts for 80 percent, and its exterior only 20 percent. Miles made the same point in 1968 when Leonard Feather played a track by Thad Jones Mel Lewis for him. "Those guys don't have a musical mind," Miles commented. ". . . They don't know what the notes mean."[38] Having a "musical mind" is about the ability to listen beyond the written notes, beyond surface appearances. As Dave Liebman put it, "[For Miles] how is more important than what."[39]

Science fiction writer Arthur C. Clarke once remarked that any sufficiently advanced technology will look like magic to those who don't understand it. The same can be said for any sufficiently advanced awareness. As discussed in Chapter 1, Miles's "knowing" was inexplicable to the musicians around him, which is why they used words like "magic," "sorcerer," or "Merlin" to describe him. Miles appears to have operated from a musical awareness ahead of his time. His exceptional alertness to both form and meaning—"exterior" and "interior," seeing and intuition/listening—as well as the fact that many of his utterings make progressively more sense to us, suggest that his was a form of the emerging "existential" paradigm.

Whether intuitively or consciously, Miles had a worldview that included a full grasp of the importance of the principle of "transcend and include" for the creative process. The tremendous significance of his aphorism "play what you know and play above what you know" now becomes immediately apparent. It is an exact translation of the principle of "transcend and include." Miles's respect for the "include" aspect showed as early as 1950, when he angrily sprang to the defense of Dixieland with, for a twenty-four-year-old, a precocious remark that could hardly be regarded as very cool by his fellow beboppers: "I don't like to hear someone put down Dixieland. Those people who say there's no music but bop are just stupid; it just shows how much they don't know."[40]

The same respect for music history has been demonstrated in the previous chapters covering Miles's innovations of January of 1965 to February of 1970. During its first three years, Miles's second great quintet methodically developed its jazz vernacular one step at a time, each time transcending and including what had been before. The quintet reached the outer limits of what could be considered jazz in December of 1967 and Miles instantly began looking for influences outside of jazz to transcend and include. Significantly, every time he brought in a new musical ingredient, he built upon the achievements of the previous session. This began with the introduction of the electric guitar and a new approach to studio postproduction on "Circle in the Round" in December of 1967. The electric piano entered on the next session three weeks later, resulting in "Water on the Pond." In May of 1968 Miles experimented with elements of soul and rock in "Stuff," and a month later with the beginnings of the pastoral/ambient/tone poem approach with "Filles de Kilimanjaro." Next came two new band members, Chick Corea and Dave Holland, followed by the idea of more than one keyboard player, and the first fulfillment of the ambient direction with "Ascent" in November of 1968. Eventually, the original *Bitches Brew* sessions transcended and included all these ingredients, incorporating influences of African and classical music, rock, free-jazz, and studio technology.

Jazz commentators have often noted how Miles tended to be "methodical" and "careful" in his jazz innovations, which really is another way of saying that he "transcended" and "included." By moving slowly, Miles made sure that he included his previous achievements with each forward step. In a perceptive passage of his Miles biography, Ian Carr described Miles's creative process in terms very analogous to "transcend and include:" "Davis had always believed in progress and development, but he had always been aware of his roots. He did not jettison; he added to what he already knew, and each stage of his development contained the essence of the previous stage."[41]

Upcoming chapters will show that Miles worked according to the notion of "transcend and include" until the end of his life. He also applied this principle to other areas of musical expression, most notably his trumpet style, which was an amalgamation of different influences, such as that of his teacher Elwood Buchanan, the St. Louis trumpet sound, the blues, bebop, and the classical tuition he received at Juilliard. However, Miles's style and music were more than the sum of these disparate parts. He infused them with a new life, a new musical vision, creating something unique. In other words, he transcended all his influences. This continuous process of "transcend and include" is one of the main secrets of Miles's musical successes. His most successful music was always familiar and fresh at the same time. His music had many layers and hence enough "depth" to obtain a timeless quality; it appealed to numerous people of many different cultures throughout many decades.

The degree to which Miles combined both traditional and revolutionary values was unusual. As was already discussed in Chapter 2, one possible explanation, given by professor Gary Tomlinson, pointed towards Miles's black middle-class background—specifically how he was steeped in the values of both white and black American cultures, which lead to "an acute fascination with difference." Miles's position on the cusp between two cultures is illustrated by his description of how, during his time at Juilliard in 1944 and 1945, he "would go to the library and borrow scores by all those great composers, like [Igor] Stravinsky, Alban Berg, [Sergey] Prokofiev. I wanted to see what was going on in all of music. Knowledge is freedom and ignorance is slavery, and I just couldn't believe someone could be that close to freedom and not take advantage of it. I have never understood why black people didn't take advantage of all the shit that they can. It's like a ghetto mentality telling people that they aren't supposed to do certain things, that those things are only reserved for white people."[42]

Few young American musicians, black or white, in the late '40s had this degree of cross-cultural openness and interest. Gary Tomlinson elaborated: "Davis's musical achievement was an acutely dialogical one, reveling in the merging of contrasting approaches and sounds, highlighting the awareness of difference that seems so crucial a part of Davis's own personality. . . . From this cultural ambivalence . . . —or better, from multivalence—arose musical dialogue. Davis's fusion music from 1969 to 1974 represents the culmination of this dialogue, a logical outgrowth of his earlier musical developments and the mediating concerns expressed in it. . . . The dialogical dimensions of Davis's fusion music, then, are numerous."[43]

Tomlinson's approach is entirely congruent with the concepts proposed by Wilber, but the principle of "transcend and include" can deepen the dialectical view. In applying

Wilber's ideas to music, each musical genre, each "difference," can be seen as a holon, and the evolution of music can be seen as the continual emerging of new holons that transcend and include previous holons. For instance, jazz is made up of musical holons like blues, ragtime, marching band music, American folk, Western classical, and African music, and yet it transcends them at the same time. Miles's "fusion" music transcended and included many musical holons, or "numerous dialogical dimensions," like blues, jazz, soul, funk, folk, classical, African, Indian, Brazilian, and Spanish music. The limitation of a dialogical view is that it purely describes the exterior aspect of music, whereas Wilber's approach also offers a window to the interior aspect and to how music can gain in significance and depth with each evolutionary step.

A word of caution is in order here. Since Wilber equates the number of "vertical" level of a holon with depth, and with meaning and significance, this could lead to the interpretation that jazz, or Miles's music, is inherently more significant than each of the musical holons it transcends and includes. But it is important to keep in mind that evolution does not always progress in such a linear and one-dimensional fashion. There's a magic to the "transcend" aspect of the creative and evolutionary process that's hard to define or predict. Sometimes what seems like a transcendence is simply what Wilber calls a "translation," a different expression of the same holon, old wine in new bottles. Sometimes a new musical holon only includes one aspect of one of the holons on which it is founded, thereby losing part of the original holon's depth. Sometimes a newly emerging holon may be akin to a Frankenstein-like grafting together of basic holons, doing little justice to its components. Much symphonic rock of the '70s was decidedly less than the sum of its classical and rock parts, for instance. The same is occasionally demonstrated in Miles's own music, with tracks like "Fun" or "Mr. Tillmon" sounding like awkwardly joined jazz and pop holons that do not manage to become more than the sum of their parts. By contrast, the original *Bitches Brew* album was so successful because the music went well beyond the many influences that went into its making, thereby creating a momentous depth and meaning that still resonate to this day.

All that can be said, therefore, is that music incorporating many levels of musical influences has the *potential* for more depth, for more meaning. Whether this potential is realized is another matter and needs careful consideration in each individual case. Similarly, musicians with superior technical skill have the potential for expressing infinitely more nuances and contrasts—i.e., depth and meaning—in their playing than musicians with limited technique. But in the end, technical skill only describes the exterior aspect of musicianship and this does not necessarily lead to more meaning. It is common in our culture to confuse span with depth, to think that quantity equals quality, and so many musicians equate more notes with more meaning. But, as Miles demonstrated and instructed throughout his career, the opposite is often the case.

Wilber's model also offers an alternative interpretation of a quote by Miles that is used by his biographer Eric Nisenson in a defense of Miles's electric music called "*Bitches Brew* and Art of Forgetting." Nisenson based his essay on Miles's assertion, "You see all those awards of mine on the wall, Eric? The reason I won them is because I can't remember anything worth a damn." Nisenson concluded, "As we all know, Miles was a master of cryptic statements, both on and off the bandstand, and this one took me a while to figure out what he was talking about. Of course, what he meant is that an artist who can forget past achievements is forced to innovate, to relentlessly forge ahead. And to plug into his own time rather than cling to the past, and it forced an artist to eschew clichés and to dig deeply both in terms of the art itself as well as his emotions and ideas. Of course for a jazz musician, who supposedly creates his music on the spot, the 'art of forgetting' is essential in order for his music to be truly spontaneous and 'in the moment,' and therefore not tethered to the past."[44]

This exchange between Nisenson and Miles took place during the latter's infamous, drug-induced silent years, from 1975 to 1980. So it may well have been a meaningless, throwaway remark. It seems dangerous to read too much meaning into it, but if it did have a deeper meaning, Miles probably referred to an idea analogous to the Zen concept of beginner's mind—a state of being fully present in the here and now, fresh and alert, without any expectations or preconceptions. But beginner's mind does not imply that we forget our skills, history, or tradition. Beginner's mind is everything but self-inflicted ignorance. In Zen, beginner's mind is a delicate balancing act between starting again in every moment and drawing on a culture and meditation practice with roots going back 2,500 years.

Similarly, as much as he or she is out on a limb, a musician improvising and coming up with brilliant new ideas is also steeped in tradition, through education, instrumental skills, and a musical awareness shaped through thousands of years of musical culture. Such a musician is the crest of the evolutionary wave, but also is still very much part of the wave, and the water from which it emerges. Had John McLaughlin really started to play as if he didn't "know how to play the guitar," Miles would have sacked him on the spot. The comment was designed to encourage the guitarist to step out of his habit energies and express his immense talent and musical training in a new way. The result was some of McLaughlin's freshest and most evocative guitar playing, exactly because it was at the same time innovative and deeply rooted in tradition.

Nisenson appears to interpret "forgetting" in such a way that it sounds like excluding the past, and in doing so he turns Miles's statement into the credo of certain sections of the free-jazz movement—which is worlds away from what Miles could have meant. Here the model of "transcend and include" comes into full focus. If Miles's development is described in dialectical terms, the option of going into free-jazz, as another "difference," would have been as attractive to him as rock, or soul, or folk, and there is no way of explaining why he preferred to focus on the music of the counterculture rather than on free-jazz.

Miles did, in fact, allow his second great quintet and the quintet following, which featured Chick Corea and Dave Holland, to experiment with free-jazz. Miles demonstrated his openness and his commitment to music by seriously trying to engage himself with the direction. Jack Chambers wrote that when Ornette Coleman had a six-month residency at a New York jazz club called the Five Spot in 1960 to 1961, "Davis and Coltrane, like nearly all other jazz musicians, were profoundly curious about [free-jazz], and both were frequent visitors at the Five Spot."[45]

Almost ten years later, despite his critical remarks about free-jazz, Miles was still curious. Chick Corea remembered that when Holland, DeJohnette, and he ventured into free-jazz territory, "Miles was waiting to see if something developed out of it. None of us will ever know what Miles was really thinking about it. All I know is that he used to listen intently from the side of the stage, and that sometimes he'd take his trumpet and join us in 'outer space' for a moment. But otherwise his role was always to bring back a focal point of melody in the group. Maybe he enjoyed that the rhythm section was playing a free-jazz manner sometimes, and then at other times it was just not enough 'form' for him, and it wasn't what he wanted to hear. So he created something more in the direction he wanted."

Miles incorporated aspects of free-jazz in his own playing, which became notably more chromatic and "out" from 1967 onwards. But his playing always retained its roots, and he preferred to surround himself with a musical context that looked forwards and backwards at the same time. In other words, he always stayed true to the principle of "transcend and include." Miles ultimately discarded free-jazz as a direction because it ran to a significant degree counter to the "transcend and include" process. To understand why this happened, the origins and deeper nature of free-jazz, and of the classical avant-garde to which it was related, need to be subjected to closer examination.

In speaking of the avant-garde in art in general, Ken Wilber wrote, "It always implicitly understood itself to be riding the crest of the breaking wave of evolving world views. The avant-garde was the leading edge, the growing tip, of an evolving humanity. It would herald the new, announce the forthcoming. It would first spot, then depict, new ways of seeing, new modes of being, new forms of cognition, new heights or depths of feeling, and in all cases, new modes of perception."[46]

In this sense, Johann Sebastian Bach, Ludwig van Beethoven, Claude Debussy, Arnold Schönberg, Charley Patton, Louis Armstrong, Charlie Parker, The Beatles, Miles Davis, and Jimi Hendrix were all avant-garde artists. All these artists "heralded the new" and were recognized for doing so when the new modes of being that they helped pioneer became mainstream. They were to music what Albert Einstein was to physics, Martin Luther King Jr. was to American race relationships, and Charles Darwin was to evolutionary theory. Almost all great and enduring works of art have to some degree gone beyond the tradition in which they emerged. Art "heralding the new" is often the freshest and the most outstanding, whereas later explorations of the same paradigm or direction may still be highly enjoyable, but they are little more than translations.

On the other hand, much avant-garde art has been forgotten by history because it either announced a worldview that never manifested, or developed in a dysfunctional manner that did not correspond with evolution's inherent process of "transcend and include." Art that does not include the past, that only tries to transcend it, has invariably been shown to have little depth or lasting value. A strong case can be made for the argument that the latter happened to some degree with the mid- to late-twentieth-century avant-garde. Only a few of the leading names of the classical music avant-garde—such as Luciano Berio, Karlheinz Stockhausen, Pierre Boulez, and Olivier Messiaen—have broken through to the general audience, while the movement's music and ideas, though influential, have not announced a new musical paradigm. The classical avant-garde's music has not become mainstream and since the end of the twentieth century the classical music world, as well as some of the above-mentioned protagonists, has increasingly been edging back to more traditional tonalities and structures.

The most likely explanation is that this particular avant-garde movement's ethos, "break with the old," was fundamentally different from that of previous avant-garde movements. The avant-garde of Bach, or Beethoven, or The Beatles, though with its head and heart in the future, was always firmly rooted with its feet in the past. In other words, it transcended and included. But in many respects the mid- to late-twentieth-century avant-garde attempted to transcend without including, and it was strongly influenced by political considerations in doing so. The movement germinated in Europe immediately after the Second World War. Confronted with the incredible devastation the war had brought, many Europeans felt deeply disappointed with their culture and political systems. They wanted to make a radical new start and some opted for systems or beliefs that appeared to throw out the old completely. (For instance, communist sympathies were at a high throughout Europe in the first years after the war.)

European artists of all disciplines were looking for ways to wholly reinvent their art, and unburden themselves of the past. The result was an avant-garde movement that attempted to make a complete break with the past. Aware of how difficult this is, many invented all sorts of techniques to thwart their habit energies, such as using the element of chance in their writings, which in some cases resulted in music without rhythm, pitch, harmony, structure, or emotional or intuitive content. In the United States, avant-garde composer John Cage experimented with dice, coins, throwing pieces of coal on music paper, or prescribing performances of randomly tuned radios.[47] The most radical classical avant-garde work, Cage's silent piece, "4:33," did away with the composer's intentions altogether. It made many important conceptual and political points about the nature of performance, about the nature of music and what distinguishes it from noise, about the sonic environment into which a performer plays, and so on. But as a piece of music, it was the flattest ever made, with no distinguishable depth or meaning in the "music" itself whatsoever. The piece was, literally and figuratively, empty.

In attempting to exclude the past, postwar classical avant-garde composers had set themselves the task of reinventing the wheel. This led to great amounts of fascinating creative efforts, and sometimes to brand-new and all-inclusive compositional systems, but since they had little or no included history (i.e., few vertical layers of holons), they were inevitably short of depth. This lack of depth, of meaning, of significance, proved to be the major shortcoming of much postwar avant-garde art. It was exemplified in the fact that there were no criteria anymore to establish whether a piece of art worked, had quality, or depth, or meaning. The result was a slide into nihilism: anything went. Although the postwar avant-garde prided itself on heralding the new, from this perspective it turned out to be an affirmation of the ancient rational paradigm in which only surfaces, and no depth, exist. In classical music, many of this avant-garde's efforts were characterized by a flatland of interesting and exciting colors, ideas, sounds, techniques, harmonies, and rhythms that are still readily applied in today's music. But in its original form its lack of meaning alienated audiences and even prompted Pierre Boulez to remark as early as 1971 that a lot of what had happened in the avant-garde was an avoidance of the composer's responsibility towards his music and his audience.

A parallel process has taken place in the free-jazz movement. When it emerged in 1959, it was in part inspired by the postwar avant-garde developments in classical music, and it attempted to "transcend and include" this influence and jazz. Many free-jazz musicians, like Ornette Coleman (who researched the blues and pre-Western harmony in

Africa), did attempt to achieve new musical structures by transcending and including old musical influences, and achieved genuinely new and inspiring syntheses. And many aspects of free-jazz still influence the way music is played and heard today, once again mostly in the radically new colors, techniques, and concepts it pioneered. Yet the size and influence of the movement has decreased as time went on, and most jazz critics appear to agree that especially its radical edge has failed to produce a substantial body of significant and enduring music.[48] The free-jazz movement also led to an audience exodus, caused by the same factor that affected the radical side of the classical avant-garde: a lack of depth and meaning, which resulted from attempts to exclude influences of the past.

Some of the champions of free-jazz have since come to not dissimilar conclusions. "At one point I felt that 'open-form' music, as I call it, gave me the most opportunity to express myself," Dave Holland remarked. "It felt like it gave unrestricted expression. But later on I realized that expression also has to happen within a form. I guess when you're younger you tend to go more into the extremes, and as you get older, you see it's actually both."

This is not to say that the postwar radical avant-garde and free-jazz were without merit. They cleaned out the ears and minds of musicians and audiences alike, extending the realm of the accepted and the possible. They added conceptual ideas and new aesthetic horizons, which have been transcended and included in today's art. And because of the many issues that it raises, "4:33" has become one of the most discussed compositions at music colleges around the world. Flawed or failed artistic experiments are part of a learning curve and regularly inspire new artistic developments. Much avant-garde and free-jazz music, as well as some of Miles's music, falls in this category. But because Miles based his whole musical approach on the principle of "transcend and include," he recognized free-jazz's limitations and how it painted itself in a corner insofar as it tried to exclude the past. Free-jazz musicians focused on playing "above what they know" and avoided playing "what they know," and this ran counter to the major principle on which Miles had built his music throughout his life.

By the late '60s there was a sense of jazz as a self-sufficient musical holon having exhausted itself. It simply had nowhere else to go but to become, in Miles's words, "a museum thing," go into free-jazz, or include outside influences. Having rejected free-jazz as a direction, and being open-minded enough to recognize the interior qualities of the music of the '60s counterculture, Miles moved toward incorporating the latter. The spotlight of the time was on this music, and for Miles to discard it because it was commercially successful was flawed reasoning. He stated, "I never thought that the music called 'jazz' was ever meant to reach just a small group of people or become a museum thing locked under glass like all other dead things that were considered artistic. I always thought it should reach as many people as it could, like so-called popular music, and why not?"[49] He also remarked, "I don't think if something is popular, it's bad."[50]

The distinction Miles made between alive and dead art is significant, because with it he distanced himself from the exterior-obsessed, rational Western paradigm, which highly values static, fossilized art that can be studied and dissected under the microscope. It was this attitude that enabled colonialists to wrench local art from its colonies, depriving it of its context and meaning and reducing it to a trophy with pure surface value. Wilber describes how one of the rational paradigm's achievements was to separate art, science, morals, and religion. These had been fused in the prerational, preindustrial paradigm, when declaring, for instance, that the earth revolved around the sun was a religious transgression, with often rather horrible consequences. While offering the freedom for a revolution in scientific thinking, this separation was hampered by the fact that scientists, and artists, practiced their vocations from ivory towers, without regard to morals or the needs of society. In art, this was expressed in the idea of "art for art's sake" and in the phenomenon of the tortured artist who only expresses what's relevant to him or her. The audience-alienating extremes of free-jazz and postwar classical avant-garde were both manifestations of this idea.

Miles, with his grounding in the worldviews of the modern, white American dream and his premodern African-American heritage, did not believe in the art for art's sake axiom. In 1969 he said that rock, "like jazz, is folk music."[51] Miles appears to use the word "folk" as in "popular music," music for and from the people, and in this sense blues is black America's original folk music. Miles wasn't into elitism. In addition to having revolutionary pretensions, he wanted to make popular, or "folk" music. The fact that he was not afraid to cover popular songs throughout his life—whether "Someday My Prince Will Come" or "Time after Time"—is an expression of this.

A communicator at heart, Miles always wanted his audience to be as large and wide as possible. He most likely took his nonelitist attitude from his African American heritage, but on a deeper level, in combination with his "knowing" and his "listening," it points once more to his living in an existential paradigm, which sees art as a highly relevant to, and integrated with, society. Attempting to make challenging and meaningful music that appeals to a wider audience can be seen as expressing this emerging worldview, whereas the "sell-out" charges appear to come from an old-fashioned "art for art's sake" worldview, an attitude that Gary Tomlinson described as "elitism pure and simple."[52] The fact that Miles's approach seemed alternatively controversial and conservative several decades ago, but makes total sense to us today, indicates how much he was ahead of his time.

In the end, what's most striking and appealing is the zest for life that permeates Miles's creative drive, as is exhibited in the aforementioned quotes: "Music comes before breathing" and "Music comes before everything." The ongoing creation of new music, moving musical boundaries forward while building on the achievements of the past, was what gave meaning to Miles's life. For him, music could never be something static, or dead, or in a museum, or without roots. Music expresses life, life expresses music, and life and music cannot but change and move forward.

Wilber describes this urge thus: "Evolution *goes beyond* what went before, but because it must *embrace* what went before, then its very nature is to 'transcend and include,' and thus it has an inherent directionality, a secret impulse, towards increasing depth, increasing intrinsic value, increasing consciousness. In order for evolution to move at all, it must move in those directions—there's no place else for it to go!"[53]

In the late '60s, there was nowhere else to go for Miles but into electric music.

Chapter Seven

"FAR-IN"

"I could put together the greatest rock and roll band you ever heard."

—MILES DAVIS[1]

The path leading Miles from his first experiments with the music of the '60s counter-culture to the creative peak of *Bitches Brew* was fairly straight. There were a few dips and detours along the way, but overall his musical direction is easy to trace. The same cannot be said for Miles's studio work after August of 1969. It is too bold to say that he lost his sense of direction, but having left the familiar landmarks of jazz behind, he sometimes seemed unsure about where to go next. Miles was probing undiscovered territory, a new musical paradigm, and even as he recognized stone circles when he saw them, it appears that he didn't necessarily know where to find them. He now traveled more as an explorer than a visionary, his musical progress sometimes taking a bewildering zigzag course. As a consequence, his studio music from November of 1969 to October of 1974 (when the last '70s session from which material was officially issued took place) is an accumulation of moments of brilliance, dreadful failures, and everything in between.

After two unsuccessful sessions in November of 1969, Miles had entered the '70s on an upward curve, gradually reducing the size of his ensemble and trying out different ideas. February 6, 1970, marked Miles's first genuinely successful session since the previous August, yielding the impressive track "Double Image." Its stop-start, hard-hitting, funk-inspired jazz-rock influenced much of Miles's music of the early '70s. Between this session and June 5, when Miles began a near two-year sabbatical from studio recording, there was a plethora of studio dates. The most important work to emerge from them was the music for the film *A Tribute to Jack Johnson,* Miles's second film score, after *Ascenseur pour l'Échafaud* from 1957.

The origins of the music for *A Tribute to Jack Johnson* have long been shrouded in mystery due to the incorrect and incomplete credits given on the liner notes. During the intervening years many details have emerged, revealing that the music featured significantly more musicians than those indicated in writer Chip Deffaa's liner notes (Miles Davis, Herbie Hancock, John McLaughlin, Steve Grossman, Billy Cobham, and Michael Henderson), and that one of the two recording dates given, November 11, 1970, is erroneous. The other date, April 7, is correct, but Teo Macero constructed the album's two tracks, "Right Off" and "Yesternow," from at least four unrelated sessions. The album was therefore even more strongly a collaborative effort between artist and producer than *Bitches Brew,* on which only "Pharaoh's Dance" and the title track were intricately edited together from material intended by Miles to become part of said tracks. Miles acknowledged Macero's central role on *Jack Johnson* with a rare public compliment in the recording's liner notes: "Dig the guitar and the bass—They are 'Far-In'—and so is the producer Teo Macero. He did it again!" The recording will be dealt with as a complete artistic work further on. In an effort to trace Miles's musical development from February 18 to June 4, 1970, the known band studio sessions from this period will first be dealt with in chronological order.

The session of February 18 featured a band whose core was the same as on the previous session of February 6: Corea, Holland, DeJohnette, and McLaughlin. Miles pared down the ensemble still further, from ten to seven, by dropping drummer Billy Cobham, sitar player Khalil Balakrishna, and percussionist Airto Moreira. In addition, Wayne Shorter was replaced by Bennie Maupin on bass clarinet, and Joe Zawinul by guitarist Sonny Sharrock. The music they recorded is based on the same material as the track "Willie Nelson," featured on the 1981 album *Directions.*

Macero pasted nearly ten minutes of the music resulting from the session of February 18 into the track "Yesternow" on *Jack Johnson,* between 13:56 and 23:56. The first half, appearing between 13:56 and 18:53, is based on a simple five-note bass riff and a staccato theme first played by Miles and Maupin in unison at 14:30. The music is underpinned by increasingly driving drumming from Jack DeJohnette and is characterized by the interplay between Miles's declamatory trumpet, McLaughlin's sololike comping in the left channel, and psychedelic noises on the right. Miles leaves big gaps between his solo statements, giving space for McLaughlin and the special effects, most likely created by Chick Corea, who fed his electric piano through various effect pedals, among them a ring modulator.[2] Maupin is set so far back in the mix that he is largely indistinguishable.

The music appearing in "Yesternow" from 18:53 till 23:56 is based on the same staccato melody line and another riff that is played in unison by Holland and McLaughlin. Corea's effects in the right channel are now enhanced by whammy-bar and echoplex effects generated by guitarist Sonny Sharrock. The latter's presence gives the track historic value as the first on which Miles featured two guitarists. Corea's controlled mayhem, Miles's dramatic and intense playing, and McLaughlin's muscular, distorted playing, beefed up with wah-wah effects, raise this session above the level of a run-of-the-mill rock jam. The musicians beautifully complement each other and jointly increase the tension. McLaughlin especially takes a star role. By inventing, as on *Bitches Brew,* a way of soloing and comping at the same time, McLaughlin once again seems to play "what he knows and above what he knows." But in this case he included more of his R&B roots.

Sharrock's addition was unexpected, because at the time he was associated with the free-jazz movement, having played with saxophonist Pharaoh Sanders and trumpeter Don Cherry. He adds a little extra color to Corea's weird effects, but does not stand out. Despite his limited contribution, the session appears to have been a momentous occasion for the guitarist, who commented, "It was the only time I ever played with the man [Miles], but it was really amazing. . . . There's something about master players, man. You learn by osmosis from them motherfuckers just being in the room. He never said shit about teaching me anything about music. But I learned more that day than any other day in my life—really, 'cause it was just being that close to him. . . . If I did something wrong he would cut his eyes at me, real sharp. Sometimes he'd say, 'No, Sonny, that's not the right note.' But he never got salty or angry. He was very giving and gentle."[3]

Miles appears to have decided that the session on February 18 hadn't quite realized the potential of the musical material, because nine days later, on February 27, he took the unusual step of recording "Willie Nelson" again. The results of this session appeared more than a decade later on *Directions,* the collection of unreleased recordings negotiated by Miles's then manager, Mark Rothbaum, to generate more income for Miles. Rothbaum managed Willie Nelson at the time (and still does today), and Miles must have named the track after the crooning country-and-western singer for the release of the 1981 album. Miles admired Nelson, and his comments on the parallels between his trumpet playing and the singer's behind-the-beat phrasing[4] echo his statements that he was influenced by the phrasing of white artists such as Frank Sinatra and the actor and director Orson Welles.[5]

On February 27, 1970, the studio ensemble was pared down to a quintet, without a keyboard player, marking another historical milestone. Miles had only once before recorded with a small band without a keyboard player, with Charles Mingus on July 9, 1955, when vibraphonist Teddy Charles handled the keyboard's rhythmic and harmonic functions. In Miles's music of the '70s these roles were increasingly given to the electric guitar and, on February 27, 1970, to John McLaughlin. Steve Grossman was on soprano saxophone and Jack DeJohnette was again on the drums. Dave Holland played only the first, five-note electric bass riff, played on February 18, for brief periods; otherwise he quickly resorted to an improvised vamp. The tempo is taken slightly faster than in the earlier version, Miles dropped the original staccato theme, and McLaughlin added some thematic interest with an interesting Arabic-flavored riff. But this second edition of "Willie Nelson" is not an improvement. The lack of structure, thematic material, and textural interest fail to raise it above the level of a studio jam by some great musicians.

A week later, on March 3, Miles tried again, with the same quintet, resulting in a very long track called "Go ahead John," which appeared in 1974 as one side of the *Big Fun* double album. "Go ahead John" shares all the shortcomings of "Willie Nelson" Mark 2, and worse, is almost three times as long, a whopping 28:24. To salvage the track Macero tried to spice things up with some studio toys, most notably two new devices invented by CBS's research department. One was an "electronic switcher," which made it possible to instantly move an instrument to specific positions in the stereo spectrum; the other was called "instant playback," a variation on tape delay that "allows entire passages or single instruments to be played back at thirty- to forty- second intervals."[6] Tape delay is normally used to double up and fatten certain parts, but the "instant playback" device had more in common with the sampling techniques emerging with digital technology in the '80s and '90s, whereby samples of sonic material are "flown" into the music.

Whether it was because Macero was trying to generate interest from undistinguished musical material or because he was one of many engineers or producers in love with new studio toys is unclear, but the producer ended up overusing the "electronic switcher" and the "instant playback" on "Go ahead John." He continuously switched the placement of Jack DeJohnette's drums between left and right for long sections of the track, making it sound like there were two drums. The application of the "instant playback" creates the impression that soloists are duetting with themselves. The section where Miles is treated this way is appealing, but while Macero's technical wizardry adds some interest, it makes the track sound like a psychedelic-era period piece.

Macero also recomposed "Go ahead John" with his usual cutting and pasting techniques, placing a fairly formless improvisation on a pedal F bass note at the front of the piece, a blues in the middle (11:47 to 24:25), and a similarly amorphous improvisation at the end. As is to be expected, the playing of the five musicians is excellent, but there's no clearly identifiable musical theme or vision to hold everything together, and the gargantuan length of the piece painfully highlights this lack of musical material and direction. When Miles plays a straight blues phrase, at 12:23, and Holland responds by cycling through blues changes, it comes as a relief: finally there is something recognizable, something with form and direction, even though it's not particularly new or innovative. Because *Big Fun* was issued several years after the music was recorded, an air of Miles fulfilling contractual obligations, or seeking additional advances, hangs over the recording. Macero was most likely sent into the vaults to conjure up something listenable, and "Go ahead John" was one of the things he came up with.

On March 17 Miles experimented with yet another combination of musicians. The resulting track was called "Duran," after the Panamanian boxing champion Roberto Duran. Miles brought back Shorter and Maupin in place of Grossman, and Billy Cobham to replace DeJohnette. The inclusion of Billy Cobham, a drummer with a more straight-ahead, rock-influenced style, says something about the direction that Miles had in mind. Another clue is Holland's circular, rocklike electric bass riff, which is repeated throughout with only the occasional variation. Miles appears to have decided that his sessions might be more successful if he used elements more idiomatic to the new territory. The role of the rhythm section is now much more clearly defined, in a manner common in rock, and the lack of a clear musical starting point that marred previous sessions is partly offset by the insistent riff, which gives the piece a solid foundation. The "Duran" riff is hummable, and Miles commented ruefully, "I thought I had a hit, but Columbia didn't release it until way later, in 1981"[7] (as part of the *Directions* set). While "Duran" is probably the closest to commercial fusion Miles ever came, the idea that a simple bass riff, without any other identifying traits, would be enough to make a piece of music climb the pop hit parades seems hopelessly naive.

A conscious attempt at breaking through to a black audience was explicitly at the heart of Miles's next recording date, on April 7, during which most of the material for *A Tribute to Jack Johnson* was recorded. The boxing theme was featured once again, since director William Clayton's eponymously titled movie told the story of Jack Johnson, the world heavyweight boxing champion at the beginning of the twentieth century. Miles commented that while recording he had the boxer's movement in mind, "that shuffling movement boxers use. They're almost like dance steps, or like the sound of a train. In fact, it did remind me of being on a train doing eighty miles an hour, how you always hear the same rhythm. . . . The question in my mind after I got to this was, well, is the music black enough, does it have a black rhythm, can you make the rhythm of the train a black thing, would Jack Johnson dance to that? Because Jack Johnson liked to party, liked to have a good time and dance."[8]

It was at this point that Miles may have consciously tried to put together "the great-est rock and roll band you have ever heard," following the adage, "the quality of music is in the musicians too. . . . If you get the right guys to play the right thing at the right time, you got everything you need."[9] To achieve a trainlike effect a rhythm section's playing has to be repetitive and very tightly circumscribed, much like in rock music, so Miles tried to assemble a rock rhythm section, inviting rock drummer Buddy Miles (who had played with Jimi Hendrix) and rock and soul bassist Michael Henderson to the ses-sion. For some reason Buddy Miles didn't work out, so Miles once more turned to Billy Cobham. Michael Henderson did make it, and turned out to be a fortuitous find. Only nineteen at the time, he was the first player Miles ever hired who was not steeped in jazz. As a Detroit native, Henderson had grown up with blues, R&B, and soul music, had been mentored by Motown's legendary bassist James Jamerson, and had played with Aretha Franklin and Stevie Wonder. So alien was the world of jazz to the young Hen-derson that he didn't know who Miles Davis was when approached by him.

"I was working with Stevie Wonder and we were playing in New York," Henderson remembered. "The Temptations were there, Mick Jagger was there, and Miles Davis was there. After the set Miles walked up to the dressing room and he told Stevie Wonder, 'I'm taking your bass player!' I didn't think anything of it because I didn't know who Miles was at the time. We were doing our R&B stuff! I had no idea that greatness had walked into the room, though I knew something was going on because everybody was paying attention. But I didn't take it that serious, until I told a friend in Detroit that Miles Davis wanted me to work for him, and my friend said: 'You fool, you better run!' So I called Miles and he said, 'I'll pay you good. Here's a plane ticket to New York. You can stay at my house.' Two weeks later we met at his brownstone in New York. Billy Cobham came over, and John McLaughlin, and Herbie and Keith Jarrett. Clive Davis was also there. And the next day we were in the studio at CBS, recording *Jack Johnson*."

The inclusion of Michael Henderson signaled a crucial shift in Miles's studio music. Henderson played with Miles until 1975, and during his tenure he became the pivot around which Miles's bands revolved. Henderson has often been derided by jazz com-mentators for his lack of skill as a jazz player and has been seen as the weakest link in the band. But this is comparable to complaining that Yehudi Menuhin was a bad folk fiddle player, or that Miles wasn't a top orchestral player. Miles did not hire Henderson for his jazz skills, but because the bassist had a very different ability, namely a remarkable talent for creating and holding down circular, repetitive grooves. Henderson recalled, "At that first meeting at his house, Miles said to me that he wanted me to hold the band down. He wanted me to hold it together. He wanted me to be a rock." Billy Cobham added, "Miles wanted Michael Henderson because he had a different feel, definitely."

The previous sessions, especially the one resulting in the track "Duran," had proven that Holland could hold his own in playing rocklike, repetitive patterns on the electric bass. But in Henderson, Miles found a player to whom this was native territory. Together, Henderson and Cobham managed to achieve the hypnotic, trainlike repetitiveness that Miles had in mind on *A Tribute to Jack Johnson*. But for all the thought and preparations that Miles put into the session, the end result may well have been very different from what he anticipated. The session turned out to be remarkably spontaneous, to the point of emerging from pure chaos.

Steve Grossman recalled that the rehearsals were as relaxed as those surrounding the *Bitches Brew* sessions. "We played a lot during rehearsals, but when we got to recording, Miles changed everything. He might keep one line from a rehearsed piece of music, or maybe nothing at all. Ninety percent of the tunes we rehearsed were never used in the studio. It seemed like everyone just felt each other out and got used to being with each other and playing with each other. Rehearsal was just hanging out together and creating something like an intimate 'family' atmosphere, a support thing."

"We rehearsed one time at Miles's house. . . . I can't remember what we rehearsed because you couldn't quite call it a rehearsal," Billy Cobham elaborated. "It was just like a gathering of minds. And something came out on a piece of paper that kind of vaguely resembled a scale, and that was the tune. And from there . . . the following day we went into the studio and all of a sudden McLaughlin got this shuffled groove happening while trying to get [recording] levels. It was really very infectious and Michael Henderson started playing it with John. Miles told us not to play, because the studio technicians were still getting a balance. Anyone who knows McLaughlin knows that if you say 'No,' he'll keep on doing it. So he kept playing, and we all joined in, and the groove got more and more infectious. Finally the red light goes on, and that became the recording session. Hence you have *Jack Johnson*. It took twenty-five minutes to make the recording date. The rest is history."

Cobham also recalled that the addition of Herbie Hancock was entirely unplanned: "He just happened to walk by! He walked past Studio B, I think it was. He looked through the window, and Miles said, 'Come in!' Imagine, the light was on, we're playing, Herbie came in with a bag of groceries, and Miles pointed him towards a Farfisa organ that was inoperative at the time. Herbie looked at what Miles is pointing at, and said, 'I can't do this.' And Miles said again, 'Play.' So while we played, Stan Tonkel, the engineer, went over and plugged the organ in. I don't know how he did it without getting either shocked or getting a couple of blips in there. Herbie dropped his grocery bag, and tried to play a solo on the organ. He couldn't get a sound, so he put his forearm across the keys, and suddenly the thing goes. . . . Wwraammm! And I'm watching all this from my drum set, as I play!"

John McLaughlin filled the gaps in Cobham's story. "The bulk of that record came out of some jamming we did in the studio. There was Herbie playing the most horrible Farfisa organ and Michael Henderson on bass, Billy Cobham on drums. We were all in the studio, just waiting for Miles. He was talking to Teo Macero in another room and that went on for 10–15 minutes, and I got bored. I started to play a boogie in E, just to have some fun, that's all. I was playing these funny kind of chords that later I used more to advantage in "Dance of Maya" [from *The Inner Mounting Flame*, Columbia, 1971]— kind of angular chords, but all really related to the blues. . . . I was really hitting the strings hard, just going for it. Billy picked it up, Michael picked it up, and in a couple of minutes we were gone. So finally the door opened and Miles ran in with his trumpet. The [recording] light was on and he just played for about 20 minutes, which I had never seen him do before. It was a situation where he just walked in and everything was happening already. And he played so fine. It was so spontaneous, such a great moment."[10]

The results of this session were compiled by Macero in the first track on *Jack Johnson*, called "Right Off." It begins with McLaughlin, Henderson, and Cobham grooving along on the "boogie in E," with McLaughlin's inspired comping at times bordering on solo guitar. At 01:38 the guitarist takes down the volume, and at 02:11 he modulates to B-flat to heighten the dramatic effect of Miles's entry. However, Henderson misses McLaughlin's modulation, and carries on playing in E. In the middle of this clash of tonalities Miles decides to make his entrance, at 02:19. He starts by playing a D-flat (C-sharp), the minor third in B-flat and the major sixth in E. It is an ingenious choice because the note is effective in either key. Miles then plays twelve staccato B-flat notes, phrasing them on the beat to drive the band on, and also as if to nudge Henderson towards the B-flat tonality. Henderson gets the message, comes into line by modulating to B-flat at 02:33, and Miles carries on, giving one of the most commanding solo performances of his career, with fast runs reaching into the higher register, and a loud, full, powerful tone.

Writer Stuart Nicholson rightly called Miles's entry in "Right Off" "one of the great moment in jazz-rock."[11] It is also one of the most impressive examples of the "there are no mistakes" adage that Miles learned from Charlie Parker in the 1940s. Most musicians would have regarded the point when Henderson and McLaughlin were clashing with two such incompatible keys as E and B-flat as an embarrassing mistake and would have either stopped the band or instructed the producer to remove the section during editing. Very few would have considered, or have had the courage, to come in at such a moment. And even fewer would have been able to make it into a resounding success.

"It's like being a visionary," Mtume, Miles's percussionist from 1971 to 1975, commented. "Miles was a master at creating a context for people to explore possibilities they had not thought about before. He used to say things like: 'What you don't play is more important than what you play.' He learned much of that from Bird, Monk, and Dizzy. He would tell me the stories about Bird. For example, at one time at a gig the piano player had overdosed and was in the hospital. So they had to get another piano player. You have to remember that back in the 1940s there were often more musicians in the audience than there were regular people. So this guy came up on stage and played, and he was fucking up so bad, that Miles walked over to Bird because he couldn't solo on top, and said, 'Bird, this motherfucker is playing all the wrong changes.' Bird looked at him and answered, 'Well, play them with him and they won't be wrong.' That's the kind of influence Miles came up under."

The anecdote Herbie Hancock told in Chapter 3, about Miles's instant reaction when the pianist played a "wrong" chord, showed that Miles had learned his lesson well. There are no wrong notes or chords, only choices. A phrase oft quoted by musicians and ascribed to Miles also exemplifies this viewpoint: "If you play a note you didn't intend to play, what determines whether it sounds like a mistake or a moment of inspiration is the note you play after it."[12]

"When you see Miles respond to situations like that, it tells you so much," Holland elaborated. "First, how much in the moment Miles was when he was playing. He wasn't just totally absorbed in his own idea, and oblivious to what the others did. Second, he didn't turn around to Herbie or Michael and say, 'That was wrong!' He completely absorbed it and made music out of it. And when you see someone doing that, it makes you think about yourself and what you're doing and how you can improve your own ways of doing things. I think anyone who had contact with Miles for any length of time came through it with some understanding that they had not had before."

From Miles's dramatic entrance in "Right Off" during a moment of clashing tonalities, an engaging piece of music emerges with enough energy and direction to compensate for the lack of formal structure and themes or riffs. As on *Bitches Brew,* Miles is the star, playing some breathtaking power trumpet. But this time the context and feel are entirely different. Miles solos for almost eight minutes, except for a brief interlude from 06:25 to 06:57, when there are no solos. Henderson and Cobham propel the groove and keep Miles on track with his train imagery. Miles's solo is striking for the amount of space he gives McLaughlin to interject little solo phrases and for the way he enhances the groove, for instance at 05:23, when he repeats an A-flat note fifteen times on the beat, and at 06:58, when he almost forces the band into jazz swing time. McLaughlin nearly switches to jazz comping style in response. Miles solos until 10:42, at which point Macero inserted about 01:33 of ambient music that consists of Miles soloing over what sounds like a ring modulator or a synthesizer. The section gives a brief respite from the shuffle groove and adds structure to "Right Off" as a whole. But the edits in and out of the ambient sections break the flow in an unmusical and ugly way.

When the shuffle groove returns, Grossman and Hancock solo effectively, and Miles returns with another solo at 16:40. At 18:29 Macero inserted a completely different section, which was based on a riff from Sly Stone's song "Sing a Simple Song," the B-side to their 1969 number one U.S. hit "Everyday People." Known as "Theme from Jack Johnson," the riff was to become a feature of Miles's live concerts during the '70s. Only McLaughlin, Henderson, and Cobham play during this section, and nothing much is done with it. Two minutes later, at 20:29, the band switches back to the same boogie groove in E that opened the piece. This effectively frames "Right Off" by creating an ABA structure, but following this the soloists run out of steam. Cutting about five minutes from the 26:52 would have enhanced the piece as a whole.

The beginning of the second track, "Yesternow," titled by Miles's hairdresser, James Finney, features the same personnel as "Right Off" and was probably also recorded on April 7. "Yesternow" has a more varied and interesting structure than "Right Off." It has more thematic material, and is therefore less dependent on incisive soloing and high energy to maintain interest. The first 12:25 are a continuous take based around a bass riff lifted from James Brown's "Say It Loud, I'm Black and I'm Proud," and slowed down. The great strength of this section is its eminent use of space. For a long stretch of time, the music is static, without harmonic development, the drums only playing accents. Miles and McLaughlin masterfully exploit this space, creating and increasing tension, until the section successfully climaxes just before Macero pastes in an excerpt from "Shhh/Peaceful" from *In a Silent Way,* which is overdubbed with the same trumpet solo as in the ambient section of "Right Off."

Following this, Macero interjects the above-described section of "Willie Nelson" that was recorded on February 18 and that features Maupin, McLaughlin, Sharrock, Corea, Holland, and DeJohnette. It fits well in this context. Finally, the most arresting moment of the album, apart from Miles's entrance in "Right Off," arrives at 23:52, when an orchestral piece called "The Man Nobody Saw" is pasted in and the same solo that Miles played over "Shhh/Peaceful" and the ambient section of "Right Off" is overdubbed once again. After nearly an hour of high-energy and harmonically and texturally simple rock music, there's a drama and grandeur to this abrupt shift in pace, texture, and harmonic complexity. The gripping atmosphere and the orchestral textures form a fitting background for the words spoken by actor Brock Peters that conclude the piece. "I'm Jack Johnson. I'm black. They never let me forget it. I'm black alright. I never let them forget it." The track's opening bass riff, taken from James Brown's song, also expresses black pride and, combined with Peter's words, creates an elegant topical ABA structure for this piece.

A Tribute to Jack Johnson was not released until the summer of 1971, and it sank without a trace. This may have been because it was a soundtrack album, which tended to be rather dire and were mostly ignored by the public. The music was also highly unusual for a black artist at the time because of McLaughlin's heavily distorted guitar sound that echoed hard rock. Despite the efforts of Hendrix in the '60s, and the hard rock-funk of bands like Mother's Finest in the '70s, it took until the '80s, when dance and rap music started to incorporate heavy-metal guitars, before this sound was widely accepted in black music. Ironically, despite trying to create music that was "black enough," Miles had in fact delivered an album way ahead of, and eminently unfashionable with, the black culture of its time. Two years later, for very different reasons, he was to be equally ahead of black music trends with *On the Corner*.

The next important step in Miles's musical development was the recruitment of pianist Keith Jarrett in May of 1970. The pianist already enjoyed some public attention, having been a member of Charles Lloyd's band and subsequently leading his own trio, with Charlie Haden on bass and Paul Motion on drums. Jarrett later said that he had been resisting Miles's invitations to join his band for several years because he did not want to play electric keyboards again, but that he eventually overruled his reluctance because he was so keen to play with Miles.[13] Jarrett's misgivings about electric instruments appear to be deeply felt. He had played electric piano on his debut solo album, *Restoration Ruin* (1968), and also with Charles Lloyd and vibraphonist Gary Burton, but would never play electric keyboards again after his stint with Miles. Nevertheless, his time with Miles provided him with a springboard from which to increase the success of his solo career, something that is unlikely to have escaped him when he decided to join Miles's band.

Jarrett's debut studio date with Miles was on May 19. The resulting track, released in 1974 on the album *Get up with It*, was called "Honky Tonk," which was a reference to the music Miles grew up on, "that roadhouse, honky-tonk, funky thing that people used to dance to on Friday and Saturday nights." The track featured McLaughlin, Jarrett, and Moreira from Miles's live band, and—as on *Jack Johnson*—Herbie Hancock was added, Cobham replaced DeJohnette, and session bassist Gene Perla stood in for Holland or Henderson. Jack Chambers wrote that the band came together to "play the unsophisticated funk of a bar band from, say, Chicago's South Side so that Davis can play a low-down blues over it."[14] To justify his derisive comment, Chambers quoted the opinions of two jazz musicians: Ron Carter, who said that the musicians "are all playing at random, and, for me, at a loss of something that's really quality,"[15] and trumpeter Blue Mitchell, who hoped that "it ain't anybody I know."[16]

These comments are worth quoting because they illustrate how different music can sound from another perspective. Listening with a rock background, "Honky Tonk" is one of the most successful jazz-rock tracks Miles ever recorded. It's a variation on the stop-start approach to playing rhythm that was introduced with "Double Image," only it is more complex and executed with more sophistication. The secret of the track's success lies in the way the musicians listen to each other, continuously opening up spaces, and filling them.

The track starts with Hancock playing a clavinet through a wah-wah pedal. Jarrett comes in on electric piano and McLaughlin answers with mouth-watering clipped chords. The guitarist is in the right channel and excitedly trades phrases with Jarrett, Hancock, and Moreira's cuica (a percussion instrument capable of making wah-wah and voicelike sounds) all on the left. At 00:57 the electric piano introduces the basic, five-note riff around which the piece centers and at 01:10 drums and bass enter, repeating the piano riff. The whole point of this stop-start riff is the amount of space it leaves for the musicians to play with, and they use it well.

Then, at 01:55, McLaughlin introduces the most clichéd rock 'n' roll riff available to rock guitarists, one that can often be heard performed by pub bands or in jam sessions around the world. Cobham and Perla immediately boogie along, for the first time playing a continuous rhythm. It is probably this section of the track that affronted Chambers and jazz purists. Had this riff been the mainstay of the track, their denouncements would have been well founded. However, they miss the way the band deconstructs this rock 'n' roll riff, transcending and including it. The riff appears three times throughout the track, and each time one expects the band to lock into this groove and remain there, at which point interest would immediately be lost because the music would be too predictable. Instead the musicians drop out of the groove again within thirty seconds, going back to the stop-start riff first stated at 00:57 and playing with space, echoing each other and creating tension by threatening to break into a funk rhythm, but never actually doing so. The track once again has an ABA structure, ending the way it began. At 05:54 "Honky Tonk" is also a masterpiece of economy, staying well clear of the major flaw of many of Miles's pieces around this time, overblown length. Miles must have judged the experiment successful because the piece became the blueprint for much of the music of the Bartz-Jarrett-Henderson live band, which existed from September 13, 1970, to March of 1972, and it remained part of the live repertoire until early 1973.

The same positive things cannot be said for Miles's next excursion into the recording studio two days later, on May 21, when he recorded a track called "Konda" with Airto Moreira, Keith Jarrett, John McLaughlin, and Jack DeJohnette. The contrast with "Honky Tonk" could not be starker. Rather than a reinvention of funk, "Konda" is an attempt to revisit ambient territory, and sadly it fails on every count. The music is dreary, sounding like gray, overcast, windless weather. When McLaughlin switches to some rather vague wah-wah playing around at 09:03 and DeJohnette joins the proceedings ten seconds later, one hopes for some more interest, but Jarrett's solo has no direction or substance either. The only moment of interest in this piece happens at 13:30, when Moreira and DeJohnette finally manage to lock into a groove that has some cohesion and inventiveness, echoing Indian percussion rhythms. But half a minute later the track is faded out. "Konda" was released on *Directions,* and seems the result of another dip into the rejects in Columbia's vaults.

Despite this failure, Miles must have felt that he was onto something because during the following two weeks he recorded several tracks in a similar atmospheric vein, with the help of the maverick Brazilian multi-instrumentalist Hermeto Pascoal. Miles and Pascoal met through Moreira; the two Brazilians had co-led a band called Quarteto Novo. Pascoal, nicknamed "O Bruxo" (The Sorcerer), is known in his home country for his innovative blend of traditional Brazilian music styles and free-jazz, and for his capacity to make music using the most unlikely sound sources (among them washbasins, teakettles, sewing machines, chickens, goats, geese, turkeys, and pigs).[17] His nickname was not the only thing he had in common with Miles; the Brazilian's bands have long been known as a breeding ground for musical talent. Apparently he and Miles struck up a friendship and are said to have considered making an album together shortly before Miles died.

The only issued music the two created together was recorded on June 3 and June 4, 1970, the tracks being Pascoal's "Nem Um Talvez" (Not Even a Maybe) and "Little Church." A third track, "Selim" (Miles's spelled backwards), is a different take of "Nem Um Talvez." Apparently Pascoal arranged all tracks. On June 3 "Selim" and "Nem Um Talvez" were recorded with an ensemble consisting of Miles, Corea, Hancock or Jarrett,[18] Holland, Moreira, and Pascoal on drums and vocals. Only Miles, Corea/Jarrett, Holland, and a whistling Pascoal recorded the track "Little Church."

Steve Grossman is not audible on the issued material but was present at the session. "There were many different, short takes," he remarked. "I remember that there was just a melody written out and we phrased it and I just tried to follow Miles the way he was phrasing it. He liked a little delayed kind of phrasing. There wasn't any beat, it was all out of time, so it was a matter of playing just a shade behind him with the soprano. I think Wayne developed that approach with him . . . just to follow him, milliseconds behind. It has a nice effect. Anyway, this one little tune that Hermeto wrote, the one with a very weird name, 'Nem Um Talvez,' is a great tune."

The intention on the three tracks is clearly to achieve a pastoral feeling of gentle music, static in time. Because they have clear melodies and are kept mercifully short, the structures of the pieces are more successful than of "Konda." But even the presence of two Brazilians cannot make the sun come through and alleviate the sense of mournful monotony. These three ear-grating tracks were released in 1971 as part of the *Live-Evil* double album, and the only thing that can be said in their defense is that they provide relief from the ferocity of the rest of the album's music. They also have some historical value as the first studio recordings on which Miles used the wah-wah pedal.

Despite Grossman's positive memories of the Pascoal sessions, from a musical perspective they meant that one of the most productive and influential eras in Miles's recording career ended on a low note. According to the currently available documentation, Miles did not enter the studio again until March or April of 1972, when he recorded another rather inconsequential track, "Red China Blues," which was followed by several sessions in early June that resulted in the revolutionary and controversial *On the Corner*. The reasons for this extensive recording hiatus remain unclear.

Perhaps Columbia discouraged him from more studio visits because of the immense amount of material they had amassed in their vaults. Perhaps Miles concluded that his studio experiments had run out of steam and was unsure of where to turn next. The inclusion of Pascoal may have been a last but unsuccessful attempt at employing his tried-and-true method of throwing different musicians into the pot and seeing what happened. Enrico Merlin quotes Macero as saying that Miles felt that the recording studio was not conducive to developing his electric music any further.

It is very possible that Miles felt uncomfortable with the increasingly schizophrenic separation between his studio and live work. If he felt forced to choose between developing a recording-only career and a concert career, as an improvising-in-the-moment musician *pur sang* he was always likely to opt for further developing his live music. Miles's move into large rock venues, often supporting famous rock acts, may have been an additional factor. Instead of playing for a few dozen people, as he had done in the late '60s, he suddenly faced thousands. There's little that will focus an artist's mind more than the sudden multiplication of his or her audience and it appears that Miles decided to concentrate all of his energies on this new challenge.

Chapter Eight

ALIVE IN THE
PRESENT MOMENT

"If you learn any of that old shit, you're fired."
— MILES DAVIS TO MICHAEL HENDERSON

As we have seen, the direction of Miles's studio and stage work began to diverge with the second great quintet in the mid-1960s. During its first studio recordings in January of 1965, the quintet embarked on a pioneering musical direction based on new material, whereas its concerts predominantly deconstructed Miles's older, '50s and early '60s repertoire. In the course of 1967, the quintet began to incorporate musical elements and compositions from its studio recordings in live performance, thereby momentarily narrowing the gap between studio and stage. But in the same year it also first played live music as continuous "musical suites," while the studio recordings remained organized in discrete tracks. The studio experiments with electric guitar, electric keyboards, electric bass, and additional musicians deepened the schism with the acoustic live quintet yet further.

The recording studio became a wholly forward-looking musical laboratory, whereas live concerts were more geared towards bringing out the potential of Miles's bands and of the new compositions recorded in the studio. Maintaining a clearer link with his musical past, the stage direction lagged in some respects behind the studio developments. This was also the case with the second great quintet's successor, called both the "lost quintet" and the "last quintet" by writer Peter Keepnews, respectively because Columbia never recorded it in the studio and because it was Miles's last band consisting of "the standard instrumentation"[1] of trumpet, saxophone, piano, bass, and drums. The "lost" quintet consisted of Miles and Shorter, who remained from the second great quintet, Corea and Holland, who joined in the summer of 1968, and DeJohnette, who became a member in the beginning of 1969.

"When I joined the band, we were still playing the kind of live music that came out of the quintet with Herbie and Ron and Tony, and from before that," Chick Corea recalled. "Later on there was a musical metamorphosis that came from the changing members. When Jack entered the band the music really started to change. As a result, the live band sounded even more different than the studio recordings. For example, the live recordings were hardly ever pastoral. They were more like free music with an occasional vamp in it, and sometimes Miles would do some unusual things and play a ballad."

In the months following the *In a Silent Way* sessions of February 18, 1969, the "lost" quintet toured the United States in a Volkswagen minibus, rock 'n' roll style. Rock influences had slowly been creeping into the music since the quintet's concerts at the Jazz Workshop in Boston in early December of 1968 (still with Tony Williams on drums), when Chick Corea switched to the electric piano and the quintet performed "Directions," recorded a week earlier. "Directions" became Miles's concert opener until November of 1971.[2]

Following this first live foray into rock-related territory, the rock-influenced tracks "Directions," "It's about That Time," "Miles Runs the Voodoo Down," and "Spanish Key" were regularly performed during the summer of 1969, including at the Juan-les-Pins Festival in Antibes, France, July 25 and 26, 1969. *1969 Miles—Festiva de Juan Pins,* recorded on July 25 and only released in Japan (in 1993), is the only official documentation of the "lost" quintet's music. The sound quality leaves a lot to be desired, but the vitality and inventiveness of the quintet is abundantly in evidence. DeJohnette and Holland continuously shift rhythms and, other than the extended swing grooves, they rarely stay in one groove the way they would a year later. There's a wild, restless, searching quality to most of the music, which is domineered by Miles's awesome tone and technique and his constant steering the quintet back to focus, using the musical cues that Merlin calls "coded phrases" (for instance at 00:00 of "It's about That Time").

Jazz repertoire makes up the majority of the sixty-three-minute-long Juan-les-Pins recording with "Milestones," "'Round Midnight," "Footprints," "I Fall in Love too Easily," "Sanctuary," and "The Theme" adding up to almost thirty-nine minutes. But by the end of 1969, rock-influenced pieces formed the majority of the quintet's live set, while the sound of the band also changed when Holland began playing electric bass as well as acoustic bass on stage. "Playing some of these tunes on acoustic bass didn't, for me, do the job that was needed," Holland explained. "Especially with the electric piano I felt that the sound of the electric bass would be a much stronger presence, more supportive in the music."

The abundance of free-jazz and rock influences in the quintet's music led Peter Keepnews to note, "Miles kept getting more and more electric, more funky, more rhythmic, and more *out,* all at the same time."[3] "This quintet was indeed extraordinary," Bill Kirchner commented. "It was the equal of its antecedent in terms of innovation and energy, and it was in the unique position of exploring three generations of Davis's repertoire: earlier pieces ("'Round Midnight' and 'I Fall in Love too Easily'), mid-1960s staples ('Masqualero,' 'Agitation,' and 'Paraphernelia'), and *Bitches Brew* fare."[4]

By the end of 1969 Miles wanted to further strengthen the influences of rock, soul, and funk in his live band and was beginning to find the traditional jazz format of the quintet restrictive. After John McLaughlin's successful contributions to *In a Silent Way* and *Bitches Brew,* Miles was especially eager to enlist a live guitarist. Canadian guitarist Sonny Greenwich was auditioned during a week of live gigs in Toronto in early December of 1969 and was invited by Miles to join, but for reasons that are unclear he failed to do so. The search for a suitable and available live guitarist would prove fruitless until the second half of 1972. Brazilian percussionist Airto Moreira, who had participated in the failed studio recordings of November, did join the live band, on December 12. His addition signified yet another step towards fulfilling Miles's aim of thickening the bottom end, as well as added a new, exotic, ethnic flavor to the music. Moreira played in Miles's live band until July of 1971 and influenced scores of '70s jazz groups. Instead of being a rarity, having a percussionist became commonplace in jazz after Moreira's stint with Miles.

In March of 1970, following the row between Miles and Columbia vice president Clive Davis described in Chapter 6, Miles began playing rock music venues and supporting rock acts. Obviously this helped Columbia in its attempts to promote *Bitches Brew* (which was released in April) to the counterculture marketplace. Miles's newcomer status in this environment meant that he did not always have an easy ride. In addition to facing mixed audience reactions, often having to play for dramatically reduced fees, and enduring the "sell-out" accusations from the jazz world, he was also attacked by sections of the black press for supposedly genuflecting to white culture.

Following Miles's first two concerts in a rock venue—at Fillmore East in New York, on March 6 and 7, 1970 (the concert on the latter date can be heard on *Live at the Fillmore East*)—Wayne Shorter left the band. Shorter wanted some time for himself after nearly five years with Miles, but soon went on to other great things: at the end of 1970 he and Joe Zawinul founded Weather Report. Shorter's replacement was Steve Grossman, a participant in the *Jack Johnson* session of April 7, as well as of the unfruitful November 1969 sessions. The inexperienced nineteen-year-old saxophonist was immediately thrown in at the deep end on April 9, two days after the *Jack Johnson* session, when the new Miles Davis sextet, consisting of Miles, Grossman, Corea, Holland, Moreira, and DeJohnette, played four concerts at the Fillmore West in San Francisco.

The second of these four concerts, of April 10, was issued in its entirety on *Black Beauty*, initially only released in Japan in 1973. Like the Juan-les-Pins recording, the sound quality and mix are substandard. Moreover, Grossman's solos are often nervous and shrill. Despite these shortcomings, *Black Beauty* is a powerful document of an exciting phase in Miles's electric explorations, when the direction of his live performances was catching up with his studio experiments. Revealing how far the band had moved into new musical territory since 1969, a mere fifteen minutes of this performance consists of material from Miles's pre-electric period. Two of these pieces, "I Fall in Love too Easily" and "Sanctuary," provide welcome breathers in an otherwise ferocious set, while "Masqualero" is treated in the same way as the rock-influenced pieces, with Holland and DeJohnette sustaining hard-hitting vamps and Corea at times playing his electric piano as if it's a rock guitar—distorting it and playing riffs. This music was indeed, as Corea had remarked, "hardly ever pastoral." A few notes from "The Theme" wind up the proceedings. (First recorded in 1955 by the first great quintet with John Coltrane, "The Theme" provided an especially strong link to the past, concluding almost all of Miles's concerts from the late 1950s till the end of 1970, when "Sanctuary" took over as the closing theme.)

The rest of the material on *Black Beauty*—"Directions," "Willie Nelson," "It's about That Time," "Bitches Brew," "Spanish Key," and "Miles Runs the Voodoo Down"—dates from after November of 1968. The last track contains a striking and amusing moment at 00:18 when the band sounds like a mix of Led Zeppelin and Jimi Hendrix, with Corea playing the main riff like hard rock and Holland supporting him with a deep, bluesy bass line. The music has done away with most of the frequent diversions into free-jazz territory that characterized the "lost" quintet's music. The musicians only delve into free territory for the last five minutes of "Miles Runs the Voodoo Down" and during the transition from "It's about That Time" to "Bitches Brew." Miles does not participate during the free sections, entering in both cases to bring the musicians back to a theme or a vamp.

Chick Corea enthusiastically recommended *Black Beauty,* "That's what the band sounded like live." Being an integral registration of a complete Miles Davis sextet performance, the recording offers the opportunity to follow the flow and logic of the music over a long period of time. Nevertheless, critics and listeners have long found it difficult to come to grips with the music. This is partly because the concert consisted of one long, continuous suite, organized on the original 1973 double LP release into four side-filling medleys called "Black Beauty 1," "Black Beauty 2," "Black Beauty 3," and "Black Beauty 4." Miles refused to specify song titles for most of his '70s live recordings, preferring to name the medleys by this kind of generic name. (Other examples are "Wednesday Miles," "Thursday Miles," etc., on *At Fillmore: Live at the Fillmore East* from 1970 and "Foot Fooler" and "Slickaphonics" on *Miles Davis in Concert* from 1972.) This obscure way of titling is one of the reasons why much of Miles's music of the '70s has been misunderstood as a largely improvised jungle with few recognizable musical markers.

"I'm not doing anything, it doesn't need an explanation," Miles told Leonard Feather regarding his music of the turn of the decade.[5] "Miles really felt that critics and people spent too much time in their mental mind, analyzing and talking for hours about something that really just is," Lydia DeJohnette clarified Miles's comment. With its focus on the exterior, conceptual musical analysis can easily distract from the "interior," or, in Miles's words, "what the notes mean." In Zen Buddhism, the focus on "exterior," or analysis, is often referred to by the analogy of a finger pointing at the moon. By focusing on the pointing finger, we may miss the moon. But conversely, if no one points, we may not notice the moon.

The latter occurred with much of Miles's '70s music, and some pointers are desperately needed. Enrico Merlin, Jan Lohmann (author of *The Sound of Miles Davis*), Peter Losin (creator of the *Miles Ahead* Web site), and Bob Belden (in his work as Columbia/Legacy reissue producer) have done much work in identifying the different vamps and pieces on which Miles's '70s music was based, making this musical territory much more transparent. Merlin's analysis of the "coded phrases" is also helpful in charting the territory, and since they were mostly used in live performance, a brief elaboration on this issue is in order here. According to Merlin, these "coded phrases" were based on the first notes of the tune, the bass vamp, or the voicings of the harmonic progressions. "As many of the compositions performed in the concerts between 1969 and 1975 were without themes, being based exclusively on a rhythmic idea or on a bass vamp, the coded phrases help us also to correctly identify the pieces,"[6] Merlin explained.

"The music would be continuous so Miles wouldn't have to speak and announce things to the audience," Jack DeJohnette commented. "He'd just speak with his horn and just cue the numbers by stating the front part of the melody, and then we automatically knew, which was great, because he wanted it to be a seamless kind of thing." Dave Holland elaborated: "Giving musical signals is a very old tradition in jazz. Back in the days with Louis Armstrong and King Oliver, the band would play and then there'd be a four-bar break, during which King Oliver or Louis Armstrong would play exactly the same improvised phrase together, in unison. Nobody knew how they could do it. It was like magic. What happened was that King Oliver would play the phrase during the bars before. Louis would hear it and so when it came around the next time he would play it. I learned from Miles how these kind of cues can be used to change direction, or introduce a new section. Miles often used phrases to show us where we'd go next. When we were playing a tune, Miles would superimpose something on top of it, and as soon as he did that we'd know that we were moving to another song, or that this or that rhythmic thing was about to happen. That's the great thing about a working band, you start to develop an intuitive sense for what's going on. You're listening all the time and you build up this language which becomes very personal to the group. But Miles did not do the hand signals when I was in the band. They came in later."

Miles's "coded phrases" are strongly in evidence on *Black Beauty,* and are one of the reasons for the almost relentless intensity of the music. Miles kept guiding the music back to vamps and themes, continually bringing the musicians back to focus. If the musicians were not fully alive in the present moment, if they were not listening with total attentiveness, they could easily have missed Miles's short cues. But they never did. The swiftness and agility with which the musicians responded to Miles's signals are remarkable, and can be heard around 00:00 of most tracks, where they invariably fall into line within seconds of Miles introducing a new song or vamp. Because the band is still playing the previous tune or vamp when Miles announces the next, the musical shifts have the effect of Macero's postproduction crossfades.[7] Macero, in fact, claimed credit for Miles's way of working, saying, "It was because of me, because we always overlapped sections in our edits. Miles also did this on stage, and only started doing these things deliberately after we did these crossfades."

The "coded phrases" can also be heard on Miles's next live recording, *At Fillmore: Live at the Fillmore East,* with Keith Jarrett, who had been added to the band in May of 1970. Using often brutal edits, Teo Macero distilled four concerts (June 17 to 20) into four suites of twenty-something minutes each. Some commentators appreciate Macero's rough approach as part of his style, but to this writer's ears the edits are not only ugly but also give the music a fragmented feel, making it hard to follow its ebb and flow, as well as the interplay between the musicians, over longer time spans. An example is the insertion of twenty-nine seconds of "Bitches Brew" into the middle of "Directions" in the first medley, which is called by the generic title "Wednesday Miles." The edit badly disturbs the flow of "Directions" and shows us nothing essential about the version of "Bitches Brew" that was played that evening. The longer sections are generally speaking more satisfying, for instance the infectious groove the rhythm section lays down in "It's about That Time" in "Friday Miles." Comic relief is once again provided, this time in "Bitches Brew" in the medley of the June 20 concert, called "Saturday Miles," when Holland distorts his bass guitar and makes the vamp sound like a heavy metal riff that would have sounded entirely idiomatic in the music of Black Sabbath. Sadly, this outrageous and exciting bit of music is cut off at 03:00 by another abrasive edit.

The reason the edits worked so well on *In a Silent Way* and *Bitches Brew* was that they were technically seamless—one had to listen very carefully to spot them—and created musical unity and flow. Through the edits the whole became much more than the sum of the parts. For *At Fillmore,* Macero had presumably taken his cue from *A Tribute to Jack Johnson,* most of which was recorded two months previously and on which he had for the first time combined totally unrelated pieces of music. On *At Fillmore,* which is also marred by a substandard recording quality, the edits are especially jarring. They give substance to the quip by writer Gary Carner that "Davis, with mad scientist Teo Macero," had become "the Doctor Frankensteins of jazz."[8]

In addition, in this case the concept of recomposing music through editing goes against the spirit of the recording. Rather than creating an aural fantasy, as was done with the studio albums, the aim of live recordings such as *Black Beauty* and *At Fillmore* is to provide an approximation of a live concert through which listeners can imagine themselves being present. Since a concert is only heard once, but a live recording may be listened to many times over, editing is justifiable to correct mistakes and to sequence the best sections of different nights into one fictitious, perfect concert. But the way in which postproduction was applied on the concerts at Fillmore East is tragic, since, insofar as can be determined from the fragmented results, the playing by the musicians is excellent, and as intense and concentrated as on *Black Beauty*.[9]

The one exception is Steve Grossman, whose contributions on the soprano saxophone once again sound shrill and uneasy. Apparently he also played tenor saxophone, but these solos were edited out, according to him because Miles only wanted to hear the soprano saxophone. This preference paralleled Miles's mounting focus on deepening the bottom end, most likely because the soprano saxophone is better able to cut through a dense rhythm section. "I always wanted to be a tenor player," Grossman commented. "So I kept the tenor on a lot of tunes, and I think a lot of my solos were cut out for that reason. Miles was really into the soprano, and I kind of disobeyed his order."

There may have been another reason for Grossman's erratic soloing. He remembered that he felt uncomfortable with the musical concept, even though "it was a very strong band, and Miles influenced me with his concept of going out of the chord harmonically, not having a harmonic concept to come back to. It's more an instinctual, melodic way of playing. He played the shit out of everything! But at Fillmore East, for the first time in my life, I didn't really know what to play. A very strange feeling. I don't know why that was. There were many things coming from each musician, maybe it was a little too busy for me."

Columbia is planning a series of live concert reissues, and releasing the unedited concerts that make up *At Fillmore* is one likely option. This will hopefully restore the coherence to these recordings and shed more light on Grossman's contribution, as well as on the exact musical relationship of keyboardists Jarrett and Corea. Jarrett plays organ in the left channel, Corea plays electric piano on the right, and together they add substantially to the density of the bottom end. "In the studio there was a definite rapport," Corea commented. "But when Keith and I played live, there really was no communication. Miles put either keyboard on each end of the stage and I could never hear what Keith was playing and I doubt Keith ever heard a note I was playing. So it was hard to really play something together."

By the end of July 1970 Miles, apparently dissatisfied with Grossman, sacked the saxophonist. Soprano and alto saxophonist Gary Bartz replaced Grossman in August. Bartz was an experienced player who had worked with pianist McCoy Tyner and drummer Max Roach, and who had one solo album to his name. The septet, now consisting of Miles, Bartz, Corea, Jarrett, Holland, Moreira, and DeJohnette, performed at the famous Isle of Wight festival on August 29, 1970, on the same bill as Jimi Hendrix, The Who, The

Doors, Joni Mitchell, and Joan Baez. Sections of the live concert were released by Columbia on two compilation CDs, *Message to Love: The Isle of Wight Festival 1970* and *The First Great Rock Festivals of the Seventies: Isle of Wight*. The two medleys—again given generic titles, "Call It Anythin'" and "Call It Anything"—are different edits from the same set and include "Directions," "It's about That Time," "Spanish Key," and "Bitches Brew." Apart from "The Theme," the selections do not include any material from Miles's jazz period, nor any free-jazz sections. The rhythm section plays noticeably funkier than two months previously, laying down very deep, one-chord, cyclical grooves that have little relationship to jazz. Miles was aiming towards the next stage in his musical development.

❖

As if on cue, Holland and Corea left towards the end of August to form Circle with drummer Barry Altschul. "Dave and I warned Miles that we would be leaving, and after that there was a transition period of some months," Corea reminisced. "Miles did ask Dave and me to stay in the band and be part of the more steady, funky rhythm direction that he was moving into, but he saw that it wasn't our desire. Dave and I wanted to play free music. It was a very natural parting of ways. I sometimes regret leaving the band, but it still seems like it was the right thing to do. But just being around Miles and the creativity that was going on has been a tremendous learning experience for me. We played a lot of concerts and being a part of them was great."

"There was a creative tension between the direction Miles was going in, the vamps and repetitive patterns, and the tendency of other members towards more freer parts," Holland elaborated. "The live records really illustrate that. It goes from this real hard rocking thing to something that suddenly opens up and is very free, and then it goes back again. I was playing a lot of fast stuff around the time, and one night Miles came up to me and said to me, 'You're a bass player, Dave, don't forget.' That was something I took away and thought about a lot. He was asking me to consider what the role of my instrument was, and not to ignore that."

"Dave Holland was always trying to push Chick to play more 'out,' but they wouldn't do it behind Miles," remarked Grossman. "Instead, they experimented behind Wayne's solos, and continued to do so behind me when I was in the band. As soon as I started soloing, they'd go free. That was when I had the most fun, because when we were playing free we were playing music that came from swing. For me, to be able to play free, it has to swing. To also play free time is more difficult."

This mixture of swing time and free playing can best be heard on the *At Fillmore* track "The Mask," which is little more than a jam in open harmony with a swing jazz bass line underneath. As far as is known it was only performed from June to August of 1970, and is an odd piece to appear at this stage in Miles's development. It may well have contributed to bringing the musical differences in his band to a head.

Miles did not replace Corea, choosing instead to carry on with only Jarrett, who graduated to playing both electric piano and organ. Miroslav Vitous stood in for Holland for a few concerts in early September until former Motown bassist Michael Henderson joined the live band on September 13, 1970. His talent for playing circular, repetitive bass riffs immediately gave Miles's music a new focus. Gary Bartz remembered that Miles had some hesitancy in hiring Henderson, "because he had never had a bassist who didn't play acoustic also."[10] Although it may seem strange for Miles to have reservations about the electric bass at this stage in his electric development, the comment fits with Miles's tendency to progress carefully, step by step, making sure he transcended and included his previous steps. But once he had chosen to go with Henderson, the instructions he gave the bassist suggest that he was planning a radical new move.

"He hired me to play just what I was playing," Henderson recalled. "He hired me to bring something new to his music. I thought that maybe he wanted me to learn some of his older stuff, but he said, 'If you learn any of that old shit, you're fired!' And he told me, 'Anytime the guys try to play any of that shit, don't follow them.' The other guys wanted to take him where he'd been before, but he didn't want me to go there. He was through with going there. Keith Jarrett used to get off on being innovative and doing off-the-wall stuff. But Miles used to come over to my side, and whisper to me, 'Don't follow that motherfucker.' I don't think the other guys understood, because Keith Jarrett sometimes got frustrated when I didn't follow. The others in the band didn't know why I was in the band, but Miles knew exactly what he wanted from me."

With Bartz, Henderson, and Jarrett in the band a very distinct and identifiable phase in Miles's electric career began. Lasting until early 1972, it featured a band with a strong musical identity as well as its own repertoire. The identity of this band has rarely been recognized. This is largely because, for three decades, only one of its concerts had been officially released: the December 19, 1970, concert at The Cellar Door in Washington, D.C., which was released on *Live-Evil*. This recording featured John McLaughlin as a guest player and didn't capture the band as it sounded during the rest of its one-and-a-half-year tenure. Columbia/Legacy is planning the release of three two-CD sets in 2002, documenting large sections of the band's entire stint at The Cellar Door, from Wednesday, December 16, to Saturday, December 19. The first three nights were without McLaughlin. Reference copies of these six CDs, kindly supplied by Seth Rothstein, senior director of Columbia/Legacy Jazz, shed much new light on this band's true nature. From the fall of 1970 to the summer of 1971 its nucleus was formed by Miles, Bartz, Jarrett, Henderson, and DeJohnette—a quintet with the same, albeit electrified, instrumentation as the second great quintet and the lost quintet. In addition there was Airto Moreira, adding bottom density and color, who was aided for a few weeks in October of 1970 by Jim Riley, who was also known as Jumma Santos and was a participant in the *Bitches Brew* sessions.

Michael Henderson was at the band's heart. Under threat of being fired, he stuck almost obsessively to his awesome, "granite-like bass vamps,"[11] on many occasions hanging on one chord for up to a quarter of an hour. Keith Jarrett often played short, funky melodies to complement Henderson's bass lines and also experimented with classical, as well as chromatic, free playing. Bartz took care of the more lyrical and melodic solos, and Miles had by now started to use a wah-wah pedal live, which became a crucial feature of his trumpet style for the next five years.

The rock influences in the Bartz/Jarrett/Henderson band were much stronger than in its predecessors. Its bottom end was denser, its playing more aggressive, its rhythms funkier, and its volume louder. One of the band's nicknames was "Miles Davis and the House Rockers," Gary Bartz recalled. ". . . We were as intense as any rock band I've ever heard and just as loud. This was the biggest hurdle I had to get over in the band. I had worked with Max Roach and Art Blakey, which were both drum-based bands. As loud and intense as these bands were, this was indeed another level."[12] Keith Jarrett dryly remarked, "We would put cotton in our ears every night—Jack and I—we couldn't stand the volume."[13]

The set list of this band remained remarkably stable throughout its existence. It included three new compositions only played live by this band, namely "What I Say," "Honky Tonk," and "Inamorata/Funky Tonk."[14] According to Jack DeJohnette, "Miles brought new pieces in and gave us a few sketches of grooves and melodies." The band's concert opener was always a frantic version of "Directions," sometimes stretching to fifteen minutes. This was usually followed by "Honky Tonk," "What I Say," "Sanctuary," "It's about That Time," "Yesternow," "Inamorata/Funky Tonk," and the theme of "Sanctuary" to close the performance. "Bitches Brew" is the only other title known to have made an occasional appearance. Despite this unusual continuity of repertoire and set structure, the band's music, like that of its predecessors, could change dramatically night by night. "Our music changes every month," Miles remarked in September of 1970. "We extend each other's ideas. I may start a phrase and not complete it, because I hear something else behind me that takes me to a different place. It keeps going further."[15]

All titles, with the exception of "Bitches Brew," feature on the six Cellar Door CDs, often repeatedly—"Directions" and "What I Say" receive five different renditions, "Honky Tonk" four. Bartz and Jarrett have commented that, due to the inclusion of John McLaughlin, the Saturday night was unrepresentative of the way the band normally played. Reissue producer Bob Belden agreed: "The newly released music is incredibly revealing. You actually hear the best fusion band Miles Davis ever had, featuring both DeJohnette and Jarrett. There's remarkable playing by Keith. When McLaughlin came on as a last-minute add-on the music completely changed."

❖

Jarrett has hinted that McLaughlin's inclusion was to the band's detriment. "They're gonna release the Cellar Door dates at Columbia," Jarrett said, "so you'll be able to hear at a good length what we sounded like. We were a lot freer than *Live-Evil* sounds like we were. You wouldn't know that from *Live-Evil*, but John [McLaughlin] only played with us one night. I think it was a marketing concept to add electric guitar. It kind of threw a curve ball into the band. I wasn't sure—nobody was sure—what the rules were."[16]

Whether this band is indeed Miles's "best fusion band" is doubtful. Although it contained near-legendary players in Jarrett and DeJohnette, there appears on the Cellar Door material a lack of chemistry between the (free) jazz polarity of the above-mentioned two players and the rock-soul sensitivity of Henderson, meaning that neither Jarrett's attempts at playing free nor the rock grooves can genuinely flourish. The best sections occur when Henderson is given space for his trademark melodic funky riffing and Jarrett and DeJohnette join in with him. The soloists, especially Miles, are in top form throughout, and the band as a whole can also be heard developing over these four nights, gradually taking more and more liberties with the material.

Jarrett used the word "free" in the free-jazz sense because, despite his comment, the curve towards more creative freedom continued on the Saturday night, when McLaughlin joined for the second and third sets (Miles had called the guitarist in New York in the morning, and he arrived halfway through the evening). The expanded freedom on this Saturday night comes mainly from the interaction between McLaughlin and Henderson, who both understand how to rock, and roll, and inspire each other to invent new funky riffs, or to deconstruct existing ones. Jarrett and Bartz therefore have a less domineering role, but ironically, in the light of Jarrett's remark, his Saturday night solo improvisation is his most imaginative of the four captured on the six Cellar Door CDs.

The recorded evidence of the second and third Saturday night concerts at the Cellar Door was edited into four tracks on *Live-Evil,* with a combined length of eighty-six minutes, and was used in conjunction with the three Pascoal tracks recorded in June, as well as with "Gemini/Double Image," recorded in February. Mercifully, after the muffled and uneven sound of the Juan-les-Pins and Fillmore albums, the sound quality and mix of the live tracks on *Live-Evil* are excellent, probably because more care was taken; the recording was clearly intended to be an important release. Graced with another eye-catching cover by Abdul Mati Klarwein, it was promoted as the follow-up to *Bitches Brew.* Miles stated that the music on *Live-Evil* transcended and included his most commercially successful recording: "I heard the same kind of musical figures for *Live-Evil* that I had heard for *Bitches Brew,* only a little bit more worked out."[17]

Macero told writer Chris Albertson that the music was "a distillation of ten to fifteen reels of tape, selected from an original working pile of thirty reels."[18] Predictably, but nevertheless frustratingly, there are elements both of Frankenstein at work and of genius in his edits, the former courtesy of several pointless edits. The latter shows in Macero's choice of material, especially in the fact that he opted to construct *Live-Evil* from the Saturday night, when the addition of John McLaughlin gave the band an edge that it lacked on the other three nights, and in his choice of the first 03:25 of the opening medley, "Sivad." Taken from the end of the performance of "Directions" of the second set, these 03:25 are arguably the most enthralling section of *Live-Evil* and a brilliant choice as an album opener. A wild, driving bass riff is complemented by a beautiful keyboard melody in one of the instances where Jarrett and Henderson bring out the best in each other. Just as on the studio recording of "Honky Tonk" earlier in May, McLaughlin creates noise and texture rather than melodic or harmonic content. He adds power and excitement to the music, as does Miles when he leaves the wah-wah alone around 02:00 and plays power trumpet à la *Jack Johnson,* as well as some of the highest notes he's ever played.

But at 03:25 of "Sivad" Macero inserted fifty-six seconds from the studio recording of "Honky Tonk" on May 19 as a lead-in to sections from the performance of "Honky Tonk" at The Cellar Door. These fifty-six seconds are out of place in terms of sound, atmosphere, and musical structure. Moreover, The Cellar Door version of "Honky Tonk" is a little pedestrian and has none of the drama, the focus, or the intricate question-answer games among instruments that made the studio version such a success.

The next live track on *Live-Evil,* "What I Say," is unedited, yet overly long at just more than than twenty-one minutes. Henderson holds down a simple one-chord groove for almost the whole track. At the beginning, Jarrett often plays thematically, for example at 02:42 when he plays a little four-note chromatic riff in unison with Henderson and during his fuguelike solo around 13:00. The track's backbone is a powerful muscular drum groove for which Miles has claimed credit. "Miles gave me that drum beat,"

DeJohnette explained. "He didn't say anything more, but I knew what to do with it. And the piece took off like a rocket. He basically wanted the groove to sit and from that rhythm he gave me, I built the piece and propelled it to the finish. I like that track a lot. Miles never told me to stay within certain parameters. He just smiled, like, 'That's right, that's it,' which was this kind of 'knowing' between us."

Another unusual aspect of "What I Say" is that, as on "Sivad," Miles played some extremely high notes. During the mid-1940s he had become aware that he couldn't play as high as his mentor, Dizzy Gillespie, and focused on the middle register notes, which allowed for a mellower, rounder tone. But on "What I Say" he moved the boundaries of his playing. "I played a lot of high notes on trumpet," Miles commented, "notes I usually don't play because I don't hear them. But I heard them a lot after I started playing this new music."[19] It is ironic that these feats of trumpet athleticism should come at a moment when Miles became increasingly interested in using wah-wah generated sound effects that required less technical skills and stamina.

Live-Evil's ensuing medley is called "Funky Tonk," after the new composition that is one of its components. The medley begins with nearly seventeen minutes of "Directions." The band tries to pull off something similar to "What I Say," sustaining a frenetic pace and energy for a prolonged period of time, but this time it doesn't work as well. Part of the reason is the less driving and engaging rhythm. Jarrett and Henderson don't complement each other rhythmically as effectively as on "What I Say." The best sections are where the rhythm section's intensity relents a little and the playing becomes more open and funky, as during Bartz's solo, around the seven and again the eight-minute mark, and during the first minute of McLaughlin's solo, starting at 08:33. At 16:52 Miles comes in with a "coded phrase," stating the theme for the composition "Inamorata/Funky Tonk," and immediately leaving the stage for Jarrett to play a lyrical and inventive unaccompanied solo on two keyboards, which was a regular feature of this composition. After Jarrett's solo, the band plays some collective accents, followed by a melodic bass riff, all of which are an integral part of "Inamorata/Funky Tonk," the composition.

"Funky Tonk," the medley, abruptly ends with another bewildering and inexplicable edit, greatly disturbing the musical flow of "Inamorata/Funky Tonk," the composition, which continues as the first 16:36 of "Inamorata," *Live-Evil*'s final medley. During the first nine minutes of this medley, McLaughlin and Henderson initiate brilliant stop-start, question-answer rhythms, similar to those so successfully explored in the studio recordings of "Gemini/Double Image" and "Honky Tonk" earlier in the year. But the playing appears to lose concentration after the nine-minute mark, jumping chaotically from riff to riff and solo to solo. Focus returns around sixteen minutes when the band, again led by McLaughlin and Henderson, settles on another infectious stop-start rhythm, only for Macero to abruptly cut this off at 16:36 by inserting the theme of "Sanctuary." Eleven seconds later Miles plays the "coded phrase" of "It's about That Time," and it sounds like at 16:58 six more minutes of the track are edited in, once more characterized by funky, stop-start rhythms, with Miles playing some excellent open trumpet. In keeping with the almost throwaway postproduction on *Live-Evil*, Conrad Roberts's narration is overdubbed starting at 23:09, while the band is still playing "It's about That Time." During the narration the music sounds very distant, apparently recorded with an audience microphone. When the narration stops, the music's volume increases, revealing an abysmal sound quality marred by lots of distortion. The last two minutes of "Inamorata" are therefore a frustrating way to conclude a record containing much excellent and pioneering music.

❖

The Cellar Door concerts marked the end of a U.S. tour that had started in October of 1970. The following year the band toured the West Coast in the spring and the East Coast during the summer, until both Moreira and DeJohnette left the group in July. "Miles was moving more and more into the direction of having a drummer play a backbeat, and I understood that and respected it, but figured it was time for another drummer," DeJohnette explained.

Percussionists Don Alias and Mtume and drummer Leon "Ndugu" Chancler replaced Moreira and DeJohnette for the European tour beginning in October. Don Alias had taken part in the *Bitches Brew* sessions, while Mtume (meaning "the messenger" in Swahili) is the son of tenor saxophonist Jimmy Heath, who had played with Miles on a few occasions in the early '50s and early '60s. Chancler was nineteen in 1971, and had played with pianist Walter Bishop and on *Mwandishi,* Herbie Hancock's 1971 mix of jazz-rock and free-jazz. The drummer only lasted a few weeks with Miles because, in Miles's words, "he did not work out."[20] Interviews with Miles's sidemen have generally been with those who played with him for a long time, or were involved in particularly important projects, and it is possible that this has painted an overly positive account of Miles's talents and influence. As a musician who "did not work out," Chancler's stories are therefore of particular interest.

Miles had spotted Chancler and Mtume in Los Angeles, in March of 1971, when playing with trumpeter Freddie Hubbard. "I didn't know Miles had come to see me play in Los Angeles," Chancler recounted. "Miles called me in L.A. half a year later, in August. When I came over to New York, he picked me up in his car, and we talked all the way to and from the first rehearsal. That's when I felt the heart and soul of Miles Davis. If I'd never played a note with Miles, just the ride was incredible. We talked about all sorts of musicians and different music genres, and I realized, 'This guy is aware of everything that's going on.' So I asked him, 'Miles, when do you have time to go see and hear all these people?' and he said, 'I just check everything out.' We didn't really play during that rehearsal. The next day we went over to Miles's house. He had cooked and he left us there, and we just talked over a few things. Those were our rehearsals. They had sent me a live tape prior to that, so I knew what was going on. But in general we just winged it during those weeks in Europe."

The European tour lasted from October 18 to November 20, 1971, long enough for Chancler to get a good impression of the inner workings of the band. "Everyone had a role in that band that was not really prediscussed," the drummer recalled. "Don and Mtume kept a lot of things going on, a lot of activity, a lot of busy stuff. Don gave an Afro-Cuban flavor, with timbals and congas, and Mtume had an African sound with a lot of colors, shakers, and bells and tuned percussion. They kept the chatter going. Michael Henderson held the groove down. He was the foundation, the anchor. Keith was the harmonic master of the band. He kept a lot of variety going harmonically on the organ and the Fender Rhodes. Sometimes you heard him and you'd think he was in a Top 40 band, other times he was playing something akin to a classical concerto against the band's groove. Gary Bartz represented the vocal aspect. What he played sounded very human, like a vocal. And Miles was the pied piper, he had the freedom to go and do whatever he wanted to do. You have to understand, in this band we didn't have a guitar player, so sometimes Miles would take on the role of a rhythm guitar player. At other times he would come out and play melody and solos, and then he'd go back to that rhythm role again, and be one of the band. Sometimes he played wah-wah, sometimes the mute. He varied. He had two mouthpieces, one connected with the electronics for the wah-wah, and one that was straight, and he would sometimes switch mouthpieces in the middle of a tune."

According to Chancler, the musical tension between Henderson sticking to his groove and Jarrett trying to play free, audible on some sections of the Cellar Door CDs, was still the major fault line in the band. "My role was to hold down a steady rhythm, or be free inside that. Sometimes I followed the percussionists, sometimes I followed Michael. I played more off Michael than he off me, because Michael had been there for a long time, and he was solid as a rock. Miles did not tell me who to follow, but he did often say to us, 'When Keith starts playing all that Catholic school shit, lay-out, don't play, don't follow him.' Keith would sometimes be playing classical-style music, which Miles called 'Catholic school stuff.' It wasn't that he didn't like what Keith was doing, but not following this was the best way to create musical diversity. It kept tension going. There was a lot of musical tension between Keith and Michael. I think Keith always felt that Michael was restricting him. Miles, Gary, Michael, the others, and myself, we all listened to commercial music. But Keith didn't respect that music, or musicians who played it, and that created the main problems. But Keith's separatist, elitist, jazz approach sometimes made the music more interesting."

Mtume remembered a salient anecdote from the same period, illustrating how Miles fostered tension and conflict. "We were doing a gig, I think it was in Milan, with the Argentinian saxophonist Gato Barbieri as the other act [this dates the concert as taking place on October 21]. I was sitting in the dressing room with Miles and Finney, his hairdresser. Gary Bartz comes in after the first set and complains to Miles, 'Man, I'm tired. I hate what Keith is playing behind me. I don't like what this motherfucker is doing, I want freedom. I don't want him to play when I play.' So Miles says, 'Okay, okay,' and sends somebody to get Keith. After Gary walks out of the room, Keith walks in, and Miles says to him, 'Gary just came in and said that he *loves* what you're playing behind him. Gary actually said, 'Play a little more!' I'm just sitting there going, 'Oh, my God!' But that's what Miles did, he loved tension. So during the next set, while Gary is playing, Keith is playing all over, smiling all over his face. After the set Gary is ready to go to blows with Keith! And Miles looks over at me and winks."

It is hard to interpret this anecdote unambiguously. One possibility is that Miles acted primarily for musical reasons. Mtume explained that Bartz was used to playing in open musical spaces with very little harmonic backing, so Miles's deception forced the saxophonist to play what he knew, and to play beyond what he knew. Miles's strategies certainly resulted in more tension-filled, and hence more alive, music. But the anecdote may also illustrate Miles's darker side, his tendency to push people's boundaries and see how far he could go.

Lydia DeJohnette's remark, that Miles could "destroy" people, is echoed by Mtume, who remembered, "Tension and trust and weakness were things he fed off. And if you were weak, he fed off that. Ndugu and I were best friends, we had played together in California. And I watched Miles give Ndugu such a hard time. Miles often left written notes for band members. So every morning you're checking, 'Oh, here's a note!' And he was leaving all these notes for Ndugu: 'Don't wear those kind of shoes.' 'Put the drum head off.' 'Put it back.' At the end of the tour Ndugu was fucked up. But when I spoke to him, he said it was the best thing that ever happened to him. He said it gave him strength and confidence."

Indeed, Chancler does not appear to have traumatic memories from his time with Miles, instead feeling that it was his making as a drummer. He ascribed any difficulties to his youth and his inexperience with this new musical direction. "Playing with Miles was definitely something I regarded as something out of my reach," Chancler said. "At that point in my life, I had geared myself up to play with Freddie Hubbard, but not for replacing Tony Williams and Jack DeJohnette. So I kind of went into shock. I was young, and I held Miles in such high esteem that I was somewhat intimidated. I think it sometimes showed in my playing. I was probably a little inconsistent, I had good nights and bad nights. I was also intimidated, because I didn't have enough awareness of that music. It was very embryonic to me. It was the beginning of a lot of that fusion stuff, so it wasn't like something that had already been established. They were trying to pull something new out of me without me knowing what they were trying to pull out."

Chancler's words describe the experiences of a musician struggling with a new musical paradigm, who had no role models, no beaten tracks to follow. Moreover, Miles was by now also getting out of step with other emerging jazz-rock bands and artists, who tended to focus more on virtuosity and harmonic complexity. Miles, on the other hand, was moving towards one-chord structures, in Chancler's words, "towards pure groove."

Every band member had to reinvent his own role, remake the mold, and for some reason, this was just beyond Chancler's reach. Miles's intuitions about his sideman's talents were nevertheless correct, because Chancler went on to an extremely successful career, playing with Michael Jackson, Stevie Wonder, Santana, George Duke, and many others. The drummer put a lot of his success down to Miles's teaching methods. "Had it not been my experience in that band, I would not have participated in the whole fusion thing the way I did. After being there I could understand why Tony Williams and Jack DeJohnette became great drummers, because Miles had a way of giving you simple words, one-liners, or whatever, that made you think about things in a different light. He did that for me. He came to me one night after the concert and said, 'You know those little phrases you play, don't finish them.' That was it. That gave me a whole other approach to fill-ins and polyrhythms. He made me hear different phrasings. Although I regarded myself as a jazz drummer at that time, Miles got me into listening to Buddy Miles, Jimi Hendrix, Sly, and James Brown. The overall awareness that he had of what everybody was doing and how they were doing it really affected me. He listened to everything and everybody. Those are the things that turned my life around. There was just so much going on there, and it was so intense and so much so soon. It was phenomenal."

Despite Chancler's troubles, the European tour was a success. Chancler recalled that "In a lot of places they loved it. I don't really remember any negative reactions. In Europe they were big on the avant-garde, and they were big on the grooves as well. We had all that covered. And this was Miles Davis."

The band returned to the United States for a concert at the Philharmonic Hall in New York, on November 26, which has become known as a poignant illustration of Miles's desperation to reach a black audience; he instructed his manager, Jack Whittemore, to spend half his fee—$2,000—on tickets, and give these to young blacks. By this stage, the internal tensions in the band manifested in a rift between Jarrett and Chancler. "Keith never liked my playing, and I can understand why," said Chancler. "He'd played with Jack for years. That was a hard adjustment for him. So Keith told Miles, 'Either he goes, or I go.' And that's all it was. In response, Miles told Keith, 'If you can get Jack [DeJohnette] back, you get him.' Miles liked me, but Keith had seniority. Keith was making the most money, he had seniority of all the guys in the band. So Jack came back for a few gigs."

Don Alias, on the other hand, offered that Miles "fired Ndugu for not fixing his bass drum. Miles wanted a funk oriented sound and Ndugu had this Tony Williams setup."[21] The truth may lie somewhere in between, but the drummer Miles enlisted in March of 1972, when he briefly revived the band, illustrated the depth of Miles's desire for a more funkier drum style. "After the concerts with Jack, we didn't work for a while," Mtume remembered, "and after that, Ramon "Tiki" Fulwood, the drummer from Parliament-Funkadelic came in for one or two gigs. I've never seen mentioned that Miles was a big fan of Parliament-Funkadelic, but he was. We all went to see them in concert. And at the time we were tightening up the rhythm, and the drummer had to have more of a funk approach. You can't be all over the place, you have to keep the shit going. So he brought in Tiki, who was as funky as you could get. But Tiki didn't work out and Miles disbanded the group."

There are many bootlegs of the band's 1971 tour, since European concerts were often broadcast by national radio and/or TV stations. As with *Live-Evil,* these bootlegs illustrate the pioneering nature of this band's music, marking the first time Miles completely released the jazz approach to playing rhythm. Michael Henderson's rock-like timing and circular riffs had irrevocably taken the band out of jazz territory. The band was now playing rhythmic structures that were reminiscent of African music and pioneered in the United States by James Brown. African music is based on rhythmic complexity and repetition rather than harmonic complexity and development. In combining these funk rhythms with jazz improvisation, rock, African, and Latin, the Bartz/Jarrett/Henderson band spearheaded a musical approach well ahead of its time.

That's not to say it was unequivocally successful, however. Due to Henderson's tendency to stick rigidly and lengthily to one bass line and one chord, there was often a coldness and rigidity to the rhythms. As a whole, the band rarely matched the scorching ensemble playing that James Brown could whip up with a few equally simple riffs. Where James Brown's band lifted off, Miles's often remained heavy on the ground. Moreover, as is evident on the new Cellar Door material, the combination of Henderson's riffs and Jarrett's "out" playing sounded like a clashing of two different worlds, rather than a blending of them. The parts only occasionally made a whole, let alone became more than their sum. A contributing reason for the mixed results may well have been Miles's experiments with his wah-wah pedal, which enabled him to express unusual colors and textures but weakened the rhythmically astute and powerful stabs with which he had been propelling and focusing his previous rock-influenced experiments.

There have been suggestions that the mixed results of this group were the major reason Miles didn't take it into the recording studio. But this seems an irrelevant argument, because Miles never took his working band into the studio around this time. Moreover, it seems unlikely that he would have kept together for fourteen months a band with which he was this dissatisfied. The slightly tainted image this band has gained over the years may also have been invoked by Keith Jarrett's repeated criticisms.

"I wasn't exactly turned on by the band," Jarrett remarked in one of *The Miles Davis Radio Project* episodes. "I wanted to play with Miles. That was already an understanding with Miles, which is why, even though it sounds weird, my direction wasn't changed. In some ways it was regressive, because you can't make an electric instrument play free, it's not sensitive enough to be pushed around. When we did those things at Fillmore that were crazy, there was an incredible amount of will involved, but I don't think of that as very interesting music."[22]

Not surprisingly, Jarrett's exhortations have drawn irritated responses from several other band members. "One of the things that insulted me more than anything was that radio special on Miles," Mtume said. "And the only motherfucker they interviewed out of that band was Keith. But whatever Keith said, the truth is, he loved what he was playing! I'll go to print with this. I saw him smiling every fucking night. And what pissed me off was that when he got to do interviews, he would say the complete opposite of what he was really doing on stage. Once he said, 'Unfortunately none of the percussionists knew the music.' It's bullshit. Keith loved it. My thought was, 'If it was that fucked up. . . . Why didn't you leave?'"

Television footage of the concerts of the European tour of 1971 indeed show a seemingly ecstatic Jarrett, often moving wildly and dramatically, and playing some of his most striking, funky, and melodic parts. "Keith was the wrong one to talk to for that radio program," Chancler stated. "I love Keith, but Keith tends to erase that time period. He went back to acoustic and said he'd never touch an electric instrument, and all of that stuff. But he was playing some of the most innovative, creative keyboard stuff going at that time with that band. There were segments where he didn't just play with the band, but alone, where he's setting up this whole synthesizer generation. Man, this guy was playing some awesome things."[23]

Mtume also denied reports that Jarrett's misgivings about electric instruments were one of the reasons for the band's demise. "It wasn't a matter of Keith leaving. Miles and I talked a lot, because we were both insomniacs, and we began to discuss where he was going. Miles always said, 'If you're going to change your music, you gotta change your band.' The next thing I know we didn't do anything until *On the Corner,* which was also the birth of a new band with only Michael and myself left from the old configuration. Everybody else was new."

Miles won *Down Beat* and *Playboy* polls for Best Jazz Musician in 1971, and his album sales and concert attendance were still considerable. He called 1971 "a good year," but added, "things seemed a little out of focus."[24] It is unclear whether he referred to his music or his personal life, but it appears that clouds had started to gather again in the latter. Although Mtume and Chancler both vouched that Miles tried to lead a healthy, vegetarian, nondrug lifestyle during the European tour of 1971, Marguerite Eskridge remembered that Miles began using drugs again during her pregnancy with Miles's third son, Erin, who was born on April 29, 1971. Eskridge was uncertain about the reasons for Miles's shift, but she explained that her separation from Miles in early 1971 was one of the results, saying "I couldn't deal with the things around his drug use."

Miles, by contrast, claimed their separation was due to the fact that "She didn't like the pace of my life and that I was going out with other women. But more than that, she didn't like just sitting around waiting for me."[25] "I never looked at the relationship with Miles as an exclusive thing, because I knew that he was together with other women," Eskridge contradicted. "That didn't bother me a lot. But Miles had a great need to have someone at his side whenever he needed them or wanted them there. That meant you could not be terribly involved in your own career, because you could always get a call saying that you needed to come to this or that place and get on this flight this afternoon. I knew this was not something I could do for a long period of time. However, Miles's return to drug use was the main reason why we separated."

The separation from Marguerite Eskridge was a tremendous shock for Miles. It came on top of the problems he had with his oldest son, Gregory. "He cost me a lot of trouble, headaches, and money while he lived with me," Miles related. I guess my two eldest sons are a big disappointment to me. . . . All I can do about it now is say I'm sorry and hope that they pull their lives together."[26] Over the years expressions of feelings of guilt and frustration about not having been a good father have cropped up in various places. It's not farfetched to speculate that Gregory's state, and the impending birth of a new son, put pressure on Miles that he found hard to handle.

Miles's physical problems also returned to haunt him. In the spring of 1971 he is said to have publicly complained of fatigue and weight loss as a result of the incessant touring.[27] He mentioned as well that his arthritic hip, caused by sickle-cell anemia, began bothering him again by the end of 1971. His sickle-cell anemia was also starting to affect his hands, making piano playing an increasingly painful experience, and leading him to compose less.

Perhaps also, as in the early '60s, the music wasn't quite happening anymore for Miles. The musical direction of late 1971 wasn't that different from that of late 1970, suggesting that he was short of new ideas. The fact that he did not try out new things in the recording studio indicates the same. Come 1972, Miles seemed at risk of going into a barren and desperate period similar to that from 1961 to 1964. But untypically, although his personal situation gradually grew worse, resulting in his total breakdown in 1975, he was still to scale some remarkable musical peaks before he succumbed to his physical ailments.

Chapter Nine

ON-OFF

"There was this musician once who came up to Miles and said, 'Miles, you're my man! But that new shit you're into, I just can't get with it.' And Miles answered, 'Should I wait for you?'"
—MARK ROTHBAUM

For those who had been involved in the '60s counterculture, the early '70s were a period of disillusionment. Following the widespread sense of expectancy and optimism in the late '60s, it gradually became clear that the "gate keepers and puppet masters" of the establishment could not be deposed through demonstrations, free love, drugs, and rock 'n' roll. Political oppression, racial discrimination, the Vietnam War, and the Cold War all continued unabated. In 1970 the deaths of two of the counterculture's musical figureheads—Janis Joplin and Jimi Hendrix—and the acrimonious dissolution of the love-and-peace era's defining band, The Beatles, added to the general sense of anticlimax.

The musical innovations and promises of the '60s also appeared to have trouble fulfilling their promise. Rock, soul, funk, and folk became more sophisticated, with bands and artists such as Led Zeppelin, The Band, Marvin Gaye, Stevie Wonder, Sly & The Family Stone, Parliament-Funkadelic, Little Feat, Ry Cooder, Van Morrison, Paul Simon, and Neil Young refining the developments of the '60s. Plus, as in classical music and jazz, rock now had its own avant-garde, which featured the likes of Frank Zappa, John Cale, Henry Cow, King Crimson, Van Der Graaf Generator, and Can. But the incredible pace of musical innovation of the '60s had slowed dramatically. Moreover, the first signs were emerging of an emphasis on virtuosity over meaning, exterior over interior, form over content. This emphasis was mirrored in the jazz-rock movement, which broke through to the rock public in 1973 with recordings like *Love Devotion Surrender* by John McLaughlin and Carlos Santana, *Birds of Fire* by Mahavishnu Orchestra, and *Headhunters* by the Herbie Hancock Group. Following their successes, many jazz-rock groups succumbed to sterile pyrotechnics and commercialization.

In keeping with the mood of the era, 1972 appears to have been a time of discontent for Miles. It is likely that he was affected not only by the general sense of disappointment surrounding him but also by the loss of his relationship with Marguerite Eskridge the previous year, and by his worsening physical condition. The unusual move of giving away tickets to young blacks for his concert in New York the previous November had demonstrated his increasing frustration with the limited inroads his music made with black Americans. Also, several of his former sidemen had become more commercially successful than he, and to his dismay he occasionally found himself playing support to some of them during the mid-1970s. Adding insult to injury, Miles seemed less than impressed with the jazz-rock that was superseding him in popularity.

"We constantly talked about music and the direction it was going," Mtume commented. "And one of the things we talked about was fusion. My view was that the fusion movement was the emphasis of form over feeling. It became about how complex you can write things. This is not writing from the heart, but writing from the head. Playing bars of 11/8 for complexity's sake is great for school, but not for music. Miles went way past that. We went straight for the feeling. We were exploring how long we could keep one chord interesting. That was infuriating to the critics, who were glorifying fusion. But we said, 'Fuck fusion.' We were into emotion."

"The other thing that we talked about was that Miles felt that his music had moved away from the pulse of African American music," Mtume continued. "He felt his shit had become too esoteric and that he had contributed to that. Miles wanted to find a way back into connecting with the black community. But the aesthetic question was, 'How do we do that?' We discussed this more than anything else. At the time Miles was listening to a lot of James Brown, Sly Stone, Jimi Hendrix, and George Clinton, and that's what he wanted to put together. Miles's idea was to get back to the root of the music—to the funk, but to funk with a high degree of experimental edge. He wanted to take it much further. Miles and I would often go to this restaurant at 125th Street in Harlem and discuss some of the influences he was hearing. It was an Indian restaurant, and obviously they were playing Indian music, and it was at that point that he was telling me about the idea of using the electric sitar and the tablas. He was a big fan of Thom Bell, the producer from Philly, who had worked with The Stylistics and The Delfonics, and who had used the electric sitar on many of his songs. Miles had had it with the direction he had been in, and he wanted to add new colors such as tablas and electric sitar to the tapestry to complete the concept. He also gave me a tape of some unreleased stuff on which he had been experimenting with sitar. I think it was his recording of 'Guinnevere,' the Crosby, Stills, Nash & Young song."

Little came of these new ideas in the first half of 1972. In addition to contending with emotional and hip difficulties, Miles "laid low" because "the IRS was creating problems."[1] And in early April he had an operation to remove a gallstone, causing another layoff. It meant that the Bartz/Jarrett/Henderson line-up was only briefly in action, in March with Ramon "Tiki" Fulwood on drums, and was dissolved immediately afterwards.

Miles now had his eyes set on his new "funk with an experimental edge" direction, and he called Paul Buckmaster in London in late April, hoping that the Briton would be able to supply the "experimental edge." The two had met on November 1, 1969, when Buckmaster had played Miles a demo tape the Briton had made with some friends for British blues singer Chris Farlowe. "It featured a bass that was keeping a basic rhythm going all the time, and some quite abstracted melodies over the top," Buckmaster explained. "Miles had listened with interest, so I think he called me on the basis of that tape. . . . I immediately packed up, went to New York, and stayed at his house until early July."

A classically trained cellist, Buckmaster had a passion for jazz, leading him to play in various avant-garde, jazz, and jazz-rock ensembles. His classical background eventually led him into a career of writing arrangements for the likes of David Bowie, Elton John, Harry Nilsson, Leonard Cohen, The Rolling Stones, Meat Loaf, and Celine Dion, and composing the music for Hollywood movies like *Twelve Monkeys* and *Murder in Mind*. Almost instantly after his arrival in New York at the end of April, Buckmaster witnessed Miles overdubbing wah-wah trumpet to "Red China Blues." "I was with Miles in the recording area when he was playing," Buckmaster recalled. "He said the track was not something he'd done. He was asked to do it, almost like a favor. He did several overdub passes one after the other. We were there for maybe ninety minutes. It was a one-off event."[2]

The session marked Miles's first return to the recording studio since early June of 1970, when he recorded the three unsuccessful tracks with Hermeto Pascoal that appear on *Live-Evil*. March 9, 1972, is the most commonly given date for the recording of "Red China Blues," which appeared in 1974 on *Get up with It*. In the light of Buckmaster's testimony it appears likely that the backing tracks for "Red China Blues" were recorded on this date and that Miles overdubbed his part nearly two months later. Consisting of little more than blues clichés, the formulaic piece is an anomaly in Miles's oeuvre. His effective wah-wah soloing is the only characteristic making it identifiable as a Miles Davis recording. This was a rare occasion during which he did not transcend the influences he included. Since the track was prerecorded without his involvement, Miles was unable to put his own stamp on the backing tracks.

Michael Henderson and Mtume, the only members of the Bartz/Jarrett/Henderson band to be retained after its dissolution in March, play on the recording, as well as, among others, drummer Bernard "Pretty" Purdie, well-known R&B guitarist Cornell Dupree, harmonica player Wally Chambers, and Wade Marcus, arranger for Motown's house band The Funk Brothers. Drummer Al Foster is also credited. If correct, this marked his first recording with Miles. Miles had met Foster when he heard him perform at a club in Manhattan, and the young drummer was to play a central role in Miles's music until 1985, and become one of his closest friends.

After the detour of "Red China Blues," Miles, with Buckmaster's help, focused on realizing the new, "experimental" funk direction he had in mind, building on the funk music influences of the Bartz/Jarrett/Henderson band and the Indian experimentations of November 1969 to February 1970. The result, *On the Corner,* was a strange, unearthly concoction of jazz improvisation, funk rhythms, Indian sounds, European avant-garde, and free-jazz. Featuring circular rhythms and bass lines repeated for more than twenty to thirty minutes, and largely devoid of distinct melodies, musical structures, or solos, *On the Corner* was—at the time of its release in the fall of 1972—Miles's most controversial and least understood recording. However, over the years it has also become one of his most influential.

Despite the attention the album has received during recent years, the exact origins of the structurally, harmonically, and melodically challenged recording have remained unclear. Buckmaster lifted some of the veil: "When I came to New York Miles wanted me to write some pieces, but he was also rather vague about what he wanted. I never really got a clear idea. I was a big fan of Stockhausen and had brought several recordings with me, particularly of two pieces, 'Gruppen' and 'Mixtur,' which involve large chamber orchestras at times processed through ring modulators. Somewhere in 'Mixtur' there is a passage for solo trumpet that startlingly reminded me of some things Miles played. I don't know if Miles knew of Stockhausen, but when I brought these records he became very interested. He immediately put them on his record player, with the automatic changer on, and for four hours he had them loudly playing all over the house."

In writing pieces for Miles, Buckmaster focused on Stockhausen's concept of contrasting electronic textures and more traditional sounds. But where Stockhausen employed classical instruments for these traditional sounds, Buckmaster's idea was to use the circular funk and rock rhythms with which he and Miles had both been experimenting.

"We were all listening to James Brown, Sly, Hendrix," Buckmaster explained. "And I wanted to combine some of these very abstract European influences with funky African American type rhythms. My idea was to alternate these street rhythms with long spaces without rhythm, totally abstract stuff, during which you'd be free-floating for a few minutes in some other space. And then through filtering and ring modulation create the effect as if you were tuning a short-wave radio. I got this idea from Stockhausen's 'Hymnen.' I remember describing this to Miles. The whole idea was based on creating a kind of 'cosmic pulse' with great abstractions going on around it. I said something to Miles like, 'Things are either on or off. Reality is made of a sequence of on and offness.' A crazy idea. But what I meant was that a sound doesn't mean anything unless it has a silence preceding it or coming after it, or next to it. Silence makes up part of music, it is in music, and that's what I was trying to get at. Like Stockhausen once said, 'Play something next to what you hear.' So I was talking to Miles about 'street music, with the cosmic pulse going on or off.' Miles took that idea and used it for the title and the cover, with the front saying 'On' and the other side 'Off.'"

As several times before in Miles's electric career, the piece "Directions," the set-opener of the Bartz/Jarrett/Henderson band, provided a starting point. "I'd heard Miles perform Zawinul's piece when he played the Royal Festival Hall in London in [November 13] 1971," Buckmaster said. "It was a very exciting concert. I always felt that Miles's studio recording of 'Directions' was a little stodgy, but the live version took off like a train, with tremendous speed and power. It sounded like Indian music because of the diminished scale they were using. It had a cosmic ambience, which was one of the ingredients I wanted to bring to this recording, and combine it with Stockhausen's influence."

"I was also practicing Bach's Prelude for the first unaccompanied cello suite at Miles's house," Buckmaster continued. "It is a nice rhythmic piece with a pedal G bass. Miles was fascinated and wanted me to play it every day. He said, 'Listen, make a piece like that. Use that as the basis for a piece.' But I was so fixated with what was maybe adolescent intensity and wanting to do this Stockhausen thing, I didn't really want to do Bach. I wish I had. It would have been an interesting departure for Miles."

Bach's influence appears to have filtered through nonetheless, but in a rather unexpected manner. Miles described how the concept of multiple voices in Bach's music reminded him of the some of the ideas of Ornette Coleman (most likely the latter's concept of "harmolodics," in which rhythm, harmony, and melody are treated as equal and independent entities). Thus musicians may play similar phrases, but in entirely different keys, or the drummer may base his rhythm on a melodic phrase, or a melody player may imitate a rhythmic pattern. Like in Bach's music, several voices can play at the same time, but unlike in Bach's music, where polyphonic voices are always subject to the overall harmony, in "harmolodics" the polyphony is usually atonal.

"Paul was into Bach and so I started paying attention to Bach while Paul was around," Miles remarked. "I had begun to realize that some of the things Ornette Coleman had said about things being played three or four ways, independently of each other, were true because Bach had also composed that way. And it could be real funky and down."[3]

As so often when dealing with musicians, Miles threw Buckmaster in at the deep end, leaving him to figure out what to do. But apparently there was some reciprocal brainstorming, such as for the theme of "Black Satin," the only genuine theme on the album. "He sang it for me and said, 'Do something like that,'" recounted Buckmaster. "I tried to transcribe what he sang. It was his spur that brought the melody about, and my interpretation of what he sang. I added some more notes, making it go from B-flat to A major and back to B-flat, all over an E bass. I also wrote something that resembled the main bass riff, plus the drum pattern and some keyboard phrases that were to occur at certain points in the piece. I still have the manuscripts somewhere. But I think Michael Henderson changed the bass line."

Buckmaster's sketches left it up to the musicians when to play the melodies, bass lines, rhythms, and keyboard patterns. Buckmaster also specified to Miles what kind of instrumentation he wanted, and once again their ideas seemed remarkably congruent. Just as they had both envisioned funk rhythms with an "experimental edge," they also both had Indian influences in mind. "I asked for tablas and sitar, two drummers, and electronic organ," said Buckmaster. "I wanted to have a Stockhausen-like thing from the organs. Chick Corea was playing a monophonic synthesizer called the ARP Axxe. I also introduced Miles to the Yamaha YC45 electronic organ, which he incorporated in his music from then on. You can hear it particularly well on 'Rated X,' and I think Herbie Hancock played it on the beginning of 'Ife.' I myself played electric cello through a wah-wah pedal, although you wouldn't be able to identify it as a cello."

On the Corner's lengthy opening track—arbitrarily subdivided in the titles "On the Corner," "New York Girl," "Thinkin' One Thing and Doin' Another," and "Vote for Miles"—was recorded on June 1. The size and instrumentation of the line-up was reminiscent of that of *Bitches Brew,* with three keyboard players (Herbie Hancock on organ, Harold "Ivory" Williams on electric piano, and Chick Corea on ARP synthesizer), John McLaughlin on electric guitar, two drummers (Jack DeJohnette, and Billy Hart from Hancock's band), and two percussionists (Don Alias and Badal Roy). In addition, there were Dave Liebman on saxophone, Collin Walcott (of the band Oregon) on sitar, Paul Buckmaster on electric cello, and Michael Henderson on electric bass.

Liebman was another important discovery for Miles. The then twenty-four-year-old saxophonist had studied with Lennie Tristano and Charles Lloyd and had experience playing with the jazz-rock band Ten Wheel Drive as well as on John McLaughlin's *My Goals Beyond.* He eventually joined Miles's live band in January of 1973. Badal Roy had come to Miles's attention three years earlier through McLaughlin. "In 1969 I was playing in an Indian restaurant with [Khalil] Balakrishna," Roy remembered. "For months we had this guitar player visiting the restaurant for vegetarian food. I never asked his name, he never asked my name, but whenever Bala and I took a break, we played together with him. One day he said, 'Miles is playing just next door at the Village Vanguard, I'd like to introduce you guys to him. Just come and play for ten minutes.' So Bala and I ran there, played for ten minutes, and came back. That was our first introduction. Then Miles asked Bala to play on some studio sessions [taking place November of 1969 to February of 1970], and John [McLaughlin] asked me to play on his album *My Goals Beyond.* In 1972 Teo got my number, I suppose from John, and asked me to come to what turned out to be the first *On the Corner* session."

Despite Buckmaster's elaborate preparations, the June 1 session went in an entirely different direction than he had intended. "For all the sessions I had said to Miles that I wanted the musicians to play like on *Bitches Brew,* with one drummer focusing on hi-hat and playing a straight snare, and the other on the ride and playing 'second line' snare, New Orleans style, the stuttering snare," Buckmaster recalled. "Jack DeJohnette is a master of this. It is the root of the funk drumming style. I had given the musicians my scores, and sang my phrases to the drummers, and they started playing them. Miles said, 'Good, leave it like that,' but I wanted to say, 'That's not what I mean!' The problem was that instead of playing the grooves I'd written, they played the fills, and they became the groove. This is why I find the end result unfree and constricting. Although I like steady grooves—they become an almost neutral backdrop that doesn't interfere—the rhythm was never intended by me to be as obsessively repetitious as it became."

"Paul Buckmaster came in with some charts, but I don't think anybody followed them. I don't think we ever did the charts," recalled Michael Henderson. "We were all set up," Badal Roy added, "and Miles came in after some time, and said to me, 'You, start.' There was nothing prepared. Zero. Since I hadn't done any rehearsals, I was a little scared. So I began this improvised groove on the tablas, and I remember that Herbie Hancock got my groove, and said 'Yeah,' and started to play, and then everybody joined in. And we just kept rolling for an hour. Miles came over to me after we had finished, and said that it sounded good. Normally, if he didn't like something, he'd stop the band abruptly, listen to the tapes, come back again, and then start again. But in this case we played easily for a whole hour nonstop. It just happened."

"I was at the doctor's office, and my mother called me there, saying that Teo Macero had called, and wanted me to be in the studio like yesterday," Dave Liebman remembered. "So I rushed to Columbia Studios, and got there by 12:30, realizing that most sessions were from ten to one. When I walked in, Miles saw me, and motioned me to come in. Lots of people were at their instruments poised to play, and I think he was instructing Jack DeJohnette. Then he signaled me to get out my horn and pushed me towards the mike, and I started playing without really knowing what was going on. I couldn't hear anything, because everybody was amplified and plugged in directly to the board, and there were no headphones available for me. I could only hear the drums, percussion, and the clicking noises of the keyboards. So you can hear me fumbling around trying to find the right key. It was just play. I only remember doing one track. Miles asked me to join his band, but I said I couldn't because I was working with Elvin Jones. And then he was gone."

The musicians' testimonies suggest that the session was as casual as the sessions for *Ascenseur pour l'Échafaud,* when Miles handed the musicians musical sketches they had not seen before, or *In a Silent Way,* when he called Zawinul the morning of the session, telling him to "bring some music." However, despite this relaxedness bordering on the offhand, it seems that Miles had made careful preparations. This is conveyed by Buckmaster's account, as well as by Henderson's recollection that by this stage Miles was rehearsing his bands in sections, spending much time with some but no time at all with others—an approach he initiated with *Bitches Brew*. Since Henderson was the linchpin of the band, Miles tended to spend the most time with him. "He often used to send for me to come to his house to teach me bass lines," Henderson said. "He often played them for me on his organ. I think he played me the bass lines for *On the Corner* as well. It's possible that we went over some of the lines of the English guy [Buckmaster]."

Through a mixture of rehearsing some musicians before the sessions, giving others written sketches, and offering no instructions for the rest, Miles allowed free improvisation to coexist with strong, repetitive, well-defined rhythmic, melodic, and/or harmonic foundations. These elements were very effective in keeping the musicians in the present and preventing them from slipping into habitual playing. "Miles insisted on minimal rehearsal in the studio," Buckmaster commented. "He wanted to catch freshness and unpredictability, catch the musicians without their 'commenting minds.' Otherwise they fall into clichés and go off and do their own thing. So Miles was keeping them on their edge, on their toes, and directed them into unexplored territory. There's a kind of Zen master quality to that, and in this way he brought out things in the musicians that they didn't even know they had themselves. If you listen to many of the works that the musicians who played with him did without him, they don't quite have that flash of inspiration in their playing, it's suddenly a bit mundane."

The remaining titles on *On the Corner*, "Black Satin," "One and One," "Helen Butte," and "Mr. Freedom X," are all based on one track that emerged from a session on June 6. The line-up was similar to that on June 1, with Lonnie Liston Smith taking over for Corea, saxophonist Carlos Garnett instead of Liebman, guitarist David Creamer replacing McLaughlin, and with the additions of Bennie Maupin on bass clarinet and of Mtume, who had recommended Garnett. The saxophonist had played with some rock bands in the '60s, as well as with Freddie Hubbard and Art Blakey, and would go on to become a member of Miles's live band during the second half of 1972. Nothing is known of David Creamer, other than Buckmaster's reminiscence: "David was from San Francisco, and played the more jazzy things. He also stayed at Miles's house during this period."

The track recorded on June 6 is based on a groove written by Buckmaster and then taken to another place by DeJohnette, Billy Hart, and Don Alias. "I had Xerox copies of my scores and handed them out," Buckmaster said. "Again, I was looking for some very spacey things to happen over the rhythms, and then for the rhythm to come in and out, maybe through copyediting later on during mixing—a little bit like was done several months later with 'Rated X,' but not quite as horrific sounding. I wasn't after a horror movie atmosphere. But I had nothing to do with the 'Rated X' session, so I don't know whether that was in any way based on my ideas."

"Miles had what he called the 'living room,' a rug on the floor where the Indian musicians sat with their tablas, etc.," Herbie Hancock remembered. "There were some minimal musical sketches laid out, a few notes and a few chords here and there, and big gaps leaving you to wonder what to do. Miles gave a lot of verbal instructions during the recording session. Just helping us to figure out the approach. The stuff was so loose that sometimes we wanted to go through a section so that we could figure out what questions to ask about it. Once we got those questions ironed out we'd go ahead and record. It was pretty daring music for that time."

In the final section of "Black Satin," called "Mr. Freedom X" on *On the Corner,* the bass and drums do drop out at times while the percussion continues, and at certain points the bass riff changes. The rhythm playing is more loose and open, leaving more space for abstract, "spacey" effects and turning it almost into an ambient piece. Although the rhythm section's on-off effects weren't as radical as Buckmaster had in mind, he remarked that this section came closer to his original vision.

"Black Satin" sounds much fuller and beefier than the other tracks, the result of an extensive overdubbing session that took place on July 7, and that featured Miles, Garnett, Mtume, Roy, and one or two of the following: Al Foster, Jack DeJohnette, Don Alias, or Billy Hart. Buckmaster recalled witnessing a rehearsal just before leaving New York in early July that was most likely a preparation for the July 7 overdub session. "There were rehearsals at Miles's home, including Al Foster and Harold Williams," the Briton said. "They were rehearsing material that I had participated in." Mtume remembered overdubbing hand claps with "Miles, Carlos, and myself. We did it after Carlos played his solo." Buckmaster also asserted that the abstract low synthesizer tones at 00:14 and 00:18 of "Black Satin" came from the ARP Axxe synthesizer played by Corea, and were therefore most likely taken from the June 1 session.

In his essay in the 2000 reissue of *On the Corner,* Bob Belden wrote, "Originally released on a 45-rpm single called 'The Molester,' 'Black Satin' was obviously influenced by Buckmaster. The whole concept of layering and multi-level rhythm was achieved on this track. First recorded on one sixteen-track tape machine, a basic mix was laid onto another sixteen-track machine and the whistles, bells, hand claps, and a second Davis trumpet part (an octave lower), were overdubbed."[4]

Belden also stressed how the tape manipulation and "looping" of Stockhausen and others in the classical avant-garde had influenced Buckmaster, and thereby Miles. But Buckmaster's ideas did not focus on the use of studio trickery. He was influenced by the result, not the method. In the case of *On the Corner,* it appears to have been Macero's initiative to cut and paste sounds in and out of a repetitive groove, in a manner suggestive of reggae dub and techno, trance, and dance music in later years.

After *In a Silent Way, Bitches Brew,* and *Jack Johnson,* Macero had once again taken studio postproduction a step further, dramatically impacting the resulting music. If the postproduction methods were a transcendence and inclusion of previous musical steps, so were the musical ingredients, which included *Bitches Brew,* the Indian experiments from November of 1969 to February of 1970, the funk elements of the Bartz/Jarrett/Henderson band, and added influences of Stockhausen, Buckmaster, and Coleman's "harmolodics." As with *Bitches Brew,* an amazing amount of influences had gone into the recording. But whereas in Miles's previous electric music it was still possible to point at musical elements idiomatic of a jazz aesthetic, these had all but disappeared with *On the Corner.* Bob Belden likened *On the Corner* to the music that emerged from

Duke Ellington's "jungle period," citing Bubber Miley's wah-wah–like trumpet as a possible inspiration for Miles. Although there may be parallels in the spontaneous execution and the influences of contemporary popular music in Ellington's "jungle period," it is hard to recognize explicit links to any jazz music in *On the Corner*.

The funk and rock aspects of *On the Corner* are much easier to distinguish, and it makes more sense to understand the recording in the context of these influences. However, these funk and rock influences were so disparate and so unidiomatic that countless people were completely bewildered by *On the Corner* when it came out, since then some have reevaluated their initial rejection. "I didn't think much of it," David Liebman said. "Definitely. I didn't know what it was. In retrospect I understand it a little better. I certainly like it a bit more, but I really did not know what was going on. Nobody knew. I'm not sure he even knew." "Honestly, when it came out, I only played it once," declared Badal Roy. "I didn't like it. Then three years ago the CD was released, and my son came from college one day, and was very excited, saying, 'Daddy, you played on *On the Corner!*' So I listened to it again, and this time I liked it."

"*On the Corner* is probably my least favorite Miles album," commented Paul Buckmaster. "It's a slightly bitter irony, because it was my opportunity to record with Miles and have some influence, and it turned out anything but what I was hoping it to be. But I have to admit that when I recently listened to it again, it didn't sound as bad as I thought it did. Parts of it sounded okay. Parts of 'Black Satin' have some redeeming features. But I still can't stand the opening track, and I still find the grooves too restrictive. I still have my critical faculties intact, and I think *On the Corner* leaves much to be desired as a street-funk-rock album, whatever you want to call it."

Predictably, the jazz world vilified the recording when it was released in the fall of 1972, graced, or disgraced in the eyes of some, by cartoons drawn by Corky McCoy on Miles's instructions. The atmosphere was indignant, filled with exclamations like "repetitious boredom," "repetitious crap," "an insult to the intellect of the people," and "that music is worthless."[5] Miles's other controversial excursion into jazz-rock territory, *Bitches Brew*, had led to a schism within the jazz community between those who liked it and those who did not. But with *On the Corner*, Miles and the jazz world parted company entirely. Only a few jazz critics sprung to its defense. One of them was the author of *Bitches Brew*'s original liner notes, Ralph J. Gleason, who wrote, "It is music which celebrates street life as well as the beauty of life itself."[6]

Some of the controversy caused by *On the Corner* was deliberate, and was due to the omission of personnel and recording details on the cover, leading to decades of confusion.[7] This exclusion was on Miles's explicit instructions, and, just like the generic titles used to identify the medleys on several of his live albums, it appears to have been another expression of Miles's efforts to confound critics, an attempt to take their attention away from the pointing finger and direct it towards the moon itself.

"It's the white folks that need those labels," Miles remarked in 1973. ". . . Here's my secret, man: I don't tell no one my secrets. *Nobody* knows all the instrumentation that I had in *On the Corner*. They're just guessing. I want to make the fuckin' critics think. Not even Teo [Macero] knows all the stuff that's on that record."[8] But the musicians involved were far from happy with the development. "I was pissed," stated Mtume. "I called Miles and said, 'What the fuck?' And he said, 'Mtume, I'm just so tired of people stealing my musicians. Every time I find a new cat, he just gets siphoned off.' Miles was slightly para-noid at that stage about the cats leaving him. I answered, 'Fuck that! What about credit-ing the musicians?' So we laughed about it, and I said, 'Okay, the thing is about the music." Michael Henderson recalled, "I told Teo Macero, if they didn't put the musicians' names on, I didn't want to be bothered. So the second release of *On the Corner* had the names of the musicians on the outside cover. I think Miles was making a statement."

On the Corner's sales were well below what Miles had hoped for, and rather than relate this to the impenetrable nature of the music, he blamed his manager Jack Whittemore, sacking him in favor of Neil Reshen, who had a reputation for handling difficult artists. Miles also attacked Columbia. "They don't do anything for you unless you're white or Jewish," he scoffed. "Except maybe when I got a new album out or something. By now I don't even talk to them anymore. For instance, when I showed 'em the new cover by Corky McCoy, they told me it won't help sell any albums. And *I* told 'em how to mer-chandise nigger music, man. Put Chinese on the covers. Put niggers on the covers, put brothers and sisters on 'em, whatever they're going to call us next, that's what you put on the covers to sell to us."9

In his autobiography Miles compared Columbia's failure to open up the black youth market with Hancock's *Headhunters* a year later, a commercially successful album with a not dissimilar musical concept. But he seemed to forget that Hancock's album was much more accessible, containing hummable hooks and vamps. Ironically, despite his aim of reaching black audiences, neither they, nor the rock world, found much resonance in the music. With the same, almost perverse, attitude that had bewildered jazz and rock fans alike during the previous two years, Miles had now created something that was an alien language for almost all music lovers in 1972, regardless of their background. Neverthe-less, according to percussionist Mtume, *On the Corner* did affect Miles's audience, a point that went unnoticed by the mainstream critics and media. "Especially 'Black Satin' connected with people who were into funk," said Mtume, "and after *On the Corner* the audience started to change. There was definitely a difference. Many young black people started coming to his concerts."

Reggae dub, which emerged in the mid-1970s, and the hip-hop, dance, techno, house, and trance music movements of the 1980s and 1990s have extensively explored the concept of repeating lengthy circular bass lines and rhythms and overlaying them with sound effects. *On the Corner* has therefore gained a new recognition and under-standing, particularly among hip-hop and dance music circles and with modern avant-garde groups and musicians such as Underworld, Leftfield, The Orb, Bill Laswell, Jah Wobble, Defunkt, Vernon Reid, and James "Blood" Ulmer. Far from being forgotten as one of the many weird '70s experiments that were only fun while they lasted, *On the Cor-ner* is increasingly being reappraised by critics around the world. "Brilliant, envelope-stretching ensemble work," wrote *Q* magazine in a four-star (out of five) review in the late '90s.10 And this was just one of many recent accolades. This newfound recognition supports the assertion that the recording pioneered a new musical paradigm that we are only now beginning to understand.

Nonetheless, despite the way our ears have been stretched during the last three decades, *On the Corner* continues to be challenging listening. The absence of musical structures, harmonic development, and melodic content poses genuine problems. One recognizable tune in fifty-four minutes is not an enticing score. As on *Bitches Brew,* the musicians blend into a complex, rhythmic collective. But the latter recording contains a number of distinctive features, such as McLaughlin's lead-rhythm playing, Maupin's bass clarinet, the coloring of the electric pianos, a great variety of vamps, grooves, and melodic themes, and most of all, the interplay between Miles's powerful playing and his ensemble. The musicians on *On the Corner,* on the other hand, have little chance to distinguish their individual identities. All solos, including Miles's wah-wah trumpet, are set far back in the mix, and Miles does not dominate the proceedings as he did on *Bitches Brew.* The groove in the opening track lacks the interest and depth to transport the listener over more than, say, ten minutes.

On the other hand, "Black Satin" has the advantages of its fairly short length and clearly identifiable groove and themes and "Mr. Freedom X" has an ambient atmosphere strong enough, and a sonic soundscape enticing enough, to compensate for the lack of more traditional musical information. The panoramic density of the rhythm section was also new for the time, as was the way instruments like percussion, sitar, and synthesizer were used. The echoes of Stockhausen in the ambient and abstract textures foreshadowed late-twentieth-century digital sampling and sound design. Saxophone, bass clarinet, electric guitar and keyboards, and wah-wah trumpet often appear to be soloing in their own universes in what appears to be an echo of Coleman's "harmolodics" concept. John McLaughlin's solo is particularly outstanding, but other than this the solo instruments only briefly surface to the top of the river of rhythm before submerging again in the rhythmic tapestry, in a manner similar to techno and dance music.

Few of the various holons included in the recording—funk rhythms, jazz improvisation, Indian sounds, and postwar European avant-garde—are transcended to a new level. The whole is less than the sum of the parts. *On the Corner* is an important, influential, visionary, and courageous work of avant-garde "heralding the new," in the sense described by Ken Wilber in Chapter 6. But even when viewed from the perspective of the musical developments in the late-twentieth and early twenty-first century, *On the Corner* remains one of those flawed experiments resulting from taking the road less traveled, where it is far easier to lose one's way than when trotting along the beaten path.

Columbia intends to eventually release a boxed set with *On the Corner* material, which may give new insights into this recording and how the end result was constructed during postproduction. *Panthalassa,* by the well-known bassist, producer, remix engineer, experimenter, and world music pioneer Bill Laswell, also sheds new light on *On the Corner,* as well as on other aspects of Miles's music from 1969 to 1974. Issued in 1998, *Panthalassa*[11] is a musical suite constructed from the original multitrack tapes of *In a Silent Way,* "Black Satin," and several other tracks recorded from 1972 to 1974. Laswell did not add any additional parts, although some of his electronic treatments sound as if he did. Instead he created a new instrumental balance and transposed various instrumental parts to other places through a process called "reconstruction and mix translation."[12]

Laswell's ambition was to reinterpret Miles's music from 1969 to 1972 via a late-twentieth-century musical perspective, using cut-and-paste postproduction techniques similar to those Macero had used. "Macero and the other people who worked on these records were from a classical and jazz background," explained Laswell. "And I can't imagine people with a background like that having a clue of what to do with the kind of stuff Miles was producing. The music Miles was making at the time had nothing to do with jazz, and there was no reference for it. *On the Corner* was the beginning of mutant hiphop for me, and I think it was too new for them. I don't think they got it. How was it supposed to sound? So one of my prime objectives was to re-mix and re-construct Miles's music from a non-jazz perspective."[13]

"People were to a large extent controlling music for which they didn't have a fitting vision," Laswell elaborated. "Miles's music was dealing with repetitive rhythms and repetitive bass lines, the same things that you would hear being developed at the time in rock and funk and R&B and reggae, and the same thing that you hear today in drum 'n' bass and techno. You have to approach that kind of music with a different sensibility, with more of a rock sensibility. You want to make the bass big and heavy, the drums powerful and hard-hitting, and in a piece with very dense rhythmic patterns you want clarity so that you can hear what's being played. Macero's editing and cut-and-paste methods were in some respects quite innovative and pioneering, and the remix culture caught up with them some twenty years later. But sadly Macero's approach was also often a kind of shuffling process, trying to construct something that could be put out as a record. It wasn't really comparable to the way people now use recording studios and technology creatively to create new music. The studio wasn't used as an instrument. It was more a matter of intuitively trying to determine a result, fairly quickly, and in some cases fairly sloppily. It could have been done better."

Laswell's criticisms of Macero's work have been ill received in some quarters. Paul Buckmaster was one of the many who sprang to Macero's defense, stating, with reason, "Macero is very creative. He was probably a jazz guy at heart, and he was dealing with music that nobody had a reference for. But he still went out there and experimented. Maybe he didn't get it 100 percent right, but for the time it was amazing."

The controversy over Laswell's remarks has led some to condemn *Panthalassa*. But whether one agrees with Laswell's comments about Macero or not, the bassist and producer managed to offer a new perspective on music that had been misunderstood and/or ignored for two to three decades, demonstrating that these sometimes freakish-sounding experiments had unrecognized meaning. Jazz and rock lovers have both acknowledged his efforts. Jazz critic John Fordham wrote, "a tautness and purpose has been brought to hours of exploratory studio time," making it sound "startlingly contemporary."[14] Music writer Richard Williams opined, "Laswell does something exceptional: he makes this music sound more like itself."[15] And Jah Wobble, rock bassist and onetime member of the postpunk band Public Image Ltd, said, "The weird thing is that when I thought of *On the Corner*, I have always heard it in my head the way Bill mixed it. That's how it really is. Bill's is the one. That's the real deal."

A number of factors contribute to *Panthalassa*'s success. Laswell created a tight musical structure, rarely sustaining grooves for longer than six or seven minutes and making sure that musical events of interest happen regularly. In doing so he took away the longueurs and noodling that marred some of Miles's music from this era. Dave Liebman has remarked, "The music had no beginnings and no endings."[16] And much of Miles's music of this era therefore sounds like a slice taken from a much larger musical tapestry. Although *Panthalassa* is organized as a continuous musical suite, Laswell created clear beginning and end points for the different sections, resulting in more satisfying musical structures. Moreover, through the use of modern studio technology Laswell was able to extrapolate sounds from the multitracks that add color and depth, and an almost orchestral texture. This gives the music echoes of the more arranged music Miles recorded in the mid- and late 1980s. Laswell also adjusted the instrumental balance in the way he described, creating clarity for bass, drums, and percussion in a way that has become a crucial feature of modern music. And finally, he added a degree of sonic subtlety and sophistication, smoothing out rough edges and making many sounds more attractive. This is Miles's late '60s and early '70s music imbued with '90s perfectionist production values. But it comes at a price: The music loses in spontaneity and here-and-now aliveness and the instant interaction between the musicians is less apparent, in some cases almost unnoticeable.

Panthalassa opens with music from *In a Silent Way*, which benefits from the improvements in sonic quality and a tighter structure, whereas "Black Satin," which follows, gains in power and attractiveness because of the substantial improvements in the clarity and depth of the many rhythm instruments. "Black Satin" is succeeded by a previously unreleased track, named "What If" by Laswell,[17] and dated by Bob Belden to June 2, 1972.[18] The personnel included Miles, Garnett, McLaughlin, Creamer, Corea, Hancock, Williams, Walcott, Henderson, Hart, DeJohnette, Roy, and Alias. "What If" is built around one groove, sounding much looser than *On the Corner*'s opening track. Although fairly inconsequential in its own right, the track is effective in the context of Laswell's medley.

The same goes for "Agharta Prelude Dub," titled by Laswell because its melody also appears on *Agharta*, Miles's 1975 live album. This tune is a development of a theme Miles played in the medleys "Funky Tonk" and "Inamorata" on *Live-Evil*, respectively at 16:51 and 00:10. The groove can also be seen as a development of the groove played at this point in "Inamorata." Like "What If," Belden dated "Agharta Prelude Dub" to June 2, 1972, but due to the differences in feel and personnel, and to the fact that the track did not make a live appearance until April of 1973, it was most likely recorded much later. Lohmann suggests November 29, 1972,[19] and this appears a more probable date. The musicians were most likely Miles, Garnett, Cedric Lawson on keyboards, Balakrishna on electric sitar, guitarist Reggie Lucas, Henderson, Foster, Mtume, and Badal Roy.

The differences between Laswell's and Macero's approaches are most extreme on the track "Rated X," recorded on September 6, 1972, with Miles, Lawson, Balakrishna, Roy, Henderson, Foster, Mtume, and guitarist Reggie Lucas. Included on *Get up with It*, "Rated X" is Miles's first-ever track on which he does not play trumpet. It was wholly constructed in the editing room by Macero, who culled Miles's Yamaha YC45 organ playing from another session and pasted it over the dense rhythm. Dominated by the ear-wrenching, dissonant, and overbearing organ clusters, the impenetrable, muffled rhythm section pounds away relentlessly for almost seven minutes. In an echo of Buckmaster's on-off ideas for *On the Corner*, the rhythm section is occasionally cut out by the mixer, leaving the organ to fend for itself.

"On vinyl 'Rated X' always sounded very, very dense and unbelievably bad and muddy, with the organ sound pushing everything else in the background," Laswell said. "But the rhythm tracks were recorded very well. It's just how they were equalized and balanced in the mix that was the problem. They clearly didn't have a clue how to deal with these dense rhythms. But for today's ears the density and detail of those rhythm tracks makes them sound very modern. In my version I mixed the organ very low to make space for the details in the rhythm track."

Laswell's mix opens up a deep sonic space for a unique and fascinating rhythmic universe in which Lucas's rhythm guitar and Balakrishna's electric sitar can be heard complementing each other. "The transcendence and essence of the music in this piece emerged with compelling relevance for contemporary times," remarked Stuart Nicholson.[20] Although improved almost beyond recognition, the rhythm remains abrasive and unrelenting. Finally, "Billy Preston," which was recorded on December 8, 1972, and "He Loved Him Madly," which dates from June 19 or 20, 1974, complete *Panthalassa.* Apart from sonic sophistication, the new versions don't add anything significant to the originals, both of which were included on *Get up with It.*[21]

In mentioning the inferior sonic quality of "Rated X" on the original vinyl release of *Get up with It,* Laswell drew attention to the important issue of the relationship between our perception of music and the quality of consumer playback equipment. As a rule of thumb, the more abstract the music is, the better the playback equipment needs to be. The essential elements of a Beatles song or a Mozart piece are usually clear, hummable melodies and easily definable chord structures, which can survive playback via a small transistor radio or a bad vinyl record. By contrast, music by Stockhausen, or Brian Eno's ambient music, or most of Miles's '70s music, will hardly come across on such equipment because these kinds of music depend on color, texture, and atmosphere for their meaning. In this situation reasonable sonic reproduction is essential. It is very possible that some listeners who couldn't come to terms with some of Miles's recordings in the '70s simply had bad vinyl pressings or bad stereo systems.

The introduction of the CD in the '80s was presented to the public as the solution to all these problems, but this proved to be misleading. Digital sound is still a very inexact science. There can be astonishing discrepancies between different CD pressings of the same album and, surprisingly, vinyl can sometimes sound better than CDs. When Sony kindly supplied me with a CD copy of *Agharta,* it sounded flat and lifeless. Puzzled, I compared the CD to my twenty-four-year-old vinyl copy. Despite having been played hundreds of times, the vinyl version still sounded infinitely better, with more punch, dynamics, depth, aliveness, and clarity. Had the CD been my first introduction, I might never have liked the album much. Sony/Columbia is addressing the problem of the varying quality of CD releases with its recent Miles Davis reissue campaign. In the case of their Master Sound series, they are raising the sound quality through a remastering and a process called Super Bit Mapping. Especially when listening to Miles's "difficult" '70s music, it is crucially to remain aware of this issue.

Returning to the narrative about the events of 1972, on June 12 there was a third session inspired by Buckmaster's sketches and ideas. Two tracks were recorded, "Jabali," the

African name of drummer Billy Hart, and "Ife," which was named after Mtume's daughter. The former has never been released, but "Ife" was issued on *Big Fun*. This time Miles had amassed Carlos Garnett on soprano sax, Bennie Maupin on bass clarinet, Harold Williams on electric piano, Lonnie Liston Smith on organ, Michael Henderson on bass, Al Foster and Billy Hart on drums, and Badal Roy and Mtume on percussion. The only confusion here concerns Buckmaster's assertion that Hancock played the YC45 organ, although he is not credited on the sleeve notes of *Big Fun*.

"'Ife' came into being through a similar process as 'Black Satin,'" Buckmaster commented. "I had written lots of keyboard phrases that were to occur at certain points in the piece. They were little fragments, phrases, or fills of two, four, or eight bars long. The musicians interpreted them, and completely distorted them. The main melody of 'Ife' and the chord accompaniment are mine. I think the bass line is Michael's. The opening phrases on organ were written by me and interpreted by Herbie."

Compared to the relentless grooves of *On the Corner*, "Ife" is a breath of fresh air. The melody and groove are light and elegant, the mix transparent, and the solos for the most part interesting and engaging. Buckmaster was happier with this piece than with *On the Corner*, saying, "It has charm to it, a little bit more space, and direction. 'Ife' breathes more. Just like 'Jabali,' for which I had also prepared some keyboard phrases."

Leaving aside any hitherto unknown sessions, the overdub session for "Black Satin" on July 7 marked the last occasion during which Miles invited a selection of his Stock Company Players for recording sessions. From this point onwards he returned to his pre-1968 working method of recording with his live band and occasionally inviting a guest musician. This meant a convergence of his live and studio directions, with studio experiments often immediately finding their way to the live stage and vice versa. There are no historical data that explain this shift in direction, but it naturally indicates that the approach of throwing together different combinations of musicians to see what would happen was no longer giving Miles the results he wanted.

In September Miles assembled a new live band, with Carlos Garnett on saxophone, Cedric Lawson on keyboards, Reggie Lucas on guitar, Khalil Balakrishna on electric sitar, plus Henderson, Foster, Roy, and Mtume. Cedric Lawson was an unknown player recommended by Mtume, whereas Reggie Lucas, then nineteen years old, was introduced to Miles by Harold Williams. "I was working as a musician in Philadelphia, having started very young playing in bars and clubs while I was studying," Lucas recalled. "Harold Williams, a friend of mine from Baltimore, and I were playing with Billy Paul. Harold found out that Miles was auditioning musicians to play in his group, and was looking for a guitarist and a keyboardist. Harold invited me to come to an audition."

For unknown reasons Harold Williams never joined Miles's live band, but Lucas was included in the new band Miles took into the recording studio on September 6, for the session that resulted in "Rated X." It was not an auspicious start, and somehow it appears that this band never quite hit its stride. Its live debut was on September 10 at the Ann Harbor Blues and Jazz Festival. The band's repertoire featured old favorites like "Honky Tonk" and "Right Off," but emphasized recently recorded material like "Ife," "Black Satin," and "Rated X" (which replaced "Directions" as the set opener). Nearly three weeks later, on September 29, the band played the Philharmonic Hall in New York. This concert was documented on *Miles Davis in Concert,* which, like *On the Corner,* featured

Corky McCoy's quirky cartoons. On the inside there was a cartoon of a white rock band, with the words "Foot Fooler" written across the bass drums. According to Mtume this was a dig at white rock music. "Miles was saying they were faking it, it was really about the funk in African music. So he's calling this rock shit 'Foot Fooler,'" said Mtume.

If Mtume's information is correct, Miles was shooting himself in the foot because *In Concert* is the weakest officially released album of his whole pre-1976 electric period, making him and the band sound like the very "foot foolers" he tried to mock. *In Concert* begins with a drawn out version of "Rated X," which surpasses the studio version because the dominant organ is removed in favor of solos by Miles and Garnett, even though the rhythm section never really locks into a satisfying groove. "Honky Tonk" is marred by the same problem. The grooves of both live sections that feature material from *Jack Johnson* also do not come close to the power of the studio versions. Although interestingly, at 02:37 in "Theme from Jack Johnson," the band follows McLaughlin's original modulation from E to B-flat, which Henderson missed, to prepare Miles's entrance. "Ife" is slightly more appealing, if only because it travels through several different bass vamps. With the new, four-note bass line that begins this version, "Ife" would become one of the most-often-played compositions of Miles's electric period, and the only one to survive his silent period, being performed until August of 1982. Finally, *In Concert* contains two brief nods to Miles's '60s repertoire with half-minute versions of "Sanctuary" (not "The Theme" as erroneously indicated on the liner notes) closing each set. They are the last-known performances of the piece by Miles.

It is unclear why there's such a stiffness and sterility to almost all the rhythms on *In Concert*. As was to be expected, jazz writers blamed the malaise on the "undeniably less talented jazz players."[22] However, this once again missed the point: Miles was not looking for highly skilled jazz players but was trying to forge a rhythmic collective. Perhaps many of the relatively inexperienced players were either, as in November 1969, playing "scared of Miles," or found themselves in a situation similar to that of Ndugu Chancler almost a year earlier, with Miles "trying to pull something new out of them without them knowing what he was trying to pull out." Also, although Miles's wah-wah playing had interesting textural qualities, on this recording he sounds nowhere as if he's capable of, in the words of Buckmaster, "Changing the whole thing with just one note. Just one note, and everything would come into line! I found that this didn't happen so much on *On the Corner,* and even less after that."

"That band was brand new at that point," offered Lucas by way of explanation. "I consider that very first record to be stiff and tentative . . . although it had some very wonderful moments. But if you had heard that same band three weeks later, we would have blown you away! The Philharmonic is just not a particularly good place to perform with a loud rock 'n' roll band, let alone record it. The acoustics were not suitable for what we were doing. It's interesting that Miles chose to introduce the new band prior to much rehearsal or even knowing each other well on a personal level."

The nonet played a few more concerts, including a concert with an offshoot of The Grateful Dead, New Riders of The Purple Sage, in Palo Alto on October 1, until Miles once again put himself out of action, this time not through drug-related illnesses, but in a car crash. At 8 A.M. on October 9, driving after taking a sleeping pill, Miles fell asleep behind the wheel of his Lamborghini, hit a traffic island, and broke both ankles. In addition to creating an enforced layoff, the accident greatly exacerbated his hip problems—a more serious consequence.

Mark Rothbaum, who worked for Neil Reshen from 1973 to 1978 and looked after Miles's affairs, recalled, "Miles had tremendous orthopedic difficulties after the car accident, and was in a lot of pain. There was an inch difference between his right and left leg, and this had a big effect on his body. After the crash he was using lots of cocaine, and any pain medication he could lay his hands on. The influx of cocaine on the West Side of Manhattan around this time was tremendous, and destroyed a lot of people's lives. Miles was a man who was obviously able to make a lot of money, and he was the prey of many people who liked to separate him from it."

All this resulted in a further nosedive of Miles's already deteriorating personal situation. He revealed, "I was making around half a million dollars a year, but I was also spending a lot of money on all the things I was doing. I was spending a lot on cocaine. Everything had started to blur after that car accident." He added that he kept his house dark all the time, because it reflected his mood. When he broke his promise to Jackie Battle, his other "spiritual woman," she, like Marguerite Eskridge, abandoned him, leaving Miles feeling "sorrier than a motherfucker."[23]

In the middle of all this turmoil, Miles still found time to record two more tracks that exemplified his "circular"[24] approach to writing (i.e., music without beginnings or endings). While walking on crutches, Miles recorded "Agharta Prelude Dub," with the same band he had put together in September. This song was most likely recorded on November 29, and "Billy Preston" on December 8. They are a moderate return to form. Both feature much more coherent rhythm playing than before his accident. "Agharta Prelude Dub" is graced with a memorable theme and a strange, lazy feel, and "Billie Preston" hangs on a mesmerizing, never-ending, circular, interlocking rhythm and bass guitar pattern. This was Miles's last-known musical activity in 1972, making for a changeable year in which he was more often off than on.

Mtume agreed that this period was musically rather indeterminate, and argued that, "*On the Corner* was the seed, and the seed can never match the plant. It was the beginning of the formation of a new direction. There was a lot of searching going on before the direction became clear." Miles's strange and uneven experimentations were to start bearing fruit in the following year.

Chapter Ten

THE FINAL FRONTIER

"We were going in directions where no one had gone before."

—Mtume

During the first months of 1973 Miles initiated several changes to his live band, such as the replacements of his saxophonist and his keyboardist, the addition of a second guitarist, and eventually the dismissal of the Indian musicians and the new keyboardist. It is unknown whether Miles evaluated the flawed, on-off results of his 1972 experiments in terms similar to those discussed in the previous chapter, but his actions suggest that he was dissatisfied and that he wanted to refocus his direction. Saxophonist Carlos Garnett was fired in the first days of the year. Since both Lucas and Mtume have asserted that his playing fit well with the band's musical direction, the only available explanation concerns Garnett's attempt to get a record deal during the layoff following Miles's October 1972 car accident. Perhaps Miles concluded that Garnett's solo ambitions carried the risk of losing his saxophonist midtour. In any case, Dave Liebman was hired as Garnett's replacement, and the new nonet immediately went into the studio on January 4, to record some as yet unreleased material. Liebman's live debut with Miles's band came eight days later, on January 12, at the Village East (formerly the Fillmore East) in New York. "I don't know what I played," Liebman recalled. ". . . Every once in a while he'd look at me . . . [from] under the glasses. I'd play. [It was] music that sounded like it came from *Star Wars* or from the future."[1]

On February 14 there was another studio session, the results of which remain unreleased. Tapes of this session were given to writer Stephen Davis, who noted that they contained "bluesy, percussive mixes dated 2/14/73 with Miles playing organ . . . similar to 'Rated X.'"[2] "I tried to show my piano player [Cedric Lawson] what was happening," Miles explained to Davis. "And it wound up sounding so good with me playing on it that Teo Macero wanted to keep it that way."[3]

The extended use of the organ was a new development in Miles's music. The electric piano had been central to his electric experiments since he first asked Herbie Hancock to play the instrument for the recording of "Water on the Pond" in December of 1967. But during the course of 1972, influenced by the ideas of Stockhausen and Buckmaster and the discovery of the Yamaha YC45 organ, Miles increasingly wanted his keyboardists to play abstract and textural sounds. Organs and synthesizers were more suited to this approach, and as a result, the concert at the Philharmonic Hall of September 29, 1972, had marked the electric piano's swan song. Lawson had played organ and synthesizer on the subsequent sessions in November and December, resulting in "Agharta Prelude Dub" and "Billy Preston."

The fact that Miles felt the need to play the organ himself on several occasions suggests that Lawson had trouble grasping what was wanted from him. And it is not surprising that the keyboardist was released at the start of an intermittent tour of the American and Canadian West Coast from March to May of 1973. His replacement, Lonnie Liston Smith, had played with Art Blakey, Pharoah Sanders, and Roland Kirk, and had also participated in the *On the Corner* sessions. On the evidence of bootlegs from Liston Smith's brief tenure with Miles's band, the keyboardist played the YC45 organ fairly conventionally, mainly comping rhythmically, adding some chordal textures, and taking very few solos. Balakrishna's contributions on the electric sitar were also essentially textural, and Lucas functioned mostly as a rhythm guitarist. By the end of March, Miles decided that he needed another solo voice in his band. Not surprisingly, given his love for Hendrix and the blues, his thoughts turned to an electric lead guitarist. "The guitar can take you deep into the blues," Miles said. "But since I couldn't get Jimi or B. B. King, I had to settle for the next best player out there."[4]

The man who fit the description was Chicagoan Pete Cosey, who had worked for Chess Records and had played with an impressive variety of artists from jazz, soul, blues, funk, and rock backgrounds, such as Chuck Berry, Billy Stewart, Fontella Bass, Etta James, Muddy Waters, Howlin' Wolf, and Gene Ammons, and had also helped found Earth, Wind & Fire. The guitarist had met most of the members of Miles's 1972 live band on September 10, after its baptism at the Ann Harbor Blues and Jazz Festival, where Cosey was soundman for the Art Ensemble of Chicago. Afterwards he jammed with Henderson, Lucas, and Mtume, and they were impressed with his playing. When Miles asked Mtume whether he knew a suitable additional guitarist, the percussionist immediately suggested Cosey.

"Miles called me from Canada the day Muhammad Ali got his jaw broken by Ken Norton [Saturday March 31]," Cosey recalled. "We agreed that I would meet him in Portland, Oregon, on Monday, when they had a day off. When I stepped off the hotel elevator his door was open, and we greeted each other. Miles was still on crutches because of the accident he'd had the year before, so they always saw to it that his room was close to the elevator. We ate fish and listened to music. Miles played me a tape of the concert of the previous night. I asked him what key each part was in, and then we moved on to the next song. That was our rehearsal. Miles looked surprised, and was smiling. I guess he surmised that I knew pretty much what was happening and did not need extensive rehearsal. The next night we played together. Years later he said that he did not want me at rehearsals because I knew what to play. It was also part of his system of rehearsing with sections of the band."

Cosey's immediate understanding was a sign that Miles had stumbled on a musician who could take his band to the next level. The guitarist's joining would prove a crucial factor in focusing and galvanizing the direction of the music. He became part of the nucleus of a band that stayed together until Miles's physical breakdown in September of 1975. He also participated in some sporadic, and as yet unreleased, recordings during 1976. Consisting of Miles, Cosey, Lucas, Henderson, Mtume, and Foster (and usually augmented by a saxophonist, such as Dave Liebman, and occasionally other musicians), this core sextet has sometimes been called the "Cosey band." However, several band members objected to this label since it distracted from the band's collective nature. The group will therefore be referred to here as "the '73–'75 band," "the funk collective," or simply "the collective." Of all his electric bands, this was arguably Miles's most adventurous, groundbreaking, and musically successful. He hinted at this in an interview in 1974, when he called it "my best band by far, because these guys can play anything."[5]

"It was the core unit," Lucas declared. "We were the ones who were closest to each other, and closest to Miles. We were the ones who conceptualized and developed the music. We had such a good intuitive understanding of what Miles wanted, it was like second nature, like breathing together. It was a very close-knit situation."

"There had been a lot of searching going on, but when Pete got in, the direction became much clearer in terms of the hardness of it, the edge," Mtume elaborated. "With Pete the rock edge really took off, because it gave us that contrast to Miles and Dave. Miles was now getting more and more clear and focused, and when the bandleader gets more focused so does the band. It was like an organic, symbiotic relationship."

The first sign of the renewed focus and direction came within days of Cosey's arrival, when an elegant and bluesy vamp, known as "Zimbabwe," was introduced at a concert in Seattle on April 5. A week later, on April 12, at a concert in Greensboro, four additional pieces had their live premiere: "Moja," "Nne," "Tune in 5," and "Agharta Prelude," a revamped, in both senses of the word, "Agharta Prelude Dub." "Honky Tonk" and "Rated X" had already been removed from the regular live repertoire in January and "Black Satin" was dropped in June, leaving "Ife" as the only remaining piece from the experiments of 1972.

More changes followed. Roy and Balakrishna's Indian instruments appeared to blunt the band's newfound hard edge, and in May Miles released them. This meant the end of his two Indian-influenced phases, November of 1969 to February of 1970 and June of 1972 to May of 1973. The experiments had resulted in a great amount of unrewarding music, and a few gems, such as "Double Image" and "Recollections." Badal Roy's tablas had always added rhythmic density and substance, but Balakrishna's sitar only played a significant role when adding texture to ambient pieces like "Guinnevere," "Recollections," and "Mr. Freedom X." Indian music does not share the common roots of blues, jazz, rock, funk, and African music, and an understanding of its inherent dynamics and structures is imperative for a successful integration with Western music. According to Roy, Miles rarely asked him about Indian culture or music, and it appears that Miles treated the Indian influence as an exotic color, with little consideration for its workings. The mixed results of Miles's Indian experiments therefore hardly come as a surprise.[6]

Lonnie Liston Smith was fired around the same time as Roy and Balakrishna, most likely because his playing was too traditional and he had problems similar to Lawson's in understanding what Miles wanted from him. In a review of a concert of the West Coast tour, writer and guitarist Eugene Chadbourne noted, "Several times Miles, perhaps dissatisfied at the sound of the organ, limped over to the instrument to demonstrate what he wanted."[7] Just as Miles had not been able to find a guitarist who understood his intentions from 1967 to 1968, he now had problems finding a suitable keyboardist. As a result he decided, for the first time in his career, not to hire a live-band keyboard player, creating a situation that continued until August of 1983.

Drawing on his experiences with "Rated X" and the unreleased blueslike track Stephen Davis had heard, Miles now played organ himself. He mostly used the instrument to cue new musical sections or to add abstract, often highly dissonant, Stockhausen-inspired clusters, in an effort to jerk his musicians out of their habit energies. Sometimes using his elbow, he carried on doing this until well into the '80s. The arthritis that was affecting his hands probably in part explained his elbow technique, as does the fact that he never played solos or technically complex parts on keyboards. "I just play it for Dave [Liebman] and different little sounds and shit," Miles asserted. "Reggie [Lucas] can play the same things that I can play. I taught him to make the same sounds."[8]

"I'll grant the old man that one, sure," chuckled Lucas when confronted with Miles's statement. "He taught me a lot. I used to play a Gibson 335 semihollow guitar. Miles wanted me to play a solid body because it looked more like a rock 'n' roll guitar. I played a wah-wah pedal occasionally, but Miles wanted me to play the wah-wah pedal a lot because he was very interested in that sound. In terms of the organ, Miles wanted to create certain surprising, nonconventional harmonic structures. So he encouraged me to do unique chordal things that were different from what anyone else was doing, and to make my playing complex and densely textured. Between Michael's bass lines and my chords there was often an extremely dissonant relationship. We had a lot of themes, textures, polyrhythms, polyharmonics, and polymelodies going on. It was about creating a sense of multiple textures on all levels, harmonic, melodic, rhythmic, all taking place coherently inside of the same composition."

The new septet first recorded on May 23 (again, nothing has been released of this session) and debuted live on a Japanese tour beginning on June 19, 1973. Bootlegs from this tour show the music at a higher level than before, more focused, elastic, and dynamic. With the ensemble pared down from ten to seven musicians the clutter had gone, revealing the revolutionary essence of the "funk with an experimental edge" in all its clarity.

"After Lonnie left, we really began to stretch the possibilities," Mtume commented. "Miles wanted to leave the music more open, and the chordal dimension in the tapestry was now filled between Pete and Reggie. We often called what we were doing 'improvisational funk.' We were dealing with a wall of sound, creating a wall of sound—a tapestry where things were coming at you so heavy, from so many different angles, that it was one motion. It was very complex. Yet the thing was to make it sound simple. That was our aim. We discussed this during rehearsals."

When queried about his mid-1970s music, Miles always emphasized the central role of rhythm. During a radio interview in Japan, broadcast in June of 1973, he suggested that there are more rhythmic than melodic possibilities. "We are dealing in rhythms rather than melodies. You can only use twelve notes when you write a melody."[9] And in 1974, in terms reminiscent of his explanation of *On the Corner* and of Ornette Coleman's "harmolodics" concept, Miles compared polyrhythms to Bach's polyphony: "I think it's time people changed where they put the melody. The melody can be in the bass, or a drum sound, or just a sound. I may write something around one chord. I may write something around a rhythm. . . . I always place a rhythm so it can be played three or four different ways. It's always three rhythms within one, and you can get some other ones in there too . . . It's almost like Bach."[10]

In his autobiography, Miles stressed that the "European sensibilities" had disappeared from the '73–'75 band, making way for a "deep African thing, a deep African-American groove, with a lot of emphasis on drums and rhythm, and not on individual solos. From the time that Jimi Hendrix and I had gotten tight, I had wanted that kind of sound because the guitar can take you deep into the blues."[11]

Never one to be concerned with consistency, Miles appeared in 1973 to de-emphasize the African aspect of the group's music when he remarked, "We don't play black, we don't play white, we just play what we know and feel."[12] Leaving aside musical considerations, the African influences were also a political statement. This was exemplified in the '73–'75 band's equipment, which was painted in the Black Panther colors—green, red, and black—despite the fact that Miles had said in 1971, "I am not a Black Panther or nothing like that. . . . I don't need to be, but I was raised to think like they do,"[13] and had always refused to align himself with any organized political movement.

Of course, the funk collective's explicit political declaration also exemplified the '70s zeitgeist, as did Miles's extravagant and sometimes rather awful sunglasses and clothing, and the funk influences and abundance of wah-wah sounds. Predictably, Miles's detractors saw all these colorful and controversial exterior signposts as evidence of his "selling out" to the culture of the day. But the origins of the political and musical direction of the funk collective stretched far back in time, all the way to Miles's youth and apprenticeship in St. Louis. He had indeed been raised with an acute awareness of racial issues, whereas the mid-1970s music was the climax of many previously integrated musical approaches.

Over the course of thirty years Miles had gradually stripped his music of its melodic and harmonic content, transferring most of its meaning to the polyrhythmic complexity of the rhythm section. The focus had shifted decisively towards the bottom end, of which Miles had an unusual awareness. "I would say that Miles was the most sensitive to the bass line of any musician I've ever heard or worked with," Dave Liebman pointed out. "As a melodic player he really responded to the bottom. Most guys don't hear the bass that way, they hear it as a function. Chords were not such a concern for him. He did not pay a lot of attention to that, his attention was usually on the bass and drums—especially on Michael [Henderson], who was the key to that band."

With its dense, funky, bluesy, and African rhythms, the music of the funk collective was the pinnacle of Miles's search for the essence of rhythm. And yet there was much more to it. It was also the outcome of Miles's blues roots, his incorporation of folk, rock, soul, and funk influences, which began in the late '60s, and his lifelong experience in organizing music. The last element had developed from his lessons in band management with Eddie Randle's Blue Devils, his improvisation with Charlie Parker, and his collective improvisation with the second great quintet. In addition, the band integrated Stockhausen influences, abstract textures, and the idea of working with short, multiapplicable musical phrases, which was introduced by Buckmaster for the recording of On the Corner, and was reminiscent of Coleman's harmolodics concept.

Miles had tried to transcend and include all of these elements during 1972, with mostly awkward results. The funk collective's success, by contrast, was due to the unique range of talents the players possessed and the chemistry between them. Henderson, Lucas, Mtume, and Cosey were all completely at home in rock, funk, and soul, and the latter two also had experience playing jazz. Cosey developed into a superlative soloist who boosted the band with a combination of Hendrix's wild energy and some of the most advanced weirdness ever performed on a guitar. Under Miles's tutelage, Lucas began hitting his stride as an infectious rhythm player, excelling in the repetitive grooves idiomatic to funk. Although a jazz drummer at heart, Foster turned out to be a natural in playing a driving, Buddy Miles–inspired, open hi-hat drum style. Locking in perfectly with the African rhythms played by Mtume, Foster kept the band focused and propelled it to lift-off. Together, Lucas, Foster, and Mtume released Henderson from his role as the band's rhythmic anchor. The bass riffs were still the "key," the pivot around which the band revolved, but Henderson now also had the freedom to vary his bass lines, which allowed him to play behind or in front of the beat, contract and expand his lines, play ornamental lines, or try out completely new parts.

Like that of the Bartz/Jarrett/Henderson band, the funk collective's regular repertoire consisted of about a dozen pieces. But it was a sign of the collective's increased creativity and versatility that its live repertoire and set order were more flexible and that it regularly tried out new pieces, as well as occasionally performed Miles's '50s material, such as "Milestones," "All Blues," and "So What." On its three officially released live albums, *Dark Magus, Agharta,* and *Pangaea,* most of the music is once again grouped in medleys, identified by generic names. In the case of *Dark Magus* these are "Moja," "Wili," "Tatu," and "Nne" (which is Swahili for 1-4, referring to the four vinyl sides of the original double album). The whole of *Pangaea* was divided into just two titles, "Zimbabwe" and "Gondwana." (Like "Pangaea," the latter title referred to one of the Earth's original supercontinents.) Once again, Jan Lohmann, Peter Losin, and especially Enrico Merlin have provided some fingers pointing to the moon, and identified and named the different pieces that make up these medleys.[14]

The typical set list of the funk collective began with a wild, cacophonous sequence consisting of "Moja" and "Nne," often with "Tune in 5" as a bridge that usually lasted half an hour or more. "Moja" and "Nne" are closely related, almost always played in tandem, and hence sometimes referred to in this book as "Moja-Nne." "Tune in 5" was the band's only musical idea that had neither a recognizable bass line nor a theme. Purely based on a polyrhythm in five over which a variety of riffs and themes were played, it could appear several times during a concert to approach a piece from a different angle, or as a springboard towards another piece. The "Moja-Nne" section had the same function as "Directions" from 1970 to 1971, overwhelming the audience with a musical knockout punch at the very beginning of the concert. During the Japanese tour of the summer of 1973 another wild and ferocious piece, "Tatu," was introduced. The piece was promoted to alternative set opener in the course of 1974, sometimes in conjunction with "Agharta Prelude." Together they had exactly the same knockout function as "Moja-Nne." These relentless and uncompromising opening sections apparently alienated many jazz lovers, leading them to dismiss the music as "another wearying exercise in spinning out a two-chord theme."[15]

The rest of the pieces or vamps were much more melodic, lyrical, and approachable. The themeless vamps of "Willie Nelson," usually played over "Tune in 5" and "Right

Off," provided nods to the past. "Zimbabwe" did not have a main melody, but its elegant, bluesy vamp often inspired lengthy blues-inspired improvisations. "Ife" became a highlight and focus point of almost every set the band played. Underpinned by a vamp based on the four-note bass riff introduced at the Philharmonic Hall in September of 1972, Buckmaster's seven-note theme was the only remaining ingredient from the 1972 studio version. The piece was sometimes stretched to over half an hour and was used as a showcase for extensive atmospheric experimentation. Merlin compared its function to that of "Dark Star" for The Grateful Dead.

The sunny "Calypso Frelimo" was introduced in July of 1973 after the band's return from the Japanese tour. Recorded in the studio in September, it will be discussed below. "Wili," also known as "For Dave" (Dave Liebman ascribes the latter title to Miles[16]), first surfaced in October of 1973 and was another slow, atmospheric piece that sometimes whipped up to a riveting funk frenzy. "Maiysha" and "Mtume" were both recorded in the studio in October of 1974 and made their way into the live repertoire from there. They, too, will be looked at more closely further ahead. The band also incorporated several references to popular music—for example, with a track that has become known as "Latin" but was, according to Cosey, titled "Mr. Foster" by Miles and was based on the Minnie Ripperton song "Loving You." Recorded in the studio on May 5, 1975, "Latin/Mr. Foster" was never officially released, neither were several other unidentified live pieces, one of which Merlin believes is based on the song "Accentuate the Positive," by Johnny Mercer and Harold Arlen.

This set of vamps and themes formed the foundation for the music of April of 1973 to September of 1975. Each vamp and theme was augmented by a range of little motifs, riffs, and rhythmic figures that the players could insert, distort, or remove at any moment of their choosing. However, these ingredients were only the framework, the exterior, the fingers pointing to the moon. The moon—the meaning, the interior, the magic—was in the way the band treated the material. It is here that the influence of the second great quintet came to the fore. The '73–'75 band reexplored and transformed these pieces through a process of seamless, highly intuitive collective improvisation. The pieces were sometimes changed almost beyond recognition from night to night, which led to the widespread misunderstanding that the music was mostly or entirely improvised.

"But it wasn't," Lucas asserted. "We had a very defined compositional basis to start from and then elaborated on it in a very structured way, yet also in a very free way. We would play the same tunes, but the tunes were loosely structured. It allowed a lot of interaction between the rhythmic components to the band. We were improvising a lot more than just the notes that were being played in the solos; we were improvising the entire song as we went along. We would get incredible grooves going that would just continually evolve in the course of an evening, and over several performances. The band was a fantastic live unit. It was an improvisational unit, but it was a structured improvisation."

"You have to start with the canvas, which is the sheet of sound you're working off," Mtume elaborated. "Then you need the brushes. Each musician is a brush with a different color. When you know what you're going for, after a period of time you know what your painting is, you know what shade of red to use on this particular cut. The bass player knows what shade of blue to play. That band was organic. It wasn't about a bunch of solos. It was the tapestry that really mattered."

"We had a magnetism, a sort of instantaneous radar, to be able to communicate with each other musically," Mtume continued. "We all knew what the others were thinking, and as a result, there was an inexplicable intimacy and intricacy to the music. It was all very natural and organic because we evolved simple frameworks into changing compositions. To this day I have never had such a great feeling as a sideman. There are very few groups that develop that sort of coherence in their collective improvisations. We were going in directions where no one had gone before. Everyone was so in tune at that point. The band was like a finely tuned engine. You just knew what you had to do. The unit was so tight we hardly rehearsed. Music is like making love; you don't rehearse it, you do it. That's how we approached it. It is all about the spontaneity of the actual act itself."

"When playing heads together, Miles and I just breathed together," Cosey added. "I learned how he phrased, and when he would sometimes phrase things differently, I knew what he was going to do just from the way he was breathing and playing. It was a form of telepathy that he developed with all players in the band, and I guess that's why they were chosen, as people with whom he could communicate telepathically."

Mtume and Cosey were rarely involved in rehearsals. But since Foster, Lucas, and Henderson laid down the rhythmic, harmonic, and often the melodic foundations of the music, Miles occasionally rehearsed them. "The rehearsals were almost always at Miles's home," explained Lucas. "They were usually quite brief. Miles felt, I think, that excessive rehearsal would just take the life out of the performances we were going to create, because this was improvisational music. The last thing you wanted to do was beat it to death before you went out and played it. And he had the confidence that we would create things on a very impromptu basis. Instead of rehearsing extensively, Miles liked to go into one of his favorite clubs, like Paul's Mall in Boston, or the Keystone Korner in San Francisco, and do club dates for seven days, three sets a night, to warm the band up before a concert tour."

Although Cosey's arrival immediately brought renewed vigor and focus, the band still had some rough edges to smooth out during 1973. There was some occasional rhythmic stiffness, with Cosey and Lucas, as well as Mtume and Foster, working out how best to complement each other, whereas Henderson had not quite liberated his astonishing vamps to the degree he was able to in 1975. Cosey, occasionally sounding disjointed and clumsy, was still in the process of developing the groundbreaking solo voice that would begin to push him into the stratosphere a year later.

This finding-form process was reflected in their initial studio recordings. A session took place on July 23, but neither of the two resulting tracks has been released. One of them was named "Calypso," and is possibly an early version of "Calypso Frelimo,"[17] which premiered live on July 8. On July 26 the band went into the studio again, and the results were released on an obscure single, with "Holly-wuud" on one side and "Big Fun" on the other.[18] The pieces are less than three minutes each, with a nondescript vamp and some fairly purposeless soloing by Miles. The tracks were little more than jams and were never played live. Their release has all the signs of Columbia demanding a single and Macero going into the vaults and almost randomly cutting out two bits of music.

Almost two months later, on September 17, the studio version of "Calypso Frelimo" was recorded. Released on *Get up with It,* it is a major work by any standard. "'Calypso' will set a new direction," Miles exclaimed in 1974.[19] And the thirty-two-minute-long studio recording indeed has all the signs of Miles attempting to document and define the band's direction. The issued version shows Macero's compositional input because he edited the three major sections together with smooth and musical edit points at 10:11 and 21:39. Miles's organ playing and wah-wah trumpet are dominant throughout. Dave Liebman played flute, and John Stubblefield soprano saxophone. The Arkansas-born saxophonist had moved to Chicago, where he met Cosey, who introduced him to Miles.

"Calypso Frelimo" is a perfect example of Miles's amazing capacity to extract a strong mood and extensive musical structures from minimal material—in this case, a couple of brief melodic motifs and one bass vamp. In the opening section the band sets up a light, fluid, calypso-influenced groove that is overlaid by sharp solos from Miles, Liebman, and Stubblefield. One of the most striking elements is Cosey's delicate, innovative, and constantly changing rhythm playing in the left channel. The tempo is halved at 10:11, and Henderson's spacious, slow bass riff conjures up associations with the riff he played at the beginning of "Yesternow" on *Jack Johnson.* Miles and the band build up the intensity, until the piece returns to the opening groove at 21:39. Cosey finally takes a solo at 22:52, but like some of his solos around this time, it alternates between excellent repeating rhythmic ideas and weird, "out" playing that sounds as if he's lost for ideas. Around 26:43 Cosey launches into an attractive two-note riff, expands on it, introduces another little motif at 28:27, and together with Miles's final solo, the piece builds to a strong climax.

Although excellent in its own right, the studio version of "Calypso Frelimo" does not capture the scorched-earth intensity and compositional fluidity that were beginning to characterize Miles's live concerts. The recording-in-sections system, and the fact that he played organ during the band's initial recordings—he overdubbed most of his trumpet parts—did not allow Miles to lead his band through the tension-release structures in which it excelled live.

"Calypso Frelimo" is well recorded and all the instruments can be heard with clarity and detail. But perhaps the sound and playing are slightly too clean. Extraneous noises are an intrinsic aspect of much African music, with rattling pieces of dirt, metal, or wood added to many instruments. Large amounts of grit were also an intrinsic part of the funk collective's live music and may well have exemplified its African leanings. But their studio recordings were usually much cleaner, most likely because Columbia's jazz studio engineers aimed for a very clean, perfect sound. By contrast, rock producers like Daniel Lanois and Rupert Hine have stressed the importance of grit in a musical sound picture, even if it is only there subliminally. Beautiful sounds alone can generate an overly smooth, kitschlike result. Grit, in conjunction with beauty, can add depth and meaning. One of Miles's strengths was the way he applied this principle to harmony, always looking for a balance between the consonant and the dissonant. But for the creation of grit in the sonic picture, Miles was dependent on the decisions of Macero and the studio engineers. In this case the only grit is provided by his slightly distorted electrified wah-wah trumpet. But, sadly, it has a penetrating, jarring, midrange sound that becomes irritating after a while.[20]

Too much grit and too little beauty can have a similarly flattening effect. This is the problem that marred the first officially released live recording of the funk collective, *Dark Magus*. Recorded at Carnegie Hall in New York on March 30, 1974, by Columbia Japan, it was released in Japan in 1977 and in the United States in 1997. The second set featured two additional musicians, saxophonist Azar Lawrence and French-Bahaian guitarist Dominique Gaumont. Miles had decided to audition them on the bandstand, a contentious move, given that he must have known that Columbia was recording the concert. According to several band members—though disputed by Liebman—Miles was dissatisfied with the saxophonist's playing at this point. Mtume had alerted Miles to Lawrence, a twenty-year-old player who had already enjoyed some success playing with Elvin Jones and McCoy Tyner.

Why Gaumont was included is a mystery. Cosey recalled that he met the eighteen-year-old guitarist in Paris in 1973 and they became "buddies." The Chicagoan then introduced Gaumont to Miles on November 15, 1973, when the band played a concert there. Cosey declared that Miles wanted "another flavor" in the band, but added, "This was not really necessary. The soloists in the band were strong enough. Miles was very conscious about people's different social, geographical, and musical backgrounds, and probably felt Gaumont had something to offer on that front."

Musicians today often cite *Dark Magus* as an influence. Jah Wobble, for example, stated, "*Dark Magus* is my favorite Miles album of that period because it is so raw, with such a hidden power, such a mixture of dark and light. When I first heard it, in 1978, it was one of those magical moments. It had an overall sound that was similar to what Public Image Ltd. was about. I couldn't believe it had been recorded several years before us. I imagine Miles deliberately threw in these new musicians at the last moment because musicians get complacent. I can imagine how he wanted to affect their psychology, and so the music. I also know that musicians can think something is not representative of their best work, and yet it's actually great and a lot of people love it."

With his last words Wobble referred to Dave Liebman's CD liner notes, in which the saxophonist suggested that the concert at Carnegie Hall was "possibly not an inspired one."[21] "My notes were surreptitiously trying to avoid mentioning the fact that it wasn't one of our great nights," Liebman explained. "Even though it sounds a little better when I listen to it now, it wasn't representative of our best playing. It was a pretty panicky night, and the vibes were never great around the band in New York because Miles tended to be a bit crazy, and weird guys would show up during the gigs, probably drug-related. Whereas in Europe things were good, depending on the city and how much dope you could get. And in Japan we usually were at our best. Miles was clean and straight there, ate good, and always had a woman with him."

Mtume, Lucas, and Cosey agreed with Liebman that *Dark Magus* does not document the band at its best. One remembered Miles being so dissatisfied with the horn playing that he initially wanted it edited out. Pete Cosey mentioned another contributing factor, stating that "Carnegie Hall was not constructed for our instrumentation. It was made for acoustic music, and we had a wall of amplifiers. The sound spread there, and had we not been a very tight band, we would not have been able to hear anything. I hated playing in that place. It was an abomination, in terms of sound."

On the aural evidence of *Dark Magus*, one has to second the musician's opinions. The first set, featuring only the collective with Liebman, began with the knockout sequence of "Moja-Nne," "Tune in 5" (called "Moja" on the CD issue), and "Funk" (or "Wili (Part 1)"). This resulted in thirty-eight minutes of dense, relentless music, with little grace, space, or depth. The recording quality, especially of "Moja-Nne" and "Tune in 5" is below par, with a soupy, midrange sound, and a bass that's not loud enough. It's difficult to distinguish the different colors in the tapestry. Miles plays the main theme of "Moja" at 01:00, and of "Nne" at 05:51 and 10:58. The most interesting moments on these tracks are Lucas's riff at 07:20 and Cosey's solo, which begins at 08:15. This was the first officially released evidence of the over-the-top, effects-ridden solo style the Chicagoan was developing.

"Funk" is reminiscent of "Tatu," which is characterized by a very similar bass riff in B-flat. However, "Funk" has a slightly different groove, and Henderson regularly goes to E-flat, triggering a series of blues-influenced variations that sets it apart from "Tatu."[22] The Stockhausen influence can be heard in Miles's dissonant organ at 05:16 and in the drum machine passing by out of time at 13:02, purely for textural effect. The final piece of *Dark Magus*'s first CD, the balladlike "Wili" (also called "For Dave"), is the best section of this set. There's space for the musicians to breathe and react to each other, and Liebman, Cosey, and Miles all solo beautifully.

The second set is weighed down by Gaumont's contributions. He takes most of the guitar solos, and his tone, feel, and approach are crude and derivative of Hendrix. On the evidence of this concert Gaumont was a talented young guitarist who still had some way to go to reach his peak. With three guitars and two saxophonists the music becomes even denser than in the first set, particularly affecting the second CD's opening track, "Tatu." Despite some infectious riffing by the guitarists, most of the music is unrelenting and impenetrable. Perhaps to try to bring some structure into the jumbled mess, Miles frequently cut out the band, leaving the soloists to play without accompaniment. It was a strategy he increasingly employed around this time, to dramatic effect. "He'd move his finger, or nod his head, and that would be it," Henderson remarked. "You'd better watch and listen, because he could do it at any moment." But in this case the effect doesn't make much difference. The band won't fly, and the music is heavy, clumsy, and far from funky.

"Calypso Frelimo" has a bit more shape and feel, and the band manages to whip up a genuinely swinging groove under Miles's solo, beginning at 04:09. But, as if the tape editor (probably Macero) insisted on joining in the general malaise, the track is cut just when the groove starts to boil. The editor treated "Ife" with similar disregard, beginning it in the middle of Cosey's solo. The piece's main theme is stated at 01:48, and Henderson begins playing the main bass riff at 02:04. Around the eight-minute mark Gaumont distinguishes himself with some phrases that betray elegance and originality, and around thirteen to fourteen minutes the band finally finds the tenderness and poise that lift bootlegs from the same era. Cosey solos on the mbira (the African thumb piano) and for forty-eight seconds "Ife" gently drifts into "Moja-Nne" (the CD mastering engineer placed the ID cue forty-eight seconds too early).

Whether the final version of "Nne" actually appeared at the end of the second set, or was put here courtesy of the editor, is unclear. But it is not an improvement on the version on the first set. The best passage begins at 03:26, with an arresting stop-start blues riff by Henderson, but eventually the groove disintegrates into a riotous, clumsy gallop that doesn't sound much more sophisticated than that of a pub rock band. The groove breaks up again at 05:52, leading to some nice funky riffing, and "Tune in 5" follows, beginning at 07:02 on the CD release. It is mostly a showcase for Mtume. Wobble was right to point to Miles's talent for the dramatic and unexpected gesture, like throwing in musicians at the last moment, to get his band to play above what they know. But *Dark Magus* illustrates that it is a high-risk strategy that can be counterproductive.

❖

Reflecting Miles's frustration with the saxophone playing at the Carnegie Hall concert, Azar Lawrence was not invited to join the live band, but Gaumont remained with the collective until the end of 1974. Cosey felt that the guitarist's inclusion "changed the dynamics of the band. It was beautiful." "Having three guitarists in the band was certainly unique from a textural point of view," Lucas agreed. "We were used to the music being a moving target. The ensemble changed shape and size as we went along, so it wasn't a problem. Also, Miles had a penchant for combining musicians from different backgrounds to achieve a desired effect." But Mtume opined, "It didn't influence the band at all. As a matter of fact, it brought tension. I don't think, with all due respect to Dominique, that he was on the same level of musicianship as Pete or Reggie. Miles liked his solo sound, and if you're the bandleader, you hire whom you want. Dominique was only there for a European flavor."

Just as he had done with John Coltrane almost twenty years earlier, Miles must have spotted a unique but not yet fully formed talent in Gaumont that was hard for others to recognize. He took Gaumont under his wing, explaining, "I teach my musicians. . . . I'm teaching a young boy now that I have in the band. . . . He's a baddd motherfucker. He's like Hendrix. I have to show him the different chords."[23]

Miles's fatherly praise lifts a little of the veil on his relationship to his musicians. In 1974 the members of the collective were all in their late teens or early twenties, with the exception of Foster and Cosey, who were in their early thirties. Miles turned forty-eight that year, and this affected their relationships considerably. "We were all Miles's surrogate sons," Lucas explained. "Miles was very nice to us. He was definitely paternal, and we were appreciative of that. He was someone we looked up to, and who helped us elevate ourselves."

"He treated me like a son," Henderson remembered. "And I felt like he was a father to me. We always got along. I can't remember a single time I was angry with him." This was despite the fact that Miles was frequently annoyed with Henderson for "fartin' around, showin' off, not being a group player,"[24] when the bassist indulged in his tendency of wearing fancy clothes and playing to the gallery.

Liebman, who turned twenty-eight in 1974, recalled that Miles rarely talked to him on stage. "But he had a lot of respect, because I've had polio and have a bad leg," Liebman said. "He was going through a particularly bad time with his hips, operations, and crutches, etc. I guess he was impressed by my ability to get around that. He'd ask, 'How do you do that?'"

Like several sidemen, Lucas observed, "Miles had a different relationship to all of us. As his surrogate sons, we were all different. He treated each one individually. He got different things from us." "It's one of the marks of a great band leader," Cosey commented. "They know the musician's likes and dislikes and how to get the best out of them." But Miles played down his leader role. "I just bring out in people what's in them," he said in 1974.[25] A year later he remarked, in a way similar to how he had once referred to the second great quintet, "You have to have a band around you which is better than you are. Only in that case do you always aim higher. You always need to have the possibility to learn from everyone in the band."[26]

Lucas remarked that Miles "was also a tough guy, and not the easiest surrogate father to have." According to Liebman, the guitarist was one of the band's main recipients of Miles's "tough" side. "This was the guy that Miles really picked on," Liebman said. ". . . This kid would get off the stage and Miles would look at him and say, 'Reggie, why did you play that?' referring to nothing, just saying that. Reggie would eventually be in tears, broken down, because he didn't know what the hell Miles was talking about. Miles never was any more specific. Reggie would start crying, and Miles would start feeling bad and he would look at me or Al Foster and say, 'Why is he crying? I didn't say anything, I didn't do anything.'"[27]

Miles's toughness sometimes degenerated into physical violence, and he regularly beat up some of the women he was with, as well as Jim Rose, his road manager. "Miles used to kick him like a punching bag," Henderson said. "I didn't think that was cool." Rose responded, "I have three stitches to show for my relationship with Miles, and that I won't go into."

The trumpeter's violent tendencies were most likely exacerbated by the drugs he was using to cope with his deteriorating physical situation. Although off crutches, he was still limping across the stage, and the pain in his hips was getting worse, occasionally leading doctors to inject him with morphine. Of course, the high heels he frequently wore on stage didn't help. Miles was also suffering from a bleeding ulcer, insomnia, nodes on his larynx, and walking pneumonia. "By mid-1974 he was having to take about eight painkilling pills a day," Ian Carr reported.[28] The insomnia meant that he alternated between taking sleep pills and speed pills, not a beneficial combination. Alcohol was also becoming a problem, and in his autobiography Miles related how he ended up in hospital during the Brazilian tour of May of 1974 after mixing vodka, cocaine, marijuana, and Percodan. The next day, Miles said, with some bravura, "I played and blew everybody's mind I was playing so good. They just couldn't believe it."[29]

Miles also went into hospital early in 1975 to have the nodes on his larynx removed. It was amazing that Miles could work with this degree of physical and emotional trouble, let alone partake in creating music of often exceptionally high quality. Spurred on, no doubt, by his amazing commitment to his art, he gave every last bit of his energy to his music. "Music is three-quarters of my life . . . ninety percent," Miles said.[30] Music most likely also became an addiction, a way of avoiding the pain in his body and personal life. This suggestion was once made to Miles by his mother.[31] An indication of this is that he sometimes took his commitment to music to unhealthy extremes. His touring schedule from 1974 to 1975 was unusually intense, and saxophonist Sonny Fortune, who replaced Liebman in July of 1974, reported that at a concert in Cleveland (probably December of 1974), Miles felt too much pain to do the second show of the night, leaving the audience "clamoring on the tables." On March 27, 1975, in St. Louis, at the end of a tour with Hancock's Headhunters, Fortune recalled, "Miles came off stage and was sick right behind the curtain." Miles was hospitalized the next day for his bleeding ulcer and had to cancel the last three dates of the tour.

"Miles was a profound trouper, in the sense of the show must go on, no matter what," Fortune added. Miles gritted his teeth and carried on performing in the face of tremendous pain, wearing a macho mask, and his sunglasses, to protect himself from the public gaze. His repeated claims that he was indifferent to his critics were another expression of this bravura. In truth, the lack of recognition he received, especially in the United States, was deeply painful for him. Just as in the mid-1960s, Miles appeared to have lost touch with the pulse of popular culture. The rock press ignored him, and the feedback from the jazz world was almost entirely venomous. Concerning a 1973 performance in Guthrie Theatre in Minneapolis, one reporter wrote: "The critics' views were unanimous—Davis stunk up the joint. . . . It was probably the worst jazz concert in Guthrie history."[32] Other jazz writers used words like "forbidding . . . austere . . . absolute nadir"[33] and "I wish I'd stayed home."[34]

In May of 1974 writer Sy Johnson told Miles during an interview, "To my ear the band seems to keep rambling around. I can't find a center." Miles reacted defensively and with hurt, and then explained, very softly, "Sy, I got into music because I *love* it. I *still* love it. All kinds."[35] Later on during the same interview Miles was close to tears when he felt that some of his former sidemen had no interest in his current band.

Embodying his role as a father figure, Miles did not share this sensitive aspect of himself with his young band members, preferring to keep up his invulnerable act. "He did not give a shit," Mtume remembered. "And neither did we. We were about exploring new things. It was a very conscious and independent group of musicians, who really did not care what the critics had to say because it was a mission. At many points it was like us against the world. But I have always been angry that this period has not been dealt with properly." This last sentence, like his irritation with the failure of the PBS radio documentary to interview any of the '73–'75 band's members, indicates that Mtume was also not immune to the incessant criticism.

Despite the critics' incomprehension and hostility, the band members all testified that audience reactions were generally speaking extremely positive and that they were finally reaching the black audience Miles had been seeking for several years. "People loved it," Cosey said. "When we did the tour with Herbie, Miles was headlining and chose to open. And people were walking out on Herbie. This happened on a regular basis." "We did have an audience," Mtume stressed. "If you listened to the critics, you wouldn't realize it, but they had no idea that this revolution was happening. We had Funkadelic in the audience, and Mick Jagger, and all sorts of other people. We were bridging something. It was new music, and we were playing to packed houses!"

On June 19 or 20, 1974, the show went on with the recording of one of Miles's most influential experiments in the musical direction that later would be called "ambient." The result was "He Loved Him Madly," of which the "Godfather of ambient," Brian Eno, has written, "Teo Macero's revolutionary production on that piece seemed to me to have the 'spacious' quality I was after."[36] Like *Get up with It,* on which it appeared,

"He Loved Him Madly" was a homage to Duke Ellington, who had died a few weeks earlier, on May 24. The title referred to the great bandleader's trademark greeting to his audiences, "Love you madly."

According to Mtume, the piece was also inspired by a curious Christmas card Miles received in the spring of 1974. "I came to Miles's house, and he opened the door with tears in his eyes," Mtume remembered. "He said, 'Man, I just got a Christmas card from Duke. Isn't that the hippest thing you can think of?' Duke had been sending Christmas cards to all his friends because he knew he wouldn't be around anymore the coming Christmas. The card said, 'Love you madly.' That became the vibe for that track."

"He Loved Him Madly" was recorded with Liebman and Gaumont, but without Cosey, who arrived from the airport just as the session began. "Rather than tune up my instrument and interfere, I just sat there and sent thoughts," Cosey said. "So I played spiritually. I played presence." "When we started working on that track there was nothing," Mtume added. "It just happened. We were playing off a mood. Forget the chords, forget everything, it is all ambience." However, as Gaumont remembered the same session: "We really rehearsed. Miles sat at the piano and showed Al and me the melodic line."[37]

From the perspective of the ambient paradigm, the thirty-two-minute-long "He Loved Him Madly" is an epic tour de force. It has a very powerful atmosphere, courtesy of a series of deceptively simple devices Miles introduced and the postproduction techniques applied by Teo Macero. With regards to the former, Gaumont and Lucas play around with some simple phrases that can barely be called 'themes' but that give identity and structure to the piece. Gaumont's main motif can be heard right at the beginning, at 00:19, whereas Lucas's motif is most clearly heard at 26:12. The other important ingredients are the unusual sonic textures of the guitars, Miles's stark, naked, sometimes dissonant organ playing, and Mtume's prominently mixed congas. Combined, these elements create a hypnotic, introspective, desolate atmosphere, particularly during the first section, which is free in rhythm, and is lengthened by Macero through an edit at 02:41, after which the first 02:38 of the piece is repeated.

At 10:48 there's another edit, and the band goes in rhythm at 10:54, creating a more outward-looking atmosphere. Liebman plays a sensitive and fluid alto flute solo, followed by a mournful and moving trumpet statement by Miles. Around the nineteen-minute mark the groove becomes more intense, and at 20:10, underneath Liebman's second solo, Lucas plays some magnificent chordal figures. The beginning of Liebman's second solo is repeated, courtesy of an edit at 22:36, and additional reverb effect is added, making the flute sound as if it was played in a cave. Miles enters on trumpet for a second time at 26:21, Foster responds by moving his hi-hat into double time at 27:00, and from here the music gets funkier, with Henderson regularly popping his bass strings. After Miles's solo, the ensemble gradually winds the proceedings down until it almost comes to a halt, sounding exactly like the beginning. Unexpectedly, Foster picks up the rhythm again, until the track is magnificently and abruptly cut off.

Macero's crucial contribution is evident from the edits, which create the structure for the piece. Many people have complained about the track's length, but it is essential for building the strong atmosphere and the track's compelling and freeing climax. This is eloquently demonstrated by Laswell's thirteen-minute version of the track on *Panthalassa*, which has neither the gravity nor tension-release impact of the original. It is unclear what

Macero's role was in the sonic picture and the instrumental balance, which may have been created by recording engineer Stan Tonkel and remix engineers John Guerriere and Stan Weiss. But it is known that the "spacious" quality to which Eno referred is courtesy of a reverb machine Macero had just acquired.

"The track was wonderful," Macero recalled. "I thought that it needed a few small extra nuances, a few smallish effects here and there, to enhance what Miles had done. I tried to apply one of my effect boxes, but we could not get it to work properly. It functioned completely differently than normal. . . . It sounded like the band of Duke Ellington. I still don't have a clue how this happened. . . . It was as if Duke had come, touched the buttons, and made everything beautiful. Something unusual, something transcendent, something that we could not explain, had messed with the machine. Until this day I have not been able to reproduce the same effect."[38]

Cosey, Mtume, Henderson, and Lucas were all proud of "He Loved Him Madly," whereas Liebman and Gaumont had mixed feelings about it. "It sounded like everyone was trying to find something. Musically there wasn't much going on," remarked Liebman. And Gaumont said, "It's not my favorite. I find it is the sort of thing you listen to only once."[39] This difference in opinion exemplified the fault line that ran between the additional musicians and the collective. The saxophonists played over the band's "living compositions" but did not partake in creating them. They were also the band members with the most unequivocal jazz backgrounds, all of which set them apart.

In the case of Liebman, there was an additional issue. He was the only white player in an all-black band that wore its militancy on its sleeve. Liebman at times felt that he was not wanted by some of the other band members. Although Miles told him to ignore this, his discomfort was a factor in his departure. According to Liebman, he was already planning his band Lookout Farm during the Brazilian tour in May of 1974. "I told Miles I was going to leave, and all he said was, 'I knew you wouldn't be here for too long,' and then something about how I will be playing bebop stuff. I answered that he had played bebop for decades and I felt I couldn't skip it."

With Liebman's departure in the air, the search for a replacement led to a hilarious incident. "After the Carnegie Hall show I told Miles that I knew a good saxophonist from Chicago, Kalaparusha Maurice McIntyre," Pete Cosey recounted. "Miles asked me, 'Is he as crazy as you?' and I said 'Yes.' Miles replied, 'Well, have him on the bandstand the next time we hit [play a concert].' As it turned out, the next gig was in Chicago, so we did not need to fly him in. But by this time Miles did not remember telling me to have him on the bandstand. So when Kalaparusha came on stage, it was a total surprise. Miles was really shocked. He thought the guy had just invaded the stage. On top of this, the song we were playing was 'Thinking of You,' which Al Green had performed, and which Miles, Michael, and Reggie had worked out in the dressing room in between sets. Everybody was in a state of confusion, trying to pay attention to this song, and Kalaparusha chose this moment to come out on stage! He did not have a clue, nobody had a clue. He appeared almost like an apparition. I played a short solo, and then Kalaparusha started blowing, and blowing, and blowing."

"Miles had the habit of cutting the band or the soloists off with a hand movement," Cosey continued. "But Kalaparusha wasn't paying attention to him, so Miles cut the band off, and Kalaparusha kept playing. Miles brought the band back in, and

Kalaparusha kept playing. Miles cut the band out again, and still Kalaparusha kept playing. This happened various times. Miles then sat down on the drum platform and listened to the guy, who kept playing. Finally Miles waved the band off. Kalaparusha told me later that when he hit the bandstand, some force grabbed him and told him to play everything he knew. His girlfriend at the time tried to send him a message from the audience to stop, but he was not receiving anything. All he heard was this message to play everything he knew. Miles was so mad, when the guy approached him after the concert and related that I had asked him to play, Miles said, 'You've just lost Pete's place in the band for him.' But when I reminded Miles of the talk we'd had, things started to flash back to him. And when he noticed that there was no malice in me, and realized he'd been wrong, he changed his mind, and I stayed in the band."

Needless to say, Kalaparusha was not asked back. Liebman's replacement, alto and soprano saxophonist Sonny Fortune, had been recommended by Mtume. An experienced jazz player who had worked with Buddy Rich, McCoy Tyner, and with Mtume in Mongo Santamaria's band, Fortune debuted during a stint at Paul's Mall in Boston from July 28 to August 3. Two of these concerts, August 2 and 3, have been bootlegged, showing the band in scorching form. For some reason Gaumont was absent for these dates.

On October 7, the band recorded two new tracks, "Maiysha" and "Mtume," which appeared on *Get up with It.* "Maiysha" was a radical departure since it featured a fully fledged theme and chord structure and was played with a relatively slick Latin beat. "Miles brought in a very sketched-out chart, which was unusual," Fortune recalled. "He played the melody on the trumpet or keyboard for us, and hummed the rhythm."

Enrico Merlin has identified the tune as a variation of the French chanson "Que Reste Til de Nous Amour." The studio version is rather stiff and has a strange instrumental balance, with Fortune's flute and Miles's trumpet mixed too far in the back and the organ too prominently to the front. The track only comes to life after 09:44, when Cosey solos over a different, rockier vamp. According to Fortune, "Maiysha" was titled after one of Miles's girlfriends, but it also means "life" in Swahili (with the spelling "maisha"). In a much grittier and more agile rendering the piece became a live highlight and a buoy for listeners drowning in the sea of vamps, rhythms, and motifs, and desperate for an extended melody.

"Mtume" has a dense, unrelenting, high-energy rhythm, reminiscent of "Rated X" and of much modern dance music. The musicians are locked in their tight, repetitive parts, and have little chance to react to each other. Gaumont plays a gawky theme in the right channel for much of the track. At regular intervals the band switches to the groove of "Right Off" and Gaumont switches to the descending chord progression of "It's about That Time." Miles's trumpet solo and Cosey's rambling guitar solo are barely audible. There's no clear vision or direction to the track, and its best moment is its brusque, off-hand ending.

"The recorded legacy of the band never came close to the live legacy," Lucas commented. "Being a record producer myself now, I attribute this to the fact that there was not really a coherent strategy for making records. Miles didn't like to spend a lot of time in the studio. He liked to get in very quickly, make the record, and get out. It was the way he'd always done jazz records, and he was working with CBS staff, including Teo, who had done a lot of jazzier type records, and very few guitar-based things. Also, we tended to go into the studio when the compositions were new, and then we'd go out and play them for a year. It wasn't like a pop song where you'd spend months and months perfecting the performance that went on record. We would only develop the compositions elaborately as we toured and performed."

Apart from his sensitive contribution to "He Loved Him Madly," Gaumont does not appear to have gained a significant musical role in the '73–'75 band. Miles sacked him before the concerts at Keystone Korner in San Francisco, on January 14 to 17, 1975, which he had booked "to warm up the band" for an upcoming Japanese tour.[40] With the guitarist's departure more textural and rhythmic space opened up for Cosey to stretch his amazing solo skills. The evidence of the band's resulting leap forward is available on the two Japanese live recordings, *Agharta* and *Pangaea.* Today, several decades later, both recordings still stand as precious documents of the high plateau Miles reached in his electric explorations. Mtume regarded *Agharta* as the flower that had grown from the seed that was sown with *On the Corner* in 1972. It had taken nearly three years to come to full bloom.

The recordings' strengths lie in a number of factors. The band members have a lot of freedom and space and use it to continuously react to each other and to Miles, giving the music an organic and fluid quality. The music has many different layers, grooves, colors, textures, and moods, making *Dark Magus* by comparison sound like a monochrome, one-groove, one-color, one-trick recording. The breaks, or total stops, which Miles commanded with a simple movement of his head or hand, were dramatic and highly effective as pivots around which this tension-release structure was organized. *Agharta* alone contains about fifty such stops. The band continuously expands and contracts in and out of these tension-release passages, alternating wild climaxes with tender, almost completely quiet sections.

"It was Miles's jazz-derived sense of dynamics, applied to another area," Lucas said. "He employed all the sensibilities and sensitivities he had learned over the years, and employed an extreme range of contrasts and dynamics in our performances. He just extended their range, and would be playing bebop trumpet while the rest of us were rhythmically playing James Brown funk, and chordally something atonal and dissonant. Extreme textures and extreme volume were as much part of the palette as the contrasting chord and rhythmic structures. Being equipped like a full rock band, we sometimes literally blew the walls out."

The direction of the music is fully realized on both recordings, but *Agharta,* recorded in the afternoon of February 1, is superior. The album's first CD opens with the high-energy ferocity of "Tatu," powered by Foster's energetic drumming and Lucas's and Cosey's prowling and growling rhythm guitars. At the first total stop, at 01:28, Miles comes in with brutal, loud, dissonant organ. At 01:44 a rhythm machine floats by on the right, increasing the density of the music. Miles plays a potent wah-wah trumpet solo, which is full of dramatic phrases and rhythmic accents. He is followed by Fortune's solo on alto sax, with a rich, muscular tone that fits well with the ensemble.

Cosey begins his first guitar solo at 11:26, imitating the figure with which Fortune signed off. In 1975 his snarling guitar style must have sounded as if it came from outer space. During a long break beginning at 14:16, and laced with collective band accents, Cosey makes some outrageous, psychedelic sounds, after which the band settles into an infectious groove that is based on Henderson's catchy bass vamp, with some great comping by Lucas. At 16:30 there's another stop, the band takes the energy down, and Cosey plays some bizarre, futuristic effects sounding as if they were recorded underwater, which was in part the result of keeping the wah-wah pedal in the upright position. Several more stops and starts follow, until Henderson plays an astonishingly inventive and infectious bass riff, beginning at 18:48. He contracts the riff at 21:11, driving the band to yet another climax, and then pops his strings, leading the ensemble into "Agharta Prelude."

Miles plays the "Agharta Prelude" theme at 22:02. During the whole of this piece, Foster and Henderson whip each other into a frenzy with a development of the kind of stop-start funk playing that inspired "Double Image" and "Funky Tonk" in 1970. Excellent solos by Miles, Fortune, and Cosey sharpen the full-frontal impact. After thirty-two overwhelming minutes, band and audience are finally allowed to relax with a superior rendition of "Maiysha," which features lyrical flute playing by Fortune and a tender, heartfelt trumpet solo by Miles. There's another astounding guitar solo, beginning at 02:32, over "Maiysha's" second vamp, with Cosey screeching and screaming his way through blues-influenced, avant-garde weirdness.

The powerful version of "Right Off" that begins the second CD is equally enticing, featuring a strong saxophone solo by Fortune, and more insanity from Cosey, until the groove almost imperceptibly shifts from boogie to jazz swing around the beginning of Miles's solo at 09:08. Miles plays a long, superbly swinging solo, which is interspersed with Cosey's more traditional blues figures. The atmosphere is buoyant and light-footed, and the band is in a good enough mood to indulge Henderson, who guesses that the risk of being fired for playing old stuff is far gone, and at 16:42 spends forty-one seconds playing the bass figure for "So What."

"Ife" begins at 17:32. Lucas plays some monstrous, roaring chords on the right, Cosey entices indescribable sounds from the EMS Synthi A, and Miles introduces the main theme of "Ife" on the trumpet at 21:15. Lucas is allowed his first solo of the night at 03:20 (30:10).[41] After another climax, and another stop, the band takes the energy down so dramatically that the music almost comes to a standstill. Miles introduces "Wili" with some organ chords at 08:39 (35:29). Cosey once again solos blisteringly, whereas Miles plays introvertedly, almost mournfully. There's a deep sadness hanging over the music now, and after eighty minutes of unbelievably concentrated and intense playing, the energy slowly drains away until there is a fade-out at 26:16 of the second CD track in the U.S. edition. (The Japanese edition includes another nine minutes of atmospheric effects, including feedback, EMS synthesizer, and percussion.)

Live concerts are commonly built towards a final climax, but Miles's '70s performances often dissolved into entropy, ending with only percussion or synthesizer. "Our concerts began like a balloon that was incredibly compressed, "Mtume explained. "After that it was a matter of gradually letting the air out. The energy it took us to play at that level was enormous. There were times that we had to lie down after we had finished playing. Before the concert we'd build this energy up. We looked at each other, and said, 'Let's go through the wall.' That was our slogan. It meant taking it as far as we could physically. To stay at that level of concentration and energy for two to three hours was going through the wall."

Pete Cosey's jaw-dropping solos on *Agharta* are a major revelation. Sometimes growling, scurrying around all corners like a caged tiger, sometimes soaring like a bird, sometimes deliriously abstract, sometimes elegantly melodic and tender, his electric guitar concept is one of the most original to have been devised on the instrument. It still sounds advanced in the twenty-first century. Like Lucas, Cosey had greatly developed in his time in Miles's band, and it is odd that his playing hasn't had more recognition or influence. Cosey was a little vague about his guitar exploits on *Agharta* because he still hopes to publish an explanation of his approach in a book. "I was not just doing weird things, I was actually playing," Cosey said. "I had developed techniques with which I could play into the spheres, beyond the notes that are on the guitar neck. I was playing into space. I used at least thirty-six different tuning systems, placed the strings in different places, and so on. One of my tunings is the E-flat tuning, which Hendrix got from me."

"Pete is a genius who never got enough recognition for his playing," Mtume commented. "He used to come on stage with five to six guitars, each guitar tuned differently. In some cases he had the strings reversed, putting the outside string inside, and vice versa. I used to fall on the floor laughing when the guitar players in the audience would watch his fingers and they didn't correspond with the notes you'd usually hear on the guitar. It was an incredible thing to watch. He played all these guitars with such fluency. Of all the cats in the band, Pete got the least attention for the amount of creativity he brought to his instrument."

Another striking aspect of *Agharta,* as well as of *Pangaea,* is the interplay of the abstract noises from Cosey's EMS Synthi A synthesizer, and, rather surprisingly, Mtume's Yamaha drum machine. The Synthi A looks like an attaché suitcase with knobs and buttons. Since it has no keyboard it is hard to play specific pitches or melodies on it and it is only suitable for abstract sounds, although Cosey attempts to play the tune of "Ife" on it in the final CD track of *Agharta,* at 00:41 (27:31).

"Our tours of Japan were sponsored by Yamaha," Mtume recalled. "[In June of 1973] they gave Miles their first drum machine. Miles handed it to me, saying, 'See what you can do with it.' We were in experimental mode, so instead of using it to create rhythm, I wanted to see whether I could use it to create texture. I played it through six or seven different pedals, phase shifters, wah-wah, and biphase mutrons and so on, while pressing down three or four rhythms at the same time. I'm also using a volume pedal, so I'm bringing the sounds in and out. It was total tapestry. Unless you were told, you'd have no idea that you heard a rhythm machine." At times, Mtume's drum machine sounds almost identical to the Synthi A. A good example of this is at 02:05 (28:55) of the last CD track on *Agharta,* where the drum machine can be heard on the right, responding to and dialoging with Cosey's Synthi A in the left channel.

Pangaea is the document of the evening concert of February 1. To perform two such intense and high-energy concerts in one day would be a challenge for any musician, but Miles was forty-eight, and physically nowhere near his peak. Moreover, Mtume recalled, "He became ill in the evening, and you can hear the difference in the energy." The evidence is abundant. Although *Pangaea* contains excellent music, Miles is much less present than on *Agharta.* There are several extended periods during which the band just plays out the grooves, waiting for Miles to give the next cue. The band also works much less with the energy-consuming tension-release structures, and takes the level of energy down after only twenty minutes. There's a sense of tiredness and drift about the later stages of the recording. On this day the balloon could not be pumped up to full power twice.

Pangaea's first CD begins with the band's usual knock-the-audience-out approach. "Moja" is the opening track, with ferocious playing by Foster, Mtume, Henderson, and Lucas. Miles enters on trumpet with a theatrical phrase at 01:18, plays the main theme together with Fortune at 01:49, and continues with a solo. Fortune follows on alto saxophone, and after the first total stop at 05:44 the band begins breaking up the rhythm in a manner similar to that on "Agharta Prelude" in the afternoon. Cosey solos in his inimitable, screeching, soaring style until a break at 10:56, into which Foster plays the rhythm of "Tune in 5." Cosey hints at the riff for "Willie Nelson" in his solo, and Lucas begins playing it at 11:22. The rest of "Tune in 5" is a succession of weird bass riffs, percussion solos, breaks, and accents. "Nne" begins at 15:68. Miles and Fortune play the theme at 16:12, and Cosey performs a blazing solo beginning at 18:02, with Foster repeatedly switching into the rhythm of "Tune in 5." Miles quotes the theme of "My Man's Gone Now" from *Porgy and Bess* at 20:57, over a gorgeously bubbling rhythm section. But, as on *Dark Magus,* the rhythms are for the most part dense and flat. Since the pieces' monochrome quality is similar on both albums, it may have as much to do with the pieces themselves as the performances or the recording quality.

The fierce level of the energy drops when Miles cues "Zimbabwe" at 21:51. Space and playfulness enter, giving the band members room to breathe and respond. An example is at 26:36, where Miles's loud flourish on the trumpet leads to an immediate response from the band. Lucas gets his second solo of the day at 30:29 and plays it to a Santana-like climax. The energy level drops still further, and Cosey's Synthi A and Mtume's drum machine add abstract textures, exemplifying the influence of Stockhausen. The set ends in total entropy, with Mtume on bells and Cosey playing autoharp and humming.

The second CD contains a repeat of the last section of *Agharta*. "Ife" is faded in, beginning with a flute solo by Fortune. Miles plays the theme at 04:51, drives the band with some staccato notes from 09:10 to 09:25, and Cosey solos on the mbira. But around eleven minutes the band already starts to sound as if it's running out of steam. One of the sections when the band is cruising, waiting for Miles to give direction, is from 14:24 to 15:33.

"Wili/For Dave" is cued in by Miles on organ and begins at 18:57, with Cosey playing a dramatic solo, accompanied by delicate, shimmering play from Lucas. Miles enters on trumpet at 28:11, with some mournful, sad playing over a gentle groove, until at 29:13, when the energy drops and everyone appears to be waiting again for the next instruction from the boss. Miles shrieks, as if to wake himself up, at 29:36, after which Henderson softly and tentatively begins walking his bass. The way Henderson and Foster gradually and gently set up a jazz swing groove is a joy to hear. Finally, Miles succumbs and pushes the groove into a glorious full-out swing with some rhythmic phrases at 33:35. His solo is followed by Cosey's, which is played delicately and with much less distortion. But once again the energy appears to drain away, and nothing happens between 38:53 and 41:34, at which point Henderson varies the groove. Lucas immediately reacts, repeating the same figure. The band plays around with this for a while before returning to the opening figure of "Wili" and quickly dissolving into entropy again, leaving Cosey alone on the Synthi A to play out the concert.

The interplay between these mostly very young musicians on these two recordings is astonishing. Miles had taught them well to focus and to listen. According to Sonny Fortune, it all happened through osmosis. "We knew his movements," Fortune explained. "Everybody watched him. I guess we all took it upon ourselves to try to read the small amount of instructions or movements he presented to us. We weren't going to say to him, 'Man, make yourself clear,' because we recognized magic. To me it seemed like Miles was the cat who gave the least and got the most in return from the band and the audience. His chops weren't the way they had been in the '50s and '60s, when chops were paramount. He even said this himself. But he knew how to get around that. He played music, he didn't play chops. And he was totally present on stage. He was a very, very, very heavy cat. Playing with him was an experience I will never forget."

On returning from the Japanese tour in late February of 1975, Miles immediately continued with a tour of the American Midwest. He appeared to be working harder than ever. Not long after he had been hospitalized with his bleeding ulcer, on March 28, he witnessed a young player from Long Island called Sam Morrison, and is reported to have said, "I haven't heard that much fire on the saxophone since 'Trane was in my band."[42] Miles invited Morrison to sit in for the second set at a concert in Paul's Mall in Boston, sometime in early April. Fortune watched the proceedings from the audience. When he saw that Morrison remained on stage for the whole set, Fortune packed his bags the next day.

"The band really advanced after the Japanese tour," Cosey asserted. "And Sam Morrison fit in very well with the band." Miles also noted, "The band was getting real hot and tight by this time."[43] The evidence of a bootleg from the Bottom Line in New York, on June 11, does indeed show the band in amazing form, alternating between hair-raising climaxes and lilting, tender passages. Like the aforementioned Boston bootleg of August 3, 1974, the standout track is "Wili." Rather than dissolving in entropy, as on *Agharta* and *Pangaea,* the track gets worked up to a funky storm, with the band seemingly on fire. It is to be hoped that Columbia has recorded some of these concerts, and will one day release them.

Miles had reached an incredible creative peak in 1975, with music that incorporated many of the influences he had integrated during his career. He had finally returned to "The sound of $1.50 drums and the harmonicas and the two-chord blues," albeit transformed to such a degree that the music appeared to come from a different universe. Miles had reached his final frontier. It's enticing to fantasize where he could have taken his music from here, but his physical condition did not allow it. Drugs, illness, relentless touring, and possibly also the unbridled hostility and criticism of the jazz community, had worn out his body and soul. In August of 1975 a hernia added to his already impressive catalog of illnesses. His final concert of the '70s was in Central Park in New York, September 5. Miles canceled a subsequent concert in Miami because he felt too sick, and when the organizers impounded the band's equipment in retaliation, he retired from touring.

"The headlines said that Miles went crazy, or that he wasn't really creative anymore," an emotional Mtume recalled. "But that's just bullshit. Yes, he was in pain, but he also played some of his highest quality work during 1975. One night he said to me, 'I know you think I'm bullshitting, but there's too much pain. I don't want to talk about it with the rest of the band, but I'm telling you.' I said, 'I understand.' We talked some more, and I remember walking over to Reggie, and saying, 'This is it!' We didn't work after that, and he did not play anymore for five years."

With this, a thirty-year-long whirlwind of creativity had come to an end. One of the most influential and controversial voices of the twentieth century had fallen silent, his penultimate musical heritage forgotten or dismissed. Only many years later did a rediscovery and reevaluation process of this heritage begin. It is still ongoing. The future is still catching up with Miles.

Miles Davis and bassist Dave Holland at a live concert in 1969. Photo by Sandy Speiser, courtesy Sandy Speiser and Sony Music

Miles Davis during a live concert in 1969.
Photo by Sandy Speiser, courtesy Sandy Speiser and Sony Music

Bassist Marcus Miller, Miles Davis, and saxophonist Bill Evans at Concertgebouw,
Amsterdam, Holland, November 1982. Photo by Rico D'Rozario, courtesy Rico D'Rozario

Drummer Al Foster, Miles Davis, and guitarist Mike Stern at Concertgebouw, Amsterdam, Holland, November 1982. Photo by Rico D'Rozario, courtesy Rico D'Rozario

Bassist Marcus Miller and Miles Davis, Jones Beach concert, September 1982. Photo by Milan Simich, courtesy Milan Simich

▲ Drummer Al Foster,
Miles Davis, and
guitarist John Scofield,
Avery Fisher Hall
concert, June 22, 1984.
Photo by Milan Simich,
courtesy Milan Simich

▶ Miles Davis and
trumpeter Bob Berg,
jazz festival in New
Orleans, April 26, 1985.
Photo by Milan Simich,
courtesy Milan Simich

Miles Davis, guitarist John McLaughlin, and composer Palle Mikkelborg during the recording session for Aura. Easy Sound Studios, Copenhagen, Denmark, February 1, 1985. Photo by Kirsten Malone, courtesy Kirsten Malone

Keyboardist Robert Irving III, Miles Davis, and drummer Steve Thornton, Lehman College concert, March 20, 1986. Photo by Milan Simich, courtesy Milan Simich

Miles Davis and saxophonist Kenny Garrett at the North Sea Jazz festival in The Hague, Holland, July 8, 1988. Photo by Rico D'Rozario, courtesy Rico D'Rozario

▲ Miles Davis with partner Jo Gelbard and Quincy Jones, backstage at Montreux concert, Switzerland, July 1991. Photo courtesy Jo Gelbard

◄ Miles Davis at Montreux concert, Switzerland, July 1991. Photo courtesy Jo Gelbard

OVERLEAF:
Miles Davis, Danbury, Connecticut, August 31, 1985. Photo by Milan Simich, courtesy Milan Simich

Chapter Eleven

HUMAN NATURE

"Miles was one of the most sensitive, intelligent, humanistic people I ever met."
—MARCUS MILLER

When Miles took time out from touring in September of 1975, he expected to make a fast comeback, but his worsening physical condition thwarted this prospect. Immediately after he took a break, his near-chronic pneumonia became acute and he was whisked off to hospital, delaying a hip operation planned in September. In the early '60s Miles's left hip had become arthritic due to his sickle-cell anemia, an illness he described graphically: "It's just a black disease where your bones get so brittle that they break off. . . . Which is very painful, you know. It's just chips. First they did a bone graft and then they put a cap on it."[1] Two operations on his hip were performed in April and August of 1965. The car crash in October of 1972 further damaged his hips, leading to three years of limping around. His third hip operation eventually took place in December of 1975, when he was one of the first people to receive an artificial hip.

Miles spent the whole fall and winter recuperating. In 1976 he was making new musical plans again. One plan involved an orchestration of the opera *Tosca* with Gil Evans, but the project never went beyond the think tank stage. In addition, three studio sessions are known to have taken place, in March, November, and December of 1976. These featured some or all members of the funk collective, as well as guitarist Larry Coryell in November. Some of the material from the December session was used for a Japanese TDK tape commercial, but nothing from these sessions has been officially released.

Columbia renewed Miles's contract at the end of 1976 and put him on a retainer, an honor only previously bestowed on concert pianist Vladimir Horowitz. The company expected Miles to be active again fairly soon, but until 1980 he could only muster a few more aborted sessions. Jan Lohmann listed two recording dates in early 1978, once again featuring Larry Coryell, with Miles on organ,[2] whereas Pete Cosey remembered two rehearsals at Miles's home in 1977. "We played at his house," Cosey recalled. "Jack DeJohnette, Sam Morrison, bassist Gerald Wiggens, and myself. We got a really good groove going, and Miles couldn't resist it, and played some horn. There was a second rehearsal around the same time with the same people, only Al Foster instead of Jack. One of the pieces we played was 'Ife.' I still have the tapes of these rehearsals."

Miles has claimed that he did not touch his horn from late 1975 until early 1980, but Lohmann's sessionography and Cosey's account suggest he played trumpet on a few occasions during these years. Either way, the break from his main instrument was dramatically long. He now also suffered from bursitis, an inflammation of the joints that made playing the trumpet painful, and this no doubt contributed to this hiatus.

With this dearth of musical activity, Miles's band members gradually drifted away. Whereas most of Miles's previous sidemen had gone on to become major players in the jazz world, Henderson, Mtume, and Lucas fulfilled the prophecy of Miles's star-making capacities in different ways. Henderson proved to be a creditable soul singer and songwriter, and was featured as a singer on hit songs such as "You Are My Starship" and "Valentine Love" by drummer Norman Connors. Henderson subsequently made several successful solo albums, including *Goin' Places* (1977), and his only gold album, *In the Night Time* (1978). Mtume and Lucas played in Roberta Flack's band before forming a songwriter/producer team, writing hits for Roberta Flack, Stephanie Mills, and Phyllis Hyman, and winning a Grammy for Best R&B Song in 1980 with "Never Knew Love Like This Before." The two parted in the early '80s, after which Mtume achieved success as a record producer and as a bandleader. Lucas wrote and produced large sections of Madonna's first album, *Madonna* (1983).

Until he rejoined Miles's new live band in 1981, Al Foster fronted his own band and worked as a successful session drummer. Strangely, Pete Cosey had the most problems capitalizing on the high profile he achieved with Miles. In the early '80s he played on Herbie Hancock's *Future Shock,* but he eventually dropped out of sight, writing and developing his own music in private, and sustaining himself by producing and arranging commercial music.

While his former sidemen moved outwards into the world, Miles collapsed inwards. His slide into a self-destructive underworld of continuous sexual excess and drug abuse, as well as occasional violence and madness, has been well documented. Miles openly shared many of the details in his autobiography. "I just took a lot of cocaine (about $500 a day at one point) and fucked all the women I could get into my house," Miles recalled. "I was also addicted to pills, like Percodan and Seconal, and I was drinking a lot, Heinekens and cognac. Mostly I snorted coke, but sometimes I would inject coke and heroin into my leg. . . . The house was a wreck, clothes everywhere, dirty dishes in the sink, newspapers and magazines all over the floor, beer bottles and garbage and trash everywhere. The roaches had a field day. . . . Mostly the house was filthy and real dark and gloomy, like a dungeon."[3]

During this time Miles was also hallucinating. In one instance he was so far gone that he mistook the snow falling into his Ferrari for cocaine, stopped the car in the middle of a busy New York street, and ran into a building and into an elevator, where a woman was also present. Thinking he was still in his Ferrari, he slapped her and told her to get out of his car.

"I was nuts," Miles told writer Cheryl McCall in 1981.[4] He added that he was also bored, "So bored that you can't realize what boredom *is.* I didn't come out of my house for four years." And he denied to her that he had been in really bad shape: "No, I was alright. It was just that I took so much medicine I didn't *feel* like playing the trumpet, didn't *feel* like listening to music."[5] These last exclamations seem to contradict the harrowing accounts in Miles's autobiography, in which he painted a picture of enough high drama to last most people a lifetime.

Mark Rothbaum, who had become Miles's sole manager in August of 1978, disputed the more sensational accounts of Miles's silent period. "I was in touch with Miles every day, and visited him regularly," Rothbaum recalled. "Many of the stories in his book did not come out of Miles's mouth. Miles simply didn't have these recollections. He didn't have a sharp anecdotal memory, although he had a sharp musical memory. But the house didn't get that dirty, and when it did, it got cleaned eventually. And the stories of all the women, they're bravado stuff. Miles did not fuck scores of women. He was at home the entire time. He was with Trixy, and he was with Loretta. And he was ill."

Vince Wilburn Jr., Miles's nephew and drummer from 1984 to 1987, disagreed with Rothbaum's assessment of the trumpeter's memory. "Miles had total recall of certain things," Wilburn asserted. "When he was doing the book, he was seeing his whole life before him, and he was ready to talk." But Marcus Miller appears to agree with Rothbaum. In reference to one of the more glaring mistakes in the autobiography (Miles's claim that none of George Duke's music appeared on *Tutu*, whereas the keyboardist provided "Backyard Ritual"), Miller stated, "That's Miles, you know, just talking. He wasn't a detailed guy—unless it came to the clothes, and also certain aspects of music." But Miller expressed surprise over Miles's other erroneous statements—that Duke did a lot of the arrangements on *Tutu*, despite the fact that most of the album was composed, arranged, and played by Miller: "That's strange, even for Miles."

These conflicting claims and factual inaccuracies raise the issue of the reliability of *Miles: The Autobiography*. Some people have suggested that parts of the book were fabricated, or did not come directly from Miles. Jack Chambers claimed, "There are scores of passages in the *Autobiography* made up of verbatim or nearly verbatim thefts from *Milestones*."[6] Quincy Troupe has explained how he spoke extensively to Miles for the book, and interviewed many others. He also consulted many previously published interviews and appears to have woven all material together to make it sound as if everything came from Miles's mouth, "sort of the way an actor becomes a character."[7] Inevitably, as do all writers, Troupe imparted his own bias, but there is little doubt that Miles was responsible for the vast majority of the book's contents.

Sometimes the stories in the autobiography differ from the accounts of others. This is not necessarily of great concern, since people's memories can vary greatly, and do so increasingly with the passing of time. Nevertheless, deliberately altering stories falls in a different category, and there is evidence of this possibility as well in the autobiography. "To tell you the truth, I think Miles made some of the autobiography up as he went along," Miles's early '80s guitarist Mike Stern remarked. "Miles either lied a lot in his autobiography, or he forgot," Lydia DeJohnette asserted. "He was losing his memory at the time he wrote the book. So some of the stories were clear, but others were rather 'stretched' to make himself look good."

One unmistakable example is Miles's account of his relationship with Jo Gelbard and how this affected his marriage to Cicely Tyson, the actress with whom he had also been involved in the '60s. Miles never mentioned Gelbard by name in his book, but described how Tyson attacked her at one point. "Cicely thought I was going with the woman; she had convinced herself I was," said Miles. "But I wasn't."[8] But he was. Later on in the book Miles implies that his relationship with Gelbard began as late as 1989. This may have been done to protect Gelbard's marriage, which did not fully dissolve until 1992, but it does not explain why he included the erroneous denial of Cicely's claim in the first place.

Glaring inconsistencies not only feature in Miles's autobiography, but they were a common feature of his public utterings in general. A striking example is his statement to Leonard Feather in 1972: "I don't believe in families. Like, if I die, my money ain't going to go to people just because they're close relatives."[9] However, a year later he revealed to Stephen Davis, "I helped send my sister through school,"[10] showing that family ties were important to him. Evidence of the same was provided by the fact that the beneficiaries of his will were his daughter Cheryl, son Erin, brother Vernon, sister Dorothy, and nephew Vince Wilburn Jr.

Perhaps Miles's many contradictory statements were efforts to make himself a moving target, preventing people from pinning him down and defining him. He may well have taken his "musical provocateur" attitude into the arena of words, deliberately being inconsistent or playing devil's advocate to undermine people's attachments to certain concepts, or their tendency to take words literally. He might well have said, to paraphrase his saying about music, "The attitude is 80 percent, the actual words 20 percent." And sometimes Miles's utterings simply had the flavor of macho bravura covering up sensitive spots.

"Just to constantly not be straightforward is a coping strategy for a person who is creative in a world that does not understand creativity," Reggie Lucas commented. "Many artists do this. Because people are mystified and threatened by what they don't understand, and try to categorize it and relegate it to a lower level, reduce it to the lowest common denominator. It's an absolute necessity for creative artists not to allow themselves to be trivialized by the establishment."

Due to Miles's disregard for verbal accountability, we may never know which of his stories were as accurate as one man's memory can be and which contain more than a trace of fantasy or exaggeration. Having said that, it appears that at least parts of Miles's accounts of his '70s excesses are correct. There are many eyewitnesses who observed his out-of-control, and sometimes-violent behavior. His violence towards road manager Jim Rose was mentioned in the previous chapter. With regards to Miles's treatment of women, Michael Henderson recalled, "In Europe, Miles knocked the teeth out of a chick's mouth. She came up to him after the gig, and kept talking to him, saying 'Look at you, look at what you have done to yourself, you should go back and play your old music.' She wouldn't leave and followed him into the elevator, and then 'Pow,' he struck her, pushed her back in the elevator, and pressed the down button."

Dave Liebman claimed that he witnessed a scene in a Parisian hotel room during which Miles poured champagne over a woman who was lying on the floor, covered with bruises. Miles was "pretty weird with women. He was not cool,"[11] Liebman commented, explaining that this behavior was related to drugs, particularly speed and cocaine. Jim Rose remembered being regularly called in to mediate between Miles and the aforementioned Loretta. "They were constantly having fights, and they were both doing a lot of cocaine," Rose said. "So they would both become unreasonable. Miles would call me in the middle of the night, and say 'Jim, get up here, I'm going to kill her.' I never thought someone would actually get killed, but she would end up with black eyes. They were both very violent. It was a very bizarre scene."

Paul Buckmaster visited Miles in August of 1979, on the invitation of Columbia vice president George Butler, who was trying to push Miles into making a comeback. Buckmaster remembered Miles "living in a mess," at one stage with the electricity cut off because Miles had failed to pay his bills. "There were food crumbs everywhere," Buckmaster reported. "Nothing had been cleaned for months, nor had the curtains and windows been open for months, so the air was very stale. We had Jewish funeral candles for light in the evening. One night it was extremely hot, and 90 percent humidity and no wind, and the whole of New York stank of rotting fish and cheese. That night Miles passed out. I checked on him, and he was breathing. But the situation had become so desperate, and Miles had reached such a degraded state, that I called his sister Dorothy in Chicago. This was around 3 A.M. New York time. I told her, 'Miles isn't very well at all. I don't want to cause a mess or a scandal, but he seriously needs looking after, and I think the only people who can do that are his family.' She said, 'I have to go to a funeral in the morning.' And I said, 'Why don't you let the dead bury the dead, and come and take care of the living?' She was taken aback, but agreed to take the first plane from Chicago to New York. I waited for her arrival on the sofa, and when I dozed off, several two-inch cockroaches ran over me."

On arriving, Dorothy's immediately called Cicely Tyson, and together the two women set about cleaning up Miles and his house. Buckmaster went back to his hotel, and returned to London a few days later. "I realized that there wasn't going to be any music at that point, this was too far gone," he recalled. The Briton speculated about the discrepancy between his and Rothbaum's stories: "It was probably only a short period that it was really bad." It is indeed likely that Buckmaster witnessed Miles at the lowest point of his silent period, the stage when drugs and sex were no longer able to distract him from his emotional and physical pain, when boredom and depression were the only remaining feelings.

The combination of incessant physical pain and excessive drug use goes a long way towards explaining Miles's depression and crazy behavior. Yet it does not clarify why he went out of control and stopped working for so long, and why he reached such levels of debauchery that he was at risk of losing his life. Miles had been a junkie before, in the early '50s. Although he had acted irrationally and destructively during that period, he kept playing, and managed to regain control of his life on his own strength. During the other period when drug use controlled his life, the early '60s, the situation was similar. So why did he run so much more dramatically off the rails in the second half of the '70s?

Mark Rothbaum believed the additional factor unique to the '70s was simply a matter of physical pain. "He literally was in too much pain to work; he was in way too much pain," said Rothbaum. Moreover, in the previous chapter it was suggested that Miles's musical activities were to some degree part of his addictive behavior. Though drugs dominated his life in the early '50s and early '60s, Miles still played music during these periods, forcing him to focus outside of himself and his habits. Since it appears that he was physically unable to engage in music during the late '70s, his addictive patterns seem to have focused entirely on sex and drugs, making it likely that they ran more out of control.

Although Miles stated that he quit playing music mostly due to his bad health, he never claimed to have been too physically incapacitated to play during his entire silent period. He offered creative exhaustion as an additional explanation for his prolonged musical nonactivity. Miles's thirty years as a professional musician had been among the most intense and productive of any twentieth-century artist. No other musician had moved the boundaries of music so often, and had so categorically refused to succumb to the temptations that face commercially successful artists: sinking in complacency, playing-it-safe, and milking the same old formula. If a certain degree of burnout is understandable, it still does not explain the depths to which Miles sank. There are, of course, different ways to regenerate and recuperate than nearly drinking and drugging oneself to death. So why did a man who appeared so fiercely independent fall to pieces to such a degree? Why did he become dependent on the care of his family and a former lover? How is it possible that there was such a dramatic discrepancy between the person and the persona, the man and the mask? Some tentative answers have been given to answer the questions this raises, but few have seriously questioned the mask, or looked deeply at the man behind it.

Discussions are often obscured by the tendency of many commentators to project a degree of hero-worship into Miles's persona, blinding them to its faults and to the deeply sensitive and vulnerable person it was protecting. Miles happily fed this macho image, not least with the occasionally bravura tone in his autobiography. However, this appeared to be counterproductive, because in response to his revelations of how he abused women, several commentators now wholly condemned him. Writer Greg Tate called Miles's stories "Gloating accounts of physical and psychological abuse" and concluded, "Miles may have swung like a champion, but . . . he went out like a roach."[12] Chambers called the autobiography a "sleazy self-portrait."[13] And Francis Davis wrote, "His treatment of women is contemptible. . . . He's peacock vain."[14]

But neither hero-worship nor the moral high ground is particularly helpful. Both focus on the exterior and ignore the interior, and in so doing dehumanize Miles. These commentators failed to recognize that the aspects they admired or condemned were different sides of the same coin, different aspects of the same persona. The only hope of understanding Miles lies in examining both persona and person, exterior and interior.

Miles's public persona had come into being during his early '50s period as a junkie. Although he had been a friendly and polite youth, Miles became distant, distrustful, and obsessed with not showing any sign of his immense sensitivity and vulnerability. He played out a macho image of invulnerability and hyperindependence, acting as if he did not need anyone, or anything. Reports of him emotionally and physically abusing others date from this point onwards.

Nevertheless, many of the seeds for his persona were sown well before his time as a junkie. Quincy Troupe pointed to the cultural climate in which Miles had grown up. "St. Louis . . . is a city founded by the French but controlled by the Germans," Troupe wrote. ". . . It is more Calvinistic than Catholic, more marching band than Mardi Gras. It is a culture where a show of emotion is considered uncouth, almost uncivilized."[15]

It is now common knowledge how deeply and inescapably family patterns are transferred from generation to generation. Miles was no exception. His addictive tendencies may have come from his Uncle Ferdinand (his father's brother) who, according to Miles, was an alcoholic. Miles inherited his massive pride and self-belief from the masculine lineage in his family. He admired Ferdinand's style and swagger, and mentioned in his autobiography how his father and grandfather instilled in him that the Davises were special. "By genetics and breeding, Miles III is always going to be ahead of his time,"[16] his father once said. This mind-set gave Miles the strength to find and manifest his direction in the world, but in his persona they were inflated to a hyperindependent, arrogant, and aloof attitude.

Miles's physical violence most likely had its roots in his mother's violence towards him; he related in his autobiography how she beat him frequently and severely, and without much provocation. Though his father didn't hit him, and sometimes even protected him from his mother's fury, Miles also witnessed scenes of violence between his parents. In addition, Miles appears to have modeled some of his violent behavior on Billy Eckstine, in whose band he played for two weeks in St. Louis in 1944 and for half a year in 1946 and 1947. It was in Eckstine's band that Miles first used cocaine, a drug that induces a hyperenergetic and hyperaware state. Miles admiringly recalled about Eckstine, "He was a rough motherfucker who didn't take no shit off no one, woman or man. He'd just knock the shit out of the first person to get out of line,"[17] and described how Eckstine beat up a woman because she asked to be called by her name.

Though regarded as objectionable today, it must be remembered that much of this kind of behavior was condoned, if not admired as the credential of a "real" man, by some of the circles surrounding Miles at the time. It is not surprising that the insecure, feminine, sensitive, and physically small Miles saw this behavior as the only route open to self-protection. "Miles was the kind of guy who was very macho," Dave Liebman commented. "It was all based on your ability to stand up to pressure. His respect was based on male virility bullshit. If he saw that you were like that, he had respect for you, and if you weren't, he took advantage of you." Marguerite Eskridge recalled, "Much of that attitude was engrained in him in his very early life. That was the way you talked and behaved."

Charlie Parker was another major influence. The young Miles not only molded his musical methods to a great extent on Parker, but also his postjunkie public persona. Parker provided an impressionable young Miles with blueprints for drug addiction, sexual excesses, and bad treatment of friends. Over the years Miles relayed dozens of portrayals of Parker's behavior that were entirely applicable to himself. Just two examples: "Bird always wore a mask over his feelings, one of the best masks that I have ever seen."[18] "One of the things I never understood about Bird was why he did all the destructive shit he used to do. Man, Bird knew better."[19]

Looking beyond Miles's mask, many who knew him well offer descriptions that are in stark contrast, such as, "He's one of the most sensitive, intelligent, humanistic people that I ever met" (Marcus Miller); "He was one of the most affectionate people I've ever met, and he was so misunderstood"[20] (John McLaughlin); "He's one of the nicest, gentlest of men"[21] (Gil Evans); "He could be the gentlest, sweetest, kindest person" (Lydia DeJohnette); and "He was really shy" (Dave Holland). Marguerite Eskridge also asserted that Miles took this persona less seriously than others: "The media made more out of it than I think he actually did. He had no problems hugging and crying and could be very nurturing."

"I knew a different side to Miles than all the macho and bravado," Mark Rothbaum elaborated. "I knew a normal guy who you hung out and watched TV with." For Vince Wilburn Jr., Miles "Was just Uncle Miles. I knew he was somebody famous, but he was also very normal. He had a soft side, and he'd be joking around. When he and his brother Vernon got together Miles was a riot! There were lots of laughs. Miles was very humorous, but it was a very private side of him." Many also commented on Miles's caring behavior, and regular offers of support and money. Dave Liebman related how he broke his leg in the early '80s, and was "pretty out of it. I had a cast up to my neck." Miles called the saxophonist and asked whether he was OK, and in need of money.[22]

Sometimes journalists peeked behind the mask. In 1981 Cheryl McCall wrote, "I've traveled with a lot with bands in my time, but I've never encountered anything like the atmosphere of reciprocity and love that Miles Davis brings with him. Cicely Tyson says he's always been like that and that the toughness is all facade."[23] McCall also spotted Miles's underlying vulnerability, writing, "There's still an air of inconsolable grief about him."[24] And in 1974 Sy Johnson observed, "That's why he wears those huge glasses. His eyes give him away. The pain, the hurt, the vulnerability, forty-eight years, all there to see. But he puts those glasses on and it's the Black Prince, who knows no pain."[25]

Jo Gelbard painted a picture of a deeply vulnerable and emotional man who was still fighting his demons, especially his loneliness and his unresolved relationships with women. "He was extremely damaged," Gelbard said. "He was just a guy who needed love, and never got it from his mother. Whatever his problem was, it started with his mother. He constantly talked about her, and about his relationships to women. I think what screwed him up with women was that he didn't get what he needed from his mother. She didn't like to be touched. She was very beautiful, well dressed, and slim, with his kind of bone structure. He looked like her. It was the classical love/hate relationship where he adored her and just couldn't get the love that he wanted. And so therefore he hated her and every woman after that."

It is easy to see how his cold, aloof, and violent relationship with his mother shaped Miles emotionally. Children who have not received emotional nurturing learn to cover up and deny their feelings and needs. As adults they often feel rage towards those in close proximity, who remind them of these repressed feelings and needs. Since these feelings and needs have to be expressed and fulfilled somehow, addictive patterns and love-hate relationships are often the result. Miles was the prototype of this condition.

While offering safety, Miles's unyielding persona also was a prison. Without the capacity for trust, genuinely nurturing human contact is virtually impossible. Miles's love-hate romantic relationships appeared to offer only temporary refuge, and it seems that his musicians were his main source of life-giving human contact and a sense of belonging. Miles said, "most of the time my best friends are the musicians in my band,"[26] and Steve Grossman recalled that the rehearsals at his home "were like an intimate 'family' kind of thing." Miles's '80s keyboardist, Robert Irving III, said, "His musicians were his closest friends. He really didn't associate with anybody else. At his home Miles was always cooking gourmet dishes, watching ball games, and going back and playing music again. Rehearsals were living, eating, sleeping, playing music, and they were a fun time."

"Miles called me when he moved out to the West Coast, in 1984," Ndugu Chancler related. "I was playing with The Crusaders, and he asked me to pick him up and bring him to the concert. I had an answer service and failed to note the number correctly, so it seemed to him that I simply had not called him back. Later, when he did an interview with Leonard Feather for *The Times* he made mention of that incident, without mentioning my name. I went to see Miles backstage in 1988/1989 at the Beverly Theatre, and the first thing out of his mouth was: 'Why did you not call me back? I want to hear from you guys.' That was the first time I felt the heart that Miles had for me."

The fact that Miles related this minor incident in a public interview with Feather, and immediately remembered it when he met Chancler again, four years later, shows the extent of his vulnerability. In the end, there was no place to hide from his humanness, especially his emotional needs and loneliness. Neither his persona, his music, his musicians, his women, nor his addictions offered an escape from the fundamental existential and emotional issues that were eating him, and on the evidence provided by Gelbard and others, he never healed his inner conflicts.

"Miles was lonely," Lydia DeJohnette commented. "He didn't easily find the stimulation he needed, except in his music. All he wanted was his musician friends around him. He would rather have one of his fellow musicians with him than the president of the country! It's sad that he wasn't able to be more loving towards himself. I don't think he found it easy to be a human being."

Miles's loneliness and inner torment broke through in much of his music, in particular the cri de coeur of his tender, almost broken trumpet sound. Writer Max Harrison observed about a solo Miles played in 1956, "We are moved by the acute sorrow that shadows the outward calm and are reminded of a comment by the English critic Michael James that 'never before in jazz had the phenomenon of loneliness been examined in so intransigent a manner' as by this musician."[27] Miles played very differently from 1966 to 1970, when he was arguably at his happiest and healthiest, courtesy of relationships with Tyson, Mabry, Eskridge, and Battle, low drug use, healthy eating, and lots of physical exercise. During this period his trumpet technique was at its peak, expressed in a virtuoso style, with a powerful tone, fast runs, and towards the end of 1970 higher notes than he had ever hit before. By contrast, the ritualistic, voodoo-istic intensity of his music from 1972 to 1975, which he elicited like a snake charmer, went hand in hand with increasingly obsessive, crazy, drug-induced behavior in his personal life. And while the superstar years of 1985 to 1991 are commonly regarded as one of Miles's happier eras, typified by striking, colorful clothes, and equally colorful, highly arranged music, Miles failed to fool one five-year-old English girl. Playing the role of the boy in the story of the emperor's clothes, she responded to the question of what the trumpet in "Tutu" reminded her of by stating, "It sounds like a little boy who's looking for his Mum."[28]

The stark contrast between the mask and the man makes a compelling dichotomy, bringing to mind the archetypal stories of the beauty and the beast, of Jekyll and Hyde. Miles's persona clearly covered up great sensitivity, kindness, loneliness, and despair. We can speculate on whether Miles seriously attempted to resolve his inner conflicts. From the evidence of his autobiography, it appears not. Although uncompromisingly open in its storytelling (exterior), the book suffers from a curious lack of introspection and reflection (interior). Miles rarely goes beyond surface observations like "See, I'm a Gemini and I can be real nice one minute and into something else the next. I don't know why I'm like that, I just am and I accept that that's the way I am."[29] Mike Stern, who was a drug addict during the '70s and early '80s, and hence spoke from experience, remarked, "It takes some time to deal with whatever got you into taking that shit in the first place. And he was definitely not dealing with that."

For a man who had an almost extrasensory perception of the interiors of music and of people surrounding him, and who always focused more on "how" (interior) than "what" (exterior), this lack of introspection is peculiar. Miles may have decided to hide behind his persona, preferring to tell the stories and reveal little about his deeper feelings and reflections. But it may also just have been the way he related to life. "I don't remember him going into why's very much," Marguerite Eskridge observed. "Everything was more action-reaction. Things just were, and he didn't reflect on where they came from."

Moreover, raised in an emotional and cultural paradigm that regarded expressing feelings and needs as weakness and that barely acknowledged the interior, Miles appears to have gone out of his way to avoid looking at his interior. His addictive patterns were one strategy. Another indication of escapist behavior was his dislike of being alone and of silence. Visitors to his house testified that he had a television set playing in every room, all the time. "Every TV in every room was always on in every house I've been in with him," Jo Gelbard said. Many musicians and acquaintances also recounted his continuous calls and invitations to come and visit him, especially late at night. "Miles had a great need to have someone at his side," Eskridge said. "He could not be alone," Dave Liebman remembered. "Much of the time Miles just wanted company—desperately,"[30] Eric Nisenson wrote.

Miles's inner turmoil and the way it was expressed in drug-related and unpleasant behavior led some to describe him in dramatic terminology. "He could be a really evil guy," said Dave Liebman. "There was a purely evil side to him," stressed Jo Gelbard. "He had no sense of morality. He had a dead zone where his sense of morality should have been." Greg Tate also referred to an absence of conscience when he called Miles's stories "gloating," just like Chambers, who remarked that *Miles: The Autobiography* was "a catalog of indiscretions without any undertones of guilt or remorse." One wonders what book Chambers and Tate read, because Miles often expressed regret, and otherwise related his craziness, violence, and drug abuse in an unemotional, factual manner. *Miles: The Autobiography* is simply, brutally, and uncompromisingly direct, and is admirable for its absence of cheap excuses and hand-wringing guilt. Miles meted out the horrors of drug use and dysfunctional relationships graphically enough to serve as a stark warning for anyone contemplating going down the same route.

On the evidence of the autobiography, Miles was less than proud of much of his behavior. He chastised himself for his incapacity to settle into a regular family life with Irene Cawthorn and their three children in the late '40s, and he realized that the reason Frances divorced him in the '60s was because he did not give her the respect and safety she wanted. Miles also repeatedly expressed feelings of guilt towards his two oldest sons, Gregory and Miles IV,[31] and for his failure to visit his parents before they died. "Miles was not in control of many things in his life," Mark Rothbaum said. "He was guilt-ridden about being a poor father, and not immune to his failures as a husband."

Miles also had considerable positive effects on the lives of many, including the musicians interviewed for this book, who almost invariably speak of him with great respect and deep gratitude. It is hard to understand how Miles could have realized this if his darkness and violence are exaggerated out of proportion. For those willing to look, all the evidence suggests that Miles was acutely aware of the difference between life-affirming and life-destroying actions, and that he valued the former more highly. Miles may often have been unable to withdraw from destructive patterns, but his awareness of these different tendencies in his life is illustrated by the fact that he did his best to keep them separate, and to protect his musicians and friends from the darker areas of his life. In effect, Miles led a double life. Jack DeJohnette recalled, "Miles had both 'good' people and not so good people around him." And Lydia added, "And it was conscious. During his heavy drug phase he wouldn't connect with people that he knew wouldn't go there. He wouldn't bother to talk to Jack or have him over. . . . He'd just say, 'This is not your shit.'"

Marguerite Eskridge says she still feels gratitude towards Miles for teaching her the difference between the two worlds. "When I met Miles, I was a very immature and extremely naive young woman," Eskridge stated. "It was the '60s, and I wanted to see flowers everywhere and the good in everyone, no matter what. Miles came into my life to help me survive, because I would not have made it. I was far too open and honest. We had constant clashes and disagreements like, 'These are my friends and they're great people.' And he would say, 'They're not great people and they're only with you for these or these reasons.' And I wouldn't believe that. But invariably I eventually came to see that he had been absolutely right, that everything he'd said was true. I needed to see how much darkness there was in life. He taught me to be streetwise. I owe much to him for that and I haven't grown bitter at all, just much more careful and conscious and so far I've survived pretty well! Miles saw straight through people, and I have learned to take on those lenses today. In many ways he was a father figure."

Marguerite Eskridge did not recall Miles ever being physically violent towards her, suggesting that whatever physical violence occurred between Miles and women was to some degree the responsibility of both people involved. Jim Rose implied as much when he recalled that Loretta also did drugs and was also violent towards Miles. And Nisenson expressed his bewilderment when the girl whose jaw Miles had broken moved straight back in after returning from hospital.[32] It appears that few, if any, of the women beaten by Miles were total victims. The women involved sought his company entirely of their own accord.

None of the above is raised to condone or belittle Miles's destructive behavior. It only serves to point out that his accounts were hardly "gloating." He had too many life-affirming values to be proud of his darker sides. Instead he was merely being honest— up to a point. Many have admired Miles's "honesty." "Honesty was one of his greatest virtues," Paul Buckmaster said. "He had a kind of nobility in this way, and he could smell bullshit a mile off." "He was the most honest person I've ever met," John McLaughlin remarked. "You could say *brutally* honest. You always knew where you were with him; there was no bullshit, he'd tell you right off."[33]

Nevertheless, as we have seen, Miles's honesty was hardly impeccable. A better way of describing the quality Buckmaster and many others have highlighted is perhaps that he possessed authenticity and fearlessness in the face of bullshit and hypocrisy. Miles could indeed "smell bullshit a mile off." He trusted his own gut instincts and had the courage of his convictions. There are many legendary tales of him violating protocol and social conventions to puncture balloons of pomposity and pretence. In one instance, during a party at the White House in 1987, Miles repeatedly and brutally cut down pretentious and patronizing exclamations. "Just a bunch of sorry motherfuckers with plastic smiles, acting all proper and shit," Miles commented later.[34] When he gave a live interview for an audience at the Studio Museum of Harlem in New York in the spring of 1989, an African American museum board member approached him. She told Miles that she hardly ever visited the museum and that she considered Miles's visit "the high point of the museum's history." Miles's response was instant and straight to the point: "This is a great place, and I wouldn't have you on my motherfuckin' board if you didn't show."[35]

There is another important area in which Miles lived life-affirming values. In race relationships he was a pioneer who contributed significantly to improvements in circumstances for African Americans. The roots of his attitude can again be found in his family origins. Although the Davis's declarations of their own superiority sound rather pretentious, they were indeed ahead of their time. With Miles's grandfather owning five hundred acres of land around the turn of the century, and his father being a landowner as well as a successful dentist, they had been comfortably middle-class for at least two generations, a highly unusual situation for a black family in the United States in the 1920s and 1930s.

Miles's father was aware of racial inequalities and willing to combat them. Miles was therefore raised with a modern outlook on race relations, which became widely accepted by the end of the twentieth century but was regarded as controversial before the '60s counterculture began to raise America's racial awareness. Before then, "Uncle Tomming" was the norm. "Every little black kid grew up seeing that getting along with white people meant grinning and acting [like] clowns,"[36] Miles remarked. By contrast, he did not think racial equality was a favor, and he demanded it as his birthright. Add to this the pride instilled in him by the male lineage of his family and the reality of racial discrimination was unusually painful to him.

"People perceived Miles as arrogant," Pete Cosey said. "But actually it was intelligence, knowing what he was supposed to have, and how he should be treated, as an equal human on this earth. But most Americans were not willing to treat him in that way. So when he refused to take flak, he was accused of being uppity, or other derogatory terms, when in fact the man was just normal. He was one of the least racist persons I've ever met, and that's why it was very painful for him to experience racism. Miles, by virtue of his age, had seen a lot of racism. We were the first generation that really did not take any crap, and the powers that be were very threatened by that. On one occasion—we had just played Toronto and were on our way to Montreal—we ran into some racism at the airport check-in. They let Dave Liebman on the plane with at least three horns and his bags, and refused to let Reggie on with just his guitar. This was perceived by everyone as a racist act. Miles turned around and said, 'We are going home.' We did not go to Montreal that night, but instead went back to New York."

Like many blacks in the United States, Miles was confronted with a daily barrage of racial prejudice in small forms, from being stopped for being a black man driving an expensive sports car to being mistaken for the janitor of his own house when an electrician called. "Miles had never become inured to such casual racism . . . running into it was still shocking and profoundly upsetting,"[37] Eric Nisenson observed. Needless to say, more extreme expressions of racism, such as his beating outside Birdland in 1959, had a deeply traumatic effect on Miles. Racial discrimination was one of the main challenges facing him and one of the main sources of the deep hurt and burning rage he carried inside. It's a topic to which he returns time and time again in virtually all published interviews. His famous 1962 interview with *Playboy* was almost solely about racial issues. "When it comes to human rights," Miles said, "these prejudiced white people keep on acting like they own the damn franchise!"[38]

The way Miles handled racism made him into a much-admired icon and role model for many blacks. Quincy Troupe explained in *Miles and Me* how Miles refused to be photographed smiling, because he associated it with black Uncle Tomming. The uproar Miles caused in conservative jazz circles because he did not introduce songs or tell stories on stage had similar grounds. "My troubles started when I learned to play the trumpet and hadn't learned to dance," he said.[39] Miles's insistence on having black women on the covers of some of his '60s albums was also regarded as breaking new racial ground.

In addition, his hard-nosed business attitudes had a great impact on the working conditions for musicians. In the '50s Miles was the first to refuse to work '40–20,' an agreement whereby musicians played for a whole evening from every twenty minutes after the hour till the hour. He reduced the maximum amount of sets played per evening to three. Miles's run-ins with promoters became the stuff of legends. When a promoter offered to pay him $2,000 for the first performance of a night and only $1,000 for the second, Miles agreed on the condition that half the auditorium was fenced off for the second performance. The promoter relented and paid the full fee for both performances.

Having inherited a knack for making money from his father and grandfather, Miles was the highest-paid jazz musician for much of his career. "There's no excuse for being poor," he said in 1972. "You see, you're not supposed to wait on anybody to give you nothing. My father taught me that."[40] In countless interviews Miles proudly announced how he made money as a teenager, doing a paper route. "[At] fourteen I was making three dollars a night. Fifteen I was making six. Sixteen I was making $100 a week."[41] But Miles not only used his business acumen to his own advantage, he also helped other black musicians get better deals, among them Horace Silver and Roberta Flack.

Presumably, Miles's detractors were provoked by the seemingly racist clichés Miles sometimes uttered, like "I can tell a white trumpet player, just listening to a record,"[42] "White groups don't reach me. I can tell a white group just from the sound,"[43] or "If a white man bothers me, man, I don't want to touch him because I don't know what I might do. I might kill him."[44] But these appear to fall in the category of deliberate inconsistencies, because Miles was resolutely color-blind when it came to his choice of musicians, friends, and women. All white musicians who worked with him testify to his non-racist attitudes. "I never had any problems with Miles about race," Steve Grossman said. "Miles would sometimes play that card, but I think it was purely to test you, to see if you were going to take bullshit or not, to see what he could get away with."

"He always treated me and other musicians that I saw him with as fellow musicians, as fellow artists," Paul Buckmaster said. "He was not locked into, 'I'm black and I have a chip on my shoulder about being black' or 'My culture is only African American.' He was fully aware of the problems of racism and had some bitter experiences. But I can evidence that he didn't have a bone in his body that could see color when it came to music. He was interested in music from all countries and all styles. He wanted to know more about classical music. He was a universal man. He had a common sense of humanity. His music reflects that. It transcends time, place, and culture."

❖

It is tempting to assume that Miles's darkness was expressed through his public persona and to see the person behind it as "the nicest, gentlest of men" or "the real Miles Davis." It's a neat and tidy division, but, of course, reality is nowhere near that simple. Both the mask and the man contained light and dark aspects, constructive and destructive tendencies. Much of Miles's violence took place in private, and many aspects of his mask found their roots in his childhood background. It is easy to have an aversion for the brutal aspects of his persona, but it is important to note that his public attitude had another, deeply inspirational side. Often referred to as "cool," it goes way beyond our common understanding of the word.

In Western culture "cool" means hip or fashion conscious and refers to a purely exterior quality, a pose conjuring up associations with superficiality and self-obsessed, narcisstic, noncaring behavior. However, the origins of the word go back to the Yoruba people of southwest Nigeria, who use it to describe an interior characteristic, serenity, expressed outwardly as composure. The anthropologist Robert Farris Thompson explains: "Coolness is the correct way you represent yourself to be a human being. . . . To the degree that we live generously and discreetly, exhibiting grace under pressure, our appearance and our acts gradually assume virtual royal power. As we become noble, fully realizing the spark of creative goodness God endowed us with . . . we find the confidence to cope with all kinds of situations. . . . This is mystic coolness."[45] In another text on Yoruban culture "coolness" is described as "The state of being composed . . . [it] is an ethical/aesthetic quality. . . . The person who is composed behaves in a measured and rational way; he or she is controlled, proud, dignified, and cool. An essential quality in a ruler, composure is particularly evident in images of kings."[46]

The writer Michael Ventura remarked, "Coolness doesn't mean coldness. Cool art is passionate art. In American culture, Miles Davis has been the exemplar of this aesthetic."[47] Ventura referred to the "cool" aspects in Miles's music, most notably the album *The Birth of the Cool*, but Miles's "coolness" permeated much more than just his music. Miles has been called "the coolest man on the planet."[48] Leaving aside the misguided macho admiration from which declarations like these sometimes emerge, this can also refer to Miles's "mystic coolness." As an artist, Miles possessed "grace under pressure," "royal power," and "dignity" in abundance. Miles may not have displayed much "coolness" in other areas of his life, but in his art he was one of the great twentieth-century protagonists of the cool attitude.

It is easy to misunderstand "coolness" for simple charisma, star quality, or hipness. The difference between this view and the deeper meaning of cool can be described as that between pose and poise. Miles's musicians repeatedly refer to his poise, his transcendent, spiritual side. "Miles had a certain way of moving and being, he had a flow," Sonny Fortune noted. "He never walked fast. The cat glided. He was always gliding. He had a certain way of moving, sitting, speaking. I've never known a person like that. People don't normally associate spiritualness with Mr. Miles Davis, but it is probably the only way to describe some of the energy that he had. He was like a little bomb of energy. He wasn't like some little flower or butterfly floating around. He possessed real awesomeness."

The question arises where Miles got his "awesomeness" and "coolness." Although there is no doubt that the degree to which he embodied this characteristic was entirely his own, his family background once again provides some clues to its seeds. Certainly the "virtual royal power" of his father's and grandfather's proud attitude was one of them, but the Native American heritage of his mother may also have played a part. Behavioral patterns can be transmitted from generation to generation without people being aware of this, and it is very possible that the young Miles assimilated Native American character traits via his mother's family line. In his book *Lila: An Inquiry into Morals,* writer Robert Pirsig described certain characteristics of the Native American manner, among them, "Silence, a modesty of manner," "Indians don't talk to fill time. When they don't have anything to say, they don't say it," "anti-snobbery," "head-on, declarative sentences without stylistic ornamentation."[49] He also claims that Native Americans were the originators of the idea that "all men are created equal."[50] Every single one of these characteristics applies to Miles.

They also fit perfectly with the Yoruban notion of "coolness." The reason is that both Yoruban "coolness" and the above mentioned qualities epitomized by Native Americans are universally recognized demonstrations of spiritual dignity. Miles embodied these with the deeper elements of his "cool" demeanor. There's something deeply "right" in the way Miles approached music, his musicians, and his audiences. The enduring culture, nation, and race-transcending interest in the man and his music illustrate the timeless nature of this quality and how deeply it resonates in our collective consciousness. It is therefore an astonishing symbol of poetic justice that *Tutu* became Miles's best-known recording of his last decade. Miles and Marcus Miller named it after the South African archbishop and antiapartheid activist Desmond Tutu, without realizing that the Yoruban word for "cool" is, in fact, "tutu."

Chapter Twelve

STAR ON MILES

"Miles could speak to the audience one to one. If you can do that to one person, you can do it to the world, and if you have the world's ear, you can do whatever you want."

—BILL EVANS

The world to which Miles returned in 1980 had evolved considerably from the world on which he had turned his back in 1975. The '70s had in many respects been a backward-looking decade, during which Western societies attempted to integrate the far-reaching political and cultural upheavals of the '60s counterculture. By the late '70s, the pendulum had swung away again from '60s values such as the classless society, racial equality, socialism, and feminism towards individualistic and hedonistic goals like getting rich, carving out high-flying careers, and being glamorous. The '80s, in short, were the era of the yuppie. This was exemplified in the ascent to power of regressive, right-wing leaders, such as Margaret Thatcher in Britain in 1979 and Ronald Reagan in the United States in 1981, paired with the emergence of glossy, vacuous rock music that emphasized form over content. MTV, founded in 1981, became the quintessence of this development.

One thing that had barely changed by 1980 was the low life expectancy for jazz musicians. Charles Mingus died at the age of fifty-seven in 1979, and pianist Bill Evans at the age of fifty-one in 1980. Miles turned fifty-four in 1980, and given the abundant rumors of his ill health, news of his death would have surprised few. Many therefore considered his return to music little short of miraculous. Various explanations have been offered, with one oft-mentioned force being that of Columbia's vice president George Butler, who began visiting Miles in 1978, hoping to push him into making music again. "My visits were frequent," Butler recalled. "We only talked about clothes, boxing, and cars. This continued for eight months, not one word about music. Then suddenly, one day Miles said, 'George, I've got some ideas.' I froze with excitement and anticipation. We walked over to the piano and he played this chord . . . nothing, absolutely no sound. None of the keys worked. That's when I decided to ask the then president of CBS Records, Bruce Lundvall, to consider giving Miles a piano for his forthcoming birthday. He consented, and I chose the piano."[1]

Following this Miles requested the presence of Paul Buckmaster, who flew over to New York in early July of 1979. "Miles wanted to do a recording of 'Love Don't Live Here

Anymore' by Rose Royce [an American group that enjoyed several hits in the second half of the '70s]," Buckmaster recalled. "I started working on an arrangement, and also wrote some things, but every time I went over to Miles's house, there'd be some friends of his with duck powder that I didn't know, and didn't want to know."

Gil Evans was also reported to have been involved in these early attempts at getting Miles to work again, but he left the scene very quickly, presumably guessing that these efforts were to come to nothing. Only one session, which took place in the summer of 1979, emerged directly from Butler's persuasions. It was organized by session contractor Gene Bianco, who gathered a band featuring the twenty-year-old bassist Marcus Miller, a rising star on the East Coast session scene. Miller had played on records by Dave Grusin, Elton John, and the Brecker Brothers, and was to play a pivotal part in Miles's music. The band recorded some of Buckmaster's arrangements, but Miles never showed up to join them.

Miles was unlikely to have been very impressed with the results, because a few weeks later he invited Pete Cosey for another studio session, which featured Buckmaster, saxophonist John Stubblefield, unknown guitarist Warne Bingham, bassist Ron Johnson (who had played with Buddy Miles, and on the 1972 album *Buddy Miles & Carlos Santana: Live!*), and Doni Hagen on drum programming. Once again Miles failed to show—this time because he had been involved in an argument in a drugstore, during which a shop attendant hit Miles with a telephone and damaged his collarbone.

Not long after these aborted sessions, the nightmarish scene in August of 1979 occurred—Miles passed out during a hot summer night—which prompted Buckmaster to call Miles's sister Dorothy, who in turn contacted Cicely Tyson. By all accounts this proved to be main turning point, the beginning of Miles's long road towards recovery. Tyson has widely been credited as the person who played the largest role in nursing Miles back into enough sanity and physical health to be able to perform again.

"She helped run all those people out of my house," Miles recalled. "She kind of protected me and started seeing that I ate the right things, and didn't drink as much. She helped me get off cocaine. She would feed me health foods, a lot of vegetables, and a whole lot of juices. She turned me on to acupuncture to help get my hip back in shape. All of a sudden I started thinking clearer, and that's when I really started thinking about music again."[2]

The renewed connection with Dorothy also played a central part in Miles's return to music. Regularly on the phone with her, Miles became intrigued with the musical activities of her twenty-one-year-old son, Vince Wilburn Jr. He had pushed Dorothy into buying Vince a drum set when he was seven, and the young man had developed into an excellent player, studying music at the American Conservatory in Chicago. "I had a band and he would call and ask my mum to hold the phone down so he could listen to our rehearsals," Wilburn recounted. "I also went back and forth to New York to see how he was doing. People think that he was just getting high, but he was always listening to music and thinking about music. He just wasn't playing the horn. I was encouraging him and trying to learn at the same time."

What is striking about these accounts is how passive Miles appears in them. He appears to have been pushed and persuaded almost every step of the way. Miles's lack of money in 1980 provided an additional and rather urgent stimulus to get back to work.

Columbia was dragging its feet over renewing his contract and continuing his retainer, and was asking for new material. Why he did not continue with the direction he had begun with Pete Cosey is unclear. "His sister worked on his conscience, saying, 'You need to do something for little Vincent and his friends,'" Cosey asserted. Miles was perhaps also anxious about working with a set of seasoned professionals at a time when his chops were almost nonexistent. The family connection and the relative inexperience of Wilburn's band provided a much less pressured return to playing music.

In addition to Vince Wilburn Jr., the core of the band featured leader and guitarist/singer Randy Hall, keyboardist Robert Irving III, and bassist Felton Crews. In April of 1980 Miles invited this quartet to New York to rehearse and record. Miles also asked Dave Liebman whether he could suggest a saxophone player. Liebman recommended a student of his, Bill Evans, who had just turned twenty-two, came fresh out of college, and had no band experience to speak of. "Miles and I became good friends," Evans recalled. "I was sort of the opposite of him, because I never did drugs. He could trust me."

Rehearsals with the young Chicago band and Evans began in May but were soon abandoned, when Miles was once again hospitalized. "There was an abscess in his knee," Mark Rothbaum said. "It was serious. But Cicely came in again, and organized his health, because he was slipping, and could have lost the leg." After this hiatus, rehearsals resumed in June.

"He was playing keyboards," Irving remembered. "I think he was a little bit reluctant to pick up his horn because he was surrounded by musicians who were into their craft. It takes time to build your embouchure, and rather than embarrass himself, he just didn't play the trumpet. We'd develop something in rehearsal, and then we'd go in the studio and record it. We recorded a total of nineteen tracks. Miles was really having fun. 'The Man with the Horn' was one of the tracks that we recorded, and Miles overdubbed trumpet to it later. But when he finally got his lip back together, he didn't overdub on the other songs. There were some other recordings that would have lent themselves to where the forthcoming album was going. Had we had a little bit more direction from him, we could have gone there."

Although Irving's regrets are understandable, the aural evidence of "The Man with the Horn," issued as part of Miles's 1981 comeback album with the same name, suggests a much more straightforward reason: the music simply wasn't good enough. The song is a mediocre ballad, played without much distinction, and featuring embarrassing lyrics paying homage to Miles. This band may well have been able to go much further, particularly given the talents Irving, Wilburn, and Crews displayed in their work with Miles later in the '80s, but its potential is not evident on this recording. Miles summed the whole direction up very neatly: "Randy Hall, and my nephew and little Bobby, they all write great music for me. If I need a bubble-gum song, I just call up Randy and say, Randy send me a bubble-gum song."[3]

Miles overdubbed his trumpet part on the recording later in the year. His technical difficulties are painfully obvious. Although his gift for melody is still evident, his sound is shrill and lacking in power, and he plays out of tune in places. Miles used his wah-wah pedal to mask his shortcomings, but it was his last session using the device. Under pressure from the other musicians he agreed to stop using it. "There was one overdub session while we were there, probably the summer of 1980, and Miles sounded terrible," Irving said. "You could tell he had ideas in his fingers and in his head, but they just weren't coming out. His lips wouldn't allow him to do it. This was his first attempt at overdubbing onto one of our tracks. Later on he tried again, and he called me around Christmas saying, 'Bobby, listen to this!' and he played me the track with him playing over it, as if to say, 'My lip is back.' But there was a general consensus among everybody that the sound of the pure trumpet was the way to go. The wah-wah was going backwards."

"Miles was still very sick," Macero recalled. "He was so fucked up on drugs and everything that he could barely play. He was breathing badly, and all bent over; it was terrible. We sometimes had to piece his playing together [during postproduction]. It was tough. On some of those tracks we had to slow the tape recorder down to half speed during recording, so he could reach those notes. The stuff with his nephew was pretty weak material. I didn't really dig it, but I accepted it. If that's what he wanted to do, we'd do it the best way we knew."

Much later, in May of 1981, Miles recorded another track, called "Shout," with the young band. Mercifully lyrics-free, it is better than "The Man with the Horn," but still no more than a bland, soul-funk exercise. The two tracks were most likely included on *The Man with the Horn* as an act of gratitude for the stepping-stone back into music the Chicago band had given to Miles. Fortunately, Miles realized they were no more than this, and after almost a year of other people pushing him, he changed course the moment his confidence and health had grown enough for him to assert his own direction. His assessment was that only saxophonist Bill Evans was advanced enough musically to be of immediate further musical use to him. He knew he wanted to work with Al Foster again, but other than this he had no idea how to proceed. Miles could easily have enlisted an all-star band at this stage, but it was indicative of his courage and commitment to music that he once again took the risk of working with unknown young musicians.

For a while Miles's plans came to nothing. He spent the rest of 1980 much as he had the previous years, indulging in drugs, alcohol, and indolence, despite a diabetes diagnosis, which offered a big warning sign that he could not carry on with his lifestyle indefinitely. During this period Bill Evans provided his main connection with normality and music. "We hung out for a whole year as friends," Evans recounted. "We'd go for lunch, I'd bring food back, we walked the streets of New York. He went through periods when he relied on certain people he felt he could trust. I happened to be that guy between 1980 and 1983. I think the only other person who spent a lot of time with him during that period was Al Foster. I was slowly chaperoning his move back into music, helping him put a band together, just being around like a friend and a musician. I knew what was going on in the New York clubs. He didn't. I was sort of his eyes with regards to what was going on. He asked me for my opinions, and he trusted me."

Miles's trust in Evans's judgements turned out to be well founded. When Miles finally did get his act together enough to lead his own band, in early 1981, the saxophonist's recommendations were extremely fortuitous. His first was bassist Marcus Miller, who had already participated in the aborted session in 1979. In addition, Miles invited guitarist Barry Finnerty, whom he had met in the late '70s and who had impressed him with a guitar synthesizer. To complete the band, Al Foster suggested Sammy Figueroa, a percussionist who had performed on Foster's 1979 solo album, *Mr. Foster*. The sextet, consisting of Foster, Miller, Figueroa, Finnerty, Evans, and Miles, went into the studio at an unknown date in the beginning of 1981. It was during the first session that the incident took place that Miller related in Chapter 1, when Miles played the bassist an F-sharp and a G and tried to intimidate him.

"In 1979 Miles didn't have anything to do with picking the musicians," Miller added. "But this second time he was in control of the session. I noticed that his chops weren't great, and later realized that he was doing a lot of cocaine. Enough to keep him in a weird state."

Despite his continuing drug use, Miles managed to coax his new band into recording several tracks that were a leap forward from the sessions with his nephew's band. Three recordings from these sessions—"Aïda," "Back Seat Betty," and "Ursula"—were included on *The Man with the Horn*. "Miles and Bill had gone over 'Aïda' before the session because they had melodies to play," Miller recalled. "He showed me the F-sharp and G bass line, and the rest was free. He'd point, he'd stop, and he conducted us right there in the studio. He had a melodic idea for 'Back Seat Betty,' but that was all. He just counted us off. Al started playing, and we fell into it. 'Ursula' was just a jam. For most of the tracks he had a few notes, just enough for everybody to unify. When we were playing, no matter how far out we got, those three or four notes would focus everybody and then we could go again. It was a cool concept."

According to Miller, the working methods Miles used during these sessions echoed the way Miles had directed his '70s bands. "Later on I went back to the '70s music, and realized that what we did was based on the same concept, the same way of approaching music," Miller said. "He was just picking up where he had left off. It all suddenly made a lot more sense. I realized that what we'd done wasn't as new as I thought it was. In the '70s Pete Cosey had been doing some crazy and amazing stuff, and Michael Henderson was probably the most underrated bass player who ever played with Miles. That music is deep. Sometimes I wish I'd understood it when I played with Miles in the early '80s because it might have given me an edge in terms of trying to figure out what to do. But in other ways it was good, because it gave me the freedom to go somewhere else, which was into more atonal stuff."

While there were a number of similarities between the two bands, Miles's early '80s band was unlike the '73–'75 band in several ways. The former did not work with the idea of "living compositions" (i.e., weaving many fragments and motifs together into an ever-changing musical tapestry). In addition, the function of the rhythm section was very different in these two bands. In the mid-1970s the music was structured around Henderson's circular and melodic bass riffs, and the hypnotic repetitiveness of Lucas's funk guitar, Foster's drumming, and Mtume's African percussion. But the early '80s music was organized along the traditional theme-solo-theme structure, while Miller's mostly linear bass lines only occasionally formed the melodic foundation. The funk-rhythm guitar is also absent, Foster drums in a more traditional, varied, jazz-like style, and the African influence has all but disappeared, with less emphasis on the bottom end and very little grit. The early '80s music is much more open, and miles away from the funk collective's all-engulfing wall of sound.

It appears that Miles did not have a strong musical direction at this stage but simply made the best of the here-and-now reality that presented itself to him. "Miles basically reacted to who he ended up with in the room," Miller said. "And then he'd say, 'I don't like this,' or he'd start shaping things. He would tell me to come up with a bass line. I'd play one, and he'd say, 'No.' I'd try another one, and again he'd say, 'No.' And on the third one he might say, 'Yeah, that's it.' Over time I tried to get into his head, so that I could give him what he liked. He'd also create environments—situations that had no precedents. So you're trying hard to find something that's appropriate for this unusual music because he's setting up things without chords or charts; he's just kind of vibing. If you're open enough and catch this vibe, you're going to come up with something that fits."

Given Miles's lack of direction in the early '80s, and the impromptu manner in which the band had come together, it is not surprising that the three tracks recorded in early 1981 are mediocre. "Back Seat Betty" opens in heavy rock style, with Finnerty repeating two heavily distorted guitar chords, after which Miller and Foster settle in a light-footed funk groove. Miles states the fairly nondescript theme at 00:30, and proceeds to solo with an open trumpet tone that's greatly improved over his efforts on "The Man with the Horn," occasionally sliding impressively into the higher register. Evans plays an adequate soprano solo, and musical structure is created by the insertion of the heavy rock power chords at several points, most likely courtesy of edits by Macero in some cases. Notwithstanding intense drumming by Foster, and some intelligent chordal playing by Finnerty, there's a sense of coldness and alienation about the music.

The same coldness hampers "Aïda," in which Miller plays around with the rudimentary F-sharp and G riff as best as he can. The graceless and embryonic ten-note motif, more riff than theme, is one of the main drawbacks. Miles again plays some very high notes, and uses space very effectively. But in this context his dramatic, declamatory phrases fail to hold interest. Evans's soprano solo is also shrill and disjointed, and as on "Back Seat Betty," there's little interplay between the soloists and the rhythm section. Finally, "Ursula" is a jam without much direction or distinction. The main interest lies in the traditional jazz-swing feel and walking bass, an unusual occurrence in Miles's electric music.

Like the tracks he recorded with his nephew's young Chicago band in 1980, these sessions were a stepping-stone. However, Miles was clearly aware of the music's limitations. He soon sacked guitarist Barry Finnerty and percussionist Sammy Figueroa, apparently deciding that they did not fit. Finnerty's "cool," controlled guitar style confined the band energetically and rhythmically. Miles needed a more versatile guitarist who could light a fire, both as a soloist and as a rhythm player, and he again turned to Evans for advice. The saxophonist suggested Mike Stern, a little-known twenty-eight-year-old guitarist who had studied at the Berklee College of Music, had played with Blood, Sweat & Tears, and was at the time a member of Billy Cobham's band. Miles and Evans caught a concert at the Bottom Line in New York to see Stern perform with Cobham. Miles was so impressed that he talked to Cobham while his band was still playing, and convinced the drummer to release the guitarist. "I was really thrilled about playing with Miles," Stern said. "I was also scared like shit, because he was such a great player, and so many great players had passed through his band. His chops were down when we first played together, but right from jump he was hitting on some great stuff."

The truth of Stern's statement was demonstrated by a session around March, which resulted in a track called "Fat Time"—the nickname Miles gave Stern. Without Finnerty, the improvement to the music is dramatic, and it is not surprising that the tune became the opening track for *The Man with the Horn*. Miller and Foster lay down an infectious, bluesy, shuffle groove over which Miles plays some stirring, suspenseful muted trumpet, with a strong tone, while Stern comps elegantly and inventively. At 01:13 there's a tension-raising shift in the rhythm as well as a modulation, with Miles playing some flamenco-like figures, followed by another modulation, again increasing the intensity of the music. At 02:15 the tension is released when the music returns to the opening key and groove. Evans solos more effectively than on any of the other tracks on the album. Miller and Foster reveal themselves to be an outstanding rhythm tandem, Stern plays an excellent solo, and Miles switches dramatically to open horn towards the end.

"Miles said, 'Al, play that New Orleans beat,' and sang it to him," Miller related. "I came up with a bass line that fit, and like the other sessions, the rest was just jammed. Teo later made sense of it during mixing and editing." "Miles really dug it," Stern asserted. "He was great at knowing when the shit was ready because I wanted to do it again, but he said, 'When you're at a party, you got to know when to leave.' Generally he was right, and this one came out really good. Teo fixed it up a little bit. During the recording Miles told me he wanted a kind of flamenco sound. So he played this flamenco thing on the keyboard, and I didn't know what the fuck he was doing. I thought I had to get a flamenco guitar, but he said, 'No, just do it your own way.' It turned out all he was after was a Spanish vibe in the middle of that tune. It didn't have to be technically correct; he was looking for a vibe. He wanted you to have your own voice, and this became a big influence on me. He really helped me find it."

With his embouchure returning, and Miller and Stern revealing themselves as top-class players, Miles's thoughts turned to playing live again. However, he still needed a more suitable percussionist. The entertaining story of how he found Mino Cinelu has echoes of the way Miles scouted Dave Holland in 1968. Originally from Martinique, Cinelu grew up in France, and had moved to New York in 1979. He expected to flourish immediately in New York's rich musical culture, but instead he found that he had to work hard to survive, often playing music with which he didn't feel great affinity. Cinelu also plays guitar and drums, but Miles witnessed him on percussion one night in the spring of 1981 at Mikell's R&B club in New York.

"He was sitting in front of the stage looking weird," Cinelu remembered. "He looked old and very unhealthy, almost like a bum, and I did not recognize him. He gave me that look, that stare, with which I was not familiar yet. I was playing relaxed, but I could feel something was going on because everybody on stage was trying to play their best licks. I was thinking, 'What is wrong with everybody tonight?' After the gig I passed in front of Miles. He grabbed me, and I tried to let him know that that wasn't a good idea. He said 'You are a bad motherfucker.' And I replied, 'Okay, thank you, but just let go of my arm.' Knowing him like I knew him since, he must have loved it. To react like that was the best introduction I could have had. I walked away, and someone said to me, 'Do you know who that is?' and I said, 'No,' and he said, 'Miles Davis.' I went, 'Oh shit,' returned, and said, 'Hi, it's a pleasure to meet you.' Miles said, 'Fuck that, give me your phone number!' I told him I'd go and get it. I went downstairs, and thought, 'I've blown the thing,' and took my time getting changed and paid. After twenty minutes I said to myself, 'Don't be stupid, you know he's not there anymore, but you told him you'd be back.' When I went upstairs he was still waiting for me. He took my card and said, 'Yeah, you're a bad motherfucker, I'll call you.' A few days later he called, told me to be at a rehearsal, and hung up."

Seeing that Cinelu gelled with the rest of the band, Miles contacted his manager, Mark Rothbaum, asking him to get a road crew together with Jim Rose at the helm and to contact promoters to organize a number of concerts. Promoter George Wein booked Miles for two concerts at the Avery Fisher Hall on July 5, 1981, for a reputed fee of $90,000. Wein refused to confirm this, but Rothbaum stated that it was "entirely possible." Similar to the way Miles had liked to "warm up" the '73–'75 band at small clubs like Paul's Mall in Boston or Keystone Korner in San Francisco, his new band was booked at Kix in Boston for four preparatory concerts, from June 26 to 29.

News of Miles's activities in the recording studio had seeped through to the media but they had not raised much interest, because there had been false alarms of a comeback before. However, the announcement in the middle of June of his imminent return to the stage made newspaper headlines around the world. For the outside world, his return to the fray was the stuff of legends, the almost archetypal story of the mysterious Prince of Darkness once again rising from the ashes, surmounting adversity with Herculean strength. As a result, all the planned concerts were instant sellouts.

With the surrounding publicity, excitement, and expectation, the pressure on the younger sextet members was enormous. The fact that Miles refused to do extensive rehearsals added to their anxiety. "We didn't rehearse much before Kix," Evans recalled. "We threw a few ideas around, but we never went through one song from beginning to end. I was scared to death before those concerts." "When we went on the road, I asked him who the keyboard player was going to be," Stern remembered. "And he said, 'No keyboards, just you.' I was doubly terrified. It was obvious that he was going for more of a lean sound, but other than that, to tell you the truth, I wasn't sure what we were doing. I would ask him what we were going to play, and he'd say, 'Just play the power chords' [meaning the opening of 'Back Seat Betty']. It was so vague. He never used to say very much to me. There was a lot of searching going on. We were still trying to find out how to end tunes, and some nights it just would not happen."

Despite their apprehension and the minimal rehearsals, the band remembered these initial concerts with great affection. "It was just us, it was like family," Evans said. "It was a special, magical time. On stage I suddenly realized that the guy who was my friend was also the guy I used to idolize." "It was magical," Cinelu recounted. "We made some unbelievable recordings, although sometimes Miles's chops were not in top shape. We had a lot of freedom and sometimes we got too excited and played too busily. Miles could then play just one note, and we immediately knew where we were. Miles could say so many things with one note. He had many talents, but that was the one that touched me the most."

Miles organized the music as he had from 1967 to 1975, playing medleys, or "continuous suites," and guiding the band through the different sections with hand movements, coded phrases on his horn, and keyboard stabs. "We used to call him 'The Claw' because he just put his hand down on the keyboard and did not bother with what keys he hit," Stern commented. "But it would always swing, so it didn't matter that he put his hand or an elbow down. We were always watching him. He would change the tune, or end your solo, and you would have to look out for that and make it work musically. You couldn't get lost in your own solo. It wasn't like at the Blackhawk in the '60s, where he'd go for a drink when the band members soloed, and came back when everybody was done. But he liked guitar, and always wanted to hear a lot of guitar. I sometimes had to play over and over again, thinking, 'What can I play next?' The music was amazingly open. It was loose as a motherfucker. Many of the initial gigs were like free-for-alls."

❖

Since Miles's recent musical undertakings had all been very short-lived, Columbia decided to take no chances and to record all six scheduled concerts. Four excerpts from these concerts, edited by Teo Macero, were released in 1982 on *We Want Miles,* with three, "My Man's Gone Now," "Aïda" (retitled "Fast Track"), and "Kix," taken from the concert at Kix of June 27. For a man who never looked back, the twenty-minute version of "My Man's Gone Now" is an astonishing revisitation of a song he had recorded in 1958 with Gil Evans as part of *Porgy and Bess.* Throughout his career Miles occasionally quoted themes from his own back catalog or from popular songs, and in the mid-1970s he regularly referred to the theme of "My Man's Gone Now." But he had not performed a whole track from his pre-1968 jazz repertoire since eliminating "The Theme" from his concert repertoire in October of 1970.

The performance of "My Man's Gone Now" on *We Want Miles* begins with a brief electric piano fragment, the first time the instrument was heard prominently in his music since the end of 1972. Miles was the main keyboardist in his early '80s live band, but he occasionally enticed the classically trained Evans into playing keyboards, and either may have played this opening. The performance continues with a monumental funk-rock bass riff, which is accompanied by graceful, textural guitar rhythm playing, one of Stern's fortes. The bass riff creates an effective contrast with the plainsonglike theme of "My Man's Gone Now." Miles plays lyrically, tenderly, and raises the tension when he switches from muted to open trumpet. At 04:24 he follows the original version's brief excursion into double swing time, and after twelve bars, egged on by a climactic shriek of the trumpet, the band takes the energy down and returns to the funk-rock vamp. The rest of the track is a continuous playing with these two rhythmic elements and with the tension-release structures that were so characteristic of the mid-1970s funk collective.

Evans and Stern both solo, but most of the solo space is taken by Miles. He is credible for much of the time, although there are some disjointed, unconvincing moments. His playing does not yet have the striking quality that immediately and irresistibly demands attention. The repeated forays into jazz-swing territory not only sound ragged, but they also destroy the focused mood set up by the funk-rock vamp. The sound is also occasionally marred by distortion on the bass and trumpet. Since this problem occurs on all the recordings on *We Want Miles,* it is most likely due to problems with the mastering. Despite these reservations, "My Man's Gone Now" is a powerful musical statement, showing that Miles was well on his way to recovery.

The same can be said for "Aïda" (or "Fast Track"), which has more energy and coherence than the original on *The Man with the Horn*. Miles plays a potent opening solo (again hampered by distortion), and Stern gets to play three solos, making the piece a showcase for his talents. At 08:05 there's a break—into which Cinelu plays a percussion solo—that is laced with several collective accents. It is the only officially released incidence of this dramatic device that Miles used so often with the '73–'75 band. After another high shriek from Miles at 12:12, Miller switches into a captivating swamplike funk groove.

The third track from Kix issued on *We Want Miles,* simply called "Kix," begins with an infectious reggaelike bass line with intelligent off-beat comping by Stern. Other highlights are Miles's open trumpet statement beginning at 02:17 and Stern's excellent solo, which begins at 07:10 and features beboplike runs, blues phrasing, and Hendrix-like licks. But this recording is disfigured by the same rhythmic schizophrenia that hampers "My Man's Gone Now," alternating between the reggaelike riff and extended jazz-swing sections that sound out of place. There's a new musical direction hidden in the funk and reggae-inspired riffs, but not in the ordinary 4/4 swing sections.

Various band members have reported on Miles's resistance to playing jazz-swing. "Miles used to say, 'I've already done that. That shit makes me feel old,'" Stern said. "Al, Mike, and Bill loved to push him in that direction," Cinelu remarked. "But Miles would say, 'No bebop.' So we eased off on that groove." Miles nevertheless relented more often than he had done since his first forays into jazz-rock in the late '60s. A possible explanation is that revisiting his past was helpful while he was in the process of relearning to play the trumpet.

"Back Seat Betty" is the only recording included on *We Want Miles* from the two Avery Fisher Hall concerts on July 5. The hard-rock two-chord opening is omitted in this version and Miles plunges straight into the theme. He proceeds to solo with a thin, unsteady sound, which, despite the high notes he hits, reveals his limitations. The main value of this recording is in the way the band sounds more together and fluid than during the Kix recordings—for instance at 05:10, where Miller introduces a new bass riff and the band seamlessly join in to whip up a storm.

Bolstered by the achievements of these early performances, Miles played several more concerts in the United States during July and August, amid reports that his stage manners had changed. "No longer aloof on stage, Davis is now openly responsive to his sidemen and the audience, and between patented glares he honestly seems to be having fun," critic Bob Blumenthal wrote.[4] Writer Cheryl McCall was present at a concert in mid-July at the Savoy, a new club in midtown Manhattan. "The concert was sensational," she noted. "Miles took more chances than he had a couple of weeks earlier at the Kool Jazz Festival. He pushed his reviving chops to the limit, freely mixing tunes like 'All of You,' with contemporary material and even . . . took an extended solo on Fender piano that had a wealth of imagination in it and more than enough technique. . . . When I went backstage, I was shocked to find Miles Davis in state of collapse, sweating like a prize-fighter between rounds and similarly attended by men with towels, drink, encouragement and aid."[5]

On September 29, 1981, Miles left for a tour of Japan, playing seven concerts from October 2 to 11 for a reported fee of $700,000. *Miles! Miles! Miles!* a Japan-only release, contains most of the Tokyo concert of October 4, with a set list consisting of "Back Seat Betty," "Ursula," "My Man's Gone Now," "Aïda," "Fat Time," and "Jean-Pierre." The upward curve of the band is audible on much of the material. The band sounds smoother and more assured, and expands on the Spanish touches to "Fat Time," while the short "Ursula" is played with a funk riff, rather than in jazz-swing time. The October 4 version of "Jean-Pierre" also appears, slightly abridged and in a different mix, on *We Want Miles*. Compared to the rest of the album, it features improved interplay, clearer role divisions among instruments, and some nice touches to the arrangements, such as a descending-chord sequence harmonizing the main melody. Although Miles is not playing strongly, Evans solos delightfully, and Stern takes a star role, accompanying inventively and performing a stirring solo with a dramatic opening. A much shorter version of "Jean-Pierre," recorded in Tokyo on October 3, completes *We Want Miles*, but does not add anything significant.

Enrico Merlin has traced the instantly recognizable tune of "Jean-Pierre" back to Miles's thirty-second birthday, on May 26, 1958, when he played it in a solo in "Love for Sale." After this the theme periodically appears in his solos. Miles named the childlike tune after his first wife's (Frances's) son from a previous marriage. (It is said to be a French children's song, but Cinelu does not remember ever hearing it in France.) Bill Evans recalled Miles first playing it to him at his home, while Stern remembered Gil Evans introducing it during a rehearsal. "Gil played the tune on a little melodica and said, 'Miles, remember this one?'" Stern recalled. "And all of a sudden Marcus went 'boom.' That was a good rehearsal day. 'Jean-Pierre' was a huge advance because it was really tight compared to the other shit. By this time we began to get things a little more together as a band, and there were a few more things we worked out, arrangement-wise. We knew each other's playing much better and things started happening more consistently."

"Jean-Pierre" was to become Miles's signature tune and concert closer until the end of 1987. It was also the concluding theme of his retrospective Paris concert in July of 1991. Miles became strongly associated with this melody during the '80s, and this has symbolic value. Because of his grounding in the blues, Miles always had a proclivity for alternating major and minor thirds, which is one of the hallmarks of the blues, and the melody of "Jean-Pierre" contains both major and minor thirds. Some have criticized the naive nature of the song, and many musicians would be reluctant to perform it for this very reason. But Miles showed courage in making the tune such an important feature of his live sets. Its childlike nature is illustrative of the childlike sense of wonder and open-mindedness with which he approached his art. These qualities led him to never dismiss any music out of hand, and to be constantly in search for the new and for the magic.

Many artists and spiritual teachers have commented on the importance of retaining our sense of wonder, and simple, unassuming openness is, of course, another way of describing Zen's "beginner's mind." It appears that Miles was acutely aware of this consideration. "He once told me he believed that great artists have to retain a childlike fascination with what they do," Troupe wrote. "They have to remain open to the world in a way that children are in order to do the work they do. Miles believed that when artists grow too adult in their thinking and emotions, they lose the ability to let their imaginations run free."[6]

In first disappearing from the limelight for nearly six years, and then making a near-miraculous comeback in 1981, Miles added dramatically to the mystique surrounding him, turning him into jazz's first superstar. This dramatic rise in interest stands in stark contrast to the fact that he was, by the time of his dropout in 1975, all but forgotten by the media, and vilified by the jazz world. But in 1981 jazz audiences around the world welcomed him back like a prodigal son. One explanation may well lie in jazz's creative drought and lack of direction. Fusion had run its course and the main development around the turn of the decade was the rise to prominence of Wynton Marsalis, who spearheaded a hardbop revival that harked back to the '50s. There was little genuinely pioneering jazz in the early '80s, and many hoped Miles could provide a new impetus.

Of course, Miles had failed to live up to the expectations of the jazz world for more than a decade, and the early '80s were no exception, but by this time it was not a case of Miles stepping into a new musical paradigm. Although the individual playing styles of Miles's sidemen gave the band a distinctive sound, and their immense talents ensured that the music never fell below the highest professional standards, Miles's early '80s music only occasionally pioneered radically new perspectives. Apart from Miles's shaky chops, or the overblown expectations of the press, it is hard to see what aspect of his music warranted the critical trouncing it received. While jazz audiences around the world responded enthusiastically to the music, the negative comments by some jazz commentators deeply unsettled his young band members, particularly Mike Stern, who bore the brunt of the attacks because he was supposedly playing "heavy rock." It was claimed that the sideman showed no "inventiveness whatever," while, "Mike Stern's guitar solos were rife with the most banal rock clichés imaginable."[7] Stern's long hair and Stratocaster guitar appeared to work like a red rag to a bull, instantly prejudicing these critics and preventing them from actually listening to the guitarist's playing, which was more informed by bebop and blues than heavy rock.

"I brought some of it upon myself, showing up with corduroy jeans, and torn and dirty clothes," Stern said. "And a Stratocaster. How jazz was that? Today nobody would frown, but at the time the instrument was rarely used in jazz. I used distortion not so much to imitate Hendrix, but to make the guitar sound more like a horn. The Hendrix stuff came out because Miles wanted it. But the critics hated it. After the Avery Fisher concerts I called Miles and read him some review. I said, 'I feel really bad about this,' and he answered, 'Fuck that shit motherfucker. Those motherfuckers don't know what the fuck they're talking about. The only review that you have to worry about is me.' He also told me that he was criticized in his beginning years in New York for being a lousy trumpet player with no sound, and that the same had happened to Coltrane, with people saying he played too much and should phrase better. So basically you can't put too much into any of that stuff. That cooled me out, and I realized it happens every time you try something new. Today people talk about how good that band was, and this was tradition for Miles. He was always ahead of his time."

In an echo of the mid-1970s funk collective's ethos, Bill Evans recalled, "It was us against the world." Marcus Miller also remembered, "We all went through the storm, so we started to say, 'Okay, we know it's only us in this little shell against everybody else. We also realized, 'How would it be if the critics loved us?' I mean, this was Miles Davis. The critics weren't supposed to like us. The last thing you want to do is make music the critics can digest. They're the slowest moving entity in the music community, much slower than the audiences. If the critics like you, you have a problem. Once I realized that, and I heard them say, 'Well, Marcus Miller is no Ron Carter,' I said, 'Okay, that's cool.'"

Columbia released *The Man with the Horn* in the summer of 1981, attempting to cash in on the wave of publicity surrounding Miles's return to the stage. This was Miles's first post–silent period release, and since all of it, with the exception of "Fat Time," was inferior to what he was playing live, most reviews were negative. Ironically, the cold, disembodied cover with mirrors and a dummy head perfectly expressed the relatively unfeeling and sterile nature of the music. *The Man with the Horn* may also not have been helped by the '80s production values of the recording, resulting in an overly clean and clinical sound.

In the middle of October, after the band's return from Japan, Mark Rothbaum managed to get Miles on the well-known American television program *Saturday Night Live*. Miles looked extremely ill, and many close to him tried to talk him out of appearing. "He was so far gone, and really really sick," Macero remembered. "So I said, 'Look at you, you play shit. Forget it, check into a hospital.' Miles answered, 'Fuck you!' I said, 'I'm trying to save your life, but it's your life, so go do it.' He did the show and I think he ended up in hospital right afterwards."

Gil Evans even took the bold step of calling and berating Rothbaum, both for the release of *The Man with the Horn* and for Miles's appearance on the show. "Gil said, 'How dare you put him on TV! You should be shot for that!'" Rothbaum recounted. "Gil thought Miles was too dazed. I got pissed at Gil in return. I'd rather have 50 percent of Miles than no Miles. The fact that he wanted to do it, and wanted to get back out on the road was all I needed. Twenty-five to thirty million people would see him on the show. It was a building block, just like *The Man with the Horn* was. The critics could say what they liked, but first, Miles was back in the studio, second, he had a future, and third, we needed the money. There was no way I could reissue more back catalog, as I had done during the late '70s. I wasn't going to say to Miles, 'You can't go into the studio, you're not up to it.'"

Although the *Saturday Night Live* show was clearly a low point, Miles's precarious health would continue to impede his musical activities until his death. In the early '80s he was particularly frail and had lost a lot of weight, which made him look gaunt and like a shadow of his former self. The arthritis was still causing him a lot of pain, and his limping on stage was a far cry from his former pantherlike gait. During some concerts in the early '80s he restlessly paced up and down to avoid being overwhelmed by pain (a practice made possible by the wireless microphone he now had attached to his horn). In September and October of 1981 he twice contracted pneumonia, and his chain-smoking did not help his problems with his lungs. To strengthen his breathing, he sometimes needed oxygen in between sets. He also wore a truss and rubber corset around his abdomen. Despite the diagnosis of diabetes, he persisted in drinking substantial amounts of alcohol, and he still regularly used cocaine.

"During the Kix concerts, and also afterwards, Al and I often massaged his hands," Cinelu said. "But he was very, very smart. He knew that he did not have the same control of his instrument as before, but even with that handicap he was able to play incredible music, and make us play incredibly. That's beyond . . . I don't want to get into mystical things, but it's like Beethoven who could write incredible music when he was deaf. Even though Miles was weak, he could hold a note for a long time, and he had a good tone. The band was also very supportive, creating atmospheres and space for him to play. And once Cicely came into the picture, he became much healthier, started to swim, and realized that if he took good care of himself, he could play better and do more."

Cinelu referred to Cicely Tyson's intervention in Miles's life, after their marriage on November 27, 1981, Thanksgiving Day. In January of 1982 Tyson had gone to Africa, and in her absence Miles indulged in more addictive and self-destructive behavior. This was despite the fact that his body was giving him strong warning signs, such as the occurrence of blood in his urine, that something was dramatically wrong. "I was snorting coke, half an ounce a day sometimes," Miles said. "I went out drinking brandy and beer around the clock. I'd get up at midnight and go out all night and half a day, smoked four packs of cigarettes. I was using sleeping pills too."[8]

Things got so bad that someone once more intervened in Miles's life. This time it was his tour manager Jim Rose. "I put him in the hospital because he was drinking so much beer that he couldn't walk," Rose recalled. "I said, 'Right, that's it. I'm putting you into the hospital.' The doctors asked him, 'Do you want to live?' He made a conscious decision, and said, 'Yes.'" A few days later Miles found that he could not open his hand. The diagnosis was a stroke, but Miles and Jim Rose speculated that he'd simply slept too long on his arm, leading to something called "Honeymoon Syndrome." "He was now going through alcohol withdrawal," Rose said. "And they'd given him liquid Valium. He'd slept so well that he didn't notice he'd been lying on his right arm, and it did some damage to the nerves."

On hearing the news, Cicely Tyson immediately returned, and when doctors told her that Miles would never play again, she convinced him to visit an acupuncturist. After an intensive treatment of acupuncture, good food, herbal medicines, physiotherapy, and physical exercise, feeling and movement began to return to his hand in March. A tour scheduled for February had been canceled. However, indefatigable, Miles now planned a new tour for April, despite the fact that his chops were in much worse shape than during 1981. As in 1973 to 1975, the show, apparently, had to go on, no matter what. Similar to the way his drug use became worse when he cut out music in 1975, now that he was forced to severely cut down on drug use, his addictive tendencies may have focused more strongly on music. One indication is that Miles went to extraordinary lengths to be able to tour again, in some instances playing from a wheelchair. "When we went to Europe in the spring of 1982, he had a brace with some rubber slings attached to each finger, which opened his fingers up after he closed them," Jim Rose added. "He could close his hand but not open it. He'd get off airplanes and the press would ask what it was, and I'd say, 'It's the Miles Davis trumpet exerciser.' He didn't want them to know that there was a question hanging above him being able to fully function again on the trumpet. But in the end he did, although it took a while for his chops to come back."

"His technique was good when we first started," Mike Stern said, "but then it was bad because he got sick, and then it got better again." "I don't think his chops ever came fully back," Evans opined. "His playing was about the vibe, about telling a story. Some nights he played one solo great; he'd nail one. He'd be really happy like a little kid who'd just played great for his teacher. At the end of the night, he'd say, 'Bill, come on over, I felt good tonight.' The next night he might have felt down because he wasn't playing so well. I think in the '80s he didn't have the chops of his whole career."

❖

During the European tour of April and May 1982, "Ife" made a brief return to live performance with a slightly modified bass line, enjoying its last performance during the U.S. tour of July and August. After the release of *We Want Miles* in the summer (it would go on to win Miles the 1982 Grammy for Best Jazz Instrumental Performance, Soloist), it became clear that Miles needed to record a follow-up album. However, Miles was still at a creative low, and short of new ideas. Miles resolved this issue by devising a new way of composing, which involved Gil Evans transcribing and arranging sections of solos by band members. "Miles relied on Gil a lot during this period," Bill Evans said. "They bounced things off each other. Sometimes Gil would bring in written lines; sometimes they were from rehearsals and he'd write out a solo and they became tunes. There was never a big arrangement, and always a lot of improvisation. The majority of the time everything was put together in the studio."

"Gil Evans was in the studio all the time, hanging out, writing down little riffs that Miles would play and turning them into arrangements," Miller added. "Because things had been so loose, we'd get a real kick out of Miles actually giving us some charts! We were having a combination of the kind of jams that Miles would orchestrate, and then he'd point and we're supposed to play the lines that Gil had written, with maybe the horn players or guitarists in unison. So it began to get a little bit more structured."

The first fruit of this approach was recorded on August 11 at Columbia Studios, and was included on Miles's next release, *Star People*. Called "Star on Cicely," it features a forceful drum groove, as well as a busy, chromatic bass line, and begins with Evans and Miles playing an excerpt of a transcribed Stern solo, which is followed by a short solo from Miles on muted trumpet. At 01:04 and 03:44 the same lengthy solo transcription is repeated, played by Evans, Stern, and Miller. Miller must have overdubbed his part because he continues playing the stirring groove as well. Stern laughed, saying, "The transcriptions were hard shit, and almost impossible to play off the page."

Having nothing in common with the focus on the bottom end, circular bass lines, and interlocking rhythms that had characterized his earlier electric explorations, this new musical direction was a radical departure for Miles. Instead, the complex, strongly chromatic nature of the music and the chromatic, linear bass playing have a parallel in some of the music of the second great quintet, although the driving rock beat naturally gives the music an entirely different feel.

The new direction also meant a dramatic overhaul of the live set. During 1981 and 1982, the live repertoire had, with the addition of "Ife," been entirely taken from *The Man with the Horn* and *We Want Miles*. By the fall of 1982 the only remaining elements were the concert closer "Jean-Pierre" and the two beginning chords of "Back Seat Betty," which were still used as a concert opener. Given how in the '70s Miles had retained and reworked several vamps and themes over periods of many years, it is another indication of the uncertainty of his direction, and that he did not regard the material on his first two '80s albums that highly.

"Come Get It," *Star People*'s opener, was constructed with the same method as "Star on Cicely" and was recorded live on August 28 at Jones Beach Theater in New York. "Come Get It" opens with the two rock chords of "Back Seat Betty" before switching into a driving rock rhythm. Miles plays electric piano and Miller comes in with a busy bass line, one of his best of the era, which Miles claimed was based on an old Otis Redding riff.[9] Miles also plays an Oberheim synthesizer, which was most likely overdubbed to the live recording. Stern alternates between playing funky one-note riffs and abstract, almost atonal comping. Miles comes in on open trumpet at 02:27, playing some declamatory chromatic phrases and occasionally some very high notes. At 03:05 he refers to the song's main theme, playing it in full at 03:20. Miller switches to a stronger funk feel, heightening the level of intensity, and Miles responds by playing fast chromatic runs, while also leaving lots of space. Around 06:49 the intensity relents, and into this break Stern begins his solo, with a clean sound and some atonal, "out" playing. It is not long before band and soloist return to the initial intensity.

The avalanche of complex, chromatic notes on "Star on Cicely" and "Come Get It" may appear at odds with the "less is more" motto that had guided Miles's musical direction until 1975. But there's an uncompromising intensity to the discordant melodies and harmonies, as well as the ferocious execution, which is immediately recognizable as Miles's. The high degree of abstraction, although not immediately easy on the ear, makes the tracks more rewarding with repeated listening. This combination of jagged, almost atonal themes, frantic funk-rock bass playing, and driving drums and percussion became a trademark of some of Miles's music until the end of his life.

Two other new tracks, called "U 'n' I" and "Star People," were also featured at the Jones Beach concert. A few days later, most likely on September 1, Miles went into the studio to record them. "U 'n' I" was twenty minutes long during the concert but is condensed to just under six minutes in the studio version. Like "Jean-Pierre," it features an almost childlike melody, which is augmented by a great, chugging bass line—giving it an understated, humorous quality. The melody gets repeated many times, and Miles, Stern, and Evans all play brief but excellent solos. "U 'n' I" may not be a pioneering musical statement but it is nevertheless novel and, due to its conciseness, focus, and coherence, it is a highlight of *Star People*.

The track "Star People" marks a return to Miles's blues roots in an unusually direct and undiluted manner. The track's opening 01:15 (repeated as an interlude at 12:38) is an atmosphere-setting statement by Miles on Oberheim synthesizer and Stern on guitar. Miles became increasingly enamored of synthesizers in general and the Oberheim in particular at this stage, but found it hard to come to terms with the technical aspects. "I haven't read the instruction book yet," Miles said about the Oberheim in 1982. "It would take someone like Paul Buckmaster or Gil [Evans] or Quincy [Jones] or J. J. Johnson, one of those writers who'd really know what to do with it."[10] Since there was no one around with the know-how or inclination to program the Oberheim, Miles simply used factory preset A1.

The Oberheim/guitar intro and interlude were recorded later, most likely on January 5, 1983, and edited in by Macero during postproduction, but both the synthesizer sound and edits are crude, making the two sections distracting. "Teo was brutal with the editing. It was part of his style, you know. Teo would just go, 'Phew!' And it became part of the music," Marcus Miller commented. The producer's rough edits worked well in most of Miles's early '80s music, and may even have salvaged some otherwise unreleasable material. But in the case of "Star People" two separate takes of the band playing the bluesy material are connected, leading to an overall length of nearly nineteen minutes, too long to sustain interest. Another problem is the irritating sound of the cymbal played by Foster for the first eleven minutes. Leonard Feather implies that it is the result of studio experimentation, "a unique and indefinably different sound to Al Foster's drums, creating a sonic illusion,"[11] but it's either an experiment gone wrong, or simply a bad recording swamped with too much digital reverb.

Other than this, there is much to enjoy in "Star People," particularly in Miles's blues soloing. He takes several extended solos on a muted trumpet, using a cap mute, which allowed him to imitate some of the variations in color he had achieved with his wah-wah pedal. Evans also plays an excellent tenor solo, and Stern's second solo is especially inventive. Whereas the guitarist's first solo is rather muddled in its direction and phrasing, his solo, which begins at 13:20, builds from delightful, thoughtful phrases to a soaring climax. Apparently the powerful, understated, and suspended feel of the track was partly caused by recording circumstances. "Miles was playing into a microphone, because his pick-up didn't work," Cinelu said. "He was also moving around a lot, and they were opening and closing the microphones as he moved, so we had to play extremely quietly."

Over the next few years Miles regularly played in this understated blues vein, and although not groundbreaking, it created enjoyable interludes in the often frenetic live sets. In his autobiography, Miles credited guitarist John Scofield with the strong blues flavor of his music around this time, but Scofield did not join the band until November, so this has to go down as one of the autobiography's inaccuracies. Miles also claimed that he brought Scofield in "to play some guitar tracks" on *Star People*, and said, "I felt that two guitarists with different styles would create a tension that was good for the music."[12]

Miles, or Troupe, may have been protecting Mike Stern, because the truth is that Stern had a severe drug problem. "I was doing drugs, alcohol, everything," Stern said. "At that point Miles was trying to get sober, and here I was, arriving fucked up at gigs, drunk and shit like that. When I think of the shit he put up with from me, I must have sounded good. But when I missed a plane, Miles said, 'Call Scofield.' It was a little awkward because Sco and I used to know each other in Boston, and he was ambivalent about taking the gig. But if Miles Davis calls, what do you do?"

Scofield was nearly thirty-one when he joined Miles, and he had worked with Charles Mingus, Gerry Mulligan, Chet Baker, Billy Cobham, Tony Williams, and Ron Carter. The guitarist had already developed a very individual guitar style, characterized by a languid feel, delicate, blues-influenced phrasing, and the capacity to construct weird solos, with many "out" notes and large, unusual intervals that at the same time contained beautifully melodic lines. His solos were therefore the perfect foils from which Miles and Gil Evans could construct new material.

The same day that Scofield got the call (on the recommendation of Bill Evans), he flew over to Cleveland where the band was playing four nights. "It was the afternoon of November 4, 1982," Scofield remembered. "I didn't know the repertoire, so I hung out with the band for three days, just listening, and the fourth night I came on stage. Miles gradually gave me more and more solos, but he also wanted Mike to keep playing. Mike and I had played together in 1982, and we were friends, so we worked out a labor divisions between us, making use of the stylistic differences between us."

"John has a tendency to play behind the beat," Miles observed. "I had to bring him up; he really changed with Al's strong beat behind him."[13] Miles has also commented that Stern had a tendency to play too many notes, and that he had to teach him to play less. "Miles was really supportive," Stern said, "and he liked my feel and timing, the way I place the notes in the groove. One thing I learned from Miles was to conceptualize about the context in which you solo, to take the rhythm and arrangement into account, and find the things to play that make you and the whole band sound the best. Another thing was to play from the heart. He always had that happening. It was the heart first and then the brain. The attitude was most important, and what you played was secondary."

The period from November 7, 1982, when Scofield entered, until June 27, 1983, when Stern left because his drug habit finally became too destructive, has a near-legendary reputation among enthusiasts of this period in Miles's career, due to the richness that came from the sparring of the two guitar players. Some of the Japanese concerts of the May 1983 tour were spectacular, with Scofield and Stern trading scorching licks and having found inventive ways of complementing each other as rhythm guitarists. As bootlegs are becoming scarcer because Columbia and the Miles Davis Estate are increasingly clamp down on them, it can only be hoped that Sony/Columbia has some of these concerts in its vaults, and will one day release them.

The only official evidence of the teaming of Stern and Scofield is on "Speak," one of the two tracks on *Star People* not yet discussed. The other track, "It Gets Better," was recorded first, in the studio on January 5, but for unknown reasons Stern is absent. "It Gets Better" was constructed in the same way as "Star on Cicely" and "Come Get It," but this time the foundation was a section of one of Scofield's solos, as well as a chord sequence borrowed from country blues guitarist Lightnin' Hopkins.

"I should have gotten a credit for that one, but okay, it's not my tune, it's me improvising," Scofield declared. "Miles was into taping everyone's solos, and then turning parts of them into melodies. Although it's not new, it's a brilliant way to compose. In the case of 'It Gets Better,' he had this great set of chord changes, taking a twelve-bar blues in B-flat and subtracting the first four bars, so you start on the fourth chord. It was simple, but so cool. Gil Evans played the bass line on the piano, and Miles told me to play along. Gil transcribed a part of it, so it was really a co-thing."

Macero edited "It Gets Better" so that it runs seamlessly into "Come Get It," using the same crude A1 Oberheim synthesizer sound as a rough bridge. Scofield introduces the delightful main theme, soon followed by Miles, who plays a delicate solo full of space, again using a cup mute. After this Scofield and Miles alternate with graceful and thoughtful solos, often referring to the main theme. The atmosphere of "It Gets Better" is almost the same as that of the restrained blues of "Star People," but because the basic material has been more condensed and defined, it has more power, focus, and originality.

"It Gets Better" was to be the last track on which Marcus Miller participated. Having written hits for Aretha Franklin, Luther Vandross, and David Sanborn, he wanted to pursue a burgeoning career as a songwriter and producer. Miller recommended Tom

Barney as a replacement. Barney played on "Speak," which was most likely recorded live in Houston on February 3, and is once again based on a transcribed Scofield solo. After a ferocious beginning, with Miles playing keyboard stabs and trumpet shrieks in unison, a feat he managed live, the theme is played by Evans, and what sounds like Scofield. Stern then takes a solo, until the theme is stated again at 02:40. After a long keyboard chord, the band takes the energy down, and opens up space for Scofield to play his second theme, at 03:24. Scofield continues to solo, using both chordal and single line figures, and is driven to greater intensity by Miles's trumpet and keyboard stabs. Miles solos only briefly on the track, preferring to direct the band and stimulate the guitar players. Nevertheless, compared to the bootleg evidence of some of the other concerts in which Stern and Scofield both feature, this is fairly tame stuff.

Featuring some of Miles's drawings on the cover, *Star People* was released in the spring of 1983. He had dabbled in painting and drawing before, and when Cicely gave him a sketchpad in late 1981, something that was initially intended as occupational therapy during stays in hospital or when traveling became an important creative outlet. First participating in the recording of mediocre pop music, then exploring a rousing funk-jazz-rock direction that was fresh but not particularly groundbreaking, Miles had been faltering in his return to musical activity. However, the stark new musical direction of the chromatic funk tracks on *Star People,* the tremendous inventiveness emanating from his band (particularly Stern and Scofield), and finally Miles's growing chops, and his almost obsessive exploration of figurative art—all indicated that his once awesome creative forces were coming back into focus again.

Chapter Thirteen

THAT'S WHAT
HAPPENED

"Miles had a great aesthetic sense. Coupled with a deep understanding of music, and a great ability to project what's inside of you, you get the results he got."
—BOB BERG

In 1983 several important changes radically altered the course of Miles's life and music. The first was the firing of his manager Mark Rothbaum at the beginning of the year. In his autobiography, Miles is vague about the reasons, simply mentioning that they had a "dispute,"[1] but there seems little doubt that Rothbaum's sacking was the result of a power battle between manager and wife. There had been friction between Cicely Tyson and the band at various occasions—for example, during the European tour of 1982, when she insisted on star treatment, and the band's roadies spent much time looking after her extensive luggage. Miles also recalled, "I found out later that when I would buy her some expensive gift, a lot of the time she would take it back and just get the money and keep that."[2] When Rothbaum confronted Miles over these things, the consequences were inevitable. As Rothbaum dryly remarked, "Naturally, he was closer to his wife than me."

Miles maintained that Tyson interfered in his business affairs, just as he claimed she had done during their first engagement in 1967. "I was losing him to this syndicate," Rothbaum explained. "It looked as if the team of people I had put together was being replaced with Cicely's people. I was pretty nervous about it." On Cicely's suggestion, Miles replaced Rothbaum with Blank & Blank, a law firm from Philadelphia. But they handled his affairs in such a way that Miles could call them "incompetent"[3] without getting sued. Despite Miles's star profile, they allegedly found it difficult to book him tours, and gradually brought in less money. During their tenure Miles was forced to sell his legendary brownstone on 312 West Seventy-seventh Street to them. He had a long association with this house, and the sale deeply unsettled him. It drove him further into the arms of Cicely, since he now lived in her apartment in New York and in her second house in Malibu, near Los Angeles.

Another far-reaching change in the "team of people" surrounding Miles was his dismissal of its longest-serving member, Teo Macero, who had produced almost all Miles's recordings since 1958. Having left Columbia in 1975, Macero had worked as an independent producer on Miles's first three '80s recordings. Macero's departure marked the end of one of the longest and most fruitful collaborations between an artist and his producer in twentieth-century history. But Miles expressed neither appreciation nor regret. When asked in 1984 about the reasons for Macero's sacking, he claimed, "Because he's like an old maid, man. I could have let Teo go years ago, but I kept him around for a while. He doesn't *do* anything so there's no reason to carry him. He never did do anything."[4] Surprised, the interviewer, Eric Snider, asked about Macero's contributions as a music editor. Miles responded, "Teo does lazy shit, man. I hate a lazy man. I can't stand that. I kept telling him to do something and it's 'Oh, no, we got a deadline.' 'I don't feel good, I gotta go to the doctor.' 'My wife this and my wife that.' . . . He eliminated himself by being so slow and backwards."[5]

Sounding like Miles's typical free-associative public utterings, these comments may have little to do with the real reasons for Teo's departure. Intriguingly, Macero also suspected Cicely's hand. "He never told me why he stopped working with me," Macero stated. "But it had something to do with his wife, Cicely. I think she told him to fire me. After all the great records we'd made together, I would have thought he would have been a little grateful. But he didn't seem to care. Yes, I was a little hurt."

Cicely Tyson has to date refused to be interviewed about her relationship with Miles, so her version of the story remains untold. However, Rothbaum's story, that with each departure of a member of Miles's old team the influence of Cicely (and of Miles's family, with which Cicely had strong ties) became stronger, appears to be confirmed by several events. When, after the Japanese tour of May of 1983, it became clear that things were not working out with bassist Tom Barney, Miles did not turn to Bill Evans for advice, as he usually did, but called his nephew Vince Wilburn Jr. in Chicago. Wilburn recommended Darryl "The Munch" Jones, a twenty-one-year-old school friend, whom Miles immediately invited to New York for a private audition. "He asked me to perform a B-flat blues, and stopped me two or three times, saying 'No, real slow.'" Jones recalled. "So I played this blues really slowly for ten minutes. Then he asked me to play to a concert tape, which I did for about twenty minutes. A little over a week later, on June 7 in St. Louis, I played my first gig with Miles."

Jones's enlistment was further evidence of Miles's gift as an astonishing talent-spotter, because the Chicagoan became, next to Miller, the most powerful bassist in Miles's '80s live bands, and went on to become one of the world's most in-demand bassists, performing with the likes of Sting and The Rolling Stones. Jones played a few concerts with the two-guitarist line-up, until Mike Stern's departure after a concert on June 26 reduced the band to a sextet consisting of Miles, Scofield, Evans, Jones, Foster, and Cinelu. Two live tracks featuring this line-up, credited as "What It Is" and "That's What Happened," were issued on Miles's next recording, *Decoy*. Both were recorded on July 7, 1983, in Montreal.

"That's What Happened" is taken from the second theme of "Speak," which had appeared on *Star People*. In this shortened version Miles restricts himself to playing accompanying stabs on the trumpet and synthesizer, while Scofield, with occasional doubling from Evans, repeats the melody over and over again. It is a succinct and powerful piece of music, although its inclusion on the already fairly short *Decoy* (which is just under forty minutes) points towards a shortage of new material. "What It Is" is in exactly the same vein. A furious bass riff, played by Jones with his trademark driving thumbing funk style, underlies an abstract, chromatic theme, once again drawn from a Scofield solo. Evans gets his only solo on *Decoy* on this track, while Miles overdubbed another trumpet to his live trumpet solo.

Additional musical material and directions were required for the new recording, and the sacking of Teo Macero may well have happened partly, or perhaps entirely, to fulfil this need. Always alert to the latest musical developments, Miles wanted to explore musical territory relevant to the '80s, particularly the sound of a new generation of affordable, easily programmable, polyphonic synthesizers. "If you're a thinking musician, like I am, you're aware of your surroundings, like cars," Miles commented. "The metal and the plastic changes, so accidents don't sound the same. My music is influenced by today's sounds. With synthesizers, there's always something new."[6]

Perhaps Miles felt that Macero, whose musical and technical outlook was grounded in previous decades, was not the right person to aid him in these explorations. In addition, it was increasingly becoming a status symbol of artistic maturity and control for rock artists to produce their own records. Given how much it rankled Miles that white men received some of the credit for his work, he may well have wanted to show that he, too, was able to produce himself.

Miles's first production effort took place on June 31, 1983, at A&R Studios in New York, where he put together one of the most bizarre tracks he ever recorded. Called "Freaky Deaky," it consists of Jones playing a laid-back, circular bass riff for almost the full duration of the track, Cinelu and Foster contributing atmospheric percussion and drums, Scofield performing some gentle figures, and Miles noodling nonchalantly on synthesizer.

"He was talking to me about a bass line that was rolling and rolling," Jones recalled. "I kept trying stuff, and every time he said, 'No, not that.' Eventually I came up with something, and he said, 'Yeah, just like that. Just play that over and over again.' It's trance music. Playing it felt so good. We all 'went under' for however long the jam lasted, which was maybe twelve to fifteen minutes. It shifted the whole atmosphere." "I love 'Freaky Deaky.' It's a totally weird kind of blues," Scofield commented. "The first take had Miles blowing an incredible solo, but they did not issue it on the record. It's still in the archives. The version on the record is just a weird, minimalist thing."

In this case it is hard to share the musicians' sentiments. The aural evidence suggests that this is one of these contradictory occasions observed by guitarist Robert Fripp when the musicians feel a strong "musical impulse" in the room but the material they're actually playing is "a real turkey." Jones's bass line is not outstanding, and neither is Miles's synthesizer playing, although he had selected a more elegant sound than on "Star People." The atmosphere is also not distinctive, and the sole importance of "Freaky Deaky" may lie in the fact that it showed Miles that production was not his forte.

Miles needed assistance, and he found it once more in a family connection. In the middle of August he called in the help of Vince Wilburn Jr. and Robert Irving III, who had both participated in the sessions from 1980 and 1981, resulting in "The Man with the Horn" and "Shout." "I had worked as an engineer," Irving explained. "And he asked me to mix his next record. He also told me to bring a tune. I immediately wrote something I called 'Outer Space,' which eventually became 'Decoy.' It wasn't clear to me what he really expected from me until I arrived in New York, when I realized that he wanted me to replace Teo Macero. He wanted to produce, and was looking for someone with technical expertise to help him."

Irving had recorded a demo of "Outer Space" in Chicago, making extensive use of music technology, most notably a Linn 9000 drum machine and various synthesizers. Like many young musicians, he enthusiastically embraced this new computer-driven technology. "I'd used a live bass, guitar, and horn player on the demo, but the rest was done by machines," Irving recalled. "Miles was amazed by what the technology could do, and he felt that the feel of the drum machine was important, and wanted Al to play alongside, and create a polyrhythmic feel. But Al didn't like playing with the drum machine at all."

Miles asked Irving and Wilburn to rerecord the demo, using a combination of the Linn 9000 and his live band, minus Bill Evans, who was replaced for the recordings by up-and-coming young saxophonist Branford Marsalis, brother of trumpeter Wynton. The rehearsals, recording, and mix took place at the well-known rock studio The Record Plant, another indication of Miles's desire to move into a more contemporary direction. Irving is credited as co-producer for these sessions, and Wilburn as associate producer. "Vince was lending his ears," Irving explained. "He was very involved in the mix, the rhythms, the percussion, in tweaking stuff. We rehearsed with the musicians and Linn 9000 for about three days, recording everything we did. Miles never attended the sessions; he delegated everything to us. The tapes always ran, and he wanted to hear everything, so every night I would take them back to his apartment to listen to. He invariably had a lot of comments. The next day we went into the studio and used his suggestions. In the end we cut 'Decoy' live, with drum machine, live drums, and musicians together, but without Miles. He overdubbed his stuff later."

Three other tracks emerged from these sessions: "Robot 415," "Code M.D.," and "That's Right." "'Robot 415' came from a 6/8 blues from a live concert over which we superimposed a whole other groove, and altered the harmonic elements," Irving explained. "'Code M.D.' was written by me during the sessions. This meant that there was less time to develop the arrangements for these tracks than with 'Decoy.'"

For this reason "Code M.D." is less successful than "Decoy," with a stiffer-sounding rhythm track and a less sophisticated arrangement. Like "Freaky Deaky," the track has a sense of dispassion and dullness, despite strong solos by Miles and Scofield. "Decoy" sounds more alive and exciting, and its abrasive, dissonant harmony, stark bass line, and driving rhythm sound like quintessential Miles. This is surprising, given that Irving wrote all these elements, but an explanation may lie in the keyboardist's exposure to Miles in 1980 and 1981, which had an importance influence on his keyboard style and compositional approach.

"When we first met he wasn't playing his horn, and he was playing a lot of piano, and there were some remarkable things that really enlightened me," Irving said. "He opened up a whole realm of possibilities for me in terms of voicings, coming in with chordal concepts of compounding chords on top of each other that were seemingly unrelated. My original bass line for 'Decoy' had a few more notes, and it occurs the way I wrote it the second time 'round in the track. Miles wanted me to take out a few notes to give it a little bit more space. There's also a melody line in 'Decoy'—appearing at 03:21 to 03:42, behind the main melody, and again at 07:23 to 07:45—which was played by the original demo guitarist, Henry Johnson. He wasn't sure how to approach the polychordal progressions, so I asked him to imagine that he could not play the guitar and play the first thing that came to his fingers. The result floored Miles so much that he listened to it over and over again, and asked me to transcribe it."

Irving claims not to have been aware that his instruction to Johnson was identical to the direction Miles gave John McLaughlin during the recording of *In a Silent Way*, making this a strange synchronicity. Miles also asked Darryl Jones to play "Decoy" with his thumb, which gave the music a harder, edgier feel. Despite the fact that he was not present in the studio, Miles's spirit clearly imbued the track. With its intricate arrangements and extensive use of synthesizers, the recording was an important new direction, laying the foundation of yet another aspect of the music of Miles's final decade.

At the same time "Decoy" and "Code M.D." cannot entirely shake off a sense of coldness and aloofness. The application of music technology is a likely culprit. Because music technology involves programming rather than playing, music created with it is always in danger of lacking spontaneity and feeling. The fact that Miles was not present in the studio during recording further impacted the end result. Delegating much of the work to Irving and Wilburn can be seen as being in line with the freedom he had always given his sidemen and with the space he had allowed Macero. But there are crucial differences. Macero was never involved in constructing material from the ground up, but invariably reworked material Miles and a group of musicians had already recorded. Moreover, when working with his bands, Miles always led with his presence, directing with trumpet, keyboard, or hand movements, and editing and exploring musical developments on the spot. By retreating from the actual recording process, he could not transmit what had always been his main strength: galvanizing and raising the creative energy of a group of musicians in the present moment.

"I think he just got very lazy, and let everybody else do all the work, and then he just came in and played over what they'd done," Teo Macero said. Others have voiced similar opinions. But Vince Wilburn sprang to Miles's defense, saying, "We were just following instructions. Miles told us what to put down and where to change things. He simply didn't want to be in the studio all day, and only wanted to be involved in making the creative decisions. That's why it was up to us to do the legwork of working in the studio and bringing the tapes back to him. The magic is in putting the shit together, not in programming synthesizers or drum machines. He was always part of what happened. We'd call him twenty times a day, and he'd call the studio, and we'd play him things over the phone. He knew what he wanted to hear, and we were constantly trying to give him that. If you presented a naked sketch of a song to Miles, the way he built on that was pure magic."

There can be no doubt that Miles was the final authority on the music on *Decoy* and that he inspired the recordings. However, it is also undeniable that the slightly neutered, disembodied results are an effect of his literally disembodied way of working. The reasons for his remoteness are unclear. What is certain is that *Decoy* marked the beginning of a divergence between Miles's live and studio work—which was similar to the period from 1965 to 1972, when he had used the studio as a forward-looking laboratory. But in the mid-1980s the studio became a repertoire-creating tool in which he delegated much of the work to others. For the last eight years of his life, his creative edge in music was most strongly expressed on the live stage. Miles showed his true colors as a performing, improvising musician, whose calling was playing music alive in the present moment.

This is beautifully demonstrated by "That's Right." Recorded live in the studio on September 10 or 11, the track is a blues very similar in mood to "Star People" but is graced by the inclusion of an arranged melody, appearing at 02:44, which is once again taken from a Scofield solo. Miles, Marsalis, and Scofield all play excellent solos on the track, and Miles's switch to open trumpet at 09:34 is an outstanding moment. The CD liner notes credit Miles and Gil Evans for the arrangement, but the latter was an acknowledgement from a young musician to a master. "Gil had been really kind to me by getting together and talking music, and being very complimentary about what I was doing with Miles," Irving explained. "He wasn't able to get involved himself, so I did the transcription and arrangement. But I wanted him to have the credit as a way of thanking him."

As on "What It Is" and "That's What Happened," Miles overdubbed synth parts to "That's Right." Irving had programmed all the synthesizer sounds on *Decoy,* creating a unity of sound between all tracks. But the album nevertheless has a markedly fractured nature, with the slow blues and the two abstract rock-funk workouts sitting uncomfortably next to the uneven, partly stilted studio recordings. For a man of fifty-seven to inspire and co-create music that sounded credible and idiomatic among current musical trends was nevertheless an impressive achievement. Proving his contemporary '80s rock credentials, Miles also recorded a promotional video for the title track.

Within weeks of the completion of *Decoy,* Miles was back on the road, playing a European tour. He wanted to enlist Branford Marsalis, but the saxophonist was committed to his brother Wynton's quartet, so Miles set off with the same band that had recorded the live tracks on *Decoy:* Foster, Cinelu, Jones, Scofield, and Evans, with the addition of Irving. Miles's relationship with his saxophonist had become tense, because Evans increasingly felt that he was not given enough space to play. It appears, however, that the friendship the two had developed in the years previously helped them to resolve their musical differences amicably.

"Yes, I was angry because I didn't get to play much," Evans said. "Sometimes he'd laugh at the end of a show, asking me, 'Are you mad?' And sometimes I was. I might spend three days waiting to play a concert, and then I hardly got to play. I'd stand there, looking like, 'For God's sake, what am I doing here?' Gil Evans told me that many of Miles's saxophonists had felt the same way during the last thirty years, even Cannonball. I told Miles in Paris [October 31, 1983] that I was joining John McLaughlin's group, and he said, 'Have a great time, at least you're leaving for a great band!' I think my last concert was at Radio City [November 6, 1983]. We stayed in touch after that. I felt very grateful for having played with him, and the main thing that I learned from him is to be yourself. That's what he did."

Mino Cinelu left the band at the same time as Evans. "I felt that the live space was disappearing," Cinelu explained. "To me, live and the studio were entirely different. *Decoy* was good, but could have been better, and live there was excitement because of the different players coming in and out. I guess he was trying different things, since there was transition after transition. But it was not for me. There were so many notes, just no space, I was unhappy. To me, it didn't make sense. But I had learned more about the concept of space from Miles than anybody else, and he taught me not to worry about the instrument I was playing. He used to say, 'Man, you could swing on a cup.'"

Yet another example of Miles's star-making capacities, Cinelu went on to play with Weather Report and developed a successful career as a bandleader. Miles replaced Cinelu with unknown percussionist Steve Thornton, but it would take him a while to find a suitable new saxophonist. The saxophonist-less band and the new percussionist took part in several studio sessions in November that were intended to be the beginning of a new joint project of Miles and Gil Evans. But another hip operation and a further attack of pneumonia in late November of 1983 interrupted the project.

Miles was back in the studio two months later for eight sessions that took place between January 26 and April 14, 1984. He recorded a number of pop hits, among them Chaka Khan's "Through the Fire," Tina Turner's "What's Love Got to Do with It?" Dionne Warwick's "Deja Vu," Cindy Lauper's "Time after Time," and several tracks by the band Toto and by singer/guitarist Nick Kershaw. "The idea was for Gil to arrange an album of pop tunes," Irving explained. "So we cut these tracks as test takes, to see if they would fit. Miles had me transcribe a lot of stuff, and we played quite a few of these tunes live as well, like 'What's Love Got to Do with It?' and 'Through the Fire.'"

Aside from these sessions, Miles spent the period from December of 1983 to May of 1984 recuperating from his pneumonia and his hip operation, mostly drawing and painting at Tyson's house in Malibu. In April, when he felt ready to go back on tour again, he had road manager Jim Rose call Bob Berg to find out whether he would fill the vacant saxophone spot. Perhaps Miles did not feel up to educating another unknown player; Berg was thirty-three at the time and already had a solid reputation as an excellent tenor and soprano saxophonist who had collaborated with Horace Silver, Cedar Walton, and with Al Foster on *Mr. Foster.* "Miles never said a word to me during our first rehearsal," Berg recalled. "After that he only ever said the bare minimum to me. Maybe he felt that my sax style was already crystallized, and he was happy with it."

Berg took part in one session in May, with a band still consisting of Foster, Thornton, Jones, Irving, and Scofield, and was immediately invited for a summer tour of the U.S. and Europe. Miles told writer Eric Snider in 1984 that he felt his trumpet technique had only fully come back during that year, saying it was, "After the operation . . . I practiced every day, and played a lot of long notes, and went swimming everyday. It was hard."[7]

"When I joined the band his chops were way up," confirmed Berg. "He was playing great. I was quite taken aback by that because I'd heard him a few times live just after his comeback and he sounded like shit. But when I went on the road with him it was like,

'Jesus Christ!' He was killing. His range was better than ever, and it was exciting to be there. I heard him practicing on many occasions, so obviously he was still interested in furthering his abilities as a trumpet player."

"It always amazes me when I hear people talk about Miles as a 'limited' trumpet player," Berg continued. "To me, that's ignorance of reality. What denotes a great player is the ability to project their musical personality and all its different aspects—musical, spiritual, emotional. If someone can play an instrument and project all those things, they're a great player, whether they play one or five hundred notes. I think Miles found a different way of expressing himself early on, and his was a different school than Dizzy's. But this had nothing to do with technical limitations. I just think Miles heard music in a different way, to me a more modern way. So I feel closer to Miles's aesthetic. Watching Miles play night after night, really close up was the biggest experience I had during my time in this band. One of his greatest assets was his amazing ability to play great phrases and his incredible use of silence. He knew when not to play! I don't think I've ever been awarded any awards for silence. It's part of my style to play a lot of notes, but when I was playing with him I was really checking out where he didn't play. I talked with him about it on a few occasions, and he mentioned that singers were a big influence on him. Less ornamentation can sometimes get you closer to the soul and the spirit."

Miles once told an amusing anecdote about how he helped rein in Berg's tendency to play a lot. "I used to tell him, 'Bob, why do you play in this spot? You're not supposed to play in this spot,'" Miles related. "He said, 'It sounded so good, Chief, I had to play to it.' I said, 'The reason it sounded so good is because you wasn't playing.' As soon as he jumps in, he fucks it up. It's a hard thing playin' with a group."[8]

The only official indication of what this band sounded like live is the title track of *You're under Arrest*. Like *Decoy*, its predecessor, *You're under Arrest* was recorded at The Record Plant and produced by Miles, Irving, and Wilburn, only now Irving was credited as being on equal footing with Miles, and Wilburn had graduated from associate producer to co-producer. Miles had waited most of 1984 for Gil Evans to complete his arrangements, but towards the end of the year he decided to complete the recording without the help of his old friend. "I guess it became apparent that Gil was moving too slow, and eventually Miles wanted to move forward with the record because it might be his last album with Columbia," Irving recalled. "He knew there were renegotiations and that he might not continue with them."

The bulk of *You're under Arrest* was recorded on December 26 and 27, 1984. The title track is based on another solo riff by Scofield, transcribed by Irving, and is a fierce funk-rock workout in the same vein as "That's What Happened" and "What It Is." The overall feeling is intense and has more depth and elasticity than some of the 1983 chromatic experiments. Scofield alternates between the wonderfully phrased theme and his inimitable solos, and both Miles and Berg take incisive and dramatic solos, supported by a simultaneously supple and tight rhythm section.

While "You're under Arrest" was intended to represent the way the band sounded live, the other tracks recorded on December 26 and 27 are studio fantasies. Again pointing to a shortage of new material, two medleys reuse previously used material. The first is "One Phone Call/Street Scenes." "One Phone Call" is based on the riff played at 18:32 in "Right Off" on *Jack Johnson*. The melodic riff of "Street Scenes" is based on the second theme of "Speak." Although Miles plays a brief but strong solo on open trumpet, and Scofield does his usual graceful-but-weird thing, the main focus is on Miles and others, including Sting as a French policeman, acting out a street scene in which Miles gets arrested and handcuffed. (The connection with Sting was made through Darryl Jones, who had been auditioning for the singer's band around the same time.)

"Miles was just having fun," Irving commented. "The whole thing was his take on the police brutality he had experienced." The problem with combining voiceovers and music is that they work on different levels, and in different time frames. A good piece of music may be listened to dozens if not hundreds of times, while even the most inspiring or engaging spoken text will not warrant more than a few listenings. The Who guitarist Pete Townshend once ruined a perfectly good solo album—*Psychoderelict* (1993)—by overdubbing a play over sections of his music. "One Phone Call/Street Scenes" suffers from the same problem. Although the music is acceptable, the best thing that can be said for the track is that it's fairly short. The themes from "Right Off" and "Speak" would nevertheless provide Miles with an effective concert opener until the end of 1987.

The other medley in part based on previously used material is *You're under Arrest*'s closing piece, made up of "Jean-Pierre," "You're under Arrest," and "Then There Were None" (a reference to the 1978 Genesis album, *Then There Were Three*). The track is another attempt at social commentary, this time sending an antiwar message. It begins with a distorted version of "Jean-Pierre," followed by Scofield disfiguring the main riff from "You're under Arrest." At 01:17 Irving enters with a gorgeous melody played on the celeste, giving the effect of a child's musical box. It is surrounded by violent noises: explosions, helicopters, crying children, and so on. The track finishes with Miles saying "I meant for you to push that other button" and the sound of a clock ticking.

"We were thinking of it as a movie," Irving explained. "We wanted to convey a picture. It was mainly done by overdubbing, and using library sound effect tapes." Despite the fact that the political symbolism is too heavily laid on the track is strangely affecting, due to the sharp contrast between the tender and melancholic celeste melody and the harsh sound effects.

Continuing his exploration of pop songs, Miles also recorded Toto's "Human Nature," which had also been a hit for Michael Jackson, and "D" Train's 1983 funk-disco hit "Something's on Your Mind," without Berg, and with Vince Wilburn Jr. on drums instead of Al Foster. "They tried recording 'Human Nature' with Al, but he left after the first take," Wilburn recalled. "I don't think he wanted to play the song. I was in the control room, and Miles said, 'You want to play?' I didn't want Al to leave, but when Miles said that, it was like, 'Yes!'" Apparently Foster not only objected to the choice of songs but also to the fact that he had to play the pop tunes to a click-track. It meant the end of his collaboration with Miles, which had begun back in 1972.

"Time after Time" is the only song included on *You're under Arrest* from the early 1984 recordings. A classic '80s hit for Cindy Lauper, it is a superb song, with an original, evocative melody. Many expressed surprise at Miles's recording of these three pop songs because they contrasted sharply with the blues-influenced funk-rock he was playing around the time. Even some of his band members raised their eyebrows, like Darryl Jones, who said, "When he first told me we were going to do 'Time after Time,' I was not pleased to hear that."

Some critics derided the inclusion of the songs as a cheap ploy for getting hits. But others pointed to the fact that Miles had often covered popular songs at the height of his jazz period, like "My Funny Valentine," "If I Were a Bell," "Stella By Starlight," and even slushy Hollywood ballads like, "I Fall in Love too Easily" and "Someday My Prince Will Come." At the time Miles's capacity for making "some unspeakable mawkish material . . . palatable by his intense involvement as he recomposes the melodies"[9] was widely admired. "If you follow my musical career I usually always play ballads that I like. It's no big thing," Miles commented in 1984.[10]

As we have seen, Miles was not subject to the elitist stance that regards mass popularity as degrading, or obscurity as a sign of artistic merit. He always wanted to reach as wide an audience as possible, and there have been several references during his electric period to him (mistakenly) hoping that one of his recordings would be a hit, such as with "Duran" in 1970 and "The Man with the Horn" in 1980. The covering of pop songs in 1984 was clearly his most conscious and deliberate attempt yet, and this time he was more successful in his aim. Miles's versions of "Time after Time" and "Human Nature" became hits in various countries around the world, while *You're under Arrest,* despite the kitsch cover, went on to become one of his best-selling albums, selling more than 100,000 copies within weeks of its release. The recordings marked Miles's breaking out of the jazz market and into the worldwide youth market, and the beginning of his final years as an international celebrity and superstar.

But are his covers good music? A worrying indicator is that Miles's versions of "Time after Time" and "Human Nature" have become staples of smooth-jazz stations around the world and are often included in the Muzak tapes played in restaurants, shopping malls, and elevators, where they can be heard among the likes of James Last and other schmaltzy kitsch. Bob Berg remarked, "I felt we were covering these tunes like a Top 40 band. Miles's history is saturated with current pop tunes, but he did something with them; they turned out completely different than the original. They evolved into what we call jazz, and they were very cutting edge at the time. Whereas I felt that 'Time after Time,' in terms of musical surroundings, was a little trite. I was disappointed by that stuff."

Miles's recordings of "Time after Time" and "Human Nature" are not particularly innovative. The band plays the backings in a manner that is similar to the originals, and Miles follows the melodies closely. Yet there is an authenticity and poise to his playing that lifts them, especially "Time after Time," out of the ordinary. One is reminded of the words of rock producer Rupert Hine, who once said of Tina Turner, "She had an amazing capacity to force any song into submission and make it entirely her own."[11] Miles did something similar with "Time after Time" and "Human Nature." The two tunes became core elements of his live sets when he and his band did "recompose" them with his "intense involvement." "After having seen him perform these tunes live, I realized that they were great vehicles for him, and that they were one of his better choices," Jones observed.

"Something's on Your Mind" falls into a slightly different category. Miles and Irving added a brief intro, called "MD 1," and a slightly longer outro, called "MD 2," both only consisting of sound effects. Scofield plays a solo with deft phrasing, tone, and choice of notes, and Miles has a striking moment at 04:46 when he switches to open trumpet. But the slick arrangements make it impossible for the recording to achieve the honesty and poignancy of the other two covers. Of course, the fact that the song itself is not on a par with "Time after Time" and "Human Nature" is a contributing factor.

After these sessions Miles still only had about thirty minutes of music, not enough to make up a whole album. A song written in the summer of 1984 by Irving and his wife offered a solution to the problem. "Miles had developed a friendship with Cindy Lauper because of having recorded 'Time after Time,'" Irving said. "She was knocked out by his version, and he offered that we write her a tune. So Morrisine and myself wrote a song called 'I Can't Stay away from You.' In January of 1985 we needed more material very quickly because we had a tour coming up. Miles suggested we did an instrumental version of the song, and called it after Morrisine."

The band had recorded a demo version of "Ms. Morrisine" on September 22, 1984, but when revisiting the track at the beginning of 1985, Miles heard that John McLaughlin was in New York, and asked the guitarist to assist him. The new version was recorded live in the studio, without Scofield, and with McLaughlin overdubbing himself. "Ms. Morrisine" is the undisputed highlight of *You're under Arrest*. The combination of a quasi-reggae beat, McLaughlin's heavy rock comping, Irving's dramatic three-note keyboard riffs, and Miles at his lyrical best, alternatively soloing and referring to the original melody, is deeply engaging. A high trumpet shriek at 03:58 cues McLaughlin's final solo, which is both one of his most straight-ahead and most thrilling solos on record.

Miles was still in need of more material, and trying to make as much use of McLaughlin as possible he asked the band to use a motif from the fifth bar of "Ms. Morrisine" as a vamp. Irving adds keyboard atmospherics, and over this backing Miles and McLaughlin slug it out, alternating solos, with McLaughlin playing in his more normal jazz-rock style. "It was a jam session," commented Irving. The track, called "Katia," after McLaughlin's partner, the classical pianist Katia Labèque, has exciting moments, with McLaughlin soloing against intense keyboard stabs and comping in staccato style behind Miles. But the vamp is not particularly interesting, and without a clear theme or other kind of direction, the excitement of the soloists sounds a little overblown.

"Katia" and a brief outtake called "Katia Prelude" complete *You're under Arrest,* which, despite the great variation in directions, is one of the most musically enjoyable recordings of Miles's last decade. There's nothing particularly new or groundbreaking, but the playing and much of the music are of high quality. The arrangements are clearer, and richer in instrumental textures and colors than before, mostly courtesy of Irving's keyboards, and Miles's return to playing ballads and extended melodies, after more than two decades of mostly abstract music, is refreshing.

❖

Since their last orchestral recordings—for *Quiet Nights* in 1962 and 1963, and the track "Falling Water" in 1968—Miles and Gil Evans had only collaborated on Miles's small-band studio albums. They regularly made plans for large-scale projects, but nothing ever materialized. Miles must have been extremely disappointed in 1984 that their latest large-scale venture had once again been aborted. However, fate unexpectedly offered him a chance to make up for the loss of an opportunity to work with orchestral material.

Exemplifying his mounting star status, Miles received honors, prizes, and accolades with increasing regularity during the '80s. The succession of Grammy Awards for his recordings and a four-hour show celebrating his career by Radio City Music Hall in New York in November of 1983, are but two examples. In addition, Denmark's prestigious Sonning Prize was awarded to him in 1984. Classical composers like Igor Stravinsky, Aaron Copland, Olivier Messiaen, and Leonard Bernstein were previous recipients, and Miles was the first nonclassical musician to be honored in this way. On learning of his illustrious predecessors, Miles traveled to Copenhagen to receive the prize and to play at a specially arranged live concert on December 14, 1984.

One of the two works performed during this concert was written by Danish trumpeter and composer Palle Mikkelborg, one of Denmark's leading musicians, who has roots in jazz and avant-garde classical music, and who was strongly influenced by Miles, Gil Evans, Charles Ives, and Olivier Messiaen. Like Miles, Mikkelborg has experimented with the electric trumpet and with synthesizers, and shares a great openness towards all music genres. The name of the composition Mikkelborg had written was "Aura," and Miles was to play for five minutes during its final movement, a blues called "Violet." Mikkelborg had also invited John Scofield as a second soloist for the live performance, which featured the Danish Radio Big Band and was recorded by Danish radio and television.

"At the time, the idea was that we would begin the concert with 'Aura,'" Mikkelborg recalled. "Gil Evans had been asked to write a piece for the second half, but he never finished anything around this time, so another American composer, Ray Pitts, who lived here in Denmark, was asked to write a piece instead. Miles arrived a couple of days before the performance for the rehearsals, and it turned out that he liked Ray's piece, but didn't want to play on it. This meant that the concert order had to be reversed, so 'Aura' became the closing piece. I had also prepared an orchestral arrangement of 'Time after Time,' which I had heard Miles play live at a concert in Finland. Miles was very impressed with that. He ended up playing for an hour, with 'Time after Time' and 'Jean-Pierre' as encores. He was so inspired!"

Miles traveled back to New York immediately after the concert to spend four days, December 17 to 20, recording a television commercial for the Japanese drink company Van Aquavit. It was his first of several excursions into the world of advertising, and another sign of his increasingly high public profile. The idea of recording an orchestral work apparently did not leave him, because in the middle of January 1985, immediately after completing *You're under Arrest,* he called Mikkelborg. "He said, 'How fast can we do this?'" Mikkelborg remembered. "It was not so much a question, more like an order: 'Get this thing together, let's do this one.' There was quite a bit of office work to be done to organize the whole thing. It took forty-eight hours to put the process in motion, but another ten days to get everyone and everything together. As soon as we were ready, Miles came over for about ten days."

The recordings took place over five days, from January 31 to February 4, 1985. Miles and Mikkelborg spent another five days discussing and altering the music. "Aura" was Mikkelborg's celebration of Miles. The work consists of nine movements, which were named after different colors in Miles's aura. "Miles had a magic aura," the Dane explained. "I saw him at a concert in 1967 or 1968, with Wayne Shorter, and we were all magnetized by him. There was something else, something more than the music. You could call it charisma, but it was more than that, something that was very hard to define."

"When he came over in January 1985, I met him in his hotel room several times," Mikkelborg continued. "He'd be sitting there in his chair, under a lamp, painting, with glasses on and wearing a nightgown and a hair weave. He looked so fragile and delicate. He was a small man, physically, and he was wearing high heels. He was also using lots of perfume, with a very special, personal scent. He had the television set on, and was talking about boxing or Clint Eastwood, very normal things. It was so abnormally normal a situation that I thought, 'Is this really Miles Davis?' But the next time I'd see him, he'd have this enormous aura around him."

In addition to taking his inspiration from Miles's aura, Mikkelborg based the main theme of the work on Miles's name. "It's a very simple system that I've used later as well, and which sometimes gives you interesting results," the composer explained. "You can make it more complex, like John Cage has done with words and poems, but what I did was take the alphabet from A to Z and assign a chromatic note to each of the letters in ascending order. Then I took the letters of Miles's name, and out came the theme. It's a very simple theme, and I started manipulating with it. That's where it became interesting. I also based some rhythmical patterns on the theme. It sounds like a complete brain construction, but it actually gave me something very beautiful to work on."

Mikkelborg structured much of the music according to one of the methods invented by twentieth-century avant-garde classical music, serialism, in which certain tone rows are rigorously repeated. He tried to explain these concepts to Miles, but the trumpeter quickly lost interest. "He asked me a few times, but when it took too long to explain, he wasn't interested," Mikkelborg said. "He was interested in how it sounded, not in how I got there. I also told him that some of the music was based on Messiaen, and asked him whether he was familiar with the composer. He said he wasn't, and asked me to play him some of his music. He listened, but never mentioned it again. I know that Miles did not really understand Stockhausen either. He called him, 'That guy Steakhausen.' I think he understood the energy, but not the method, and I think this was a conscious choice. He wanted his relationship to music to be entirely intuitive."

Mikkelborg emphasized that Miles's influence was not only implicit, in the way he had inspired the aesthetic values of "Aura," but also explicit, in the way Miles directly influenced many musical decisions. "Some of his ideas were so beautiful and clear,"

Mikkelborg said. "I'd written some sections that were very complicated, very constructed. He said, 'I'm not sure I like this section too much.' He was very polite. I think he understood that they had taken me the longest time to write. It was a huge section for saxophones, and I knew from the beginning there was something wrong. The thinking was right, but the orchestration was wrong. Miles said it was clumsy and had no flow, and I agreed with him, so I took it out. I found that the parts of 'Aura' where I'd been most meditative and had not written so many notes were the best parts. Miles often tried to strip things to basics. He didn't like a lot of ornaments. He said many times, 'When a guy composes a theme, it's because he wants it to be played. If there's a theme, there's a reason for that theme. So play the theme.'"

"In another section, he wanted some bassoon and low flutes, like Gil Evans wrote on *Sketches of Spain,*" Mikkelborg added. "I said, 'It's not possible at this short notice,' and he looked at me and said, 'Alright.' I had the feeling he was kind of testing me. But he was very sweet and very cooperative, and very inspiring. Throughout the project he was delicate, diplomatic, and never got angry. I never saw any of his dark side. Yes, he could be demanding. He gave orders. 'I need a comb' meant 'Give me a comb.' But he was also prepared to accept refusals."

Miles's influence also showed in other ways. Continuing their work on *You're under Arrest* a few weeks earlier he invited John McLaughlin and Vince Wilburn Jr. to the sessions. "I wasn't supposed to play drums at all," Wilburn recalled. "I just went to co-produce with Miles, but then he ordered some Simmons [electronic] drums. I guess he was going through his electronic drum thing where he wanted to hear certain reinforcements on the rhythm."

The inclusion of McLaughlin on *Aura,* the recording, is especially fortuitous, because the guitarist plays extremely well on the three pieces on which he features, adding a powerful solo voice to Miles's. The Briton has a strong impact on the opening movement, called "Intro," in which he introduces the theme based on Miles's name, starting at 00:36.[12] The band comes in at 01:45 with a syncopated, heavily accented staccato rhythm, over which McLaughlin plays a short but stirring solo with a beautiful distorted tone. Miles enters at 02:21 with some fast phrases, and guitarist and trumpeter duet compellingly for the rest of the movement.

It's an intense opening, and the gentle, playful, dreamlike "White" that follows it comes as a surprise. "White" was not originally intended to be part of *Aura.* "I don't like the sound of a band or orchestra warming up," Mikkelborg explained. "So I had created some music that could be played via a tape before the first performance of 'Aura' in December [of 1984]. The tape consisted of eight meditations on Miles's scale, which I had asked a synthesizer friend to improvise over with electronic sounds. One day in the studio Miles remembered it from the rehearsals, and said, 'Put on that electronic tape. At first I didn't know what he was talking about, but once I understood him I realized we had a fifteen-inch copy in the studio. He said, 'Put it on, and open the microphone,' and suddenly we had to work very fast. I had no idea what he wanted to do. I asked the oboe player to be ready to play a little theme I had when I gave him some cues, and I said to [percussionist] Marilyn Mazur that she could play her poetic percussion any way she wanted."

"So the engineer and Miles were sitting in complete darkness, with headphones on," Mikkelborg continued. "And then Miles started playing. It was a first take, and we all felt as if an angel was passing through the room. It was very atmospheric, very touching, and very pure. I knew this was one of these magical creative moments, the moment before the intellect comes in and asks what is being played. When we finished, Miles was very touched, too, and completely quiet. Then he said, 'Did you hear my calypso, to break the ice?' It was the phrase he'd started with. And then he told us, 'Put it on again,' and he did another take, once again with that little B-flat theme in it. It was a very powerful moment. Somehow Miles sounded like a little boy with his mute. I used the recording as it was, with both takes, although there were a couple of cracked notes, which I took out."

"White" is a stunning ambient piece, with a potent glacial atmosphere, calling up images of an endless white desert, perhaps explaining Miles's comment that he tried to "break the ice." With its stark, original synthesizer sounds and Miles's exquisite playing, the track is one of *Aura*'s highlights. The third track, "Yellow," again has a strong ambient tendency, led by harp, oboe, and eerie, unearthly synthesizer textures. The ambient textures breathe in and out with cool serenity, but the mood is periodically disturbed by heavy, almost gothic brass and drums rhythms. Miles does not appear on the track.

The fourth piece, "Orange," illustrates the main shortcoming of *Aura,* the sometimes heavy-handed and stiff approach to rhythm. This is, in part, due to the stodgy sound of the electronic Simmons drums, which dates the music in the '80s, but also to the arrangements. Both Miles and McLaughlin are in excellent form, but the band only starts to catch fire when an interesting melody is introduced at 06:02, with voicings suggestive of Gil Evans, and a funky electric piano and rhythm guitar that add a little playfulness to the rhythm.

"Red" is based around a heavy, driving rock rhythm. The tension is gradually increased with modulations and brass chords and stabs. Miles plays open trumpet, beginning the piece with a descending figure to which extensive studio effects have been added. He plays tenderly, hesitantly, and playfully, as if to offset the dark power of the rhythm. At 04:18 the tension is released by an electric guitar break, followed by the same syncopated rhythm as featured in "Intro." There's a passion to this piece, exemplifying its subject matter, which was, according to Mikkelborg, "fire."

The intensity of "Red" is followed by the cool, ambient quality of "Green," which was recorded on the same night as "White." The atmosphere is softer and more pastoral, partly because of the warm sound of the two extended bass solos, one acoustic, by Niels-Henning Ørsted Pedersen, one fretless, by Bo Stief. "Green" is based around a number of delicate, haunting, slow-moving chords, which are reminiscent, according to *Aura* CD liner notes writer Khephra Burns, of Charles Ives's "The Unanswered Question" and also of Gil Evans.[13] Miles only plays in the second section, sparring on muted trumpet with Niels-Henning Ørsted Pedersen and gradually building the track to more intensity. Accompanying them is a sixteen-voice female choir, which is the overdubbed voice of Eva Thaysen. Mikkelborg used a female voice because, "The feminine is very present in Miles's art. His attraction to the female universe came out strongly in his trumpet sound and in his clothes, which were often women's clothes around this time, and which suited him fantastically."

"Blue" begins with some abstract synthesizer sounds, over which Miles plays a few chromatic phrases. At 00:38 the music switches into a reggaelike rhythm, accentuated by synthesizer chords and muted horns. Miles solos exuberantly on open horn throughout, and the music has a joyous, extrovert feel until Mikkelborg subverts the mood with dissonant brass and woodwind. Following this the reggae rhythm gradually fades in the background and the wind instruments take over, with Miles soloing very chromatically. Rhythmically "Blue" is one of the most assured sections of *Aura* although there's still a stiffness to the arrangement and playing.

Miles liked "Red" so much he soloed again over a shortened version, this time using a mute. This version is called "Electric Red." Its main attraction lies in the way Miles dances like a butterfly over the rhythm, with childlike phrases defying the gravity of the groove. The following track, "Indigo," has five seconds of brass added in the 2000 rerelease. The brass functions like a wake-up call, after which the band plays five minutes of deconstructed jazz, without Miles, but featuring Thomas Clausen on piano, in almost avant-garde fashion. This kind of music has been done many times before, and the track only gains genuine interest at 05:14, when wild brass phrases and electronic drums produce some unusual effects.

Finally, the blues "Violet" is based on two chords from Olivier Messiaen's book *My Musical Language*. "Those two chords have followed me all my life," Mikkelborg revealed. "They were even on my earliest records. You can hear them when the rhythm begins. They sound bluesy, and yet very different. Miles never found out what they were, but he played some very strange things over the top." The dissonant chords add significantly to the atmosphere of "Violet," and set up a challenging context for Miles and McLaughlin to solo against. They both play well, but the deliberately disjointed atmospheric ending, which begins at 07:53, could have come earlier.

"After we had finished recording Miles said to me, 'You produce this, you mix this, I believe in you,'" Mikkelborg remembered. "I had never produced such a complicated thing before, and there were so many takes, he had done so many solos on top of each other, it was not easy. He wanted me to select the best parts. There were four or five solos on some tracks, and sometimes he missed a lot of notes, and some of them were very beautiful misses. I used my intuition in selecting the best takes. But he didn't hit the notes with the same power as in the '50s and '60s, and he seemed very weak physically. When I saw him a few years later, he looked a lot better and walked stronger."

Miles was, by all accounts, extremely pleased with *Aura*. When he heard the fruits of Mikkelborg's work he phoned the Dane with the message, "It's a motherfucker!" and he called the recording a "masterpiece"[14] in his autobiography. Despite its flaws, *Aura* is arguably the best studio album to have come out of Miles's last decade, combining unusual harmonies with a unique mixture of synthesizers, rock rhythms, and jazz bigband arrangements. Miles can also be heard at his most varied, with daring chromatic playing—this despite the fact that his tone is rarely strong enough to impose his presence entirely convincingly on the music.

Aura is a perfect complement to the much-easier-on-the-ear tunefulness of *You're under Arrest,* making late 1984 to early 1985 a high point of Miles's '80s musical output. *Aura* is also an honorable continuation of Miles's late 1950s to early 1960s orchestral experiments with Gil Evans, and restored Miles's reputation as a groundbreaking musician. Miles predicted to Mikkelborg that it would change the Dane's life, and today Mikkelborg indeed has legendary status in Scandinavia as "The Man Who Worked with Miles Davis."

However, all this was not to occur for several more years. For unknown reasons, Columbia refused to release the work. The company is said to have withdrawn funding halfway through the recording, and refused to pay for a digital remix Miles requested. It was completed courtesy of a $1,400 grant from the National Endowment for the Arts, and some of Miles's own money.[15] "The Danish radio, which did a film portrait of this session, also invested some money," Mikkelborg added. "And so did the Danish radio big band organization. There was a lot of politics going on behind the scenes. But one day in the late '80s George Butler called me and said that he'd listened to the tape because a lot of people had been asking about it. He said he thought it was fantastic, that everything Miles had done since was nothing in comparison, and that he was looking forward to releasing it. Of course, I was very pleased to hear that."

Aura was released in 1989, benefiting from the publicity surrounding *Miles: The Autobiography,* which was published around the same time. It was, generally speaking, well received, especially in jazz circles. Critic Francis Davis, who teaches jazz at the University of Pennsylvania, called it "so shockingly good that you're slightly disappointed in it for not being perfect."[16] Miles received two Grammies for *Aura,* one in the Best Jazz Instrumental Performance, Soloist category, the other for Best Jazz Instrumental Performance, Big Band. The turmoil surrounding *Aura* contributed to the growing schism between Miles and Columbia, and in May of 1985 he moved to Warner Bros., terminating a working relationship that had lasted thirty years. This dramatic change in the team surrounding Miles once again radically changed the course of his life and music.

Chapter Fourteen

GRACE UNDER PRESSURE

"I make music that I like, but I found out that usually what I like, somebody else will like too. If you're sincere about it, somebody else can see it."

—MILES DAVIS[1]

Miles's move to Warner Bros. in 1985 is one of the big mysteries of his career. The reasons for his departure from Columbia have never become entirely clear. When queried for an explanation, Miles often cited two incidents: Columbia's treatment of *Aura,* and its handling of its other trumpet star, Wynton Marsalis. "[It was because of] different reasons," Miles said in late 1986. "When we did this [*Aura*] I wanted $1,400 for a digital remix and Columbia wouldn't pay it. And then George Butler calls me up. He says to me, 'Why don't you call Wynton?' I say, 'Why?' He says, ''Cause it's his birthday.' That's why I left Columbia."[2]

Columbia's initial refusal to support the *Aura* project is mystifying, given Miles's stature as a musician and his thirty-year-long relationship with the company. It's understandable that Miles perceived it as a slap in the face, and the star-treatment Columbia meted out to Wynton Marsalis most likely added insult to injury. While Miles may well have felt hurt and angry by what appears to be careless treatment by Columbia, it seems insufficient reason for him to leave. "I do not believe for a second that the way *Aura* was handled was the reason he left Columbia," Mark Rothbaum said. "There was no reason for Miles to leave Columbia. I also think the rivalry between Wynton and Miles is blown out of proportion. Miles ruled at Columbia. He broke their hearts when he left. It came as a terrible shock to them."

In attempting to unearth the real reasons for Miles's change of record company, there are once again suggestions of Cicely Tyson's influence. In early 1985 Miles sacked Blank & Blank as his management. However, apparently not having learned from his previous mistake, he again appointed someone on his wife's recommendation. This time it was David Franklin, who managed Tyson, as well as Roberta Flack and Richard Prior.

According to Jo Gelbard, Miles was at a financial and personal low when they first met in 1984, at the end of the Blank brothers' tenure. "He was broke when I met him, and in a mess," she recalled. "A total mess. I don't think there was one reason for him to be alive. Everything was wrong with him. His hips. His diabetes was out of control. His heart. Everything. It was a very gloomy period."

Franklin apparently tried to plug Miles's financial hole, and distracted by his problems, or perhaps desperate for any change in his circumstances, Miles accepted the deal his new manager negotiated with Warner Bros. Records, the record company, and Warner Chappell Music, the music publishers; the contracts were signed in May and June of 1985 respectively. Astonishingly, half the copyrights of Miles's existing compositions as well as half of the material he was to write in the future were awarded to Warner Chappell. These were unusually high amounts.

"David fucked up the negotiations by giving up too much to Warner's, like the rights to all my publishing," Miles complained. "They gave us a lot of money to come over to Warner Bros., in the seven figures, just to sign. But I didn't like the idea of giving up my publishing rights to them."[3]

The question remains why Miles, once known for his business acumen, signed. "I think Miles did it because he was scared, and wanted his own money," Rothbaum commented. "Miles was terribly afraid of being poor. Miles had choices, but often didn't know he had choices. He could have had everything, but instead moved wildly one way and then the other. The deal with Warner Bros. was, in my opinion, totally mishandled. I spoke to people at Columbia, and they said, 'We would have given him the money!' Alternatively, he could have gotten a bank loan for one million dollars on the strength of his back catalog. When I looked after Miles's affairs, I lent him probably five times as much money, without collateral, without even a handshake."

With the Warner Bros. contract in place, Miles was much less likely to put his own compositions on his albums. Of course, Miles's main strength and calling was never compositional, despite the fact that he had written several classic jazz tunes. "Miles was not a composer," Bob Berg stated. "He didn't write many tunes, but he was a great stylist, a great forger of musical style. His aesthetic sense and values and outlook on what was hip was his strongest suit, and consequently what he did throughout his career was to surround himself with people who could project a similar kind of aesthetic." "Miles was not really a great composer, or writer," Dave Liebman added. "He was an arranger in the theater sense, a director sort of thing. He wasn't the kind of guy that would say 'You play an E here, and an F over there and at the third beat play this chord.' That wasn't his thing."

Nevertheless, several of Miles's creative peaks—such as *Ascenseur pour l'Échafaud, Kind of Blue,* the period with the second great quintet of December of 1967 to June of 1968, *Bitches Brew,* and much of the material of the '73–'75 band—coincided with prolific periods in his own writing. Whether his writing inspired these peaks or exemplified them is unclear, but the deal with Warner Chappell precluded a recurrence. Instead, Miles had now made himself entirely reliant on others for new studio material, strongly influencing his future output.

As he had often done when attempting to forge a new musical direction, Miles began work on a new studio recording by drawing upon his past. In 1985 he went back to the methods by which "Decoy" and "Code M.D." had come into being (i.e., young musicians writing material for him with the aid of music technology). Following the involvement of Bob Irving and Vince Wilburn Jr., he now approached guitarist Randy Hall, who had also participated in his first comeback sessions in 1980 and 1981. Hall was now living in Los Angeles and recording an album called *Love You like a Stranger*. He was aided by Adam Holzman, who was establishing himself as a keyboardist of some repute, playing in the fusion band The Fents.

"I also worked in a music store," Holzman said, "and had access to lots of instruments and learned how to program them. So when I met Miles I was at the cutting edge of the midi revolution, and worked as a synthesizer programmer and studio musician. Randy said he was going to use me for the session with Miles, not so much to play, but to program synthesizers. We did the first session in October 17, when we worked on a song called 'Rubber Band.' It also featured Mike Stern, who Miles had flown in. Miles was intrigued by synthesizers, which were beginning to sound pretty good in 1985. He was also intrigued by the whole approach of layering tracks in the studio, of doing one thing at a time, which seemed contrary to what you'd expect. Because of his fascination with synthesizers he immediately hired me for his live band. I flew over to New York the next day, and two days later I was on a European tour with Miles."

The October session also featured Zane Giles, Hall's writing partner, on guitar and drum programming, as well as Steve Reid on percussion. When returning from the European tour in November, Miles continued to develop the direction set in October, with the help of Holzman, Hall, Zane, Reid, and Vince Wilburn Jr. Other players, such as keyboardists Wayne Linsey and Neil Larsen and saxophonist Glen Burris, were also involved. According to Holzman, "Miles wanted to try many people. And I know that he had a lot of little irons in the fire, working with different writers."

Miles was actively seeking out musicians who could write material for him during this period. By the beginning of 1986 Miles was, or had been, in touch with at least four: Prince, Bill Laswell, Paul Buckmaster, and keyboardist George Duke. "Prince wrote me a letter and along with the letter he enclosed a tape of instrumental tracks he'd recorded by himself in the studio," Miles said. "In this letter he wrote, 'Miles, even though we have never met . . . if this tape is of any use to you, please go ahead and play whatever you feel over it. Because I trust what you hear and play.'"[4]

Miles communicated with Laswell, Buckmaster, and Duke on his own initiative. He had first met Laswell in January of 1984 in Paris, when the bassist was working on an album with Manu Dibango that featured go-go rhythms. From 1984 to 1986 Laswell and Miles occasionally discussed collaborations, but Laswell was too deeply involved in other projects to follow up on their plans. Buckmaster did respond to Miles's request and recorded three "simple, floaty" tracks using midi equipment, based on a bass line that Miles hummed him over the phone. They were never used.

"I first met Miles in 1971, when I was playing with Cannonball Adderley," Duke remarked. "I had taken over the keyboard spot from Joe Zawinul. When I came offstage, Miles came up to me, and said, 'Hey, you think you can play with me?' I said, 'Sure, give me a call.' I didn't hear from him for years. He finally called me at the end of 1985, asking me to write a song for him. I initially thought it was a prank, one of my friends impersonating him. So I didn't do anything, and a week later he called again. I said, 'Who is this?' and he started swearing at me, 'Motherfucker, write me a song.' So I said, 'This is no joke?'"

In the mid-1980s George Duke was a writer, producer, and solo artist of considerable repute. He had begun as a jazz pianist, moved into jazz-rock, funk, rock, and soul music, and enjoyed hit singles and albums. With the help of a Synclavier, a combination of a synthesizer, sampler, sequencer, and thirty-two-track hard disk recorder, Duke wrote three tracks for Miles. Duke's inspiration was twofold: R&B and the Cuban band Irakere, which mixes Cuban folk music with jazz, salsa, classical, and funk rock influences.

"Miles wanted me to do something that resembled Irakere," Duke explained. "I'd never heard of them, so Miles sent me a tape, and said, 'Give me something with this vibe.' I loved it, and it inspired me to write a piece called 'Fumilayo,' which was eventually covered by Dianna Reeves and nominated for an Oscar. The other two songs were 'Tribute' and 'Backyard Ritual.' The last piece was R&B–inspired because Miles was always influenced by stuff that had an R&B edge. I also lean that way, which is why I think he called me. My recordings were all intended as demos, with sampled and synthesizer instruments, and I sent them off, thinking he was going to re-record them with his band. But Miles said, 'We're not going to re-record it, I like it the way it is, it sounds funny.' I said, 'But you're going to at least replace the synthesizer sax, right?' And he replied, 'No, I like it.'"

Tommy LiPuma, head of the jazz division at Warner Bros. in the mid-1980s, was acutely aware of Miles's trial-and-error approach to the creation of his first studio album for the company. LiPuma gradually shifted from following the project from a distance to hands-on involvement, and he ultimately co-produced the project with the writers involved. After Miles's recent efforts at co-producing his own records, this was a radical shift in direction. Also, contrary to the relative production inexperience of Vince Wilburn Jr. and Robert Irving, LiPuma was, and is, one of the American music industry's heavyweights. He had worked with Barbra Streisand, David Sanborn, and Al Jarreau, propelled George Benson to smooth-jazz fame, and won numerous Grammys.

LiPuma was more likely to give Miles strong direction than Wilburn and Irving, and sifting through the variety of material that had emerged, the producer decided that only George Duke's "Backyard Ritual" and Prince's track "Can I Play with U" showed promise. The material from the "Rubber Band" sessions was rather crude, tarnished by stiff rhythms and a lack of melodic material or distinguished vamps. LiPuma and Miles began the second week of February of 1986 by overdubbing to the twenty-four-track of "Can I Play with U" and to George Duke's "Backyard Ritual." But two songs did not constitute a musical direction. LiPuma and Miles were still at a loss as to how to proceed, throwing up names for other possible collaborators. LiPuma suggested keyboardists like Lyle Mays, who had worked with Pat Metheny, or Thomas Dolby. As luck would have it, LiPuma received a phone call from Marcus Miller around this time. "I knew Tommy, and had heard that Miles had moved to Warner Bros.," Miller recalled. "I didn't know Tommy was working with Miles, but since he was head of jazz at Warner, I told him that I felt I might contribute something if Miles was ever looking for songs. Tommy barely let me finish, and said, 'Great! We've been talking about where we're going, and the direction isn't quite there yet. But there's a song by George Duke that I think is a good point of departure.'"

"When I heard the track, I thought, 'Wow, if Miles is willing to start using drum machines and stuff, let me show my take on that,'" Miller continued. "So I wrote 'Tutu,' 'Portia,' and 'Splatch,' and demo-ed them using synthesizers and drum machines, as well as bass guitar and bass clarinet. I wasn't directly musically influenced by George's track, but it gave me a direction. It showed me that it was okay to use machines, to make music the way we were making it at the time. So I used the machines to create lots of colors, samples, all kinds of things."

Marcus Miller was living in New York at this time, working in close collaboration with keyboardist and synthesizer programmer Jason Miles, who didn't play but who programmed most of the sounds for the three songs. "When we were finished, I called Tommy, and he told me to come to L.A.," Miller said. "I arrived with the tapes, feeling a little strange to present a demo, but it turned out not to be a presentation at all. They were like, 'Let's hear it.' And then, 'That's great, let's start recording.' Miles wasn't even there. I said, 'Where's the band?' And they said, 'It sounds great on the tape, just do it.' So I rented a lot of equipment, and proceeded to record 'Tutu.' Miles came in on the third day, and said, 'I love it, keep going.' It was great to see him again. He looked a completely different person. He wasn't dying anymore, but was healthy, alert; he looked fantastic, to the point that I couldn't stop mentioning it to him and he told me to shut up."

When Miller began recording in Los Angeles, he wanted to have Jason Miles at his side, but was told that the budget didn't stretch this far. Perhaps Warner Bros. was reluctant to make another sizeable investment after the large advance they had paid Miles. In response to Miller's wish to work with a keyboard player and synthesizer programmer, Miles suggested Adam Holzman. As a consequence, the basic tracks for "Tutu," "Portia," and "Splatch" were laid down in the beginning of February by a cast consisting of several synthesizers, a Linn 9000 drum machine, and Miller, Holzman, and LiPuma.

"We recorded the three tracks in the course of three or four days," Holzman recalled. "Marcus and I did some synthesizer programming, and I also played a solo on 'Splatch,' bringing a little bit of the live-band vibe to the record. Those early days were a very hip time to be there because Tommy and Marcus were guiding the ship, and there was a creative buzz that you get when you're working on something that's really good and unique. It was a special project, with a new sound, and it was an exciting and very charged time."

It was LiPuma's decision to work without Miles's live band, and it would have an enormous impact on the shape and sound of the album. The producer felt that Miller's use of drum machines and synthesizers was very innovative and that the recordings sounded perfect as they were. In the often-erroneous section on the making of *Tutu* in his autobiography, Miles remarked that he found taking his band into the studio "too much trouble" because some musicians might not feel so great on a particular day. He claimed that the new studio technology would compensate for any lack of spontaneity or enthusiasm. He also said, "Nowadays, you walk into the studio, there's these machines that'll do it all for you. . . . I love 'em!"[5] But everyone who has recorded using the overdubbing process knows that retaining aliveness and spontaneity is one of the main problems, since musicians inevitably have to follow the tape, and cannot lead or interact.

For a musician who had always prided himself on being in control and giving the lead, and who was fiercely and tirelessly committed to music, the above utterings are barely credible. Miles's explanations once again have the whiff of a smokescreen. Something of the veil is lifted when Miles wrote that Tommy LiPuma's taste in music was different from his. LiPuma has gone on record as stating that he looks at his association with "smooth-jazz" with pride. Implications that he attempted to push Miles into making a more commercial form of jazz have cropped up with some regularity.

"Rather than get myself, the working band, and Tommy into all kinds of hassles by trying to bring my working band in the studio to record music I might like, but Tommy doesn't, we do it this way,"[6] Miles recounted. Although "this way" referred to working with studio technology, it appears more appropriate to simply lose the "t"—to avoid "too much trouble" Miles preferred to record things LiPuma's way.

"I don't think they knew what to do with Miles at Warner Bros. around this time," Jason Miles commented. "And that's where Marcus came in. Was there some political shit going on between what Tommy and Miles wanted to put on the record? Absolutely. People say *Tutu* was a Marcus Miller solo record, but if anybody was the puppet master, knowing which strings to pull, it was Tommy. It was not Marcus's idea not to work with the live band. He wanted to have live musicians."

"I wasn't party to the decision not to use the live band," Miller added. "And I'm sure Tommy recognized when I played him my demo of 'Tutu' that he could get it on the radio, make it a hit." But the bassist stressed, "Tommy didn't push me in any direction. He let me do my thing. He suggested things, but never to smooth the music out. He more just enjoyed what we were doing."

Miles's involvement was minimal during the early stages. "Miles came in and played over what I had laid down," Miller explained. "I basically directed him through it, which was weird at first. Imagine telling Miles what to do! When he came in, I just told him to do his thing, but he said, 'No man, you got to tell me what you need me to do.' Eventually I got comfortable giving him directions. He only did two takes on 'Tutu,' and I think we used take number one. His chops were a little shaky. There were some cracked notes that you can hear, and we edited some out. After he left we overdubbed other things to support what he'd done, to make it sound more cohesive."

"I won't forget when he put his solo in 'Tutu,'" LiPuma said. "It was the first time down. Bam, that was it. I kept looking around to the tape machine, making sure it was recording, because it was so good. The next day I told him how excited I was over what we had gotten down. I asked him whether he was coming over, and he said that he needed to take a couple of days off. I realized that he had given it his all, to the point of exhaustion. There's nothing more you can ask of any artist, to give it everything he's got."[7]

Miller demonstrated the twenty-four-track tape for "Tutu" in *The Miles Davis Radio Project*, explaining the different elements of the arrangements. He revealed that the bass line was inspired by Miles's Prince of Darkness image, the chords based on the voicings Herbie Hancock used in the second great quintet, and the synthesizer trombone ensemble inspired by Gil Evans's arrangements of *The Birth of the Cool*. Miller also related that it was his idea to title the track "Tutu" after Archbishop Desmond Tutu, and that he had images of South Africa in his mind while writing. "The people there were still struggling," Miller said. "I wanted to make sure that the titles were short and to the point. 'Portia' is just a beautiful name, and 'Splatch' is just a word I used to say."

On March 1, Miles and Holzman added more overdubs to Prince's track, "Can I Play with U." Miles and Holzman worked again on the track two weeks after that. Later on, when he heard Miller's material, Prince decided that his track didn't fit, and he withdrew it. ("Can I Play with U" eventually appeared on Prince bootlegs as "Red Riding Hood.")

LiPuma, happy with Miller's direction, asked the bassist to write and record more material to complete the project. Back in New York between March 12 and 25, and together with Jason Miles and LiPuma, Miller recorded three new tracks, titled "Tomaas" (Miles's nickname for LiPuma), "Don't Lose Your Mind," and "Full Nelson." The third of these songs had an intense, staccato rhythm similar to Prince's song. "I intended 'Full Nelson' to be a bridge between what I'd been doing and the Prince stuff," Miller explained. The title is a play on Nelson Mandela, Prince (whose last name is Nelson), and Miles's composition "Half Nelson," which the trumpeter first recorded with Charlie Parker in 1947.

LiPuma had also been looking for a pop song for Miles to cover. "Tommy had given Miles a ton of records to listen to," Jason Miles recalled. "And Miles came back with the message, 'I want to do this Scritti Politti tune, "Perfect Way." Tommy was stunned that Miles had found this song among all these records, had come up with the perfect match, the perfect way."

Adam Holzman was not involved in the New York sessions. The only additional musicians were drummer Omar Hakim, who overdubbed on "Tomaas," Bernard Wright, who played some synthesizers on "Tomaas" and "Don't Lose Your Mind," and Michael Urbaniak, who performed an electric violin solo on the latter track.[8] Marcus Miller recounted that Miles was by now more involved in the actual creation of the music. "He'd given me a tape with a melody he'd played on a keyboard," Miller said. "This was the basis for 'Tomaas' and the reason why the track is credited to both of us. He also told me on that track, 'I don't like the piano, use something else.' He was still Miles, you know, he still made sure it was all his."

Tutu was released in the fall of 1986. The album's radical new musical direction, characterized by the striking and dominant use of synthesizers and drum machines, as well as the fact that most instruments, arrangements, and music were by Marcus Miller, led to criticism that it was a Marcus Miller solo album in all but name. A similar criticism was levied at *Aura* when it was issued three years later. Others pointed to the parallels with Miles's orchestral works with Gil Evans, which were billed as Miles Davis solo albums with a credit for Gil Evans on the front cover. A comparable construction might have been more appropriate for *Tutu* and *Aura*. There are strong analogies among the musical environments created by Evans, Mikkelborg, and Miller. Miles was featured soloist in all these contexts, and Miller's arrangements, despite mostly being performed on synthesizers, were as strongly orchestral in nature as those on Evans's and Mikkelborg's works.

"Gil also set up the band and did all the arrangements," Miller commented. "But these recordings are still Miles's records. As soon as Miles walked into the studio and played his first three notes, it became his. It was the same with *Tutu*. I did everything with Miles in mind, and would never have done this music had it not been for him. I mean, with who else would I have been able to get away with these harmonies, or these kinds of rhythms? Nobody. Also, as much as I like *Tutu*, I would never say that it compares to the albums of the '50s. For me, the records Miles made in the '50s were his purest expression. Other stuff is great, but it always stands in relation to the '50s. In the radio program [*The Miles Davis Radio Project*], they had a voice-over, 'Miles Davis, from the past to the future,' and they played 'So What,' and then edited to 'Tutu.' I loved that, because it's also the line that I hear."

"I'm really committed to making music for now, although the problem with that is that you never know how dated it will sound ten years later," Miller added. "But I can't worry about that when I'm doing it. With *Tutu* I did a full-out version of what I saw as '80s music, using all the machines and so on. I thought, 'This will be different for him. It will create controversy.' Controversy needs to happen when a Miles album comes out. A Miles album should make you go one way or the other! If you're lukewarm to it, it's not doing its job. So it was like, 'Let's go all the way, and see what we get.' And it definitely made people take sides."

"Many jazz critics did not like the machines and the overdubs; it was like sacrilege to them. When I played it for people, most over thirty-five hated it, while the rest went, 'Yeah, man, we've been waiting for Miles to do something like this. It sounds like Miles to me.' Their ears were not distracted by the electronic instruments, and the voice samples and stuff. It was a normal backdrop to them. So it was a language issue."[9]

With all these considerations in mind, how does *Tutu* stand up in the twenty-first century? Has it become hopelessly dated, like most '80s electronic music, or is it still transcending its era, and relevant today? The answer is that *Tutu* is a mixed bag. The title track remains a masterpiece. The dark, brooding, mammoth bass line calls up associations with a walking giant, while the staccato orchestral samples and the mysterious synthesizer chords add to the ominous atmosphere, which is lightened by the beautiful, silky texture of the synthesizer sounds. In the middle of this sonic canvas, the fragile, darting sound of Miles's muted trumpet may indeed call up associations with "a little boy looking for his mother." Aside from mood and textures, the most striking aspects of this piece are the strength of Miller's themes, the fact that the synthesizer textures still sound fresh and original today, and the cohesiveness of the musical concept. The album as a whole is lifted by Miles's muted trumpet sound, which is the main humanizing element. If one imagines *Tutu* without Miles, it immediately loses a significant part of its shine. In addition, a plethora of samples, and the rigid feel of the drum machines, date some of the tracks strongly in their time.

"Tomaas" has an atmosphere similar to "Tutu," with long, evocative, breathy synthesizer lines. "Portia" has a mellower theme and mood, reminiscent of late-night jazz. It features a charming duet of Miles with Miller on soprano saxophone. "Splatch" is most strongly marred by the album's shortcomings, in particular heavy-footed rhythms and an overload of samples. There's no clear mood, and the track stumbles from interesting effect to interesting effect, with the musicians seemingly in love with their newfound musical toys. In terms of moods, sounds, and arrangements, Duke's "Backyard Ritual" is *Tutu*'s most buoyant selection. There's an attractive playfulness and directness not present in Miller's material, even while the melodic content is rather slight. The atmospheric beginning and ending, in which Duke experiments with the characteristic, glassy Synclavier sounds, are especially interesting, and one wishes that he or Miller had experimented more in this direction.

"Perfect Way" fits in well with the other material, but is weighed down by dense and heavy drum machine programming, leaving Miles little space to impose himself on the material, as he had done on the pop songs "Human Nature" and "Time after Time." There exists a piece of film footage that illustrates how he struggled with the track, attempting to overdub with headphones on, then gesturing at the engineer to stop the tape, and joking loudly, "Weird . . . it's weird, it's weird, it's weird! Strange . . . ! Shit! Okay, just let me play something that I like, and I'll bow out gracefully."[10]

The reggaelike rhythm of "Don't Lose Your Mind" adds some much-needed bounciness. There's a great moment around the four-minute mark, after Urbaniak's violin solo and during Miles's only substantial passage on the open trumpet on *Tutu*, when the music genuinely lifts off. "Full Nelson" is characterized by a gorgeous, infectious melody, and some terrific, festive rhythm playing, but Miles's muted horn begins to sound irritatingly uniform by this stage. It was the first indication of his overuse of the mute during the late '80s. "It seems as if it's easier to get the tone more uniform," Miller speculated. "If your chops aren't strong you don't have to blow as much air. And I think there's something comforting about the sound of the mute."

Despite the fact that jazz fans balked at the usage of synthesizers, *Tutu* was generally well received. It turned into one of the hippest and most-talked-about releases of 1986, crossing over hugely into the rock and pop market and winning Miles yet another Grammy for Best Jazz Instrumental Performance (it was also awarded a Grammy for Best Recording Package). Whether or not LiPuma had in any way smoothed out or commercialized the music is unknown, but the producer certainly helped bring a focus and consistency to the recording. This was exemplified in his suggestion for the snappy, trendy title for the album. (The recording was originally to be called *Perfect Way*.)

In combination with the striking close-up picture of Miles on the cover, and the unique, ultramodern, unearthly music, the whole package captured the zeitgeist as perfectly as *Bitches Brew* had sixteen years earlier. For the next few years *Tutu* was regularly to be heard in trendy cafés, clubs, and coffee shops the world over, and in late 1989 jazz critic Michael Zwerin called it "The best jazz record of the decade."[11] In combination with Miles's Columbia hits "Time after Time" and "Human Nature," *Tutu* was another important factor in raising his public status to that of a superstar. At the same time, since the '80s were very much about surface values and looking "cool," and very little about spiritual ideals, it is ironic that the Yoruban word for spiritual "coolness," or "grace under pressure," is the hidden meaning of the recording's title.

❖

One of the consequences of Miles's rising public profile was the increasing number of invitations he received to guest star on other artist's records and to participate in various media events. He had always received such invitations, but he only now began to accept them with regularity. This occurred in tandem with a general loosening up of Miles's persona, almost beyond recognition from the brooding, austere, menacing image he had projected earlier. In the second half of the '80s he was wearing a hair weave, and loose-fitting, lush, glittery, and often very colorful clothes that reflected the bright colors he used in his paintings and drawings. He also spoke to his live audiences and appeared in promotional videos (*Tutu* spawned two), granted more interviews than he had done in his entire previous career, and appeared on talk shows, as well as in commercials, movies, and television series. In addition, he signed a book contract in the spring of 1986, around the same time as his signing with Warner Bros., to work with poet and writer Quincy Troupe on his autobiography.

On one occasion Miles ascribed his newfound approachability simply to his improving health,[12] but it appears that the feminine presence in his life was once more a significant factor. By 1986 Miles was deeply involved with Jo Gelbard, an artist, who, at thirty-six, had a great awareness of current fashions, clothing styles, and artistic directions. "We met in an elevator in 1984, when I was thirty-four," Gelbard recalled. "I was married, with one little son, and he was married to Cicely Tyson. He was on crutches because of having his hip done, and generally falling apart. When he found out I was a sculptor and an artist he asked me to give him painting lessons. At the time he was sketching a lot, which was a kind of therapy for him, and so I started to teach him how to paint. Our relationship developed from there. It was rocky in the beginning, because his marriage was disintegrating, and he was going to California a lot. I was a clean, regular, nice Jewish girl, who gave him vitamins, made him dinner, and took him swimming, so I balanced him in terms of a straight, healthy lifestyle, which is probably why he fell in love with me."

Several other people played a part in the way Miles changed his life and image during the mid- to late 1980s, encouraging him to dress differently, give more interviews, and generally be more media-friendly. Clothing designers Gianni Versace and Koshin Satoh impacted his dress sense, and Dorothy Weber, partner in the law firm that represented Miles from 1987 onwards and still looks after the Miles Davis Estate today, worked together with him on improving his relationships with the press. Gelbard also had a significant impact on these fronts. "I pushed him all the time," Gelbard commented. "It was like, okay, let's Hollywood this up a little. After all, it's show bizz. The hair weave? If you're going to do it, do everything! And he looked beautiful in Versace clothes because his dark skin was so beautiful. He could wear these bright colors. The colors were also in his house. I did his apartment in similar candy colors. When I met him everything was gray and dark and gloomy, so I was painting his whole life, candy-coloring it up. The apartment that he lived in towards the end was in those colors, too. It was like a candy palace, so he was in a happy, bright, white atmosphere, all marble and light. Of course, the reality of him was not that."

Miles's '80s sidelines had begun with the commercial for the Japanese drink company Van Aquavit in 1984, followed by his participation in 1985 in a Honda scooter commercial and in an episode of *Miami Vice,* playing a pimp. (Both were broadcast in 1986.) In October of 1985 Miles and Robert Irving also collaborated on the writing of a soundtrack for an episode of *Alfred Hitchcock Presents* called "The Prisoner," which, said Irving, "consisted mainly of sequencers with Miles overdubbing." Also in that year, Miles participated in guitarist Little Steven's "Artists United Against Apartheid" project, which also featured Peter Gabriel, Bono, Bob Geldof, Lou Reed, Bruce Springsteen, and others. An album called *Sun City* contained Miles's participation on three tracks. These included two rather boring funk-disco workouts called "Let Me See Your I.D." and "Revolutionary Situation," on which he can only be heard in the background. The third track, "The Struggle Continues," reunited him with, among others, Herbie Hancock, Ron Carter, and Tony Williams. Although Miles takes some proficient muted solos, it is little more than a formless jam.

Miles's second known excursion on other artists' recordings took place in 1986, when he guested on Toto's *Fahrenheit,* playing on the instrumental track "Don't Stop Me Now," and adding to the compliment he had paid the band by covering their "Human Nature." The gentle, jazzy, melodic rock track is pleasant but not very exciting, and Miles's bluesy muted soloing is the best thing about it. He would include "Don't Stop Me Now" in his live repertoire on a few dozen occasions. In October of 1986 Miles and Irving supplied the soundtrack for *Street Smart,* a movie starring Christopher Reeve, Morgan Freeman, and Mimi Rogers. Written by Irving, the music featured Miles, Mike Stern, Bob Berg, Robert Irving, Adam Holzman, Darryl Jones, and Steve Thornton, plus Bob Mintzer on saxophone, Alex Blake on acoustic bass, and Adam Nussbaum on drums. The music was never released separately from the movie. Irving explained, "Because of what the director demanded, most of the pieces were not a very typical Miles thing, and there wasn't enough material to warrant a soundtrack."

Towards the end of 1986 there was another invitation. "Someone called Miles and said, 'Look, we're doing a movie, and we've dropped in *Sketches of Spain* as temporary music, but we'd like you to write new music,'" Marcus Miller recounted. "Miles sent me a copy of the rough draft of the movie, and told me, 'Write some music, it should sound something like this.' He had one line for a piece that became 'Theme for Augustine.' I recorded two or three songs, and the next thing I knew I was landed with the whole score, and had to get it finished in two weeks. So I holed myself up in a studio in Burbank, and basically knocked it out."

The film, shot in Spain, was called *Siesta.* It was directed by Mary Lambert and featured such well-known actors and actresses as Ellen Barkin, Gabriel Byrne, Isabella Rossellini, Martin Sheen, and Jodie Foster. After having written a kind of '80s *The Birth of the Cool* with *Tutu,* Miller now found himself making a *Sketches of Spain* for the '80s. He once again played and programmed most instruments, with help from Jason Miles on synthesizer programming. Miller also called in John Scofield and Earl Klugh on classical guitars, Omar Hakim on drums, and James Walker on flutes. Miles is featured soloist on most, but not all, tracks.

"I invited Miles whenever I needed a trumpet," Miller said. "He was less involved and less present than with *Tutu.* He encouraged me, and said, 'When you need a trumpet, just let me know.'" "Miles only showed up occasionally on *Siesta,*" Jason Miles added.

"He blew a few times, and then left, 'Hey, see you later.' Marcus was orchestrating the whole thing and was 90 percent there, which is why his name is on the cover."

In the last part of this comment, Jason Miles was referring to the controversy over whether the collaborations between Miles and Miller could justifiably be billed as Miles Davis recordings. *Siesta* was also intended as a Miles Davis recording, but Miller's manager protested. "He said to me, 'Listen, you should have some credit,'" Miller explained. "And he fought a battle for me." *Siesta* was issued in 1987 under a joint Marcus Miller—Miles Davis heading, the first time Miles had shared the billing for a recording since his collaborations with Gil Evans between 1957 and 1963.

Film score recordings are notoriously fragmented and uneven because composers are writing in the service of visual cues rather than following the logic of the music. *Siesta* suffers to some degree from this, most notably in the shorter tracks on which Miles does not play, such as "Submission," "Lost in Madrid, Part III," and "Afterglow." The often artificial-sounding use of the synthesizer is another flaw of the recording. The most likely reason is that Miller often used synthesizer sounds to imitate "real" instruments. By contrast, the sounds on *Tutu* were intended as abstract aural fantasies that had little, if any, relation to regular instruments, and thus did not have an ersatz quality.

Despite these limitations, *Siesta* contains some deeply evocative music, mostly courtesy of Miller's melodies and the abundance of Miles's gorgeous open horn playing. His melancholy yet powerful sound and phrasing is reminiscent of that in *Sketches of Spain*, and it carries especially "Lost in Madrid, Part I," "Siesta," "Lost in Madrid, Part V," and "Los Feliz" to great heights. Had this music been recorded with a real orchestra, it would have been on a par with Miles's work with Gil Evans. The real flutes in "Los Feliz," for example, immediately lift the piece. These five tracks—particularly "Siesta," featuring John Scofield on classical guitar—are highlights of Miller and Miles's late '80s collaborations. The debt to Gil Evans for the orchestral-sounding arrangements was acknowledged in the dedication on the sleeve: "To Gil Evans, The Master."

In 1987 there were more important changes concerning the people surrounding Miles. First he fell out with road manager Jim Rose. In Miles's account this was the result of Rose turning over money for a particular concert to manager David Franklin's assistant. Miles got angry because, in his words, "Some funny things were happening to my money lately."[13] When Rose refused to return the money, Miles hit him. It was the end of a working relationship that had stretched back to 1972. Later in the year Miles broke with David Franklin, and also with Cicely.

Miles also appointed his business lawyer Peter Shukat (partner in the same law firm as Dorothy Weber) in Franklin's place. "He called me up one day and said, 'You're now my manager,'" Shukat recalled. "So I was responsible for touring and dealing with agents. But when you're handling a legend like Miles, you're not reinventing the wheels. My job was to make sure the wheels kept turning. We hired Gordon Meltzer as a tour manager, and worked very closely with him."

In addition, three musicians who became part of Miles's live band also played a central part in Miles's next studio recording. In February of 1987 twenty-two-year-old alto saxophonist Kenny Garrett was brought in. A rising star in the jazz world, he had already played with the Mercer Ellington Orchestra, Art Blakey's Jazz Messengers, and Freddie Hubbard, as well as Blue Note's band, Out of the Blue. With a muscular tone, a keen melodic sense, and elegant phrasing, Garrett had shadows of Miles's '70s alto saxophonist Sonny Fortune, and turned out to be the most appropriate saxophonist of Miles's '80s live bands.

The addition of drummer Ricky Wellman in March dramatically changed the rhythmic foundations of Miles's music. Together with "the godfather of go-go," Chuck Brown, Wellman is the coinventor of the go-go rhythm that emerged in Washington, D.C., during the '70s. The rhythm has a relaxed, slow-burning but driving feel based on R&B and funk, and appears to rush a little inside of the beat, giving it a slightly skipping swing feel. Miles recounted that the go-go beat reminded him of the drumming of Art Blakey, Max Roach, and Kenny Clarke. "I love the beat," he said. "Go-go is like Max [Roach] used to play; the beat swings."

Miles scouted the third musician, a completely unknown guitarist/bassist from Cincinnati, Joe "Foley" McCreary, in a rather unlikely manner, demonstrating again how deeply Miles trusted his intuition. "Somebody gave me a tape of this guy," Marcus Miller explained. "Miles called when I was listening to it, and asked, 'What's playing?' I told him it was a tape I'd received from some guy. Miles said, 'He plays too many notes.' I replied, 'You're probably right.' So we ended our conversation. Five minutes later Miles called me back, and said, 'What's the guy's name?' I said, 'Foley,' and Miles said, 'Give me his number.' I did, and a few minutes later the phone rings again, and it's this kid from Ohio, who asks me, 'I've just got a call from someone who says he's Miles Davis. Is it possible that it's true?'" Foley joined Miles's live band in May. Inspired by his love of Bootsy Collins and Eddie van Halen, he had adapted a bass guitar in such a way that it could function as a lead guitar, playing it for the most part like a very fat-sounding electric guitar.

In June of 1987, with the sales and reputation of *Tutu* riding high, Miller, LiPuma, and Jason Miles began work on a follow-up recording. Eventually titled *Amandla,* in another reference to the South-African anti-apartheid struggle ("amandla" means "power" in the Zulu language), the album was composed through a process similar to that of *Tutu.* Only this time Miles gave the direction that he wanted the music to be informed by go-go rhythms and zouk.

Zouk is Creole for "party." The dance music originated in the French Antilles, especially the islands Guadeloupe and Martinique. It is influenced by African, Caribbean, funk, and rock music and is typified by a driving beat, often with a four-to-the-floor bass drum and rolling, lilting guitars, cheerful accordions, and punchy brass. Its most famous exponent is the band Kassav, which came to prominence with the electrified world music that emerged from Paris during the middle of the '80s.

"I remember bringing by the music of Kassav for him to listen to one afternoon when he was feeling down . . . ," Quincy Troupe wrote. "As soon as he heard them, Miles almost jumped out of his skin with excitement, leaping up from the couch he was lying on and yelling, 'Who is that and what are they playing?' . . . Kassav's music completely freaked him out."[14]

Following the success of *Tutu,* Miller was given more leeway on *Amandla,* and he decided to bring in additional musicians. "I felt a need to go back to a more live sound, which is why you see Ricky Wellman, Kenny Garrett, and Foley appearing," Miller said. With the help of the three live band musicians the basic tracks of "Catémbe," "Big

Time," and "Hannibal" were recorded. They were, in the words of Jason Miles, "really cooking." But after these June 1987 sessions Miller and Jason Miles became preoccupied with writing, programming, and producing material for several other artists, and the recordings for Miles's new album were put on hold for more than a year.

Meanwhile Miles recorded a track for the movie *Scrooged* towards the end of 1987, with David Sanborn on alto saxophone, Paul Shaffer on keyboards, Larry Carlton on guitar, and Marcus Miller doing arrangements and drum programming. The movie, featuring Bill Murray, Karen Allen, and Robert Mitchum, was complemented by a soundtrack with contributions by artists like Annie Lennox, Al Green, Robbie Robertson, and Natalie Cole. Miles plays on "We Three Kings of Orient Are," which is one of his better collaborations. It is graced by an elegant, slightly limping jazz rhythm, a fine melody, and excellent soloing by Miles, Sanborn, and Carlton. The band also appeared on *Late Night with David Letterman* on December 11, playing "We Three Kings." In addition, Miles overdubbed around the same time to "Oh Patti" by Scritti Politti, whose "Perfect Way" he had covered a year and a half earlier. "Oh Patti (Don't Feel Sorry for Loverboy)" is schmaltzy, effeminate '80s English synthesizer pop, and Miles's muted contribution, in both senses of the word, does nothing to alleviate the tedium.

In early 1988 Miles played on "In the Night" by the electronic dance-funk band Cameo. The track, which later appeared on their recording *Machismo,* has a hard disco/funk beat with a reggae twinge, and Miles plays strongly on open trumpet before switching to the mute. On June 29, Miles was involved in the recording of two tracks for Chaka Khan's *C.K.* "Sticky Wicked" was written and partly performed by Prince, and is a typical frantic throwaway tune of the kind that he was able to turn out thirteen to the dozen. Miles, on muted trumpet, seems at a loss how to contribute. "I'll Be Around" is a slushy jazz ballad with syrupy strings. Miles, again on mute, would have been better advised living by his own adage: "If you don't know what to play, play nothing."

Work resumed on *Amandla* in September of 1988 and continued until January of 1989. An unknown twenty-three-years-old guitarist, John Bigham, contributed the track "Jilli," and George Duke wrote, arranged, and recorded a track called "Cobra." "I now realized that they might use the track exactly the way I would record it," the keyboardist commented, "so I decided to take more care over what I put on tape. Michael Landau, a friend of mine, did some guitar parts, and Tommy and Marcus later added a few things. But they left the track pretty much as it was."

Miller wrote and arranged the remainder of the album. He began with adding more overdubs to the tracks recorded in the previous year, "Catémbe," "Big Time," and "Hannibal." Still determined to make the forthcoming album sound more live than *Tutu,* Miller not only used some of the members of Miles's live band, he also brought in several session musicians. "Around that time I was in the habit of working with cats from all over to play on the albums I produced, which is why musicians appear like Omar Hakim, Jean-Paul Bourelly, and so on. Also, Miles's chops were in much better shape to my ears. He was playing what he heard, and going for it. On *Tutu* he was often just trying an idea. On *Amandla* there were a few great solos."

"'Mr. Pastorius' was the biggest surprise," Miller enthused. "I'd written the main head—the main melody—and we were playing through it, and I was thinking of playing a funk-blues after it. Miles didn't play changes anymore, so I assumed he'd ignore them. Suddenly he held up four fingers, which means playing in four, in jazz-swing. I started walking the bass, and he just went! Chorus after chorus, all improvised. I was looking at the engineer, going, 'Please tell me you're recording this. Please don't let this go out in the air.' When you make music, you have to take the magic when it comes. There was a gap in the middle, because the engineer had to switch tapes, so I had to edit the two tape sections together. It was just Miles and me in the studio, and after he left, I called Al Foster. Al said, 'Oh, my goodness, I've been waiting for Miles to play something like this.' Al turned the lights off, put headphones on, and as far as he was concerned, he was playing there with Miles. Later on I orchestrated the last section, and added some keyboards to it. It was cool, I loved it."

Amandla was released later in 1989, and although it sold respectably, it failed to make an impact similar to *Tutu,* perhaps because the album's multicolored optimism did not capture the stylish, sophisticated, but nihilistic '80s zeitgeist. The cover is designed in Gelbard's bright "candy colors" and features a drawing made by Miles and Gelbard together, as well as a black-and-white photograph of an improbably young-looking Miles in one of his colorful outfits. It points towards music that is worlds away from the dark, brooding, introspective atmosphere of *Tutu.* The music on *Amandla* is indeed as bright and colorful as the cover, with mostly an upbeat feel and a plethora of instrumental colors. The rhythms are loose and elegant, courtesy of the influence of zouk and go-go, as well as the talents of the musicians involved. Like Miles, Miller had recognized the jazz-swing element in the go-go rhythms he was creating. "Go-go has a swing to it," Miller said, "and I thought it would be interesting for Miles to superimpose some of the swing phrasing from his earlier days over this beat. The sound is a little like a throwback, yet completely new."

All of these ingredients show in the opening track, "Catémbe," which was named after a stretch of the coastline south of the Mozambican capital Maputo. Driven by Don Alias and Mino Cinelu on percussion, an infectious groove carries Miller's beautiful melody. Miles and Garrett both solo incisively, with considerable amounts of swing to their phrasing. George Duke's "Cobra," graced by an engaging duet between Miles and Garrett, has a rhythm similar to that of "Catémbe," and a surly theme reminiscent of "Tomaas." "Big Time" features Ricky Wellman, and the go-go rhythm comes noticeably alive because of his contribution and that of percussionist Don Alias. Miles plays the childlike theme over the drums and percussion before the band comes in. Miles, Garrett, live-band lead bassist Foley, and Miller all play strong solos.

But by this stage some problems with the music become obvious. As a whole, the unique and fresh musical direction of *Amandla* is superbly conceived and executed, and over a decade after its making the recording sounds less dated than some of *Tutu.* But the motifs, arrangements, and atmosphere of many of the tracks on *Amandla* are too similar. In addition, the musical direction and arrangements sometimes appear to be more born from the head than from the heart; the mood of a few of the tracks is not well defined, leading the soloists to perform without purpose. A contributing factor is that Miles, the main humanizing force on *Tutu,* becomes a strand in a web of many colors in *Amandla* and distinguishes himself much less. Marcus Miller remarked that a Miles

Davis album needs to court controversy, and since there is nothing on the agreeable *Amandla* that offends or challenges, it isn't, by Miller's standards, quite doing its job.

"Hannibal" has a go-go-like shuffle rhythm, with Omar Hakim on drums, and samples of Caribbean steel drums adding color and echoes of zouk. The tune is taken at a slightly slower pace than the previous three tracks, and is built around an effective tension-release structure, which holds the attention effectively. Nevertheless, the theme Miles plays at 00:53 is almost identical to the theme he introduces on "Big Time," and the multitude of colors is so overwhelming that everything becomes shades of gray. "Jo-Jo," named after Jo Gelbard, is one of the most attractive songs on *Amandla,* courtesy of the interplay between the contagious go-go rhythm, which is driven along by syncopated synth stabs, and an inventive melody. Jean-Paul Bourelly, at the time an up-and-coming guitarist in the jazz-funk-grunge vein of James "Blood" Ulmer and Vernon Reid, plays a great solo, as do Miles and Garrett. Rick Margitza, who briefly replaced Garrett in the live band in the summer of 1989, supports on tenor saxophone, and co-creates some nice sax choirs with Garrett.

"There was a lot of politics around Miles at that time," Bourelly commented on his participation. "[Miles's] operation was more radio-oriented, not like the records that made me get into his music in the first place. Sessions where the cats were just playing mistakes and all. That session was done under very controlled circumstances; no mistakes saw the light of day. There was a lot of computer automation going on, and I think they [the producers] were trying to highlight Miles's working group and Marcus as a composer, and so they mixed and edited the session that way. It turned out to be a nice record, but I could see I wouldn't be highlighted too much because a few times I cut loose on some takes and I saw one of the producers' face kind of look down at the floor. I knew then my shit was up."[15]

The title song, an outstanding ballad, would have been better placed earlier on in the track order. It is well constructed, breathes beautifully, and allows Miles to spread out and make his mark. "Jilli" is the most disappointing track on *Amandla,* mainly due to the mediocre theme and an irritatingly skipping go-go beat that leaves Miles little room to maneuver. Finally, "Mr. Pastorius" is a triumph. Miller's theme is magnificent, and his arrangements conjure up orchestral textures reminiscent of Gil Evans. Miles, freed from the constraints of the mute and the up-tempo rhythms, solos expressively and touchingly, and dominates the proceedings. This is his track, even as it is named in honor of the bassist Jaco Pastorius, who had died on September 21, 1987. Following Gil Evans's death on March 20, 1988, *Amandla* is, like *Siesta,* dedicated to Miles's close friend and colleague.

Immediately after the completion of *Amandla,* Miles continued with his guest performances. He played on Marcus Miller's "Rampage," which was issued on the bassist's solo effort *The Sun Don't Lie.* The track is a spectacular hard-funk workout, and Miles offers some relief in the more melodic, softer, interludes. Early in 1989 Miles also appeared on two tunes on sideman Kenny Garrett's solo album, *Prisoner of Love.* "Big 'Ol Head" is a funk tune, performed by Miles's live band, with Mino Cinelu playing a percussion solo and Miles on mute duetting with Garrett, who also plays keyboards. "Free Mandela" features an African choir and a nice flowing rhythm, courtesy of

Garrett's keyboard and drum programming and Miles once again on mute. Around the same time Miles also took part in the recordings of two tracks for Quincy Jones's *Back on the Block,* which also features Dizzy Gillespie, James Moody, Joe Zawinul, George Benson, Ella Fitzgerald, and Sarah Vaughan. Jones's busy arrangements of "Jazz Corner of the World" and "Birdland" give Miles little space to make a difference.

These are Miles's only known studio recordings in 1989. By contrast, 1990 turned out to be a more productive studio year during which Miles recorded with Michel Legrand, John Lee Hooker, Paolo Rustichelli, and Shirley Horn. Miles and Legrand were jointly billed as composers of the soundtrack for the feature movie *Dingo,* recorded in March. Miles was once more ensnared in the trappings of success because, like many rock stars, he accepted an acting part. Whereas his role in *Miami Vice* was purely supportive, *Dingo* was virtually built around him. Miles is center stage in about a third of the movie playing a famous trumpeter called Billy Cross. The touching, though sentimental, movie charts his relationship with, and the artistic aspirations and struggles of, an unknown Australian trumpeter called Dingo Anderson.

Miles/Billy Cross performs extensively on muted trumpet, while trumpeter Chuck Findley performs Anderson's parts on open trumpet. Miles had worked with Legrand before, in 1958, when he performed on four tracks appearing on the French bandleader, arranger, and composer's recording *Legrand Jazz,* which was well received in jazz circles. *Dingo* revisits similar big-band territory, at times played in deliberately ramshackle fashion, but also includes several funk workouts featuring members of Miles's live band. Despite the superfluous sections of movie dialog, the soundtrack for *Dingo* is an engaging listening experience. The recurring haunting main theme lodges in the memory, and there's great vitality to the tracks, and Miles plays well throughout.

Miles's collaboration with John Lee Hooker took place in May of 1990 when the two, along with Taj Mahal and Roy Rogers on guitars, Earl Palmer on drums, Tim Drummond on bass, and Bradford Ellis on keyboards, recorded the soundtrack for the motion picture *The Hot Spot.* Directed by Dennis Hopper and featuring Don Johnson, Virginia Madsen, and Jennifer Connolly, the movie is a nihilistic and empty effort at film noir set in the sweltering American South. Hopper, who was friendly with Miles, invited his involvement, and contracted composer Jack Nitzsche to write the music. Nitzsche's contribution is unclear, because for the most part the tracks are standard blues schemes, over which John Lee Hooker moans and groans and Miles displays his blues credentials. Although he sounds entirely at home in these authentic blues surroundings, and the music is pleasant enough, other than the novelty interest of the combined billing of Miles with some blues greats, there's little that raises the level of the music to great heights.

Keyboardist and composer Paolo Rustichelli made slightly better use of Miles's talents when the latter visited the Italian's studio in Rome in July of 1990. Rustichelli is fairly unknown, despite the fact that he is able to muster an all-star cast for many of his recordings. On *Mystic Jazz* these included Herbie Hancock, Carlos Santana, Wayne Shorter, Andy Summers, and Miles. Several members of Miles's live band, including Garrett and Wellman, are also featured on the recording. Miles plays on "Capri," with Rustichelli performing on the Waveframe Audioframe, an instrument capable of effects like those of the

Synclavier. The track is gorgeous ambient jazz of the highest caliber, and Miles's switch from muted to open trumpet has, as so often, a dramatic effect. The trumpeter also appears on five tracks on Rustichelli's later album *Mystic Man* (issued on Santana's label Guts & Grace Music), but most are spoiled by bombastic, New Age–influenced effects, like opera singers singing "Kyria," lots of sampled voices, and flat rhythms. Only the lazy, late-night "Rastafario," on which Miles duets with Santana, escapes the kitsch treatment.

On August 13, 1990, Miles recorded what is arguably his most effective and moving guest performance, the title song for Shirley Horn's *You Won't Forget Me*. A jazz singer and pianist, Horn was a protégé of Miles in the '50s, and in playing the classic Goell/Spielman jazz song they both revisited their pasts. The performances by Horn and Miles are exquisite, deeply melancholic, and perfectly balanced and supported by drummer Steve Williams's driving rimshot snare. Miles plays on mute throughout, and his poise, phrasing, sense of space, and choice of notes are outstanding.

In the course of 1991 Miles participated in the sessions for his last solo album, *Doo-bop*. The recording ended his last ten years on a similarly dubious artistic note as when he had begun them. The story of *Doo-bop* is explained in the CD liner notes, written by road manager Gordon Meltzer, who also acted as the recording's associate and executive producer. Miles had a great variety of collaborations in mind for *Doo-bop*, among them Prince, New York producer Sid Reynolds, John Bigham, Easy Mo Bee, as well as a reworking of the "Rubber Band" sessions. Without LiPuma's input, Miles appeared to want to do it all, and talked of creating a double CD. Bigham had prepared three tracks, while Prince sent Miles eight instrumental tracks, three of which he performed with his live band during his 1991 European tour—"Penetration," "A Girl and Her Puppy," and "Jail Bait." Miles also unexpectedly went into a German studio with his live band in the summer of 1991 to record these three Prince tracks, despite the fact that discussions were still ongoing about whether Prince would be involved in the recordings.

Miles's death on September 28 thwarted these plans. He had overdubbed on only six tracks by Easy Mo Bee, a young and unknown hip-hop and rap artist who had been suggested to him by Russell Simmon, head of Def Jam Records. To finish the incomplete album, Easy Mo Bee (née Osten Harvey) was asked to use two performances by Miles from the "Rubber Band" sessions and build new backing tracks around them. By reprising one of the songs, Mo Bee stretched the uncompleted recording to just over forty minutes.

There are, of course, ethical issues involved in completing an unfinished project by someone who cannot partake. But Matt Pierson, head of A&R at Warner Bros. at the time, and associate producer of the recording, attested that Miles heard the finished tracks and was "very happy" with the results. In addition, he stressed that the decision to record two tunes posthumously was made in close collaboration with the Miles Davis Estate.

In the end, the music speaks for itself. Sadly, most of the arrangements and sounds on *Doo-bop* are bland, and the fairly embarrassing raps that glorify Miles and Easy Mo Bee also lower the quality level. Had Miles not allowed the similarly humiliating lyrics of "The Man with the Horn," one might feel sure that these lyrics were added after his death. If one accepts the validity of Miles's now well-established formula of blowing over backing tracks created by others, there is nothing amiss with the musical direction of *Doo-bop* as such. Founded on extended circular and repetitive grooves without changes, it is based on an approach similar to that of *On the Corner*. However, in the case of *Doo-bop*, the grooves are played by machines, created by Easy Mo Bee sampling and looping sections of other people's recordings, and adding drum machines and keyboards. This could have worked well, but Mo Bee's execution is for the most part mediocre: The rhythms are not particularly engaging, there's an almost complete absence of themes and ear-catching bass riffs, and the keyboard sounds are glossy and plastic-sounding.

The cover of *Doo-bop* features a photograph of Miles in his "candy-colored" apartment, but with a sullen expression on his surreally youthful face that is reminiscent of that of a teenager. It may well be that with the awareness of his impending death, he tried too hard to be a hip part of the youth culture of the day. Like the songs he had recorded with his nephew's Chicago band in 1980, the songs on *Doo-bop* are mostly "bubble-gum" teenage music. The only tracks with real distinction are "Mystery," courtesy of a pleasant, lazy groove and some nice keyboard riffs, "Chocolate Chip," with its industrial-sounding rhythms and nice syncopated sample (appearing for the first time at 00:48), and "Sonya," because it contains the recording's only memorable bass riff. "Fantasy" has a striking circular background sound, and some interest is provided by the chord changes, but sadly it is destroyed by the juvenile lyrics of Mo Bee's rap. Another short-coming of *Doo-bop* is the lack of additional soloists. As if to compensate, Miles plays extremely well on the whole recording, improvising with inventiveness, precision, and great focus. It earned him a posthumous Grammy in 1992 for Best R&B Instrumental Performance.

One nevertheless wishes that Shirley Horn's version of "You Won't Forget Me" had indeed been Miles's last issued studio recording. With its high level of musicianship, his poignant and moving soloing, and the song's wistful, longing lyric, it would have been a deeply fitting studio swan song:

"You won't forget me,
though you may try,
I'm part of memories,
too wonderful to die."

Chapter Fifteen

ALIVE AROUND
THE WORLD

*"People were mesmerized. To see people's faces glued
to him, their eyes following him like he was a pied
piper, it was awesome."*

—VINCE WILBURN JR.

The preceding chapter charted all of Miles's officially released studio recordings from 1985 to 1991. However, it does not complete the story of his music. Just like the period from 1965 to 1972, his last six years were characterized by a strong divergence between his live and studio music. And, as has already been alluded to in previous chapters, during his Warner Bros. years Miles's most powerful and creative musical expressions occurred in concert. As from 1965 to 1972, the studio music from 1985 to 1991 strongly influenced the live music, providing repertoire and new ideas, but the live music followed its own logic and direction.

The earliest origins of Miles's live direction during his Warner Bros. years go all the way back to his two periods of collaboration with Gil Evans—from 1949 to 1950 and from 1957 to 1962. Miles was eager to perform this music on stage with his live band, but because it involved an orchestra, this was neither practical nor affordable. Having never quite forgotten this desire, Miles quickly understood the potential of the synthesizers that emerged in the late '60s and early '70s. "I'm crazy about the way Gil Evans voices his music, so I wanted to get me a Gil Evans sound in a small band," Miles remarked. "That required an instrument like the synthesizer, which can get all those different instrumental sounds.[1] . . . [It] was the only thought I had: What can I get to give me a cheap Gil Evans sound in a small band?"[2]

However, the synthesizers that Miles's sidemen began using in 1972 were still monophonic, and unable to hold sounds in storage. Sounds had to be manually programmed for each usage, a time-consuming process that made them impractical for live performance. Only in the early '80s, with the emergence of the cheap, preprogrammable, polyphonic synthesizer, with hundreds of sounds immediately available at the touch of a button, did the instrument become sophisticated enough for the realization of Miles's dream.

The sessions in 1980 and 1981 with the young Chicago band featuring Vince Wilburn Jr. and Robert Irving, which resulted in the tracks "Shout" and "The Man with the Horn," may have been an additional inspiration. The songs were strongly melodic, entirely arranged, and recorded using synthesizers and overdubbing. When, in 1983, Miles wanted to explore synthesizer technology, as well as produce his own recordings, he turned to Wilburn and Irving for help. The recordings they midwifed, *Decoy* and *You're under Arrest,* contained the first studio actualizations of Miles's old dream. This melodic, highly arranged musical direction, with limited space for improvisation, was further developed on *Tutu* and *Amandla,* and gradually integrated into the live music.

The earliest move towards a more arranged live direction occurred when Robert Irving joined the band on August 15, 1983. The first keyboardist to be enlisted in the live band since May of 1973, Irving was not only made musical director but was also given the task of providing what can be called the "orchestral" parts with a battery of synthesizers. Irving's role was different in nature from that of John Scofield, Mike Stern, Marcus Miller, Al Foster, Mino Cinelu, or Darryl Jones, who had all been hired on the strength of their consummate instrumental skills. Miles once pointed to Irving's supportive role when he said, "If you can hear him [Irving], he was too loud. You're supposed to be able to feel him, not hear him."[3]

The line-up of Miles, Bob Berg, John Scofield, Robert Irving, Darryl Jones, Vince Wilburn Jr., and Steve Thornton existed from March to August of 1985 and straddled both the Columbia and Warner Bros. eras. Its repertoire and approach covered the strongly improvised blues and chromatic funk directions that Miles had pursued from 1981 to 1983, as well as much predominantly arranged music, including some of the pop ballads he had recorded in 1984. Sections of this band's concerts were officially released on a little-known video and laser disc, *Live in Montreal,* which was recorded on June 28, 1985. The chromatic funk direction is in evidence on the track "Speak," the highlight of the recording. Scofield and Berg play the main theme, which is more developed than in the version on *Star People,* while Miles solos impressively for five minutes on open horn. Scofield's inventive, well-constructed solo functions as an effective climax. The recording also includes a shadow of "Hopscotch"—a chromatic funk track inspired by one of the themes of "Star on Cicely," performed regularly by the live band since October of 1982 but never included on an official recording. "Maze," which explores a similar direction, was edited out, leaving the remainder of the video to consist of the band's more heavily arranged direction, with an emphasis on the pop songs "Something's on Your Mind," "Time after Time," and "Human Nature." These last two were performed in a relatively short and straightforward manner. They had not yet become the epic workouts of later years.

Miles solos at length throughout the concert registration, but his playing is disjointed at times, and the band sounds leaden. In comparison with other bootlegs of the same era, this does not appear to capture the band on a good night. Notwithstanding his excellent soloing, Scofield looks and sounds ill at ease, and his idiosyncratic and behind-the-beat rhythm playing doesn't gel with the on-the-beat rock feel of the rest of the band. "When you're in a band like this," Miles commented, "it's got to sound . . . on top of the beat all the time. John Scofield . . . would play so far behind the beat, I'd say, 'John, goddamn.'"[4]

Scofield left the band soon afterwards, his last concert being in Tokyo, on August 7. "I had been with him for three years and did three albums," Scofield explained, "and I thought he might fire me. He kept saying, 'Listen to Eddie van Halen. Why don't you listen to Eddie?' I was thinking, 'Wow, I'm not Eddie van Halen. I guess Miles is hearing something different.' Also, playing behind Miles in songs like 'Human Nature' or 'Time after Time' means repeating the same thing over and over again. There's an art to playing rhythm guitar, but it's not what I wanted to do for the rest of my life."

Scofield's departure inaugurated the plethora of personnel changes that characterized Miles's live bands during his Warner Bros. years. An amazing thirty-two musicians are known to have been members of Miles's bands from the summer of 1985 to his final concert in August of 1991. There may appear to be a parallel with the large number of Miles's Stock Company Players in the early '70s, but the '80s situation was entirely different. Most of the Stock Company Players only took part in studio sessions and, more crucially, were always hired for the individual sound they could bring to the recordings. But in the second half of the '80s many players were hired as "orchestral" players, performing parts in an arrangement and laying down the foil for the soloists. Whereas most personnel changes in the '70s and early '80s bands led to instantly recognizable changes in the music, the effects of changes in the "orchestral" players of the late '80s bands were often too subtle to make a significant difference.

The repertoire Miles chose to play live during his Warner Bros. years necessitated this approach. He is known to have performed a staggering total of more than fifty tunes in live performance, more than twenty-two of which have never been officially released. About a dozen of these fifty-plus tunes were pop songs with catchy melodies and fairly straightforward chord schemes. A similar number were chromatic funk compositions with ferocious bass lines, highly abstract melodies, and a lot of space for the band to stretch. The rest of the repertoire moved somewhere in between these two extremes, but sophisticated arrangements and clearly recognizable themes and bass lines characterized all material.

John Scofield suggested that, having played highly abstract music between 1968 and 1983, Miles wanted to go back to what was once his main forte—his lyricism and his tremendous melodic gift. "It was great to hear him play tunes again after making the really 'out' music for years," Scofield said. "People were so happy to hear him play a melody again. He hadn't really done that since the '60s. Miles needed to do something else than his darker stuff, and it's important to realize that he wanted to have a hit, wanted to be popular. Miles saw it as a necessary way to expand his audience."

The enormous amount of material in the live repertoire during the Warner Bros. years suggests that he was not resting on his laurels and was still expanding creatively. The large number of band members Miles recruited may be another sign of his appetite for expansion, as well as the fact that he gradually enlarged the size of his live band. The addition of Danish percussionist Marilyn Mazur occurred in Miles's trademark intuitive and unorthodox manner. Half a year after she had contributed to *Aura,* the two met again during one of Scofield's last concerts with the band, on July 28, 1985, in Molde, Norway. "I had rushed to the concert and was late and there were no seats left," Mazur recalled, "so I was sitting in front of the seats. In the middle of the concert Miles suddenly spotted me, and said in his microphone, 'Marilyn, come and play with us.' I went on stage and had a lot of fun. A few weeks later he called and said, 'When can you be here?' And I asked, 'What do you mean?' And he replied, 'Be here Wednesday.'"

"I dropped everything and went to New York," Mazur continued. "We rehearsed for three days, but he didn't say much to me, and pretty much left me to do what I wanted to do. He had much more strict ideas for some of the others in the band, like for Vince, who I think had a hard time, because Miles wanted him to be really dead on, locking into the groove. The role division between Steve [Thornton] and me was that he would play more grooves and Latin stuff, while I could do more sound paintings with percussion. I also used some electronic percussion, for which I made all kinds of weird samples. I had a mat with triggers on the floor, and danced around on the mat, which would trigger the samples."

Of mixed race and born in the United States, Mazur moved to Denmark with her parents when she was six. She is the only woman ever to have been a member of Miles's live bands. Mazur's first concert with Miles was at Hudson River Pier, in New York, on August 17, an occasion that also marked the return of Mike Stern. Miles had not been able to find a replacement for Scofield, and he turned to his erstwhile guitarist for help. "The music wasn't amazingly different," Stern commented. "There were still a lot of vamps, and things were much more stretched than on the studio recordings. What was different was that there wasn't so much reaction from the rhythm section, who were more locked into a straight backbeat kind of thing. If you played too free over that, it sounded out of context. But there were plenty of nights where we cranked it up and tried to play as free as we could."

The band played an American tour in August and September of 1985, during which Darryl Jones left to join Sting. Bassist Angus Thomas replaced Jones on September 19. After the "Rubber Band" session of October 17, Adam Holzman joined the live band for the European tour, beginning on October 24. The band had now expanded to a nonet, the largest live group since the nonet of April and May of 1973. Consisting of Miles, Berg, Stern, Holzman, Irving, Thomas, Wilburn, Thornton, and Mazur, it played Copenhagen on October 28. This concert was recorded and broadcast on Danish radio, resulting in many excellent-sounding bootlegs. The repertoire included a large amount of unreleased material, like "Hopscotch," "Maze," "Pacific Express" (a John McLaughlin composition arranged by Miles and Irving), Irving's and Randy Hall's hard-rock–like effort "Burn" (from the unreleased sessions for *The Man with the Horn*), "Stronger than Before" (a ballad also covered by Chaka Khan), and "Rubber Band" by Randy Hall and Zane Giles. The recording displays a coherent band full of vitality and inventiveness, with Mike Stern taking scorching solo after scorching solo, Miles in good lip, and Mazur and Holzman adding many interesting colors. The only dissonant element is perhaps the all-too-frequent and overly mechanical backbeat.

"It was just the way he had set it up, where the drummer would play an exact groove which wasn't that flexible," Marilyn Mazur remarked. "It didn't keep the music open in the way I liked, but Miles's magic remained. He definitely gathered the energy of the musicians, and functioned as a power center. I think I listened differently after playing with him. I was more conscious of grooves and how they can really focus the music than I was before."

Holzman functioned as an "orchestral" player, hired to supplement Irving's synthesizer textures and colors. The two did not repeat the same parts every night but, in an approach not dissimilar to the idea of a "living composition" in the Cosey band, wove ever-changing webs from certain motifs. "Bobby and I worked stuff out during sound checks, and in hotel rooms, and at rehearsals," Holzman said. "We'd figure out how to orchestrate the stuff, and we also were doing spontaneous improvisations, where we would start with different elements that could be superimposed or pushed around. The tunes became canvases for ideas, and it was no longer a matter of simply running down a pop tune and Miles playing on top of that."

"I came from a fusion/jazz-rock background when I joined the band," Holzman continued, "and playing with Miles pushed me into creating soundscapes with an almost film score–like approach. I learned to play more economically, creating a mood with just a few notes, or a sample, or superimposing different chords over static bass lines. All these things were new to me, and became part of my personal style. It's become a cliché, but it's true that Miles was able to weed out all the crap, and unearth the essence of a song. John McLaughlin's 'Pacific Express' was a good example. It appeared on *Mahavishnu* as an up-tempo tune with a vague Latin-like feel, but Miles slowed it way down, used only two or three fragments from the melody, and created this incredible 'moody' piece."

The nonet remained together until March of 1986, when Angus Thomas left. His replacement, Felton Crews, was the third member of the young Chicago band with which Miles had worked in 1980 and 1981 to become part of the band. Two weeks after Crews's first concert, on March 12, Mike Stern departed to refocus on his solo career, and Robben Ford took his place. Ford had already built up a considerable reputation as a fusion-blues guitarist, playing with Joni Mitchell, George Harrison, and the Yellowjackets.

"When I met Miles, the only thing he asked me was, 'Robben, what are you going to wear on stage?'" Ford recalled. "I thought I was going to throw up! That first night I played with him, I figured the guy wants Mike Stern, who has ridiculous single-note facility. So the second night I just said, 'Robben, be yourself. Don't try to fill anybody else's shoes.' And Miles was grinning at me. That's what he wanted. . . . When you took a solo it might go on for a long time. He would nod at you to play—it's your turn, go. It wasn't up to you when it ended. It ended when he was ready for it to end—and he'd end it by playing. You might be finished with a solo as far as you were concerned, but you still had to go and go. I was amazed at times; he was leaving me out on a limb. But as he said, that's what Charlie Parker used to do to him. But you're dying out there!"[5]

Until this point Warner Bros. had not taken much notice of Miles's live performances, but during 1986, in the wake of the publicity surrounding *Tutu,* the company worked hard to maximize Miles's commercial potential. Miles gave an interview for a one-hour PBS television program called *Miles Ahead: The Music of Miles Davis,* appeared on *The Dick Cavett Show,* and participated in French and German documentaries on his life and work. Following the addition of Robben Ford there was also a feeling of excitement at Warner Bros. over the capacities of the live band, and between July 13 and 30 the company recorded five live concerts of the European summer tour. This included the concert at the Montreux Jazz Festival on July 17, 1986, for which George Duke and saxophonist David Sanborn were invited as guest performers.

Miles felt confident enough about the results to announce his next album to an interviewer a few weeks after the shows. "I did it live with George Duke and David Sanborn," Miles said. "It sounds hot, y'know. This new stuff I'm coming out with is better than anything I've recorded in the past. Hell, I don't *think* so, I *know* so! I want my shit to get out to people. That's why I left Columbia, see."[6]

Ironically, the recordings were never released, and Robert Irving's comment "Miles was frustrated with Warners Bros." is hardly surprising. "The official word was that there were technical flaws on the recording," Adam Holzman added, "but with such a front line, the company should have recorded at least one concert of every tour. They knew he wasn't going to live forever." With five shows on record, "technical flaws" were unlikely to be the real reason why Warner Bros. shelved the concert, although no other explanations have been forthcoming. Bootlegs indicate a band in blazing form and Ford in a starring role. The repertoire is similar to that of the Copenhagen concert of October of 1985, with some of the lesser-known tunes—such as "Pacific Express," "Rubber Band," "Hopscotch," and "Stronger than Before"—replaced by material from *Tutu.*[7]

More personnel changes followed. Marilyn Mazur had already left the band at the end of April, leaving Steve Thornton as solo percussion player, and in September Robben Ford departed to return to his solo career. Miles again had problems finding a replacement on guitar, and Ford recommended Garth Webber, a capable pupil who lacked personality in his playing and never fitted well with the band. Webber's first concerts were in September; he left the band in December. In October Darryl Jones returned after completing his tour with Sting. For a series of concerts in Los Angeles between Christmas and New Year's Eve, Miles enlisted both guitarist Dwayne "Blackbyrd" McKnight, who had played with Herbie Hancock, and Gary Thomas as an additional saxophonist. The latter had been an opening act for one of Miles's concerts in Baltimore in 1985.

Bob Berg was increasingly feeling—and sounding—out of place among the new developments. "Gary's inclusion was my invitation to leave, I think," Berg commented. "I don't like to play in one key, and a lot of the stuff Miles was playing was based on one-chord vamps. I just played the way I always played, and the more pop tunes we played, the less input I had in the music. Sometimes I played only fifteen minutes on a night, and I told him that wasn't enough for me. I wasn't really enamored with the *Tutu* stuff either. It was a cool concept, and Marcus is a great writer, but it bugged me that I didn't play on the record, and that the live music became more and more controlled. I never found out what the capabilities were of most of the other members in the band because Miles had them padlocked to doing their parts. Consequently, when you were soloing, you never felt the rhythm section was following you. It felt like playing over a set track. It must have been what Miles wanted because I'm sure the guys could do more."

Berg, McKnight, and Steve Thornton all left after the concerts at the end of 1986. Hiram Bullock, who had played with Al Foster, David Sanborn, and Paul Shaffer and had gained some fame as the barefoot guitar player in the mid-1980s on *Late Night with David Letterman,* was the new guitarist, but only lasted for four concerts.

Thornton's replacement was another former band member, Mino Cinelu. "At first I wasn't excited about the music, which was very organized, with lots of keyboards," Cinelu said. "During my first time with the band everybody was a virtuoso, and that was not the case with the '87 band. It's another concept when you have almost ten people in the band. You have to play much more restrained. There was less room to show off if you wanted to. You had to be more concentrated on the groove and play less. But then I opened up, and a lot of great things happened. Sometimes it was very powerful and really deep music."

Both Cinelu and Bullock joined the band on January 24, 1987. In February there were yet more changes. Chicagoan funk and blues–inspired jazz guitarist Bobby Broom replaced Bullock, and Kenny Garrett was added, playing alongside Thomas until the latter left in the end of March. This continual coming and going of musicians could be taxing on the band members. But Miles, in another display of his skills as a bandleader, allowed new musicians time to find their feet.

"He was not fast to fire guys," Darryl Jones recalled. "I remember sometimes thinking, 'Come on Miles, lose this guy!' But he would wait and give a guy a chance to get his stuff together. Whether it was working or not, he didn't seem to mess with them a lot. He would give you a chance to find your own place, and after he felt you were secure enough, he began to work on you. In my case he was very particular about what bass lines I played. He just wanted something strong and not too busy because he really believed in space. He would come up to me after the show and say, 'Play again what you played last night,' or 'Don't answer yourself there, play half of that.' One of the big lessons I learned in playing with him was that generally you don't need to play nearly as much as you think you do. Working with Miles was definitely the doctorate course."

Miles's willingness to give a lot of freedom to his musicians apparently did not extend to his drummers. Jones related an anecdote illustrating how important rhythm was to the bandleader. "I remember one night on stage he was standing close to me, and we both had our heads down," Jones said. "Suddenly the timing moved. I'm talking here about a very small amount, barely noticeable. When it moved, I raised my head. He looked at me and said, 'You felt that?' I replied, 'Yeah.' And he said, 'Nobody ever feels that small a change.' He looked at me excitedly, with an expression in his eyes saying, 'I always thought I was the only one who feels these things.' I realized that his listening sense was not just geared towards harmony and melody, but also very strongly towards rhythm. He always referred to rhythm when talking about musicians. I remember concerts where he would stop the band straight after it began playing a song because the tempo wasn't right. He cared more about the music than giving a perfect show. He was very tough on drummers, whether it was Al, Vince, or Ricky [Wellman]. Miles was always standing right in front of them, giving them directions throughout the set, something he never did with other guys."

"I enjoyed it when Miles was hard on me because it made me stronger," Vince Wilburn Jr. commented. "He just wanted to bring the best out of you. I've been told he was harder on Ricky than on me. Miles always wanted me to keep 'locked in,' and encouraged me to listen to James Brown and Buddy Miles." These musical references may explain why the rhythm section with Wilburn was so strongly geared towards a straightforward backbeat. Miles, however, seemed to imply that Wilburn's drumming skills were at issue. He sacked his nephew in March of 1987, and remarked, "I still wasn't pleased with the way my nephew Vincent was playing the drums because he was always dropping the time, and if there's anything I can't stand in a drummer it's to drop time."[8] Yet this version of the events was disputed by Mike Stern. "Vince is a naturally talented drummer with a really strong groove," Stern explained. "Sometimes I think that he'd have been better off if Miles had given him less direction and allowed him more musical freedom."

Most likely it was simply a matter of Miles's penchant for change. In the beginning of 1987 he had become interested in the go-go music coinvented by Ricky Wellman in Washington, D.C. The drummer's first concert with Miles's band was in Minneapolis on March 25, which was followed by a concert in Chicago two days later. Why Miles chose to dismiss his nephew right before a home concert remains unclear. It was a hard lesson for Wilburn, who had hoped to perform for his family and friends from Chicago. "It was painful," Wilburn commented. "But then I said to myself, 'I still want to be all right with my uncle. It's his band and his decision.' And I had a great ride. It was a once in a lifetime experience."

The live band for the Minneapolis concert consisted of Miles, Garrett, Thomas, Broom, Irving, Holzman, Jones, Wellman, and Cinelu. It was immediately clear that the addition of Wellman changed the feel of the live band from the rock backbeats to a more playful, light-footed, yet very powerful swing. But the problems with the guitarists continued: Broom preferred a clean jazz sound and refused to use distortion. "All I needed now . . . was a guitar player who could play what I wanted," Miles remarked.[9] However, he first took two months off, most of which he spent, as had become usual by this stage, with the two other loves in his life—Jo Gelbard and painting.

❖

"The last four years of his life, he was either painting or making music," Peter Shukat, Miles's manager from 1987 to 1991, recalled. "He'd spend time in Malibu, and in New York, and if he wasn't on the road, he'd paint and paint and paint. If you walked into his apartment there'd be a canvas ten by ten feet long, and paint was everywhere. And if he was touring, Gordon [Meltzer] made sure that he always had his pencils and his drawing books. He painted, or drew, or played music. That's what he did."

Although the original impulse to draw and paint was his own, it followed a familiar pattern in Miles's life that he was strongly influenced by his romantic partners in this creative endeavor. While Cicely Tyson had handed him sketchpads in the early 1980s, several years later he regularly collaborated artistically with Jo Gelbard. "He was sending me paintings through the mail, and then I'd add my parts, and we'd talk about it," Gelbard said. "We did many of the paintings together, and we started to do exhibitions, and this 'career' began to run away with us. The relationship ended my marriage because it was no longer containable. Eventually I started to do everything for Miles, decorating his home, buying his clothes, being with him every day."

Gelbard revealed how some of Miles's approaches to art were very similar to the way he worked with music and musicians. "When we met, I had no self-confidence and a terrible self-image. And he thought I was fantastic. . . . 'Miles Davis thinks I'm fantastic!' So he created me, like he created his musicians. He had no ego in that sense. It wasn't like, 'I'm the greatest, back me up!' It was more like, 'Let's do it together.' That lack of ego has created many great musicians and also created our art. I don't meet many people who could possibly paint with another person, because it's all about what their ego wants to say."

"Miles was bored artistically all the time," Gelbard continued. "He moved real fast creatively. Whether it was lousy or valid, as long as it moved he was happy. But as a painter he was totally different from the way I had imagined him to be. In his drawings he was very light-handed and whimsical, but the moment he got a paintbrush in his hand he was so heavy-handed. He just loved pouring on paint, like a child, mixing it, getting things heavier and thicker. All his expensive clothes would be full of paint. But he liked to buy clothes so it didn't bother him. He could drop fifty grand in a shop like that! Without blinking. He'd come home in the afternoon, and there'd be twenty leather jackets for me. He was a compulsive buyer. He loved fabrics, clothes. I think that's where his feminine side came out. He was delicate, skinny, soft spoken, and had a light touch as a lover, but otherwise there was nothing feminine about him."

Miles's "compulsive" buying habits were another indication of the addictive side of his personality, which manifested in ways that bewildered Gelbard. "He'd stopped smoking and drinking," she commented, "but he was on painkillers, a lot of painkillers. And on sleeping pills. And on things that woke him up. He would go to sleep at four in the morning, if he went to sleep at all. I would often find him sitting alone in a dark room at night. Just sitting there, with the TV on. I never slept in the same bed as him the time I was with him. He'd fall asleep on the couch, passing out from exhaustion during the day. It was never a regular life like, 'It's night, let's go to bed.' I think this was a residue of his time as a drug addict, and he would do things that were totally foreign to me. He might be cooking a pot of chili, and drop it, and the chili was all over the kitchen floor, and he'd never touch it. When he came back from tour, it might still be there. It just didn't exist. It was something to do with being able to shut out physical reality.

"Miles could be really violent. The stuff that he took to keep him up, in combination with lack of sleep, made him nuts. He was capable of unspeakable cruelty. I don't think he had a sense of morality. Everything was possible. When he wanted to hurt there was no stopping him. I'm an athlete, and very strong, so I was never scared of him, but at times it was like hell, like a nightmare. We were locked in a room for most of five, six years. There were no parties, and no presents, just us, painting. We were like tigers in a cage, circling each other, following each other's tail. There was a very heavy atmosphere, very intense, and no music. He never played music in the house, ever. We didn't really have to talk, we just instinctively went, 'Yes, I get it,' whether it was the song, or the painting, or the clothes, or how you want to live. We had such a strong artistic connection, it was like a force of nature. And at a certain point, when I knew he was going to die, I felt that I owed him. I didn't want him to die alone. He was afraid of dying, and wasn't ready to die. His rage was about dying. To be okay with myself for the rest of my life, I needed to give him a good death."

It was a paradoxical situation. On the one hand Miles became aware of his impending death, on the other his relationship with this strongly artistic woman twenty-four-years his junior greatly rejuvenated him, to the point where he began to look increasingly youthful. This also surprised Gelbard.

"I don't know what happened to his skin; it began to look like a baby's," she said. "And he did nothing to it, no face lift or collagen, or whatever bullshit people do. Although keeping up his own image became very tiring in the end. I called him Dewey, and he often made fun of how terrible he looked at home, and what an effort it was to become Miles Davis, with the hair and the outfits and his clothes. But when I look at where he went when he was with me, the art and Montreux, and being knighted, and all the honors, the movies, he was definitely moving up, to a higher level than he ever was before. He reinvented himself."

There have been suggestions that during Miles's final years, painting became more important to him than music, but Gelbard strongly disputed this. "He loved the art, but nothing came up to the music," she asserted. "There was always a song in his head. His awareness of sound, music, it never stopped. That subconscious thing that related to music was never not there. But it's true that he didn't practice much on the trumpet. Right before a tour a little bit. He worked on musical ideas in his head, and sometimes wrote them down, but didn't actualize much. We had set up a music room for him, and this is where he did his work with Jason [Miles]. But never on his own."

Having fallen in love with technology during the making of *Tutu* and *Siesta*, Miles had bought an Akai four-track cassette recorder, some synthesizers, and a drum machine, and invited Jason Miles to help him use it. "I went to his place," Jason Miles recalled, "and Miles just looked at me and said, 'Man, you do this shit. What the fuck is going on?' So I told him, 'If you want to change this, press from there to there to there,' but he never really understood it. We worked on stuff together until a few months before he died, creating drum grooves and so on, and actually wrote a few tunes together that were played by the live band, like 'Funk Suite' and 'Heavy Metal.' One day I programmed a drum pattern for him, and when I came back three days later, it was still going. He had chaos going, with TVs on everywhere. Another time he was in the New York hospital for special surgery for three weeks with renewed hip problems. He had his gear in hospital, so I went there three times a week to record with him in his room."

In May of 1987 Miles was back on the road with a live band consisting of Kenny Garrett, Adam Holzman, Robert Irving, Darryl Jones, Ricky Wellman, Mino Cinelu, and Foley on lead bass. Regarding Foley's playing style, Marcus Miller said that the tape Foley had sent him, and that Miles had heard over the phone, contained material in which the guitarist "really let rip, like Pete Cosey." But in the live band the Cincinnati player was much more restrained, taking traditional, melodic, bluesy solos and comping in fairly nondistinct fashion as part of the "orchestra." While his playing with Miles was lacking in originality, Foley's sensitive, rhythmic touch and excellent blues phrasing fitted well with Wellman's go-go rhythms.

The repertoire of the '87 band remained fairly similar to that of the '85–'86 band. The concerts usually began with the sequence "Right Off" and "Speak" (aka "One Phone Call/Street Scenes"), "Star People," and "Perfect Way." Following this there was a mixture of the signature pop songs "Time after Time" and "Human Nature," complemented by a sprinkling of tracks from *Tutu*, plus tunes like "Wrinkle," "Burn," Foley's "The Senate" and "Me and You," Neil Larsen's "Carnival Time," Toto's "Don't Stop Me Now," and Prince's "Movie Star." The regular set closer of the previous six years, "Jean-Pierre," was dropped.

The game of musical chairs in Miles's live band continued when Mino Cinelu left to play with Sting in September of 1987 and was replaced by Rudy Bird, who debuted for the European tour beginning October 19. Darryl Jones, who had left the group for Sting in September of 1985, was now in turn sacked by Miles after the concert of February 22, 1988. Miles claimed that Jones started "getting dramatic, too show biz for my band."[10] Irving added, "Miles told me that he was hearing the role of the bass more sparse, like Prince's 'Kiss,' which was a hit at the time, and had almost no bass, and that it was a drag to ask Darryl to play much less."

That same month Miles revised his set list, introducing "In a Silent Way" as the new opener, followed by a new composition, "Intruder." "Right Off" and "Speak" were removed from the live repertoire soon afterwards. Hawaiian-born bassist Benny Rietveld replaced Jones for the next concert, on April 9. Rietveld had played with Sheila E., supporting Prince, and was recommended to Miles by Prince's road manager. On the same day Rudy Bird made way for Marilyn Mazur, who had been performing with Wayne Shorter's band in the interim. After Stern, Cinelu, and Jones, she was the fourth ex–band member to return. "It was easier this time because I was the only percussionist," Mazur said, "but it also meant I had to be more groove orientated."

This band, consisting of Miles, Garrett, Foley, Holzman, Irving, Rietveld, Wellman, and Mazur, was officially documented with two tracks on *Live around the World*, which was released in 1996 and compiled by Gordon Meltzer and Adam Holzman. The recordings on the album were selected from hundreds of hours of two-track recordings made by live engineer Patrick Murray, who owned a portable DAT machine and connected it to his mixing board every evening. Murray's job was taken over in late 1990 by Don Kurek, who recorded to lower-quality compact cassette. This was the reason why only one track from his tenure, "Hannibal," was included on the album.

"Gordon did the actual selection," Holzman explained. "He spent a year judiciously listening to the tapes and narrowing it down to a couple of choices for each song. Then I came in and we weeded it down a little more, and I came up with a few more adventurous songs that hadn't been selected, like 'Wrinkle,' 'Intruder,' and 'Full Nelson.' We tried to put together the best representation of a concert that we could."

The two tracks from the above-mentioned band to appear on *Live around the World* were an abridged version of "Full Nelson," which was recorded on August 7, 1988, in Tokyo, and an altered version of "Star People," called "New Blues," which was from a concert in California a week later, on August 14. "New Blues/Star People" is brought alive by the sharp keyboard accents, animated soloing by Miles, first on muted then open trumpet, a blistering and very elastic blues solo by Foley, and attentive responses from the band. Aside from its truly scorching groove, the truncated "Full Nelson" does little justice to the way the band could stretch this song in live performance.

In September of 1988 Robert Irving left the group. "Miles got sick in September," Irving said. "He was in hospital and the doctors had advised him to retire. Everybody thought that was the end, and I began work on another project. When Miles called by the end of the month to tour again, I had to make a choice. I'd been there five years, and the music had become really structured and confining, so I decided not to go."

Miles's disregard of his doctors' advice can be interpreted as admirable courage in the face of adversity, or as reckless behavior. Jo Gelbard reckoned it was both. "Even as he was scared of it, he absolutely invited death," she said. "You can take good care of yourself and be okay, or you can live hard until you die. And that's what he did in his last years. He decided, 'I'm going to do whatever I want to do and be creative and look good, and when I die, I die. For example, he was a bad diabetic, and he abused that. He would have Gordon come in the middle of the night and bring him ice cream and cookies. He'd eat the whole box, and then he'd be in a sugar shock. You can think this or his return to touring irresponsible, but you know, when you're as sick as he was, what are you going to do? Laps in the pool? Jog in the Park? Taking care of yourself is a preventative thing. When you're that sick, why bother? I don't think he would have prolonged his life much more than a year or two if he had left out the cookies and the pills."

As if to remind Miles of the choice he was making, Gil Evans had died in March of 1988, an event that had a deep impact. "The evening Gil died was the saddest moment I ever spent with him. He was devastated," Gelbard said. A more positive moment was Miles's knighting into the Order of St. John, a religious group founded during the time of the Crusades, on November 13, 1988. But when Miles was made a Chevalier of the Legion of Honor, the highest honor the French government can bestow, on July 18, 1991, it was a deeply unsettling experience. "No one called him," Jo Gelbard explained. "There were no flowers, there was nothing. It was a horrible night because it occurred to him that he was truly alone, that everyone who worked for him was making money from him, and that apart from me, there was no one who was just there because they wanted to be with him."

The years 1988 to 1991 were entirely informed by the tension between Miles's creative drive and the personal challenges facing him. Depending on how strong he felt physically, his powers on the trumpet varied greatly from night to night. "The trumpet must be the physically hardest instrument to play," Holzman noted. "Miles had strength and power, and I think later in the '80s he definitely did get the same chops back he'd had in the '60s. But at the same time his health seemed to go up and down. And towards the end of my tenure with the band [late 1989], his energy level definitely declined." "His health started to fail him in the last one and a half years of his life," Wellman seconded. And Rietveld noted, "A lot of the time he would leave straight after the show, and sometimes he'd go home, even if it was just for a day. He just wanted to play, and save all his energy for that."

Despite his varying health and chops, and the increasingly regimented nature of the musical arrangements, Miles was still capable of transcendence and of inspiring his band. All band members interviewed concurred that even on occasions when his playing was below par, he was entirely present with the music and his band. "Miles would suggest changes just before the gig," Holzman said, "and sometimes it would be difficult to achieve what he wanted. But if you tried, and fucked up, at least you made an attempt to address what he was talking about, and he was happy to see you go in that direction, as opposed to doing things by routine. He didn't want people to feel too comfortable. There were a couple of times when the band became like one big, happy family, and the first thing that would happen is that someone would be axed. He wanted people thinking about the music, and doing something fresh with it. He was very serious about performing, and he would always get on my case about jumping in too quickly, and trying to play a lot of shit too soon, instead of taking my time to find my pace, and develop a solo logically and musically. Listening back to the stuff now, he was 100 percent right."

"In the beginning I had a hard time in the band, mainly because I had to follow Darryl Jones, who is a phenomenal player," Rietveld revealed. "Of course they were disappointed, and I more or less had to relearn to play the bass. But there was never anything negative coming from Miles. He'd let me know if it wasn't happening, but always in a positive way, like 'Let's try this feel on this song.' You had to really pay attention, and be right in the moment all the time. He had an incredible presence, which was like a mystical part of him, drawing everyone in. His presence kept everybody on their toes, so that the music was still alive. When musicians play something they know already, the initial spark goes. He never liked that. So he would change things every night, not really radical changes, but things that kept the music fresh, as if you were playing it for the first time. It was like having a Zen mind-set: everything is always now, there is no before or after, you should be totally immersed in what's happening in the moment. He didn't talk much. There is not a lot that needs to be said anyway, and he knows that people usually don't listen. So why talk? But he sometimes made these short, cryptic comments, and they were like a nut you had to crack open, and find the meaning on your own."

Ricky Wellman, an experienced player with a well-developed style, recalled, "Miles brought out qualities in my playing that I never thought I had, just by giving me different signals, or humming me nursery rhymes. In the beginning I thought he was crazy. How was I going to learn from 'Humpty Dumpty fell off the wall, Humpty Dumpty had a great fall'? How was I going to apply that to this music? But if you really put your mind to it, suddenly you'll go, 'Oh, that's what he means!' Like in certain sections of 'Tutu,' which is a very slow cut, he wanted that Humpty Dumpty part played. So you're playing a rhythm on top of or inside a 4/4 rhythm, and it changes the feel, and how the musicians improvised. Miles was always directing the band to improvise, to keep it exciting, to keep the element of surprise. And if you don't know what to play, don't play, because otherwise you're getting in the way. He loved to communicate and express these points to his musicians. It delighted him, and put a spark in his eyes. You could see that on stage when he was directing the band."

With the departure of Robert Irving in late September of 1988, Adam Holzman was promoted to the role of musical director, while Joey DeFrancesco became second keyboard player. Three selections played by the new octet were included on *Live around the World*—a performance of "Human Nature," which was recorded in Austria on November 1, and "In a Silent Way" and "Intruder," which were the two opening tunes from the band's second concert on December 17, 1988, in New York." "In a Silent Way" and

"Intruder" were effective concert openers, since both have a suspended feel that never resolves. "In a Silent Way," harking back to the studio recording of 1969 and never played live by Miles, sounds otherworldly, as if coming from another musical universe. The band played "Human Nature" lightly and delightfully during Miles's touching and delicate solo. But the piece had become a showcase for Garrett, whose wild and lengthy saxophone solo drives the music, which towards the end was built on a rising chord sequence taken from "Milestones," to an astonishing climax.

After the New York concert, Miles was laid low for several weeks with bronchial pneumonia and only returned to touring in late March of 1989. A sign of his decreasing powers was that the number of concerts he played in that year, thirty-one, was almost half that of the previous years. Unsurprisingly, the band changed again. Marilyn Mazur returned to Denmark and was replaced by Munyungo Jackson, and keyboardists Kei Akagi and John Beasley had taken over from Joey DeFrancesco and Adam Holzman, who was suffering from "tour fatigue."

Amandla was issued in the spring of 1989, and the following European tour was the first to feature material from this album. One tune from this tour is included on *Live around the World.* The wistful, melancholic "Mr. Pastorius," recorded on April 12, showcases Miles on open trumpet. Frustratingly, the recording is abridged, and Miles also cracks a few notes, but otherwise a strong atmosphere permeates the occasion.

In June Beasley made way again for Holzman. For the next European tour, Kenny Garrett wasn't available, and was replaced for three weeks by tenor saxophonist Rick Margitza. According to Adam Holzman, Margitza never quite gelled with the band, which led Miles to play much more than he normally did.

Bootlegs from 1989 illustrate that, with the inclusion of material from *Amandla,* the highly arranged live direction had reached a pinnacle, and was in danger of toppling over into kitsch. An admirable quality of *Amandla* was the lightness of the synthesizer sounds, but when live keyboards were mixed too far up-front in live performances, the sound became syrupy. Moreover, the band's playing was beginning to display a certain slickness. Fortunately, Holzman and Meltzer included two recordings from 1989 on *Live around the World* on which the keyboards are kept well under control. "Time after Time," recorded on June 5 in Chicago, with Garrett on flute, is a touching treatment of what had become Miles's signature song, while "Amandla" is both tenderly and dynamically performed.

The other new development in 1989 was the substantial amount of solo space given to the virtuoso Kei Agaki. This is in evidence on the only other live recording Warner Bros. has issued of Miles, the video *Miles in Paris,* recorded on November 3, 1989, without Holzman, who had decided to pursue his career elsewhere, and with John Bigham on electric percussion, instead of Munyungo Jackson. (The two personnel changes had occurred in October and September respectively.) The music on the video is in parts excellent. "Tutu" and "New Blues" feature great solos by Foley, and Miles plays at length, and well. At the same time the slickness that is noticeable on bootlegs also permeates this event. The extensive light show and the populist holding up of signs with the names of his band members add to an impression of Miles's concerts being on a slide towards toothless, middle-of-the-road entertainment.

Sadly, the makers of the video treat the music in exactly this fashion, by cutting out some of the more exciting parts of the concert and, most of all, pasting an interview with Miles over sections of the music. It belies Miles's comment on the sacredness of music: "Every phrase should matter, that's why I don't waste any phrases." In the light of this declaration, the editor's cuts are farcical, and seemingly born from the whole sad and destructive MTV-era idea that a piece of music is boring without ever-changing visuals, and when it lasts for longer than four minutes.

After a break of two months, Miles was back on the road again in February of 1990. April 19 saw the debut of bassist Richard Patterson, another young Chicagoan, who had preceded Felton Crews as bassist in the band featuring Randy Hall, Vince Wilburn Jr., and Bobby Irving. In early June there was yet another change, when Miles's twenty-year-old son, Erin, replaced John Bigham. Erin had often been on the road with Miles in previous years, working as a roadie. Although he had some experience as a drummer, he felt nowhere near ready to be promoted to membership in Miles's live band.

"I had a hard time," Erin recalled. "Instead of just being Erin, I now suddenly had to deliver. I much more enjoyed listening and being part of the crew. If he'd asked me to play drums, at least I'd have known what to do, but I didn't know how to play an Octopad, didn't know what the buttons did, and wasn't really familiar with samples and stuff. The problem was figuring out something creative to play. I thought my playing was horrible, but my Dad said, 'It's not.' He helped me a lot, and was pretty easy about it. I guess he just wanted me to play in his band and develop."

Perhaps after having felt a failure as a father with his two other sons, Gregory and Miles IV, Miles tried to make up for his previous shortcomings with Erin. Not only did Miles add Erin to the band, he also credited the compositions "Wrinkle" and "Intruder" to his son, even though the first was a reworking of "Star on Cicely." "We worked on some stuff at his home," Erin said. "He had a little four-track, and he'd play parts, and I'd write drum beats and so on. We worked on 'Wrinkle' and 'Intruder,' and he gave me full credit for them." Obviously, by giving all credit to Erin, Miles also avoided handing half of his publishing to Warner Bros.

Two tracks from the band with Patterson and Erin—"Wrinkle" and "Tutu," both recorded at Montreux, on July 20, 1990—are included on *Live around the World*. Like Darryl Jones, Patterson proved to be a natural, and his driving influence can be heard on the fierce "Wrinkle," which is a variation on the chromatic funk direction, intensely and tightly played by the band. Based around a staccato theme and a deeply funky bass riff, the recording showcases not only Patterson, but also Akagi, who takes a long solo at the beginning, with Miles's elegant chromatic phrasing dancing over the cross-rhythms. Miles briefly duets with Garrett before the latter lets rip on alto. "Tutu" had become Miles's theme song of his Warner Bros. era and features some great supportive lines and an exciting solo by Foley, with Miles drawing laughter from the audience for some humorous trumpet phrases.

After the European tour, the band didn't perform live from November of 1990 till March of 1991. For Miles's final concert performances a new keyboard player, Deron Johnson, replaced Akagi, and the group was without a percussionist. The band now consisted of Miles, Garrett, Foley, Johnson, Patterson, and Wellman. Although this shrinking to a sextet in Miles's final six months has been interpreted as a winding down of creative focus, the evidence of bootlegs does not bear this out. In fact, this final band was perhaps his best in several years. Johnson played less as an "orchestral" player and more in the free soloing and comping style of the electric piano players Miles had around 1970, while Wellman and Patterson were a formidable and very funky rhythm tandem. The smaller band format allowed more interplay and freedom, and did away with the borderline kitsch slickness that had sometimes marred the bands of 1988 and 1990. Sadly, the only officially issued evidence of this lineup is "Hannibal," the final track of *Live around the World*, which was recorded on August 25, 1991, at the Hollywood Bowl. It amply demonstrates the band's tightness, lightness, and economy of means.[11]

The concert at the Hollywood Bowl turned out to be Miles's final concert. "Not long after the Hollywood Bowl concert Miles started spitting blood and was rushed to hospital," Wellman recalled. Virtually all who heard about Miles's latest hospitalization were not unduly worried, since pneumonia, hospitalizations, and unlikely recoveries had become a habitual pattern. Miles, with his "knowing," appears to have been the only one who was aware that his time was up, even before he had the stroke.

"We went into hospital on Labor Day weekend in September of 1991," Jo Gelbard said. "It was a long weekend, and no one was around. I was in the hospital with him throughout. He was Miles Davis, so they let us do what we wanted. He was in a rage. The first week I was in the hospital with him he was ripping the I.V. drips out of his arm, and walking around. On the last day before the stroke, he was standing naked in the room, furious. He just wanted to get out of there and not die. He knew that it was his last day."

Ian Carr reports that Miles had his stroke as a result of his anger at some doctors who insisted on trying to put a tube down his throat to assist his breathing,[12] but Gelbard disputes this version of the events. "He went into a coma after his stroke, was moved to intensive care, and never came out of it. For the next weeks he was sometimes squeezing our hands, and we were playing him music. But other than hand movement, there was nothing. His brother [Vernon], his sister [Dorothy], his daughter [Cheryl], and Vince were regularly there."

Erin was the only son who visited Miles. "I generally had a good relationship with him," Erin said, "but we had had a falling out after I left the band, and we weren't really talking. Luckily I went to see him in hospital a month before he died, and we started talking again."

Miles eventually had a second stroke, and died on September 28. His cause of death has been given by different sources as respiratory failure, diabetes, heart failure, pneumonia, a stroke, and/or AIDS-related illnesses. A Dutch pop encyclopedia, for instance, simply mentions that Miles died of "AIDS complications."[13] Peter Shukat commented, "I won't discuss Miles's medical history, but he died of complications from diabetes."

The mention of AIDS in relation to Miles has become a source of controversy in the United States, most likely in part because Western attitudes towards AIDS still involved a degree of stigmatization and blaming and shaming the victim, but probably also because of Miles's vehement and furious denials. In his autobiography he wrote, "That story made me madder than a motherfucker when I found out about it. It wasn't true, of course."[14] In an interview in 1989 Miles blamed Cicely Tyson for the rumor. "I think an ex-wife must have something to do with that," he said. " . . . I don't have AIDS now. I don't think I'm going to sue."[15] Of course, the inclusion of the word "now" and Miles's reluctance to sue are notable.

Jo Gelbard refused to address the issue, saying "Miles's death is his own. I don't speak about what killed him. But some people have a knowing about their destiny that includes their death. Instinct is stronger than people think and goes into places we can't explain. So my feeling is that it was his time to die . . . period." Dorothy Weber, by contrast, felt that Miles was not aware of his impending death before going into hospital. She asserted that Miles was "actively planning his future" and pointed towards his plans for a two-CD set as well as the fact that Miles had already agreed to dates for a 1992 tour.

Quincy Troupe raised the AIDS question in his book *Miles and Me.* In a section called "a mysterious virus" Troupe related that Miles was taking AZT,[16] a drug developed to delay or suppress the onset of full-blown AIDS. And in 1991, when Troupe, in the context of Miles's retrospective concerts in Montreux and Paris, jokingly reminded Miles of his oft-made statement, "If I look back, I'll die," a sore spot was clearly touched. "He was livid, his face flushed, spit coming out of the side of his mouth," Troupe wrote. "I had never seen him this mad before. He was almost crazed."[17]

Another taboo issue, related to allegations that Miles had AIDS, is his sexual orientation. There have been rumors of a homosexual side, to the point that he has occasionally been treated as a gay icon. Ian Carr claims that Miles was bisexual,[18] but strangely fails to back this up with any details. Quincy Troupe mentions the existence of rumors that suggest Miles had homosexual relationships.[19] But like any questioned for this book, Troupe never witnessed a homosexual relationship. "He may have had sex with men in his lifetime," Jo Gelbard commented, "but his preference was definitely with women." Miles did have many gay friends, but in the end, given how indiscreet Miles was, it seems unlikely that he would have been able to keep a strong homosexual side under wraps. And if a possible explanation must be provided for his alleged AIDS, there are plenty of alternatives, such as dirty needles during his period of drugs use, or the plethora of blood transfusions Miles received during the '70s and '80s. And Jim Rose offered that during the '80s, "He had acupuncture everywhere he went in the world. There is no telling how clean those needles were."

We are unlikely to ever know with certainty the exact cause of Miles's death. This is of no great concern. Gelbard's testimony—that Miles was aware for several years that his remaining time was limited, and that this informed his choices—is of more importance. Although Dorothy Weber disagrees, it seems likely that Miles's untypical participation in the retrospective concerts in Montreux and Paris in July of 1991, described in Chapter 2, was inspired by a foreknowledge of his death. Gelbard also related that Miles did not find this "knowing" an easy burden to carry, especially as the world was finally giving him the recognition he wanted, while he seems to have found in Jo Gelbard arguably the most fulfilling and stable relationship of his life.

"He died right before we were about to get it all together," Jo Gelbard said. "I was about to get divorced, and the last summer tour of Europe was like our honeymoon, because I was finally free, finally completely his. He was happier all the time, but as he got happier, he got more tormented, because he knew he was going to die. The last year of our relationship turned out to be the worst, because of his dying. It was Shakespearean in its tragedy."

A memorial service was held in New York on October 5, 1991. Among the speakers were Quincy Troupe, Herbie Hancock, Bill Cosby, and Jesse Jackson, while a letter from Prince was read. Miles's final resting place is Woodlawn Cemetery in the Bronx, New York, where he was buried with one of his trumpets and other personal belongings. The silence that he used so effectively throughout his career has since been his only note.

CODA

"I have to change, it's like a curse."
—MILES DAVIS IN 1969

"Now I know it's not a curse, it's a blessing!"
—MILES DAVIS IN 1986[1]

Although Miles was unable to see his final and most radical change as a blessing, he gave the issue of his own impermanence serious thought. "When the time comes, I don't think I'll really die," Miles said in 1987. "The spirit will still be there."[2] Two years later he remarked, "I don't think people really die. . . . I don't know what happens; they have to come back and be around somewhere. . . . I don't believe that thoughts get lost. . . . The thoughts are still there. . . . [Like] music's floating around, and one day somebody's going to be able to pick it up."[3] Quincy Troupe also related in *Miles and Me* how Miles routinely talked to those close to him who had died—his parents, Gil Evans, other musicians—as if they were still alive.

The idea that people don't die is also central to Zen, but is usually taken less literally. Rather than imagining a person's spirit surviving physical death, in Zen our immortality follows from the recognition of the interconnectedness of everything. Our actions affect everything and everyone, and their effects ripple into eternity. Our immortality is established in the everlasting marks we make. Miles's death in 1991 demarcated him as a twentieth-century artist, yet the marks he made with his music and his method, his awareness and teachings, live on in the twenty-first century. Fittingly, just as Miles enhanced the power and depth of his music with a virtuoso use of silence, his legacy has resounded with increasing power and meaning in the silence he left us with since his death. On the basis of his combined acoustic and electric legacy, Miles is increasingly being remembered as one of the major musicians of the twentieth century, on a par with greats like The Beatles and Igor Stravinsky.

Miles has long been acknowledged as one of the greatest jazz artists of all time, but the reevaluation of his electric music is a fairly recent phenomenon. *In a Silent Way* and *Bitches Brew* stand alone among Miles's electric oeuvre in being recognized as important and influential milestones soon after their release. Towards the end of the twentieth century *On the Corner* also gained understanding and recognition as its sonic experi-mentations and circular rhythms were name-checked in dance music circles. In addition, Bill Laswell's *Panthalassa* has drawn fresh attention to the electric music of 1969 to 1975; and trumpeter Mark Isham has paid tribute to and further developed this music—with *Miles Remembered: The Silent Way Project* (1999)—as have guitarist Henry Kaiser and trumpeter Wadada Leo Smith, with *Yo Miles!* (1998) and *Yo Miles!—Upriver/Downriver* (2001).

In an article entitled "Return to the Music That Time Forgot" writer Jonathan Rom-ney observed about Miles's music from 1969 to 1975 that: "Milesian fusion wasn't a style or genre, but an attitude, a way of thinking about music in terms of time, space, and density."[4] Mark Isham seconded Romney's opinion, saying, "The whole idea of the music is that it's so open that it demands of the players that they really listen, really play together 100 percent of the time. You have to be completely present every second, because if you're just going through the motions this music can be utterly boring. But if the band is there, it's the most exciting stuff in the world."

"This music comes alive in live performance," Henry Kaiser concurred. "It is inter-esting to really experience what happens when you approach that stuff in the same way Miles did, as a door to go through to find new things. Each time we play it there are moments of discovering different feelings, new colors, and new musical territories, and different relationships between players."

"I always felt Miles's music of 1973 to 1975 was some of the most important music ever made," Leo Smith added. "Miles took a direction that was different than that of almost all his colleagues. His compositions are based on conceptual structures that are unique for any music in any time zone. Probably the most brilliant part of it is that the notion of phrasing changed completely. No longer were long, arced phrases sought after. In his music there was the notion of using short nuclei of notes as a basis for improvisa-tion, as opposed to the language of harmonic progression. It's a whole other conceptual design where the actual material that's being used is as short as your five fingers, while the piece of music may be quite long. This is a new language, with roots in African music. The reason it's being looked at today is that there's not much happening. People are quite bored, and alienated from the notion of inspiration, so they are looking at things that people already did. And this music is important and powerful."

From an entirely different musical discipline, Karl Hyde, of the British dance band Underworld, commented: "The music is about pure sound, of tunes and timbres, in a similar way that perhaps dub was or dance music is. It also has a fantastic, magical sense of space, which is a big influence on the way I play guitar and the way I think about space."

While the process of rediscovering and reevaluating Miles's electric experiments of the '60s and '70s is ongoing, no similar interest is discernible regarding his music from 1981 to 1991. The simplest explanation is that the music of 1981 to 1991 did not announce a new musical paradigm and hence does not invite belated reevaluation. It was, in the words of Ken Wilber, a "translation," not a "transcendence." The only exception was Miles's chromatic funk approach, which had elements of transcendence. But it remained just one of the many strands in his '80s repertoire.

Although there is little disagreement today that Miles's music from 1981 to 1991 was not transcendent, the question remains why this was so. One reason offered is that Miles, after the horrors of his five-year absence from the music scene, had neither the requisite trumpet technique, physical stamina, nor creative drive to reach his previous heights. There may well be substance to this claim. Mtume asserted that Miles told him on his final birthday, May 26, 1991, that he was "coasting." The percussionist played a central part in the most controversial and groundbreaking of all Miles's bands, the '70s funk collective, and all Miles's later bands seem relatively tame by comparison. The density and intensity of the extremes of music from the mid-1970s put great demands on the minds and bodies of the performers, and it would be understandable if Miles no longer had the stomach for such radical forays after his comeback.

However, there is a more fundamental reason why Miles was unlikely to achieve genuine transcendence from 1981 to 1991, regardless of whether or not his physical, creative, and trumpet powers were at a similar level as before 1976. This explanation goes to the heart of his working methods described in earlier chapters. Throughout his career, one of Miles's main strengths was his ability to have his finger on the pulse of the zeitgeist and to both transcend and include the music of his era. He did not invent the directions of which he was at the forefront—bebop, hardbop, modal bop, orchestral jazz, avant-bop, ambient jazz, or jazz-rock—but applied his John Aubrey–style talent: to recognize stone circles where others merely saw random collections of rocks. Western, and particularly American, music culture of pre-1976 was a maelstrom of musical innovation. Different genres and new directions emerged with stunning regularity. In other words, there were plenty of stone circles for Miles to recognize, explore, and transcend. But during the '70s this waterfall of innovation began to run dry. Consequently, when Miles returned to the world of music after his silent years, there were few new stone circles to transcend and include.[5]

Given these limiting circumstances, Miles appears to have done the best he could. It was a demonstration of his continuing drive for change that he incorporated the three new musical developments that did occur during the '80s. The first was the coming of age of midi technology, the second was the blending of world music with rock and jazz, and the third was the development of rap and dance music. As was briefly alluded to in Chapter 13, the fact that Miles was able to integrate midi technology and world music in a credible way was a remarkable achievement. Rock stars who are in their forties and fifties often begin to look and sound like parodies of their former selves, especially if they suddenly attempt to appear trendy by jumping on the latest musical bandwagon. Conversely, if these artists keep repeating themselves, they cease to be interesting. Although Miles attained only occasional transcendence in his last decade, one of his great achievements was that he still sounded modern and fresh while in his sixties, still played excellent music, still retained his artistic dignity, still displayed grace under pressure. In doing so, Miles fulfilled one of the '60s counterculture's mottos: at sixty-five, he died before he got old.

Miles was once asked during a mid-1980s interview, "How many times in your life did you feel you were starting a new career?" With a look of exasperation Miles snarled, "I only have one career, and that's music. I made up my mind when I was about seven years old that I wanted to be a musician. And that was it." "So there's one line all the way through?" the questioner asked insistently. "That's right," Miles retorted.[6]

As with his pre-1976 music, the roots of Miles's music from 1981 to 1991 can be traced to his childhood in St. Louis. Adam Holzman has argued that Miles's late '80s live bands presented an "overview" of his career. "We did a couple of tours that were almost bordering on jazz, where 'Mr. Pastorius' had almost a swing feel on the drums and a walking bass line," Holzman remarked. "There would be everything ranging from that to the percussion frenzies of 'Carnival Time' and the freak outs of songs like 'Heavy Metal' and 'The Senate.' In addition there were the more melodic things like 'Time after Time' and the more orchestral Marcus Miller's stuff, which was in turn influenced by Gil Evans. I think that in some ways you have elements of his whole career appearing in the sets that we were playing in the late '80s. Without claiming to know what was on his mind, it may be that he was wrapping things up."

In other words, Miles's final period was a translation of the different directions he had pursued throughout his career. The symmetry of Miles's first attempts at charting his own musical course with *The Birth of the Cool* in 1949 and 1950 and his return to a highly arranged, orchestral-sounding direction in his last years is indeed remarkable. Moreover, this "one line all the way through" is not only visible in Miles's music, but also in his attitude and his musical methods.

"Until the end of his life, Miles believed in the necessity of not repeating oneself, and not allowing the critics or the public or the record companies to force you into a rut," Reggie Lucas commented. "Miles's idea of an artist was very pure in the sense that he believed in the idea of the musician, the artist, serving his own muse. I think he correctly identified that as the true creative spirit, and he was appalled by the constraints placed upon him by his legendary status as a jazz musician. He didn't wish to play the same standards over and over again till he died.

"Miles's personality and his music challenge one to think and to reevaluate one's basic conceptions of what life is and how it's to be lived, what music is and how it's to be created. That's difficult for some people. They like terra firma. They're threatened by change. Their goal in life is to create as much definiteness, irrespective of how much mediocrity they have to embrace in order to achieve it. Miles was the enemy of this. His goal was to create individuality and innovative expression at any time that he could. He was most contemptuous of artistic complacency and mediocrity."

Understood in the context of the relentless critical onslaught and the incessant physical pain Miles endured, as well as the obvious problems Miles faced in being a human being, his ongoing commitment to "individuality and innovative expression" has heroic qualities. This invites an interpretation of Miles's musical legacy and life in the mythological framework outlined by author and scholar Joseph Campbell's in his famous book *The Hero with a Thousand Faces*. Campbell explained how the hero's journey is a timeless story that appears in all human cultures. The hero leaves the safety of his daily existence to give his life to a cause bigger than himself or other than himself. He steps outside the normal range of human experience, deals with trials, temptations, and tribulations, and attains a transformation in his consciousness, a change in the way he thinks and views the world. Finally, the hero returns home to share his discoveries and the gift of his new consciousness.

Miles was one of the thousand faces of this mythological hero. The cause to which he gave his life was music, the undiscovered country he traveled, and the trials and tribulations he underwent have been described at length in this book. And true to the hero's story, Miles did his best to share the consciousness he attained—in his music, in his methods, and in his expanded listening awareness. On another level he also pioneered and taught, by example, a modern awareness of racial equality. We only now begin to recognize that his consciousness exemplified the currently emerging existential worldview. Miles was one of the harbingers of this twenty-first-century paradigm.

Miles's working methods, the way he taught his musicians, can also be interpreted as a form of a new, spiritual type of leadership. He was not an old-fashioned leader who expected slavish followers or who coerced his band members into doing what he wanted. Neither was his leadership designed to aggrandize himself. There were no big speeches or other attempts at convincing his band members of his righteous cause. Instead he expected them to join him in the service of the sacred aim of making meaningful here-and-now music. Rather than using external pressures, Miles utilized his leadership to mobilize unknown inner forces in his musicians. And although few of his sidemen were able to reach similarly high peaks on their own as they had reached with Miles, their growth and self-discovery were genuine: they always played better after having played with Miles than they had before. He helped them to unearth undiscovered countries, to develop different levels of consciousness.

The testimonies of the musicians who played with Miles from 1981 to 1991 indicate that his presence and leadership were as inspiring to them as they had been to his musicians prior to 1976. Yet, Miles's role does appear to have changed somewhat towards the end. With the second quintet and the bands immediately following, he was a leader among equals. Although he was looked at as a father figure by the young musicians in his '73–'75 and '81–'83 bands, there was still a strong element of reciprocity, of collective music making. But as virtuoso players like Marcus Miller, Mike Stern, John Scofield, and Bob Berg began leaving his band, this reciprocity gradually dissolved. Miles more and more stepped into the role of musical mentor, and his one-liners made way for elaborate and explicit instructions to musicians who often were not one, but two, generations younger than he.

David Liebman interpreted Miles's many interviews during the '80s as a very public sign that Miles was taking on this musical mentor role. "In the '80s he acted more like a grand master of the art than he had before," David Liebman commented. "Before, he was still trying, he was still in there, trying to be young still, and now he was in his 50s to 60s. The fact that he gave so many interviews, that he wrote his autobiography, that he really talked. . . . He was so much more outgoing, and it seemed like he was giving out the great knowledge and great wisdom he had."[7]

This "great knowledge and great wisdom" is still an inspiration to musicians today. "The way Miles would turn things around live and the way he reinvented himself was really important for me," Karl Hyde remarked. "The phrase that I always attribute to him is: 'Concentrate but be completely free.' Miles's gigs were about forgetting your preconceptions. It was like: 'Tonight we're doing this for the first time. Forget the record, forget the way you heard it, forget about anything that's precious and the way you think about music.' That idea has become one of the central aspects of our own shows. Miles showed us that."

While Miles has been tremendously successful in translating his heightened consciousness into his music and his methods, it is clear from the stories of his personal life that he was also a wounded hero, a pain-ridden and lonely man, who succumbed to some of the temptations that test the hero on his journey—power, lust, hedonism—and hence prevent him from truly transcending the personal challenges of his origin. The evidence is in the stories of his dark side, his drug abuse, his verbal abuse, his physical violence, as well as in the rage he still carried when he died. The question arises: is his dark side relevant to our assessment of his art? Looking at Miles from the existential paradigm he announced, the answer is affirmative. Ken Wilber has outlined, in the currently dissolving rational paradigm, how art, science, religion, and morals are quite separate, giving rise to the science-for-science's sake and art-for-art's-sake attitudes, with often narcissistic and nihilistic results.

However, the first signs of the emerging existentialist paradigm can be recognized in the demands that scientists take responsibility for the moral and social implications of their discoveries and inventions. The same is also increasingly being asked of artists. A few decades ago the private lives of artists were deemed to have no bearing at all on their art. But more recently revelations of the private shortcomings of artists (as well as other public figures) have become commonplace. Although in part born from a deplorable tendency towards sensationalism, this development nevertheless exemplifies the idea that the personal and the political are interrelated, that separating art, science, morals, and religion into unconnected entities is self-defeating and destructive. Yet the challenge is not to equate these different spheres of human experience again, as was done in the prerational era, but to integrate them while retaining their individual natures and independence.

From this perspective, the attacks on Miles's personal behavior that have emerged since the publication of his autobiography are a step forward. What Miles did in his personal life does matter. But dismissing his musical legacy because of his violence against some women means a regression to the prerational paradigm. From the twenty-first-century existential worldview, an integrated view of Miles is needed—one that encompasses all aspects of his being, and that neither dismisses the greatness of his achievements nor airbrushes some of the depths to which he sank.

Singer Joni Mitchell did her best to do this by making a balance of all of Miles's life. "My two patron saints, Miles and Picasso, are both monsters," she remarked, "but I love them to death. Because they are restlessly creative, they're long runners, they're lifers, they have the potential to reinvent themselves until they snuff. They have to reinvent themselves. That means they need fuel, I think those monsters eat things up around them, in a way therefore appearing monsters to others. Picasso stirred up trouble, anything to keep the flame. In the divinity of it all, they have to be forgiven, because they're monsters in their devotion to their art, which makes them appear extraordinarily selfish.

But it's odd in a way, it's like yin-yang, it's selfless and selfish. It must be done."[8]

From the testimonies in this book and the accompanying analysis of Miles's electric music and its influence, a similar conclusion can be drawn. Despite his destructive sides, Miles Davis had an overwhelmingly life-giving impact on the vast majority of the people who knew him, and on people and musical cultures around the world. In the end, the balance of the life of the Prince of Darkness was greatly biased towards the Light. We may wonder about the strange juxtaposition of a life of sex 'n' drugs 'n' rock 'n' jazz with his unusual musical and spiritual awareness. We may consider the mystery of why he sometimes sank so deeply on a personal level yet soared to such heights in his art. We may ask that final, simple, but utterly unanswerable question: "Who was Miles Dewey Davis III?" But in the end, we can do nothing but, in the words of Rainer Maria Rilke, "live the questions now. Perhaps you will then gradually, without noticing it, live along some distant day into the answer."[9]

We live these questions by holding up the mirrors he showed us of our potential, by taking heed of his directions on how to reach for more than we know. And we live them by listening, between the lines of his words, his music, and his continuing presence.

ENDNOTES

INTRODUCTION

1 Quincy Troupe, "Overview Essay—*Bitches Brew*," in *The Complete* Bitches Brew *Sessions* (Columbia/Legacy, 1998), 41.

2 Joel Lewis, "Running the Voodoo Down," *The Wire* (December 1994): 21.

3 They filter through, for instance, in Geoffrey C. Ward and Ken Burns's *Jazz: A History of America's Music*. For a brief discussion, see Chapter 3, page 40.

4 I am aware of the debates in the field of music aesthetics about the parallels between music and language. I use the word "language" here purely as an analogy, and do not intend to make any implications about these debates.

5 Miles Davis and Quincy Troupe, *Miles: The Autobiography* (London: Picador, 1990), 313.

6 Jack Chambers, *Milestones II: The Music and Times of Miles Davis Since 1960* (New York: Da Capo Press, 1998), 237.

7 Ibid., "Introduction, Freaky Deaky 1980–91," vii.

8 Bill Kirchner, ed., *A Miles Davis Reader* (London: Smithsonian Institution Press, 1997), 3.

9 Gene Santoro, "Miles Davis, Part 1: The Enabler," *Down Beat* (October 1988): 24.

10 For more information, read Marshall B. Rosenberg, *Nonviolent Communication: A Language of Compassion* (Del Mar, California: PuddleDancer Press, 1999).

CHAPTER ONE

1 In 1986 to Ben Sidran. See Sidran, "Talking Jazz," in *The Miles Davis Companion: Four Decades of Commentary* ed. Gary Carner (London: Omnibus Press, 1996), 196.

2 As quoted by Todd Coolman in "The Quintet," *Miles Davis Quintet 1965–1968* (Columbia/Legacy: 1998), 58. Gary Peacock was one of several regular stand-ins during the mid-1960s, when regular bassist Ron Carter could not make a live performance with the second great quintet.

3 To Dave Holland, passed on during an interview with the author. All unannotated quotations in this book are from interviews conducted by the author.

4 To Dave Holland, as quoted by Ian Carr in *Miles Davis: The Definitive Biography* (London: HarperCollinsPublishers, 1998), 247.

5 To saxophonist Wayne Shorter, passed on by the saxophonist in an interview with the London edition of *Time Out* in May of 1999.

6 Nat Hentoff, "Miles's Jazz Life," in Carner, *Miles Davis Companion*, 71.

7 In 1968 to Leonard Feather. See Feather, "The Blindfold Tests," in Kirchner, *Miles Davis Reader*, 134.

8 James Rotondi, "In a Not So Silent Way: The Guitar Legacy of Miles Davis," *Guitar Player* (March 1992): 91.

9 Ibid., 88.

10 Amiri Baraka, "Miles Davis: 'One of the Great Motherfuckers,'" in Kirchner, *Miles Davis Reader,* 68.

11 *Days with Miles,* directed by Per Møller-Hansen, Danish Television, 1986, video.

12 Keith Jarrett, Gary Peacock, and Jack DeJohnette, from the liner notes of the CD *Bye Bye Blackbird* (ECM, 1993). The CD is a tribute to Miles and was recorded two weeks after his death.

13 *Miles & Quincy: Live at Montreux,* directed by Gavin Taylor, Rudi Dolezal, and Hannes Rossacher, Warner Music Vision, 1991, video.

14 Chris Albertson, "The Unmasking of Miles Davis," in Carner, *Miles Davis Companion,* 195.

15 Davis and Troupe, *Miles,* 302.

16 Chambers, *Milestones II,* 192.

17 Ibid., 192.

18 *Miles Ahead: The Music of Miles Davis,* written and directed by Mark Obenhaus, Public Broadcasting Service, 1986, video.

19 Davis and Troupe, *Miles,* v and viii.

20 John Ephland, "Miles to Go," *Down Beat* (October 1988): 19.

21 Bob Doerschuk, "Miles Davis: The Picasso of Invisible Art," *Keyboard* (October 1987): 71.

22 *Miles & Quincy, Live at Montreux.*

23 Jarrett, Peacock, and DeJohnette, *Bye Bye Blackbird.*

24 In *Echoes of a Genius: Miles Davis in Europe,* documentary made by Ulli Pfau, and produced by Brilliant Media in Hamburg, Germany, 1999.

25 Note by Palle Mikkelborg in *Aura's* original notes, reprinted on page 7 of the CD liner notes to the 2000 reissue.

26 Rotondi, "Not So Silent Way," 91.

27 Joachim-Ernst Berendt, *The World Is Sound, Nada Bhrama: Music and the Landscape of Consciousness* (Rochester, Vermont: Destiny Books, 1991), 139.

28 Ibid., 140.

29 Ibid., 148–149.

30 Davis and Troupe, *Miles,* 401.

31 Eric Nisenson, *'Round about Midnight: A Portrait of Miles Davis* (New York: Da Capo Press, 1996), xix.

32 Quincy Troupe, *Miles and Me* (Berkeley, California: University of California Press, 2000), 71.

33 Robert Fripp, *The Act of Music* (Charlestown, West Virginia: Guitar Craft Services, 1989), 10. Fripp has written a series of self-published educational monographs and articles on music, guitar tuition, and music performance that attempt to capture in a methodical way many of the things Miles taught by intuition. Significantly, Fripp is strongly influenced by spiritual ideas and his writings have strong overtones of Zen. He also employs the Alexander technique in his teaching methods. Alexander technique—

an awareness of how we move, sit, and stand—has often been called "the Zen of the West."

34 Leonard Feather, "Miles Smiles," in Carner, *Miles Davis Companion,* 121. The assessment as to whether any of these changes in course can truly be called a paradigm shift is better left to writers fully idiomatic with the jazz idiom.

35 Quincy Troupe, Steve Rowland, Jay Allison, and Danny Glover. *The Miles Davis Radio Project* (Washington, D.C.: National Public Radio, 1990), episode 3.

36 Ibid., episode 1.

37 For instance with Charlie Parker, on December 21, 1947, in "Bird Gets the Worm," take D833-1. Enrico Merlin pointed me towards this gem.

38 Peter Watrous, "Miles Davis: Rebel without a Pause," *Musician* (May 1989): 51.

39 Michael Zwerin, "Miles Davis," *International Herald Tribune* (April 18, 1983).

CHAPTER TWO

1 Hollie I. West, "Black Tune," *Washington Post* (March 13, 1969); quoted by Carr, *Miles Davis,* 209.

2 I have been unable to find a source for this, but it's one of several aphorisms attributed to Miles that does the rounds among musicians.

3 Larry Fisher, *Miles Davis and Dave Liebman: Jazz Connections* (Lewiston, New York: The Edwin Mellen Press, 1996), 176.

4 Called *Miles and Friends* and directed by Renaud le van Kim, it was broadcast in the United States by the Bravo Cable Channel. There also exists a bootleg CD of the full concert, called *Black Devil.*

5 Davis and Troupe, *Miles,* 7.

6 Ibid., 101.

7 Troupe, *Miles and Me,* 59.

8 Gary Tomlinson, "Miles Davis: Musical Dialogician," in Kirchner, *Miles Davis Reader,* 240.

9 In his autobiography Miles names the woman he fell in love with as the French singer Julliette Greco. According to writer John Szwed, author of the exhaustively researched forthcoming book *Dig: A Biography of Miles Davis,* Miles most likely overstated the nature and duration of his relationship with Greco.

10 Davis and Troupe, *Miles,* 126.

11 Irene Cawthon is referred to as Irene Birth in all previous publications on Miles, including his autobiography. However, John Szwed discovered that Birth was the name of her stepfather.

12 Baraka, "Great Motherfuckers," in Kirchner, *Miles Davis Reader,* 64.

13 Davis and Troupe, *Miles,* 79.

14 Davis and Troupe, *Miles,* 258.

15 Les Tomkins, "The Classic Interview: Miles Davis," *Crescendo International* (circa late 1969/early 1970): 28.

CHAPTER THREE

1 Cheryl McCall, "Miles Davis," *Musician* (March 1982): 45.

2 Davis and Troupe, *Miles*, 252.

3 Ibid., 262.

4 Kirchner, *Miles Davis Reader*, 164.

5 Nat Hentoff, "Afternoon with Miles Davis," in Carner, *Miles Davis Companion*, 91.

6 Doerschuk, "Picasso of Invisible Art," 70.

7 Davis and Troupe, *Miles*, 384.

8 Ibid., 263.

9 Bill Milkowski, liner notes to Joe Henderson's *So Near, So Far (Musings for Miles)* (Verve Records, 1993).

10 Ibid., np.

11 This is "Petits Machins," which shows up on recordings by Gil Evans under the title "Eleven." These nine compositions exclude "Teo's Bag," which is credited to Miles, but is actually Hancock's "The Collector."

12 Doerschuk, "Picasso of Invisible Art," 69. Zawinul in turn had become interested in the electric piano when he, as a member of Dinah Washington's band, was touring on the same bill as Ray Charles, who on occasion used a Wurlitzer electric piano.

13 See Chapter 2, page 31.

14 Davis and Troupe, *Miles*, 280.

15 Geoffrey B. Ward and Ken Burns, *Jazz: A History of America's Music* (London: Pimlico, 2001), 448.

16 Ibid., 449.

17 Feather, "Blindfold Tests," in Kirchner, *Miles Davis Reader*, 136.

18 Stanley Crouch, "Play the Right Thing," in Carner, *Miles Davis Companion*, 23.

19 Stanley Crouch, "The Presence Is Always the Point," in Ward and Burns, *Jazz*, 420.

20 In 1968. See Arthur Taylor, "'I Don't Have to Hold the Audience's Hand,'" in Carner, *Miles Davis Companion*, 106. These two sentences are repeated almost word for word in Davis and Troupe, *Miles*, 279.

21 Ibid., 106. Once again, these lines are repeated, with a few words changed, in Davis and Troupe's *Miles*, immediately following the lines mentioned under the previous annotation.

22 Davis and Troupe, *Miles*, 267.

23 Eric Olsen, Paul Verna, and Carlo Wolff, eds., *The Encyclopedia of Record Producers* (New York: Billboard Books, 1999), 844.

24 Chambers, *Milestones II*, 150.

25 The extensive editing applied in the construction of *Miles Ahead* (produced by George Avakian), *Porgy and Bess* (produced by Cal Lampley), and *Sketches of Spain* (produced by Teo Macero and Irving Townsend) is detailed by reissue producer Phil Schaap in the booklet accompanying *Miles Davis and Gil Evans: The Complete Columbia Studio Recordings* (Columbia/Legacy, 1996).

26 Unless otherwise indicated, the track timings in the narrative are based on those in the sessionography—for which Merlin lists the timings of the music itself, rather than the CD track timings. Since most CD tracks are followed by a few seconds of silence, this means that most of Merlin's entries are slightly shorter than those given on the CDs.

27 Davis and Troupe, *Miles*, 279.

28 Quoted by Chambers, *Milestones II,* 119–120. Chambers added that Miles blamed the white color of Beck's skin, which supports allegations of Miles's supposed racism. This issue is dealt with in Chapter 11.

29 *Guitar Player,* 1996, other details unknown.

30 It is unclear whether Beck or Benson participated in the January 25 session. On the basis of the aural evidence, Merlin and I think it was Beck. See sessionography, page 307.

31 Bob Belden, "Annotations," *Miles Davis Quintet, 1965–1968,* 95.

32 Don Demicheal, "Miles Davis," *Rolling Stone* (December 13, 1969): 24.

CHAPTER FOUR

1 Other boxed sets issued to date are *Miles Davis and John Coltrane: The Complete Columbia Recordings, 1955–1961* and *Miles Davis and Gil Evans: The Complete Columbia Studio Recordings.* They are numbered "one" and "two" respectively, while the second great quintet boxed set is numbered "four" and the *Bitches Brew* boxed set "six," meaning that Columbia still has to fill the gaps. This gives an indication of how far ahead the company is planning these sets.

2 Davis and Troupe, *Miles,* 281.

3 Quoted by Howard Mandel in "Sketches of Miles," *Down Beat* (December 1991): 17.

4 Carlos Santana, "Remembering Miles and *Bitches Brew*," *The Complete* Bitches Brew *Sessions* (Columbia/Legacy, 1998), 7.

5 Davis and Troupe, *Miles,* 295.

6 An in-depth portrayal of the origins of jazz-rock can be found in Stuart Nicholson's excellent book *Jazz-Rock: A History* (Edinburgh, Scotland: Canongate Books, 1998). Exhaustively researched, it places Miles and other jazz-rock luminaries in a larger context, while excavating many now-forgotten pioneers of the jazz-rock genre, such as Jeremy Steig, Compost, Mike Mainieri, and John D'Andrea & The Young Giants.

7 Ibid., 79.

8 There is a widespread story that Miroslav Vitous subbed as bassist in between Ron Carter and Dave Holland, but this is incorrect. According to Vitous, in conversation with Enrico Merlin, he only played with Miles in August of 1967, when he was a stand-in for Carter, and in September of 1970, when he filled the gap between Holland and Michael Henderson.

9 The correct title was given by Bob Belden and will be used in the *In a Silent Way* boxed set, which at the time that this book was going to press, was scheduled for release in September of 2001. The track has long been credited to a W. Process and mistitled as "Dual Mr. Tillman Anthony" on the *Water Babies* sleeve. The error is probably based on a misunderstanding. The track was written by Tony Williams, whose full name was Anthony Tillmon Williams, and he must have given the track its long name. Someone, somewhere, probably thought the name was overly long and guessed that the last two words referred to the writer.

10 The mention of Carter in various releases is a mistake.

11 Brian Eno, cover notes for *Music for Airports* (EG Records, 1978).

12 Brian Eno, cover notes for *On Land* (EG Records, 1982).

13 Joe Zawinul's piece had already been played by Cannonball Adderley's band, and was recorded by Weather Report in 1971. It is therefore an important piece in the early development of jazz-rock.

14 From *Downbeat* (July 18, 1974): 35; quoted by Nicholson, *Jazz-Rock*, 137.

15 Davis and Troupe, *Miles*, 286.

16 Chick Corea explained that the remarks in which he put down Miles's leadership capabilities—which were ascribed to him in the *New Musical Express* in February 8, 1975, and quoted by Carr in *Miles Davis* on page 247—were "made up."

17 "This" was performed live a few times by the Miles Davis Quintet between April of 1969 and April of 1970. It narrowly missed being registered for posterity when it was played at Fillmore West in San Francisco on April 9, 1970, the day before the recording of *Black Beauty* at the same venue.

18 Demicheal, "Miles Davis," 23.

19 Andy Widders-Ellis, "John McLaughlin," *Guitar Player* (January, 1992): 80.

20 Leonard Feather on June 13, 1968. See Feather, "Blindfold Tests," in Kirchner, *Miles Davis Reader*, 134.

21 Don Heckman, *Stereo Review* (November 1974); quoted by Nicholson, *Jazz-Rock*, 98.

22 Peter Keepnews, "The Lost Quintet," in Kirchner, *Miles Davis Reader*, 186.

23 Robert M. Pirsig, *Lila: An Inquiry into Morals* (London: Corgi Books, 1992), 50.

24 H. G. La Torre, "A Session with Miles Davis," *Modern Recording* (February/March 1976): 37–38. In addition to the two hours of material recorded on February 18, 1969, there was also the music to consider from another session, on February 20, 1969, featuring exactly the same ensemble as on the eighteenth, during which two tracks, "The Ghetto Walk" and Joe Zawinul's "Early Minor," were recorded. These two tracks were rejected, but will appear as part of Columbia's *In a Silent Way* boxed set.

25 Eric Olsen et al, *Encyclopedia of Record Producers*, 486. The edit points are detailed in Enrico Merlin's sessionography in the back of this book.

26 Quincy Troupe claimed that there were also many overdubs on the album (see page 78 of *The Complete* Bitches Brew *Sessions*), but none are discernible. Moreover, Teo Macero has asserted that, though many studio production techniques were used on Miles's albums, overdubbing was generally speaking not one of them, saying, "How can you possibly get anything but a sterile performance?"(La Torre, "Session with Miles Davis," 37). The final form of *In a Silent Way* was created exclusively through tape editing.

27 Bill Milkowski, *Rockers, Jazzbos & Visionaries* (New York: Billboard Books, 1998), 177.

28 Stephen Davis, "My Ego Only Needs a Good Rhythm Section," in Carner, *Miles Davis Companion*, 155.

29 Dan Morgenstern, "Miles in Motion," in Carner, *Miles Davis Companion*, 114.

CHAPTER FIVE

1 Carlos Santana, "Remembering Miles," 7–8.

2 Tomlinson, "Musical Dialogician," in Kirchner, *Miles Davis Reader*, 247.

3 Greg Hall. "Teo . . The Man Behind the Scene," *Down Beat* (July 1974): 14.

4 Quincy Troupe, "Overview Essay," 92.

5 Dan Ouellette, "*Bitches Brew*: The Making of the Most Revolutionary Jazz Album in History," *Down Beat* (December 1999): 32.

6 *The Miles Davis Radio Project,* episode 5.

7 Phil Sutcliffe, "Radiohead: An Interview with Thom Yorke," in *Q* magazine, October 1997, republished in *Rock's Back Pages* on http://www.rocksbackpages.com/library/files/sutcliffe/00887 sutclif_radiohead.html.

8 Jon Hassell, "Forbidden Fruit," *The Wire* (December 1994): 28.

9 Hall, "Man Behind the Scene," 14.

10 Davis and Troupe, *Miles,* 302.

11 Ibid., 289.

12 Ouellette, "*Bitches Brew,*" 34. Miles also claimed in his autobiography to have met and been influenced by Paul Buckmaster, an English composer and cellist with a classical music background who was exploring jazz and rock at the time. However, Buckmaster does not remember meeting Miles until November 1, 1969, after the trumpeter's concert at Hammersmith Odeon in London. Given that the *Bitches Brew* sessions happened two-and-a-half months earlier, it is difficult to see how the then little-known Buckmaster could have influenced Miles. Miles must have misconstrued the sequence of events in his memory. These inconsistencies demonstrate that not everything in the autobiography can unquestionably be accepted as the definitive truth. See also Chapter 11, 179–180.

13 Davis and Troupe, *Miles,* 289–290.

14 Lenny White claimed that he played on this version, but only Jack DeJohnette is credited, and the aural evidence only reveals one drummer.

15 Bob Belden, "Session-by-Session Analysis," *The Complete* Bitches Brew *Sessions* (Columbia/Legacy, 1998): 125.

16 Strangely, Bob Belden's annotations in *The Complete* Bitches Brew *Sessions* mentions nineteen edits, but only lists sixteen in the detailed editing chart (page 129). Enrico Merlin distinguishes eighteen edits in his sessionography, pages 312–313. Incidentally, all track timings in this chapter refer to *The Complete* Bitches Brew *Sessions.*

17 Lewis, "Voodoo Down," 24.

18 Hall, "Man Behind the Scene," 14–15.

19 This may be the reason Teo Macero displayed a certain bitterness upon reaching old-age—he "knows how to hold a grudge" noted Carlo Wolff in Eric Olsen et al's *The Encyclopedia of Record Producers* (page 485)—and why he refused to be interviewed unless paid substantial sums of money. Although he graciously took this writer out for lunch and answered some brief questions over the phone, since no funds were available, many valuable observations and anecdotes sadly remained off the record.

20 Hall, "Miles: Today's Most Influential Contemporary Musician," *Down Beat* (July 1974): 14.

21 Lewis, "Voodoo Down," 24.

22 Olsen et al, *Encyclopedia of Record Producers,* 486.

23 Davis and Troupe, *Miles,* 290.

24 Davis, "Good Rhythm Section," in Carner, *Miles Davis Companion,* 155.

25 Olsen et al, *Encyclopedia of Record Producers,* 487.

26 Hall, "Man Behind the Scene," 13.

27 There has been some controversy around Billy Cobham's claims that he played on the original *Bitches Brew* sessions, something that was hotly denied by Lenny White. When asked about this, Cobham answered that he felt that the whole issue was blown out of all proportion, because he's not sure what sessions he played on at all. Apparently Miles gave him a copy of *Bitches Brew* with his compliments. Since the album came out several months after the November 1969 and January and February 1970 sessions, of which Cobham had been a part, and the music was radically altered through editing, the drummer genuinely believed for a long time that he had played on the original album. Since Joe Zawinul did not recognize *Bitches Brew* when it was played to him (see page 72), such confusions are understandable. Many musicians had no idea on which sessions they had actually played—or when and whether and how the material was released. Cobham also doesn't remember playing triangle, although he is credited as having played the instrument on the session of February 6, 1970. As so often, the mists of time appear to have covered a lot of historical detail.

28 Merlin elaborated on his concept of "coded phrases" in a lecture called "Code MD: Coded Phrases in the First 'Electric Period,'" which was given during a conference called *Miles Davis and American Culture II,* at Washington University in St. Louis, Missouri, on May 10 and 11, 1996. A transcript, including musical examples and a details analysis of "Spanish Key," is available at Peter Losin's *Miles Ahead* site, at http://www.wam.umd.edu/~losinp/music/code_md.html.

29 Ouellette, "*Bitches Brew,*" 37.

30 Ralph J. Gleason, "Original LP Liner Notes to *Bitches Brew,*" in *The Complete* Bitches Brew *Sessions* (Columbia/Legacy, 1998): 35.

31 Davis and Troupe, *Miles,* 301.

32 Belden, "Session-by-Session Analysis," 135.

33 Ibid., 135.

34 Davis and Troupe, *Miles,* 296–297.

35 Fisher, *Davis and Liebman,* 78.

36 Hall, "Man Behind the Scene," 15.

37 Lee Underwood, "Airto and His Incredible Gong Show," *Down Beat* (April 1978): 16; quoted by Chambers, *Milestones II,* 192.

38 James Isaacs, liner notes for CD reissue of *Circle in the Round* (Columbia, 1979): 9.

CHAPTER SIX

1 Demicheal, "Miles Davis," 25.

2 Trumpeter Freddie Hubbard to Leonard Feather. See Feather, *The Pleasures of Jazz: Leading Performers on Their Lives, Their Music, Their Contemporaries* (New York: Horizon Press, 1976): 45; quoted by Chambers, *Milestones II,* 214.

3 Crouch, "Right Thing," in Carner, *Miles Davis Companion,* 34.

4 Amiri Baraka, "Where's the Music Going and Why?" *The Music: Reflections on Jazz and Blues* (New York: Morrow, 1987), 177–180; quoted by Gary Tomlinson in "Musical Dialogician," in Kirchner, *Miles Davis Reader,* 237. Baraka's remark was made in reference to jazz-rock in general, viewing *Bitches Brew* as one of its main expressions.

5 Feather, "Miles Smiles," in Carner, *Miles Davis Companion,* 131.

6 Tomlinson, "Musical Dialogician," in Kirchner, *Miles Davis Reader,* 234–249.

7 John Litweiler, *The Freedom Principle: Jazz After 1958* (New York: DaCapo, 1982), 111–223; quoted by Tomlinson, "Musicial Dialogician," in Kirchner, *Miles Davis Reader,* 235.

8 Crouch, "Right Thing," in Carner, *Miles Davis Companion,* 34.

9 Ibid., 22.

10 Carner, *Miles Davis Companion,* 21.

11 Chambers, *Milestones II,* 175.

12 Davis and Troupe, *Miles,* 310.

13 Tomkins, "Classic Interview," 26.

14 Demicheal, "Miles Davis," 23.

15 Clive Davis, *Clive: Inside The Record Business* (New York: William Morrow, 1975), 260; quoted by Carr, *Miles Davis,* 226.

16 Gary Giddins, "Miles's Wiles," in Kirchner, *Miles Davis Reader,* 218.

17 Ibid., 221.

18 Chambers, *Milestones I,* 187.

19 Leonard Feather, CD liner notes to *Star People* (CBS, 1983): 5.

20 Ibid., 3.

21 Davis and Troupe, *Miles,* 306.

22 Ibid., 278–279.

23 Demicheal, "Miles Davis," 25.

24 *Washington Post* (March 13, 1969); quoted by Carr, *Miles Davis,* 251.

25 *The Miles Davis Radio Project,* episode 1.

26 Ibid., episode 3.

27 Ibid., episode 5.

28 Ibid., episode 3.

29 Mark Rowland, "Miles Davis Is a Living Legend, and You're Not," *Musician* (March 1987): 87.

30 Fisher, *Davis and Liebman,* 123–124.

31 Davis and Troupe, *Miles,* 60–61.

32 Ibid., 309.

33 Tomlinson, "Musical Dialogician," in Kirchner, *Miles Davis Reader,* 245. The reference to Greg Tate is from "Electric Miles," *Down Beat* (July 1983): 16–18.

34 Tomkins, "Classic Interview," 28.

35 Davis and Troupe, *Miles,* 91.

36 Feather, "Miles Smiles," in Carner, *Miles Davis Companion,* 138.

37 The existential paradigm is sometimes called "postmodern" and the rational worldview is called "modern." Please note that these terms refer to consciousness

paradigms and not to the "modern" artistic style, which is a particular artistic aesthetic that emerged during the twentieth century as a transcendence of the romantic style.

38 Feather, "Blindfold Tests," in Kirchner, *Miles Davis Reader,* 134.

39 Fisher, *Davis and Liebman,* 129.

40 Pat Harris, "Nothing but Bop? 'Stupid,' Says Miles," in Kirchner, *Miles Davis Reader,* 16.

41 Carr, *Miles Davis,* 216.

42 Davis and Troupe, *Miles,* 51.

43 Tomlinson, "Musical Dialogician," in Kirchner, *Miles Davis Reader,* 241–242, 246.

44 On the *Milestones* Web site, http://miles.rtvf.nwu.edu/~miles/sivadselim/nisenson96.html.

45 Chambers, *Milestones II,* 19.

46 Ken Wilber, *One Taste: The Journals of Ken Wilber* (Boston: Shambhala, 1999), 265. With ideas delivered in bits and pieces in a diary format, *One Taste* is even more accessible than Wilber's *A Brief History of Everything* (Boston, Shambhala, 1996), but it is not as systematic and comprehensive.

47 Famously, John Cage experimented with the *I Ching,* a Chinese oracle that can be consulted through throwing coins. However, in attempting to write random, or aleatory, music, Cage made the elemental mistake of assuming that throwing coins for the *I Ching* results in random results. But for the user of the *I Ching* throwing coins is a way of attuning to a wider cosmic order and results in more depth and meaning, rather than less. There's nothing arbitrary or random about it.

48 Acknowledging my own limited, and nonjazz, perspective, I found many of the free-jazz concerts I witnessed in Amsterdam in the early '80s, by Archie Shepp, Misha Mengelberg, Han Bennink, and many others, were entertaining from a theatrical point of view. However, the recordings I bought by them invariably went forever unplayed after at most one listen, because I recognized little or no inherent meaning.

49 Davis and Troupe, *Miles,* 195. Geoffrey C. Ward claims that Miles also said that jazz was "dead." (*Jazz: A History of America's Music,* page 448). However, Ward gives no reference for this. Neither John Szwed nor I have encountered the quote during our research. Ironically, by objecting to a museum approach, Miles did not declare jazz dead, but tried to prevent it from dying.

50 Watrous, "Miles Davis," 51.

51 *Washington Post* (March 13, 1969); quoted by Carr, *Miles Davis,* 251.

52 Tomlinson, "Musical Dialogician," in Kirchner, *Miles Davis Reader,* 238.

53 Wilber, *Brief History of Everything,* 41.

CHAPTER SEVEN

1 To Don Demicheal. Demicheal, "Miles Davis," 25.

2 Chick Corea makes similar sounds on the two live albums that were also recorded during the first half of 1970, *Black Beauty* and *At Fillmore.* For example, check at 10:24 in "Directions" on the former album or around 03:00 in "Saturday Miles" on the latter.

3 Rotondi, "Not So Silent Way," 89–90.
4 McCall, "Miles Davis," 42.
5 Davis and Troupe, *Miles,* 60.
6 La Torre, "Session with Miles Davis," 37.
7 Davis and Troupe, *Miles,* 305.
8 Ibid., 305.
9 Demicheal, "Miles Davis," 25.
10 Milkoswki, *Rockers, Jazzbos & Visionaries,* 177.
11 Nicholson, *Jazz-Rock,* 117.
12 I remember reading this in an interview many years ago. Several of Miles's
   musicians confirmed that they heard Miles say something to this effect, or that he
   could easily have said it, but I have not been able to trace the quote.
13 Julie Coryell and Laura Friedman, *Jazz-Rock Fusion: the People, the Music* (New
   York: Dell Publishing Co., 1978), 172–173; quoted by Chambers, *Milestones II,*
   207.
14 Chambers, *Milestones II,* 208.
15 Leonard Feather, "Blindfold Test: Ron Carter," *Down Beat* (December 1975): 18;
   quoted by Chambers, *Milestones II,* 208–209.
16 Leonard Feather and Ira Gitler, *Encyclopedia of Jazz in the Seventies* (New York:
   Horizon Press, 1976), 33; quoted by Chambers, *Milestones II,* 209.
17 For more information on Pascoal, an article by Bruce Gilman at
   www.brazzil.com/musdec96.htm is informative.
18 Both players are given in the *Live-Evil* CD credits, but only one keyboardist is audible.

CHAPTER EIGHT
1 Keepnews, "Lost Quintet," in Kirchner, *Miles Davis Reader,* 185.
2 Miles briefly reformed his live band of 1971 in March of 1972 after a layoff since
   November. Little is known about what occurred in March of 1972, and it is
   unknown whether "Directions" was performed.
3 Keepnews, "Lost Quintet," 189.
4 Kirchner, *Miles Davis Reader,* 184.
5 Feather, "Miles Smiles," in Carner, *Miles Davis Companion,* 135.
6 See Chapter 5, note 28.
7 The starting point of any new new piece is therefore ambiguous. On the
   Sony/Legacy releases the CD track starting points are given where producer Bob
   Belden considers them most logical from a musical perspective: sometimes at the
   start of a "coded phrase," sometimes when the band falls in behind Miles,
   sometimes at a point in between. Enrico Merlin acknowledges these musical
   considerations, but feels that in this case consistency is most important, and has in
   his sessionography consistently taken the moments Miles begins his "coded phrases"
   as the starting points of the tracks in question.
8 Carner, *Miles Davis Companion,* 82.
9 Merlin has a very different opinion on this issue, see the sessionography entry for
   June 20, 1970.

10 Gary Bartz, "The Hardest Working Band in the Jazz Business," liner notes to *Live-Evil* (Columbia, 1971), 8.

11 Merlin, "Code MD: Coded Phrases in the First 'Electric Period.'" See Chapter 5, note 28.

12 Bartz, "Hardest Working Band," 5.

13 David Rubien, "Keith Jarrett," in *Salon Magazine* (December 2000), at http://www.salon.com/people/conv/2000/12/04/jarrett/index.html.

14 At the time this book went to press the Complete Cellar Door producers, Bob Belden and Adam Holzman, were intending to call this tune "Inamorata." Merlin and I favor the name "Funky Tonk"—see Merlin's note on December 19, 1970, in the sessionography. Since Belden and Holzman hadn't entirely made up their minds yet, it is referred to here as "Inamorata/Funky Tonk."

15 Morgenstern, "Miles in Motion," in Carner, *Miles Davis Companion,* 116.

16 Rubien, "Keith Jarrett."

17 Davis and Troupe, *Miles,* 307.

18 Albertson, "Unmasking of Miles Davis," in Carner, *Miles Davis Reader,* 197.

19 Davis and Troupe, *Miles,* 307.

20 Ibid., 311.

21 Bob Belden, "Introduction," on page 6 of the Columbia/Legacy 2000 reissue of *On the Corner.*

22 *Miles Davis Radio Project,* episode 5.

23 It would have been interesting to hear Jarrett's reaction to his former band member's comments, but the pianist declined to be interviewed for this book, citing health reasons.

24 Davis and Troupe, *Miles,* 311.

25 Ibid., 315.

26 Davis and Troupe, *Miles,* 304.

27 Chambers, *Milestones II,* 228.

CHAPTER NINE

1 Belden, *On the Corner,* 6.

2 This account of the origins of "Red China Blues" was confirmed by saxophonist Dave Liebman in "The Music in General" in the liner notes for the 2000 reissue of *Get up with It* (Columbia/Legacy 2000), 11.

3 Davis and Troupe, *Miles,* 312.

4 Belden, *On the Corner,* 8.

5 Collected and quoted by Bill Milkowski on page 4 of in his liner notes for the first CD issue of *On the Corner.*

6 Ralph J. Gleason, "Miles & Carlos: Music of Philosophy and the Street," *Rolling Stone* 123 (1972): 62.

7 See my note in Enrico Merlin's sessionography for details of the confusion that resulted, page 323.

8 Davis, "Good Rhythm Section," in Carner, *Miles Davis Companion,* 160.

9 Ibid., 154.

10 Mat Snow, review was available on http://www.qonline.co.uk.

11 Panthalassa is the name of the primordial ocean that surrounded Pangaea, the original, unbroken continent. *Pangaea* is, of course, also the name of the live recording Miles made in 1975.

12 *Panthalassa,* front cover.

13 Some of Laswell's quotes can be found in a *Sound on Sound* article by this author on the making of *Panthalassa,* available at http://www.tingen.co.uk/words.htm and http://www.sospubs.co.uk/sos/may98/articles/billlaswell.html.

14 John Fordham, "Miles Ahead," *The Guardian* (February 13, 1998).

15 Richard Williams, "Fixing It in the Mix," *The Guardian* (January 23, 1998).

16 Liebman, "Music in General," 8.

17 Laswell initially did not know from what time period the recording came, and so he imagined, "What if it was [guitarist] Pete Cosey?"

18 According to Jan Lohmann, there are no records of a session on June 2. This makes June 1 a more likely date, because of John McLaughlin's presence.

19 Jan Lohmann, *The Sound of Miles Davis: The Discography: A Listing of Records and Tapes, 1945–1991* (Copenhagen, Denmark: JazzMedia, 1992), 140. This was also confirmed during correspondence with Lohmann.

20 Nicholson, *Jazz-Rock,* 125.

21 There was a follow-up, called *Panthalassa: The Remixes* (Columbia, 1999). This was a remix too far. Dance and techno representatives DJ Cam, DJ Krush, King Britt & Philip Charles, Doc Scott, and Jamie Myerson remixed some of the material Bill Laswell had used on *Panthalassa,* but failed to give any new insights into the music. Laswell's own sixteen-minute remix of "Black Satin" is the most successful, extending on the ideas presented in *Panthalassa.*

22 Chambers, *Milestones II,* 247.

23 Davis and Troupe, *Miles,* 318.

24 Davis and Troupe, *Miles,* 319.

CHAPTER TEN

1 Fisher, *Davis and Liebman,* 89–90.

2 Davis, "Good Rhythm Section," in Carner, *Miles Davis Companion,* 152.

3 Ibid., 153.

4 Davis and Troupe, *Miles,* 319.

5 *Encore,* 1974. No more information is available. The quote was related by both Cosey and Mtume.

6 Miles was not alone in his trouble with successfully integrating Indian and rock influences. During the '60s and '70s the combination of fragile-sounding Indian instruments and the raw power of rock often sounded mismatched. One of the few bands that successfully combined Western and Indian music was Oregon, which included the sitar and tabla player Collin Walcott, who performed on *On the Corner.* But Oregon was an acoustic band. It took until the '80s and '90s for genuinely satisfying hybrids between Indian music and electric instruments to emerge, with bhangra music in Britain, and artists such as Bally Sagoo, Asian

Dub Foundation, U. Srinivas, and the amazing Jai Uttal.

7 Eugene Chadbourne, "Heard and Seen, [Miles Davis in Calgary]" *Coda* (June 1973); quoted by Chambers, *Milestones II,* 254.

8 Sy Johnson, "An Afternoon at Miles's," in Kirchner, *Miles Davis Reader,* 207.

9 NHK TV broadcast, June 20, 1973.

10 Johnson, "Afternoon at Miles's," in Kirchner, *Miles Davis Reader,* 204.

11 Davis and Troupe, *Miles,* 319–20.

12 NHK TV broadcast, June 20, 1973.

13 Albertson, "Unmasking of Miles Davis," in Carner, *Miles Davis Reader,* 192.

14 Sometimes the names they give to the pieces vary. For example, what Merlin calls "Moja" is also known as "Turnaround," or "Turnaroundphrase," after Dave Liebman's description of the tune. These were, however, not titles used by Miles or the band. This book follows Enrico Merlin's logic of naming untitled pieces after the official medley in which they first appear. If a medley consists of more than one vamp, the vamp that has not yet been titled receives the medley's name. For example, "Zimbabwe" consists of four vamps. Three have been previously identified as "Moja," "Nne," and "Tune in 5." The remaining vamp is therefore called "Zimbabwe." Assuming that the generic titles of the medleys on his official releases were Miles's, the advantage of Merlin's method is that the titles given to the individual vamps are also Miles's.

15 Chambers, *Milestones II,* 276.

16 Dave Liebman, "The Miles Experience," liner notes for *Dark Magus* (Columbia/Legacy, 1997): 13.

17 "Frelimo" was a reference to the left-wing liberation movement, founded in 1962, that fought for Mozambican independence from Portugal, and formed the governing party of newly independent Mozambique in 1975.

18 The latter track bears no relation to the double CD of the same name. Mtume has said that "Agharta Prelude" was also once called "Big Fun," but admitted that the titles the various pieces were given changed over time, whereas others never received any titles.

19 Hall, "Most Influential Contemporary Musician," 19.

20 A quarter century later guitarist Henry Kaiser and trumpeter Ishmael Wadada Leo Smith recorded an homage to Miles's '70s music, called *Yo Miles!* Although the recording contains much excellent music and a worthwhile introduction to this music, the production and some of the playing have the same problem as Miles's version of "Calypso Frelimo." It's often too clean, too tidy, and too controlled.

21 Liebman, "The Miles Experience," 11.

22 "Funk" is only known to have been played one other time, in Rio de Janeiro in May of 1974.

23 Hall, "Most Influential Contemporary Musician," 18.

24 Johnson, "Afternoon at Miles's," in Kirchner, *Miles Davis Reader,* 205.

25 Hall, "Most Influential Contemporary Musician," 17.

26 Stephen Davis, "Ich habe keine Ahnung wie man das Ding wirklich spielt," *Stereo* 17 (1975): 32. Translated back from German.

27 Fisher, *Davis and Liebman,* 160–161.

28 Carr, *Miles Davis,* 323.

29 Davis and Troupe, *Miles,* 320.

30 McCall, "Miles Davis," 40.

31 Davis and Troupe, *Miles,* 128.

32 Ron Johnson, "Around the World [Miles Davis in Minneapolis]," *Coda* (March 1973): 37; quoted by Chambers, *Milestones II,* 251.

33 Carr, *Miles Davis,* 319 and 324.

34 John Orysik, "The Scene: Montreal [Miles Davis in Minneapolis]," *Sound* (April 1973): 32; quoted by Chambers, *Milestones II,* 251.

35 Johnson, "Afternoon at Miles's," in Kirchner, *Miles Davis Reader,* 203.

36 Eno, *On Land.*

37 Dominique Gaumont, "Comme j'ai rencontré Miles," *Jazz Hot* (September 1981); quoted by Chambers, *Milestones II,* 270.

38 Antoni Roszczuk, "Ein Producent muss den Kuenstler zu neuem anregen," *Jazz Forum* 50 (1977): 39–40. Translated back from German.

39 Gaumont, "Rencontré Miles," quoted by Chambers, *Milestones II,* 270.

40 Sadly Gaumont died in the late '70s or early '80s, reportedly from a drug overdose.

41 For the reader's convenience, the timings for *Agharta* and *Pangaea* are given as they appear on the CDs, and don't refer to the song starting points as analyzed in Enrico Merlin's sessionography. However, while the music on the second CD of the American issue of *Agharta* is split in two (the ID code falls in the middle of "Ife"), on the superior-sounding Japanese Master Sound edition it is presented as one long medley. In the double timings given here, the first relates to the two tracks on the U.S. edition, the second to the medley on the Master Sound edition.

42 Flibbert J. Goosty, "Sam Morrison," *The Buffalo Weekly* (January 6, 1996), which can be found at http://www.allaboutjazz.com/fringes/a0300_01.htm.

43 Davis and Troupe, *Miles,* 321.

CHAPTER ELEVEN

1 McCall, "Miles Davis," 40.

2 Lohmann, *Sound of Miles Davis,* 165. The date of the first session and the names of bassist and the drummer are unknown. The second session is dated March 2 and featured Miles (organ), Larry Coryell (guitar), Masabumi Kikuchi and George Paulis (keyboards), T. M. Stevens (electric bass), Al Foster (drums), and Bobby Scott (horn charts).

3 Davis and Troupe, *Miles,* 325.

4 McCall, "Miles Davis," 40.

5 Ibid., 40.

6 See page xxi of Chambers's introduction, "Freaky Deaky, 1981–1991," in *Milestones II.*

7 Troupe, *Miles and Me,* 93.

8 Davis and Troupe, *Miles,* 356.

9 Feather, "Miles Smiles," in Carner, *Miles Davis Companion,* 143.

10 Davis, "Good Rhythm Section," in Carner, *Miles Davis Companion,* 162.

11 Fisher, *Davis and Liebman,* 164.

12 Greg Tate, "Silence, Exile, Cunning," in Carner, *Miles Davis Companion,* 236.

13 See pages viii and x of Chambers's introduction in *Milestones II.*

14 Francis Davis, "Miles Antagonists," in Carner, *Miles Davis Companion,* 208–209.

15 Troupe, *Miles and Me,* 6.

16 Feather, "Miles Smiles," in Carner, *Miles Davis Companion,* 121.

17 Davis and Troupe, *Miles,* 84–85.

18 Ibid., 110.

19 Ibid., 66.

20 Mo Nazam, "Northern Soul," *The Guitar Magazine* (November 1994): 30.

21 Quoted by Ian Carr. See Carr, *Miles Davis,* 327.

22 Fisher, *Davis and Liebman,* 166.

23 McCall, "Miles Davis," 40.

24 Ibid., 40.

25 Johnson, "Afternoon at Miles's," in Kirchner, *Miles Davis Reader,* 210.

26 Davis and Troupe, *Miles,* 347.

27 Michael James, *Jazz Monthly* (February 1958); quoted by Max Harrison in "Collector's Items," in Kirchner, *Miles Davis Reader,* 51.

28 British Miles Davis enthusiast Martin Booth's daughter Jeannie in 1990.

29 Davis and Troupe, *Miles,* 257.

30 Nisenson, *'Round about Midnight,* xvi.

31 See Chapter 8, page 128.

32 Nisenson, *'Round about Midnight,* xxvi.

33 Nazam, "Northern Soul," 30.

34 Davis and Troupe, *Miles,* 371.

35 Troupe, *Miles and Me,* 80.

36 Alex Haley, "Miles Davis: A Candid Conversation with the Jazz World's Premier Iconoclast," *Playboy* (September 1962): 58.

37 Nisenson, *'Round about Midnight,* xii.

38 Haley, "Candid Conversation," 62.

39 Ibid., 58.

40 Feather, "Miles Smiles," in Carner, *Miles Davis Companion,* 122–123.

41 McCall, "Miles Davis," 45.

42 Tomkins, "Classic Interview," 26.

43 Demicheal, "Miles Davis," 23.

44 Feather, "Miles Smiles," in Carner, *Miles Davis Companion,* 142.

45 Robert Farris Thompson, *Flash of the Spirit* (Random House, 1984). Quoted by Michael Ventura, "Hear That Long Snake Moan," *Whole Earth Review* (Spring 1987): 30. Ventura's fascinating essay traces the origins of rock and jazz back to voodoo culture.

46 Susan Mullin Vogel, *Aesthetics of African Art: The Carlo Monzino Collection* (New York: Center for African Art, 1986), 21. Quoted by George P. Landow in "Tutu in Yoruba Aesthetics," available at http://landow.stg.brown.edu/post/africa/tutu.html.

47 Ventura, "Hear That Long Snake," 30.

48 Richard Williams, *The Man in the Green Shirt* (London: Bloomsbury, 1993), back cover.

49 Pirsig, *Lila*, 54, 58, 5, and 62.

50 Ibid., 62.

CHAPTER TWELVE

1 Takao Ogawa, "The Doctor Talks about Miles," *1969 Miles: Festiva de Juan Pins*, (Sony, 1993), 7.

2 Davis and Troupe, *Miles*, 330.

3 McCall, "Miles Davis," 43.

4 Bob Blumenthal, "Miles Gloriosus," in Kirchner, *Miles Davis Reader*, 215.

5 McCall, "Miles Davis," 38.

6 Troupe, *Miles and Me*, 45.

7 Robert Palmer, "Jazz Scene: Miles Davis Comeback," *The New York Times* (July 7, 1981): 17.

8 Zwerin, "Miles Davis," *International Herald Tribune* (April 18, 1983).

9 Feather, *Star People*, 5.

10 Richard Williams, "On Top of all That Beat," *The Times* (April 28, 1983).

11 Feather, *Star People*, 4.

12 Davis and Troupe, *Miles*, 344.

13 Feather, *Star People*, 5.

CHAPTER THIRTEEN

1 Davis and Troupe, *Miles*, 345.

2 Ibid., 355.

3 Ibid., 345.

4 Eric Snider, "Miles," *Jazziz* (January/February 1985): 9–10.

5 Ibid., 9–10.

6 Doerschuk, "Picasso of Invisible Art," 69.

7 Snider, "Miles," 9.

8 Ephland, "Miles to Go," 19.

9 Jazz critic Martin Williams, quoted by Chambers, *Milestones I*, 285.

10 Snider, "Miles," 9.

11 To the author.

12 All timings are based on the 2000 reissue of *Aura*.

13 Khephra Burns, liner notes, *Aura* (Columbia/Legacy: 2000): 6.

14 Davis and Troupe, *Miles*, 379.

15 Ephland, "Miles to Go," 54.

16 Francis Davis, "Miles Antagonists," in Carner, *Miles Davis Companion*, 206.

CHAPTER FOURTEEN

1 Watrous, "Miles Davis," 50.

2 Rowland, "Living Legend," 92.

3 Davis and Troupe, *Miles,* 352. Miles and Troupe were mistaken in writing that the rights to "all" publishing were sold. The 50 percent figure comes from Peter Shukat, Miles's business lawyer.

4 Nick Kent, "Prince of Darkness," *The Face* (October 1986): 23.

5 Ibid., 20.

6 Davis and Troupe, *Miles,* 361.

7 *The Miles Davis Radio Project,* episode 5.

8 Some sources have also mentioned sessions spread over two days towards the end of March, featuring Miles, Marcus Miller, Chaka Khan, Prince, and Lenny White, but no other details are available, and nothing has been released. Adam Holzman offered the most likely explanation, which is that the sessions never occurred.

9 Miller referred here to the discussion concerning different musical languages featured in the introduction.

10 Shown in a BBC program aired days after Miles's death.

11 Mike Zwerin, "Top Records of the Decade," *International Herald Tribune* (November 14, 1989).

12 Snider, "Miles," 10.

13 Davis and Troupe, *Miles,* 372.

14 Troupe, *Miles and Me,* 57–58.

15 Interview at Jean-Paul Bourelly's Web site http://www.bourelly.com.

CHAPTER FIFTEEN

1 Davis and Troupe, *Miles,* 285.

2 Doerschuk, "Picasso of Invisible Art," 69.

3 Ibid., 71.

4 Ibid., 72.

5 Rotondi, "Not So Silent Way," 91.

6 Kent, "Prince of Darkness," 128.

7 Indicating the intense interest among Miles fans, in the fall of 2000 a CD bootleg of the Montreux 1986 concert was auctioned for $700 at ebay.com.

8 Davis and Troupe, *Miles,* 367.

9 Ibid., 367.

10 Davis and Troupe, *Miles,* 380.

11 Warner Bros. intends to issue sections of the concert in Paris of July 11, described in Chapter 2, as part of a six-CD boxed set. In addition to featuring the many famous guest performers, the concert also showcases Miles's final live band. The concert included an excellent performance of Prince's magnificent "Penetration."

12 Carr, *Miles Davis,* 545.

13 Frans Steensma, ed., *Oor's Eerste Nederlandse Pop Encyclopedie,* eleventh edition (Amsterdam: Telegraaf Tijdschriften Groep, 1998), 87.

14 Davis and Troupe, *Miles,* 378.

15 Watrous, "Miles Davis," 98.

16 Troupe, *Miles and Me,* 77.

17 Ibid., 107.

18 Carr, *Miles Davis*, 481.

19 Troupe, *Miles and Me*, 77.

CODA

1 Kent, "Prince of Darkness," 128.

2 Rowland, "Living Legend," 86.

3 Watrous, "Miles Davis," 97.

4 Jonathan Romney, "Return to the Music That Time Forgot," *The Guardian* (February 20, 1998).

5 This problem confronted everyone in the '80s, whether working in the areas of rock, jazz, soul, or funk music. At best, artists such as Van Morrison, Lou Reed, Bill Frisell, Herbie Hancock, George Clinton, Marvin Gaye, Ry Cooder, and Tom Waits responded by creating innovative individual styles. But few would argue that they fostered musical directions during this era that transcend what came before them to such a degree that their work could be called a new genre, or could be used as a blueprint for others to base their work on. Like Miles, these artists translated, but did not transcend.

6 Unidentified piece of '80s footage from the video collection of Enrico Merlin.

7 Fisher, *Davis and Liebman*, 170–171.

8 *The Miles Davis Radio Project*, episode 3.

9 Rainer Maria Rilke, *Rilke on Love and Other Difficulties: Translations and Considerations of Rainer Maria Rilke* (New York: W. W. Norton, 1994), np.

BIBLIOGRAPHY

BOOKS:

Berendt, Joachim-Ernst. *The World Is Sound, Nada Brahma: Music and the Landscape of Consciousness.* Foreword by Fritjof Capra. Rochester, Vermont: Destiny Books, 1991.

Buckley, Jonathan, and Mark Ellingham, eds. *Rock: The Rough Guide.* London: The Rough Guides, 1996.

Carner, Gary, ed. *The Miles Davis Companion: Four Decades of Commentary.* London: Omnibus Press, 1996.

Carr, Ian. *Miles Davis: The Definitive Biography.* London: HarperCollinsPublishers, 1998.

Chambers, Jack. *Milestones: The Music and Times of Miles Davis.* New York: Da Capo Press, 1998.

Cugny, Laurent. *Électrique Miles Davis, 1968–1975.* Marseille, France: André Dimanche, 1993.

Davis, Miles, and Scott Gutterman. *The Art of Miles Davis.* New York: Prentice Hall, 1991.

Davis, Miles, and Quincy Troupe. *Miles: The Autobiography.* London: Picador, 1990.

Fisher, Larry. *Miles Davis and David Liebman: Jazz Connections.* Introduction by Phil Woods. Lewiston, New York: The Edwin Mellen Press, 1996.

Fripp, Robert, *The Art of Craft.* Charlestown, West Virginia: Guitar Craft Services, 1988.

Fripp, Robert, *The Act of Music.* Charlestown, West Virginia: Guitar Craft Services, 1989.

Fripp, Robert, *An Introduction to Guitar Craft.* Charlestown, West Virginia: Guitar Craft Services, 1990.

Hardy, Phil, and Dave Laing. *The Faber Guide to Twentieth-Century Popular Music.* London: Faber and Faber, 1990.

Kirchner, Bill, ed. *A Miles Davis Reader.* Washington, D.C.: Smithsonian Institution Press, 1997.

Kuyper, Ruud. *Miles Davis Dichterbij.* Utrecht, Netherlands: Uitgeverij Luitingh, 1988.

Lohmann, Jan. *The Sound of Miles Davis: The Discography: A Listing of Records and Tapes, 1945–1991.* Copenhagen, Denmark: JazzMedia, 1992.

Milkowski, Bill. *Rockers, Jazzbos & Visionaries.* New York: Billboard Books, 1998.

Nicholson, Stuart. *Jazz-Rock: A History.* Introduction by Bill Laswell. Discography by Jon Newey. Edinburgh, Scotland: Canongate Books, 1998.

Nisenson, Eric. *'Round about Midnight: A Portrait of Miles Davis.* Updated edition. New York: Da Capo Press, 1996.

Olsen, Eric, Paul Verna, and Carlo Wolff, eds. *The Encyclopedia of Record Producers.* New York: Billboard Books, 1999.

Pirsig, Robert M. *Lila: An Inquiry into Morals*. London: Corgi Books, 1992.

Rilke, Rainer Maria. *Rilke on Love and Other Difficulties: Translations and Considerations of Rainer Maria Rilke*. New York: W. W. Norton, 1994.

Rosenberg, Marshall B. *Nonviolent Communication: A Language of Compassion*. Del Mar, California: PuddleDancer Press, 1999.

Steensma, Frans, ed. *Oor's Eerste Nederlandse Pop Encyclopedie*, eleventh edition. Amsterdam: Telegraaf Tijdschriften Groep, 1998.

Toop, David. *Ocean of Sound: Aether Talk, Ambient Sound and Imaginary Worlds*. London: Serpent's Tail, 1995.

Troupe, Quincy. *Miles and Me*. Berkeley, California: University of California Press, 2000.

Ward, Geoffrey C., and Ken Burns. *Jazz: A History of America's Music*. London: Pimlico, 2001.

Williams, Richard. *The Man with the Green Shirt*. London: Bloomsbury, 1993.

Wilber, Ken. *A Brief History of Everything*. Boston: Shambhala, 1996.

Wilber, Ken. *One Taste: The Journals of Ken Wilber*. Boston: Shambhala, 1999.

ARTICLES:

Atkins, Ronald. "A Trumpet Fallen Silent." *The Guardian* (September 30, 1991).

Becker, Rob. "Bebop is de moeilijkste muziek." *De Muziekgids* (circa 1995).

Behrendt, Joachim-Ernst. "Miles Davis und seine soehne." Part 1. *Frankfurter Hefte* (December 1971).

Behrendt, Joachim-Ernst. "Miles Davis und seine soehne." Part 2. *Frankfurter Hefte* (January 1972).

Bos, Andy. "Een ijle trompetklank vervlogen in de eeuwigheid." *Music Maker* (November 1991).

Cook, Richard. "Miles Runs the Voodoo Down." *New Musical Express* (July 13, 1985).

Davis, Stephen. "Ich habe keine Ahnung wie man das Ding wirklich spielt." *Stereo* 17 (1975).

Demicheal, Don. "'And in This Corner, the Sidewalk Kid....'" *Down Beat* (November 1969).

Demicheal, Don. "Miles Davis." *Rolling Stone* (December 13, 1969).

Dery, Mark, and Bob Doerschuk. "Miles Davis, His Keyboardists, Present." *Keyboard* (October 1987).

Doerschuk, Bob. "Hancock, from Miles Davis to Interactive Media." *Keyboard* (June 1995).

Doerschuk, Bob. "Miles Davis: The Picasso of Invisible Art." *Keyboard* (October 1987).

Ephland, John. "Miles to Go." *Down Beat* (October 1988).

Fordham, John. "Miles Ahead." *The Guardian* (February 13, 1998).

Gleason, Ralph J., "Miles and Carlos: Music of Philosophy and Street." *Rolling Stone* 123 (1972).

Goosty, Flibbert J. "Sam Morrison." *The Buffalo Weekly* (January 6, 1996).

Haley, Alex. "Miles Davis: A Candid Conversation with the Jazz World's Premier Iconoclast." *Playboy* (September 1962).

Hall, Greg. "Miles: Today's Most Influential Contemporary Musician." *Down Beat* (July 1974).

Hall, Greg. "Teo . . The Man Behind the Scene." *Down Beat* (July 1974).

Hassell, Jon. "Forbidden Fruit." *The Wire* (December 1994).

Keepnews, Orrin. "Miles Davis, His Keyboardists, Past." *Keyboard* (October 1987).

Kent, Nick. "Prince of Darkness." *The Face* (October 1986).

Lake, Steve. "A Not-So-Silent Way." *The Wire* (January 1991).

La Torre, H. G. "A Session with Miles Davis." *Modern Recording* (February/March 1976).

Lewis, Joel. "Running the Voodoo Down." *The Wire* (December 1994).

Lubin, David. Review of Jack Johnson. *Rolling Stone* (July 8, 1971).

Mandel, Howard. "Sketches of Miles." *Down Beat* (December 1991).

McCall, Cheryl. "Miles Davis." *Musician* (March 1982).

Nazam, Mo. "Northern Soul." *The Guitar Magazine* (November 1994).

Nugteren, Hugo van. "Miles Davis doet navolgers verbleken." *NRC Handelsblad* (June 6, 1976).

Ouellette, Dan. "*Bitches Brew*: The Making of the Most Revolutionary Jazz Album in History." *Down Beat* (December 1999).

Palmer, Robert. "Jazz Scene: Miles Davis Comeback." *The New York Times* (July 7, 1981).

Resnicoff, Matt. "McLaughlin: Fulfilling the Promise." *Guitar Player* (April 1996).

Romney, Jonathan. "Return to the Music That Time Forgot." *The Guardian* (February 20, 1998).

Rotondi, James. "In a Not So Silent Way: The Guitar Legacy of Miles Davis." *Guitar Player* (March 1992).

Rotondi, James. "Mastering the Musical Moment." *Guitar Player* (July 1992).

Roszczuk, Antoni. "Ein Producent muss den Kuenstler zu neuem anregen." *Jazz Forum* 50 (1977).

Rowland, Mark. "Miles Davis Is a Living Legend and You're Not." *Musician* (March 1987).

Rubien, David. "Keith Jarrett." *Salon Magazine* (December 2000).

Rule, Greg. "Chick Corea: A Trip Through Time." *Keyboard* (November 1995).

Santoro, Gene. "Miles Davis, Part 1: The Enabler." *Down Beat* (October 1988).

Snider, Eric. "Miles." *Jazziz* (January/February 1985).

Stratton, Bert. "Miles Ahead in Rock Country." *Down Beat* (October 1970).

Tate, Greg. "The Electric Miles." *Down Beat* (August 1983).

Tingen, Paul. "Master of Arts." *Guitarist* (October 1986).

Tingen, Paul. "Miles into the Future: Bill Laswell, Re-shaping the Music of Miles Davis." *Sound on Sound* (May 1998).

Tomkins, Les. "The Classic Interview: Miles Davis." *Crescendo International* (circa late 1969/early 1970).

Ventura, Michael. "Hear That Long Snake Moan." *Whole Earth* 54 (Spring 1987).

Watrous, Peter. "Miles Davis: Rebel without a Pause." *Musician* (May 1989).

Williams, Richard. "Fixing It in the Mix." *The Guardian* (January 23, 1988).

Williams, Richard. "On Top of All the Beat." *The Times* (April 4, 1983).

Zwerin, Mike. "Rio, Women and Colourful Squares by Miles Davis the Painter." *International Herald Tribune* (July 11, 1988).

Zwerin, Mike. "Top Records of the Decade." *International Herald Tribune* (November 14, 1989).

Zwerin, Mike. "Miles Davis." *International Herald Tribune* (April 18, 1983).

LINER NOTES:

Bartz, Gary. "The Hardest Working Band in the Jazz Business," *Live-Evil* (Columbia/Legacy: 1997).

Belden, Bob. "Annotations." *Miles Davis Quintet, 1965–1968* (Columbia/Legacy: 1998).

Belden, Bob. *On the Corner* (Columbia/Legacy: 2000).

Belden, Bob. "Session-by-Session Analysis." *The Complete* Bitches Brew *Sessions* (Columbia/Legacy: 1998).

Burns, Khephra. *Aura* (Columbia/Legacy: 2000).

Corea, Chick. *Black Beauty* (Columbia/Legacy: 1997).

Coolman, Todd. "The Quintet." *Miles Davis Quintet, 1965–1968* (Columbia/Legacy: 1998).

Deffaa, Chip. *A Tribute to Jack Johnson* (Columbia/Legacy: nd).

Eno, Brian. *On Land* (EG Records: 1982).

Feather, Leonard. *Star People* (CBS: 1983).

Gleason, Ralph J. "Original LP Liner Notes to *Bitches Brew*," in *The Complete* Bitches Brew *Sessions* (Columbia/Legacy: 1998).

Isaacs, James. *Circle in the Round* (Columbia: 1979).

Jarrett, Keith, Gary Peacock, and Jack DeJohnette. *Bye Bye Blackbird* (ECM: 1993).

Jeske, Lee. *Agharta* (Columbia: nd).

Liebman, Dave. "The Music in General." *Get up with It* (Columbia/Legacy: 2000).

Liebman, Dave. "The Atmosphere at a Miles Davis Recording Session" and "The Music" *Get up with It* (Columbia/Legacy: 2000).

Liebman, Dave. "The Miles Experience." *Dark Magus* (Columbia/Legacy: 1997).

Maupin, Bennie. "Bennie Maupin on Big Fun." *Big Fun* (Columbia/Legacy: 2000).

Merlin, Enrico. *Yo Miles!* (Shanachie: 1998).

Milkoswki, Bill. *On the Corner* (Columbia: nd).

Milkowski, Bill. *So Near, So Far (Musings for Miles)* (Verve Records: 1993).

Ogawa, Takao. "The Doctor Talks about Miles," *1969 Miles: Festiva de Juan Pins* (Sony: 1993).

Previte, Bobby. *Miles Davis in Concert* (Columbia/Legacy: 1997).

Santana, Carlos. "Remembering Miles and *Bitches Brew.*" *The Complete* Bitches Brew *Sessions* (Columbia/Legacy: 1998).

Stern, Chip. *Filles de Kilimanjaro* (Columbia: 1990).

Troupe, Quincy. "Overview Essay—*Bitches Brew.*" *The Complete* Bitches Brew *Sessions.* (Columbia/Legacy: 1998).

Whitehead, Kevin. *Pangaea* (Columbia/Legacy: nd).

RADIO PROGRAMS:

Troupe, Quincy, Steve Rowland, Jay Allison, and Danny Glover, *The Miles Davis Radio Project.* Washington, D.C.: National Public Radio, 1990. Seven-episode radio series.

VIDEOS:

Days with Miles, directed by Per Møller-Hansen, Danish Television, 1986. Video.

Echoes of a Genius: Miles Davis in Europe, directed by Ulli Pfau, Hamburg, Germany: Brilliant Media, 1999. Video.

Miles Ahead: The Music of Miles Davis, written and directed by Mark Obenhaus, Public Broadcasting Service, 1986. Video.

Miles and Friends, directed by Renaud le van Kim. Video.

Miles & Quincy: Live at Montreux, directed by Gavin Taylor, Rudi Dolezal, and Hannes Rossacher, Warner Music Vision, 1991. Video.

MILES DAVIS'S LIVE-BAND PERSONNEL, 1963–1991

This personnel listing is taken from the moment the first musicians relevant to the electric period joined Miles's live band. It also lists guest performers for dates that are considered to have particular historical and/or musical importance. Unless followed by "only" or "ⓖ," the entries give the starting date of a musician's tenure with Miles's band. For clarity, we also give the entire band line-up at the top of the page and when the band returns to action after lay-offs of more than three months.

KEY	
ⓖ	guest performer
☐	no musician fills this spot
◇	the whole band is not in action

Date	Drums	Percussions	Bass	Guitar	Keyboards	Horn
May 1963	Tony Williams	☐	Ron Carter	☐	Herbie Hancock	George Coleman
July 1964		☐				Sam Rivers
September 1964		☐		☐		Wayne Shorter
January to November 1965	◇	◇	◇	◇	◇	◇
1966 to 1968	Tony Williams	☐	Ron Carter or replacement	☐	Herbie Hancock	Wayne Shorter
January to March 1967		☐		☐		Wayne Shorter and Joe Henderson
April 1967		☐		☐		Wayne Shorter only
early August 1968		☐	Dave Holland	☐		
late August 1968		☐		☐	Chick Corea	
early 1969	Jack DeJohnette	☐		☐		
December 1 to 6, 1969 only		☐		Sonny Greenwich ⓖ		
December 12, 1969		Airto Moreira		☐		
February 1970				occasionally John McLaughlin ⓖ		
April 10, 1970				☐		Steve Grossman
May 1970				☐	Chick Corea and Keith Jarrett	
August 18, 1970				☐		Gary Bartz
early September 1970			Miroslav Vitous	☐	Keith Jarrett only	
September 13, 1970	Airto Moreira and Jumma Santos (Jim Riley)		Michael Henderson	☐		
November 1970	Airto Moreira only					

Date	Drums	Percussions	Bass	Guitar	Keyboards	Horn
December 19, 1970	Jack DeJohnette	Airto Moreira	Michael Henderson	John McLaughlin ⒢	Keith Jarrett	Gary Bartz
early 1971				occasionally John McLaughlin ⒢		
October 18, 1971	Leon "Ndugu" Chancler	Mtume and Don Alias		☐		
November 27, 1971, to March 1972	◇	◇	◇	◇	◇	◇
March 1972	Ramon "Tiki" Fulwood	Mtume only	Michael Henderson	☐	Keith Jarrett	Gary Bartz
March to September 1972	◇	◇	◇	◇	◇	◇
September 1972	Al Foster	Mtume and Badal Roy	Michael Henderson	Reggie Lucas and Khalil Balakrishna[1]	Cedric Lawson	Carlos Garnett
January 12, 1973						Dave Liebman
March 1973					Lonnie Liston Smith	
April 1973				Reggie Lucas, Pete Cosey, and Klalil Balakrishna		
June 1973		Mtume only		Reggie Lucas and Pete Cosey only	☐	
March 30, 1974				Reggie Lucas, Pete Cosey, and Dominique Gaumont	☐	Dave Liebman and Azar Lawrence ⒢
July 1974					☐	Sonny Fortune
January 1975				Reggie Lucas and Pete Cosey only	☐	
April 1975					☐	Sam Morrison
September 6, 1975, to June 25, 1981	◇	◇	◇	◇	◇	◇
June 26, 1981	Al Foster	Mino Cinelu	Marcus Miller	Mike Stern	☐	Bill Evans
November 7, 1982				Mike Stern and John Scofield	☐	
February 3, 1983			Tom Barney		☐	
June 7, 1983			Darryl Jones			☐
June 29, 1983				John Scofield only		
August 15, 1983					Robert Irving III	
November 7, 1983, to May 31, 1984	◇	◇	◇	◇	◇	◇
June 1, 1984	Al Foster	Steve Thornton	Darryl Jones	John Scofield	Robert Irving III	Bob Berg
March 1985	Vince Wilburn Jr.					

[1] Rather than dedicate a whole column to the electric sitar, we have included Khalil Balakrishna in the electric guitar column.

Date	Drums	Percussions	Bass	Guitar	Keyboards	Horn
July 22, 1985	Vince Wilburn Jr.	Steve Thornton and Mino Cinelu Ⓖ	Darryl Jones	John Scofield and John McLaughlin Ⓖ	Robert Irving III	Bob Berg
August 17, 1985		Steve Thornton and Marilyn Mazur		Mike Stern		
September 19, 1985			Angus Thomas			
October 24, 1985					Robert Irving III and Adam Holzman	
March 1986			Felton Crews			
April 4, 1986				Robben Ford		
May/June 1986		Steve Thornton only				
September 8, 1986				Garth Webber		
October 21, 1986			Darryl Jones			
December 28 to 31, 1986 only				Dwayne "Blackbyrd" McKnight		Bob Berg and Gary Thomas
January 24, 1987		Mino Cinelu		Hiram Bullock		Gary Thomas
February 26, 1987				Bobby Broom		Kenny Garrett and Gary Thomas
March 25, 1987	Ricky Wellman					
March 27, 1987				Alan Burroughs Ⓖ		
May 15, 1987				Joe "Foley" McCreary[1]		Kenny Garrett only
October 19, 1987		Rudy Bird				
April 9, 1988		Marilyn Mazur	Benny Rietveld			
October 7, 8, and 9, 1988		Marilyn Mazur and Steve Thornton Ⓖ		Joey DeFrancesco and Adam Holzman		Kenny Garrett and Gary Thomas Ⓖ
December 19, 1988	◇	◇	◇	◇	◇	◇
March 25, 1989	Ricky Wellman	Munyungo Jackson	Benny Rietveld	Joe "Foley" McCreary	Kei Akagi and John Beasley	Kenny Garrett
June 3, 1989					Kei Akagi and Adam Holzman	
July 5, 1989						Rick Margitza
August 24, 1989						Kenny Garrett
September 10, 1989		Munyungo Jackson or John Bigham				
October 29, 1989		John Bigham			Kei Akagi	
April 19, 1990			Richard Patterson			
poss. June 8, 1990		Erin Davis				
November 17, 1990	◇	◇	◇	◇	◇	◇
March 13, 1991	Ricky Wellman	□	Richard Patterson	Joe "Foley" McCreary	Deron Johnson	Kenny Garrett

[1] Foley played (lead) bass, but musically he functioned as a guitar player, which is why he is listed in the guitar column.

DISCOGRAPHY, 1967–1991
by Enrico Merlin

Album titles are listed in chronological order. All the albums are issued under the name of Miles Davis except where noted. The editions given are those that we rate highest in terms of musical and historical importance, completeness, sound quality, and packaging. Where possible we have also given preference to editions that are available in the U.S. market.

1	*Miles Davis Quintet, 1965–1968* (6 CD)	Columbia C6K 67398
2	*Circle in the Round* (2 CD)	Columbia C2K 46862
3	*Directions* (2 CD)	CBS/Sony CSCS 5135/6
4	*Miles Davis & Gil Evans: The Complete Columbia Studio Recordings* (6 CD)	Columbia C6K 67397
5	*Filles de Kilimanjaro*	Columbia CK 46116
6	*Water Babies*	Sony SRCS 5710
7	*In a Silent Way*	Columbia CK 40580
8	*1969 Miles—Festiva de Juan Pins*	Sony SRCS 6843
9	Chick Corea: *Music Forever & Beyond: The Selected Works of Chick Corea 1964–1996* (5 CD)	GRP GRD-5-9819
10	*The Complete* Bitches Brew *Sessions* (4 CD)	Columbia C4K 65570
11	*Bitches Brew* (2 LP/2 CD—first edition)	CBS 66236
12	*Big Fun* (2 CD)	Columbia C2K 63973
13	*A Tribute to Jack Johnson*	Columbia CK 47036
14	*Isle of Wight*	CBS 450472 1
15	*Black Beauty: Miles Davis at Fillmore West* (2 CD)	Columbia C2K 65138
16	*Get up with It* (2 CD)	Columbia C2K 63970
17	*Live-Evil* (2 CD)	Columbia C2K 65135
18	*At Fillmore: Live at the Fillmore East* (2 CD)	Columbia C2K 65139
19	Various Artists: *Message to Love: The Isle of Wight Festival 1970*	Castle Communications EDF CD 327 (2 CD)
20	Various Artists: *Message to Love: The Isle of Wight Festival 1970* (Video)	Castle Communications 054140-3
21	*On the Corner*	Columbia CK 63980

49	Miles Davis & Michel Legrand: *Dingo, Selections from the Motion Picture Soundtrack*	Warner Bros. 9 26438-2
50	John Lee Hooker, Miles Davis, Taj Mahal . . . *The Hot Spot (O.S.T.)*	Antilles 261 140
51	Paolo Rustichelli: *Mystic Jazz*	Polygram/Changes 513 415-2
52	Paolo Rustichelli: *Mystic Man*	Guts & Grace 161-531 065-2
53	Shirley Horn: *You Won't Forget Me*	Verve 847 482-2
54	*Doo-bop*	Warner Bros. 9 26938-2

SESSIONOGRAPHY, 1967–1991

by Enrico Merlin

This sessionography contains information about officially released Miles Davis studio sessions and live performances from December 4, 1967, to August 25, 1991.

The basic format for the entries in the sessionography is as follows:

(1) Date, location, and recording/live/video/post-production/rehearsal

(2) Listing of musicians and the instruments they play

(3) Five columns describing different aspects of the issued track:

Track Title	Attributes	Time	Album	Details
track title	attributes of the issued track (editing details, i.e., whether master or alternate take, etc.)	length of the issued track	release(s) on which the track is issued	variations in the personnel & instrumentation

(4) Explanatory notes, editing charts, and/or musical analysis

For instance:

NOVEMBER 11, 1968   **NEW YORK CITY—COLUMBIA STUDIOS**   **RECORDING**

Miles Davis (tp); Wayne Shorter (ts); Herbie Hancock (el. p) on left channel; Chick Corea (el. p) on center; Dave Holland (b); Tony Williams (d, cowbell)

Track Title	Attributes	Time	Album	Details
Dual Mr. Anthony Tillmon Williams Process	poss. editing	13:20	(6)	TW d; add MD voice
Two Faced	edited mst	18:00	(6)	add MD voice

The above describes a studio session that took place on November 11, 1968, at Columbia Studios in New York City. During this session two tracks were recorded, "Dual Mr. Anthony Tillmon Williams Process" and "Two Faced," with personnel consisting of Miles, Shorter, Hancock, Corea, Holland, and Williams, who play the instruments given. (The key on page 304 explains all abbreviations that may occur.)

The five columns are self-explanatory, with the exception of the "Details" column on the right. In order to present a sessionography that is transparent, sufficiently detailed, and yet concise, I have chosen to use the following formula: under (2) all the instruments are given that the musicians play during the session. The "details" column specifies any changes per track. If nothing is noted in this fifth column, the musicians play all the instruments given under (2). However, if the musician's initialized name appears in the "details" box, the instruments given here take precedence over the data provided under (2). In other words, the musicians only play the instruments given in the fifth column. The only exception to this rule is when an entry is preceded by "add," in which case it is an addition to what is written under (2). So "add MD voice" means Miles's voice is audible on the given track, in addition to any instrument he may play. Finally, "out" means a musician does not play on the track in question at all.

In the above example, "Miles Davis (tp) and Tony Williams (d, cowbell)" are given in (2), meaning that Miles played trumpet on the session and Williams played drums and cowbell. On "Dual Mr. Anthony Tillmon" Miles's voice is also audible, and Williams only plays drums. On "Two Faced" Miles's voice is once again audible, in addition to his trumpet, and Williams plays both drums and cowbell.

A number of aspects demand attention:

• To further musical understanding, and to correct errors in the officially issued releases, the details provided in the sessionography refer to the music itself, rather than to details given in CD booklets. For instance, the track times given refer to the length of the music itself, not to the CD track timings, which are often longer, because CD tracks tend to be followed by a few seconds of silence.

• The same song titles are maintained for different version of the same song, even when different performances are issued with new titles. In these cases, the song's original title is given first, followed by the issued title in brackets. If the two titles refer to essentially the same musical material, the issued title is preceded by a = sign. For instance, "Wili (= For Dave)." If the musical material of the new version is substantially different than the original version, the issued title is preceded by a ~ sign. For instance, "Star People (~ New Blues)." An entry in parentheses that is not preceded by a symbol denotes a normal song subtitle, for instance "Petits Machins (Little Stuff)."

• Many of the vamps and tunes Miles played in his live medleys from 1970 to 1975 had no titles at all. Unless a valid alternative is available, any untitled tune/vamp is named after the first officially released medley in which it appears. See also Chapter 10, note 14.

• For subsequent sessions with identical personnel and instrumentation, the listing under (2) is not repeated.

• When two tracks or musical sections are crossfaded, both the starting point of the fade-in section and the ending point of the fade-out section are given.

• Where the coded phrases occur that Miles often used to cue his band for the next musical section, they are taken as the starting point of the relevant track. (This system was preferred over the alternative—taking the moment the band falls in behind him as the starting point. See also Chapter 8, Note 7.)

• When two editing charts appear side by side under category 4, the chart on the left is always of the most complete version, regardless of when it was released. This makes comparisons between the left and right charts easier.

The information in this sessionography is taken from my day-by-day history of Miles Davis's musical career, in which I list and analyze more than 2,000 issued and unissued live and studio dates, from 1945 to 1991, resulting in 8,246 separate track entries. The information provided in this sessionography amounts to 5 percent of this chronicle.

KEY

afl	alto flute	ss	soprano sax
ann	announcer	synth	synthesizer
arr	arranger	tb	trombone
as	alto sax	tp	trumpet
b	acoustic bass	ts	tenor sax
bars	baritone sax	tu	tuba
bcl	bass clarinet	v	violin
bgo	bongos	voc	vocals
btb	bass trombone	w	assorted woodwinds
cga	congas	wah tp	trumpet with wah-wah effect
cl	clarinet		
co-arr	co-arranger		
comp	composer	add.	additional
cond	conductor	alt	alternative, alternate
d	drums	cont.	continue
dm	drum machine programming	ec	cut at the end of the track
dir	director	exc	excerpt
el. b	electric bass	ic	initial cut, (i.e., cut at the beginning of the track)
el. d	electronic drum		
el. p	electric piano	incl.	including
el. perc	electronic percussion	iss.	issued
el. v	electric violin	mc	cut in the middle of the track
engh	english horn	mst	master
fl	flute	occ.	occasional
flh	flugelhorn	poss.	possibly
frh	french horn	prob.	probably
g	electric guitar, unless otherwise specified	rpm	rounds per minute
		tk	take
k	assorted keyboards	w.	with
m.c.	master of ceremonies	✄	editing point
narr	narration	▶	change of a musical section (i.e., from THEME to solo)
org	organ		
p	acoustic piano	▷	musical change inside a musical section
perc	assorted percussion		

Miles Davis (tp, tubular bells); Wayne Shorter (ts); Joe Beck (g); Herbie Hancock (celeste); Ron Carter (b); Tony Williams (d)

Track Title	Attributes	Time	Album	Details
Circle in the Round	Teo Macero edited mst	33:30	(1)	
Circle in the Round	Stan Tonkel edited mst	26:10	(2)	add MD voice

These are two different masters edited from the same recordings. All material issued on (1) was remixed by Mark Wilder.

In 1968 Teo Macero combined many different takes to assemble a 33:30 master, issued for the first time on (1). Editing chart:

✂ 00:00   INTRO by rhythm section ▶ THEME by Shorter (00:26)

✂ poss. 00:52   THEME by Shorter & Miles (00:52) ▶ Williams first solo (01:19) ▶ THEME by Shorter & Miles (01:45) ▶ Williams first solo cont. (02:13)

✂ 03:14   End of Williams first solo ▶ THEME by Shorter (03:36)

✂ 04:02   THEME by Shorter & Miles ▶ Williams second solo (04:28) ▷ drums out & groove by bass, celeste & guitar (04:47) ▶ THEME by Shorter & Miles without drums (05:02) ▶ Williams third solo (05:27) ▶ THEME by Shorter & Miles (06:18)

✂ 07:01   Hancock solo

✂ 08:42   Miles first solo

✂ 09:07   Miles first solo cont. ▶ Shorter first solo (09:58)

✂ 10:44   Miles second solo

✂ 11:34   Miles second solo cont.

✂ 12:07   Miles second solo cont.

✂ 12:12   Miles second solo cont.

✂ 12:59   Shorter second solo

✂ 13:51   Miles third solo

✂ 15:59   Miles third solo cont.

✂ 16:31   Miles third solo cont.

✂ 18:09   Miles third solo cont.

✂ 19:45   Shorter third solo

✂ 21:22   Miles fourth solo

✂ 22:08   Miles fourth solo cont.

✂ 23:49   Carter solo

✂ 25:26   Williams fourth solo

✂ 27:03   Miles fifth solo

✂ 28:48   Miles sixth solo

✂ 29:54   Shorter fourth solo

✂ 30:50   Miles seventh solo

✂ 31:35   Interplay by Miles & Shorter

✂ 32:05   Interplay by Miles & Shorter

✂ 32:35   Interplay by Miles & Shorter

✂ 33:02   Interplay by Miles & Shorter

Issued on (2) in 1979, this version was assembled by Stan Tonkel, using Teo Macero's master as a starting point. Tonkel cut 07:20 from the original two-track master. Editing chart:

✂ 00:00   INTRO by rhythm section ▶ THEME by Shorter (00:26)

✂ 00:52   First part of THEME by Shorter & Miles

✂ 01:09   End of THEME by Shorter & Miles ▶ Williams first solo (01:19)

✂ 02:22   End of Williams first solo ▶ THEME by Shorter (02:23)

✂ 02:49   THEME by Shorter & Miles ▶ Williams second solo ▷ drums out & groove by bass, celeste & guitar (03:34) ▶ THEME by Shorter & Miles (03:49) ▷ drums out ▶ Williams third solo (04:14) ▶ THEME by Shorter & Miles (05:05)

✂ 05:48   Hancock solo

✂ 07:29   First phrase of Miles first solo

✂ 07:30   Miles first solo cont.

✂ 08:21   Shorter secnd solo

✂ 09:12   Miles third solo

✂ 10:01   Miles third solo cont. (from this point onwards Stan Tonkel's version is identical to Macero's version, starting at 17:19, with the exception of the addition of Miles's voice—see below)

✂ 10:51   Miles third solo cont.

✂ 12:27   Shorter third solo

✂ 14:04   Miles fourth solo

✂ 14:50   Miles fourth solo cont.

✂ 16:31   Carter solo

✂ 18:08   Williams fourth solo

✂ 19:44   Miles fifth solo

✂ 21:29   Miles sixth solo

✂ 22:35   Shorter fourth solo

✂ 23:31   Miles seventh solo

✂ 24:16   Interplay by Miles & Shorter

✂ 24:45   Interplay by Miles & Shorter

✂ 25:16   Interplay by Miles & Shorter

✂ 25:42   Interplay by Miles & Shorter

✂ 26:11   Miles voice

In Macero's master tubular bells (prob. played by Miles) are audible several times between 07:33 and 08:31 and again at 26:57 (the latter stroke is also audible at 19:38 of Tonkel's master).

DECEMBER 28, 1967   NEW YORK CITY—COLUMBIA 30TH STREET STUDIO   RECORDING

Miles Davis (tp, chimes, tubular bells); Wayne Shorter (ts); Herbie Hancock (Wurlitzer el. p, clavinet); Joe Beck (g); Ron Carter (b); Tony Williams (d) on right; unknown (overdubbed snare drum) on left

Track Title	Attributes	Time	Album	Details
Water on the Pond	edited mst, fade out	07:01	(1)	

There's one editing point, at 02:14. Miles plays tubular bells in the bridge. During solo sections Hancock plays only electric piano. During the theme statement, he accompanies on two keyboards.

- Clavinet: 00:09/00:26–00:51/01:01–01:20/01:25–06:37/06:53

- El. piano: 00:32/00:51–01:08/01:19

JANUARY 12, 1968   NEW YORK CITY—COLUMBIA STUDIO B   RECORDING

Miles Davis (tp); Wayne Shorter (ts); Bucky Pizzarelli (g); Herbie Hancock (el. harpsichord); Ron Carter (b); Tony Williams (d)

Track Title	Attributes	Time	Album	Details
Fun	original mst	04:05	(1)	
Fun	edited mst	04:05	(3)	

On (1), Macero's edits described to the right do not occur. No other cuts are audible.

On (3) a twelve-second rhythm-section-only excerpt, occurring immediately after the opening theme statement, is copied and used to replace eight bars of Shorter's solo.

- 00:00   THEME ▶ Shorter solo (00:29)
- ✂ 02:44   excerpt taken from 00:16 to 00:28
- ✂ 02:56   Shorter solo cont. ▶ rhythm section only (03:21) ▶ drum fill (03:27) ▶ rhythm section only led by Herbie Hancock

JANUARY 16, 1968   NEW YORK CITY—COLUMBIA STUDIO B   RECORDING

Miles Davis (tp); Wayne Shorter (ts); Herbie Hancock (p); George Benson (g); Ron Carter (b); Tony Williams (d)

Track Title	Attributes	Time	Album	Details
Teo's Bag (= The Collector)	alt. take; poss. editing	05:56	(1)	GB out
Teo's Bag (= The Collector)	complete mst	05:50	(1)	GB out
Teo's Bag (= The Collector)	edited mst	05:54	(2)	GB out
Paraphernalia		12:36	(1)	add MD voice

The unedited master take of "Teo's Bag," as well as a previously unissued alternate take, were both issued on (1). An edited version of the original master was first issued on (2). Its only edit occurs at 05:37, where the final statement of the theme was replaced by another, better performed statement, lasting four seconds longer.

JANUARY 25, 1968   NEW YORK CITY—COLUMBIA 30TH STREET STUDIO   RECORDING

Miles Davis (tp); Wayne Shorter (ts); Herbie Hancock (p); Joe Beck (g); Ron Carter (b); Tony Williams (d)

Track Title	Attributes	Time	Album	Details
I Have a Dream	rehearsal sequence	06:43	(1)	add MD voice
Speak like a Child	rehearsal tk	02:25	(1)	JB & GB out; add MD & TM voices

On page 109 of the booklet of (1) the guitarist is given as Joe Beck or George Benson. The aural evidence suggests Beck.

FEBRUARY 15, 1968   NEW YORK CITY—COLUMBIA STUDIO B   RECORDING

Miles Davis (tp); Wayne Shorter (ts); Herbie Hancock (p); George Benson (g); Ron Carter (b); Tony Williams (d)

Track Title	Attributes	Time	Album	Details
Sanctuary		08:46	(1)	add MD voice
Side Car I	mst #1	04:56	(1)	GB out
Side Car II	mst #2	03:31	(1)	

FEBRUARY 16, 1968   NEW YORK CITY—COLUMBIA STUDIO B   RECORDING

Miles Davis (tp); Julius Watkins, Ray Alonge (frh); Howard Johnson (tu); Wayne Shorter (ts); Hubert Laws (fl); prob. Danny Bank (fl, alto fl); Romeo Penque (engh); prob. Karl Porter (bassoon); Gloria Agostini or Betty Glauman (harp); Herbie Hancock (Wurlitzer el. p); Herb Bushler (Hawaiian g); Joe Beck (g); Lawrence Lucie (mandolin); Ron Carter (b); Tony Williams (d); Warren Smith (marimba, timpani); Gil Evans (arr, cond); Teo Macero (co-dir)

Track Title	Attributes	Time	Album	Details
Falling Water	tk 4	03:42	(4)	
Falling Water	tk 6	04:22	(4)	
Falling Water	tk 8	04:14	(4)	
Falling Water	tk 9	04:18	(4)	

MAY 15, 1968   NEW YORK CITY—COLUMBIA STUDIO B   RECORDING

Miles Davis (tp); Wayne Shorter (ts); Herbie Hancock (p); Ron Carter (b); Tony Williams (d)

Track Title	Attributes	Time	Album	Details
Country Son	tk 1, mst, ic	13:48	(1)	unknown (voice)
Country Son	tk 3, alt	14:37	(1)	

The beginning of the master take was lost.

MAY 16, 1968   NEW YORK CITY—COLUMBIA STUDIO B   RECORDING

Track Title	Attributes	Time	Album	Details
Black Comedy	tk 2, alt, fade out	06:23	(1)	
Black Comedy	tk 12, mst	07:23	(1)	

Miles Davis (tp); Wayne Shorter (ts); Herbie Hancock (el. p); Ron Carter (el. b); Tony Williams (d)

Track Title	Attributes	Time	Album	Details
Stuff	edited mst	16:57	(1)	add MD voice

The long opening theme statement was created through editing. There may be more edits than are detailed below.

✂ 00:00   INTRO by rhythm section ▷ 00:18 Miles whispers something ▶ THEME by Miles & Shorter (00:30)

✂ poss. 00:54   THEME by Miles & Shorter (cont.)

✂ 01:50   THEME by Miles & Shorter (cont.) ▶ Miles (05:54); Shorter (09:06); Hancock (12:13); Williams (14:00) ▶ THEME by Miles & Shorter (14:35) ▶ Coda by rhythm section (15:53)

Track Title	Attributes	Time	Album	Details
Petits Machins (Little Stuff)		08:04	(1)	add prob. Gil Evans (arr)

Miles is credited as composer of "Petits Machins (Little Stuff)," but the theme is identical to that of "Eleven," performed by Gil Evans and his orchestra. The song was most likely either co-written by Miles and Gil or written by Gil Evans alone.

Track Title	Attributes	Time	Album	Details
Tout de Suite	tk 5, alt	14:35	(1)	
Tout de Suite	tk 9, mst	14:03	(1)	

Track Title	Attributes	Time	Album	Details
Filles de Kilimanjaro (Girls of Kilimanjaro)		11:59	(1)	

Miles Davis (tp); Wayne Shorter (ts); Chick Corea (RMI el. p); Dave Holland (b); Tony Williams (d)

Track Title	Attributes	Time	Album	Details
Mademoiselle Mabry (Miss Mabry)	edited mst	16:29	(5)	
Frelon Brun (Brown Hornet)	ec	05:35	(5)	

Miles Davis (tp); Wayne Shorter (ts); Chick Corea (Wurlitzer el. p) on left channel; Herbie Hancock (Fender Rhodes el. p) on center; Dave Holland (b); Tony Williams (d, cowbell)

Track Title	Attributes	Time	Album	Details
Dual Mr. Anthony Tillmon Williams Process	edited mst	13:20	(6)	TW d; add MD voice
Two Faced	edited mst	18:00	(6)	add MD voice

Editing chart for "Two Faced":

• THEME #1 by Miles & Shorter (00:00) ▶ THEME #1 rhythm section arrangement only (00:22) ▶ THEME #2 paraphrase by Miles (00:42) ▶ Miles first solo (01:18) ▶ rhythm section only (01:44)

✂ 01:56   THEME #1 rhythm section arrangement only (two times) ▶ Interplay by Corea & Hancock (02:37)

▶ THEME #1 rhythm section arrangement only (04:56) ▶ THEME #1 by Shorter (05:16) ▶ THEME #2 by Shorter (05:37—two times) ▶ Shorter first solo (06:17) ▶ THEME #1 by Shorter (07:40—two times)

✂ 08:22   THEME #2 by Miles & Shorter (canon—three times) ▶ Interplay by Corea & Hancock (09:22) ▶ Miles second solo (12:02); Shorter second solo (14:30)

✂ prob. 15:39   THEME #1 rhythm section arrangement only (two times) ▶ Interplay by Corea & Hancock (16:19) ▶ THEME #2 by Miles & Shorter (17:18—canon—two times)

| NOVEMBER 12, 1968 | NEW YORK CITY—COLUMBIA STUDIO B | | | RECORDING |

Miles Davis (tp); Wayne Shorter (ts); Chick Corea (Wurlitzer el. p) on left channel; Herbie Hancock (Fender Rhodes el. p) on right; Dave Holland (b); Tony Williams (d)

Track Title	Attributes	Time	Album	Details
Splash	edited mst	08:30	(2)	

| NOVEMBER 27, 1968 | NEW YORK CITY—COLUMBIA STUDIO B | | | RECORDING |

Miles Davis (tp); Wayne Shorter (ss, ts); Chick Corea (Wurlitzer el. p); Herbie Hancock (Fender Rhodes el. p); Joe Zawinul (Fender Rhodes el. p, org); Dave Holland (b); Jack DeJohnette (d); Teo Macero (tamb on "Ascent, part 1")

Track Title	Attributes	Time	Album	Details
Directions I	tk 1	06:46	(3)	JZ el. p; add MD voice
Directions II	tk 2	04:49	(3)	WS ss, ts; JZ el. p
Ascent	edited mst	14:38	(3)	JZ org

Note: There were three takes of "Ascent," edited together as follows:

✂ 00:00   Keyboard prelude

✂ 04:35   Shorter first solo ▶ Keyboard interlude (07:09) ▶ Shorter first solo (09:18)

✂ 09:39   First part of Miles solo

✂ 12:03   Second part of Miles solo

| FEBRUARY 18, 1969 | NEW YORK CITY—COLUMBIA STUDIO B | | | RECORDING |

Miles Davis (tp); Wayne Shorter (ss); Chick Corea (Wurlitzer el. p) on left channel; Herbie Hancock (Fender Rhodes el. p) on center; Joe Zawinul (org) on right; John McLaughlin (g); Dave Holland (b); Tony Williams (d)

Track Title	Attributes	Time	Album	Details
Shhh/Peaceful	edited mst	17:58	(7)	

✂ 00:00   INTRO by McLaughlin & Zawinul

✂ 00:06   McLaughlin first solo

✂ 01:33   Miles solo ▶ Interplay by rhythm section (05:16)

✂ 05:55   McLaughlin second solo (no drums)

✂ 06:14   McLaughlin second solo cont.; Shorter solo (09:12)

✂ 10:42   Interplay by Corea, Hancock, Zawinul & McLaughlin

✂ 11:55   Duplication of first, second, and third sections (00:00/05:54) followed by fade-out (00:09)

Miles develops his solo starting from a phrase he often used, for instance in "Country Son" and "Petits Machins."

Track Title	Attributes	Time	Album	Details
In a Silent Way	edited mst	04:15	(7)	
It's about That Time	edited mst	11:28	(7)	add MD voice

The two compositions are edited together as follows:

✂ 00:01   In a Silent Way

✂ 04:15   It's about That Time

✂ 15:43   In a Silent Way

The final version of "In a Silent Way" is a duplication of the opening statement.

"It's about That Time" is based on three basic elements, called "#1," "#2," and "#3" below, which Joe Zawinul has claimed were written by him. Sections "#1" and "#2" share the same bass vamp in F mixolydian, but "#2" is characterized by a descending chord progression of three bars recalling the first phrase of Miles's solo in "Directions I." The mood of section "#1" is more relaxed than of "#2," which is more funky and syncopated. Section "#3" has a longer, highly melodic bass vamp on the F myxolidian scale and is played by several instruments. In some cases one section fades into the next one (e.g., during Miles solo).

Editing chart for "It's about That Time":

✂ 04:15   Miles solo on "#1." This excerpt is duplicated from 13:58 to 14:45 of the issued master

✂ 05:02   Electric piano plays chord progression of "#2" (unidentified voice at 5:13)

✂ 05:36   Different excerpt of "#2" McLaughlin solo (05:47) first on "#2" then on "#3" (08:24)

✂ 09:14   Electric piano playing chord progression of "#2" Shorter solo on "#2" (09:36) and "#3" (10:33)

• 11:56   Miles solo on following sections:

• 11:56   "#2" changes gradually back to "#1"

• 12:46   "#3" changes slowly into in "#1" (the process begins at 13:50 and is completed at 13:58)

• 14:45   Miles solo on "#3," ending at 15:18, rhythm section continues to groove on "#3" until the end at 15:42

JULY 25, 1969	JUAN-LES-PINS FESTIVAL, ANTIBES (FRANCE)— PINEDE GOULD "FESTIVAL DU JAZZ"			LIVE

Miles Davis (tp); Wayne Shorter (ss, ts); Chick Corea (el. p); Dave Holland (b); Jack DeJohnette (d)

Track Title	Attributes	Time	Album	Details
Directions		06:00	(8)	WS ts
Miles Runs the Voodoo Down		09:16	(8)	WS ss
Miles (= Milestones)		13:45	(8)	WS ts
Footprints		11:36	(8)	
'Round Midnight		08:23	(8)	WS ts
I Fall in Love too Easily		00:36	(8)	WS out
It's about That Time		09:31	(8)	WS ss
Sanctuary		04:15	(8)	WS ss
The Theme		00:13	(8)	WS ss

JULY 26, 1969	JUAN-LES-PINS, ANTIBES (FRANCE)—PINEDE GOULD "FESTIVAL DU JAZZ"			LIVE
Track Title	Attributes	Time	Album	Details
Spanish Key	exc	00:11	(9)	WS ss
I Fall in Love too Easily		02:54	(9)	WS, DH, JDJ out

Note: The original master of "Spanish Key" was 10:32.

AUGUST 19, 1969	NEW YORK CITY—COLUMBIA STUDIO B			RECORDING

Miles Davis (tp); Wayne Shorter (ss); Bennie Maupin (bcl); Joe Zawinul (el. p) on left; Chick Corea (el. p) on right; John McLaughlin (g); Harvey Brooks (el. b) on left; Dave Holland (b) on center; Lenny White (d) on left; Jack DeJohnette (d) on right; Don Alias (cga, poss. bgo); Jim "Jumma Santos" Riley (pandeiro, shaker, perc)

Track Title	Attributes	Time	Album	Details
Bitches Brew	edited mst	26:56	(10)	add MD voice

From the liner notes by Bob Belden in *The Complete* Bitches Brew *Sessions* (10) we know that the track "Bitches Brew" was originally conceived as a five-part suite. Only three sections ended up on (10). The issued master of "Bitches Brew" is composed from two of these sections: the first section is used as Intro, Interlude, and Coda, the second section as a vamp for soloing. The third section became "John McLaughlin." All material issued on (10) was remixed by Mark Wilder in 1998.

INTRO
- 00:00 Bass vamp #1
- 00:41 THEME by Miles w. echo ▷ THEME by Miles & Shorter

SOLOS SECTION #1
- ✂ (a) 02:50 Bass vamp #2 by Brooks & Alias
- (b) 02:56 Bass vamp #2 by Brooks, Maupin & Alias
- ✂ (b) 03:01 Duplication of (b)
- ✂ (b) 03:07 Duplication of (b)
- ✂ (b) 03:12 Duplication of (b)
- ✂ (ab) 03:17 Duplication of (a) & (b) in straight sequence
- ✂ (b) 03:27 Duplication of (b)
- 03:32 The rest of the rhythm section comes in and the tape rolls without any cuts until 10:36
- Solos: Miles (03:54/06:20); McLaughlin (06:32/07:26) ▷ Groove ▷ McLaughlin (07:50/08:55); Miles (08:55 . . .)
- ✂ 10:36 Duplication of last brief passage (from 10:31 through 10:36) and new fragment (five notes by Miles tp) until 10:42
- ✂ 10:42 Duplication of last brief passage (from 10:36 through 10:42) and new fragment until 10:52
- ✂ 10:52 Duplication of last brief passage (from 10:42) and continuation of Miles solo until 11:28; Shorter (11:39/12:36); brief Holland solo (12:36 . . .)
- ✂ 12:42 Groove ▶ Corea (12:49 . . .)
- ✂ 13:28 Corea cont.

INTERLUDE
- ✂ 14:36 Bass vamp #1 ▶ THEME by Miles w. echo (15:55)

SOLOS SECTION #2
- ✂ 17:20 Bass vamp #2 ▶ Solos: Holland (17:29/19:18); Miles (19:23/20:11) ▷ Groove ▷ Miles (20:58/21:48)
- ✂ 22:01 Groove ▶ Zawinul (22:31)

CODA
- ✂ 24:04 Duplication of the introduction (00:00 to 02:50)

During the first solo section, Dave Holland improvises beneath the main soloists. From 18:02 onwards the "subterrean"-improviser role goes to Bennie Maupin. At 05:51 Miles quotes and disfigures the theme of "Spinning Wheel" by Blood, Sweat & Tears. In fact, Miles's entire solo of 03:54/06:20 can be interpreted as a parody of the theme of "Spinning Wheel."

Bennie Maupin (bcl); Joe Zawinul (el. p) on left; Chick Corea (el. p) on right; John McLaughlin (g); Harvey Brooks (el. b); Dave Holland (b); Lenny White (d) on left; Jack DeJohnette (d) on right; Don Alias (cowbell, pandeiro, perc); Jim "Jumma Santos" Riley (shaker, perc); Miles Davis (dir, comp)

Track Title	Attributes	Time	Album	Details
John McLaughlin	edited mst	04:22	(10)	

Miles Davis (tp); Wayne Shorter (ss); Chick Corea (el. p); Dave Holland (b); Jack DeJohnette (d); Don Alias (bgo, cga); Jim "Jumma Santos" Riley (shaker)

Track Title	Attributes	Time	Album	Details
Sanctuary	two takes edited together	10:55	(10)	

Editing point at 05:13.

Miles Davis (tp); Wayne Shorter (ss); Bennie Maupin (bcl); Joe Zawinul (el. p) on left; Chick Corea (el. p) on right; John McLaughlin (g); Harvey Brooks (el. b) on center; Dave Holland (el. b) on left; Don Alias (d, perc, poss. cga) on left; Jack DeJohnette (d) on center; Jim "Jumma Santos" Riley (shaker, perc) on left

Track Title	Attributes	Time	Album	Details
Miles Runs the Voodoo Down edited mst		14:03	(10)	

Miles Davis (tp); Wayne Shorter (ss); Bennie Maupin (bcl); Joe Zawinul (el. p) on left; Larry Young (el. p) on center; Chick Corea (el. p) on right; John McLaughlin (g); Harvey Brooks (el. b); Dave Holland (b); Lenny White (d) on left; Jack DeJohnette (d) on right; Don Alias (cga, pandeiro, perc); Jim "Jumma Santos" Riley (shaker, perc)

Track Title	Attributes	Time	Album	Details
Spanish Key	tk 4, mst	17:32	(10)	add MD voice
Pharaoh's Dance	first edited mst	20:03	(11)	DA cg pe
Pharaoh's Dance	second edited mst	20:03	(10)	DA cg pe; add MD voice

For unknown reasons, on the original vinyl edition (11), "Pharaoh's Dance," has a four-second keyboard passage not occurring on every CD reissue I have heard, with the exception of the very first CD reissue, CDCBS66236, which is the only one identical to the original vinyl version. The additional four seconds appear at 08:29/08:33 in the left-hand table. The altered version of "Pharaoh's Dance" in the right table compensates for the lost four seconds with a longer fade-out at the end. Differences in analog tape speed cause some of the slight time differences between the left and right tables in the third and fourth sections.

Original LP version—Editing chart:

SECTION 1 (Theme sequence)

✂ (a) 00:00   Intro & THEME #1 (00:03) two times

✂ (b) 00:15   Vamp #2 & THEME #2 (00:20)

✂ (c) 00:46   THEME #2

✂ (b) 00:56   Duplication of Vamp #2 & THEME #2 (b) starting from 00:15

✂ (c) 01:29   Duplication of THEME #2 (c) starting from 00:46

✂ (a') 01:39   Duplication of an exc of (a) from 00:03 through 00:15 (THEME #1)

(THEME #1)

✂ (b) 01:50   Duplication of THEME #2 (c) starting from 00:46

✂ (c) 02:22   Duplication of THEME #2 (c) starting from 00:46

SECTION 2 (Solos first sequence)

✂ 02:32   Miles solo briefly

✂ 02:54   THEME #1 ▶ Miles solo (03:31); Maupin (05:41) ▶ THEME #1 by Corea & Maupin (07:33)

✂ 07:55   Vamp #1 & Interplay by Zawinul, Young, Corea & McLaughlin

SECTION 3 (Interlude & microediting sequence)

✂ poss. 08:29   Brief keyboards passage

✂ 08:33   INTERLUDE: delay effects added to trumpet (08:40)

✂ 08:46   Duplication of exc between 08:44 & 08:46

New, remixed master on (10)—Editing chart:

SECTION 1 (Theme sequence)

✂ (a) 00:00   Intro & THEME #1 (00:03) two times

✂ (b) 00:15   Vamp #2 & THEME #2 (00:20)

✂ (c) 00:46   THEME #2

✂ (b) 00:56   Duplication of Vamp #2 & THEME #2 (b) starting from 00:15

✂ (c) 01:29   Duplication of THEME #2 (c) starting from 00:46

✂ (a') 01:39   Duplication of an exc of (a) from 00:03 through 00:15 (THEME #1)

✂ (b) 01:50   Duplication of Vamp #2 & THEME #2 (b) starting from 00:15

✂ (c) 02:22   Duplication of THEME #2 (c) starting from 00:46

SECTION 2 (Solos first sequence)

✂ 02:32   Miles solo

✂ 02:54   THEME #1 ▶ Miles solo (03:31); Maupin (05:41) ▶ THEME #1 by Corea & Maupin (07:33)

✂ 07:55   Vamp #1 & Interplay by Zawinul, Young, Corea & McLaughlin

SECTION 3 (Interlude & micro-editing sequence)

✂ 08:29   INTERLUDE: delay effects added to trumpet (08:40); at 08:39 the accurate new remastering reveals a voice, prob. Miles, saying "Hey Joe!" not audible in previous editions

✂ 08:42   Duplication of exc between 08:40 & 08:42

≫ 08:48   Duplication of exc between 08:33 & 08:41

≫ 08:57 to 9:05   A fragment of around one second (taken from 08:43 to 08:44 of the issued mst) is looped five times

SECTION 4 (Solos second sequence)

≫ 09:06   Miles solo cont. ▷ Interplay by Miles & Maupin (10:41) ▷ Interplay by Maupin & electric pianos (11:06) ▶ Shorter (11:51); McLaughlin (12:58) ▶ electric piano paraphrases the THEMES #1 & #2 (14:09)

≫ 15:24   INTRO of CLOSING THEME by Zawinul, Young, Corea ▷ at 16:07 Bennie Maupin join in ▶ CLOSING THEME (eight times) by Miles (16:43)

≫ 08:44   Duplication of exc between 08:29 & 08:37

≫ 08:53 to 09:00   A fragment of around one second (taken from 08:39 to 08:40, and with a voice calling "Hey Joe!" audible in the new mix) is looped five times

SECTION 4 (Solos second sequence)

≫ 09:00   Miles solo cont. ▷ Interplay by Miles & Maupin (10:37) ▷ Interplay by Maupin & electric pianos (11:01) ▶ Shorter (11:47); McLaughlin (12:53) ▶ electric piano paraphrases the THEMES #1 & #2 (14:04)

≫ 15:19   INTRO of CLOSING THEME by Zawinul, Young, Corea ▷ at 16:01 Bennie Maupin join in ▶ CLOSING THEME (eight times) by Miles (16:38)

NOVEMBER 19, 1969   NEW YORK CITY—COLUMBIA STUDIO E   RECORDING

Miles Davis (tp); Steve Grossman (ss); Bennie Maupin (bcl); Herbie Hancock (el. p) on left; Chick Corea (el. p) on right; John McLaughlin (g) on left; Khalil Balakrishna (sitar, tampura) on right; Ron Carter (b) on left; Harvey Brooks (el. b) on center; Billy Cobham (d, triangle); Airto Moreira (wood blocks, cuica, sheep bells, berimbau, cuica, guiro, agogo bells, perc, voc) on left; Bihari Sharma (tabla, tampura) on right

Track Title	Attributes	Time	Album	Details
Great Expectations	edited mst; two exc on 45 rpm	13:43	(10)	KB si, prob. tam; BC d; AM wo cu sh pe

Note: The theme is performed eighteen times by tp & bcl:

• 00:00   Three times (muted tp); three times (open tp)

≫ 04:38   Four times (muted tp); seven times (open tp); one time (muted tp)

"Great Expectations" and "Orange Lady" were originally issued on *Big Fun* (12) as one track called "Great Expectations." On (10) the two tracks were separated and given their respective titles. The four original tracks of the 1974 release of (12)—"Great Expectations," "Ife," "Go ahead John," and "Lonely Fire"—were reissued in identical form on the 2000 rerelease of *Big Fun*. From the aural evidence (12) is indistinguishable from the 1997 Japanese Master Sound edition.

Track Title	Attributes	Time	Album	Details
Orange Lady (Mulher Laranja)	edited mst 1; exc on 45 rpm	13:45	(12)	AM be cu gu pe; add MD voice
Orange Lady (Mulher Laranja)	edited mst 2	13:45	(10)	AM be cu gu pe; add MD voice

The master on (12) runs faster, but the length of the two versions is identical because the version on (12) contains a six-second edited repeat not present on (10).

On (12) "Orange Lady (Mulher Laranja)" was edited together with "Great Expectations" and begins at 13:37 of the combined track.

Editing chart:

≫ 13:37   Intro ▶ THEME A (14:04) ▶ THEME B (14:56/16:25/18:05/19:55) ▶ Groove (21:19)

≫ 25:00   Duplication of 24:54 to 25:00 ▶ THEME A (25:06)

≫ 26:00   Intro ▶ THEME A (26:08) ▷ fade out (27:22)

Miles's voice at 24:54 is duplicated at 25:00.

An excerpt of "Orange Lady (Mulher Laranja)" was used to create a 45 rpm, mistitled "Great Expectations" on (14).

Editing chart of master on (10):

• 00:00   Intro ▶ THEME A (00:27) ▶ THEME B (01:19/02:49/04:30/06:20) ▶ Groove (07:45) ▶ THEME A (11:28)

≫ 12:22   Intro ▶ THEME A (12:31) ▷ fade-out (13:45)

Miles's voice has become audible in Wilder's remix, at 11:23 and at 13:43.

Track Title	Attributes	Time	Album	Details
Yaphet		09:38	(10)	AM be cu pe; add MD voice
Corrado		13:11	(10)	AM ab pe voc; add MD & TM voices

NOVEMBER 28, 1969   NEW YORK CITY—COLUMBIA STUDIO E   RECORDING

Miles Davis (tp); Steve Grossman (ss); Bennie Maupin (bcl); Herbie Hancock (el. p) on left; Larry Young (org, celeste) on center; Chick Corea (el. p) on right; John McLaughlin (g); Khalil Balakrishna (sitar) on left; Dave Holland (b) on right; Harvey Brooks (el. b) on left; Jack DeJohnette (d) on right; Billy Cobham (d, triangle, sheep bells, pandeiro) on right; Airto Moreira (cuica, perc) on left; Bihari Sharma (tabla, tampura) on left

Track Title	Attributes	Time	Album	Details
Trevere		05:55	(10)	BC tr sh; AM cu; add MD voice
The Big Green Serpent	mc at 1:58	03:35	(10)	BC sh pe ▷ left; BS tab
The Little Blue Frog	tk 3, alt	12:13	(10)	JDJ out; BC d tr; add MD voice
The Little Blue Frog	tk 4, mst; edited mst (2:36) on 45 rpm	09:09	(10)	BC d tr; add MD voice only on 45 rpm

JANUARY 27, 1970   NEW YORK CITY—COLUMBIA STUDIO B   RECORDING

Miles Davis (tp); Wayne Shorter (ss); Bennie Maupin (bcl); Joe Zawinul (el. p) on left; Chick Corea (el. p, ring modulator) on right; Khalil Balakrishna (sitar, tampura) on right; Dave Holland (el. b); Billy Cobham (d, vibraslap, perc) on left; Jack DeJohnette (d, sheep bells, shaker, perc) on right; Airto Moreira (agogo bells, guiro, sheep bells, berimbau, cuica, pandeiro, perc)

Track Title	Attributes	Time	Album	Details
Lonely Fire		21:18	(10)	BC d pe; AM ab gu sh pe
Guinnevere	complete mst	21:07	(10)	CC elp; BC ▷ center; add MD voice
Guinnevere	edited mst	18:03	(2)	as above— MD voice out

Complete master issued on (10):

- 00:00   INTRO ▶ THEME A (02:50/03:44/04:34) ▶ THEME B (05:26) ▶ Miles first solo (05:56) ▶ THEME A (06:40) ▶ Miles second solo (07:10) ▶ THEME A (08:35) ▶ Miles third solo (09:06) ▶ Holland changes bass vamp slightly ▶ THEME A (10:08) ▶ Miles fourth solo (10:36) ▶ THEME B (11:32) ▶ Miles fifth solo (12:01) ▷ Groove w. Zawinul & Corea Interplay (12:34) ▶ THEME A (13:00) ▷ Groove (during this section Moreira switches from pandeiro to cuica) ▶ THEME B (14:56) ▶ Miles sixth solo (15:20) ▶ THEME B on bass vamp of A section (15:49) ▶ Miles seventh solo (16:20) ▶ THEME A (17:08) ▶ Miles eighth solo (17:38) ▶ Miles quotes the theme of B section) ▶ Groove w. Balakrishna (sitar) solo (18:09) ▶ The tune ends with Airto's cuica (19:08) ▶ Groove Reprise (19:10) with Moreira (cuica), Cobham (vibraslap), DeJohnette (shaker ▷ d) ▶ THEME A (20:12) ▶ End (21:07) ▶ Miles's voice (21:12)

Edited master issued on (2):

- 00:00   INTRO (taken from 00:00 to 00:18 of the complete mst)
- ✂ 00:18   INTRO (taken from 01:32 to 02:50 of the complete mst) ▶ THEME A (1:35/2:28) ▶ THEME A (03:16) ▶ THEME B (04:09) ▶ Miles first solo (04:40) ▶ THEME A (05:24) ▶ Miles second solo (05:53) ▶ THEME A (07:16) ▶ Miles third solo (7:47) ▶ Holland changes bass vamp slightly ▶ THEME A (08:45) ▶ Miles fourth solo (09:16) ▶ THEME B (10:11) ▶ Miles fifth solo (10:40) ▷ Groove w. Zawinul & Corea Interplay ▶ THEME A (11:40) ▷ Groove (during this section Moreira switches from pandeiro to cuica) ▶ THEME B (13:33) ▶ Miles sixth solo (13:57) ▶ THEME B on bass vamp of A section (14:25) ▶ Miles seventh solo (14:57) ▶ THEME A (15:44) ▶ Miles eighth solo (16:13) ▶ Miles quotes the theme of B section) ▶ Groove (16:43) w. Balakrishna (sitar) solo (taken from 18:09 to 18:22 of complete mst)

✂ 16:56   Groove (taken from 19:45 of the complete mst) w. Moreira (cuica), Cobham (vibraslap), DeJohnette (shaker ▷ d) ▶ THEME A (17:11)
✂ 18:03   End

JANUARY 28, 1970   NEW YORK CITY—COLUMBIA STUDIO B   RECORDING

Miles Davis (tp); Wayne Shorter (ss); Bennie Maupin (bcl); Joe Zawinul (el. p) on left; Chick Corea (el. p) on right; John McLaughlin (g); Dave Holland (el. b); Billy Cobham (d, perc) on left; Jack DeJohnette (d, perc) on right; Airto Moreira (cuica, perc) on left

Track Title	Attributes	Time	Album	Details
Feio		11:49	(10)	
Double Image		08:25	(10)	

FEBRUARY 6, 1970   NEW YORK CITY—COLUMBIA STUDIO B   RECORDING

Miles Davis (tp); Wayne Shorter (ss); Chick Corea (el. p, ring modulator) on right; Joe Zawinul (el. p, org) on left; John McLaughlin (g); Khalil Balakrishna (sitar); Dave Holland (el. b); Jack DeJohnette (d); Billy Cobham (triangle, perc); Airto Moreira (cuica, cymbals, sheep bells, perc)

Track Title	Attributes	Time	Album	Details
Recollections (~ In a Silent Way)	tk 4	18:54	(10)	add MD & TM voices

Miles Davis (tp); Wayne Shorter (ss); Chick Corea (el. p); Joe Zawinul (el. p, org); John McLaughlin (g); Khalil Balakrishna (sitar or el. sitar); Dave Holland (el. b); Jack DeJohnette (d); Billy Cobham (triangle); Airto Moreira (cuica, cymbals, sheep bells, perc)

Track Title	Attributes	Time	Album	Details
Take It or Leave It		02:13	(10)	

Miles Davis (poss. two overdubbed tps); poss. Wayne Shorter (ss); Chick Corea (el. p, ring modulator) on left; Joe Zawinul (el. p) on right; John McLaughlin (poss. two overdubbed gs); poss. Khalil Balakrishna (el. sitar); Dave Holland (el. b); Jack DeJohnette (d); Airto Moreira (cuica, tambourine, perc)

Track Title	Attributes	Time	Album	Details
Double Image	ec	05:53	(10)	

FEBRUARY 1970   NEW YORK CITY—COLUMBIA STUDIOS   RECORDING

poss. Miles Davis (tp); unknown (brasses); unknown (b); unknown (d); Teo Macero (arr, poss. cond)

Track Title	Attributes	Time	Album	Details
The Man Nobody Saw	edited mst	01:43	(13)	

According to Teo Macero, "The Man Nobody Saw" is part of an old movie score. Whether Macero used an old recording, or re-recorded the arrangement on this day, is unknown, but a recording session with brass ensemble is listed by Jan Lohmann. Whether Miles played trumpet with the ensemble, overdubbed at a later date, or whether his trumpet solo was taken from elsewhere, is also unknown. The brass ensemble recording, Miles's solo, and Brock Peters's narration were combined as the fourth part of "Yesternow" (see below).

FEBRUARY 18, 1970   NEW YORK CITY—COLUMBIA STUDIOS   RECORDING

Miles Davis (tp); Bennie Maupin (bcl); prob. Chick Corea (el. p, ring modulator) on right; John McLaughlin (g) on left; Sonny Sharrock (g) on right; Dave Holland (el. b); Jack DeJohnette (d)

Track Title	Attributes	Time	Album	Details
Willie Nelson	fade-in, mc, fade-out	10:00	(13)	

This master was used as the third part of the "Yesternow" medley on (13). Editing chart:
• 13:56   E-flat Bass Vamp #1—Intro ▶ THEME played by tp & bcl ▶ Miles solo.

✂ 18:49   Electric piano chord

✂ 18:53   Cm Bass Vamp #2—Interplay between Sharrock & Corea (ring modulator) ▶ THEME played by tp & bcl ▶ Miles solo.

| FEBRUARY 27, 1970 | NEW YORK CITY—COLUMBIA STUDIOS | | | | RECORDING |

Miles Davis (tp); Steve Grossman (ss); John McLaughlin (g); Dave Holland (el. b); Jack DeJohnette (d)

Track Title	Attributes	Time	Album	Details
Willie Nelson	tk 2, remake, ic	10:19	(3)	

| MARCH 3, 1970 | NEW YORK CITY—COLUMBIA STUDIOS | | | | RECORDING |

Track Title	Attributes	Time	Album	Details
Go ahead John	edited mst	28:24	(12)	
Go ahead John	45-rpm mst	02:32	(14)	

In this track Teo Macero abundantly used two electronic devices made by CBS's research department, the "electronic switcher," which can instantly switch instruments in the stereo spectrum, and the "instant playback," which can play back instruments with a thirty-second delay. The doublings in SECTION #2 of the solos by Miles and Grossman were created with the "instant playback." Since a rhythm guitar can be heard during McLaughlin's solos in SECTIONS #1 and #3, he most likely overdubbed his solos, after which Macero applied the "electronic switcher" in places. The "electronic switcher" can also be heard extensively on DeJohnette's drums.

Master issued on (12):

SECTION #1 (Vamp in F)

• 00:00/11:53   Solos: Grossman (00:16); Miles (01:43); McLaughlin (06:36); Grossman (10:39)

SECTION #2 (Slow blues)

✂ 11:47/24:25   Solos: Miles (11:47); Grossman (21:41)

SECTION #3 (Blues progression of #2 in tempo of #1)

✂ 24:20/28:24   Solos: Grossman (24:46); McLaughlin (26:56)

Master issued on 45 rpm & (14):

✂ 00:00   Excerpt from 00:01 to 00:13 of (12)

✂ 00:14   Excerpt from 01:44 to 02:38 of (12)

✂ 01:08   Excerpt from 03:25 to 03:43 of (12)

✂ 01:27   Excerpt from 05:09 to 06:14 of (12)

On (14) this master is wrongly titled "The Little Blue Frog."

| MARCH 17, 1970 | NEW YORK CITY—COLUMBIA STUDIOS | | | | RECORDING |

Miles Davis (tp); Wayne Shorter (ss); Bennie Maupin (bcl); John McLaughlin (g); Dave Holland (el. b); Billy Cobham (d)

Track Title	Attributes	Time	Album	Details
Duran	tk 2, mst	10:54	(3)	add MD voice

| APRIL 7, 1970 | NEW YORK CITY—COLUMBIA STUDIO B | | | | RECORDING |

Miles Davis (tp); Steve Grossman (ss); Herbie Hancock (org); John McLaughlin (g); Michael Henderson (el. b); Billy Cobham (d)

Track Title	Attributes	Time	Album	Details
Right Off, part 1	edited mst	10:52	(13)	SG & HH out
Right Off, part 3	edited mst (original mst 09:16)	06:32	(13)	
Right Off, part 4	edited mst	08:21	(13)	MD out
Yesternow, part 1	edited mst (original mst 15:29)	12:25	(13)	

The parts of "Right Off" and "Yesternow" are numbered in accordance with their placement in Macero's final edit of "Right Off" on *A Tribute to Jack Johnson* (13) and do not necessarily correspond with musical contents or with the order in which the material was recorded. The E-flat riff in the beginning of "Right Off, part 4," inspired by Sly Stone's "Sing a Simple Song," appears to have been pieced together by Macero from different segments, maybe because McLaughlin and Henderson had trouble with the riff—they regularly fumble and miss notes. Evidence of Macero's work can be heard at 19:32, where the edit is mistimed, creating an additional half beat, and at 19:22 and 20:04, where McLaughlin repeats an identical mistake. The E-flat riff of "Right Off, part 4" also appeared on Agharta (25), and was again recorded on December 26 and 27, 1984, as "One Phone Call."

The bass line of "Yesternow, part 4" is taken from the James Brown song "Say It Loud, I'm Black and I'm Proud, part 1."

UNKNOWN DATES IN 1970	NEW YORK CITY—COLUMBIA STUDIOS	POST-PRODUCTION & RECORDING

The following three sessions are combined because the date(s) when they occurred are unknown, and because the same trumpet solo is used in all cases. Since Macero used the material from these sessions as interludes in his final edit of (13), it is likely that he compiled this material after the main sessions of April 7, when he was attempting to make all the pieces of the *Jack Johnson* puzzle fit.

Miles Davis (tp); unknown, poss. Chick Corea (ring modulator)

Track Title	Attributes	Time	Album	Details
Right Off, part 2	edited mst	01:33	(13)	

Perhaps Miles played to Chick Corea's ring modulator, and Macero then copied and inserted Miles's solo into the other two pieces mentioned below. Alternatively, Macero may have taken Miles's solo from the recording of "The Man Nobody Saw" and inserted it over the ring modulator.

Miles Davis (tp); Brock Peters (narr—overdubbed speech); Teo Macero (arr)

Track Title	Attributes	Time	Album	Details
Yesternow, part 4	edited mst	01:43	(13)	

Macero used "The Man Nobody Saw," possibly recorded in February, as a basis for this section (timings refer to "Yesternow"):

✄ 23:52/25:34   Cross-fade and insertion of "The Man Nobody Saw"
• 23:56/25:27   Miles solo, played with ensemble, overdubbed or copied
• 25:18/25:30   Peters overdub

Miles Davis (tp) on a prerecorded tape

Track Title	Attributes	Time	Album	Details
Yesternow, part 2	edited mst	01:48	(13)	

Macero used two excerpts from "Shhh/Peaceful" for this Interlude (the timings refer to "Yesternow"):

✄ 12:23/13:26   Cross-fade and insertion of an excerpt of "Shhh/Peaceful" moving from the right channel to the left
✄ 12:31/13:27   Miles overdubbed or copied solo
✄ 12:54/14:12   Cross-fade and insertion of a different excerpt of "Shhh/Peaceful," this time moving from left to right

UNKNOWN DATE IN 1970	NEW YORK CITY—COLUMBIA STUDIOS	POST PRODUCTION

Final mix and editing of the *Jack Johnson* album (13).

"Right Off " medley (26:50)

✄ 00:00/10:52   part 1
✄ 10:42/12:15   part 2
✄ 11:57/18:29   part 3
✄ 18:29/26:50   part 4

"Right Off" contains three bass vamps:

"Yesternow" medley (25:34)

✄ 00:00/12:25   part 1
✄ 12:23/14:12   part 2
✄ 13:56/23:56   part 3 ("Willie Nelson," recorded on February 18, 1970)
✄ 23:52/25:34   part 4

- #1 in E-flat—beginning at 18:44
- #2 in E—beginning at 00:00 and again at 20:29
- #3 in B-flat—beginning at 11:57, but already appearing in embryonic form at 2:33

(The vamps occur in this order during live performances of "Right Off," which is why they are numbered as given.)

APRIL 10, 1970   SAN FRANCISCO, CALIFORNIA—FILLMORE WEST   LIVE

Miles Davis (tp); Steve Grossman (ss); Chick Corea (el. p, ring modulator); Dave Holland (el. b); Jack DeJohnette (d); Airto Moreira (cuica, cowbell, guiro, agogo bells, tambourine, vibraslap, perc)

Track Title	Attributes	Time	Album	Details
Directions		10:46	(15)	AM cu pe
Miles Runs the Voodoo Down		07:17	(15)	AM cu co pe
Willie Nelson		11:27	(15)	CC el. p; AM cu pe
I Fall in Love too Easily		01:34	(15)	SG out; CC el. p; AM cu pe
Sanctuary		04:01	(15)	AM, cu pe
It's about That Time		09:59	(15)	CC el. p; AM, cu pe
Bitches Brew		12:53	(15)	AM cu, gu ab ta pe
Masqualero		09:07	(15)	CC el. p; AM cu pe
Spanish Key		11:08	(15)	CC el. p; AM ta pe
The Theme		00:37	(15)	SG out; AM vi ta pe

MAY 19, 1970   NEW YORK CITY—COLUMBIA STUDIOS   RECORDING

Miles Davis (tp); Keith Jarrett (el. p); Herbie Hancock (clavinet); John McLaughlin (g); Gene Perla (el. b); Billy Cobham (d); Airto Moreira (cuica)

Track Title	Attributes	Time	Album	Details
Honky Tonk	edited mst	05:54	(16)	

MAY 21, 1970   NEW YORK CITY—COLUMBIA STUDIOS   RECORDING

Miles Davis (tp); Bennie Maupin (bcl); Keith Jarrett (el. p); John McLaughlin (g); Jack DeJohnette (d); Airto Moreira (berimbau, perc, cuica)

Track Title	Attributes	Time	Album	Details
Konda	tk 3, edited mst	14:04	(3)	

Miles's solo was doubled and transposed two octaves down electronically.

JUNE 3, 1970   NEW YORK CITY—COLUMBIA STUDIO B   RECORDING

Miles Davis (wah tp); Chick Corea, Herbie Hancock, or Keith Jarrett (org); Dave Holland (el. b); Airto Moreira (perc); Hermeto Pascoal (d, voc overdub)

Track Title	Attributes	Time	Album	Details
Nem Um Talvez	tk 1, mst	04:03	(17)	
Selim	tk 2, mst	02:12	(17)	AM out

NEW YORK CITY—COLUMBIA STUDIO B

Miles Davis (tp); Keith Jarrett or Chick Corea (org) ; Dave Holland (el. b); Hermeto Pascoal (whistling, voc overdub)

Track Title	Attributes	Time	Album	Details
Little Church		03:14	(17)	

JUNE 17 TO 20, 1970 NEW YORK CITY—FILLMORE EAST **LIVE**

These four concerts were issued in edited form on *At Fillmore: Live at the Fillmore East* (18). Macero abridged and edited each concert into medleys called "Wednesday Miles," Thursday Miles," "Friday Miles," and "Saturday Miles." All CD reissues have followed the same procedure, until the 1997 Columbia/Legacy edition, which was the first to identify individual song titles. Some errors were made in this process that are corrected below. After the track titles and details, editing charts are given for the three main CD editions: the Sony Japanese Master Sound edition, the original Columbia CD issue, and the Columbia/Legacy edition. Other differences in timings between the Sony and Columbia editions are due to variations in the speed of the original analog tape.

JUNE 17, 1970 NEW YORK CITY—FILLMORE EAST **LIVE**

Miles Davis (tp); Steve Grossman (ss, ts); Chick Corea (el. p, ring modulator) on right; Keith Jarrett (org) on left; Dave Holland (el. b, b); Jack DeJohnette (d); Airto Moreira (cuica, guiro, sheep bells, wood blocks, tambourine, triangle, perc, fl, kazoo, whistle, voc); poss. Bill Graham (m.c.)

During "The Mask" a second drum set can be heard, probably played by Corea (in the center). Dave Holland plays acoustic bass only on "The Mask," and electric bass on the remainder of the medley.

"Wednesday Miles":

Track Title	Attributes	Time	Album	Details
Directions	exc 1 & 2 (ed. at 02:04)	02:29	(18)	SG out; AM cu gu pe
Bitches Brew	insert	00:29	(18)	SG out; AM gu pe
Directions	exc 3	00:13	(18)	SG ts; AM gu pe
The Mask	edited mst	01:45	(18)	SG ss; AM gu pe
It's about That Time	ic	08:10	(18)	SG ss; AM gu sh pe fl voc
Bitches Brew	edited mst	10:33	(18)	SG ts; AM cu sh wo pe fl voc
The Theme		00:20	(18)	SG out; CC elp; AM pe wh

Description	Sony SRCS9121/2	Columbia 476909-2	Columbia/Legacy C2K 65139
• Directions exc 1	00:01	00:01	Track 1—00:01
✂ Directions exc 2	02:04	02:04	Track 1—02:03
✂ Bitches Brew insert	02:30	02:30	Track 2—00:00
✂ Directions exc 3	03:00	03:00	Track 2—00:29
• The Mask	03:14	03:13	Track 2—00:42
✂ It's about That Time	04:59	04:59	Track 4—00:00
• Bitches Brew	13:09	13:09	Track 4—08:07
✂ Bitches Brew exc 2	16:44	16:42	Track 5—03:29
✂ Brew Brew exc 3	19:33	19:31	Track 5—06:17
• The Theme	23:44	23:40	Track 5—10:25

During "Directions" and "The Mask" a second drum set can be heard, probably played by Corea (in the center); Dave Holland plays acoustic bass only on "The Mask" and "Bitches Brew," and electric bass on the remainder of the medley; DeJohnette plays additional tambourine on "It's about That Time."

"Thursday Miles":

Track Title	Attributes	Time	Album	Details
Directions	edited mst	05:37	(18)	SG ts; AM cu pe wh
The Mask		09:51	(18)	SG out; AM cu pe
It's about That Time	mc & editing	09:40	(18)	SG ss; AM gu ab pe fl wh
Bitches Brew	2 exc on record	00:25	(18)	SG out; CC el. p; AM tr pe
The Theme		01:05	(18)	SG ss; AM pe wh

Description	Sony SRCS9121/2	Columbia 476909-2	Columbia/Legacy C2K 65139
• Directions	00:01	00:00	Track 6—00:01
✄ Directions exc 2	01:33	01:33	Track 6—01:33
✄ Directions exc 3	01:47	01:47	Track 6—01:47
• The Mask	05:37	05:37	Track 7—00:00
• It's about That Time	15:28	15:28	Track 7—09:49
✄ It's about That Time exc 2	21:28	21:28	Track 8—05:58
• Bitches Brew	25:08	25:08	Track 8—09:37
✄ Bitches Brew exc 2	25:28	25:28	Track 8—09:57
• The Theme	25:33	25:33	Track 8—10:03

Dave Holland plays only electric bass and Steve Grossman plays only soprano sax on this recording.

"Friday Miles":

Track Title	Attributes	Time	Album	Details
Band setting	excerpt	00:13	(18)	SG out
Unidentified Tune (poss. Directions)	excerpt	00:06	(18)	
It's about That Time		08:41	(18)	AM sh gu cu ta tr pe wh
I Fall in Love too Easily		02:02	(18)	SG out; CC el. p; AM pe
Sanctuary		03:43	(18)	CC el. p; AM pe
Bitches Brew	edited mst, loops	12:28	(18)	SG out; AM sh cu pe wh
The Theme		00:26	(18)	SG out; pe wh

Description	Sony SRCS9121/2	Columbia 476909-2	Columbia/Legacy C2K 65139
• Band Setting	00:00	00:00	Track 1—00:00
✄ Unidentified Tune	00:13	00:13	Track 1—00:13
• It's about That Time	00:19	00:19	Track 1—00:19
• I Fall in Love too Easily	09:00	09:01	Track 1—08:59
• Sanctuary	11:02	11:03	Track 3—00:00
• Bitches Brew	14:45	14:47	Track 4—00:00
✄ Bitches Brew loop 1	15:57	15:59	Track 4—01:11
✄ Bitches Brew loop 2	16:35	16:37	Track 4—01:49
✄ Bitches Brew exc 2	19:47	19:49	Track 4—05:00
• The Theme	27:13	27:16	Track 4—12:26

Editing chart of Macero's treatment of "Bitches Brew" (timing refers to the Columbia/Legacy edition):

- 00:00   Coded phrase by Miles, after which he plays the theme
- ✂ 01:11   Duplication of 00:53/01:11
- ✂ 01:49   Duplication of 00:10/01:49 (without the previous duplication), following which the tape continues without edits
- ✂ 05:00   Cut to free section

In my opinion, the version of "Bitches Brew" included in this medley is a brilliantly conceived reconstruction of reality through editing, aimed at doing away with the concept of a live recording as a literal registration of an event. It eloquently demonstrates Macero's "postcomposition" approach.

JUNE 20, 1970   NEW YORK CITY—FILLMORE EAST   LIVE

There's possibly a second drum set on "It's about That Time," once again most likely played by Chick Corea (in the center). Steve Grossman (ss) is only audible on "Willie Nelson." Dave Holland plays acoustic bass only on the first twenty seconds of "It's about That Time," and electric bass on the remainder of the medley.

"Saturday Miles":

Track Title	Attributes	Time	Album	Details
It's about That Time	edited mst	03:44	(18)	AM cu ab sh ka voc
I Fall In Love too Easily	ec	00:54	(18)	CC el. p; AM cu pe wh
Sanctuary	ic	02:49	(18)	CC el. p; AM ab sh pe wh
Bitches Brew	edited mst	06:58	(18)	CC el. p; AM cu sh pe wh
Willie Nelson	edited mst	07:15	(18)	CC el. p; AM pe
The Theme		00:24	(18)	CC el. p; AM pe wh

Description	Sony SRCS9121/2	Columbia 476909-2	Columbia/Legacy C2K 65139
• It's about That Time	00:00	00:00	Track 5—00:00
• It's about That Time exc 2	00:20	00:20	Track 5—00:20
• I Fall in Love too Easily	03:44	03:44	Track 6—00:00
✂ Sanctuary	04:38	04:38	Track 7—00:00
• Bitches Brew	07:27	07:27	Track 8—00:00
✂ Bitches Brew exc 1	10:27	10:27	Track 8—02:59
• Willie Nelson	14:25	14:25	Track 9—00:00
✂ Willie Nelson exc 2	14:34	14:34	Track 9—00:09
• The Theme	21:40	21:40	Track 9—07:11

AUGUST 29, 1970   ISLE OF WIGHT (GREAT BRITAIN)—"ROCK FESTIVAL"   LIVE

Miles Davis (tp); Gary Bartz (ss, as); Chick Corea (el. p) on left channel; Keith Jarrett (org) on right channel; Dave Holland (el. b); Jack DeJohnette (d); Airto Moreira (cuica, perc, whistle, voc); unknown (m.c.).

Gary Bartz (ss) is audible only in "Directions."

Three different medleys were assembled from the live recording.

TITLE	"Call It Anythin'" (14)	"Call It Anything" (19)	Excerpt of video (20)	Details
Directions	06:31	06:08		AM cu pe voc
Bitches Brew	00:05	03:45		AM pe voc
It's about That Time	04:37		01:41	AM pe voc
Sanctuary			00:14	AM pe voc
Spanish Key	05:31	03:12	00:27	AM pe
The Theme	00:41	01:23		AM pe wh

"Call It Anythin'" (17:25)

✂ 00:01 "Directions"—first pt of MD solo)

✂ 01:39 "Directions"—secnd pt of MD solo

✂ 02:11 "Directions"—last note of the "THEME" GB solo; KJ & CC Interplay

• 06:31 "Bitches Brew"—coded phrase

✂ 06:36 "It's about That Time"—MD solo

✂ 11:13 "Spanish Key"—exc of MD solo

✂ 12:01 "Spanish Key"—conclusion of KJ & CC Interplay; closing solo by MD "The Theme"

✂ 17:02 "The Theme"—CODA

"Call It Anything" (14:34)

✂ 00:00 "Directions"—fade-in "MD solo" THEME (x2) "GB solo"

✂ 04:10 (prob. cut) "Directions" (end section)

• 06:08 "Bitches Brew"—coded phrase "THEME" MD solo

✂ 09:22 (prob. cut) "Bitches Brew"—THEME to end

✂ 09:59 "Spanish Key"—closing solo by MD

• 13:11 "The Theme"—(complete)

Excerpt of video (02:22)

✂ 00:00 "It's about That Time"—exc taken starting from 09:34 of "Call It Anythin'," but in this version the piece continues where the other master was cut

• 01:41 Miles plays the coded phrase for "Sanctuary" (not present in the two other masters)

✂ 01:55 "Spanish Key"—exc 16:09/16:36 of "Call It Anythin'"

DECEMBER 19, 1970   WASHINGTON, D.C.—THE CELLAR DOOR   LIVE

Miles Davis (tp & wah tp); Gary Bartz (ss, as); Keith Jarrett (el. p, org); John McLaughlin (g); Michael Henderson (el. b); Jack DeJohnette (d); Airto Moreira (cuica, guiro, cabaca, cowbell, agogo bells, sheep bells, vibraslap, perc, bamboo fl, whistle, voc); unknown (m.c.)

Musical elements of *Live-Evil* in the live set playing order:

Second set:

Track Title	Attributes	Time	Album	Details
Directions	final exc	03:25	(17)	GB out
Honky Tonk	edited mst	11:49	(17)	GB out
What I Say		20:53	(17)	GB ss
Sanctuary Theme	exc	00:17	(17)	GB as

Third set:

Track Title	Attributes	Time	Album	Details
Directions		16:52	(17)	GB ss
Inamorata/Funky Tonk		23:11	(17)	GB as
Sanctuary	exc	00:12	(17)	GB as
It's about That Time	two edited excerpts	09:22	(17)	GB as
Sanctuary Theme	fade out	00:29	(17)	GB out

Teo Macero edited these selections into four medleys. Editing charts:

"Sivad" medley (15:15):

✂ 00:01 "Directions"—final excerpt from second set

✂ 03:26 "Honky Tonk"—excerpt from the studio recording of May 19, 1970

✂ 04:15 "Honky Tonk"—excerpt from

"Whay I Say" medley (21:10):

• 00:01 "What I Say"

• 20:53 "Sanctuary Theme"—fragment

"Funky Tonk" medley (23:27):

• 00:01 "Directions"—excerpt from third set

• 16:52 "Inamorata/Funky Tonk"—coded phrase by Miles, and Jarrett solo

"Inamorata and Narration by Conrad Roberts" medley (26:31):

• 00:01 "Inamorata/Funky Tonk"—continuation from "Funky Tonk" medley

✂ 16:36 "Sanctuary"—end of THEME

• 16:47 "It's about

second set (fade out
at end)

That Time"—coded
phrase by Miles

✄ poss. 16:58   "It's
about That Time"—
excerpt from the
solo section &
narration overdub

• 26:10   "Sanctuary
Theme"

There have been debates over what to call the tune "Inamorata/Funky Tonk." On the forthcoming Cellar Door releases it is marked as "Inamorata," according to reissue co-producer Adam Holzman, because the majority of the track, 16:36, appears inside the "Inamorata" medley on (17). But the tune's musical material first appears in the "Funky Tonk" medley. It is also entirely unrelated to the Conrad Roberts's narration, which occurs during a performance of "It's about That Time." Since the tune "Inamorata/Funky Tonk" has nothing to do with the "Inamorata" narration, it makes more sense to call it "Funky Tonk."

MARCH 9, 1972	NEW YORK CITY—COLUMBIA STUDIOS				RECORDING

Miles Davis (wah tp) w. an unknown brass band incl. Joe Newman (tp); Wally Chambers (harmonica); unknown (org); Cornell Dupree & unknown (g); Michael Henderson (el. b); Al Foster, Bernard "Pretty" Purdie (d); Mtume (perc); Wade Marcus (brass arrangement); Billy Jackson (rhythm arrangement)

Track Title	Attributes	Time	Album	Details
Red China Blues	fade-out	04:05	(16)	MD tp overdub

The date most likely refers to the recording of the basic track. Paul Buckmaster, who did not arrive in New York until the end of April 1972, stated that he was present when Miles overdubbed to the finished backing track.

JUNE 1 & 6/JULY 7, 1972	ON THE CORNER SESSIONS		RECORDING

The exact discographical details for this album have long been a source of confusion. Miles ordered that no personnel and recording details were to be printed on the cover for the first release of On the Corner in the fall of 1972. After protests from the musicians, a credit list was supplied on the next vinyl edition, but it contained several mistakes and omissions. Since then, the information given on different vinyl and CD reissues has conflicted. The 2000 Columbia/Legacy reissue of On the Corner does not clear up these confusions and actually introduces some new ones. Al Foster is given as one of the drummers on all tracks, but it is unlikely that he was present at the June sessions. Mtume and Don Alias were forgotten in the personnel listing, although the latter is mentioned in Bob Belden's essay in the CD booklet. Khalil Balakrishna is given on electric sitar on "Black Satin," but there is no reason for there to be a sitar player in addition to Collin Walcott. The aural evidence and the session track sheet also suggest an acoustic sitar, rather than an electric sitar. And Bennie Maupin is credited on "Black Satin" but only plays on "One and One." To make matters even more confusing, the memories of those involved often conflict with the available evidence, and with each other. Below we give our best guesses about the exact discographical details of these sessions. In the case of conflicting evidence we have relied on 1) the aural evidence of the issued material, 2) the original track sheets for the sessions of June 1 and 6, and July 7, and 3) Buckmaster's testimony, since he appeared to have to sharpest and most complete recollections of all involved. Our most important assumption is that the session of July 7, on which "Black Satin" is said to be recorded, was in fact an overdub session to the "Black Satin" master, recorded on June 6. The tracks sheet for July 7 clearly indicates that this was an overdub session to a prerecorded stereo master. Overdubbed parts include whistles, handclaps, trumpet, bells, and percussion. In addition, "Black Satin," "One and One," "Helen Butte," and "Mr. Freedom X" are all based on the same musical material, have very similar instrumentation, and an almost identical sound and feel. It makes sense to assume that they were all recorded during one long session, which is why the material is listed as "Black Satin, parts 1, 2, 3, and 4." (Paul Tingen)

JUNE 1, 1972	NEW YORK CITY—COLUMBIA STUDIOS		RECORDING

Miles Davis (wah tp); Dave Liebman (ss); Chick Corea (synth) on left; Harold "Ivory" Williams (el. p, ring modulator) on center; Herbie Hancock (org) on right; John McLaughlin (g); Collin Walcott (sitar); Paul Buckmaster (wah el. cello); Michael Henderson (el. b); Jack DeJohnette (d); Billy Hart (d, perc); Don Alias (cga, shaker) on right; Badal Roy (tabla) on left; unknown (cowbell, cabaça) on right.

Track Title	Attributes	Time	Album	Details
On the Corner	edited mst	19:53	(21)	

On the Corner is seemingly arbitrarily divided into "On the Corner," "New York Girl," "Thinkin' One Thing and Doin' Another," and "Vote for Miles."

- ✂ 00:32 at this point the stereo image is reversed. The stereo placements given above apply to after this point.
- ✂ 11:12 edit point given in Belden's essay in the 2000 reissue of (21). Nothing musically significant changes at this point.

The unknown percussionist could be Mtume, because there is a hint of waterdrum at one stage when the cowbell drops out. However, he claimed not to be present at this first session. On the aural evidence, Collin Walcott plays acoustic sitar. Far in the background, in the left channel there is occasionally an unidentified instrument, which may well be Buckmaster's wah-wah electric cello. According to Buckmaster, Corea played an ARP Axxe synthesizer.

POSS. JUNE 2, 1972	NEW YORK CITY—COLUMBIA STUDIOS	RECORDING

The information provided for this session is based on a fax from Bob Belden to Bill Laswell for the latter's use during the making of *Panthalassa* (22). Since Paul Buckmaster does not recall a recording date immediately following June 1, the date given may be incorrect. However, the studio track sheet for the June 1 session refers to an overdub session on June 2. Since McLaughlin is also present on "What If," perhaps the basic tracks were recorded on June 1, and Creamer, Garnett, and Henderson overdubbed their parts on June 2. (Paul Tingen)

Miles Davis (wah tp); Carlos Garnett (ts); Chick Corea (synth) on left; Harold Williams (el. p, ring modulator) on center; Herbie Hancock (org) on right; John McLaughlin, David Creamer (g); Collin Walcott (sitar); Michael Henderson (el. b); Jack DeJohnette (d); Billy Hart (d, cowbell, perc); Don Alias (cga) on left; Badal Roy (tabla)

Track Title	Attributes	Time	Album	Details
What If	Bill Laswell edited mst	07:18	(22)	

Title given by Bill Laswell.

JUNE 6, 1972	NEW YORK CITY—COLUMBIA STUDIOS	RECORDING

Miles Davis (wah tp); Carlos Garnett (ss, ts); Bennie Maupin (bcl); Herbie Hancock, Harold Williams (el. p, org, synth); Lonnie Liston Smith (org); David Creamer (g); Collin Walcott (sitar); Michael Henderson (el. b); poss. Paul Buckmaster (el. cello); Jack DeJohnette, Billy Hart (d); Don Alias (cowbells, sheep bells, perc); Mtume (waterdrum, sheep bells) on left; Badal Roy (tabla) on right

Track Title	Attributes	Time	Album	Details
Black Satin, part 1	edited mst	05:14	(21)	BM out; CG ss

Editing chart:
- ✂ 00:00   Percussion introduction
- ✂ 00:34   Vamp & theme
- ✂ 03:41   Possible edit point
- ✂ 04:31   Duplication of the opening percussion introduction via a crossfade

An edited version of "Black Satin" was issued as "Molester" on 45 rpm.

Track Title	Attributes	Time	Album	Details
Black Satin, part 2	fade-out	06:08	(21)	CG ss; JM wd
Black Satin, parts 3 and 4	fade-out	23:18	(21)	BM out; CG ts; JM wd

Parts 2, 3, and 4 of "Black Satin" were issued as "One and One," "Helen Butte," and "Mr. Freedom X," respectively. The 2000 reissue gives Balakrishna on sitar for "Black Satin, part 1" and Collin Walcott on sitar on "Black Satin, parts 2, 3, and 4." Since we regard this as all the same track, recorded on June 6, it is logical to assume that there's only one sitar player, most likely Walcott.

NEW YORK CITY—COLUMBIA STUDIOS

Miles Davis (tp & wah tp); Carlos Garnett (ss); Bennie Maupin (bcl); Harold Williams (el. p, prob. synth) poss. on left; Lonnie Liston Smith (org) poss. on right; Michael Henderson (el. b); Al Foster, Billy Hart (d, poss. perc); Mtume (cga, waterdrum, sheep bells, perc) on right; Badal Roy (tabla) on left

Track Title	Attributes	Time	Album	Details
Ife	edited mst	21:33	(12)	add MD voice

Editing point at 08:06

JULY 7, 1972   **NEW YORK CITY—COLUMBIA STUDIOS**   **RECORDING**

Overdub session to "Black Satin, part 1"

Miles Davis (tp & wah tp, handclaps); Carlos Garnett (ss, handclaps); Mtume (waterdrum, perc, handclaps) on left; Badal Roy (tabla, handclaps) on right; Al Foster, Jack DeJohnette, Don Alias, and/or Billy Hart (whistles, perc)

SEPTEMBER 6, 1972   **NEW YORK CITY—COLUMBIA STUDIOS**   **RECORDING**

Miles Davis (org); Cedric Lawson (synth); Reggie Lucas (g); Khalil Balakrishna (el. sitar); Michael Henderson (el. b); Al Foster (d); Mtume (cga, perc); Badal Roy (tabla)

Track Title	Attributes	Time	Album	Details
Rated X	Macero edited mst	06:50	(16)	RL left; KB right
Rated X	Laswell edited mst	05:58	(22)	RL right; KB left

The dense organ clusters were created with tape loops.

SEPTEMBER 29, 1972   **NEW YORK CITY—PHILHARMONIC HALL**   **LIVE**

Miles Davis (wah tp); Carlos Garnett (ss); Cedric Lawson (el. p, org, synth); Reggie Lucas (g); Khalil Balakrishna (el. sitar); Michael Henderson (el. b); Al Foster (d, prob. sheep bells where noted); Mtume (cga, waterdrum, sheep bells, perc); Badal Roy (tabla)

Track Title	Attributes	Time	Album	Details
Foot Fooler		05:57	(23)	CG out; JM cg
Rated X		06:12	(23)	JM cg
Honky Tonk		09:21	(23)	JM wd
Right Off		10:13	(23)	JM cg
Black Satin		13:36	(23)	JM cg wd; AF prob. sh
Sanctuary Theme		00:28	(23)	CG out; JM cg
Ife		27:59	(23)	JM cg wd; AF prob. sh
Slickaphonics		09:52	(23)	JM cg
Sanctuary Theme		00:32	(23)	CG out; JM pe

NOVEMBER 29, 1972   **NEW YORK CITY—COLUMBIA STUDIOS**   **RECORDING**

Track Title	Attributes	Time	Album	Details
Agharta Prelude (= Agharta Prelude Dub)	Laswell edited mst	04:09	(22)	JM cg; RL left; KB center

DECEMBER 8, 1972   **NEW YORK CITY—COLUMBIA STUDIOS**   **RECORDING**

Track Title	Attributes	Time	Album	Details
Billy Preston	fade-out	12:33	(16)	MD tp wtp; JM cg; RL right; KB left
Billy Preston	Bill Laswell edited mst	14:34	(22)	MD tp wtp; JM cg; RL right; KB left

Miles Davis (wah tp); Reggie Lucas (g) on left channel; Pete Cosey (g) on right channel; Michael Henderson (el. b); Al Foster (d); Mtume (cga)

Track Title	Attributes	Time	Album	Details
Big Fun	fade-out	02:31	(14)	
Holly-wuud	fade-out	02:52	(14)	

Some sources list Dave Liebman and John Stubblefield, but neither is audible.

Miles Davis (wah tp, org); Dave Liebman (fl); John Stubblefield (ss); Reggie Lucas (g) on right channel; Pete Cosey (g, twelve-string g) on left channel; Michael Henderson (el. b); Al Foster (d); Mtume (cga, cymbals, sheep bells, tambourine, perc, whistle)

Track Title	Attributes	Time	Album	Details
Calypso Frelimo	edited mst	32:06	(16)	

Editing chart:

SECTION #1 (Vamp in C)

- 00:00   Miles (wah tp) solo

✂ 00:28   THEME by Miles (org)

✂ 00:37   Miles (wah tp) solo ▷ Interplay by Miles (wah tp) & Cosey ▶ Solos: Liebman (04:57/06:57); Miles (wah tp, 6:35); Stubblefield (7:33/9:39); Miles (wah tp, 09:42)

SECTION #2 (Same vamp in C, but half tempo)

✂ 10:11   C-sharp chord by Miles (org) ▷ Groove ▶ Solos: Miles (org, 10:40); Liebman (15:20); Miles (wah tp, 16:57)

SECTION #3 (Same as #1)

✂ 21:39   Intro by Miles (org)

✂ 22:52   Cosey solo (g) ▷ Groove ▶ Miles (wah tp, 25:59/31:05) ▷ Groove ▶ THEME by Miles (org, 31:35), fade-out

The theme appears also at 00:08, 09:19, 14:24, 22:13, 23:39, and 24:45.

Miles plays organ throughout "Calypso Frelimo." Because he uses the instrument to give musical cues, he most likely played it when the basic tracks were recorded and later overdubbed his wah-wah trumpet parts.

Miles Davis (tp & wah tp; org only when noted); Dave Liebman (ss, ts); Reggie Lucas (g) on mid-right; Pete Cosey (g, mbira, cowbell, agogo bells, sheep bells, perc) on left; Michael Henderson (el. b); Al Foster (d); Mtume (cga, waterdrum, mbira, rhythm box, perc)

First set:

Track Title	Attributes	Time	Album	Details
Moja	edited mst	05:50	(24)	MD wtp; PC g; JM cg
Nne	edited mst	06:38	(24)	MD wtp; PC g; JM cg
Tune in 5		12:35	(24)	MD wtp; DL ts; JM cg wd mb rb pe
Ife	coded phrase only	00:02	(24)	MD org alone
Funk		14:21	(24)	DL ss; PC g co sh pe; JM cg rb
Wili (= For Dave)		10:39	(24)	DL ts; PC g ab sh pe; JM cg wd

Second set. Dominique Gaumont (g—stereo floating, on right when steady) and Azar Lawrence (ts) join the band.

Track Title	Attributes	Time	Album	Details
Tatu	fade-in	18:50	(24)	DL ss; PC g co pe; JM cg
Calypso Frelimo	fade-out	06:28	(24)	DL ss; PC g co mb pe; JM cg wd voc
Ife	ic	16:07	(24)	DL ss; PC g mb sh pe; JM cga wd rb; DG in center
Nne		06:13	(24)	DL ss; PC g sh pe; JM cg pe; DG in center
Tune in 5		2:53	(24)	MD & DL out; PC g mb ab sh pe; JM cg pe voc; DG in center

The two-second entry for "Ife" in the recording of the first set occurs in the Japanese release, but has been deleted in the Columbia/Legacy edition.

Only "Ife" and "Calypso Frelimo" were titles used by the band, since these tunes had already been recorded in the studio. Many of the tunes that were only played and recorded live were never given titles by Miles or the band. The untitled tunes/vamps the '73–'75 band played have been identified by the logic explained in the Introduction, which is to name any previously untitled tune/vamp after the first officially released medley in which it appears. If a medley consists of more than one vamp, the untitled vamp receives the medley's name. For instance, "Calypso Frelimo" appears in the medley "Tatu" on (24), and the remainder of the medley is titled "Tatu." This approach would be problematic if more than one untitled vamp occurred in one medley, but the only instance in which this occurs is in "Moja." Dave Liebman and I decided to call its middle section with a 5/4 polyrhythm simply "Tune in 5." In discussions between Henry Kaiser, Paul Tingen, and myself it was agreed that since "Moja" has a second theme, and this second theme is the only theme to appear in the medley "Nne" (other than "Tune in 5"), we would call this second theme "Nne." However, "Moja" and "Nne" often appear together, and are hence sometimes referred to by us as "Moja-Nne." "Funk" was a name given by Dave Liebman, and since it only officially occurs on (24), I have chosen to retain the name. Miles told Liebman that the music in the second section of the "Wili" medley was called "For Dave." This tune has therefore become known by both names.

JUNE 19 OR 20, 1974   NEW YORK CITY—COLUMBIA STUDIO E   RECORDING

Miles Davis (tp & wah tp, org); Dave Liebman (fl); Dominique Gaumont (g) stereo floating; Reggie Lucas (g) on right; Michael Henderson (el. b); Al Foster (d); Mtume (cga)

Track Title	Attributes	Time	Album	Details
He Loved Him Madly	edited mst	32:14	(16)	DG floating

Add Bill Laswell (reconstruction, remix, studio effects, samples)

Track Title	Attributes	Time	Album	Details
He Loved Him Madly	Bill Laswell edited mst	13:35	(22)	DG left

Original master (16):

SECTION #1
- 00:00   Intro by Miles (org)
- 00:19   Gaumont plays motif ▷ Gaumont solo
- ✂ 02:41   Duplication of 00:03/02:41

Gaumont is the only guitar player in section #1
- ✂ 10:48   Organ insert

SECTION #2

Secnd Movement (10:54/32:14)
- ✂ 10:54   Reggie Lucas enters on right channel.

Solos: Gaumont (11:26); Dave Liebman (12:49) ▶

Laswell master (22):
- 00:00   Studio effects
- 00:06   Whale sample
- 00:13   INTRO by Miles (org), with studio effects
- 01:16   Gaumont plays motif
- 01:25   Lucas enters
- 01:32   Henderson enters ▷ Liebman solo (01:33/03:44)
- 01:58   Foster enters
- 03:45   Gaumont solo
- 05:03   Groove
- 05:31   Miles (wah tp)

Guitar Interlude (14:46) ▶ Miles (wah tp—16:06) ▶
Guitar Interlude (20:01) ▶ Dave Liebman (20:10)
✂ 22:36   Duplication of 20:10/22:36

Solos: Liebman (22:36, repeat of previous solo) ▶
Guitar Interlude (25:02) ▶ Miles (wah tp & org, 26:21)
▷ Foster's hi-hat goes into double time (27:00);
Gaumont (30:06)

- 09:14   Gaumont solo
- 11:18   Rhythm section out and organ coda

Laswell has moved individual instrumental parts around in the arrangement, rather than editing the whole band arrangement, as Macero used to do. For instance, in Laswell's version Lucas's guitar appears before Foster's drums, whereas in the original Lucas and Foster enter simultaneously. For this reason, it is impossible to provide an editing chart for (22).

OCTOBER 7, 1974   NEW YORK CITY—COLUMBIA STUDIOS   RECORDING

Miles Davis (wah tp, org); Sonny Fortune (fl); Dominique Gaumont, Reggie Lucas (g); Pete Cosey (g, cowbell, bottles, claves, agogo bells, perc); Michael Henderson (el. b); Al Foster (d); Mtume (cga)

Track Title	Attributes	Time	Album	Details
Mtume	edited mst	15:07	(16)	SF out; PC g co bo pe

The track contains two different sections, alternated throughout. The first section is characterized by a motif played by Gaumont at 00:23 and a theme introduced by Miles (wah tp) at 06:47. In the second section Henderson plays the B-flat vamp (#3) of "Right Off," transposed to "G," while Gaumont and Lucas play the descending chord progression of "It's about That Time."

Track Title	Attributes	Time	Album	Details
Maiysha	ec	14:49	(16)	PC g cl ab pe

"Maiysha" has two sections. The first section combines a Latin rhythm with a melody reminiscent of the French chanson "Que Reste Til de Nous Amour." The second section has an R&B feel and is based on the same two chords as "Honky Tonk" (E7 & A7). Henderson plays an ascending, four-note chromatic vamp. In live performance Miles often quoted the riff of "Tramp," a song by Fulsom & McCracklin sung by Otis Redding and Carla Thomas in 1967, during the second section.

FEBRUARY 1, 1975   OSAKA (JAPAN)—FESTIVAL HALL, AFTERNOON CONCERT   LIVE

Miles Davis (wah tp, org); Sonny Fortune (ss, as, fl); Reggie Lucas (g) on right channel; Pete Cosey (g, synth, autoharp, mbira, chimes, cowbell, bottles, agogo bells, claves, triangle, perc) on left channel; Michael Henderson (el. b); Al Foster (d); Mtume (cga, waterdrum, rhythm box, sheep bells)

Track Title	Attributes	Time	Album	Details
Tatu		22:01	(25)	SF as; PC g co bo pe; JM cga rb
Agharta Prelude		10:02	(25)	SF ss; PC g au co bo pe JM cga wd rb
Maiysha		13:06	(25)	SF ss fl; PC g ab cl; JM cg sh
Right Off		16:42	(25)	SF as; PC g co ab pe; JM cg
So What		00:41	(25)	SF out; MD org; PC g; JM cg
Ife		17:35	(25)	SF fl; PC g sy pe
Wili (= For Dave)		25:48	(25)	SF fl; PC g sy ab mb ch tr pe; JM + voc

"Maiysha" and "Wili" are issued complete on (25). In all other editions the tracks are faded out at 12:19 and 16:51 respectively.

Track Title	Attributes	Time	Album	Details
Moja		11:05	(26)	SF ss as; PC g; JM cg
Willie Nelson on Tune in 5		04:53	(26)	SF out; MD wtp; PC g co bo sh pe; JM cg
Nne		05:53	(26)	MD wtp; SF ss; PC g co pe; JM cg
Zimbabwe		19:45	(26)	SF ss; PC g au co bo sh pe
Ife		18:57	(26)	SF fl; PC g mb cl ab pe; JM cg wd
Wili (= For Dave)		30:42	(26)	SF out; PC g sy ab bo pe; JM cg rb

"Ife" and "Wili " are issued complete on (26). In all other editions "Ife" is faded in at 00:18, while "Wili" is faded out at 28:10. During "Nne" Miles quotes "My Man's Gone Now" (20:57).

MAY/JUNE 1980   NEW YORK CITY—COLUMBIA STUDIOS   RECORDING

Miles Davis (tp); Bill Evans (ss); Robert Irving III (p, synth); Randy Hall (g, celeste, Mini Moog synth, lead & background voc); Felton Crews (el. b); Vince Wilburn Jr. (d)

Track Title	Attributes	Time	Album	Details
The Man with the Horn		06:32	(27)	

PROB. JANUARY 1981   NEW YORK CITY—COLUMBIA STUDIOS   RECORDING

Miles Davis (tp); Bill Evans (ss); Barry Finnerty (g); Marcus Miller (el. b); Al Foster (d); Sammy Figueroa (perc)

Track Title	Attributes	Time	Album	Details
Back Seat Betty	edited mst	11:14	(27)	
Aïda	fade-out	08:10	(27)	
Ursula	edited mst	10:50	(27)	add MD voice

C. MARCH 1981   NEW YORK CITY—COLUMBIA STUDIOS   RECORDING

Miles Davis (tp); Bill Evans (ss); Mike Stern (g); Marcus Miller (el. b); Al Foster (d); Sammy Figueroa (perc)

Track Title	Attributes	Time	Album	Details
Fat Time	edited mst	09:53	(27)	add MD voice

Also issued on 45 rpm, shortened to 04:45.

MAY 6, 1981   NEW YORK CITY—COLUMBIA STUDIOS   RECORDING

Miles Davis (tp); Bill Evans (ss); Robert Irving III (el. p, synth); Randy Hall (synth); Barry Finnerty (g); Felton Crews (el. b); Vince Wilburn Jr. (d); Sammy Figueroa (perc)

Track Title	Attributes	Time	Album	Details
Shout	edited mst	05:52	(27)	

Two longer masters of "Shout" were issued on 12" (Columbia AS 1274).

Miles Davis (tp, el. p); Bill Evans (ss, ts, el. p); Mike Stern (g); Marcus Miller (el. b); Al Foster (d); Mino Cinelu (perc)

Track Title	Attributes	Time	Album	Details
My Man's Gone Now	fade-out	20:05	(28)	BE ss
Aïda (= Fast Track)		15:03	(28)	MD tp; BE ss
Kix	ic	18:35	(28)	BE ts el. p

Macero inserted ten seconds of the bass vamp of "My Man's Gone Now" at the beginning of the track "Aïda" as an intro. The origins of these ten seconds are unclear.

Track Title	Attributes	Time	Album	Details
Back Seat Betty	edited mst	08:12	(28)	BE out; MD tp

The complete master of this track was 21:00. This track issued on (30) was edited at 03:02 and 05:02, then faded out at 08:12. A longer master was issued on 12" (Columbia AS 1367).

Track Title	Attributes	Time	Album	Details
Jean-Pierre	mc	03:48	(28)	MD tp; BE ss

Editing point at 03:13.

Track Title	Attributes	Time	Album	Details
Back Seat Betty		19:45	(29)	MD tp; BE ss
Ursula		02:00	(29)	BE out; MD tp
My Man's Gone Now		15:44	(29)	BE ts
Aïda		12:07	(29)	BE ts
Fat Time		12:51	(29)	BE ss
Jean-Pierre	complete mst	11:01	(29)	BE ss

An edited master of "Jean-Pierre" of 10:39 was issued on (28). During his opening solo on "Back Seat Betty" Miles quotes the theme of "Bess You Is My Woman Now" (02:32). At 00:57 in "Ursula" he quotes the first phrase from his solo in the studio version of "It's about That Time."

Track Title	Attributes	Time	Album	Details
Star on Cicely	edited mst	04:30	(30)	MD tp; el. p prob. MD; BE ss; poss. Gil Evans (arr)

From the evidence of live performances "Star on Cicely" is based on three different themes that almost always appear in the same order in live performance. (THEME #1 later inspired "Hopscotch" and THEME #2 became the theme of "Wrinkle.") Macero entirely recomposed the version on (30) through editing, removing THEME #1 and most of THEME #2.

- 00:01 Opening statement by guitar and soprano sax in unison (end of THEME #2)
- ✂ 00:05 Miles solo
- ✂ 01:04 THEME #3, played by guitar, overdubbed bass, and soprano sax in unison (a muted trumpet is briefly overdubbed)
- 01:49 Stern quotes part of THEME #2 ▶ Interplay Miles and Stern
- ✂ 02:40 Duplication of the opening statement

- 02:44   Miles solo
- 03:44   Duplication of THEME #3 appearing at 01:04, fade-out

AUGUST 28, 1982   LONG ISLAND, NEW YORK—JONES BEACH THEATRE   LIVE

Track Title	Attributes	Time	Album	Details
Come Get It	ec	11:21	(30)	BE out; add MD synth

The original master was 13:18.

"Come Get It" has the same introduction as "Back Seat Betty." Miles plays the riff of "Tramp" during his solo (05:10/05:29).

PROB. SEPTEMBER 1, 1982   NEW YORK CITY—COLUMBIA STUDIOS   RECORDING

Miles Davis (tp, synth, el. p); Bill Evans (ss, ts); Mike Stern (g); Marcus Miller (el. b); Al Foster (d); Mino Cinelu (perc)

Track Title	Attributes	Time	Album	Details
Star People	edited mst	18:47	(30)	BE ts; add MD voice
U 'n' I	ec	05:55	(30)	MD tp; BE ss

JANUARY 5, 1983   NEW YORK CITY—RECORD PLANT STUDIOS   RECORDING

Miles Davis (tp); Bill Evans (ss); John Scofield (g); Marcus Miller (el. b); Al Foster (d); Mino Cinelu (perc)

Track Title	Attributes	Time	Album	Details
It Gets Better	edited mst	09:48	(30)	

POSS. JANUARY 5, 1983   NEW YORK CITY—RECORD PLANT STUDIOS   RECORDING

Miles Davis (Oberheim synth); Mike Stern (g)

Track Title	Attributes	Time	Album	Details
Intro	exc 1	00:33	(30)	add MD voice
Interlude	exc 2	00:41	(30)	

Excerpt 1 is edited into "Star People" at (00:01/00:34), excerpt 2 at (12:39/13:20).

POSS. FEBRUARY 3, 1983   POSS. HOUSTON, TEXAS—UNIVERSITY OF HOUSTON,   LIVE
CULLEN AUDITORIUM, SECOND CONCERT

Miles Davis (tp, synth); Bill Evans (ss); John Scofield, Mike Stern (g); Tom Barney (el. b); Al Foster (d); Mino Cinelu (perc)

Track Title	Attributes	Time	Album	Details
Speak	edited mst	08:33	(30)	

"Speak" is made up of two parts: part one consists of a theme and bass line in F, appearing at 00:12, 02:40, and 05:36; part two consists of a theme and bass line in D-flat, occurring at 03:07. The date and location are given by Jan Lohmann and the Master Sound edition of (30), but the above piece of music does not appear on a bootleg of the Houston concert credited to this date.

JUNE 31, 1983 & JULY 1, 1983   NEW YORK CITY—A&R STUDIOS   RECORDING

Miles Davis (synth); John Scofield (g); Darryl "The Munch" Jones (el. b); Al Foster (d); Mino Cinelu (perc)

Track Title	Attributes	Time	Album	Details
Freaky Deaky	ic	04:30	(31)	add MD voice

Miles Davis (tp, synth); Bill Evans (ss, ts, fl); John Scofield (g); Darryl Jones (el. b); Al Foster (d); Mino Cinelu (perc)

Track Title	Attributes	Time	Album	Details
Speak (~ That's What Happened)	edited mst	03:29	(31)	BE ss ts

The original master was 12:18. On (31) only a part containing the second section of "Speak" is selected and issued as "That's What Happened."

Track Title	Attributes	Time	Album	Details
What It Is	edited mst	04:31	(31)	BE ss fl; MD tp overdubs

The original master was 07:03. Some studio overdubs were added.

Miles Davis (tp, synth); Robert Irving III (synth, synth-bass, dm, co-arr); Mino Cinelu (perc)

Track Title	Attributes	Time	Album	Details
Robot 415		01:08	(31)	

Miles Davis (tp); Branford Marsalis (ss); Robert Irving III (synth, dm, arr); John Scofield (g); Darryl Jones (el. b); Al Foster (d); Mino Cinelu (perc)

Track Title	Attributes	Time	Album	Details
Decoy		08:33	(31)	
Code M.D.		05:56	(31)	MD tp overdubs; add MD voice
That's Right	fade-out	11:11	(31)	add MD synth; dm out

Miles Davis (tp, arr); Robert Irving III (synth, co-arr); John Scofield (g); Darryl Jones (el. b); Al Foster (d); Steve Thornton (perc)

Track Title	Attributes	Time	Album	Details
Time after Time	edited mst	04:29	(32)	

A longer version of "Time after Time" was issued on 12" (CBS TA 4871).

Miles Davis (tp, arr); Robert Irving III (synth); John Scofield (g); Darryl Jones (el. b); Vince Wilburn Jr. (d); Steve Thornton (perc)

Track Title	Attributes	Time	Album	Details
Human Nature	ec	04:29	(32)	RI co-arr
MD 1		00:10	(32)	Train sounds only
Something's on Your Mind		06:41	(32)	MD tp overdubs
MD 2		00:32	(32)	Synth & perc effects only

"MD 1" crossfades into "Something's on Your Mind," which is why the total time of the three combined tracks overruns the total track time given on the CD sleeve, 07:17.

Miles Davis (tp, police & MD voices, arr); Bob Berg (ss); Robert Irving III (synth); John Scofield (g); Darryl Jones (el. b); Al Foster (d); Steve Thornton (perc)

Only on "Speak": Steve Thornton (Spanish voice); Sting ("French policeman's voice"); Marek Olko (Polish voice); James "J.R." Prindiville (handcuffs)

Track Title	Attributes	Time	Album	Details
Right Off (= One Phone Call)		00:54	(32)	
Speak (= Street Scenes)	mc	03:41	(32)	MD tp overdubs

These two tracks were combined and issued as "One Phone Call/Street Scenes." "One Phone Call" is based on Vamp #1 of "Right Off"; "Street Scenes" is based on the D-flat theme and bass line of "Speak."

Track Title	Attributes	Time	Album	Details
You're Under Arrest		06:12	(32)	JS co-arr
Medley: Jean-Pierre/ You're under Arrest/ Then There Were None		03:22	(32)	RI co-arr; add MD voice

---

FIRST TWO WEEKS IN 1985   **NEW YORK CITY—RECORD PLANT STUDIOS**   **RECORDING**

Miles Davis (tp, arr); Robert Irving III (synth, co-arr); John McLaughlin (g); Darryl Jones (el. b); Vince Wilburn Jr. (d); Steve Thornton (perc)

Track Title	Attributes	Time	Album	Details
Ms. Morrisine	ec	04:55	(32)	JML g overdubs
Katia		08:23	(32)	add MD synth

McLaughlin overdubs a second guitar part on "Ms. Morrisine."

FROM JANUARY 31 TO FEBRUARY 4 1985   **COPENHAGEN (DENMARK)— EASY SOUND STUDIO**   **RECORDING**

Miles Davis (tp); Benny Rosenfeld, Palle Bolvig, Jens Winther, Perry Knudsen, Idrees Sulieman (tp, flh); Vincent Nilsson, Jens Engel, Ture Larsen (tb); Ole Kurt Jensen (btb); Alex Windfeld (btb, tu); Jan Zum Vohrde, Jesper Thilo, Per Carsten, Uffe Karskov, Bent Jaedig, Flemming Madsen (saxes, w); Niels Eje (oboe, engh); Lillian Toernqvist (harp); Thomas Clausen, Ole Koch-Hansen, Kenneth Knudsen (k); John McLaughlin, Bjarne Roupé (g); Bo Stief (el. b); Niels-Henning Ørsted Pedersen (b); Lennart Gruvstedt (d); Vince Wilburn, Jr. (el. d); Marilyn Mazur, Ethan Weisgaard (perc); Eva Thaysen (voc); Palle Mikkelborg (comp, arr, cond, additional tp & flh)

Track Title	Attributes	Time	Album	Details
Intro		04:47	(33)	
White		06:04	(33)	JML out
Yellow		06:47	(33)	MD & JML out
Orange		08:37	(33)	
Red		06:04	(33)	JML out
Green		08:10	(33)	JML out
Blue		06:35	(33)	JML out
Red		04:16	(33)	JML out
Indigo		06:04	(33)	MD & JML out
Violet		09:02	(33)	

A five-second brass section is added at the beginning of "Indigo" in the 2000 edition of *Aura* (33). The new edition also corrects the erroneous banding of "Red" and "Green" on the first edition.

Miles Davis (tp, synth); Bob Berg (ss); Robert Irving III (k); John Scofield (g); Darryl Jones (el. b); Vince Wilburn Jr. (d); Steve Thornton (perc)

Track Title	Attributes	Time	Album	Details
Right Off		01:56	(34)	BB out
Speak		11:18	(34)	
Star People	excerpt	00:02	(34)	BB out
Human Nature		05:30	(34)	add BB poss. k
Something's on Your Mind		12:31	(34)	
Time after Time		08:01	(34)	add BB k
Code M.D.	ec	07:08	(34)	
Hopscotch	excerpt	01:34	(34)	BB ts
Medley: Jean-Pierre/ You're under Arrest/ Then There Were None		08:21	(34)	BB ts

Miles Davis (tp); Richard Scher (synth); Doug Wimbish (el. b); Sonny Okosuns (talking drum, voc); Ray Barretto (cga); Little Steven, Ben Newberry, Keith Le Blanc (dm); D.J. Cheese (scratcher); Gil Scott-Heron, Peter Garrett, Malopoets, Peter Wolf, Granmaster Melle Mel, Duke Bootee (voc); Annie Brody Dutka (background voc)

Track Title	Attributes	Time	Album	Details
Let Me See Your I.D.	edited mst	07:19	(35)	

Three different mixdowns were issued on 12" (EMI/Manhattan V56015).

Miles Davis (tp); Herbie Hancock (p & poss. synth); Richard Scher (synth); Stanley Jordan (g); Ron Carter (b); Tony Williams (d); Sonny Okosuns (talking drum)

Track Title	Attributes	Time	Album	Details
The Struggle Continues		07:03	(35)	add MD voice

Miles Davis (tp) overdubs; Malopoets (voc); Nelson Mandela, Desmond Tutu (voices); rest unknown

Track Title	Attributes	Time	Album	Details
Revolutionary Situation		06:16	(35)	add MD voice

Miles Davis (tp); Mike Stern (g—in October only); Zane Giles (g, dm, sampler); Randy Hall (g, voc); Adam Holzman (k); Vince Wilburn Jr. (d, perc); Steve Reid (perc). Occasionally: Glen Burris (saxophone); Neil Larsen, Wayne Linsey (k)

These sessions, about a dozen in total, have become known as the "Rubber Band Sessions," after one of the tunes recorded. Two of Miles's solos from these sessions were used on (54), to create "High Speed Chase" and "Fantasy."

Miles Davis (tp); David Sanborn (as); Steve Porcaro (k, electronics); David Paich (k); Steve Lukather (g); Michael Porcaro (el. b); Jeff Porcaro (d, perc); Joe Porcaro (perc)

Track Title	Attributes	Time	Album	Details
Don't Stop Me Now		03:06	(36)	

The following four entries list the known dates for the recording of four tracks for *Tutu* (37). Since George Duke and Marcus Miller spent considerable time writing, programming, and recording the basic tracks, these four February 1986 dates most likely only refer to final overdubbing sessions.

FEBRUARY 6, 1986   LOS ANGELES, CALIFORNIA—CAPITOL RECORDING STUDIOS   RECORDING

Miles Davis (tp); George Duke (sampled ts, k, el. b; dm); Marcus Miller (el. b); Paulinho DaCosta (perc)

Track Title	Attributes	Time	Album	Details
Backyard Ritual		04:48	(37)	

FEBRUARY 10, 1986   LOS ANGELES, CALIFORNIA—CAPITOL RECORDING STUDIOS   RECORDING

Miles Davis (tp); Marcus Miller (ss, synth, fretted & fretless el. b, g, dm); Adam Holzman (synth solo); Paulinho DaCosta, Steve Reid (perc)

Track Title	Attributes	Time	Album	Details
Splatch	ec	04:43	(37)	

FEBRUARY 11, 1986   LOS ANGELES, CALIFORNIA—CAPITOL RECORDING STUDIOS   RECORDING

Miles Davis (tp); Marcus Miller (ss, synth, el. b, dm); Paulinho DaCosta (perc)

Track Title	Attributes	Time	Album	Details
Tutu	fade-out	05:15	(37)	

There are two trumpet parts on "Tutu."

FEBRUARY 13, 1986   LOS ANGELES, CALIFORNIA—CAPITOL RECORDING STUDIOS   RECORDING

Miles Davis (tp); Marcus Miller (ss, synth, fretless & fretted el. b, g, dm); Paulinho DaCosta (perc)

Track Title	Attributes	Time	Album	Details
Portia		06:18	(37)	

FROM MARCH 12 TO 25, 1986   NEW YORK CITY—CLINTON RECORDING STUDIOS   RECORDING

Miles Davis (tp); Marcus Miller (ss, bcl, el. b, synth, g, dm); Bernard Wright (synth); Omar Hakim (d, perc)

Track Title	Attributes	Time	Album	Details
Tomaas	ec	05:35	(37)	

Miles Davis (tp); Marcus Miller (ss, bcl, synth, g, el. b, dm)

Track Title	Attributes	Time	Album	Details
Perfect Way		04:34	(37)	add MM voice

Miles Davis (tp); Marcus Miller (ss, bcl, synth, g, el. b, dm); Michael Urbaniak (el. v)

Track Title	Attributes	Time	Album	Details
Don't Lose Your Mind	ec	05:49	(37)	

Miles Davis (tp); Marcus Miller (ss, synth, g, el. b, dm)

Track Title	Attributes	Time	Album	Details
Full Nelson	ec	05:06	(37)	add MD voice

Miles Davis (tp); Marcus Miller (ss, bcl, synth); John Scofield (classical g); Omar Hakim (d)

Track Title	Attributes	Time	Album	Details
Siesta		05:08	(38)	
Theme for Augustine		04:26	(38)	JS & OH out

Miles Davis (tp); Marcus Miller (synth)

Track Title	Attributes	Time	Album	Details
Lost in Madrid, part I		01:47	(38)	
Kiss		00:31	(38)	
Lost in Madrid, part IV		00:21	(38)	add MM bcl
Lost in Madrid, part V		04:31	(38)	add MM bcl elb pe

Miles Davis (tp); Marcus Miller (synth, fretless el. b, perc); Earl Klugh (classical g)

Track Title	Attributes	Time	Album	Details
Claire		02:25	(38)	

Miles Davis (tp); Marcus Miller (ss, bcl, sampled harp sound, synth); James Walker (fl)

Track Title	Attributes	Time	Album	Details
Los Feliz		04:34	(38)	

Miles Davis, Kenny Garrett, Joe "Foley" McCreary, Marcus Miller, Ricky Wellman, lay basic tracks for, "Catémbe," "Big Time," and "Hannibal," issued on (44). This information was provided by Jason Miles. We do not know what material from these sessions ended up on (44).

Miles Davis (tp); David Gamson (k, arr); Dan Huff (g); Fred Maher (dm); Green Gartside (lead voc); Eric Troyer, Rory Dodd (background voc); John Mahoney, Ray Niznik (Synclavier)

Track Title	Attributes	Time	Album	Details
Oh Patti (Don't Feel Sorry for Loverboy)		04:20	(39)	MD overdub

It is unknown where Miles added his parts.

Miles Davis (tp); David Sanborn (as); Paul Shaffer (k); Larry Carlton (g); Marcus Miller (co-arr, prob. dm)

Track Title	Attributes	Time	Album	Details
We Three Kings of Orient Are		04:41	(40)	

Miles Davis (tp); Kenny Garrett (as); Merv De Peyer (k, dm); Larry Blackmon (voc; poss. perc & b); Tomi Jenkins (voc); Nathan Leftenant (voc)

Track Title	Attributes	Time	Album	Details
In the Night		04:43	(41)	MD

JUNE 29, 1988   NEW YORK CITY—THE HIT FACTORY   RECORDING

Miles Davis (tp); Atlanta Bliss (tp); Eric Leeds (ts); Prince (synth, g, sampled bass, dm); Chaka Khan (voc)

Track Title	Attributes	Time	Album	Details
Sticky Wicked		06:51	(42)	add MD voice

Miles Davis (tp); Margaret Ross (harp); Dave Grusin (p, arr); Rob Mounsey (synth); John Tropea (g); Marcus Miller (fretless el. b); Steve Ferrone (d); Chaka Khan (voc); David Nadien (concertmaster); String orchestra arranged by Dave Grusin & conducted by Ettore Stratta

Track Title	Attributes	Time	Album	Details
I'll Be Around	ec	05:23	(42)	

AUGUST 7, 1988   OSAKA (JAPAN)—EXPO PARK, "LIVE UNDER THE SKY" FESTIVAL   LIVE

Miles Davis (tp, synth); Kenny Garrett (as); Adam Holzman, Robert Irving III (k); Joe "Foley" McCreary (lead el. b); Benny Rietveld (b); Ricky Wellman (d); Marilyn Mazur (perc)

Track Title	Attributes	Time	Album	Details
Full Nelson	edited mst	02:45	(43)	MD tp

The original master was 03:31.

AUGUST 14, 1988   LOS ANGELES, CALIFORNIA—GREEK THEATRE   LIVE

Track Title	Attributes	Time	Album	Details
Star People (~ New Blues)		05:26	(43)	add MD voice

Miles began performing "Star People" on August 28, 1982, and the tune became a staple of his live recordings. My research has unearthed 339 versions of "Star People," performed between August 28, 1982, and Miles's last concert, August 25, 1991! The performance of the tune gradually developed over the years, although the basic chord scheme and feel remained the same. On (48) it is retitled "New Blues," a practice repeated on (43).

SEPTEMBER 1988 THROUGH JANUARY 1989   NEW YORK CITY—   RECORDING
CLINTON RECORDING STUDIOS

Miles Davis (tp); Kenny Garrett (as); Marcus Miller (ss, bcl, k, g, el. b, dm); Don Alias, Mino Cinelu (perc)

Track Title	Attributes	Time	Album	Details
Catémbe	ec	05:35	(44)	

Miles Davis (tp); Marcus Miller (ss, bcl, k, el. b); Kenny Garrett (as); Jean-Paul Bourelly (g) on right; Joe "Foley" McCreary (lead el. b) on left & solo; Ricky Wellman (d); Don Alias (perc)

Track Title	Attributes	Time	Album	Details
Big Time	ec	05:40	(44)	

Miles Davis (tp); Kenny Garrett (as); Marcus Miller (bcl, k, blues g, el. b); Joe "Foley" McCreary (lead el. b); Omar Hakim (d); Paulinho DaCosta (perc)

Track Title	Attributes	Time	Album	Details
Hannibal	ec	05:49	(44)	

Miles Davis (tp); Kenny Garrett (as); Rick Margitza (ts); Marcus Miller (k, el. b, dm); Jean-Paul Bourelly (g); Paulinho DaCosta (perc)

Track Title	Attributes	Time	Album	Details
Jo-Jo	fade-out	04:51	(44)	

Miles Davis (tp); Kenny Garrett (as); Joe Sample (p); Marcus Miller (k, fretless el. b, prob. g); Omar Hakim (d); Don Alias, Bashiri Johnson (perc)

Track Title	Attributes	Time	Album	Details
Amandla	ec	5:20	(44)	

Miles Davis (tp); Kenny Garrett (ss); Marcus Miller (bcl, k, el. b); George Duke (k, synclavier, dm); Joey DeFrancesco (k); Michael Landau (g)

Track Title	Attributes	Time	Album	Details
Cobra	ec	05:15	(44)	

Miles Davis (tp, synth); Kenny Garrett (as, fl); Joey DeFrancesco, Adam Holzman (k); Joe "Foley" McCreary (lead el. b); Benny Rietveld (el. b); Ricky Wellman (d); Marilyn Mazur (perc)

Track Title	Attributes	Time	Album	Details
Human Nature	edited mst	12:29	(43)	add MD voice

The original master was 14:23.

Track Title	Attributes	Time	Album	Details
In a Silent Way		01:54	(43)	KG out
Intruder		04:51	(43)	MD tp; KG as

Miles Davis (tp); Kenny Garrett (as); Marcus Miller (bcl, k, g, el. b); John Bigham (k, g, dm); Billy "Spaceman" Patterson (wah-wah g); Joe "Foley" McCreary (lead el. b); Ricky Wellman (d)

Track Title	Attributes	Time	Album	Details
Jilli	fade-out	05:05	(44)	

Miles Davis (tp); Marcus Miller (bcl, k, el. b); Al Foster (d)

Track Title	Attributes	Time	Album	Details
Mr. Pastorius	mc	05:41	(44)	

Miles (tp); Sal Marquez (add. tp); Marcus Miller (k, rhythm g, el. b, dm); Vernon Reid (g); Will Calhoun (d)

Track Title	Attributes	Time	Album	Details
Rampage	edited mst	05:46	(45)	add MD voice

Some of Miles's trumpet lines sound sampled.

Miles Davis (tp); Kenny Garrett (ss, k, synth b); Joe "Foley" McCreary (lead el. b); Darryl Jones (el. b); Ricky Wellman (d); Mino Cinelu (perc & solo); Rudy Bird (perc)

Track Title	Attributes	Time	Album	Details
Big 'Ol Head		04:52	(46)	add MD voice

Miles Davis (tp); Kenny Garrett (as, k, d, perc, whistle); Rudy Bird, Mino Cinelu (perc); Mikel Dean, Mia Dean, Chananja Bryan, Akira Frierson, Myisha Hollaway, Eric Myers, Erin Myers, Mysheerah Durant, Bonnie Bozeman, Katrina Anderson, Duane Thomas, Noel John, Cie Romeo, Ideka Romeo, Akalier Soogrim (voc)

Track Title	Attributes	Time	Album	Details
Free Mandela		06:05	(46)	

Miles Davis, Dizzy Gillespie (tp); James Moody (ts); Joe Zawinul (synth); George Benson (g); Bill Summers (perc, rhythm arr); Ella Fitzgerald, Sarah Vaughan (voc); Big Daddy Kane, Kool Moe Dee (rappers); Quincy Jones (rhythm arr)

Track Title	Attributes	Time	Album	Details
Jazz Corner of the World		02:53	(47)	

Miles Davis, Dizzy Gillespie (tp); James Moody (ts); George Benson (g); Ella Fitzgerald, Sarah Vaughan (voc) w. Jerry Hey, Gary Grant (tp); Bill Reichebach (tb); Larry Williams (ts, k); Nathan East (el. b); Quincy Jones, Rod Temperton (handclaps, rhythm arr); Ian Underwood (handclaps); Ian Prince (rhythm co-arr); Quincy Jones, Jerry Hey (horn arr)

Track Title	Attributes	Time	Album	Details
Birdland		05:34	(47)	

Miles Davis (tp); Kenny Garrett (ss); Kei Akagi, John Beasley (synth); Joe "Foley" McCreary (lead el. b); Benny Rietveld (fretless el. b); Ricky Wellman (d); Munyungo Jackson (perc)

Track Title	Attributes	Time	Album	Details
Mr. Pastorius	edited mst	03:32	(43)	

The complete master was 08:43.

Miles Davis (tp); Kenny Garrett (fl); Kei Akagi, Adam Holzman (synth); Joe "Foley" McCreary (lead el. b); Benny Rietveld (el. b); Ricky Wellman (d); Munyungo Jackson (perc)

Track Title	Attributes	Time	Album	Details
Time after Time		09:37	(43)	

Track Title	Attributes	Time	Album	Details
Amandla		05:52	(43)	add MD voice

Miles Davis (tp); Kenny Garrett (as, fl, only when specified); Kei Akagi (synth); Joe "Foley" McCreary (lead el. b); Benny Rietveld (el. b); Ricky Wellman (d); John Bigham (el. perc)

Track Title	Attributes	Time	Album	Details
Star People (~ New Blues)	ic	13:15	(48)	
Hannibal		07:05	(48)	
Human Nature		16:06	(48)	add KG fl
Mr. Pastorius	edited mst	02:07	(48)	KG, JFMC & JB out
Tutu		12:33	(48)	KG fl
Jilli		05:19	(48)	
Star on Cicely (~Wrinkle)	edited mst	03:54	(48)	
Don't Stop Me Now	ec	04:10	(48)	KG fl
Amandla		06:32	(48)	

The video features an interview with Miles. The theme of "Wrinkle" is THEME #2 of "Star on Cicely" combined with a new bass vamp.

Miles Davis (tp); Chuck Findley (tp); poss. Kei Akagi or Alan Oldfield (synth); Michel Legrand (p, arr); Benny Rietveld (el. b); Ricky Wellman, Harvey Mason, or Alphonse Mouzon (d); John Bigham (el. perc)

Track Title	Attributes	Time	Album	Details
The Arrival		02:07	(49)	CF out
The Departure		01:58	(49)	add MD voice
The Dream		03:50	(49)	CF out
The Jam Session		06:09	(49)	

Miles Davis (sampling k); prob. Chuck Findley (tp); Colin Fries (voice)

Track Title	Attributes	Time	Album	Details
The Music Room		02:41	(49)	add MD voice

Miles Davis (tp); Chuck Findley, Nolan Smith, Ray Brown, George Graham, Oscar Brashear (tp); Jimmy Cleveland, Dick Nash, George Bohanan, Thurman Green, Lew McGreary (tb); Vince de Rosa, David Duke, Marnie Johnson, Richard Todd (frh); Kenny Garrett (as); Buddy Collette, Jackie Kelso, Marty Krystall, Bill Green, Charles Owens, John Stephens (w); Kei Akagi, Alan Oldfield (synth); Michel Legrand (p, k, arr); Mark Rivett (g); Joe "Foley" McCreary (lead el. b); Benny Rietveld (el. b); Ricky Wellman, Harvey Mason or Alphonse Mouzon (d); John Bigham (el. perc);

Track Title	Attributes	Time	Album	Details
Concert on the Runway		04:13	(49)	add unknown (choir); add MD voice
Trumpet Cleaning		03:57	(49)	
Paris Walking II		03:16	(49)	
Going Home		02:09	(49)	MD tp overdubs

"Departure," "The Dream," and "Going Home" are different arrangements of "The Arrival."

Miles Davis (tp); John Lee Hooker (el. g) on left & (voc); Taj Mahal (dobro) on center; Roy Rogers (slide g) on right; Tim Drummond (el. b); Earl Palmer (d)

Track Title	Attributes	Time	Album	Details
Coming to Town	ec	03:08	(50)	

Miles Davis (tp); Taj Mahal (dobro) on left & (voc); Roy Rogers (slide g) on right; Tim Drummond (el. b)

Track Title	Attributes	Time	Album	Details
Empty Bank		02:21	(50)	
Sawmill		03:05	(50)	add RR tremolo el. g

Miles Davis (tp); John Lee Hooker (el. g) on left & (voc); Taj Mahal (dobro) on center; Roy Rogers (slide g) on right & (tremolo el. g); Tim Drummond (el. b)

Track Title	Attributes	Time	Album	Details
Harry and Dolly		02:51	(50)	

Miles Davis (tp); John Lee Hooker (el. g) on left; Taj Mahal (dobro & voc); Roy Rogers (g) on right; Tim Drummond (el. b); Earl Palmer (d)

Track Title	Attributes	Time	Album	Details
Bank Robbery		04:34	(50)	

Miles Davis (tp); Bradford Ellis (k)

Track Title	Attributes	Time	Album	Details
Gloria's Story		03:25	(50)	

Miles Davis (tp); Bradford Ellis (k); John Lee Hooker (el. g) on left & (voc); Roy Rogers (slide g) on right; Tim Drummond (el. b)

Track Title	Attributes	Time	Album	Details
Murder		04:11	(50)	

Miles Davis (tp); John Lee Hooker (el. g) on left; Taj Mahal (dobro) on center; Roy Rogers (slide g) on right; Tim Drummond (el. b); Earl Palmer (d)

Track Title	Attributes	Time	Album	Details
End Credits		05:21	(50)	

Longer versions of "Empty Bank," "Sawmill," and "Harry and Dolly" and four extra tracks are audible in the movie score.

JULY 1990	ROMA (ITALY)—RUSTICHELLI STUDIO	RECORDING

Miles Davis (tp); Paolo Rustichelli (synth, Waveframe Audioframe, dm)

Track Title	Attributes	Time	Album	Details
Capri	mst 1	03:56	(51)	
Capri (reprise)	mst 2	03:38	(51)	

UNKNOWN DATES BETWEEN 1990 & 1991	ROMA (ITALY)—RUSTICHELLI STUDIO/ LOS ANGELES—NIGHTINGALE STUDIO	RECORDING

Track Title	Attributes	Time	Album	Details
Wild Tribes	2 mst (04:22 & 04:32)	04:32	(52)	add PR voc

Miles Davis (tp); Paolo Rustichelli (synth, dm); Mario Leonardi (ten, voc)

Track Title	Attributes	Time	Album	Details
Kyrie		04:11	(52)	add MD voice

Miles Davis (tp); Paolo Rustichelli (synth, dm); Carlos Santana (g); unknown (female voc)

Track Title	Attributes	Time	Album	Details
Get On		04:06	(52)	
Rastafario		04:49	(52)	

Miles Davis (tp); Paolo Rustichelli (synth, dm, voc); Brenda Lee Eager (voc)

Track Title	Attributes	Time	Album	Details
Love Divine		04:52	(52)	

JULY 20, 1990	MONTREUX (SWITZERLAND)—CASINO, "TWENTY-FOURTH MONTREUX JAZZ FESTIVAL"	LIVE

Miles Davis (tp, synth); Kenny Garrett (as, fl); Kei Akagi (synth); Joe "Foley" McCreary (lead el. b); Richard Patterson (el. b); Ricky Wellman (d); Erin Davis (el. perc)

Track Title	Attributes	Time	Album	Details
Star on Cicely (~Wrinkle)	edited mst	07:12	(43)	KG as; add MD voice
Tutu	edited mst	08:48	(43)	KG fl

The original master of "Star on Cicely" was 08:04, of "Tutu" 13:30.

AUGUST 13, 1990	NEW YORK CITY—CLINTON RECORDING STUDIOS	RECORDING

Miles Davis (tp) ; Shirley Horn (p, voc); Charles Ables (b); Steve Williams (d)

Track Title	Attributes	Time	Album	Details
You Won't Forget Me		07:12	(53)	add MD voice

Miles Davis (tp); Deron Johnson (k) on most tracks; rest unknown

Track Title	Attributes	Time	Album	Details
Mystery	edited mst	03:55	(54)	tp overdubs
Mystery (Reprise)	edited mst	01:25	(54)	tp overdubs
Chocolate Chip	edited mst	04:38	(54)	tp overdubs
Sonya	edited mst	05:30	(54)	tp overdubs
Duke Booty	edited mst	04:54	(54)	tp overdubs, add MD voice
High Speed Chase	edited mst	04:40	(54)	
Fantasy	edited mst	04:35	(54)	

Miles's solos on "High Speed Chase" and "Fantasy" were recorded during the "Rubber Band Sessions" from October of 1985 to January of 1986.

Miles Davis (tp); Deron Johnson (k); R.I.F. "Rappin' Is Fundamental": J. R., A. B. Money, Easy Mo Bee (rappers)

Track Title	Attributes	Time	Album	Details
The Doo-bop Song	seven edited masters	04:59	(54)	

Miles Davis (tp); prob. Deron Johnson (k); Easy Mo Bee (rap voc); Peter Daou, Cavin Fisher (k, perc & remix on "mst #2"); unknown female (bgr voc)

Track Title	Attributes	Time	Album	Details
Blow	eight edited masters	05:05	(54)	add MD voice

The January/February date is given by Jan Lohmann. According to Jo Gelbard and Deron Johnson, Miles and Johnson recorded most of their parts after coming back from the European tour. If this is correct, these sessions must have occurred between July 24 and Miles's final two live dates in Los Angeles, on August 24 and 25.

Miles Davis (tp); Kenny Garrett (as, bars); Deron Johnson (k); Joe "Foley" McCreary (lead el. b); Richard Patterson (el. b); Ricky Wellman (d)

Track Title	Attributes	Time	Album	Details
Hannibal	edited mst	07:20	(43)	

The original master was 17:28.

EDITOR'S NOTE:

Due to lack of space, we were unable to include the details for the following recording dates:

- Louis Armstrong: *What a Wonderful World* (CD) One track with Miles (voice), recorded on May 29, 1970.
- Betty Davis: *Nasty Gal* (CD) One track directed by Miles, recorded in 1975.
- Various Artists: *DOC Anthology* Vol. 1 (Video) Three tracks by Miles's band from an Italian RAI TV Broadcast, recorded on April 6, 1989.
- Various Artists: *Tribute to Nesuhi Ertegun* (Video) and Various Artists: *Montreux Jazz Festival, 25ème Anniversaire* (4 CD Box) One track by Miles's band, recorded on July 21, 1989 (same track for both items)
- Miles Davis & Quincy Jones: *Live at Montreux* (Video) and Miles Davis & Quincy Jones: *Live at Montreux* (CD) Complete show recorded on July 8, 1991. The video contains some extra excerpts from the rehearsals of the band.

Details of these sessions—as well as of future electric Miles Davis releases—can be found at www.miles-beyond.com.

INDEX

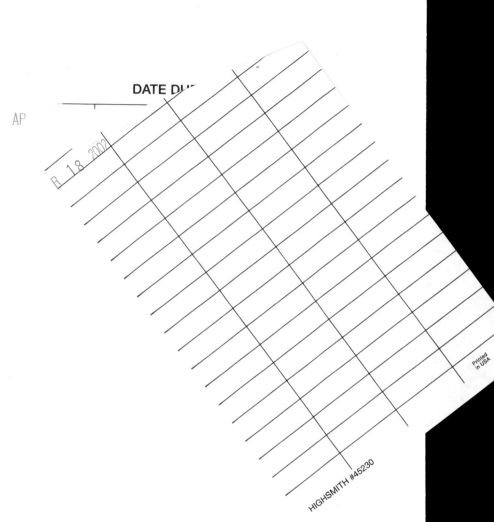

DATE DUE

AP

R 18 2002

Printed
in USA

HIGHSMITH #45230